Toby and Character Jugs

of the 20th Century
and their Makers

Editorial Consultant: Kevin Pearson

Design and Layout: Dana Benedetto

Cover Photo and Photo Consulting by Frank Held of Held Images

Interior Design: The Lee Allison Company

Photo Processing: Perfect Photo Labs

Printing Coordination: Allison and Associates, LLC

Publisher: Kevin James Publishing

Printed and bound in China

© David C. Fastenau and Stephen M. Mullins, 1999

© Kevin James Publishing, 1999

A current price guide may be obtained from the publisher by mailing the enclosed card at the back of this book. If the card is missing, please contact the publisher at the address below.

Further copies of this book may be obtained directly from Kevin James Publishing, 917 Chicago Avenue, Evanston, Illinois, 60202, U.S.A. Telephone: (800) 634-0431 or (847) 570-4867; fax (847) 570-4871; email – britcol@MSN.com.

Authors with book ideas on other antique and collectible subjects are welcome to contact us.

ISBN # 1-928938-01-9

Frontpiece Photo: Royal Doulton's George Robey Toby Jug, Leonard Jarvis' Winston Churchill Toby Jug, and Grimwades' John Bull Character Jug

Title Page Photo: Staffordshire Fine Ceramics' Abraham Lincoln Toby Jug

This book is dedicated to my mother, whose interest in antiques and things old created an environment for me to learn to appreciate them; and to my grandmother, whose small collection of Royal Doulton jugs got me started on my passion for collecting and learning about Toby Jugs.

David

This book is dedicated to my wife, Carol, who for thirty-six years has endured the collection of "shrunken heads" that adorn our home ("not another one"); as well as the long forgotten camp counselor in Canada who, in 1947, enticed me with a Royal Doulton brochure to use the balance of my camp candy account money, all of $9, to buy six small Character Jugs. Two thousand jugs later, he knew not what he wrought.

Steve

Authors Steve Mullins on left and David Fastenau on right; World's Largest Toby Jug in center, produced by LJB Ceramics in a limited edition on commission for the American Toby Jug Museum.

Acknowledgments

Particular thanks to those who have devoted their time and knowledge to making this book more complete and accurate, helping us along the way.

To our new acquaintances and old friends around the Stoke-on-Trent area: Albert Arrowsmith, Lionel & Lorna Bailey, Roger & Brenda Bairstow, Judi Bland, Bill Buckley, Dave Coup, Chris Davenport, Rhodri & Rhys Davies, Kristine Fernandez, Jim Fryer, Peter Goodfellow, Arthur Griffiths, Phil Jaram, Diana Keates, Roy Kirkham, D. Barry Leigh, John Pointon, Paul Singh, Deborah Skinner, Chris Slater, Mavis Whieldon, Sanchia Wood, and Tony & Jackie Wood.

To the North American Royal Doulton specialists for their knowledge and generous photographic opportunities: Arnie Berger, Bill Cross, Gillian & Jim Denmark, Joan & Charles Dombeck, Ann & Joe Nemes, Ed Pascoe, Bea & John Vitkovics, Betty & Dean Weir, Princess & Barry Weiss, and Stan Worrey.

To the staff of Royal Doulton for their timely cooperation in keeping the Doulton section current and complete: Joan Barker, Michael Doulton, Cath Hickling, Fiona Lawton, Julie McKeown, Maureen Murphy, and Nicole Tripp.

To other friends, potters and patient souls for their help and encouragement: Grace Apgar, James Brannan, Helen Cunningham, Peter Dunn, Judith Fox, Ray & Diane Ginns, Gordon & Irene Hopwood, John Love, Joyce McGowan, Ray Noble, Kevin Pearson, Mike Pender, Tom Power, Frank Salmon, Vic Schuler, Ron Smith, Rita Smythe, Robin Tinkler, Betty & Bob Wheeler, Diane Wilkinson, and Kent Yozie.

Special thanks to all of those collectors who willingly shared their enthusiasm and collections with us: Virginia Brisco, Bill Cumming, Stuart Dawkins, Mike Doyle, Bill & Pam Foster, Brian Heckford, John Hobbs, Jay Hunzinger, John Johnson, Robert Keylock, Emmett Mathews, William McIntyre, Andrea & Mike McNamara, Muriel Miller, Bob Palmer, Guadalupe Pequeno, Sharon & Steve Roots, John Sanderson, Ed Weinstein, Edna & Graham Wilkinson, and Charles Wood.

Most special thanks to the following who exhibited extraordinary patience while allowing us to photograph their world class Royal Doulton collections, without which this book would be incomplete: Tony D'Agostino, Neil Galatz, and Irene & Vern Rouf.

This book wouldn't be possible without those who assisted with its production: Lee Allison, Richard Allison, Bryce Bastian, Dana Benedetto, Frank Held, Zee Bradshaw-Pittman, Sandy Johnson, Steve Mayer, George Nwia, Abdol Sabbagh, Ralph Smith, and Joan Sollers.

Betty - thanks for introducing the two of us, we're sure you could not have known what would come of it.

Kevin - thanks for providing the push to turn our idea into a work in process.

Toby and Character Jugs of the 20th Century and their Makers

I was quite honored when asked to do a preface for this book. My three editions of *British Toby Jugs* were sadly lacking in the detail of the 20th century, which this book makes up for in its comprehensive detail.

I am impressed with the time and research that has gone into this book, not only with reference to past literature on the subject, but by direct contact with potteries still in production and heirs of now defunct potteries, as well as individual Toby and Character Jug collectors.

The last hundred years have covered almost half of the life of the Toby Jug, which was born in roughly 1770. It is often more difficult to find records and research material of deceased potteries from the past one hundred years than for those of the 18th and 19th centuries, simply because no one before now has attempted to develop an in depth history of the 20th century Toby and Character Jug.

I have learnt much from this book. I feel sure that others will also. I feel that it will be regarded as an important piece of 20th century ceramic literature.

Vic Schuler

Authors Steve Mullins on left and David Fastenau on right with Vic Schuler

Political Jugs Of The 20th Century

Character Jugs left to right: Winston Churchill, Prime Minister of Great Britain, 1940-45, 1951-55 (Kevin Francis Ceramics); Jan Christian Smuts, Prime Minister of the Union of South Africa, 1919-24, 1939-48, (Burgess & Leigh); Franklin D. Roosevelt, President of the United States, 1933-1945 (Grimwades-Royal Winton); John G. Diefenbaker, Prime Minister of Canada, 1957-63 (J. Fryer & Co.)

Toby Jugs left to right: Theodore Roosevelt, President of the United States, 1901-1909 (Lenox); David Lloyd George, Prime Minister of Great Britain, 1916-1922 (Wilkinson,Ltd); Mikhail Gorbachev, General Secretary and President of USSR, 1985-91 (Kevin Francis Ceramics).

This book is organized alphabetically by the name of 20th century makers of Toby and Character Jugs. Many of these potters have long histories dating back one or more centuries. Potteries that produced Toby Jugs in the 18th or 19th century, but not the 20th, are not included here. However, some of the jugs listed originated in the 19th century, with production continuing into the 20th century. For each potter, a brief history is provided, along with considerably more details about jug production than was previously available. For each potter, jugs are listed alphabetically with Character Jugs and Toby Jugs separated. Where considered an important part of the genre, Toby and Character Jug derivative items are also included.

Following the alphabetical list of potteries is a section on jugs that have been identified by country of origin when known. This section also includes makers of jugs that are considered less important or for which there is little known. Jugs produced by a completely unknown potter are listed in the Unattributed section. Be sure to check these sections if you cannot find your prized jug under a specific pottery.

About the Market Values of Character and Toby Jugs

In the companion Price Guide to this book, we provide an indication of the prevailing market values for the identified Toby and Character Jugs. As with any collectibles market, where there is ever changing supply and demand, as well as trends in what is hot and periodic changes in taste, the true value of any jug is what is agreed upon between a buyer and a seller for a given piece and on a given day.

Supply and demand of collectibles can be surprisingly elastic. An item in significant, but unquantifiable, demand and scarce supply may be priced as low as a similar, readily available piece. This paradox has been the norm for the Toby and Character Jug market, and occurs even in the well-documented collecting world of Royal Doulton. The lack of readily available information for identification and valuation of Character and Toby Jugs has ensured just this sort of irreconcilable pricing of jugs. Many are priced out of lack of knowledge, or simply priced based upon what one paid for the jug.

Another interesting phenomenon of jug collecting is that it is quite common to find excellent 18th and 19th century jugs for less than one might pay for similar, yet inferior, 20th century jugs. Several key factors contribute to this. Identifying older jugs is more difficult because most were unmarked. This, plus the existence of modern reproductions, warns the collector to exercise caution. Also, the range of characters portrayed during the 18th and 19th centuries was much more limited. Many of these characters were produced in great numbers by numerous potters and are relatively available to the collector. Finally, as with the collectibles field in general, today's collectors seem to be more interested in 20th century limited edition collectibles than true antiques from our past. This is not to say that 20th century jugs are more valuable in general. Only the rare and more collectible pieces are pricier, while the most rare 18th and 19th century jugs also can command extraordinary prices.

One's selling and purchasing of Toby and Character Jugs should be based on the value one places on the piece, and the value placed on it by the seller or buyer. Overall, values have increased in varying degrees over the past decade. In the next millennium, we expect the value of 20th century jugs to continue to appreciate at least on par with 20th century collectibles in general.

The purpose of collecting anything is the enjoyment derived from displaying your collection, finding new pieces, and learning about your hobby. We hope this book helps you do exactly that.

It is the intention of the authors to offer an updated Price Guide regularly. Such guides may be obtained on a subscription basis by mailing the return card enclosed with this book or writing the authors in care of the American Toby Jug Museum at the address on the next page.

Regarding the Compiled Jug Listings in this Book

The listings within this book consist of only those jugs that have been positively identified by the authors. Where the lists are considered comprehensive, they are so indicated. However, despite the author's combined seventy years of collecting and researching, some of these listings remain incomplete. There are undoubtedly many additional jugs of which neither of the authors are aware. Also, historical information on some potteries is much more limited than on others.

In particular, hundreds of Japanese produced jugs commonly appear in the market, such as at antique malls and on Internet auction sites. The authors have not made extensive efforts to catalog this production. Rather we list those jugs that we consider more interesting and of better quality.

To better complete these listings and continue their research, the authors invite readers to provide feedback on individual potteries or with details of jugs not included herein.

Detailed information about a pottery or jugs, including description, character name, height, coloring, marks and photographs, may be sent to the authors at:

The American Toby Jug Museum
917 Chicago Avenue
Evanston, Illinois 60202 USA

Two rooms of the American Toby Jug Museum

Is it a Jug or a Mug?

More and more, the authors have noticed both the novice collector and experienced dealer referring to Toby and Character Jugs as "toby mugs" or "character mugs". This is incorrect nomenclature. Webster's defines a jug as "a container for liquids with a handle and a narrow mouth for pouring." A mug is defined as "a drinking cup, usually cylindrical and with a handle." Collectors will note that virtually all jugs listed in this book have a narrow mouth or spout for pouring. Those that do not, we correctly identify as mugs, or in cases of taller containers, tankards.

The key is to look at the top rim. If the opening has a spout, it's a jug, not a mug.

Lancaster and Sandland
Scottie Jug

Lancaster and Sandland
Scottie Mug

Toby Jugs versus Character Jugs

A Toby Jug is defined as a jug or pitcher in the form of a full-bodied character, while a Character Jug comprises only the head or face, and often shoulders. For the purposes of this book, we include any jug that depicts a half-body to the waist or more as a Toby Jug. Bust jugs, those showing a subject from above the waist up, are listed with Character Jugs, while half and three-quarter bodied jugs are listed under Toby Jugs.

Royal Doulton Falstaff Toby Jug

Royal Doulton Falstaff
Character Jug

Collecting Toby and Character Jugs

Collecting anything can be a very rewarding hobby. In fact, most people begin many different collections during their lifetime. As children, the habit of collecting can begin with paperclips, bottle caps, or other easily found items. It is likely some childhood collections, such as baseball cards, stamps or coins, carry right through to adulthood.

Why would anyone begin collecting something as unusual as Character or Toby Jugs? There are probably as many answers to this question as there are jug collectors. However, the common denominator is likely the humorous characterizations depicted in the jugs.

Jug collections may be started unintentionally. Many collections begin when someone receives a Character Jug as a gift, often one of the many Royal Doulton jugs. They may find it amusing or meaningful, and begin searching for more. Others may inherit a small collection or buy one or two jugs on impulse.

Some jug collectors get started more indirectly. For example, a collector might be focused on building a collection of goods produced by a particular manufacturer such as Shorter & Son. In building a broad collection of Shorter pottery, several Toby Jugs are purchased, and somehow, branching away from Shorter specifically, Toby Jugs become the focus for a new collection. This same scenario could happen to military collectors, advertising collectors, brewery collectors, history buffs, or Occupied Japan collectors, just to name a few. Fads and keenly peaked collecting niches, such as a Nursery Rhyme collection, can also play a part in launching a jug collection.

Whatever has started your jug collecting fever, our best advice is not to fight it. Many common Character and Toby Jugs can easily be found today for reasonable prices. Of course, some rare jugs are difficult to find and very expensive when they do come to market. The best approach to building any collection is to buy pieces you like for prices you are willing to pay.

Don't worry too much about adding damaged pieces to your collection, assuming the price is appropriately lower to compensate for the damage. Damaged pieces are a good way to fill out your collection quickly. Over time these pieces can be restored to new condition, or replaced with pristine jugs and then resold to other collectors. With the exception of Royal Doulton and Beswick, professionally repaired jugs often sell at close to the same price as perfect pieces.

The same reasoning can be applied to reproduction jugs. Fill out your collection with reproductions for completeness, and gradually upgrade, as you are able, with the harder to find, and typically more expensive, originals.

Your collecting interests are also likely to change over time. Again, don't fight your desires. Portions of your collection can be sold to make room for, and fund, new and exciting additions or directions.

When entering into any new collecting genre, it is common to be a bit overwhelmed by the possibilities and choices. Given that you cannot collect everything within a specialty or, certainly for the more prolific potters, not even all the jugs produced by one company, we find one of the most rewarding ways to build a collection is through series, sets or even pairs. A series generally consists of a number of jugs in a single theme issued over a period of time, often on a subscription basis. A set consists of a number of similar jugs issued at the same time, and a pair is just that - a pair of jugs issued together. Following the lists of makers and jugs at the end of this book you will find our suggestions and favorites for collecting series, sets and pairs.

Over the years we have found the best sources of finding new jugs are auctions, antique shows, fairs, malls and shops, and reputable mail order dealers. The latter is true particularly for Royal Doulton and Beswick jugs. A new and exciting source of goods for the collector has emerged over the past few years: The Internet. Through both Internet antique and collectible shops and on-line, interactive auctions, a wealth of possibilities can be discovered. Watch out though, you might be bidding against one of us!

One of the most fulfilling aspects of collecting is meeting and networking with others who share your same enthusiasm. It is through such networking that this book was made possible, and the display cases at the American Toby Jug Museum continue to fill with new additions.

Happy Collecting!

The unique type of a jug in human form, now known as the Toby Jug, was created by an unknown Staffordshire potter during the middle to late part of the 18th century. The jovial, squat-bodied container for pouring ales embodied the convivial spirit of the age in which it was born.

Within a few years of its innovation, the Toby Jug became one of the most popular jugs using the human form ever produced. The Toby Jug's popularity spread quickly throughout England, and then to the European Continent and abroad. Tobies were being used in Williamsburg, Virginia by the end of the 18th century. Today, Toby Jugs, and their derivative cousin the Character Jug, are prized and sought after by collectors throughout the world.

A Little About Toby's Lineage

While today's 20th century Toby Jug had its origins in the middle of the 18th century, it is descended from a long line of anthropomorphic figures and vessels from ancient times. Long before recorded history, images of living things were being made from clay. Archeologists have found evidence of pottery figures dating back to the Stone Age, and some think such figures were being made even before utilitarian earthenware pots and pitchers.

Pottery figures over 6,000 years old have been found in Egypt, and figural jugs over 4,000 years old have been discovered in Crete, home of the Ancient Minoan civilization. Numerous examples of ancient jugs, cups, pots and other vessels made in the likeness of humans and mythical beings have been unearthed in Greece and Italy and other parts of the Roman Empire, including Britain.

Although little pottery has survived in England from Anglo-Saxon times, a few jugs exist from that era that were molded in human shape, including those of kings. Some of these 14th and 15th century medieval jugs provide the same spirit of whimsical fun so evident in the 18th century Toby Jug.

Over this same period of historic time, ancient Peruvian and other South American civilizations produced a wide range of hand molded figural jugs and vessels. In North America as well, many examples of bowls, jugs and bottles made in human likeness have been discovered. Terra-cotta burial figures, vases and water vessels made by Mayan and Toltec potters are also well documented.

Key Potters of the Mid-1700s

The mid-1700s were a critical period in English pottery history. The poorly modeled, amateurish pots of the past were quickly replaced by high quality ceramics. Items both for everyday use and decorative accessories were produced.

It was the potters of this era who were primarily responsible for the British pottery industry of today. Key Staffordshire potters of this time included John Astbury (1686 - 1743), Thomas Whieldon (1719 - 1795), Ralph Wood (1715 - 1772), Ralph Wood II (1748 - 1795), Aaron Wood (1717 - 1785), Enoch Wood (1759 - 1840), Josiah Wedgwood (1730 - 1795), and John Voyez (dates unknown).

As early as 1725, John Astbury operated at a small single-kiln pottery in Shelton. Astbury previously worked for the Elers where he learned their secrets of lead glazed earthenware. From the 1740s Astbury created distinctive earthenware figures, groups of people, and animals. Astbury's groupings of several people participating in everyday events became quite popular and were known as pew groups. Other potters quickly copied these. By adding flint and using other new processes, Astbury produced better modeled, lighter pots which were more durable. He was the first Staffordshire potter to bring white pipe clay in from Devon, producing whiter bodied wares. Astbury also experimented with sprigging, the application of hand formed threads of clay to the unfired body using this white pipe clay. Astbury's son Thomas continued producing this type of ware, now widely known as Astbury-ware.

Thomas Whieldon of Fenton Low arguably was the best potter of his day. He refined the process of sprigging by decorating unfired earthenware with pre-molded reliefs and threads of thinly rolled clay. He produced this ware primarily between 1740 and 1745. It was so successful that it was widely copied by his contemporaries. Whieldon produced two unique types of multi-colored pottery bodies: tortoiseshell ware and agate ware. Agate ware was the result of combining multicolored clay slips. Whieldon perfected this ware in the 1740s using white clays stained with metallic oxides.

Whieldon greatly influenced his contemporaries and educated the next generation of Staffordshire potters. He took in Ralph Wood as an apprentice, later worked with Aaron Wood, and partnered with Josiah Wedgwood from 1754 to 1759. Wedgwood's

Traditional 18th Century Ordinary Toby Jug

18th Century Bacchus Jug. Forerunner of today's Character Jug

Mezzotint of Toby Philpot by Bowles and Carver 1761

Astbury Toby Jug

Ralph Wood Ordinary Toby inscribed #51

Whieldon Ordinary Toby

famed book of experiments began during this partnership. This book held the secrets of Wedgwood's success.

Ralph Wood, known as the Miller of Burslem, was the father of Ralph Wood the Potter, who apprenticed with Astbury in 1730 and later worked with Thomas Whieldon, learning the manufacture of colored glazes. In 1754, Ralph Wood the Potter began producing his own salt-glazed earthenware goods. Wood was making high quality, very detailed figures in nicely colored glazes by 1760. These figures had a white earthenware body and translucent hand painted lead glazes with metal oxides for color. He was among the first Staffordshire potters to sign his work, impressing R Wood. He married into the Wedgwood family, linking the two names forever in the history of English pottery.

Ralph Wood the Potter had two sons who also became potters: John and Ralph II. John Wood (1746 - 1797) eventually started his own pottery in Brownhills in 1787. Ralph Wood II also became an accomplished potter, carrying on with his father's work as well as creating his own designs. For a time Ralph II was in partnership with his cousin Enoch Wood. Ralph Wood III (1781 - 1801) carried on the family pottery tradition for a short time after his father's death.

Aaron Wood, Ralph Wood the Potter's younger brother, apprenticed with Thomas Wedgwood II from 1731 until 1746, when he went to work for Thomas Whieldon. In 1750 he opened his own pottery. Aaron's two sons, William and Enoch, also became potters. Both apprenticed with Wedgwood at an early age. William Wood (1746 - 1808) remained with Wedgwood as a modeler.

After a short apprenticeship with Humphrey Palmer, Enoch Wood left Wedgwood and founded a pottery in Burslem with Ralph Wood II. Enoch entered into a partnership with James Caldwell in 1790, forming Wood & Caldwell. Enoch then started his own pottery, Enoch Wood & Sons, in 1818 and produced popular earthenware and porcelain. This pottery closed in 1846. Enoch built a reputation as the finest modeler and block cutter of his day.

After his father's death, Josiah Wedgwood started working in his father's factory at the Churchyard Pottery at the age of nine. In 1744, Josiah was apprenticed to his older brother Thomas. In 1754, Josiah went into partnership with Thomas Whieldon. As Whieldon was considered one of the greatest English potters of his time, this partnership allowed Josiah to

further develop his skills and begin experimenting with colored creamware. Josiah Wedgwood ended his partnership with Whieldon and established his own pottery at the Ivy House factory in Burslem in 1759, founding what has become today one of the two largest ceramic conglomerates in England.

John Voyez was a Frenchman transplanted to England. He is believed to have been from the Amiens region of France. Voyez first went to London, where he built a reputation as a fine modeler while working as a carver for architect John Adams. Josiah Wedgwood enticed Voyez to Staffordshire in 1768, but then dismissed him the next year for alleged misconduct. After serving a three-month prison term, Voyez was offered pay from Wedgwood on the condition he leave Staffordshire never to return. Voyez instead chose to work for Wedgwood's competitors. While it has not been substantiated, specific wares have been found which indicate Voyez might have worked for a time with Ralph Wood the Potter. Without question Voyez was influential in the modeling of Staffordshire figures, and some credit him with modeling of the first Toby Jug. Not only was he a gifted potter, the enigmatic Voyez also built quite a reputation as a classic toper and womanizer.

The interrelationships among all of these renowned potters greatly contribute to the mystery of the Toby Jug's creator.

The Genesis of Toby Himself

Sometime in the period between 1730 and 1750, Staffordshire potters were hand crafting small earthenware figures and figural jugs, typically standing between six and eight inches high and portraying midshipmen, soldiers, musicians and other common characters dressed in the everyday garb of the period. Today these types of pieces are collectively referred to as "Astbury" wares, though they were most certainly made by many different potters. These Astbury figural jugs were undoubtedly the immediate forerunners of the Toby Jug. In these figures the Staffordshire potter revealed a sense of whimsy and humor, as well as the more commonplace aspects of everyday life. The "Astbury" type Toby Jug reflects the style of these figural jugs and many historians attribute it to be the forerunner of the traditional Ordinary Toby. However, it seems likely that such jugs were modeled in the "Astbury" fashion after the creation of the first Toby Jug.

Perhaps the most well known of all jugs made in human form, the original Toby Jug, referred to in this book as the Ordinary Toby, depicted a jovial seated drinking man, who holds a jug of ale in his left hand balanced on his knee. Toby was dressed in the common costume of the day wearing a full-length coat with low large pockets, a broad waistcoat, cravat, knee breeches, stockings, buckled shoes and a tri-corn hat, the corners of which formed the spout of the jug. Virtually overnight the Toby Jug became a popular figure in homes and taverns throughout Staffordshire and England. Shortly his fame spread throughout the British Empire and beyond.

It is not conclusively known who truly created the first Toby Jug. Various historians have bestowed this honor on several key potters mentioned previously: John Astbury, Thomas Whieldon, Ralph Wood the Potter, Aaron Wood, and John Voyez. Although some researchers date the creation of the Toby to as early as 1750, the general consensus dates it between 1760 and 1770. No concrete data has been found which accurately pinpoints when Toby was created and by whom.

The early Toby Jugs were not marked, nor were accurate records kept at most of the small thatched pot-works that had sprung up throughout the Staffordshire area. Also, it is not accurate to assume that the most primitive forms of the Toby Jug are the earliest. Some potters who may have copied the design of the original Toby were simply less advanced or skilled to effectively reproduce the quality of the better craftsmen they were attempting to rival. Ralph Wood the Potter is most commonly credited as the Father of the Toby Jug, possibly creating it among his many other figures in the early 1760s. Certainly the jugs attributed to him are the most sought after. However, we tend to favor Thomas Whieldon for the honor of Toby's creator.

Equally obscure is the origin of the name Toby as it is applied to these figural jugs. Again, various experts have different theories on this subject. The French word tope means to drink to excess and the English derivation therein of a drunkard is a toper. Given the British inclination to assimilate words, a toper could have become a toby.

The name Toby was associated with heartiness and a good drink by Shakespeare in the per-son of Sir Toby Belch. Toby Fillpot could have been in common use in the mid-1700s as a moniker for infamous local drinkers. Legend has it that Harry Elwes is reputed to have drunk two thousand gallons of ale in his lifetime, and was nicknamed Toby Fillpot. Paul Parnell, a Yorkshire farmer, had the reputation of drinking nine thousand pounds sterling worth of Stingo ale. The name Toby Fillpot appears in Reverend Francis Fawkes' 1761 song The Little Brown Jug, which told of a thirsty old soul who was known to drink large quantities of ale. It is possible that the mezzotint of the rotund and jolly seated toper holding a mug of ale, which was printed by Bowles and Carver and included Fawkes' verse inscribed below, served as the inspiration for the first Toby Jug. This last theory seems the most plausible.

In the later 1700s, Toby Jugs became common drinking and pouring vessels at local pubs and taverns. Early tobies had a hollow cap that fitted into the brim of the tri-corn hat, completing the crown of the hat. These small cups may have been used to pour into, creating a cup from which to drink. Today most of these caps, or crowns, are not found with an 18th century Toby, being damaged, discarded or destroyed over the years.

Toby's Evolution

Toby's service as a toping vessel continued well into the 19th century. In Hughes' Tom Brown's Schooldays, published in 1857, one can find the phrase "pouring out his ale from a Toby Philpot jug." Probably better known, Dickens' Barnaby Rudge contains a passage in which Gabriel Varden asks his daughter Dolly to "put Toby this way, my dear." Gabriel's Toby was a "goodly jug of well-browned clay, fashioned into the form of an old gentleman ... atop whose bald head was a fine froth answering to his wig, indicative beyond dispute of sparkling home-brewed ale."

It was not long before a menagerie of congenial cronies joined the Ordinary Toby. Many other humorous, eccentric or historical figures have been created in the fashion of Toby Fillpot. However, it has become common to use the general term Toby to refer to any full-bodied figural jug of this type. The majority of early tobies measured around ten inches in height, although some fine miniatures six inches tall were made by the Woods and other potters. Beside the

Ordinary Toby, examples of some of the best known Toby Jugs of the 18th and 19th centuries are the Thin Man, Squire, Hearty Good Fellow, Snufftaker, Sailor, Man on a Barrel, Lord Howe, Collier, Drunken Sal, Gin Woman, and Martha Gunn. Yes, even women became part of the Toby tradition early on.

Left to right: Drunken Sal, Gin Woman, and Martha Gunn Toby Jugs

Thin Man Toby Jug

Squire Toby Jug

Snufftaker Toby Jug

Sailor Toby Jug

Toby Jug production and the creation of new characters grew through the 19th century, producing interesting jugs like the Cross-legged Toby and Sir John Falstaff. However, mass production by the middle of the 1800s had reduced the quality of pottery in general and the Toby Jug as well, with inferior modeling, painting and glazing. Notable exceptions to this trend were Samson Smith, which produced well modeled Punch and Town Crier tobies around 1860 and 1880 respectively, and Minton, which produced excellent Quaker Man and Quaker Woman tobies from 1865 into the 20th century. These are more commonly known as the Barrister and Lady with Fan.

William Kent was a prolific manufacturer of Toby Jugs in the late 19th century and into the 20th century. Kent produced interesting characters such as Punch, Judy, Admiral Lord Nelson, the Cavalier and the Man on a Barrel. The William Kent models are used today at the Bairstow Manor Pottery. Potters also began branching out into animal Toby Jugs around this time, an exciting new development in the range of Toby Jugs.

Character Jugs, the derivatives of the Toby Jug that depict only the head and shoulders of its figure, got their start as early as the late 18th century. However, the production of Character Jugs throughout the 19th century was limited. It is appropriate that the first Character Jug produced in today's modern style was probably by Doulton and Watts in 1820. John Doulton's hero was Admiral Lord Nelson and, in honor of this great leader, Doulton and Watts created stoneware Character Jugs in Nelson's likeness.

By the end of the 19th century the popularity of the Toby Jug had risen such that Toby Jugs were being produced around the world, although in smaller quantities on continental Europe and in the Americas than in England.

The 20th century also contributed to the evolution of the Toby. Between 1914 and 1918, F. Carruthers Gould designed one of the most significant series of Toby Jugs ever created. This series depicted eleven World War I heroes and was produced by A. J. Wilkinson. In the 1920s, Harry Simeon at the Royal Doulton Lambeth factory designed an extensive range of stoneware Toby Jugs and derivatives. Derivatives are defined as any non-jug toby style container, for example ashtrays, book-ends, liquor decanters, salt shakers, teapots, wall plaques, or humidors.

Even though Character Jugs had their beginning much earlier, Charles Noke of Royal Doulton can be called the Father of the Character Jug. It was he, perhaps inspired by Simeon's designs, who created a series of Character Jugs in the 1930s based on British folklore and the lively characters that parade through the works of Charles Dickens. From Noke's important first steps, Character Jugs have exploded in terms of variety and collectability, being manufactured by scores of potteries during the past half century.

In 1949, Shorter and Son introduced the figural Toby Jug through its D'Oyly Carte Opera series, yet another bold step in Toby's development. This exciting collection featured characters from Gilbert and Sullivan operas dressed in authentic D'Oyly Carte costumes and depicting action poses. Later examples of figural tobies include a set of Dickens figural jugs offered by Franklin Porcelain. However, Kevin Francis Ceramics has further elevated the creative use of the figural jug, most notably in its Artists and Potters series and Star Trek series.

For a more complete review of the evolution of the Toby Jug and the early characters created, particularly during the 18th and 19th centuries, please refer to Vic Schuler's *Collecting British Toby Jugs*.

The Changing of the British Pottery Industry

As the Toby Jug is uniquely a British creation, it is interesting to examine the evolution of the

British pottery industry as well. Early English potters, unrecorded by history, created pottery for use by the local population out of readily available resources and using crude techniques. This is often referred to as the period of peasant pottery. By the 1700s, the pottery industry was based on family potting lore and knowledge passed down from generation to generation. Familiar family names such as Wood and Wedgwood had their start during this era through the entrepreneurial spirit of a few individuals. The Wood family is sometimes credited as the driving force behind England's peasant potteries evolving into an industry.

By the 19th century family potteries and traditions were the backbone of the British pottery industry. However, many potteries did not survive or were taken over by others. Others survived and potted for more than 75 years, the family business managed by three, four, or more generations. Today, firms such as Bairstow Manor and Burgess & Leigh can proudly boast of their family traditions. During the 1800s, primary production was still for local use and export within the British Empire.

The 20th century brought much change to the pottery industry; changes such as public tastes, accessibility of new markets, improvements in design and production techniques, and the broad affordability of quality goods. Also changing was the makeup of the industry itself. While family potteries flourished in England after the turn of the century, and new entrepreneurs were still beginning their own traditions, large pottery corporations began to take shape. The groundwork for this had been laid in the industrial revolution, as new, more mechanized processes replaced hand craftsmanship with no decrease in quality.

Due to the economic trials of the first half of the 20th century, beginning with the First World War, followed quickly by the Great Depression and then World War II, many small family potteries went out of business completely. It was certainly difficult to invest in technology to modernize a factory when the demand for products had fallen drastically, and the overall economy was suffering. Other potteries merged amicably with another similar or complimentary pottery for survival. These friendly mergers were embraced in the pottery industry, and the number of these sorts of mergers increased in the face of continued economic hardship.

Immediately after WW II, global markets outside the British Empire opened and became more easily reached. Also, consumers demanded new distinctive designs in larger volumes at lower prices. Many potteries were poised to capitalize on this, primarily those with talented artists and modern facilities with large production capacity. Others were not so prepared and the merger/buyout trend accelerated as firms' fought for survival by expanding product offering and capacity. Earthenware firms bought out fine china specialists, or firms producing high-end goods acquired large volume makers of everyday, low cost wares. Many of these purchases were hostile and not friendly, as in the past. Other potteries turned to the equity markets as a way to raise capital to fund factory modernization or acquisitions.

Britain's Clean Air Act of 1956 forced potters to find efficient alternatives to coal burning kilns, a governmental factor requiring additional capital investment by the potteries. In the Staffordshire area the result was a dramatic drop in the number of coal fired kilns from 2000 in 1938 to 550 in 1957. Over the same time, the number of gas fired kilns increased fivefold from 61 to 326, and electric kilns from 16 to an astounding 386.

This shakeout in the pottery industry paved the way for the emergence of the pottery Group or Holding Company, a conglomeration of several independent potteries into one business unit. While less family and tradition oriented, the Group had the benefit of providing capital resources and yet allowing a pottery to remain somewhat independent and preserve the family name, both attractive benefits to a proud family pottery on the brink of failure.

The 1980s added speculation to the merger and buyout trend in the industry. Factories were bought and sold more for their short-term profit potential than for any long-term ceramic goal. The result of this evolution of the pottery industry was that by the 1990s very few family owned potteries remained in Britain. A long-standing exception to this trend is Burgess & Leigh, a thriving family owned pottery that has been in business for over a century and a quarter. However, even Burgess & Leigh eventually stumbled, encountering severe economic hardship in the late 1990s.

Today two major conglomerates dominate the British ceramic industry: the Wedgwood Group and Royal Doulton. There are many similarities

Lord Howe Toby Jug

Cross-legged Toby

Sir John Falstaff Toby Jug by Edward Steele

Pewter Character Jug

Toby biscuit tin (from the collection of Vic Schuler)

Two foot tall outdoor cement Toby

Toby Cigarette Card

between these two companies. Both are long standing firms, each founded by a potter with vision and drive. Both firms have exemplary reputations for high quality, well-modeled products. Both firms have experienced continuous growth, more recently through aggressive acquisitions and diversification. However, there always seems to be room for new entrepreneurial family potters to successfully enter the market. Peggy Davies Ceramics, founded in 1987, and Cortman Limited, started in 1996, are two fine examples of this.

Summary

Since his birth around the mid-1770s, the Toby Jug, or Ordinary Toby, has fathered a long list of characters who have been immortalized in Toby form. Many of these characters were real people; heroes, politicians, royalty or other notable individuals. Other characters were derived from fictional and literary works, poems, songs or simply the potter's imagination. In the authors' estimation, the most popular 20th century jug characters are Winston Churchill, Henry VIII, and Dickens' Mr. Pickwick and Sairey Gamp.

The Toby form itself has evolved from a full-figured pouring vessel into the Character Jug and more recently the figural jug. A staggering variety of derivative Toby forms can also be found, including ash pots, teapots, plates, boxes, salt and pepper shakers, figural steins, liquor containers, and condiment sets to name but a few. Toby's medium has also broadened. Today Toby and Character Jugs can be found produced from glass, leather, wood, brass, other metals, plaster of Paris, and even plastic. While this book addresses only ceramic Toby

and Character Jugs, these other derivative works are occasionally discussed.

Today Toby has become so universally famous that he has a nebula surrounding a red giant star named for him. More down to earth, Toby is the subject of several paintings and has made his way into children's stories, films and television shows. From Bangkok to South Africa, North America to Europe, numerous inns, pubs and restaurants carry the name Toby Jug. The Charrington Toby Jugs and earlier Hoare tobies, produced by about a dozen different potters, have become synonymous with Charrington Ale in pubs around the world. Toby Fillpot is the logo on cans of Charrington ale, and Great Britain also produced a Toby lager beer in honor of the notorious toper. A government building in the London Area is referred to as the Toby Jug site. A British champion bulldog is named Toby Jug. The backstamp of the London retail firm of Hales, Hancock & Godwin included a Toby Jug, as does the logo for an English soccer team.

The remainder of this book is devoted to providing detailed information on 20th century ceramic Toby Jugs and Character Jugs, their makers and history. In spite of all the research and theories which have been painstakingly accumulated to date, and excluding the extensive information available regarding Royal Doulton and Beswick, one of the great ironies regarding the history of the Toby Jug is that, over his past one hundred year life, published information on Toby and his makers has been scant. This is also a period that has experienced possibly the greatest production and diversification in Toby's two hundred plus year history.

Postcard ca. 1920

Two Standing Toby Jugs and a Female Toby made from glass

Collection of brass Character Jugs; top - graduated set of Toby Philpots and Farmer's Wife; bottom - Parson Brown and Capo-di-Monte

Painting of Three Tobies Conversing, circa 1820

Toby
&
Character Jug Makers

A. A Importing
St. Louis, Missouri

Character Jug Name	Height, inches
Colonial Man	5 1/2
Equestrian	5 1/2
King Arthur	5 1/2
Pirate	5 1/2

Toby Jug Name	Height, inches
Mermaid	8 3/4
Monkey	9
Pirate on chest	9
Sinbad	9 1/4

Tankard Name	Height, inches
Pirate	10
Postillion	9 3/4
Servant	9 3/4
Soldier	10

Mark found on Toby Jugs

History

The A. A. Importing Company of St. Louis, Missouri has been importing goods from the Far East for many years. The company mostly purchases goods for resale stateside, but it also commissions goods of its own from overseas manufacturers.

Character Jugs and Toby Jugs

In the 1970s, A. A. Importing commissioned many items from Japanese manufacturers for import and sale in the United States. These items included several Character Jugs, Toby Jugs, and tankards in toby form. The Character Jugs have a crown stamped underglaze in blue ink and originally came with a sticker that read "A. A. Importing Co., St. Louis, MO. Made in Japan".

In addition to this same sticker, the Toby Jugs carry a stamped blue ink mark on the base consisting of a shield emblazoned with a chevron, all under a Staffordshire knot and flanked by a wolf and griffin. This is a very elaborate mark that, without the additional sticker, might make one think the item was of English manufacture. The Mermaid and Monkey are three-quarter bodied jugs.

Character Jugs from left to right: King, Robin Hood and Equestrian

Monkey and Mermaid three-quarter body Toby Jugs

Pirate Toby Jug on left and Sinbad Toby Jug on right

Toby-type tankards with flip tops, from left to right: Pirate, Servant, Postillion, and Soldier

Aidee International Limited
Devon, England

Toby Jug Name	Height, inches
The Doctor #7	9 1/2

History

Aidee International was located in Bovey Tracey, Devon on Newton Road, an industrial street. Aidee began operating in the early 1950s as a ceramics manufacturer. Much of its production was under contract for the toiletry giftware trade. Through the purchase of the local Devon Tors Pottery in 1970, Aidee branched out into high quality limited edition ceramics, with wares being hand crafted and hand-painted. Previously Aidee was a scent bottle customer of Devon Tors Pottery. Aidee eventually demolished the Devon Tors factory and built a perfume factory on the site.

By the 1990s, the firm was a subsidiary of Price's Patent Candle Company. In 1993 Aidee added specialty teapots to its range of products and opened a factory shop where visitors could view production and make purchases. In 1994 the firm went out of business while in the midst of plans to begin conducting factory tours, offer food in a tea room, and open a teapot museum. One of the last known contacts at the firm was a Mrs. Julia Vittle, the Museum and Exhibition Coordinator.

Toby Jug

Aidee International made only one known Toby Jug. By manufacturing a Toby Jug of The Doctor, the main character in the popular British science fiction television serial *Dr. Who*, the firm completed production of a set of seven Toby Jugs. The first six jugs in the series were produced by Bovey Pottery of Devon. It is believed that Bovey Pottery went out of business before the seventh jug went into production, and nearby Aidee was selected to produce jug number seven.

The Doctor was a Time Lord from the far away planet of Gallifrey. The Time Lords were an ancient and powerful race who had the ability to time travel. The Doctor, he never did have a name, fled Gallifrey travelling to Earth in his timeship, TARDIS. The television series chronicles The Doctor's adventures on Earth and time travelling to exotic locations. The Time Lords have the unique ability to regenerate themselves, changing both their physical body as well as personality. The Doctor Toby Jug series depicts the first seven different, regenerated Doctors from the series. These regenerations conveniently occurred at the same time a new actor assumed the role of The Doctor in the series. Each jug was made in a limited edition of 750 jugs. The entire set makes a very interesting collection, and is a "must have" for the serious Dr. Who fanatic. Aidee produced the seventh jug in the series. The Doctor #8 was never produced. Also refer to Bovey Pottery.

The Doctor #7 played by Sylvester McCoy (from the collection of Sharon and Steve Roots)

Albert Stahl
See Jugs Marked by Country of Manufacture under Germany

Alfred Evans
Philadelphia, Pennsylvania

History

Alfred Evans was a retail distributor located in Philadelphia, Pennsylvania. The firm distributed both domestically manufactured goods as well as ware imported from abroad.

Toby Jug

Around the turn of the century, most likely between 1896 and 1910, Alfred Evans sold a Napoleon Toby Jug. These Napoleon Toby Jugs were actually produced by Morris and Willmore of Trenton, New Jersey for Evans. Five sizes of Napoleon in several different colorways have been found.

Those in full colorway (though mostly cream colored body) are consistently found marked on the base "Napoleon Jug Pat. apl. for Alfred Evans, Phila. Pa.". Monocolor jugs are typically not marked and may not have been distributed by Evans, but reached the market through Morris and Willmore itself, or another retailer.

These jugs are highly prized by collectors, with the full colorway versions commanding a higher market value than monocolor. Because it was marketed around the time of President McKinley's reelection campaign, this jug is commonly, but mistakenly, referred to as a McKinley Toby.

Toby Jug Name	Height, inches
Napoleon	9 1/2
	7
	6 1/2
	5 1/4
	4 1/2

Alfred Evans mark found on Napoleon Toby Jugs

Napoleon Toby Jug in 9 1/2", 7", 6 1/2", 5 1/4", and 4 1/2"

Allertons Limited
Longton, England

Character Jug Name	Height, inches	Production Life
Woodrow Wilson	6 1/2	1903-1912
	2 1/2	

Toby Jug Name	Height, inches	Production Life
Ordinary Toby	8	1929-1942
	4 1/2	1929-1942
Snufftaker	6 1/2	1929-1942
	2 1/2	1929-1942
Standing Toby	3 3/4	1929-1942
Squat Toby	5 3/4	1903-1912
	5	1903-1912
	4 1/2	1903-1912
	4 1/8	1903-1912
	3	1929-1942

Toby Jug Derivatives	Height, inches
Standing Toby-salt	
Squat Toby-teapot	
-bank	
-creamer	
-sugar	

Allertons laurel wreath backstamp

Woodrow Wilson Character Jug

History

Allertons Limited traces its roots back to the pottery founded in Longton, Staffordshire in 1860 by Charles Allerton. Charles was previously in partnership with two other gentlemen, operating the Allerton, Brough and Green pottery. Branching out on his own, he purchased the Park Works factory and began Charles Allerton & Sons. Park Works was an existing factory in Longton that was built in 1831. Unfortunately, Charles died in 1863, leaving the firm to his four sons, William, John Bill, Charles Bradbury, and Frederick James.

The sons operated the family business together for a number of years. By 1887, only William and Charles Bradbury remained with the firm. Charles retired in August of 1887. William continued running the factory until 1895 when he passed away and willed the pottery to his two eldest sons. In 1912, Cauldon Potteries purchased Allerton & Sons, changing the name to Allertons Limited.

The firm produced a wide variety of both bone china and earthenware products. Much of the ware was exported to North America with the distributor's name included in the backstamp. Allertons is probably best known for its gilded flow blue and lusterware production. The pottery continued active production under Cauldon until 1942.

The firm used several backstamps over the years. The two most common 20th century marks are of interest here. The Allertons mark used between 1903 and 1912 is a stamped "Allertons" in a banner, with a crown above it and below "England". After Cauldon Potteries assumed control of the business, the common mark became an "A" in a laurel wreath, with "Allertons England" underneath and the phrase "est 1831". This date has no correlation to when an item was actually produced, but simply refers to the founding of the original Park Works factory.

Character Jugs and Toby Jugs

Allertons' made an eclectic group of Character and Toby Jugs. These are of average modeling, but each has unique and interesting attributes that make it desirable to the collector. The Woodrow Wilson Character Jug was a satirical piece made during the height of Wilson's political career. The jug depicts Wilson with a wide-eyed, open-mouthed expression that is not becoming. The jug was made in an earthenware body finished with a sprayed green paint on both the jacket and hat, and in the firm's gilded flow blue finish. The jug is stamped with "Allertons" in a banner.

Allertons' Toby Jugs have porcelain bodies, and were made in its gilded flow blue, with accent decorations in lively greens and yellows, and often with copper luster rims. The Standing Toby and Snufftaker have red hats. Tobies have also been found in an all over copper luster finish. Derivative Squat Toby teapots and sugars were also made. The most common mark found on Allertons' tobies is "A" in a laurel wreath with "Allertons England" underneath. Allertons also produced a version of its Squat Toby Jug on commission for a group in Glendale, California. These are marked "Made in England for the Scottish Village Glendale California." Other jugs may also exist.

Group of Snufftaker Toby Jugs in three sizes

Group of four Squat Tobies and a miniature Standing Toby Jug

Toby Jug derivatives: Squat Toby teapot and creamer, Standing Toby salt, and Squat Toby sugar bowl and bank

Americraft Products
See Grace S. Apgar

Anton Potteries
See Jugs Marked by Country of Manufacture under United Kingdom

Applause Incorporated
Woodland Hills, California

History

Applause is a contemporary maker and importer of gifts, collectibles, figurines, dolls and stuffed toys located in Southern California. Applause plans to continue its successful line of PVC miniature figures, limited edition dioramas, and figural Character Mugs. The majority of its products is produced in Korea and Indonesia, and is imported into the United States.

Character Mugs

Applause produced several series of well-modeled decorative Character Mugs of contemporary subjects. It is more accurate to refer to these as mugs, not jugs, since they lack a spout. The first series was a cartoon character series issued in the early to mid-1990s and licensed by Warner Brothers. The 1990s brought a Star Trek series authorized by Paramount Pictures, and a Dick Tracy series based on the characters of the 1990 Disney movie, *Dick Tracy*, starring Warren Beatty, Madonna, Al Pacino and Dustin

Hoffman. In 1994, a limited edition series based on *Star Trek: The Next Generation* was released.

Most recently, Star Wars mugs were produced in three series, inspired by the twentieth anniversary re-release of the Star Wars movies. The first series consisted of Darth Vader, Stormtrooper, Boba Fett, and C-3PO. Han Solo, the Emperor Palpatine, Tuskin Raider, Gamorrean Guard, and Bib Fortuna comprised the second series. The third series included Chewbacca, Luke Skywalker, Obi-Wan Kenobi, and Princess Leia. The Darth Vader mug was also issued in a striking chrome finish, limited edition version. Applause issued most of these mugs in limited editions; however, multiple limited edition sets were released. The first edition mugs are the more valuable.

The following list is quite extensive, but not complete. Applause also intends to continue with its production of ceramic Character Mugs, so look for more characters in the future.

```
APPLAUSE INC.
WOODLAND HILLS, CA 91365
TM & © 1995 WARNER BROS.
MADE IN INDONESIA
SKU # 29375    CE
MICHIGAN J. FROG
NOT DISHWASHER SAFE
DO NOT MICROWAVE
```

Common Applause backstamp

Character Mug Name	Height, inches	Model Number	Year Issued & Edition Size
Batman	3 7/8	45669	1991
Bib Fortuna	5 1/2	46225	1996
Big Boy	5		
Boba Fett	4 3/4	46045	1995
Borg	5 1/2	45849	1994 Limited Edition of 7500
	5 1/2	45849	Limited 4th Edition of 20000
	5 1/2	45849	1996
Boss	5 1/2	662270	
Breathless Mahoney	5 1/2		
Bugs Bunny	3 1/4	29125	1995
C-3PO	4 3/4	46047	1995
	4 3/4		1997
Captain America			
Captain Janeway	5	42703	1997
Captain Kirk	5 1/2		1994 Limited 1st Edition of 7500
Captain Sisko	5 1/4	42696	1997

Character Mug Name	Height, inches	Model Number	Year Issued & Edition Size
Cardassian	5 1/2	45851	1994 Limited 1st Edition of 7500
	5 1/2	45851	1994 Limited 2nd Edition of 15000
Chewbacca	5	42679	1997
Daffy Duck	3 7/8	29374	1993
	3 7/8	29374	1995
Darth Vader chrome finish	5	46044	1995
	5	42692	1997
	5		1997
Data	5	45853	1994
	5	45853	Limited 3rd Edition of 10000
Dax	5 1/4	42695	1997
Deanna Troi	5 3/4	45958	1994 Limited Edition of 15000
	5 3/4	45958	1994 Limited Edition of 7500
Dick Tracy	5 1/2	662267	
Djali			
Donald Duck		33569	
Dopey			

Character Mug Name	Height, inches	Model Number	Year Issued & Edition Size
Dr. Crusher	5 1/2		1994 Limited Edition of 7500
Dr. Doom	6	42727	1997
Dr. McCoy	5		
Elmer Fudd	5 1/2		
Emperor Palpatine	5	46235	1996
Esmerelda	5	42206	
Flat Top	5 1/2		
Foghorn Leghorn	3 1/2	29181	1994
Gamorrean Guard		46226	1996
Geordi La Forge	5 1/4 5 1/4	45848 45848	1994 Limited 2nd Edition of 15000
Goofy		33504	
Gorn	5 1/4	46127	1996
Grumpy	4	45592	
Han Solo	5 1/4	46227	1996
Incredible Hulk	4 1/2	42729	1997
John Smith		41891	
Kazan	5	42704	1997
Kermit the Frog	5	32453	
Luke Skywalker	5 1/4	42680	1997
Mad Hatter			
Marvin the Martian	3 1/4		1995
Michael Jordan	5		1997
Michigan J. Frog	4 3/4	29376	1995
Mickey Mouse	4	61082	
Minnie Mouse	4 1/4	33568	
Miss Piggy	5 3/8	32533	
Neelix	5 1/2	46129	1994
Obi-Wan Kenobi	5	42681	1997
Odo	5 1/2		1994 Limited Edition of 7500
Pepe Le Pew	4	29158	1993
Phoebus			
Princess Leia	5	42682	1997
Q	5 3/4	46128	1996
Quark	5 5		Limited 3rd Edition of 10000
Quasimodo			
Queen (from Snow White)	4 5/8	45590	
Rafiki	5 1/2	41712	
Riker	5	45960	1994 Limited Edition
Road Runner	3 1/4	29128	1991
Rover Dangerfield			1990
Scar			
Simba			
Speedy Gonzales			1993
Spiderman			
Spock	5 1/2 5 1/2		1994 Limited 2nd Edition of 15000 Limited 4th Edition of 20000
Stormtrooper	4 1/2	46046	1995 Limited Edition
Sylvester			

Character Mug Name	Height, inches	Model Number	Year Issued & Edition Size
Tasmanian Devil	4 1/2 3 5/8	29373	1992 - 1995
Tusken Raider			1997
Tweety	3 1/4	29375	1995
Ursula	4 1/2	41643	
Wiley Coyote	4	29127	1989 - 1992
Woodstock	4	36124	1965, 1972
Worf			1994

Star Wars Character Mugs: top row left to right – Luke Skywalker, Princess Leia, and Han Solo; bottom row left to right – C-3PO, Obi-Wan Kenobi, and Chewbacca

Star Wars Character Mugs: top row left to right – Darth Vader chrome finish and Emporer Palpatine; bottom row left to right – Stormtrooper, Boba Fett, and Bib Fortuna

Disney Character Mugs: top row left to right – Mickey Mouse, Minnie Mouse, Goofy, and Esmerelda; bottom row left to right – Grumpy, Witch, Ursula, and Beast

Warner Brothers' Character Mugs: top row left to right - Daffy Duck, Pepe Le Pew, Foghorn Leghorn, Roadrunner, Marvin the Martian, and Wiley Coyote; bottom row left to right - Michigan J. Frog, Tasmanian Devil, Bugs Bunny, Tweetie, and Sylvester

Jim Henson's Muppet Character Mugs; Miss Piggy and Kermit the Frog

Dick Tracy Movie Character Mugs: top row- Waren Beatty as Dick Tracy, Madonna as Breathless Mahoney; bottom row-Al Pacino as Big Boy and William Fordyce as Flat Top.

Marvel Comic's Spiderman and Captain America Character Mugs

Star Trek Character Mugs: top row left to right - Captain Janeway and Neelix; bottom row left to right - Dax, Captain Sisko, and Dr. McCoy

Star Trek Character Mugs, left to right - Data, Deanna Troi, Geordi La Forge, Borg, and Dr. Crusher

Marvel Comics Incredible Hulk, Batman, and Marvel comics Dr. Doom Character Mugs

Lion King Character Mugs, left to right - Simba, Rafiki, and Scar

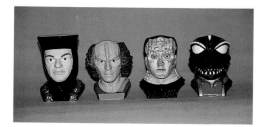

Star Trek Character Mugs, left to right - Q, Kazan, Cardassian, and Gorn

Arcadian China
See Arkinstall & Sons

Arkinstall & Sons Limited
Stoke, England

History

Arkinstall & Sons was a contemporary and competitor of W. H. Goss for bone china. The firm operated at the Trent Bridge Pottery from 1904 until 1925. For the majority of this time, the site was known as the Arcadian Works. Arkinstall was purchased by Robinson & Leadbetter in 1908, but remained an independent operation. Arkinstall was then sold to Cauldon Potteries in 1925. Arkinstall used the trade names "Arcadian" and "Arcadian China" in marking its wares.

Toby Jugs

Like Goss, Arkinstall included high quality, china Toby Jugs as a part of its production, offering both plain and crested jugs. Its crested jugs are of fine translucent porcelain in a basic cream finish with the lip of the jug often gilded. The Ordinary Toby is listed in an Arkinstall catalog as model number 317 in the D series of ware. The Standing Toby is model 515 from the F series.

Arkinstall marked its tobies with "Arcadian". The small Ordinary can also be found with the following special backstamp: "This jug is an exact copy in miniature of the Old Toby jug 'No toungue can tell No heart can think O how I love a drop of drink.'" Wherein the same jug can be found as both plain or crested, the crested versions have a market value at the high end of the range and the plain at the lower Opposite is a complete list of Arkinstall's Toby Jugs.

Toby Jug Name	Height, inches
Black Boy	4
Ordinary Toby	3 3/8
	2 1/2
special backstamp	2 1/2
Sailor	4
Standing Toby	

Arnart
New York, New York

Character Jug Name	Height, inches
Aramis	5 1/8
Captain Henry Morgan	5
Civil War Soldier	5 1/2
Doctor	4 1/2
Izaak Walton	5
Legionaire	4
Long John Silver	4 3/4
Man with pipe handle	4 1/2
Minuteman	4
Pirate	4 1/2
Sailor	4
Sea Captain	4

Arnart Royal Carlton backstamp

History

Arnart is a New York City based importer of goods primarily manufactured in the Far East. The firm was founded in the mid-20th century with A. Tamchin a principal of the firm. Today Leonard Tamchin and Stephen Didimamoff manage the firm.

Character Jugs

In the 1970s, A. Tamchin designed a series of Character Jugs that were produced in Japan and marketed under the tradename of Royal Carlton. Royal Carlton Character Jugs stand approximately five inches tall and are of good quality and detail with decorative handles in the Royal

Doulton fashion, unusual for jugs produced in Japan. These were stamped underglaze with "Copyright A. Tamchin Royal Carlton" and have crossed arrows with the character's name underneath and the number 8070. Aramis is incised "All for one and one for all" across his back. The jugs pictured are direct copies of Royal Doulton jugs, although in a different size.

A four-inch group of Character Jugs can be found marked Royal Crown 2301. Originally these jugs also had a sticker that read "Original Arnart Creation Japan", but these stickers are typically no longer affixed. More recent Character Jug imports by the firm are of lesser quality and are marked "arnart 5th avenue handpainted".

Left to right - Long John Silver, Izaak Walton, and Aramis Character Jugs with Royal Carlton Backstamps

Minuteman on left and Legionaire on right with Royal Crown Backstamps

Arthur Bowker
Fenton, England

Character Jug Name	Height, inches
Henry VIII	3 1/4
Lady Clementine Churchill	4 1/4
Sandy	3 3/4
Scotsman	5 1/4
Winston Churchill	3 1/4

Toby Jug Name	Height, inches
Ordinary Toby	8 1/4
	5 1/2

Arthur Bowker stamped mark

History

Arthur Bowker Pottery operated at King Street in Fenton, Staffordshire from 1948 to 1958, producing bone china ware.

Character Jugs and Toby Jugs

Only a few Arthur Bowker Character and Toby Jugs have been identified, but there were likely more. These are all fine china jugs with very good modeling. These jugs were produced between 1950 and 1958, and are stamped in black ink with the below backstamp.

The Winston and Lady Clementine Churchill jugs were issued in 1951 when Churchill became Prime Minister of England for the second time. The Henry VIII jug appears to be from the same mold as the earthenware version produced by Shaw & Sons under its Burlington tradename. Most likely Shaw & Sons purchased the Henry VIII mold from Bowker when it closed. Henry VIII has his name stamped on the base of the jug in addition to Bowker's regular backstamp.

Henry VIII and Sandy Character Jugs flanking a 5 1/2 inch Ordinary Toby

Winston Churchill and Lady Clementine Churchill Character Jugs

History

Working through a partnership established in 1884 called Capper and Wood, Arthur Wood began his potting career producing a line of teapots. Around 1900, Arthur Wood became the owner of the firm and in 1904 he renamed it Arthur Wood. The pottery enjoyed much success and sustained growth during the early part of the 20th century.

By the 1920s, Arthur Wood was producing hand painted transferware and other typical designs of the period as a part of its expanding business. By 1928 Arthur's son, Gerald Wood, joined the business after graduating from college. The firm's name was again changed this time to Arthur Wood and Son.

Arthur and Gerald branched out into other potting endeavors, forming the Arthur Wood & Son Group to more effectively manage their broad pottery interests. Arthur Wood and Son was the major factory within the Group. Additions to the Group included Collingwood Brothers, renamed Collingwood China, and Winterton Pottery in the mid-1940s. Gerald Wood took over Price Brothers in the early 1930s and merged it into the Group in the early 1950s. Kensington Pottery was merged with Price Brothers in 1962, and Carlton Ware was purchased in 1967.

Around 1970, Gerald took over from his father as Chairman of the Arthur Wood Group. Gerald's son Anthony succeeded him as the Managing Director of Arthur Wood and Son, while continuing his other responsibilities at Price & Kensington. When Gerald died in 1986, Anthony Wood became the Chairman of the Group.

Arthur Wood and Son was successful for many years and was still operating in the 1990s.

Character Jugs and Toby Jugs

The early mark of Arthur Wood and Son has the words "Arthur Wood" in a ribbon across a globe and "England" in a ribbon below it. Later marks replaced the England ribbon with the words "Made in England".

Character Jug Name	Height, inches
Falstaff	5 1/4
Jolly Roger	2 3/4

Toby Jug Name	Height, inches
Ordinary Toby	8 1/4

Artone Pottery
Burslem, England

History

George Lawton and Bob Hardman founded the Artone Pottery at the site of the original Ellgreave Pottery in Burslem, England. The Ellgreave factory dates back to 1921 and at one time was owned by the Wood family, with Wood and Sons operating at the site for a period. When Wood and Sons moved to a new location on Newport Lane in 1946, Artone Pottery leased a part of the Wood's facility and began producing earthenware ceramics. The folklore behind the name of the firm is that it was to be called Manton, a combination of the two surnames; Man from Hardman and Ton from Lawton. However, Mintons voiced an objection based on the close similarity. The pair then settled on Artone, the Art from artist, and the firm's mark incorporated an artist's palette.

George Lawton came from a pottery family. His father worked at Royal Doulton, and he joined his father there as a caster. George left Royal Doulton and, partnering with Hardman, started Artone Pottery to produce ceramic floral items, china, and figures. Both of their wives also worked at the pottery. George's wife was a paintress, and Bob's wife made ceramic flowers by hand. Bob was the primary caster, and George dipped the biscuit into the glazes and fired the kiln. They developed a unique process whereby earthenware and china pieces were fired together in the same kiln at a higher than normal temperature for earthenware. This resulted in ware stronger than typical earthenware products. Tom Davis, a moldmaker at Royal Doulton, worked on a freelance basis for Artone and was known for his work with blocks and cases.

Initial ware focused on floral decorated ceramics that relied heavily on the skills of the two wives. However, these items required a large amount of handcrafting, so there continually was empty space in the kiln. To fill this space and increase production volume, other ceramics were soon added, including Toby and Character Jugs. Over the next several years, Artone expanded its offerings, and produced a variety of pottery ware consisting mainly of giftware and decorative items. Included in these were figures, figural teapots, jugs, bookends, piebirds, bells, and chained ceramic tags for spices and liquors. By the late 1970s, the bulk of the floral production was shipped to Bermuda for the tourist trade there.

Sadly, Bob's wife died unexpectedly. Shortly thereafter he left England and moved to Canada. Bob continued in the pottery business in Canada, managing a casting department for a subsidiary of a British pottery. Jack Lawton, George's younger brother, then left Doulton, and joined George at Artone, replacing Bob Hardman as partner and primary caster. In 1978, George Lawton sold the Artone Pottery to Phil Jaram, who assumed a workforce of fourteen and the lease arrangement at the Ellgreave factory. Jack remained at the factory for a short time until Jaram became established, at which time Jack retired.

Phil enthusiastically took charge of the firm with initial plans to phase out ceramics and convert the factory to glass production. Even though his background was in the glass industry and he had no prior potting experience, Jaram liked pottery and enjoyed challenging himself. He continued making pottery at the factory, producing the same basic Artone ware. He added his own designs over time, tending to select traditional subject matter. Tom Davis freelanced again for Artone under Jaram, working with Jaram to expand some existing lines and create new ones, such as the figural teapot range. Jaram also focused on the United States market and hired Lionel Goldsmith as his representative there. Goldsmith was also the U.S. representative for Staffordshire Fine Ceramics.

Jaram operated the pottery until 1993. At this time, Phil was ready to sell the pottery and retire; however, he had a difficult time finding a buyer. Eventually most of the molds and assets were sold to an importer of Far East goods that shipped Artone's molds and other assets off to the Philippines. So far, no new items produced from these molds have appeared on the market.

After the sale, Jaram destroyed the remaining blocks, cases, and stock on hand. The Ellgreave factory remained vacant for a few years until Cortman Limited leased the facility in 1996 to produce pottery under the tradename LJB Ceramics. By early 1998 the Ellgreave factory was again dormant as Cortman moved to larger facilities nearby.

Artone pottery can be found with two similar, but slightly different, marks. The original backstamp was derived from an artist's palette with the words "Artone England" across it. This mark was used from 1946 to 1978 and was stamped underglaze in green ink. Upon taking over the pottery, Phil Jaram retained the basic backstamp design, but used a smaller version underglaze in black ink from 1978 to 1993. A third green ink mark has been found which is simply "Artone England". The Lawton brothers most likely used this mark before 1978.

Character Jugs and Toby Jugs

From the beginning, Artone produced a large selection of Character Jugs and a smaller number of Toby Jugs, capitalizing on the successes of Royal Doulton and others. Artone jugs are of very good quality, and well convey the human traits of their subject. Some can be found with a musical movement in the base.

From 1978 onward, Phil Jaram continued producing jugs from original molds, and added new characters of his own creation. Jugs added by Jaram include the large and tiny Dickens Character Jug series, and the Scotsman 3/4 body Toby. The tiny Dickens Character Jugs were created from an unpopular series of busts by simply removing the head from the bust model and re-molding the top to create a jug shape. The jugs proved much more popular than the busts.

The Character Jugs based on the seven travelers from the song *Widecombe Fair* were produced exclusively for Mr. Middleweek, the owner of a gift shop in Widecombe who wanted to sell them as souvenirs. Artone produced these jugs for a while, then Middleweek claimed the blocks and cases to continue production elsewhere.

Artone produced the Sherlock Holmes Tiny Character Jug series initially for Widecombe Pottery. This project never reached production with Widecombe, so Phil's son produced a small number of these jugs under the Artone name. The firm also created a Bookkeeper Character Jug as a promotional item for the Bank of England to be sold in the Bank's shop. This jug proved to be not very popular, selling only a dozen or so. The Dr. Bernardo Toby was made in the 1980s to commemorate the generous work of Dr. Bernardo (1845 - 1905), who established a well-known charity for orphan children.

The last series of jugs created by Artone was the Working Man Series. Tom Davis procured the designs for these jugs and produced the blocks and cases. This series consisted of the Postman, Cooper, Newspaper Seller, Blacksmith, Cobbler, Saddler, and Miner. The firm produced very few of these jugs and so they are quite difficult to find today.

In the early to mid-1980s, Phil also was asked

to reproduce small D'Oyly Carte Toby Jugs from molds provided by Mark Bolton. These were produced, numbered specifically, and stamped with another firm's mark. Speculation is that Artone was producing replacement jugs from original Shorter & Son molds for Sherwood

Pottery's D'Oyly Carte limited edition sets after Sherwood closed. Following is a comprehensive list of the Artone jugs produced. An occasional new jug might still surface in the market. Today a collection of Artone jugs can still be assembled at reasonable prices.

Common Artone backstamp

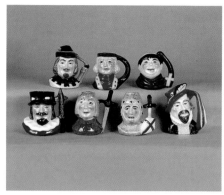

Group of small size Character Jugs: top row left to right - Robin Hood, Maid Marian, and Friar Tuck; bottom row left to right - Beefeater, Crusader, Knight, and Sir Walter Raleigh

Bill Sykes Character Jug in large, small, miniature, and tiny sizes

Small sized Sir Francis Drake Character Jug on left and Captain Patch on right

Farmer's Wife Character Jug in small, miniature and tiny sizes

Fortune Teller Character Jug in small, miniature, and tiny sizes

Granny Character Jug in miniature and tiny sizes

Tony Weller Character Jug in small, miniature, tiny and extra tiny sizes

Robin Hood and Friar Tuck Character Jugs in medium size

Character Jug Name	Height, inches	Production Life
Artful Dodger	5 1 1/4	1978 - 1993 1978 - 1993
Beefeater	3 1/2	1978 - 1993
Bill Brewer	3 1/4 1 3/4	1946 - 1978
Bill Sykes	4 1/2 2 1/2 1 1/2	1946 - 1993 1946 - 1993 1946 - 1993
Bookkeeper		1978 - 1993
Buzz Fuzz	5	1978 - 1993
Captain Ahab	3 3/4	1946 - 1978
Captain Cuttle	1 1/4	1978 - 1993
Captain Patch	3 1/2 2 1/2 1 1/2	1946 - 1993 1946 - 1993 1946 - 1993
Crusader		
Dan'l Whiddon	3 1 3/4	
Dick Whiddon	1 1/2	1946 - 1978
Dr. Watson	1 1/4	1978 - 1993
Fagin	5 1/2 1 1/4	1978 - 1993 1978 - 1993
Farmer's Wife	3 1/2 2 1/2 1 1/2	1946 - 1993 1946 - 1993 1946 - 1993
Fortune Teller	4 2 3/4 1 1/2	1946 - 1993 1946 - 1993 1946 - 1993
Friar Tuck	5 3	1978 - 1993 1978 - 1993
Granny	3 1/2 2 3/4 1 1/2	1978 - 1993 1946 - 1993 1946 - 1993
Harry Hawke	3 1 1/2	
Inspector Lestrade	1 1/2	1946 - 1993
Jan Stewert	3 1 3/4	
Jock	4	1978 - 1993

Josh
  two faced jug
  two faced jug
	
	2
	1 1/2
		
		1946 - 1993
		1946 - 1993

King Harold	5	1978 - 1993
Knight	3 3/4	1978 - 1993
Little John	5 1/2	1978 - 1993
Maid Marian	3	1978 - 1993

Character Jug Name cont.	Height, inches	Production Life
Mr. Beadle	4 3/4 1 1/4	1978 - 1993 1978 - 1993
Mr. Micawber two faced jug two faced jug	5 2 1 1/2 1 1/4	1978 - 1993 1946 - 1993 1946 - 1993 1978 - 1993
Mr. Pickwick two faced jug two faced jug	4 2 1 1/2 1 1/4	1978 - 1993 1946 - 1993 1946 - 1993 1978 - 1993
Oliver Twist	1 1/4	1978 - 1993
Peter Davey	2 3/4 1 1/4	1978 - 1993
Peter Gurney	3	1 3/4
Professor Moriarty	1 1/4	1946 - 1993
Robin Hood	5 1/4 3 1/2	1978 - 1993 1978 - 1993
St. George	3	1946 - 1993
Sarah Gamp two faced jug two faced jug	3 3/4 2 1 1/2 1 1/4	1946 - 1978 1946 - 1993 1946 - 1993 1946 - 1993
Scrooge	5 1/2 1 1/4	1978 - 1993 1978 - 1993
Sherlock Holmes	1 1/4	1946 - 1993
Sir Francis Drake	3 1/4	1946 - 1993
Sir Walter Raleigh	3 3/4	1946 - 1993
Tom Pearce	3 1 1/2	
Tony Weller	4 1/4 3 1/2 1 1/4	1946 - 1993 1946 - 1993 1946 - 1993
Uncle Tom Cobleigh	3 1/2 1 3/4	1946 - 1978
Uriah Heep	5	1978 - 1993
William the Conqueror	4 1/2	1978 - 1993
William Shakespeare		1978 - 1993
Winston Churchill		1978 - 1993

Toby Jug Name	Height, inches	Production Life
Artful Dodger	3	1946 - 1993
Bill Sykes	3	1946 - 1993
Blacksmith	5 1/2	1978 - 1993
Captain Cuttle	3	1946 - 1993
Coachman	5 1/2	1946 - 1993
Cobbler	5	1978 - 1993
Cooper	5	1978 - 1993
Dr. Bernardo	5 5/8	1980s
Fagin	4	1946 - 1993
Fat Boy	2 1/2	1946 - 1993
Highwayman	2 3/4	1946 - 1993
Miner	5 1/2	1978 - 1993
Mr. Pickwick	3	1946 - 1993
Newspaper Seller	5	1978 - 1993
Oliver Twist	3	1946 - 1993
Ordinary Toby	7	1946 - 1978
Postman	4 3/4	1978 - 1993
Saddler	5	1978 - 1993
Scotsman	6 1/4	1978 - 1993
Smoker	2 1/4	1946 - 1993
Swordsman	2 1/2	1946 - 1993
Tony Weller	3	1946 - 1993

Medium size Character Jugs top row left to right: Uriah Heep, Fagin, and Scrooge; bottom row left to right: Beadle, Mr. Micawber, and Artful Dodger

Tiny Character Jugs: top row left to right - Fagin, Artful Dodger, Oliver Twist, Mr. Pickwick, and Bill Sykes; bottom row left to right - Captain Cuttle, Tony Weller, Mr. Bumble, and Scrooge

Widdecombe Fair miniature Character Jugs: top row left to right - Bill Brewer small and tiny, Uncle Tom Cobleigh small, Peter Gurney tiny and small, and Jan Stewert tiny; bottom row left to right - Peter Davey small, Harry Hawke tiny, Tom Pearce small, and Dan'l Whiddon tiny and small

Small Character Jugs of King Harold on left and William the Conqueror on right

Tiny two-faced Character Jugs, top row 2" size, bottom row 1 1/2" size: left to right - Mr. Micawber, Sairey Gamp, Mr. Pickwick, and Josh

Toby Jugs left to right - Cobbler, Saddler, Blacksmith, and Cooper

Tiny Character Jugs, from left to right - Sherlock Holmes, Inspector Lestrade, and Professor Moriarty

Dr. Bernardo Toby Jug

Large Ordinary Toby on left and Coachman Toby Jug on right

Left to right miniature Toby Jugs – Smoker, Swordsman, and Highwayman

Miniature teapots: top row left to right - Postman, Beefeater, Guardsman, London Bobby, and Farmer; bottom row left to right - Fireman, Old Salt, Nurse, and Traffic Warden

Miniature teapots, top row left to right - Oliver Twist and Sailor; bottom row - Mr. Pickwick, Sairey Gamp, Mr. Micawber, and Josh

Salt and pepper shakers: Captain Cuttle and Mr. Pickwick

Toby Jug Derivatives	Height, inches
Beefeater teapot	3
Captain Cuttle salt	2 1/2
Farmer teapot	3 3/4
Fireman teapot	3 1/2
Guardsman teapot	3 1/2
Josh teapot	2
London Bobby teapot	5
Mr. Micawber teapot	2
Mr. Pickwick teapot pepper	2 2 1/4
Nurse teapot	3 1/2
Old Salt teapot	3 3/8
Oliver Twist teapot	2 1/2
Postman teapot	3 1/2
Sailor teapot	2 1/4
Sairey Gamp teapot	2 1/2
Traffic Warden teapot	3 1/2

Ashtead Potteries Limited
Surrey, England

History

Ashtead Potteries Limited registered as a limited company on December 7, 1922. The firm began production with four employees in April of 1923 at the Victoria Works factory, and opened for retail business in 1924. Victoria Works was built in 1900 in the charming village of Ashtead, Surrey.

The pottery was founded by Sir Lawrence Weaver to provide new careers for British World War I disabled veterans. Lady Kathleen Weaver, Sir Lawrence's wife, led the fundraising efforts for the pottery, with help from others including F. Carlyle-Mitchell. The British Red Cross and the Order of St. John provided some of the initial funding. By 1926, Ashtead Potteries employed thirty to forty men in the production of a broad range of earthenware decorative products. The firm also produced a large number of advertising wares on commission.

Several years after it began production, the firm also was sponsored in a fashion by English Royalty, who were always interested in causes oriented toward disabled veterans. Queen Mary and the Duchess of York purchased products from Ashtead at the 1924 Wembley Exhibition. King George V and Queen Mary visited the factory itself the next year and bought more ware. This attention brought sales from other nobles. The Duchess of York created the most publicity for the pottery when she visited in 1928, accompanied by a large press corps. The Duchess praised the pottery for its products, as well as its cause of providing productive careers for veterans. The paparazzi's coverage of the visit was widespread.

Several respected designers and modelers worked for the firm, including Phoebe Stabler, who designed figurines, and artist Percy Metcalfe, one of Ashtead's first modelers. Percy Metcalfe (1895 - 1970) was a sculptor, medal and stamp designer. He created many of the firm's political items, plaques, putto bookends, and animal figures, including the highly sought after Wembley Lion. He also modeled a popular bust of a child in the likeness of one of his own children.

Lawrence Weaver and his wife ran the company together until 1927, when Lady Kathleen passed away. Lawrence continued the factory, but he died a few years later in 1930. Succeeding Weaver as the Director was Sir Stafford Cripps, who, with the assistance of others, continued production. The early 1930s brought severe competition and a poor economic climate that adversely impacted the company. Finally, on January 9, 1935, Ashtead Potteries ceased operations under working manager Mr. Over, and many of the firm's molds were sold to other potteries. The Victoria Works was demolished in 1985.

Of a First Edition Strictly Limited to Five Hundred Jugs bearing the Signatures of the RIGHT HON. SIR DOUGLAS McGAREL HOGG K.C.M.P. And the ARTIST. This Is No. 134.

Percy Metcalfe.

Ashtead backstamp on Douglas Hogg jug

Character Jugs and Toby Jugs

Ashtead Toby Jugs are highly sought after, high quality jugs. Most notable is a group of political tobies designed by Percy Metcalfe and consisting of the Right Honorable S. M. Bruce, David Lloyd George, Lord Halisham Douglas M. Hogg, and two models of Stanley Baldwin. These jugs have a unique design of oversized heads and smaller body features. To enhance their striking appearance, the jugs had a creamware finish, with only the subject's signature in black decorating the jug. These jugs were issued in limited editions of 1000 and marked on the base with the common black Ashtead backstamp and Metcalfe's signature. A Stanley Baldwin jug has also been found in an all over blue glaze.

Also designed by Percy Metcalfe, the Johnny

Samuel Johnson Character Jug

Walker Toby was produced in a limited edition in 1925. The exact quantity is not known, but since each Johnny Walker jug was numbered, and numbers above 400 have been verified, the edition size may have been 500. Around the end of the 1920s, Ashtead Potteries produced several limited edition Toby Jugs specifically for export to North America. Also designed by Metcalfe, the subjects of these tobies were historical figures from United States' history. To date, only the Benjamin Franklin Toby has been identified. Franklin is seated holding the Liberty Bell on his knees. It was also issued in a limited edition with number 77 the highest numbered one known. The only known Ashtead Character Jug was of Samuel Johnson, produced in a solid green colorway as advertising piece for Barclay's Ales, Stouts and Lagers.

Left to right - S. M. Bruce, Douglas M. Hogg, Stanley Baldwin, and David Lloyd George Toby Jugs

Benjamin Franklin Toby Jug

Johnny Walker Toby Jug

Character Jug Name	Height, inches	Production Life
Samuel Johnson	3 1/2	1920s

Toby Jug Name	Height, inches	Model Number	Production Life
Benjamin Franklin	9 1/2		1929 - 1930s
David Lloyd George	7 1/2	J45	1926 Ltd Ed of 1000
Douglas M. Hogg	7 1/2	J47	1926 Ltd Ed of 1000
Johnny Walker	14 1/2		1925 Ltd Ed
S. M. Bruce	7 1/4	J28	1926 Ltd Ed of 1000
Stanley Baldwin	7 1/2	J24 and J25	1926 Ltd Ed of 1000

Audley Porcelain Company
Goldenhill, England

Common Audley mark

Studio 'D'
Sovereign Cottage
Sovereign Lane
Ashley
Market Drayton TF9 4LS

Audley Studio D sticker

History

In the 1950s, Diana P. Capener studied pottery and design, and graduated from the Newcastle School of Art. In the early 1970s, she was a freelance designer and figure modeler at various potteries in the Staffordshire area. In 1975, Diana founded the Audley Porcelain Company as a small home-based studio pottery in the village of Audley.

Diana's initial products were large craftsman figures sold under the tradename Studio D. Small Character Jugs were quickly added to production as a means to fill the kilns for firing.

These were marketed as the Kilnfiller range. In 1978 Diana married Malcolm Keates and he joined her at the pottery. As the business grew, the couple purchased a building from a bakery in Goldenhill, Stoke, and moved the pottery to the site where it still operates today.

Tom Walker joined the thriving pottery as a partner in 1980 and the three operated the pottery as an equal partnership, naming the firm Audley Porcelain Limited. Audley Porcelain's slogan was "Made entirely in Britain by the British." At its peak, the pottery employed fifteen ex-Royal Doulton paintresses on a freelance basis. The paintresses were paid for every dozen decorated pieces. The pottery produced a variety of porcelain, but production shifted toward lighting ceramics and other product lines became a lower priority. The bulk of the firm's production was sold in the UK through direct sales to gift shops and retailers, and in Australia through commissioned agents.

Tom Walker purchased Malcolm Keates' share in the pottery in 1985 and the next year he bought Diana's share. By 1990 Audley was almost exclusively making lighting ceramics. Walker liquidated the firm in May of 1990.

The factory remained dormant until October of 1990, when Tom Walker, the former Audley Porcelain manager, entered into a partnership with John Pointon. The pair reopened the pottery as the Audley Pottery Company, focused solely on lamp base production.

Pointon purchased full control of the firm in 1994 and three years later, sold the business to Village Lighting Limited of Cheshire, Audley's largest customer. The firm is still active today, producing ten to twelve thousand lamp bases per week under the guidance of Managing Director John Pointon. Diana Capener Keates and Tom Walker retain ownership of the physical factory to this day.

Character Jugs and Toby Jugs

Audley's Kilnfiller range of porcelain Character Jugs was modeled over a ten year period from the mid-1970s to the mid-1980s. Audley advertised these as an "endless range for the collector." Diana Capener modeled all of the jugs except for two,

Smoker and Richard Ingrams. The Smoker was the first Character Jug produced by Audley, the mold for which Diana purchased from a local craft store. Fluck and Law modeled the Richard Ingrams jug.

Early examples of Audley's jugs can be found marked with the "Studio D" tradename. Early jugs were shipped in brown boxes with a cellophane window, but the bulk of production came in a dark green box. Later production carried a backstamp of "Audley Staffordshire England" surrounding a co-joined A and P. The original Character Jug block molds and cases remain at the factory today.

The Winston Churchill jug was produced on commission for Blenheim Palace, Churchill's birthplace. In the early 1990s, the Hospital of London ordered production of the Chelsea Pensioner jug in his best hat. The Victorian Railway Guard was made in a limited edition for Isle of Man Productions. The Viking jug was also done on request. Fluck and Law, the founders of the now famous Spitting Image television series, commissioned the Richard Ingrams jug. Richard Ingrams was the editor of Private Eye, a satirical British newspaper.

The four ashtrays preceded their Character Jug counterparts. The jugs were remodeled from the ashtray molds and handles added. The entire collection of small Character Jugs is constantly on display, hanging around the bar at the Coopers Arms, a small pub in Woore, England, only a few miles from Stoke-on-Trent. The photographs are from the collection of Diana Keates. The list of Audley jugs is complete.

Character Jug Name	Height, inches
Baker	3 3/4
Beefeater	2 3/4
Chelsea Pensioner in Best Hat	3 3/4 3
Coachman	3
D.H. Lawerence	3
Fisherman	2 3/4
Guardsman	3 3/4
Highland Piper	3
Huntsman	3
Leprechaun	3
Mad Hatter	2 3/4
Pirate	3 1/4
Pixie	3 1/4
Policeman	3 1/2
Richard Ingrams	9
Robin Hood	3 1/4
Sailor	3 1/4
Scotsman	3 1/4
Smoker	2 3/4
Sweep	3
Teacher	3 1/8
Towncrier	2 1/2
Victoria Railway Guard	3 1/2
Viking	3
Watchman	
Welsh Lady	3 1/2
William Shakespeare	3 1/4
Winston Churshill	3
Yachtsman	2 1/2

Toby Jug Name	Height, inches
Bowls	1 3/4
Cards	1 3/4
Darts	1 3/4
Dominos	1 3/4
Drinker	1 3/4
Snooker	1 3/4

Ashtray Name	Height, inches
Beefeater	4
Chealsea Pensioner	4
Mad Hatter	4
Town Crier	4

Character Jugs top row left to right - Victorian Railway Guard, Teacher, Pixie, and Guardsman; bottom row left to right - Policeman, Sweep, Watchman, and Baker

Character Jugs top row left to right - Winston Churchill, William Shakespeare, D. H. Lawrence, and Chelsea Pensioner in Best Hat; bottom row left to right - Welsh Lady, Leprechaun, Scotsman, and Viking

Character Jugs top row left to right - Chelsea Pensioner, Town Crier, Beefeater, and Mad Hatter; bottom row left to right - Robin Hood, Highland Piper, Sailor, Fisherman, and Smoker

Coachman Character Jug on left and Huntsman Character Jug on right

Tiny Toby Jugs, top row left to right - Bowls, Darts, and Dominoes; bottom row left to right Piper, Cards, and Drinker

Richard Ingrams Character Jug

Diana Capener Keates, founder of Audley Porcelain, with two of her Character Jug creations

Ault Potteries Limited
Burton-on-Trent, England

Toby Jug Name	Height, inches	Production Life
Peace Toby	9 1/4	1919
Tit Bits Toby	9 1/4	1917

Tit Bits Toby on left and Peace Toby on right

History

Ault Potteries opened in 1887 in Swadlincote, near Burton-on-Trent, under the direction of William Ault.

William Ault was born on October 23, 1842 and was orphaned as a young boy. In 1858 at the age of fifteen, he joined Henry Wileman's Foley Pottery in Longton as a packing boy. Ault soon became the warehouse manager at Foley. Through the recommendation of Christopher Dresser, Ault obtained a position with T. G. Green at its Church Works. He moved from there to the Gresley Pottery as the factory manager, but left Gresley in 1867 to study accounting. Upon completing his studies, Ault went to work again for Green as the manager at Green's new factory, Winthorpe Pottery.

It was at Winthorpe Pottery that William Ault met Harry Tooth. Tooth asked Ault to join him in a pottery partnership and Ault agreed. In 1883 the pair left Winthorpe to form their own pottery, Tooth & Ault, with Tooth the artist and Ault the businessman. The partners operated at the Bretby Art Pottery.

William left Tooth & Ault in 1886 to start his own pottery, called William Ault. His factory opened in 1887 and a London showroom was opened in 1888. The factory's primary production was earthenware goods, such as pots and vases. Grotesques were introduced in 1909. Beginning in 1910 the firm began to market some ware as "Ault Faience", or "Ault's English Art Pottery." William experimented with different glaze recipes, winning the gold medal at the 1893 Chicago World Exposition for his efforts. One of the key early artists employed by the pottery was Ault's friend and advocate Christopher Dresser, who created unique designs for the firm between 1891 and 1896, sometimes adding his signature to the firm's mark.

Ault's nephew, Edward Stuart Rowley, joined the firm in 1907 as a manager. He became the Director in 1919. The firm was named William Ault from its founding until 1922 when William Ault retired. Through an amalgamation with the Ashby Potters' Guild that same year, and a partnership with Mr. Tunnicliffe, the company was renamed Ault & Tunnicliffe Limited. The Ashby Potters' Guild focused on increasing exports, but by 1927 the firm had incurred serious debt and Mr. Tunnicliffe left late that year. W. H. Gile, Ault's son-in-law, carried forward on a much smaller scale. By 1937 the debt was completely paid off and the firm reorganized again as Ault Potteries Limited.

Gile retired in 1962 and the Pearson Group took over Ault Potteries. The Pearson Group's history dates back to 1810 with stoneware tile production. Mr. Illsley was the Managing Director of the Pearson Group at the time, which also owned Allied English Potteries. Illsley retired in 1974, the Pearson Group was broken up, and the Allied English Potteries merged with Royal Doulton. The original Ault factory was destroyed in 1976.

Toby Jugs

Ault Potteries produced two solid color glazed Toby Jugs in limited quantities near the end of World War I. The first jug was a standing Toby commissioned by George Newnes for the *Tit Bits* newspaper as a promotional item. The jug depicted a standing man reading a newspaper with the Tit Bits banner. This jug was a prize awarded to winners of the Tit Bits' Dittoes Competition. It is glazed in an all over greenish tan color and dated December 15, 1917.

The second jug is very similar to the first, and was produced to celebrate the end of the World War I, proclaiming peace to the world on Toby's newspaper. The Peace Toby is actually more like a liquor container, having a small opening in the top with an attached rubber stopper and chain. The chain and stopper are rarely found with the jug. This jug is finished in a brown glaze.

Neither jug was produced in large quantities, probably no more than one hundred each, with Peace being the rarer jug. The mark on the Tit Bits Toby is "Ault England Reg applied for," and on the Peace Toby "Ault England 9". The firm used these marks between 1887 and 1922.

Avon Art Pottery Limited
Longton, England

History

Avon Art Pottery was founded in 1930 at the Jubilee Works in Longton, England. The firm produced mainly utilitarian pottery, and used the tradename "Avon Ware" on many of its products. The pottery operated until 1969, when it merged with Elektra Porcelain Company as a part of Elektra's diversification.

The tradename "Avon Ware" appeared in marks of two different styles. A mark with "Avon Ware" in printed block letters inside of a circle, either stamped or impressed, was used from 1930 to 1939. A stamped mark with a script "Avon Ware" in an oval was used from 1947 until the firm ceased production in 1969.

Character Jugs and Toby Jugs

Avon Art Pottery offered a range of Character and Toby Jugs, the Character Jugs based on the popular Dickens' characters. Most of the Avon Ware jugs bear the more recent script mark. Some of the Avon ordinary tobies were produced as advertising items; one, for example, has been found marked with Niagara Falls. Advertising jugs command a slightly higher value in the marketplace. To date, the following jugs have been identified; certainly others exist. In 1998, Bairstow Manor began reproducing Avon's Charles Dickens' Character Jugs on commission from an individual who also supplied the molds. These are slightly smaller and more darkly painted. They are marked simply with a crown above the words "Made in England".

Character Jug Name	Height, inches
Buz Fuz	4 1/2
Fagin	4 1/2
Fat Boy	4 3/4
Little Nell	4 3/4
Mr. Micawber	4 3/4
Mr. Pickwick	4 1/2
Tony Weller	4 5/8
Uriah Heep	4 3/4
Winston Churchill	4 1/2

Toby Jug Name	Height, inches
Ordinary Toby	9
	6 1/2
	5

Common Avon Art Pottery mark

Small size Winston Churchill Character Jug

Character Jugs top row left to right - Fagin, Mr. Pickwick, Little Nell, and Tony Weller; bottom row left to right - Mr. Micawber, Uriah Heep, Fat Boy, and Buz Fuz

Ordinary Toby Jug

Bairstow Manor Pottery Limited
Hanley, England

Fancies Fayre Jugs

Character Jug Name	Height, inches
Mr. Bumble	2 1/4
Robin Hood	2

Toby Jug Name	Height, inches
Ordinary Toby	3 1/2
	2 3/4
	2
	1 1/2
Scottie	3
Snufftaker	2 1/4
	1 3/4
Standing Toby	2 1/4
	1 1/2

Fancies Fayre Backstamp

Bairstow Manor Jugs

Character Jug Name	Height, inches	Production Life
Judy (Kent)	4 1/2	1994–current
Nigel Mansell		1991
Paddy Hobkirk		1992
Punch (Kent)	4 1/2	1994–current
Toby Tavern	7 1/4	1998

Roger and Brenda Bairstow at the Bairstow Manor Pottery

History

The history of Bairstow Manor Pottery dates back to the end of World War II, and an enterprising young potter named Percy Edward Bairstow. Percy apprenticed at Twyford's Limited, making porcelain fittings. Even though he had a promising career with Twyford's, possibly as the future factory manager, Percy left the firm and started his own pottery.

Percy Bairstow founded the Fancies Fayre Pottery at the Britannia Works in Hanley in 1946, producing earthenware goods, figures, and bone china. Around 1951, Fancies Fayre moved to the Mount Pleasant site and, in 1953, Percy renamed the firm P. E. Bairstow & Company. During the 1940s and 1950s, Percy operated the factory in partnership with R. T. Buckley. Bairstow & Company continued using the Fancies Fayre name as a tradename.

In 1958, Percy Bairstow purchased the Trent Walk Pottery in Hanley to continue expanding its production. The Mt. Pleasant site was eventually sold in the mid-1960s. Percy's two sons joined the firm almost as soon as they finished school. One son remained only a short time before relocating to Sydney, Australia, where he did some studio pottery work. The other son, Roger, remained at Bairstow working with his father and learning the business.

In 1979, Percy retired and Roger assumed ownership of the pottery. The firm changed its name to Bairstow Manor Pottery Limited and began marking its wares with the tradename "Manor Pottery." In 1987, the firm moved again to the Blackhorse Works in Hanley. In 1994, the firm obtained old molds from the William Kent pottery on loan from John Kent, William's grandson. The molds had previously been loaned out to several other factories. The terms of the loan specified that all wares produced from these molds be marked with the Kent backstamp.

Bairstow Manor continues operating today at the Blackhorse Works site under the direction of Roger Bairstow and his wife, Brenda. Sadly, Percy Bairstow passed away at the age of 89 in 1997.

The pottery still produces ware with the Kent molds. In 1997 it began potting Carlton Ware on behalf of the new Carlton owner, Francis Salmon. It also launched new ranges of figurines and jugs, and started making teapots on commission for Totally Teapots, the Novelty Teapot Collectors Club organized by Vince and Linda McDonald. The first teapot produced by Manor was a two-sided teapot modeled by Ray Noble, depicting Queen Elizabeth on one side and Queen Victoria on the other.

Character Jugs and Toby Jugs

P. E. Bairstow produced a range of Character and Toby Jugs through the 1950s, sometimes using the tradename Fancies Fayre in script for its backstamp. Included in this offering were a Robin Hood series, and a set of tiny Toby Jugs standing between two and four inches tall. Most of these molds were discarded in the 1960s; however, the tiny tobies are being produced again. Fancies Fayre jugs can be found marked with "Fancies Fayre England" or, from 1949 onward, more simply "Staffordshire F. F. England".

As Bairstow Manor Pottery, the firm again began producing several series of its own Toby Jugs beginning in 1980. Mick Abberly from Royal Doulton designed the first six of the Traditional Series Toby Jugs as well as one from the Dickens series. Grant Palmer modeled others. The Nigel Mansell Character Jug was designed in 1991, the year he won the Formula 1 championship. Paddy Hopkirk was piloted after the Mansell jug, but never released. The Centurion Toby was made on commission for Mansell PLC and is marked "Mansell 1998 Contractor of the Year."

Ray Noble and Andy Moss modeled the Winston Churchill Toby Jugs: Ray the Knight and Lord, Andy the Artist. All three were produced as both figurines and tobies. Toby Taverns, a chain of 250 pubs, commissioned the Toby Tavern Character Jug. Designer Anthony Cartlidge presented the first fifteen jugs to the new manager of the pub chain. Russian Merchant Ltd of Moscow commissioned the Russian Merchant Toby Jug. The following jugs are all marked Manor and include the following series. All are still being produced today.

Traditional Toby Series: Blacksmith, Cavalier, Coachman, Crusader, Friar, Highwayman, Innkeeper, Jester, Medieval King, Puritan, Squire, and Town Crier

Traditional Series: John Bull, Toby Philpot, and mini tobies

Dickens Series: Artful Dodger, Bill Sykes, Fagin, Mr. Bumble, Nancy, and Oliver Twist

Military Series: Montgomery and Rommel

Sporting Series: Bowler, Cricketer, Fisherman, Footballer, Golfer, Lady Golfer, Tennis Player, and Lady Tennis Player

Race Car Drivers: Nigel Mansell and Paddy Hobkirk

Bairstow Manor also purchased other manufacturer's toby molds and began using them in the late 1980s. An Ordinary Toby mold in two sizes was purchased from Carlton Ware in 1988. Others include a Little Old Lady mold from Wood & Sons, and a Toby Philpot mold bought in 1992. The Shorter & Son John Bull mold was purchased at an auction from Wood Potters of Burslem, and put into production in 1996. In 1998, Manor also began reproducing Avon Art Pottery's Charles Dickens' Character Jugs on commission from an individual who also supplied the molds. These are slightly smaller than the originals and marked simply with a crown above the words "Made in England".

The following William Kent molds were consigned in 1994 from John Kent, William's grandson: Cavalier, Squire, Hearty Good Fellow, Jolly Miller, Judy, Mr. Pickwick, Nelson, Punch, and Snufftaker. All but the Snufftaker have been put into production. Other future plans for Bairstow Manor possibly include offering an Australian Series by the turn of the 20th century, consisting of a Prospector, Bushranger, Stockman, and Sheep Shearer. This Series may not be produced however, as demand for Toby Jugs does not result in high production volume.

Common backstamp

William Kent mark used with permission

Toby Jug Name	Height, inches	Production Life
Artful Dodger	4 1/4	1985 - current
Bill Sykes	4 1/4	1985 - current
Blacksmith	6 1/4	1980 - current
Bowler	6 1/4	1988 - current
Cavalier (Kent)	10 1/2 6 1/4	1994 - current 1982 - current
Centurion (3/4 quarter body)	6 3/4	1998 Ltd Ed
Coachman	6 1/4 5 3/4	1980 - current
Cornish Tin Miner	7 1/2	
Cricketer (W. G. Grace)	6 1/4	1988 - current
Crusader	6 1/4	1984 - current
Fagin	4 1/4	1985 - current
Fisherman	6 1/4	1988 - current
Footballer	6 1/4	1988 - current
Friar	6 1/4	1982 - current
Golfer	6 1/4	1988 - current
Hearty Good Fellow (Kent)	11 1/4	1994 - current
Highwayman	6 1/4	1980 - current
Innkeeper	6 1/4	1980 - current
Jester	6 1/4	1984 - current
John Bull (Kent) (Shorter & Son)	10 6	1994 - current 1996 - current
Jolly Miller (Kent)	9	1994 - current
Lady Golfer	6 1/4	1988 - current
Lady Tennis Player	6 1/4	1988 - current

Toby Jug Name	Height, inches	Production Life
Little Old Lady (Wood & Sons)	6 1/4	
Medieval King	6 1/4	1984 - current
Montgomery	6 1/2	1986 - current
Mr. Bumble	4 1/4	1985 - current
Mr. Pickwick (Kent)	7 3/4	1994 - current
Nancy	4 1/4	1985 - current
Nelson (Kent)	11 1/2	1994 - current
Oliver Twist	4 1/4	1985 - current
Ordinary Toby (Carlton) (Carlton)	7 1/2 6 1/2 3 3/4 3 2	1988 - current 1988 - current 1988 - current 1988 - current 1988 - current
Puritan	6 1/4	1982 - current
Rommel	6 1/4	1986 - current
Russian Merchant	9 1/2	1998
Sam Weller	4 1/4	1985
Squire (Kent)	11 6 1/4	1994 - current 1980 - current
Tennis Player	6 1/4	1988 - current
Toby Philpot	8 3/4	1975 - current
Town Crier	6 1/4 5 3/4	1980 - current
Winston Churchill Knight of the Garter Lord Warden of the Cinque Ports Artist	9 1/2 9 1/4 9	1999 1998 1999

Centurion special commission Character Jug for Mansell PLC

Toby Tavern special commission Character Jug

Roger Bairstow at work in the Bairstow Manor Pottery

Top row Original 18th-19th century Toby Jugs, left to right - Squire, Cross-Legged Toby, and Hearty Good Fellow; bottom row Manor reproductions from original William Kent molds, left to right - Squire, Jolly Miller, and Hearty Good Fellow

Top row Original 19th century William Kent Toby Jugs, left to right - John Bull, Mr. Pickwick, Cavalier, and Lord Nelson; bottom row Manor reproductions from original William Kent molds, left to right - John Bull, Mr. Pickwick, Cavalier, and Lord Nelson

Montgomery Toby Jug on left and Rommel Toby Jug on right

Graduated set of three small Ordinary Toby Jugs

Traditional Series Toby Jugs: top row left to right - Squire, Town Crier, and Highwayman; bottom row left to right - Innkeeper, Coachman, and Blacksmith

Traditional Series Toby Jugs: top row left to right - Crusader, Medieval King, and Jester; bottom row left to right - Cavalier, Puritan, and Friar

Cornish Tin Miner Toby Jug

Sporting Series of Toby Jugs: top row left to right - Bowler, Tennis Player, Lady Tennis Player, and Fisherman; bottom row left to right - Cricketer, Golfer, Lady Golfer, and Footballer

Dickens Series left to right - Fagin, Oliver Twist, Artful Dodger, Bill Sykes, Nancy, and Mr. Bumble

Russian Merchant Toby Jug

Pair of Toby Jugs marked Fancies Fayre, 2" and 2 1/4" tall

Old Lady Toby Jug from Wood and Sons mold

Winston Churchill Lord Warden of the Cinque Ports Toby Jug, front and rear view

Winston Churchill the Artist figurine, also made as a Toby Jug

Large and small teapots from Shorter and Son molds

Fancies Fayre Robin Hood and Mr. Bumble Character Jugs flanking a Fancies Fayre Ordinary Toby Jug

John Bull Toby Jug from Shorter mold flanked by Punch and Judy Character Jugs from Kent molds

Ceramic Punch doorstop made from original metal mold

Clay model of Winston Churchill Knight of the Garter figurine, also to be made into a Toby Jug

Large two-sided teapot of Queen Victoria and Queen Elizabeth, both sides shown

Barina Potteries
See Jugs Marked by Country of Manufacture under United Kingdom

Barrington
See Jugs Marked by Country of Manufacture under United Kingdom

Barum
See Brannam Limited

Belleek Pottery Works Company
Fermanagh, Ireland

Toby Jug Name	Height, inches
Young Girl	4 1/2

Young Girl Toby Jug

History

John Caldwell Bloomfield founded the Belleek Pottery in 1858. John inherited the Castlecaldwell estate from his father in 1849. The estate included the village of Belleek, Ireland. With the potato famine recently ended and unemployment high, John wanted to develop productive labor for the folk of Belleek. A geological survey of the area revealed the necessary raw ingredients for pottery production. He recruited two partners, Robert Armstrong, a London architect, and David McBirney, a wealthy businessman, and then successfully lobbied for a railroad stop in Belleek.

Construction of the factory began on November 18, 1858. To launch the factory, Bloomfield hired fourteen craftsmen from the Stoke area to develop products for the firm. Even though the goal of the firm was to produce quality porcelain, its early products were mainly everyday tableware, hospital ware, tiles, and industrial ceramics. The pottery was a success and the firm quickly was exporting products abroad. The first parian ware was produced in 1863, and porcelain products were featured for the first time at the 1872 Dublin Exposition. However, utilitarian pottery remained the staple of the pottery until 1920.

David McBirney died in 1882, followed two years later by Robert Armstrong. Local investors purchased the factory in August of 1884 and continued production as Belleek Pottery Works Company Limited. The firm expanded its porcelain production, creating the ivory colored, thin porcelain it is renowned for today. Production was drastically reduced due to World War I, with exports dropping to virtually nothing by the end of the war.

In 1920, Bernard O'Rourke purchased the factory for ten thousand pounds. Production was again reduced during World War II, but O'Rourke successfully operated the factory through this troublesome period, falling back to primarily everyday earthenware production. After the war, two new kilns were added to the factory and Belleek again focused exclusively on porcelain. Success came quickly as orders from around the world began flooding in.

The business grew steadily for many years. In 1990, Erne Heritage Investments purchased the pottery and has been expanding its markets. Following the acquisition trend in the ceramics business, Belleek purchased Galway Irish Crystal in 1993 and Aynsley China of Stoke in 1997.

Toby Jugs

To date, only one Belleek Toby Jug has been identified. This delicate porcelain jug depicts a kneeling young girl in a flowing dress. It is marked with the first green Hound, Harp and Castle mark, dating it between 1946 and 1955, and has a registration number of 0857.

Beswick Limited
Longton, England

History

The roots of the Beswick family and potting can be traced back to 1840, when Robert Beswick, proprietor of a coal mine, purchased a plot of land in Tunstall. In partnership with John Leese, Robert built a pottery on this site. The pair produced earthenware products until 1857, when the pot bank, known as Churchbank, was leased out to local potters with the provision that the potter use coals from the Beswick mine. In 1891, Churchbank was sold to Thomas Booth, who built it into a respected earthenware manufacturer.

As is well known, this was not the end of the pottery business for the Beswick family. In 1894, James Wright Beswick (1845 - 1920), Robert Beswick's son, took over a lease on a pottery in Longton. This was the beginning of the Beswick pottery that we know today. Over the next three generations, the Beswick factory thrived under the careful business basics practiced by the family, which created intense dedication and loyalty from the employees, and a high degree of community spirit in the surrounding area.

Beswick's early ware included majolica, earthenware, jugs, figures, pots, spittoons, and some special lines in Jet, China and Rockingham finishes. Within only a few years, Beswick built a reputation for quality goods at a fair price. The Gold Street Works, the long term site of Beswick production, was leased in

1898 and described as a very modern factory. Expansion at this site began almost immediately, and volume production continued there for over fifty years.

James Wright's son, John Beswick, joined the firm in 1905. His early contribution to the family business was keeping the company solvent through World War I and the subsequent depression, as well as catering to the vast change in consumer tastes during this period. James Wright Beswick died in 1920, passing on the leadership of the company to his son John. Albert Hallam (1910 - 1976) joined Beswick in 1926 as a mold maker and remained with the firm until 1975. He quickly became head mold maker and modeler, and was regarded as one of the most talented mold makers of his time in Staffordshire. John Beswick passed away in 1934 and his son John Ewart assumed the position of Chairman and Managing Director, becoming the third generation to manage the company.

The early 1930s ushered in an era of new products. The finest modelers and artists available were brought in, allowing Beswick to create a wide range of new products and raise the level of quality. It was during this time that many of the now highly regarded figures and animals were first introduced, along with other product families such as wall masks, Dickens ware, and lines of jugs, vases and novelties. These new products started a growth spurt that was fueled by several takeovers throughout the decade. Beswick became a limited company in 1938.

For jug collectors, an important milestone in Beswick history occurred in 1939 when Arthur Gredington (1903 - 1971) joined the company as a sculptor, having recently graduated with distinction from the Royal College of Art. Gredington's impact at Beswick was immediate with his design of Bois Russell (model number 701), the firm's first naturalistic animal design. Gredington continued to work for Beswick as a modeler and sculptor until his retirement in 1968.

The post World War II era was another time of expansion for Beswick. At the suggestion of John Ewart's wife Lucy, perhaps the most famous Beswick line was launched in 1947, the very popular Beatrix Potter characters, of which Jemima Puddle-Duck was the first of many produced by Beswick. The firm continued to introduce new products and manufacture old favorites for fifteen more years. However, by the mid-1960s, John Ewart Beswick was ready to retire, but had no heir to whom he could pass along the company; no fourth generation. John Ewart eventually sold the firm in June of 1969 to Royal Doulton, as a part

of Doulton's expansion into new areas of ceramic production.

Up to the present, Royal Doulton has kept Beswick focused on its specialties, operating it as the John Beswick Studio. The Studio produces primarily the animal series, maintaining its reputation for quality and attractive ware that the Beswick family had created over three generations. Under Studio Manager Graham Tongue, who joined the firm in 1966, the John Beswick Studio is also responsible for production of Royal Doulton's Character and Toby Jugs at the Beswick Longton Works.

Character Jugs and Toby Jugs

Beswick produced its first Character Jug, Tony Weller, in 1935 to capitalize on the growing popularity of Royal Doulton's jugs. Following Tony Weller, other captivating figures from the pages of Dickens' novels soon appeared. The Dickens jugs were also produced in related derivative pieces such as creamers, sugars, salt shakers, pepper shakers, teapots, and preserves.

Three successive modelers were responsible for the majority of Beswick's Character and Toby Jugs. Mr. Watkins was the first, designing the line of large Dickens Character Jugs starting with Tony Weller and through Scrooge. He also created the Winston Churchill Toby Jug in 1941, an exceptional tribute to an exceptional man, as well as the Patriotic Jug Series. The Winston Churchill Toby Jug has a detachable crown that is formed by a part of Winston's bald head, and a scroll that reads "We shall fight on the beaches, on the landing grounds, in the fields and in the hills. We shall never surrender." This jug is often found missing its crown, detracting substantially from its value.

Arthur Gredington modeled the line of traditional Toby Jugs, selecting traditional Toby Jug subjects and recreating them true to their original form. He also designed the Dickens' teapot, sugar and creamer sets, and many of the derivative items. Albert Hallam produced the final series of Dickens Character Jugs in 1965, this time creating characters not previously produced by Royal Doulton. Hallam also designed the final two Beswick Character Jugs in 1967, large versions of Henry VIII and Falstaff. Hallam's designs had only a brief production life as Royal Doulton terminated production of all Beswick jugs in 1973. It is interesting that, after purchasing Beswick, Royal Doulton turned over design and production of its Character and Toby Jugs to the Beswick studio.

A unique contribution of Beswick to jug

collecting was the production of the Patriotic Character Jug Series: Air Force, Navy and Old Bill. These were produced during World War II when patriotism was at its height in England and the United States. The Tony Weller and Mr. Micawber Character Jugs were re-modeled by Graham Tongue in 1969, but were only produced for a few short years. There are clear differences in design and coloring between the original designs and the new versions.

Beswick produced three promotional advertising jugs on commission. The Lord Mayor Toby Jug was an advertising jug for Bass Ale, designed by Albert Hallam in 1961 before the firm's incorporation into Royal Doulton. This jug had only limited production, but was re-released in 1985 by Royal Doulton. The Double Diamond Character Jug was produced as a promotional item for Double Diamond Brewery, and comes with a hat as the attached lid. Other Double Diamond items were produced including a teapot. These were designed by Albert Hallam and Jim Hayward in

1958, and produced until 1970. Peter, Griffin, Woodward Inc., a United States department store, commissioned the PGW Colonel Character Jug in 1967 to celebrate its 35th anniversary.

Lastly, under Royal Doulton's direction, a series of six Peter Rabbit Character Jugs was designed and sold by Beswick between 1989 and 1992. While these were not commercially successful at the time, they have become quite collectible today. The characters produced were Peter Rabbit, Jeremy Fisher, Old Mr. Brown, Mrs. Tiggy-Winkle, Tom Kitten, and Jemima Puddle-Duck.

Beswick's jugs are marked rather simply with "Beswick England" stamped on the base, typically forming a circle, and with the model number incised. All Beswick jugs are highly sought after today, with the Toby Jugs, patriotic jugs, and Peter Rabbit series being especially scarce. The Peter Rabbit jugs may also be found with a Royal Albert backstamp. Following is a complete list of Beswick jugs and derivatives.

Winston Churchill Toby Jug with removable pate

Mr. Micawber Character Jug, original design with green hat left and black hat center, remodeled design on right with eyes looking to the right

Scrooge Character Jug on left and Sairey Gamp Character Jug on right

Tony Weller Character Jug, original design with green hat left and yellow hat center, remodeled jug on right with whip touching his hat

Character Jug Name	Model Number	Height, Inches	Production Life
Air Force	737	4 3/4	1939 - 1954
Barnaby Rudge	1121	4 1/2	1948 - 1969
Betsy Trotwood	2075	5	1966 - 1973
Captain Cuttle	1120	4 1/2	1948 - 1973
Double Diamond	1672	6 1/4 small	1960 - 1965
Falstaff	2095	6 3/4	1967 - 1973
Henry VIII	2099	7	1967 - 1973
Jemima Puddle-Duck	3088	3 1/4	1988 - 1992
Jeremy Fisher	2960	2 1/2	1987 - 1992
Little Nell's Grandfather	2031	5 3/8	1965 - 1973
Martin Chuzzlewit	2030	4 3/4	1965 - 1973
Mr. Bumble	2032	4 7/8	1965 - 1973
Mr. Micawber re-modeled creamer	310 310 674	8 1/4 8 1/4 3 1/2	1935 - 1973 1969 - 1973
Mr. Pecksniff creamer	1117	3 1/2	1948 - 1973
Mr. Pickwick creamer	1119	3 1/4	1948 - 1973
Mr. Vardon creamer	1204	3 1/4	1950 - 1973
Mrs. Tiggy-Winkle	3102	3	1988 - 1992
Navy HMS Wink	736	4 3/4	1939 - 1954
Old Bill	735	4 3/4	1939 - 1954
Old Mr. Brown	2959	2 3/4	1987 - 1992
Peter Rabbit	3006	3	1988 - 1992
PGW Colonel		5 1/8	1967
Sairey Gamp	371	6 1/2	1936 - 1973
Scrooge	372	7	1936 - 1973
Tom Kitten	3103	3	1988 - 1992
Tony Weller re-modeled	281 281	6 3/4 6 3/4	1935 - 1973 1969 - 1973

Henry VIII large Character Jug on left and Falstaff large Character Jug on right

Pair of advertising jugs; Lord Mayor Toby Jug for Bass Ale on left and PGW Colonel Character Jug on right

Teapots; top row left to right - Dolly Varden and Sam Weller, bottom row two colorways of Sairey Gamp flanking Peggoty

Old Bill Character Jug alongside Japanese reproduction (from the collection of Bill Cumming)

Old Bill, Navy (H. M. S. Wink), and Air Force Character Jugs

Toby Jug Name	Model Number	Height, Inches	Production Life
Lord Howe on barrel	1114	3 1/2	1948 - 1966
Lord Mayor	1741	8 5/8	1961 - 1967
	1741	8 5/8	1985 - current
Martha Gunn	1113	3 1/2	1948 - 1966
Midshipman	1112	5 1/4	1948 - 1973
Toby Philpott	1110	8	1948 - 1973
	1111	6 1/2	1948 - 1973
Winston Churchill	931	7	1941 - 1954

Small Character Jugs; top row left to right - Mr. Bumble, Betsy Trotwood, and Martin Chuzzlewit; bottom row left to right - Little Nell's Grandfather, Barnaby Rudge, and Captain Cuttle

Peter Rabbit miniature Character Jugs; top row left to right - Miss Tiggy-Winkle, Jemima Puddle-Duck, and Tom Kitten; bottom row left to right - Old Mr. Brown, Peter Rabbit, and Jeremy Fisher

Double Diamond Advertising ware; large Character Jug on left and teapot on right

Laurel and Hardy three piece cruet set

Large and small Toby Philpott Toby Jugs

Left to right Lord Howe, Midshipman, and Martha Gunn miniature Toby Jugs

Lord Howe and Martha Gunn miniature Toby Jugs in special colorways

Wall Masks	Model Number	Height, Inches
Indian	282	7 1/2 6 3/4
Jester	279	5 1/4
Mr. Micawber	280	9
Tony Weller	274	7 1/2

Indian wall mask

Mr. Micawber wall mask

Tony Weller wall mask

Sugar Bowls	Model Number	Height, Inches	Production Life
Mrs. Varden	1205	3	1950 - 1973
Pecksniff	1129	3 1/2	1948 - 1973
Pickwick	1198	3 1/4	1948 - 1973
Tony Weller	673	2 3/4	1939 - 1973

Preserve Pots	Model Number	Height, Inches	Production Life
Sairey Gamp	1206	3	1950 - 1973
Tony Weller	1207	3	1950 - 1973

Cream pitcher and sugar bowls; top row left to right - Mr. Micawber, Tony Weller, Mr. Varden, and Mrs. Varden; bottom row left to right Mr. Pecksniff pair and Mr. Pickwick pair

Teapots	Model Number	Height, Inches	Production Life
Dolly Varden	1203	6 1/4	1950 - 1973
Double Diamond	1517	8	1958 - 1970
Peggoty	1116	6	1948 - 1973
Sairey Gamp (2 colorways)	691	5 3/4	1939 - 1973
Sam Weller	1369	6 1/4	1955 - 1973

Tony Weller and Sairey Gamp preserves jars; Mr. Micawber and Sairey Gamp salt and pepper shakers

Tony Weller and Mr. Micawber sugar and creamer flanking copies in treacle glaze (from the collection of Bill Cumming)

Busts "Thunderbirds"	Model Number	Height, Inches	Production Life
Brains	3339	4	1992
The Hood	3348	4	1992
Lady Penelope	3337	4	1992
Parker	3346	4	1992
Scott Tracy	3344	4	1992
Virgil Tracy	3345	4	1992

Cruet Set	Model Number	Height, Inches	Production Life
Laurel & Hardy cruet	575	4 1/2	1938 - 1969
Mr. Micawber salt shaker	690	3 1/2	1939 - 1973
Sairey Gamp pepper shaker (2 colorways)	689	2 1/2	1939 - 1973

Set of Thunderbird busts, top row left to right - Scott Tracy, The Hood, and Virgil Tracy; bottom row left to right - Parker, Lady Penelope, and Brains

History

Lawrence A. Birks, Charles Goodfellow, who came from a family of potters, and Adolphus Rawlins, a financial advisor, founded the firm of Birks, Rawlins & Company in 1898. The company operated at the Vine Pottery in Stoke and was originally named L. A. Birks with Lawrence Birks serving as the Managing Director. Before founding this pottery, Birks apprenticed at the Minton factory under the renowned M. L. Solon in the 1870s and became an internationally known pate-sur-pate artist. The firm produced a variety of fine china and porcelain, including the popular crested ware, but really specialized in pate-sur-pate production. In 1900, the name changed to Birks, Rawlins & Company.

Frederick Rhead worked at Birks, Rawlins briefly from 1910 until 1912, when he left to become the Art Director for Wood and Sons. At the 1911 International Exhibit in Turin, the firm displayed pate-sur-pate wares decorated by Frederick Rhead and Adolphus Rawlins. Also on display were tube lined porcelain pieces designed by Frederick's daughters, Charlotte and Dollie Rhead.

The pottery used a variety of tradenames on its products including Carlton China, Savoy China and Birks China. Savoy China was the tradename used for the firm's crested novelty products. The pottery was purchased by Carlton Ware Limited in 1932.

Toby Jugs

Birks, Rawlins & Company produced full colored, china Toby Jugs under the tradename Savoy China in the 1920s and 1930s. More jugs than those listed likely exist.

Toby Jug Name	Height, inches
Bagpiper	5
Ordinary Toby	2

Blue Ridge China
See Southern Potteries

Bovey Pottery
Devon, England

History

Bovey Pottery dates back to the Bovey Tracey Pottery that operated in Bovey Tracey, Devon from 1842 until 1894. After the demise of Bovey Tracey, the production at the factory resumed in 1894 as Bovey Pottery. A wide range of earthenware products, including the signature cottage ware and motto ware the Devon region is famous for, were produced for many years.

The Bovey Pottery firm closed in 1957. However, production at the factory continued, probably on a much smaller scale. The Bovey Pottery name continued to be used, now as more of a tradename.

Toby Jugs

One of the commissioned projects undertaken by someone working at the Bovey Pottery was the production of a series of Toby Jugs based on the *Dr. Who* British television series. For a few years in the early 1980s, the pottery produced the first six in a series of seven Toby Jugs of The Doctor, the main character in the popular and long-running British science-fiction television serial, *Dr. Who*. The Doctor was a Time Lord from the far away planet of Gallifrey. The Time Lords were an ancient and powerful race who had the ability to time travel. The Doctor, who never did have a name, fled Gallifrey travelling to Earth in his timeship, TARDIS. The television series chronicles The Doctor's adventures on Earth and time travelling to exotic locations. The Time Lords have the unique ability to re-generate themselves, changing their physical body as well as personality.

The Toby Jugs depict the seven different, regenerated Doctors who appeared in the television series. These re-generations conveniently occurred at the same time a new actor assumed the role of The Doctor in the series. The Doctor Toby Jug series was designed and sculpted by Peter Rogers with each Doctor having a detachable hat. Each jug was made in a limited edition of 750 and priced at 75 pounds. Bovey Pottery manufactured the first six jugs in the series, but must have closed before the seventh jug was made. Aidee International produced the seventh jug in the series.

Interestingly enough, there have been eight different actors who portrayed The Doctor, but only seven jugs produced. Could the eighth jug

Toby Jug Name	Height, inches
Ordinary Toby	5 1/2
The Doctor #1	9 1/2
The Doctor #2	9 1/2
The Doctor #3	9 1/2
The Doctor #4	9 1/2
The Doctor #5	9 1/2
The Doctor #6	11

Ordinary Toby Jug

depicting the actor Paul McGann never have been intended, or could the demise of first Bovey Pottery and then Aidee have eliminated production plans for the eighth jug? The entire set makes a very interesting collection, and is a "must have" for the serious Dr. Who fanatic.

See also Aidee International.

Bovey Pottery also produced an Ordinary Toby.

Photos of The Doctor jugs are from the collection of Sharon and Steve Roots.

The Doctor #6 portrayed by Colin Baker

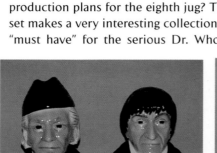

The Doctor #1 portrayed by William Hartnell on left and The Doctor #2 played by Patrick Troughton on right.

The Doctor #3 portrayed by Jon Perthee on left and The Doctor #4 played by Tom Baker on right

The Doctor #5 portrayed by Peter Davison

Brannam Limited
Devon, England

History

Thomas Backway Brannam (1815 - 1897) was born into a family with potting history. Ancestors on his mother's side of the family, the Backways, were potters in Bideford. Thomas apprenticed at the Cleavehouse Potteries in Bideford. In 1837 he left Cleavehouse and founded his own pottery on Litchdon Street in Barnstaple in partnership with John Rendell. In 1848, Thomas assumed Rendell's lease on a pottery in North Walk, and in 1853 he purchased the Litchdon Street facility outright. Production consisted mainly of everyday wares, brick, and tile. However, Thomas was accomplished in sgraffito pottery, one of his pieces winning a medal at the 1851 Great Exhibition.

Charles Hubert Brannam (1855 - 1937), Thomas' only son, was trained by his father in the production of pottery. He further developed his education through a variety of studies and occupations. In 1879, Charles began creating his own pottery under the name Brannam Limited. In 1881 he also took over management of the Litchdon Pottery from his father upon Thomas' retirement.

Charles soon developed an art pottery department, recruiting skilled artists and designers. One of these early designers was Owen Davis, a Barnstaple native, who happened upon Brannam's studio pottery in 1881 quite by accident, where he saw a pot with one of his drawings on it. Queen Victoria placed an order with the pottery in 1885 that greatly raised interest in the firm's products. Production at this time included jugs, vases and toilet sets. Much of the art pottery carried the tradename "Barum Ware". Barum was an early Roman name for Barnstaple. In 1885, the tradename changed to "Royal Barum Ware".

At the beginning of the twentieth century, Brannam's products were distinguished by their colorful slips, carving, and sgraffito decoration of birds, fish and flowers. A key designer working with Brannam was F. Carruthers Gould, a renowned British political cartoonist. Gould would later design the famous World War I series of Toby Jugs for A. J. Wilkinson.

Although Charles took an active interest in the pottery until his death in 1937, he turned over the family pottery to his two sons, Charles William Brannam and John (Jack) Woolacott Brannam, in 1913. In 1914, the firm was renamed C. H. Brannam and Sons and became a limited partnership. The brothers faced the difficult challenge of managing the firm through the Great Depression and then World War II. Several exciting new glazes were introduced during this time, including a radioactive orange glaze. Joe Vernon, a respected designer formerly of the Liverton Art Pottery, where he designed Toby and Character Jugs, and Stoke-on-Trent, came to the Brannam factory and worked, there with his sons and daughter in the 1930s. After World War II ended, Jack's son Peter led an effort to modernize the factory and eventually ended up owning the pottery.

The firm was owned and operated by four generations of the Brannam family through 1979. Peter retired that year and sold the pottery to Candy Tiles of Newton Abbot. Candy Tiles grew out of the Brannam facility, and in 1990 the pottery moved from the Litchdon Pottery to a new factory at the Roundswell Industrial Estate. The old Litchdon factory still remains today, most recently being used as a health center.

Character Jugs and Toby Jugs

Brannam produced a variety of Character and Toby Jugs in the early twentieth century. Brannam's jugs are typically marked with an incised "Brannam" or "Barum" or both, and sometimes include a date. The firm may have produced additional jugs to those listed here.

The President Kruger jug was modeled by F. Carruthers Gould and shows an elderly Kruger smoking a pipe with a boar's head for the handle. Joe Vernon's daughter credits the design for the Winston Churchill Toby Jug to her father Joe Vernon; however, this has not been substantiated. The Ordinary Toby jug came in solid colors of browns or less commonly oranges. It is often referred to as a Blackamoor due to its facial features. A full colored version was also produced.

Character Jug Name	Height, inches	Production Life
Franklin D. Roosevelt		1930s
President Kruger (of S. Africa)	6 1/4	1930s

Toby Jug Name	Height, inches	Production Life
Admiral Beatty Lloyd George Lord Kitchner Ordinary Toby	9 1/2	1909 - 1920
	6	1909 - 1920
	3	1909 - 1920
Squat Toby	3 3/4	
	3	
Winston Churchill	7 3/4	1941 - 1950

Winston Churchill Toby Jug

Large and small Ordinary Tobies Flanking two small squat tobies and illustrating four different colored glazes

Bretby Art Pottery
Derbyshire, England

History

Two men, who together and separately made significant contributions to the British potting industry, founded the Bretby Art Pottery. Henry Tooth was born in Newport in 1842. In the 1860s, he worked with a London architectural firm decorating buildings. From there he moved to Derbyshire, eventually ending up working for Thomas G. Green in his Winthorpe Pottery.

William Ault worked at several potteries in the mid-1800s. His first position was at Linthorpe Pottery through the recommendation of Christopher Dresser. Ault then went to work for Thomas G. Green at his Church Works factory. He moved from there to Gresley Pottery, but left Gresley in 1867 to study to become an accountant. Upon completing his studies, Ault

went to work again for Green at his new factory, Winthorpe Pottery, as the manager.

It was at Winthorpe Pottery that William Ault met Harry Tooth. Tooth asked Ault to join him in a pottery partnership and Ault agreed. In 1883 the pair left Winthorpe to form their own pottery, Tooth & Ault, with Tooth the artist and Ault the businessman. The factory in which the pair operated was the Bretby Art Pottery, which was registered as the pottery's tradename in 1884 and later became the firm's legal name. Artist and modeler George Mellor joined the firm from Linthorpe Pottery through the urging of Tooth. The partnership however was short lived and in 1886 William Ault left to found a pottery on his own; see Ault Potteries, Limited.

In 1887 Henry Tooth brought in John Downing

Character Jug Name	Height, inches
Edward VIII w/ music box George VI w/ music box	4 1/4

Toby Jug Name	Height, inches
Ordinary Toby	6 3/4

Edward VIII Character Jug

Wragg as his new partner and continued operating as Tooth & Company. The firm made a wide variety of art pottery and other ware, including figures, busts, vases, jugs, umbrella stands, jardinieres, and tea sets. Along with its wonderful designs and models, unique glazes were also created at the firm.

Wragg left the firm in 1912 and Henry's son W. E. Tooth became his new partner. The firm now operated as H. Tooth & Company Limited. Henry died on September 19, 1918 and the family continued operating the pottery.

In 1932 the Tooth family sold the pottery to Mr. Parker, who renamed it Bretby Art Pottery. Parker continued producing the existing ware and added novelty items to production in the 1930s. During the Second World War, the factory was closed between 1940 and 1945 and used by the Ministry of Food as a warehouse. The Bretby Art Pottery reopened in 1946, but was limited by the government to export production only. In 1947, all restrictions were lifted, and by 1951 the firm was producing over two thousand different items. Mr. Parker's sons continued production at the firm.

Character Jugs and Toby Jugs

The Edward VIII Character Jug was produced around 1937 in preparation for Prince Edward's coronation as King, an event that never happened. It had an E shaped handle and came in a semi-matte cream or an all over green finish. The George VI character jug was made at the same time. Both jugs were fitted with a musical movement. The George VI jug plays God Save the King. In November 1938, Neville Chamberlain presented a creamware George VI jug to Adolf Hitler. A photograph taken of Hitler's office shortly after the fall of the Third Reich shows the George VI jug displayed on Hitler's desk.

The Ordinary Toby was produced over a long period of time.

Brush-McCoy Pottery
See Brush Pottery

Brush Pottery
Zanesville, Ohio

Davy Crocket Toby Jug

History

George Brush founded his first pottery on December 10, 1906. Unfortunately the factory was completely destroyed by a fire on November 26, 1908. Brush then invested significantly in the J. W. McCoy Pottery Company in 1909, becoming its General Manager. Through a proposal by Brush to the Board of Directors, a new company named Brush-McCoy Pottery was spun off from J. W. McCoy on December 13, 1911. Brush-McCoy produced McCoy wares and added many new art pottery products of its own. Much of the pottery by Brush-McCoy is unmarked.

In 1925, the McCoy family sold its interest in the Brush-McCoy Pottery and focused fully on Nelson McCoy. On December 9, 1925, Brush-McCoy was renamed Brush Pottery. The pottery operated through World War II, but production levels were cut in half by 1945 due to the lack of gas to fire the kilns. New equipment was installed in 1946 and the pottery introduced a large number of new products, including its now widely sought after cookie jars.

Character Jugs and Toby Jugs

Brush Pottery produced a small number of Character and Toby Jugs. The Sarreguemines-like jug is marked "Brush USA #88A", and can be found decorated in gold highlights. Introduced in 1956 were sets of nicely modeled matching cookie jars and mugs, or Toby Jugs. The known Toby Jugs from these sets are listed a few others might also exist.

Character Jug Name	Model Number	Height, Inches
Santa		
Sarreguemines style	88A	7 1/2

Toby Jug Name	Model Number	Height, Inches
Davy Crockett		5
Little Boy Blue	K250D	5
Little Red Riding Hood	K240D	5
Peter Pan	K230D	4 1/2
Peter Peter Pumpkin Eater		5

History

Burgess & Leigh grew out of another pottery, Hulme & Booth, which was founded in 1851. Retirements of some of the principals of Hulme & Booth in 1862 resulted in the firm resting in the hands of three gentlemen: Frederick Rathbone Burgess, William Leigh, and Frederick Lownds Good. The company was soon renamed Burgess, Leigh & Company, and operated out of the Hill Pottery Works from 1868. Edmund Leigh joined his father at the firm in 1867 at the young age of 13. Edmund quickly became influential in the firm, and by the age of 18 he was representing the pottery in London and throughout Britain. Frederick Good retired in 1877, and the pottery's name was again changed, this time to the familiar Burgess & Leigh.

From the start, the company catered to the local demand for earthenware products, producing bowls, jugs, tea ware, and kitchen items. The credo of the pottery was high quality in every step of production. Burgess & Leigh expanded quickly as demand for its ware grew, moving to larger facilities once owned by Samuel Alcock, and purchasing some of Alcock's best known molds and the rights to its beehive mark.

Fueled by continued growth, Edmund Leigh led the construction of the Middleport Pottery in 1888, using state-of-the-art equipment. In 1889, Burgess & Leigh moved into its new factory in Middleport, a rural district of Burslem, which is where the firm still operates today. This site is situated on a small canal that was critical for transportation of raw material to the pottery and finished goods to market. This seven-oven facility became a model of the modern factory in Staffordshire.

From 1900 into the 1920s, the bulk of the pottery's production was dedicated to toilet sets. In 1938, the firm's seven bottle ovens consumed one hundred tons of coal every seven days, turning thirty-five tons of clay into finished ware weekly. The firm used the bottle ovens until 1965, when they were finally replaced with more modern electrical kilns.

With the death of William Leigh in 1889, Frederick Burgess continued the pottery with his and William's sons involved as partners. The sons, Edmund Leigh and Richard Burgess, carried on the daily activities of the pottery. Through the passing of Frederick Burgess in 1898, and Richard in 1912, Edmund Leigh assumed sole control of the company and continued managing design and production with his three sons, William, Kingsley and Edmund Denis Leigh. In 1919, the firm became a private limited company with the first directors being Edmund and his three sons.

Burgess & Leigh's Middleport loading dock where in earlier times large quantities of raw materials such as clay and coal were unloaded, and finished goods were loaded for their journey down the English canal system and to market.

Edmund Leigh passed away in 1924 and control of the firm passed to his sons. Edmund Leigh had become well known and respected as a master potter with great vision, tremendous energy and an engaging personality. Not only did he develop a very successful pottery, but he was also very active in the pottery trade, leading the formation of the Pottery Manufacturer's Federation, and other social and civic concerns. In his honor, Burgess & Leigh developed the Edmund Leigh Gallery in the 1990s, a series of reproduction antique blue and white plates from Edmund's personal collection. For the company's centenary, it also produced a commemorative figural relief jug depicting Edmund.

The noted artist Charlotte Rhead joined Burgess & Leigh in 1926 from Wood and Sons, and designed a new line of pottery marked Rhead Ware. This was a continuation of her work at Wood and Sons. This new ware used a time consuming production method called tube lining to decorate the pottery, resulting in a unique richness. Charlotte had learned this process from her father, Frederick Rhead. Charlotte left Burgess and Leigh after a number of years for a position with Crown Ducal.

In 1925, Ernest T. Bailey was an apprentice modeler who was given freedom to explore new novelty items for Burgess & Leigh, resulting in a series of novelty jug lines. Perhaps the most famous were the Flower Jugs with animal handles. Other series included the sporting jugs, animal jugs and Art Deco Lozenge jugs. Some of the Alcock molds were also resurrected to produce a line of Victorian jugs.

William, Kingsley and Edmund Denis Leigh continued to operate the firm. They brought the fourth generation of the Leigh family onto the Board of Directors, Edmund Robert Leigh and Denis Barry Leigh, who joined the firm in 1938. Denis Barry Leigh volunteered for duty with the armed services and in November of 1939 entered the British Army at the age of 20. Barry served for one and one-half years in Italy, supporting the British 8th Army and American 5th Army. Ernest Bailey was conscripted into the British Navy in 1942, serving his country during World War II until 1946. Bailey's service to his country inspired him to design many figures and jugs of heroes and leaders of the war after he returned. Bailey remained at the firm until retiring in 1980. He passed away in the early 1990s.

World War II brought much change to the pottery industry. Before the war, England was largely a manufacturer, and its colonies agricultural. England swapped goods with its colonies for food. During the war, this trade did not continue sufficiently. Therefore, England started an agricultural economy with government subsidies, and the colonies began producing the goods they could not get from England. This greatly evaporated the potteries' export markets.

As with many other British firms, the production of fancy goods was halted at Burgess & Leigh during World War II. Instead, the firm centered production on hotel dinnerware for the armed forces. Burgess and Leigh resumed production of fancy goods shortly after the war was over, but found that the market had changed. Demand was high, and the public wanted new and colorful designs. However, the colonies no longer required large volumes of imported pottery due to increased local production. Also, many small English potteries started and flourished during this time. Due to the implementation of import tariffs and quotas by other countries, around 1953 the market slowed.

Burgess & Leigh has continued to design and introduce new wares to the present day. Much of its current production is centered on traditional dinnerware designs decorated with transfers. The firm built and maintains a well-deserved reputation for consistently high quality. Its tradename, Burleigh Ware, still enjoys this reputation today. Burgess & Leigh has also been blessed with the loyalty of many employees, including the roughly one hundred working there today.

The Leigh family still manages the pottery more than one hundred and forty years after its founding. The fifth generation, consisting of Alan Leigh, Kingsley Leigh and Mary Leigh Babb, are now actively involved in the business. Burgess &

Leigh still produces a broad range of high quality ceramics at its Middleport site. One of the seven original bottle ovens is still standing and is registered as an historic site.

Character Jugs and Toby Jugs

Sole remaining bottle kiln at the Burgess & Leigh plant. This kiln is now an historical landmark. Those few that remain stand as landmarks of the Potteries' gritty past.

Burgess & Leigh introduced its first series of Toby Jugs in August 1941. This series was based on the characters of Charles Dickens, and consisted of a jug of Dickens himself plus ten of his literary characters. These were sold between 1941 and 1985. This popular series was followed by a Shakespearean series, introduced in April of 1950 and also produced until 1985. This series consisted of William Shakespeare and eight figures from his various works. The Dickens and Shakespeare jugs themselves are rarer than the others. The most popular of the Shakespeare jugs was Midsummer Night's Dream. The firm used the Burleigh Ware tradename on these jugs.

Some characters in these two series proved not too popular, so they were phased out and replaced with new characters. Therefore, some Dickens and Shakespeare jugs reached the market in limited quantities. Other jugs reached the prototype stage but were never released. For example, Juliet, Malvolio, and Othello were modeled, but did not go into production, yet small quantites are known to have been found in the market. Julius Caesar, Hamlet, Ophelia, Mrs. Bardell, Fat Boy, Oliver Twist and Sairey Gamp went into production, but for only a brief time. As a result, about fifteen different Shakespearean characters and fifteen Dickens characters were modeled over time. Burgess & Leigh hand mixed the enamel facial paint for these jugs, a difficult task that resulted in a variety of skin tones across the range. All of these jugs were modeled by Ernest Bailey and are incised with his name.

Also designed by E. T. Bailey, Burgess & Leigh produced a group of wartime Character and Toby Jugs of Winston Churchill during the 1940s. All of these jugs sold very well. The most popular jug was the "Victory" jug released in 1941. This jug depicts a squat Churchill making a V for victory and the letter V in Morse Code on the front of the base. Bailey greatly admired Churchill and designed the Churchill Bulldog Toby based on a John Bull-like stance to convey Churchill's stern demeanor. Bailey's Churchill Character Jug had a naval theme, but Churchill displays the same severity. Incised on the bottom of the Churchill Character Jug is "We shall defend every village every town and every city', Churchill Premier 1940." A few of the large size Character Jugs were reissued in 1965 following Churchill's death. The reissued jugs have a brown handle instead of green. The smallest Churchill Character Jug is very rare.

Additional wartime Character Jugs of other World War II leaders were modeled. Prototypes were produced in limited quantities of some, but these jugs were not introduced to the general market. The series includes Field Marshal Jan Smuts, Neville Chamberlain, General Douglas MacArthur, Sir Stafford Cripps, and Joseph Stalin. Stalin proved to be unpopular and was not produced. The Smuts jug was commissioned by a South African firm to honor its Prime Minister. However, the firm did not check into copyrights and encountered problems. Therefore, only a few Smuts jugs were made, mostly in a cream finish. Full colorway jugs are rare and command a much higher market value than the creamware versions. Also, a limited number of MacArthur jugs were marketed in the United States.

Two other exceptional tobies modeled by Bailey, the Beefeater and Chelsea Pensioner, were introduced in the late 1940s. The Beefeater backstamp has a commemorative dedication to "Ye Old Yeoman of the Guard". The Chelsea Pensioner jug commemorates the founding of the Chelsea Royal Hospital and the declaration of "Oak Apple Day" by King Charles. The Toby Philpot jug came as part of a set with a sugar, creamer, preserves pot, and squat teapot. Mr. Quaker was an advertising jug designed by Bailey

and produced in a limited edition of 3500 for the Quaker Oats Co. Mr. Quaker has a detachable hat. A Toby Jug of Flint McCullough has been found which depicts the character portrayed by Robert Horton from the television western, *Wagon Train*. It is believed this was made on commission for the television show or someone associated with it.

The Burgess & Leigh jugs are all well modeled, typically with a droll and comical posture, and depict each character in excellent detail and coloring. Mary Harper, the principal paintress on most of the Toby Jugs, is due credit for her wonderful artistry. An occasional cream white jug has been found, which most likely was produced during World War II when use of colors for decorative painting was restricted. Three different backstamps can be found on the Dickens and Shakespeare jugs. The earliest is from the 1940s and features the Alcock bee mark. The second backstamp was used beginning in 1960 and was created by adding "Ironstone" to the Alcock bee mark. The third mark, "Burleigh Ironstone" in block letters, is the most recent. The Churchill, Chelsea Pensioner, and Beefeater jugs carry different, more detailed marks.

The bulk of the Toby production occurred during the 1950s, but tobies were made for almost fifty years. Burgess & Leigh discontinued production of all Toby Jugs in 1985 because demand had fallen off, and the high cost of hand painting made them unprofitable. One estimate suggests that fifty percent of the painter's time was spent on the faces of these jugs. The remaining Toby bisque stock on hand in 1985 was finished with a blue and white spray, and sold off at a discount. Numerous examples of these can be found on the market today.

The firm still has all of the Toby molds. Perhaps it will resume production of these jugs, and hopefully add new jugs, some time in the future. Following is an exhaustive list of all of Burgess & Leigh's jugs, although a rare additional jug may still surface.

D. Barry Leigh, the fourth generation of Leighs to manage the pottery, with two of his favorite Toby Jugs

Burgess & Leigh bee backstamp

Later Burgess & Leigh mark

World War II leader Character Jug of Joseph Stalin (courtesy of Ron Smith)

Character Jugs of World War II leaders from left to right - Winston Churchill in small and miniature sizes, General MacArthur, and Jan Christian Smuts

World War II leader Character Jug of Chamberlain in cream colorway

Character Jug Name	Height, inches	Production Life
American Indian	5 1/8	
General MacArthur	4 1/4	1942 Limited
Jan Christian Smuts	5	1941
Joseph Stalin	5 3/4	1941 prototype
Mr. Quaker	8	1980s Ltd Ed of 3500
Neville Chamberlain	6 3/4	1938 prototype
Winston Churchill	5 1/4	1940 - 1955
	3 1/4	
	2	

Toby Jug Name	Height, inches	Production Life
Beefeater	7 1/4	late 1940s
Caesar	5 3/4	Limited
Cardinal Wolsey	5	1950 - 1985
Charles Dickens	7	1941 - 1985
Chelsea Pensioner	7 1/2	late 1940s
Dan'l Peggoty	5 3/4	1941 - 1985
Falstaff	5 1/2	1950 - 1985
Fat Boy	6	Limited
Flint McCullough	6	1950s
Juliet		Limited
Hamlet		Limited
MacBeth	5 1/2	1950 - 1985
Malvolio		None
Marley's Ghost		
Midsummer Night's Dream	4 3/4	1950 - 1985
Mr. Micawber	5 3/8	1941 - 1985
Mr. Pecksniff	5 3/4	1941 - 1985
Mr. Pickwick	5 1/2	1941 - 1985
Mrs. Bardell	5 3/8	Limited
Nicholas Nickelby	5 7/8	1945 - 1985
Oliver Twist	5 7/8	1945 - 1947
Ophelia		None
Othello		None
Owl	9 1/4	
Portia	5 3/4	1950 - 1985
Romeo	5	1950 - 1985
Sairey Gamp	4 3/4	1941 - 1947
Sam Weller	5 1/2	1945 - 1985
Scrooge	5 3/4	1945 - 1985
Shylock	5 3/4	1950 - 1985
Sir Stafford Cripps		Limited
Toby Philpot	4 1/2	1950s
Tony Weller	5 1/4	1941 - 1985
Touchstone	5 1/2	1950 - 1985
William Shakespeare	6 1/2	1950 - 1985
Winston Churchill "Bulldog" "Victory"	11 5 1/4	1940 - 1955 1941 - 1955

Figural Relief Jug Name	Height, inches
Edmund Leigh	7
Queen Elizabeth	7

Toby Jug of World War II leader Sir Stafford Cripps, the British Ambassador to the USSR (Courtesy of Ron Smith)

Mold for American Indian Character Jug found in Burgess & Leigh's mold room, unknown if jug ever was produced

Winston Churchill Victory Toby Jug

Winston Churchill Bulldog Toby Jug

Charles Dickens Toby Jug on left and William Shakespeare Toby Jug on right

Beefeater Toby Jug on left and Chelsea Pensioner Toby Jug on right

YE OLD YEOMAN OF THE GUARD "BEEFEATERS" FORMED BY KING HENRY VII 1485 FOR HIS PERSONAL BODYGUARD —LATER— DEFENDERS OF THE TOWER · OF LONDON · BURLEIGH·ENGLAND

Detailed Beefeater backstamp

"CHELSEA PENSIONER" THE ROYAL HOSPITAL CHELSEA. FOUNDED BY CHARLES II. AT THE WISH OF NELL GWYNN. DESIGNED BY WREN. COMPLETED 1690 ON KING CHARLES' BIRTHDAY "OAK APPLE DAY. 29TH MAY" PENSIONERS WEAR A SPRIG OF OAK LEAVES TO COMMEMORATE CHARLES' ESCAPE FROM CROMWELL BY HIDING IN AN OAK TREE BURLEIGH, ENGLAND

Chelsea Pensioner descriptive mark

Left to right: Oliver Twist, Scrooge, Dan'l Peggoty, and Sam Weller Toby Jugs

Left to right: Mr. Pickwick, Tony Weller, and Mr. Pecksniff Toby Jugs

Left to right: Mr. Micawvber, Sairey Gamp, Nicholas Nickelby, and Fat Boy Toby Jugs

Left to right: Romeo, Midsummer Night's Dream, and MacBeth Toby Jugs

Left to right: Shylock, Touchstone and Falstaff Toby Jugs

Left to right: Portia, Ceasar, and Cardinal Wolsey Toby Jugs

Group of blue and white finished tobies from 1985; top row left to right - Midsummer Night's Dream, Nicholas Nickelby, Tony Weller, Mr. Micawber, and Touchstone; bottom row left to right - William Shakespeare, Shylock, Cardinal Wolsey, and MacBeth

Mrs. Bardell Toby Jug (from collection of Bill and Pam Foster)

Flint McCullough Toby Jug, a television character from *Wagon Train* played by Robert Horton; hat removable (from collection of Bill and Pam Foster)

Mr. Quaker limited edition Character Jug produced for Quaker Oats (from collection of John Hobbs)

Owl Toby Jug

Toby Philpot creamer or jug on left and sugar bowl on right

Edmund Leigh commemorative figural relief jug

Queen Elizabeth II coronation figural relief commemorative jug

Burleigh Ware
See Burgess & Leigh

Burlington or Burlington Ware
See Shaw & Sons

Camark
Camden, Arkansas

Character Jug Name	Height, inches	
Admiral's Cup	5 1/4	135

Toby Jug Name	Height, inches	Model Number
Parrot	4	137

History

Samuel (Jack) J. Carnes, an Ohio native, founded Camark in 1926 as the Camden Art Tile and Pottery Company. The pottery was located in Camden, Arkansas. John Lessell was to be the Art Director for the company, bringing with him the designs and experience of his prior positions at Owens China and Weller. While in Ohio, Lessell made the first Camden Art Tile products using imported Arkansas clay. These pieces were marked "Lessell". Unfortunately, Lessell died unexpectedly in December of 1926 before relocating to Arkansas; however, his wife and daughter, Billie, proceeded as planned and joined Carnes at the Camark pottery.

The Camark plant opened in the Spring of 1927, producing a variety of pottery goods. Some of these were patterned after the successful products of other firms including Weller, Muncie and Owens. Stephen J. Sebaugh, a friend and colleague of John Lessell, and his two sons were also hired from Owens China to help launch the firm. The pottery's key early product line was LeCamark. In December of 1927, the firm introduced its daring Modernistic line designed by Alfred P. Tetzschner, preceding Roseville's similar Futura line by one year. Frank Long created the hand thrown pottery produced by the firm, and Boris Trifonoff, a former Muncie employee, helped the pottery produce pieces in the drip and mottled glaze style of Muncie.

After 1930 the factory turned toward pastel colored products for the mass market. Mary Daniel purchased Camark in the 1960s. She stopped all production in 1983.

Character Jugs and Toby Jugs

Although Camark produced a wide range of distinctive art pottery in only a few years, the firm produced only two documented Character and Toby Jugs. Designed at roughly the same time, the Admiral's Cup is marked "Camark 135" and the Parrot "Camark 137". Interestingly, model 136 is a drinking glass or vase in the form of a woman's head. Had she a handle, she would be considered a Character Jug.

Capo-di-Monte
See Jugs marked by Country of Manufacture under Italy

Carlton Ware Limited
Stoke-on-Trent, England

Character Jug Name	Height, inches
Albert Tatlock	5 1/4
Ena Sharples	5 1/4
Harrods's Doorman	4 1/4
Henry VIII	3
Ordinary Toby with verse	4 1/2
Pigeon Fancier	5 1/4
Stan Ogden	5 1/4
Toby Philpot	3

History

The Wiltshaw and Robinson Company established the Carlton Works factory in 1890 through the partnership of James F. Wiltshaw, W. H. Robinson and J. A. Robinson. James Wiltshaw was raised in the pottery business, his father worked for Macintyre & Company in Burslem. James worked at the Macintyre factory with his father for several years, reaching the position of manager before leaving to start his own pottery. Wiltshaw and Robinson was registered as a pottery in 1893, with the tradename Carlton Ware being adopted in 1894.

Wiltshaw and Robinson pottery became widely known for its variety of products ranging from very high-end quality gilded ware to tableware items for everyday use, as well as advertising pieces. Also included in early production was a wide variety of lusterware in many different colors. Bone china crested ware was introduced in 1902.

Operations continued smoothly until April of 1911, when the company principals split, leaving James Wiltshaw as the sole proprietor. In November 1911 he registered the firm as Wiltshaw and Robinson Limited. A new designer, Horace Wain, joined the firm around this time and was a key contributor to revitalizing the company with exciting new products of eye-catching shape, design and color. The most popular and longest lived product lines were the floral embossed range, more commonly known as chintz, and the salad ware. Carlton's chintz offered many different brightly colored floral patterns and has remained popular with collectors today. Salad ware was introduced in the 1920s and remained a mainstay through the mid-1970s.

James Wiltshaw was killed in an accident at the Stoke railway station in 1918. His son Frederick C. Wiltshaw took over the business and brought renewed energy to the pottery. More new products were introduced in the 1920s, such as cruets, earthenware, and advertising pieces. The business prospered and its luster wares became unparalleled in quality and variety. This continued growth precipitated the purchase of Birks, Rawlins and Company in 1932 to provide additional production capacity for the popular Carlton Ware china.

Another era of expansion for the firm began after the end of World War II. Electric kilns, ovens and dryers were first installed in the mid-1940s to reduce production time and increase both the quality and yield of the products. Additional modernization was done in the mid-1950s. During this decade, the firm turned toward more sophisticated designs, re-styled many of its older ones, and added new whimsical items including the Guinness advertising toucan.

In January of 1958, the firm's name was officially changed from Wiltshaw and Robinson Limited to Carlton Ware Limited with Cuthbert Wiltshaw as Director. The Wiltshaw family owned and operated the firm until 1967, when it was sold to Arthur Wood and Sons. Because of its reputation for fine quality products, Arthur Wood and Sons operated Carlton Ware semi-independently as a part of the Arthur Wood Group. It continued using the Carlton Ware tradename under Managing Director Anthony Wood.

Under the direction of the Wood Group, export sales rose rapidly in the 1970s. Designed by Danka Napiorkowska and Roger Michell, Carlton's famous Walking line was introduced in 1975. The firm also produced comical characterizations, some in cooperation with Fluck and Law, the creators of the Spitting Images puppets. Interest in Carlton Ware products eventually waned. By the late 1980s, Carlton Ware had lost money for several years and was floundering. Finally Carlton Ware went into receivership and the Arthur Wood Group ceased production in 1987, selling the pottery in December of that year to County Properties PLC. County Properties combined Carlton Ware with James Kent Limited, also recently acquired, and

renamed the result Carlton & Kent.

In March 1989, Carlton and Kent went into receivership with County Properties hoping to sell the assets of the firm, including the tradename, pattern books, and some existing molds, as an ongoing concern. Grosvenor Ceramic Hardware purchased Carlton and Kent from County Properties in May of 1989 and attempted to continue producing the firm's signature products using the Carlton Ware name. Grosvenor relaunched Carlton Ware in February of 1990 with a limited edition vase to celebrate the centenary of the founding of Wiltshaw and Robinson. Unfortunately, Grosvenor also met with little success and ended production in 1992.

Francis Salmon, formerly a partner in Kevin Francis Ceramics, purchased the remaining assets of Carlton Ware and its tradename in early 1997 from John McClusky, the Director of Grosvenor Ceramics. He reissued some favorite Carlton Ware designs in late 1997, which were produced by Bairstow Manor Pottery. Salmon also started issuing new, high quality designs under the Carlton Ware tradename. An exciting figurine called Hollyhocks was the first of these new issues and was produced by Peggy Davies Ceramics. In 1998 a Mephisto figurine was introduced, produced by Bairstow Manor. All production offered by Salmon carries the familiar Carlton Ware name in script with a U.S. trademark symbol at the end of the words "Carlton Ware" to differentiate it from earlier production.

Today the popularity of Carlton Ware is growing dramatically. In February of 1997 a large amount of unauthorized reproduction Carlton Ware was seized at a small factory in Longton. According to authorities, none of the reproduction pottery reached the market.

Character Jugs and Toby Jugs

Carlton Ware made only a few jugs, modeling some of its ordinary and female tobies after the Royal Worcester jugs. Like Worcester, Carlton Ware made a complete Toby cruet set. Perhaps the most interesting jugs produced by the firm depicted characters from a popular British television comedy. Six Character Jugs portrayed the main characters from Coronation Street and were produced with the permission of Granada TV Limited in 1986. The three identified to date are Albert Tatlock, Stan Ogden, and Ena Sharples. Other likely jugs in this series are Kent Barlow and Hilda Ogden.

The Carlton Ware Humpty Dumpty Toby Jug came with a musical movement in its base. Less than 1000 were produced, making it very desirable to both Carlton and music box collectors

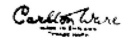
Original Carlton Ware mark

HAND PAINTED
MADE IN ENGLAND
Late 1990s backstamp with trademark symbol

Coronation Street series backstamp

Pigeon Fancier Character Jug

Pair of gilded Character Jugs made by a factory worker and carried out of the factory; Henry VIII on left and Toby Philpot on right

Harrod's Doorman Character Jug

Stan Ogden Character Jug from
Coronation Street

alike. Carlton also produced some crested ware Toby Jugs with verses in the 1930s. The mold for Harrod's Doorman somehow made its way to Carlton from Shaw & Copestake during the 1980s, most likely through Wood and Sons. In 1998 the Old Chintz Company commissioned the Pigeon Fancier jug in a limited edition of 500 with two colorways, a brown pigeon or a gray pigeon handle. Some of Carlton's Character Jugs have been found in an all over gold luster finish.

Until 1927 the firm primarily used the initials of

Wiltshaw and Robinson in its backstamp with the crown and flying swallow; however, the trade-name Carlton Ware was used sporadically as early as 1894. From 1930 to 1934, the trade-name Carlton Ware in large font was used exclusively. Between 1935 and 1945, to discourage Far East reproductions, the backstamp was changed to a smaller version of Carlton Ware in script, often with registration marks added. Bairstow Manor reproduced the Harrod's Doorman and Ordinary Toby in the latter 1990s.

Albert Tatlock and Ena Sharples Character Jugs from Coronation Street

Humpty Dumpty musical Toby Jug

Two Ordinary Toby Jugs, new production from the Bairstow Manor factory

Toby Jug Name	Height, inches	Model Number
Humpty Dumpty	8	1213
Ordinary Toby	7	2747/7
	5 7/8	1149/6
w/ verse	4 1/2	
Standing Lady		
Standing Toby crested	3	

Toby Derivatives	Height, inches
Man & Woman salt, pepper, and mustard	
Ordinary Toby ashtray	

Ordinary Toby ashtray

Toby cruet set; Woman Mustard, Man Salt, and Woman Pepper

Carson Pirie Scott & Company
Milwaukee, Wisconsin

Character Jug Name	Height, inches
Nutcracker	5 3/4

History

Carson Pirie Scott & Company is a family oriented full-line regional department store chain with locations throughout the Upper Midwest portion of the United States. Officially founded in 1889, the beginning of the firm dates back to 1854 when Samuel Carson opened a dry goods store in Amboy, Illinois after immigrating to America from Ireland. The firm almost went out of business in 1871 when a disastrous fire struck, destroying sixty percent of its stock. Carson Pirie, as it was known then, survived the fire and

continued to grow, adding more stores to its chain.

Carson Pirie Scott merged with another large retailer, Donaldsons, in 1987, further expanding its business and geographic coverage. In 1989 an Illinois competitor, P. A. Bergner, acquired Carson Pirie Scott. In 1991 Bergner filed for Chapter 11 bankruptcy, and two years later a reorganized public trading company emerged named Carson Pirie Scott & Company. Since then the firm has grown steadily through further penetration of target markets, and strategic buying and selling of store locations.

Today Carson Pirie Scott has annual revenues over $1 billion from fifty-three department stores and four furniture galleries. The firm holds the number one or two market position in each of its target markets.

Character Jugs

In the 1970s or 1980s, Carson Pirie Scott offered a Character Jug for the Christmas holidays. It is not known who potted this jug for the retailer.

Nutcracker Character Jug produced for Carson Pirie Scott by an unknown potter

Carson Pirie Scott backstamp

Cauldon Potteries Limited
Hanley, England

History

Cauldon Potteries was originally known as Cauldon Limited and was located at Cauldon Place in Hanley, England, operating there from 1905 to 1920. This site traces its roots back to the factory established by John and William Ridgway in 1813. John Ridgway retired and sold the factory to Brown-Westhead, Moore & Company around 1858. Brown-Westhead operated successfully for many years and included high quality majolica in its production. In 1905, Brown-Westhead reorganized and became the Cauldon Potteries, producing goods marked "Cauldon". The firm's initial production was a variety of earthenware and porcelain products.

In 1920, Harold T. Robinson purchased Cauldon Potteries. That year he moved the pottery from Cauldon Place to Bristol, at the same time rearranging the firm as a limited company and changing its name to Cauldon Potteries Limited. The pottery was granted the Royal Warrant in 1924, and use of the Royal Cauldon tradename began. Business expanded rapidly in the 1920s and 1930s, during which time Cauldon Potteries produced a wide range of tableware and other lines. Purchasing and absorbing other potteries fueled the firm's expansion. Arkinstall & Sons was purchased in 1925, followed by Hewitt Brothers in 1926. In 1929, Cauldon Potteries purchased W. H. Goss for two thousand pounds. Cauldon renamed the pottery Goss China Limited and continued using the Goss name for production of tea sets, cottage sets, and commemorative items.

Pountney & Company of Bristol purchased Cauldon in 1962 and split up the firm. The porcelain production was sold to E. W. Brain & Company, which in turn became part of Coalport, a member of the Wedgwood Group. Pountney retained the trade-style earthenware portion of the business and production was moved to Bristol where earthenware products labeled Cauldon Bristol Potteries were manufactured until 1969. Kingston Pottery purchased the Cauldon factory and assets in the mid-to-late-1970s and continued producing its bone china pudding ware products. The Kingston Pottery closed in 1985 and the Cauldon pottery was sold to the Perks Ceramic Group of Yorkshire, which added Cauldon Potteries Limited to its Group.

Toby Jugs

Cauldon Potteries tobies were produced in porcelain from Goss molds with the most common mark being a crown with "Royal Cauldon, England, Est. 1774" in script below. "Made in England" was typically found as well. The usage of 1774 in the date is most likely a reference to the historic significance of Cauldon's initial Hanley pottery. The Ordinary Toby was produced in three known colorways: orange and blue, orange and green, and blue and orange.

Toby Jug Name	Height, inches	Production Life
Cross-legged Toby w/arm handle	3 1/2	1930s - 1950
Ordinary Toby	2 5/8	1930s - 1950
	1 5/8	1930s - 1950

Royal Cauldon backstamp

Cross-legged Toby and two sizes of Ordinary Tobies, all produced from Goss molds

Ceramic Arts Studio
Madison, Wisconsin

Toby Jug Name	Height, inches	Production Life
Colonial Man	3 1/2	1952 - 1956

Colonial Man Toby Jug

History

Ceramic Arts Studio was founded in Madison, Wisconsin in 1940. Lawrence Rabbit, a University of Wisconsin student, researched the clay found locally in Wisconsin for a class project and produced hand thrown pottery from it, which he sold locally in the Madison area. In January 1941 Lawrence entered into a partnership with Reuben Sand, another University of Wisconsin student, to expand the pottery. Rabbit continued designing and producing pieces, while Reuben took charge of marketing and distributing the firm's products.

The next major step in the evolution of Ceramic Arts Studio occurred in 1942, when Betty Harrington visited the studio and asked to have a kneeling nude figurine fired that she had sculpted from clay in her backyard. This figurine demonstrated clearly the raw talent of Harrington. Instead of firing the figurine for a fee, Reuben asked Betty to model figurines for the Studio. This was the beginning of Harrington's

career as a modeler for Ceramic Arts Studio. Over the next fourteen years, she designed more than six hundred figures.

Ceramic Arts Studio was in active production from 1940 to 1956, producing decorative figurines, wall plaques, salt and pepper sets, and head vases among other items. The Studio's products were sold at retail outlets and gift shops in the local Madison area, as well as by traveling salespeople. Ceramic Arts products are well known for their distinct style and high quality. During its peak years in the mid-1940s, Ceramic Arts Studio produced over 400,000 pieces annually and employed 100 people.

Toby Jugs

Ceramic Arts Studio produced one Ordinary Toby Jug. Ceramic Arts collectors commonly refer to this jug as the Colonial Man. The jug was produced in a variety of colorways, including a polychrome version and solid colors of blue, cream and others.

Cerno
See Crown Winsor

Charrington Toby - earlier versions known as the Hoare Toby
See Fielding & Company, Hancock & Corfield, Hoare & Company, Lancaster & Sandland, Price & Kensington, Royal Doulton, Shelley Potteries, Staffordshire Fine Ceramics, Tony Wood, Wade Ceramics, Wood and Sons

Charrington Toby Jugs originally commissioned by Hoare and Company as the image for its Hoare Toby Ale; later from several different potters by Charrington Ales, after purchase of Hoare and Co; top row left to right - Royal Doulton, Wade, Wood & Sons, and Royal Doulton; bottom row left to right - Staffordshire Fine Ceramics, Hancock & Corfield, Lancaster & Sandland, and Fielding's Crown Devon

Charrington Toby at the
entrance to a London pub

Charrington Toby Ale Bar Towel

Charrington Toby Ale beer can

Charles Ahrenfeldt & Son
Alt-Rohlau, Austria

History

In 1886, Charles Ahrenfeldt founded a porcelain factory in the town of Alt-Rohlau in Bohemia. The firm produced primarily porcelain items, typically decorated with floral designs, and distributed its ware locally through a decorative porcelain retail shop. It also exported ware to the United States through the Van Heusen Charles Company of Albany, New York. Ahrenfeldt also owned a porcelain factory in Limoges, France. The Alt-Rohlau factory closed in 1917, most likely due to the impending political changes in the area.

Alt-Rohlau's physical location in Europe resulted in the town changing its country of allegiance as a result of the two World Wars. In the late 19th century, the town was a part of Bohemia. From 1900 through 1918, it became part of the Austrian Empire. Through the political changes as a result of World War I,

Alt-Rohlau then became a part of the new country of Czechoslovakia in 1918, and most recently the Czech Republic in 1990.

Toby Jugs

The Ordinary Toby has a light porcelain body and depicts a seated gentleman with his legs crossed and both hands enclosed in a muff. In his muff and long overcoat, he appears dressed for cold weather. He bears a stamped green underglaze mark of a shield with "Altrohlau Austria" across diagonally and the initials of Charles Ahrenfeldt, a "C" and "A", in the upper left hand corner and lower right hand corner of the shield respectively. The Cross-legged Toby has been found in gilded white porcelain with the Ahrenfeldt mark and "4100/1127" stamped on the base. The Van Heusen mark has also been seen on these jugs.

Toby Jug Name	Height, inches	Production Life
Cross-legged Toby	6 1/8	1900 - 1917
Ordinary Toby	7	1900 - 1917

Ordinary Toby with muff on left and Cross-legged Toby on right

Clay Art Company
San Francisco, California

History

Michael Zanfagna and Jenny McLain founded the Clay Art Company in San San Francisco, California in 1979. Michael and Jenny were teachers at Mission High School in San Francisco and decided to start a pottery business together. Their goal was to produce attractive, affordable ceramic art. The first item produced was a ceramic hook in the form of a cherub's bottom. Today the pottery employs fifty people and produces a variety of collectible items,

including salt and pepper sets, wall masks, and, most notably, figural cookie jars.

Character Jugs

Clay Art produced two known Character Jugs. Its Marilyn Monroe Character Jug was introduced in 1988 and produced at least until 1996. It was approved by Marilyn's estate and was part of a set along with Marilyn salt and pepper shakers and a cookie jar. The James Dean jug was sold in 1996 as well.

Character Jug Name	Height, inches
James Dean	4 3/4
Marilyn Monroe	4 1/2

Clay Art Marilyn Monroe backstamp

James Dean and Marilyn Monroe Character Jugs

Clayton Bailey Ceramics
Port Costa, California

Toby Jug Name	Height, inches
Clayton Bailey	10
Fred Chavez	8 1/2

Clayton Bailey self portrait Toby Jug

History

Clayton Bailey Ceramics is the Northern California studio pottery of Clayton Bailey, a well-known professor of ceramics at the California State University in Hayward, California from 1968 through 1996. Born in 1939, Clayton has been potting whimsical jugs, figures, gargoyles, and even a Big Foot over a thirty-year period. Since moving to California from Wisconsin in 1967, he has exhibited often, both in groups and as a solo artist, receiving many honors and awards. Bailey's work can be found in public and corporate collections around the world.

Clayton's work is not all fun and games. He produced a Pyrograph, a ceramic vessel that records sunshine by focusing sunlight onto a wooden board inside the Pyrograph and burning a record of the sun's path onto the board. In 1987, Bailey was commissioned to produce ceramic tiles for use at a station platform in Sacramento's new light rail system. He created tiles of $16 bills that were installed in the pavement near public telephones. Bailey claims that passengers who notice the money are uplifted by their good fortune of finding a fortune. This moment can create a positive attitude to last the day.

Clearly stating his personal politics, Clayton produced ceramic guns that have been fired once, but will never shoot. These guns also have the unique feature of aiming backwards at the bearer. Not satisfied to be limited to pottery, Clayton also creates robots out of discarded electronics and appliances, one of which is owned by Microsoft executive Bill Gates.

Toby Jugs

In 1972, a student in Bailey's University ceramic class named Fred Chavez owned a Staffordshire Snufftaker Toby that Bailey wanted to purchase. A deal was struck in which Bailey would create a Toby Jug of Chavez in exchange for the Snufftaker. When the work was completed, Clayton Bailey had created two tobies, one of himself and one of Fred Chavez.

Bailey produced these two tobies in the Ordinary Toby style to resemble the thin walled slip cast English tobies of the 18th century. His self-portrait Toby wears a T-shirt with "SPECIMEN" on the front, proclaiming Bailey's obsession at the time with finding the remains of mythical animals like Big Foot. Another unique feature of this jug is the life-sized phallus inside, one of the artist's recurring recreational interests. The Fred Chavez jug depicts a seated Fred dressed in denim pants and jacket.

Clayton also produced a relative of the Character Jug between 1989 and 1993. Called the Jugheads, these are based on the face jugs created in the early 1800s by slave potters in the southeastern United States for use in burial ceremonies. His sense of humor not allowing him to leave well enough alone, Clayton's Jugheads have a unique hidden feature; they all run (pour) from the nose. As with all of Bailey's work, his Toby Jugs are one of a kind.

Group of face jugs

History

Cliff Adkins is an amateur studio potter residing in Chippenham, Wilts, England with his wife and three sons. Cliff designs and models his creations and a potter friend fires his ware.

Toby Jugs

Cliff is also a Toby Jug enthusiast and collector, so it was natural that his collecting hobby turn into potting Toby Jugs himself. His first toby creation was in 1997 of Sleeping Toby, produced in a limited edition of thirty. Cliff's focus is on traditional subjects with whimsical quirks, as demonstrated by the mice playing around the Sleeping Toby. He plans to design one or two limited edition Toby Jugs a year. Cliff is hard at work on his second Toby Jug, a traditional Toby Philpot holding a teapot.

Toby Jug Name	Height, inches	Production Life
Sleeping Toby	8	1997
Toby Philpot		1999

Cliff Adkins backstamp

Sleeping Toby Jug

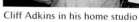

Clay model of the large Toby Philpot with teapot

Cliff Adkins in his home studio

Clinchfield Artware Pottery
Erwin, Texas

History

Clinchfield Artware Pottery was located in Erwin, Texas and was closely coupled with Southern Potteries. This pottery opened in 1945 and was managed by Ray and Pauline Cash. The couple initially produced pottery with molds purchased from Southern Potteries and also developed their own Blue Ridge pattern. In 1984, the Cashes sold the pottery. Today the factory produces only statuary and lamp bases.

Goods produced by the Cashes may carry several different marks. Some are stamped "Clinchfield Artware", while others are marked simply "Made by the Cash Family".

Character Jugs and Toby Jugs

Clinchfield most likely reproduced all of the jugs made by Southern Potteries. So far Paul Revere is the only one of these identified. The Ordinary Toby has a handle on the side of the jug and is typically finished in a cream glaze with powder blue and black detailing on the jacket, shoes, jug, and hair.

Character Jug Name	Height, inches	Production Life
Paul Revere	6	1945-1960

Toby Jug Name	Height, inches	Production Life
Ordinary Toby	5	1945-1960

Clough's Royal Art Pottery
Longton, England

History

The history of Clough's Royal Art Pottery dates back to 1913 and the pottery founded by Alfred Clough. At the beginning of the 20th century, Alfred Clough was a street peddler of household goods in the Staffordshire area. As he sold a great deal of pottery, Clough became interested in potting. To learn the business, he took a job at the Melbourne Works in Longton and then moved to the Smithfield Works.

Alfred Clough entered into a brief partnership with Mr. Lester in 1913. After the partnership ended, he founded Alfred Clough Limited and began operating the Carlton Works, Garfield Works, and Winterton Pottery. Alfred Clough Jr. joined his father at the Carlton Works in

Toby Jug Name	Height, inches	Production Life
Standing Toby	3	1951-1960s
Standing Woman w/ unbrella	3	1951-1960s

1923. In 1928, during a barbershop conversation, Clough reached an agreement with Harvy Aynsley to purchase the St. Louis Works in Longton. This factory produced a range of everyday earthenware. In 1930, Alfred Jr., along with brothers Aubrey and Astor Clough, took over operations at the Garfield Works. Alfred also purchased the large nine-kiln Royal Art Pottery from Harvy Aynsley in 1937.

The Royal Art Pottery became the hub of Clough's pottery conglomerate. Aubrey Clough was Managing Director of Royal Art Pottery. Alfred Jr. was in charge of production at both the Royal Art Pottery and the Garfield Works. Astor Clough was the Managing Director of the St. Louis Works.

World War II stalled production at the St. Louis Works, but Royal Art Pottery continued through the war and rebounded robustly after the war ended. Alfred Clough died in 1948 and the business was passed along to his three sons.

Through postwar expansion and diversification, the firm became the parent company to many factories by the 1950s. These other potteries included Barker Brothers, Cartwright & Edwards, W. H. Grindley, Royal Art Pottery, and Sampson Smith. Alfred Clough went public and became a limited partnership in January of

1954. The Directors of Cartwright and Edwards, a pottery focused on teaware, purchased the entire Alfred Clough Limited Group in 1955 and soon sold off the aging St. Louis Works. The pottery moved to Bedford Street in Longton in 1961 and changed its name again, becoming Clough's Royal Art Pottery. The firm continued operating into the 1980s.

Toby Jugs

To date, a pair of unremarkable Toby Jugs has been attributed to Clough's Royal Art Pottery. Both jugs carry the mark "Royal Art Pottery" above a crown and "England" below. The Royal Art Pottery used this mark between 1951 and 1961, when it operated independently from its parent. Clough's used the mark as well from 1961 onward. Toby's jacket is brown and the woman has been found in two colorways.

This pair is very similar to the numbered, unknown English jugs listed in the Unattributed Section. These are the Standing Toby and Standing Woman jugs with numbers like 750/1. This pair is also very similar to standing Peasant Village jugs. Some relationship certainly exists between these three, but what it is remains unknown.

Compton Potters Art Guild Limited
Surrey, England

Toby Jug Name	Height, inches
Ordinary Toby	7 5/8

History

The Compton Potters Art Guild began in 1899 as the Compton Pottery. Located in Compton, Surrey, the pottery was established by Mary Seaton Watts (ca 1850 - 1938), the wife of the well known artist and painter George Frederick Watts (1817 - 1904), and a gifted artist in her own right. The couple literally lived their art, residing in Limnerslease, a house built for George Watts in 1891. The name comes from Middle English and means "painter's final place."

Mary Seaton developed her skills at the Slade and South Kensington Schools of Art before marrying George Watts. In addition to her talents with pottery, she was also an accomplished architect. Mary designed the Watts Chapel in 1895 as a needed expansion for the local church graveyard. The Chapel was constructed between 1896 and 1904 with volunteer labor for construction and decorating provided by the local villagers. It was consecrated in 1898. After her husband's death in 1904, Mary designed an expansion of the Watts Gallery, a building that housed the works of

George Watts. Most notable of her architectural projects, Mary Watts designed and led the construction of The Cloisters in 1911, an Italian styled structure that houses George Watts' tomb and memorial. All of these buildings remain popular tourist attractions in the Compton area today.

Compton Pottery's initial products were focused on terra–cotta garden and ornamental figures. The pottery used clay dug near Guildford and the Watts' estate. While much of the labor for the pottery came from local amateur potteries, several noted designers worked at the pottery during its production life. These included Lincoln Holland, Ralph Lindsey and Harry Yalden. Due to declining health, Mary sold the pottery to new owners, and from 1936 to 1956 the firm operated under the name Compton Potters Art Guild Limited.

Toby Jugs

The 1920s were a boom period for the Compton Pottery, during which time it produced the Ordinary Toby, its only known Toby Jug.

History

The Co-operative Wholesale Society operated from 1922 to 1971 in Longton, Stoke-on-Trent. Operating at the Windsor factory, initial manufacturing was focused on bone china products. The firm expanded into earthenware production in 1946 at the Crown Clarence factory on King Street in Longton.

The company used many tradenames in marketing and distributing its wares, including "Windsor" and "Clarence Bone" for bone china, and "Balmoral" and "Crown Clarence" for earthenware. In 1971, Anton Potteries acquired the firm. When Anton Potteries closed in 1975 the Crown Clarence factory and assets were sold to Churchill Pottery, which operated a subsidiary, Churchill China Limited, at the site.

Character Jugs and Toby Jugs

A collection of Character Jugs called the Just So Series was produced by the Co-operative Wholesale Society under its Crown Clarence tradename. To date, only a few jugs in this series have been found, others certainly exist. These jugs are identical to Westminster Pottery's Just So Series. Although the connection between these two firms is not known, Co-operative most likely purchased the molds after Westminster closed in 1956 and produced jugs from them into the 1960s. Please refer to Westminster, Anton Potteries and Staffordshire Fine Ceramics for additional Just So Series production. Toby Jugs from Westminster's Tavern Series are found with the Crown Clarence backstamp, indicating that these molds were used by the Society as well.

Character Jug Name	Height, inches
Big Chief	4 1/2
Outlaw	3 1/4
Paddy	4
Tam O'Shanter	4 1/2

Toby Jug Name	Height, inches
Mine Host John	8 7/8
Mine Hostess	8 3/8

Co-operative Wholesale Society's Crown Clarence backstamp

Just So Series Character Jugs of Big Chief, Paddy, Outlaw, and Tam O'Shanter

Cooper Clayton Characters
See Sterling Pottery

Cooper Clayton Pottery
England

History

A pair of acquaintances, Mr. Clayton and Miss Cooper founded Cooper Clayton Pottery. The two had experience working in the potteries and shared a desire to own and operate their own pottery. They launched a pottery together using a chivalrous combination of their last names.

In the midst of potting together, romance bloomed and marriage followed. In the mid-1960s, roughly coinciding with the birth of their daughter, the couple closed the business and apparently sold it to Sterling Pottery which continued using the Cooper Clayton name.

Cooper Clayton's backstamp is "Staffs Cooper Clayton England" all enclosed by a large C.

Character Jugs

Cooper Clayton produced many well-modeled Character Jugs; however, only a few are known with the Cooper Clayton backstamp. Sterling produced jugs from these molds, using the tradename "Cooper Clayton Characters by Sterling" on its production. These are more common today than original Cooper Clayton jugs. See Sterling Pottery for a more complete list of Cooper Clayton jugs.

Character Jug Name	Height, inches
Bill Sykes	3
Burns	4 3/4
Friar Tuck	2 1/4
Granny	1 1/2
John Bull	1 3/4
Mr. Merry	2 1/2
	2
Mr. Micawber	1 1/2
Mr. Monty	2
Mr. Pickwick	1 1/2
Pirate	6
Robin Hood	2 1/2
Sam Weller	3 1/4
	1 1/2
Skipper	2 1/2
Tam O'Shanter	3 3/4
Will Scarlett	2 1/2
William Shakespeare	2 3/4

Cooper Clayton backstamp

Left to right - small Robert Burns, miniature William Shakespeare, and small Tam O'Shanter Character Jugs

Group of Character Jugs; top row left to right - Mr. Merry in small and miniature, Will Scarlett, and Robin Hood; bottom row left to right - Skipper, William Shakespeare, a tiny John Bull, and Sam Weller

Coopers Art Pottery Company
Hanley, England

Character Jug Name	Height, inches	Production Life
Josiah Wedgwood	5 3/8	1936-1958

Toby Jug Name	Height, inches	Production Life
John Bull	4 7/8	1911-1958
	2 1/2	1911-1958

Josiah Wedgwood Character Jug in three colorways

History

The Coopers Art Pottery Company traces its beginnings back to the firm of Physick & Brassington, which began operations in 1892 at the Anchor Works in Hanley. Mr. Cooper became a partner in the firm in 1899, and for one year the pottery operated as Physick & Cooper. In 1900, the company changed its name to the Art Pottery Company, and operated as such until 1911, when it became Coopers Art Pottery Company. The pottery ceased operations in 1958.

Character Jugs and Toby Jugs

Production of only two jugs by the Coopers Art Pottery is known, although there are probably more. The first is a well-done Character Jug of Josiah Wedgwood. Wedgwood is most commonly dressed in a brown jacket and hat, but is also found in an all over thick green glaze. Josiah is impressed with "C. Ltd England" on the back of the jug.

The second known jug is a three-quarter bodied John Bull Toby similar in style to Shelley's Intarsio John Bull jug. Cooper's John Bull has a flat, unglazed base with "Made in England" stamped on it. Like Wedgwood, John Bull is also impressed with "C. Ltd England" on its back. The handle is located on the side of the jug, not on the back as found on poorer reproductions. Another similar John Bull jug has "J. Bull" embossed on the bottom. The makers of these reproductions are not known.

H. F. Coors Company
Inglewood, California

Character Jug Name	Height, inches
Old Salt	5

History

In 1935, Herman Coors, the third son of brewery legend Adolph Coors, founded the H. F. Coors Company in Inglewood, California. Herman had worked at the Coors Porcelain Company in Golden, Colorado, serving as the plant manager from 1916. Coors Porcelain was started by Adolph to diversify the family business. Although primarily focused on producing quality industrial porcelain items, Coors Porcelain produced porcelain dinnerware during World War I, taking advantage of the lack of imported German porcelain.

In California, H. F. Coors produced tiles, plumbing ceramics, doll heads, hotel ware, and commercial pottery. The firm developed a thin, sturdy porcelain tradenamed "Coorsite Pottery". The factory was still active in the 1980s.

Character Jugs

Only one Character Jug made by H. F. Coors has been identified to date. This jug is marked with the Coorsite tradename. The firm most likely produced other jugs.

History

The history of W. T. Copeland & Sons envelops the activities of two great potters, Josiah Spode and William Taylor Copeland.

Josiah Spode founded a small pottery in the early 1760s. By 1770, he had quit his small pot and returned to Stoke to found the firm that has become famous the world over. He perfected the process of manufacturing blue underglaze earthenware in 1774. By 1800, he was making quality porcelains with applied transfers of an eastern design. A few years later, his son Josiah II had joined the firm, and together they perfected a mixture of kaolin, feldspar and ash to create a fine bone china, arguably Spode's most significant contribution to European pottery, and the product upon which the firm build its reputation.

Josiah II operated the firm's London showroom and warehouse with William Copeland, who joined Spode in 1784. When his father died in 1797, Josiah II returned to Stoke and took control of the pottery. Josiah II sent his son William to learn the business under Copeland in London. William Spode retired in December 1811, selling three-quarters of his interest to Copeland and the other one-quarter to his father. In 1826, William Copeland died, passing along his interest in the pottery to his only son, William Taylor Copeland, who had already become a partner in the firm.

With the deaths of Josiah Spode II in 1827 and his son Josiah Spode III shortly thereafter, the Spode family sold the Spode Works in Stoke to William Taylor Copeland in 1833. William Copeland took in Thomas Garrett as his partner in 1834, operating as Copeland & Garrett. Thomas Garrett immediately went to Stoke to take over the daily operations of the factory. Driven by an outstanding art department headed by Thomas Battam, the firm continued producing a wide range of high quality ware and introduced new porcelain statuary, ornate figures, and decorative tiles.

Between the late 1790s and 1816, the factory produced ware marked Spode & Copeland. In 1835 the firm signed an exclusive contract with the Hudson Bay Company to be its sole earthenware supplier. This contract lasted into the 1870s, during which time over one hundred different patterns were sold to Hudson Bay. In 1843 the pottery was one of the largest in the Stoke area, employing over 1000 laborers. In 1829, William Copeland became Alderman for the Bishopsgate ward of London and in 1935 he was named Lord Mayor of London.

On June 24, 1847, Thomas Garrett retired and the firm became simply W. T. Copeland. William continued operating the Spode Works, producing a wide range of fine quality porcelain and earthenware. Between 1847 and 1867, the firm used the mark Copeland, late Spode.

The business continued to grow rapidly. By 1861 it employed over eight hundred workers, 241 of them children. William's four sons joined the firm in 1867 as partners, and the company became W. T. Copeland & Sons, or more commonly just Copeland. The sons were William Fowler Mountford Copeland, Edward Capper Copeland, Alfred James Copeland, and Richard Pirie Copeland.

Copeland built a large business in parian ware and bone china while continuing production of Spode's popular transfer ware. On December 31, 1867, William Copeland retired and left the firm in the capable hands of his four sons. He died suddenly the next year. In the 1870s, Copeland introduced majolica products to take advantage of the widespread demand for these colorfully glazed traditional items. A range of stoneware was introduced in the 1880s. Crests, badges and logos became popular in the latter 19th century, and Copeland eagerly met the demand. The popularity of parian continued into the 20th century.

Upon the death of Richard Pirie Copeland in 1913, the firm was passed along to his two sons, Richard Ronald Copeland and Alfred Gresham Copeland. In the 1930s, Art Deco became the rage and modeler Eric Olsen joined the firm from Wedgwood to create exciting new Art Deco designs. During the 1930s, Copeland revived the Spode name and used it in conjunction with Copeland or by itself on bone china. After the end of World War II, the firm heavily emphasized its connection with Spode.

In 1956, the next generation of Copelands, Spencer and Robert Copeland, assumed control of the firm. In the later 1950s, the firm experienced serious financial difficulties due to several factors including the rising cost of production. The firm was offered for sale in 1963. Josiah Wedgwood & Sons considered purchasing the company but did not. Copeland remained for sale until July of 1966 when the Carborundum Company bought it. Carborundum was a United States-based maker of industrial ceramics that wanted to expand into dinner-ware production. The firm was renamed Spode Limited in 1970, completing a two hundred year cycle. Carborundum offered Spode for sale in 1974 and, after an unsuccessful bid by Josiah Wedgwood, Worcester Royal Porcelain Company acquired Spode. The two potteries fully merged in 1976, becoming Royal Worcester Spode Limited.

Between 1983 and 1988, Royal Worcester Spode was owned by Crystalate Company, then London International PLC, and finally Derby International, a North American investment group. In December 1988, Derby reorganized its British operations, renaming itself The Porcelain & Fine China Companies Limited and began operating Spode Limited and Royal Worcester Limited as independent companies. In the 1990s, the firm began offering high quality reproductions of Spode's early giftware, beginning with pattern 1166, which was first introduced in the 1810s. Today the company is most noted for its wide range of Christmas Tree pattern dinnerware and accessories.

Toby Jugs

From the start of the twentieth century until the 1930s, Copeland produced several different styles of Toby Jugs. Information transcribed from the potter's notes for these jugs follows.

Model Number and Description

9301 A china Toby with delicate flowers to body, some gilding, gilt base and burgundy hat.

9302 A china Toby with the body in ground cobalt blue with a gilt base and hat.

9303 A china Toby, spotted body on light blue, gilt base and black hat.

9304 A china Toby, blue bells painted on the body, gilded line to the base and handle with a burgundy hat.

5652 Toby with a blue hat, the body with a claret/brown underglaze and various coloured overglaze decoration.

5653 Hat printed with green and coloured underglaze body, face, and hands in overglaze various decoration.

5654 Daniel Lambert jug holding a small cup not a jug. Body in underglaze pink, cobalt blue hat, overglaze to face, hands and body.

T/609 Toby in underglaze green, peacock and parsley back crowns, a bird painted on one side of the Toby.

6061 Spode Imperial body Toby Jug. Bangup bead and sprigs in magazine blue. Stars in cobalt blue underglaze print. Underglaze colours of deans pink, orange, claret, jaffers blue, black, olive green, yellow. Black and claret for hair. Onglaze colours of purple. Brown edges, blue, new rose colours, yellow peacock, indian red and black, stark grey, 2 sprigs inside and 4 sprigs outside of jug.

6062 Spode Imperial Toby Jug printed in royal brown inside and oak on cap. 2 sprigs inside, 2 outside. Jacket printed in pink underglaze. Edge of hat in purple brown. Onglaze fox colours, new rose colours, yellow, peacock, indian red, baltia, stark grey. Underglaze colours of deans pink, orange, claret brown, jaffers blue, bert black, olive green, yellow, black and claret mixed for hair.

6597 Toby Jug printed in green with a blue handle.

6748 Toby with body painted with primular wild flower pattern.

7332 Toby with blue coat, green hat, yellow waistcoat, pink trousers.

7698 Spode Imperial body jug pencilled in orange, pink, green, black, cobalt blue, grey, all in underglaze. Face and hands coloured in red on glaze. Black handle, hat and base. Blue and green mottled coat.

7699 Spode Imperial Toby Jug. Pencilled sprigs in yellow, orange, pink, cobalt blue, and green on jug. Black and light green on sprigs. Face and hands coloured on glaze in red. Blue handle, hat and base with handcraft roses.

7700 Spode Imperial Toby Jug. Pencilled in green, cobalt blue, yellow, orange, pink, brown, black and grey underglaze. Face and hands coloured on glaze. Green coat, blue handle and hat and base.

7701 Toby Jug pencilled in green, pink, orange, cobalt blue, black, brown and grey underglaze. Face and hands coloured on glaze. Blue coat, handle and base, green hat back and legs.

9189 Large size Daniel Lambert Toby. Wisteria printed in pink and coloured underglaze. Face and hands coloured on glaze. Wisteria coat and hat, blue handle and base.

9700 Spode King of Hearts Toby. Pencilled in cobalt blue, green, pink, orange. Pale black underglaze. Face and hands pencilled in pale red on glaze. Hair and ermine in very pale black.

These jugs are found with the common Copeland Spode mark, or unmarked. Copeland Spode introduced excellent Toby Jugs of Winston Churchill and Franklin Roosevelt in 1945, both of which were designed by Eric Olsen in 1941. The Churchill jug proved to be very popular, selling at least until 1952. The Roosevelt jug did not meet with the same level of success so was produced in smaller quantities, making it more scarce today. Fully colored and white creamware versions of these two jugs were produced.

It is possible that the Squat Toby is actually the Daniel Lambert jug; further investigation is required. The large Squat Toby has been found with a Copeland Late Spode backstamp. The smaller Squat Toby is marked "Spode Royal Jade." The Chinaman is marked "Copeland China England", a backstamp used between 1892 and 1920.

Copeland Spode backstamp

Toby Jug Names	Height, Inches	Model Number	Year Introduced
Chinaman	4		1892
Daniel Lambert		9189	1930
		5654	1906
Franklin D. Roosevelt	8 1/2		1945
King of Hearts	7 1/2	9700	1930s
Ordinary Toby	7 7/8	5652, 5653	1906
	7 7/8	T/609	1907
		6597	1913
		6748	1915
China body		7332	1919
Imperial body	6 1/4	9301, 9302, 9303, 9304	1898
Imperial body	6 1/4	6061, 6062	1908
		7698, 7699, 7700	1923
	6 1/4	7701	1923
Squat Toby	6 3/4		
	5 1/2		
Winston Churchill	8 1/2		1945

Winston Churchill Toby Jug and the much rarer Franklin D. Roosevelt Toby Jug

Squat Toby and Ordinary Toby in decorative chintz colorways

Cortman Limited
Burslem, England

History

Lionel Bailey and his partner Geoff Stanway founded Cortman Limited in 1995. The firm operates with a Board of Directors consisting of Lionel and Jennifer Bailey, Geoff Stanway and his wife, and Lorna Bailey. The pottery's tradename, LJB Ceramics, is named after Lionel's daughter, Lorna Jennifer Bailey. Lionel, an antique dealer, helped his daughter realize her dream of becoming a ceramics designer by opening LJB Ceramics. Lorna, 18 years old at the time the pottery opened, earned a national diploma in ceramic design and specializes in art deco ware. Lorna's designs are fast gaining acclaim in the ceramics and collecting world.

Cortman began by leasing 1000 square feet at the Ellgreave Pottery, the same site where only a few years earlier the Artone Pottery was operating. The Ellgreave Pottery site had been owned and operated by Wood and Sons prior to Artone and dates back to 1921. To quickly launch its new business, Cortman bought a number of Shorter & Son and Wood Potters of Burslem molds at auction. Business did grow quickly and, to keep up with the increased production volume, the firm moved into the Crownford Works site on New Castle Street at the end of 1997. Crownford Works is a larger and more modern facility of approximately 5500 square feet located at the other end of Ellgreave Road.

Cortman purchased the Old Court Pottery portion of the J. Fryer Pottery when Fryer ceased operations on November 22, 1998. Cortman obtained additional space across the street from the Crownford Works to accommodate Old Court production. Under the direction of James Fryer and his daughter Marianne, production of Old Court's art pottery, luster ware and limited edition figurines and jugs have resumed with the Old Court Pottery name.

In addition to Lorna Bailey, several noted designers have done work for the firm. Tom Davis and Anthony Cartlidge are two of these. Tom, a mold maker from Royal Doulton, had previously done freelance designs for the Artone Pottery at the same site. Anthony also modeled for Bairstow Manor and Staffordshire Fine Ceramics. In addition to exciting new designs sold under the label of LJB Ceramics, Lorna Bailey, and Old Court, the firm also produces goods under the names of Shorter, Old Ellgreave Pottery, and Woods Potteries.

Founder Lionel Bailey and his daughter Lorna Bailey standing in front of a kiln at the Cortman factory. Lionel is holding the Lorna Bailey prototype Character Jug and Lorna is holding one of her art deco design vases.

Character Jugs and Toby Jugs

Cortman created exciting new Character and Toby Jug designs under the Old Ellgreave Pottery tradename. On commission from the American Toby Jug Museum, the company designed a giant Toby Philpot jug. Standing over three feet tall, this jug surpassed Roy Kirkham Pottery's giant Toby Philpot as the largest Toby Jug in the world. Cortman's Toby Philpot was modeled by Anthony Cartlidge and hand painted by Lorna Bailey. Originally, Toby was planned as a limited edition of fifty jugs, with the first delivered to the Museum in 1999 and others available by special order only; however, less than ten were actually made.

On commission, Cortman produced a large Toby Jug of Eleazer Wheelock, the founder of Dartmouth College in 1769. Co-author Steve Mullins, a Dartmouth College graduate, commissioned this jug in 1998. The first jug was presented to retiring President James O. Freedman. The Eleazer Wheelock Toby was also offered to Dartmouth alumni in a limited edition of 150. The handle of the jug depicts Samson Occum, a Native American Indian who was Dartmouth's first fundraiser.

The Lorna Bailey Character Jug is a one-of-a-kind prototype that was modeled by Anthony Cartlidge for Lorna herself. In spite of the fact that Lorna does not think it is a good likeness, it may be put into production one day.

Another exciting Toby Jug series is the Alice in Wonderland Series. This collection consists of twelve characters including Alice, the March Hare, and the Mad Hatter among other favorites. This series was produced from Tony Wood molds and distributed with the Old Ellgreave Pottery backstamp. LJB's Tubby Toby and Toby Philpot both come in a variety of colorways and sizes.

Through Cortman's successful bidding at auctions and other acquisitions, Lionel estimates that the firm now owns about one-third of the Shorter & Son Toby and Character Jug molds, including all of the small D'Oyly Carte molds. Some of the jugs currently in production are easily recognized as Shorter favorites. For example, LJB's Clay Pipe Toby is Shorter's Mr. Farmer. Until 1996, Cortman used a mark with "Shorter" in block letters on jugs produced from Shorter & Son molds. Thereafter, it changed the mark to "Hand Painted by Shorter."

The catalogue sheets on pages 70 - 72 are courtesy of Lionel Bailey.

Eleazor Wheelock backstamp

Old Ellgreave Pottery backstamp

Prototype Character Jug of Lorna Bailey, inspirational designer of the rapidly expanding Lorna Bailey Art Deco line

Alice in Wonderland Toby Jugs from original Tony Wood molds, top row left to right - Ugly Duchess, Mad Hatter, Jabberwocky, and Queen of Hearts; bottom row left to right - White Knight, Lion, Walrus, and Black Knight. All jugs carry Old Ellgreave backstamp

Character Jug Name	Backstamp	Height, Inches	Production Life
Admiral	Shorter	3 1/2	1995 - Current
Beefeater	Shorter	2	1995 - Current
Clown	Shorter	4 1/4	1995 - Current
Irish Mike	Shorter	3 3/4	1995 - Current
Lorna Bailey	Old Ellgreave	6 1/4	1998
Mountaineer	Shorter	4	1995 - Current
Smuggler	Shorter	3 1/4	1995 - Current
Winston Churchill	Shorter	5 1/2	1995 - Current

Front and rear views of Eleazer Wheelock Toby Jug, founder and first President of Dartmouth College; special commission for the Dartmouth Alumni by Steve Mullins; rear view shows handle of Samson Occom, Darmouth's first fund raiser.

Toby Jug Name	Backstamp	Height, Inches	Production Life
Aaron	Wood Potters	6 1/2	1995 - Current
Alice	Old Ellgreave	3 1/2	1997 - Current
Beefeater	Shorter Shorter	5 1/2 4	1995 - Current 1995 - Current
Benjamin	Wood Potters	7 5/8	1995 - Current
Betsy	Wood Potters	5 3/4	1995 - Current
Black Knight	Old Ellgreave	3	1997 - Current
Carpenter	Old Ellgreave	3	1997 - Current
Caterpillar	Old Ellgreave	3 3/8	1997 - Current
Clay Pipe Toby	Shorter	4 1/2	1995 - Current
Clerk		mini	1995 - Current
Coachman	Wood Potters Shorter	8 small	1995 - Current 1995 - Current
Dick Whittington	Shorter	4 1/4	1995 - Current
Drunken Parson	Old Ellgreave	3 1/8	1995 - Current
Eleazer Wheelock	Old Ellgreave	10	1998 Ltd Ed of 150
Father Neptune	Shorter	9 1/2	1995 - Current
Flower Seller	Shorter	5	1995 - Current
Friar Tuck	Shorter	extra large	1995 - Current
Gamekeeper	Old Ellgreave	3 1/4	1995 - Current
Gardener	Shorter Shorter	8 4 1/4	1995 - Current 1995 - Current
Guardsman	Shorter	4 1/2	1995 - Current
Haymaker		mini	1995 - Current
Hearty Good Fellow		9 1/2 small	1995 - Current 1995 - Current
Highlander	Old Ellgreave	8	1995 - Current
HMS Cheerio	Shorter	7	1995 - Current
Jabberwocky	Old Ellgreave	3	1997 - Current
Jabez	Wood Potters	7 1/2	1995 - Current
Jester			
John Bull	Shorter	5 1/2	1995 - Current
Jolly Miller		9 1/2	1995 - Current
Judy			
Lion	Old Ellgreave	3 1/4	1997 - Current
Long John Silver	Shorter	small	1995 - Current
Lord Howe		5 3/4	1995 - Current

Toby Jug Name	Backstamp	Height, Inches	Production Life
Lord Mayor		7	1995 - Current
Lover		mini	1995 - Current
Mad Hatter	Old Ellgreave	3	1997 - Current
March Hare	Old Ellgreave	3 3/8	1997 - Current
Martha Gunn	Old Ellgreave	5 3/4 3 1/4	1995 - Current 1995 - Current
Moses	Wood Potters	5 3/4	1995 - Current
Musician		mini	1995 - Current
Newsboy			
Pearly King	Shorter	6 1/2	1995 - Current
Pearly Queen	Shorter	7	1995 - Current
Piper	Old Ellgreave	7 1/2	1995 - Current
Policeman	Shorter	5	1995 - Current
Queen of Hearts	Old Ellgreave	3	1997 - Current
Ralph Wood		mini	1995 - Current
Royal Volunteer	Shorter	7 1/2	1995 - Current
Sailor	Old Ellgreave	5 3/4 3 1/8	1995 - Current 1995 - Current
Shepherd	Old Ellgreave	3	1995 - Current
Shepherdess	Old Ellgreave	3 1/2	1995 - Current
Toby Philpot	Old Ellgreave	39 7 6 5 3/4 5 3	1998 1995 - Current 1995 - Current 1995 - Current 1995 - Current 1995 - Current
Trumpeter	Shorter Shorter	7 4 1/2	1995 - Current 1995 - Current
Tubby Toby		6 1/2 5 1/2 4 3 1/2	1995 - Current 1995 - Current 1995 - Current 1995 - Current
Tweedle Dee & Dum	Old Ellgreave	3 1/8	1997 - Current
Ugly Duchess	Old Ellgreave	2 7/8	1997 - Current
Uncle Sam	Old Ellgreave	10	1999
Walrus	Old Ellgreave	3	1997 - Current
White Knight	Old Ellgreave	3	1997 - Current
White Rabbit	Old Ellgreave	3 1/2	1997 - Current

World's largest Toby Jug, standing three feet tall, commissioned by author Steve Mullins for the American Toby Jug Museum in Evanston, Illinois

Assortment of Toby and Character Jugs from original Shorter & Son molds produced by Cortman; all jugs carry the modern Shorter marks used by Cortman

Assortment of Toby and Character Jugs from original Wood & Sons, Tony Wood and Wood Potters of Burslem molds and produced by Cortman; all jugs bear the "Wood of Burslem" backstamp

Set of small size Gilbert and Sullivan D'Oyly Carte Toby Jugs from original Shorter & Son molds produced by Cortman; all jugs carry the modern Shorter marks used by Cortman

Assortment of teapots and creamers from original Wood & Sons, Tony Wood, and Wood Potters of Burslem molds, produced by Cortman; all jugs carry the modern "Wood of Burslem" backstamp

Coventry Pottery
Barberton, Ohio

Character Jug Name	Model Number	Height, inches
English	5556A	4 7/8
Jolly Fellow	5557A	4 7/8
Mephistopheles	5558A	4 1/2

Toby Jug Name	Model Number	Height, inches
Junk Man	5561A	5 1/2
Monk	5560A	5 3/4

History

Mrs. Carrie Daum founded Coventry Pottery in Barberton, Ohio in 1932. Coventry Ware was the tradename used by the firm on a variety of ware, including chalk figurines. Coventry also produced a wide range of porcelain Hummel-like figures and animal figurines, many of which were produced in gilded porcelain.

One of the key designers for the firm was Elaine Carlock, who worked there in the 1940s and 50s. At its peak, Coventry employed only thirty people and therefore its output was relatively low compared to other firms. The firm remained in active production through the late 1960s.

Character Jugs and Toby Jugs

Coventry produced a few Character and Toby Jugs beginning in the 1940s, as documented in a company catalog page from the later part of that decade. The English and Jolly Fellow Character Jugs are reproductions of the popular Sarreguemines jugs.

Coventry gold ink backstamp

Mephistopheles Character Jug

Monk and Junk Man Toby Jugs

Creek Pottery
Checkotah, Oklahoma

History

The Creek Indian Nation in Checkotah, Oklahoma founded the Creek Pottery. The small pottery was short lived, operating only from 1970 until 1976. Chief Dede McIntosh managed the pottery and was aided by John Frank of the nearby Frankoma Pottery. Frank loaned molds and provided raw materials and his expertise to the Creek Pottery. At its peak, Creek employed around fifteen workers.

Character Jugs

Creek Pottery produced an Indian Chief Character Jug with a tomahawk handle. He has been found in an all over turquoise blue glaze with red and green highlights. The jug is incised on the base with a triangular teepee and "Creek" in angular letters.

Character Jug Name	Height, inches
Indian Chief	4 1/2

Crown Clarence
See Co-operative Wholesale Society

Crown Devon
See Fielding & Company Limited

Crown Staffordshire Porcelain Company Limited
Fenton, England

History

The Crown Staffordshire Porcelain Company has a long family tradition dating back to the early 1800s and an enterprising young potter named Thomas Green.

Thomas Green (1798 - 1859) was the son of a potter who, aside from learning from his father as a child, apprenticed at Minton beginning in 1822 and from there moved to Copeland. Branching out on his own, Green founded the Minerva Works in Fenton in May of 1833 along with Mr. Richards, his partner and brother-in-law.

Operating as Green & Richards, the pottery flourished. Over the years, Thomas brought four of his eight sons into the business, two as sales representatives, one as an artist, and another as the Production Manager. The 1840s was a period of great growth and expansion for the firm. The pottery operated as T. Green between 1847 and 1859, when Thomas Green died. The family continued production under the direction of Thomas' widow Mary and their son Spencer, operating as Mary Green & Company. In 1877 Mary passed away and Spencer carried on the family pottery as T. A. & S. Green, along with his brother Thomas A. Green and two sons Alfred and Samuel Green.

The pottery continued to prosper and construction at the site resulted in a new warehouse in 1880. Thomas A. Green assumed full ownership of the firm in 1889 and changed its name to Crown Staffordshire in 1897. Around the turn of the century, Alfred Green, who was very interested in china production, led the introduction of a wide range of china ware, resulting in the firm's name changing to Crown Staffordshire Porcelain Limited in 1903 to reflect this popular new range.

The 1910s were a difficult decade for the firm. Alfred Green died in 1913. World War I reduced demand for fine china significantly. A fire in the factory caused a setback, but production was not too impacted. In 1919, Samuel Green and his younger brother Douglas Green formed a partnership and rededicated the firm to high quality bone china production. Three new directors were added to the firm as well, Alfred's son Richard Green and Samuel's sons Frank Green and Samuel Sinclair Green.

Crown Staffordshire Porcelain emerged from World War I reenergized and entered into a very prolific period, producing a huge selection of primarily bone china tableware, figures, and other porcelain fancy items. The factory specialized in hand molded, delicate, applied porcelain flowers. As an indication its overwhelming number of designs, by 1922 Crown Staffordshire Porcelain had exceeded pattern number 10,000.

Both before and during World War II, the factory produced a large amount of china for the British Armed Forces. Samuel Green died in 1940 and Douglas Green was named the new Managing Director. After World War II, export demand for fine china escalated quickly. Crown Staffordshire Porcelain purchased the

Toby Jug Name	Height, inches
Betsy Prigg	3
Little Dorrit	3
Mr. Pickwick	3 1/4
Ordinary Toby	7
Snufftaker	1 3/4
Standing Toby	3 3/4
Squire	4 1/2
Trotty Veck	2 7/8

Crown Staffordshire backstamp

Tiny Snufftaker Toby Jug and four inch tall Standing Toby

Heron Cross factory in Fenton to keep up with this export demand and then rebuilt the Minerva plant, replacing the old bottle kilns with more efficient and high volume tunnel kilns. The pottery's name was changed to Crown Staffordshire China Company Limited in 1948, perhaps representing a focus on bone china dinnerware. By the 1950s, the pottery had built an international reputation for its decorative china flowers and had added two North American subsidiaries for distribution.

Samuel Sinclair Green was named Chairman and Managing Direction of the pottery in 1954. The Green family retained control of Crown Staffordshire China until 1964, when the Semart Importing Company purchased the factory and continued operating it. Semart Importing became the Automatic Retailers of America in 1966. In November of 1973, the Wedgwood Group took over the pottery and, under the direction of Mr. Brain, used the Crown Staffordshire tradename on selected products until 1985. The majority of the firm's marks included a crown and the words "Crown Staffordshire", "Staffordshire", or "Staffs".

Toby Jugs

Crown Staffordshire produced good quality, small porcelain Toby Jugs of traditional Toby characters, including the popular Dickens characters. These Dickens tobies have the same appearance as those by Sitzendorfer, Sandizell, and Crown Winsor, including the character's name impressed across the lower front of the jug. An unanswered question is the relationship between these firms and whether one firm acquired molds from another. The mark on these jugs indicates production from the 1930s onward.

Left to right - miniature Standing Toby, Squat Toby inkwell, two tiny Snufftakers, Betsy Prig, and Trotty Veck

Crown Winsor
Longton, England

Toby Jug Name	Height, inches
Leprechaun	4 3/4
Mandolin Player	6

Crown Winsor Staffordshire Character Jugs backstamp

History

Crown Winsor was the operating name of a pottery owned by the North Midland Co-Operative Society. The North Midland Co-Operative Society was formed in 1982 to purchase the land, buildings and business of Shaw and Copestake, which had gone out of business in May of that year. The Society acquired the Shaw and Copestake designs, facilities and tradenames, including SylvaC and Falcon Ware. After a failed lease to a worker's co-operative named Longton Ceramics, the Society reorganized and took over the pottery business itself in early 1984 as the United Co-Operative Society. The firm produced goods marked "Crown Winsor" until 1989, when it closed and the assets were sold to Portmeiron.

Character Jugs and Toby Jugs

Among other Shaw and Copestake goods, Crown Winsor immediately began producing Shaw and Copestake Toby and Character Jugs under its own tradename. Therefore, it is possible to find the same jug with Crown Winsor, SylvaC or Kelsboro Ware backstamps. All of these jugs carry the same inscribed model numbers used by Shaw and Copestake. In a few cases, Crown Winsor jugs have surfaced that appear to be cast from Grimawades' Royal Winton molds. While a documented connection has not been found between these potteries, Billy Grindy likely carried the designs or molds with him from Grimwades to Shaw and Copestake, where he modeled many of its Character and Toby Jugs.

Crown Winsor designed and issued a collection of Character Jugs beginning in 1984 called the Series of American Presidents. The firm also created Working Man Series of Character Jugs. The Crown Winsor backstamp is a crown over a Staffordshire knot and often includes the phrase "Staffordshire Character Jugs." "CERNO" is sometimes found as well.

Working Man Series of Character Jugs; top row left to right: Farmer and Miner; bottom row left to right: Game Keeper, Sweep, and Shoemaker

Top row left to right: Shakespeare, Henry VIII, Mr. Winkle, and Chelsea Pensioner; bottom row left to right: Yeoman of the Guard, Lifeguard, and Grenadier Guardsman

Character Jug Name	Height, inches
Auld Mac	4 1/2
Cavalier	
Chelsea Pensioner	4 1/2
Dwight D. Eisenhower	4 3/4
Farmer	4 3/4
Fisherman	5 1/4
Game Keeper	4 5/8
George Washington	5
Grenadier Guardsman	5 1/4
Henry VIII	4 1/4
King Neptune	3 1/4
Lifeguard	5 1/2
Miner	4 1/2
Mr. Pickwick	3 1/4
Mr. Winkle	3 1/4
Sam Weller	
Santa Clause	4 1/4
Seafarer	2 1/2
Shakespeare	5 1/2
Shoemaker	4 5/8
Sweep	5 1/4
Watchman	3 1/2
Winston Churchill	4 1/2
Yeoman of the Guard	5 1/4 4 1/2

Winston Churchill and Dwight D. Eisenhower Character Jugs

Leprechaun Toby Jug

Mandolin Player Toby Jug

Dartmouth Pottery Devon, England

History

Dartmouth Pottery began operating in Dartmouth, Devon in 1947 and is still active today. The firm initially produced traditional torquay cottageware that was hand–thrown and hand-painted. Later the firm changed to molded products with transfer decorations. Dartmouth started Britannia Designs in 1958 as a subsidiary focused on souvenir goods. Dartmouth continues production today offering a variety of earthenware goods based on a red clay body finished in traditional torquay glazes. Mottoware is one of its primary products.

The firm's ware can be found with one of several marks, as well as commonly found unmarked. The most basic mark is "Dartmouth Hand Made in England Pottery" incised or stamped. A more ornate printed circular mark includes the words "Dartmouth Pottery Devon Made in England". Often the tradename Britannia Designs was used. The Dartmouth Pottery remains active under its present owner Samuel Heath.

Toby Jugs

As with all of its production, Dartmouth Toby Jugs were done in red earthenware and torquay finish. Its tobies are hard to find and, even if unmarked, can be easily identified by their red clay bodies and a very distinctive handle. The handle is plainly decorated but has a knob on top where one's thumb can rest. The Black Friar Toby was an advertising piece commissioned by the Black Friar Distillery. It was produced in both a full colorway and an all over brown finish. The Mermaid has only been found in a solid dark brown glaze.

Toby Jug Name	Height, inches
Black Friar	6 3/4
Mermaid	6 3/4
Ordinary Toby	5 1/2
	4 1/4
	3
Standing Toby	4
Town Crier	2 3/4

Mermaid Toby Jug

Two very different Ordinary Toby Jugs

Black Friar Toby Jug commissioned by Black Friar Distillery (from the collection of Virginia Brisco)

Dave Grossman Creations
St. Louis, Missouri

Dave Grossman backstamp for the Little Doc mug

History

Dave Grossman is a designer of collectible and limited edition works of art. After graduating from college, Dave, a St. Louis native, was commissioned to do a variety of architectural sculptures for various firms. One of his pieces can be seen in New York's Lincoln Center. He was also commissioned to sculpt busts of Presidents Johnson and Nixon.

Dave founded his own company, David Grossman Designs, in St. Louis in 1968, creating metal sculptures. In 1973, Dave Grossman Creations was launched. This firm's offerings were limited edition collectibles, most notably figurines and Christmas ornaments inspired by the work of Norman Rockwell. His was the first firm to produce collectible Rockwell figurines. From this successful start, the firm expanded into other licensed collectible figures and other collectibles, including The Wizard of Oz water globe collection, the Emmett Kelly Collection, Gone With the Wind figurines and bronze scenes, Bill Bell's Happy Cats, and most recently

Spencer Collin Lighthouses. Dave creates the designs and most of the firm's production is done in the Far East.

The company is still active and dedicated to offering high quality collectibles. The firm's plans include expanding the current lines of collectibles and adding new licensed limited editions. A Spencer Collin Lighthouse Collector's Club was recently started to bring together the admirers of these one-of-a-kind treasures. Dave Grossman remains the creative and artistic force behind the firm.

Character Mugs

Dave Grossman Creations released a high quality set of Character Mugs in 1979 and 1980 based on famous Saturday Evening Post cover art by Norman Rockwell. The issue price for these mugs was $35 each, except for NRM-7 that sold for $40. These mugs were produced in Japan and are well designed with a matte finish. They hold true to the Norman Rockwell artwork.

Character Mug Name	Height, Inches	Model Number	SEP Cover Date
Cowboy	4 1/4	NRM-2	August 13, 1927
Fisherman	4 1/4	NRM-6	August 4, 1929
Hobo	4 1/4	NRM-5	October 18, 1924
Jester	4 1/4	NRM-4	February 11, 1939
Little Doc	4 1/4	NRM-1	April 23, 1938
Merry Christmas	4 1/4	NRM-3	December 3, 1921
St. Nicholas	4 1/4	NRM-7	December 4, 1920

Top row left to right - Merry Christmas, Jester, and Cowboy; bottom row left to right - Fisherman, Little Doc, Hobo, and St. Nicholas

Davenport Pottery Company Limited
Longport, England

History

The Davenport pottery of Longton, Staffordshire has a long and enviable history dating back to 1793. Over the years, the pottery produced an impressive array of products in every imaginable ceramic body.

While Davenport did not produce any known Character or Toby Jugs, the firm did produce a limited edition set of high relief collector plates based on popular Toby Jug personalities. The Original Toby Plate Collection was sponsored by the Gladstone Pottery Museum and consisted of a set of six plates issued between 1984 and 1987.

Toby Plate Name	Diameter, inches
Falstaff	8 3/4
Friar Tuck	8 3/4
Jack Tar	8 3/4
Long John Silver	8 3/4
Mr. Pickwick	8 3/4
Toby Philpot	8 3/4

The Original Toby Plate Collection presented in order of issue; from top left to bottom right - Toby Philpot, Falstaff, Jack Tar, Mr. Pickwick, Long John Silver, and Friar Tuck

Delft
See France under Country of Manufacturer

Denby Pottery
See Joseph Bourne & Son

Denton China Limited
Longton, England

History

Denton China Limited operated in Longton, England from 1945 until 1968, producing fine china dinnerware, figures, jewelry and other bone china items. Denton China was purchased by the Aynsley Group in 1969, which, after an unsuccessful hostile takeover bid by Spode Limited, was taken over by the Waterford Glass Company in October of 1970.

Toby Jugs

The Denton mark found on Toby Jugs is "Best Bone Denton China England". Thus far, only the Ordinary Toby and Punch have been found. Others certainly exist, most likely a Judy.

Toby Jug Name	Height, inches
Ordinary Toby	4 1/8
Punch	2 1/4
	1 3/4
	1 3/8

Denton China mark

Ordinary Toby Jug with two sizes of Punch Toby Jugs

Desvres
Desvres, France

Character Jug Name	Height, inches	Production Life
Pierrott	6 1/2	ca 1915

Toby Jug Name	Height, inches	Production Life
Dog Soldier "392"		1903 - 1934
Man with Cane	5	post 1934
Soldier 3/4 body		1903 - 1934

History

Jean Francois Sta founded the Desvres factory in 1760. The factory remained in family control until 1887 with Sta's three sons assuming control of the pottery, one after another. During the late 19th Century, Desvres was best known for its faience production .

In 1903, Francois Masse bought the site and began producing majolica figures. After Francois died, his wife Marguerite ran the factory for awhile before passing control to their son, Robert. Desvres majolica produced by Masse is marked with an intertwined FM inside of a shield, a mark used until 1934. More recent production from the Desvres area, possibly dating from Post World War II, is marked simply with "Desvres".

Character Jugs and Toby Jugs

During Masse's ownership of the Desvres factory, a few majolica or faience jugs were produced. As majolica figures were only produced for a relatively short time by the firm, any pieces would be considered rare. The Pierrott Character Jug is a well-done comical character. It was potted in the Desvres area, but likely not at Masse's pottery. The Man with Cane is a modern Toby Jug also produced in the Desvres area.

Devon Tors Art Pottery
Devon, England

Character Jug Name	Height, inches
Uncle Tom Cobleigh	6

Toby Jug Name	Height, inches
John Bull - 3/4 body	4
Ordinary Toby	
Squat Toby	11
	6 1/2
	4 1/2
	4
	3 3/4
	3
	2 1/2

History

Brothers William and Frank Bond and Robert Fry founded the Devon Tors Art Pottery in 1921, right after the end of World War I. The pottery was located on Newton Abbot Road in Bovey Tracey, Devon. It produced mainly hand thrown red earthenware using local clay. The pottery began in a few small wooden buildings with foot-powered potter's wheels. Two larger buildings were constructed during 1936 and 1937 for decorating and glazing, with two new bottle kilns between them. Shortly thereafter, two showrooms were added.

Supplies of the local clay were scarce during the Second World War, so production was forced to scale back. Devon Tors' main production during this period was brown undecorated utilitarian ware. Devon Tors was renowned for its black and lapis lazuli blue colors, and its kingfisher designs, cottages, Toby Jugs, and earthenware pitchers. The firm also specialized in commemorative pieces for hotels, inns or special occasions. The pottery was sold in 1970 to Aidee International of Torquay. Aidee was previously a scent bottle customer of Devon Tors. It demolished the site and built a perfume factory.

Character Jugs and Toby Jugs

Devon Tors produced several Character and Toby Jugs. As with other Devon area potters, the pottery made a nice Character Jug of Uncle Tom Cobleigh. The Ordinary Toby came with or without a music box in the base. The Squat Toby was done in the Allertons style at the Bovey Tracey factory. It was produced in many sizes and with a variety of jacket colors including green, yellow, rust, brown, and light blue. The large Squat Toby mold was also used as a lamp base.

Uncle Tom Cobleigh Character Jug

John Bull 3/4 body Toby Jug

Squat Toby Jugs in various sizes and colorways

Extra large eleven inch tall Squat Toby
along with several smaller Squat Tobies

Devon Ware
See Fielding & Company

Devonia
See Torquay Pottery

Devonmoor Art Pottery Limited
Devon, England

History

The Devonmoor Art Pottery grew out of momentum started in Liverton by the Devon Ball Clay Company. Through backing from Farrows Bank Limited, Devon Ball Clay was incorporated on January 31, 1913 in Liverton at Newton Abbot, near Bovey Tracey, Devon. This backing was assured, as the three founders of Devon Ball Clay were also Directors of Farrows Bank. Devon Ball Clay was formed to take economic advantage of the reserves of clay at Halford, which were found by German nationals mining for lignite. With a small brickworks and separate pottery, Devon Ball began making pots and pans. The firm wanted to expand into art pottery and hired designer and mold maker Joe Vernon from Stoke to do so. Vernon arrived in Devon toward the end of 1913.

With the outbreak of World War I, the German management closed the factory in 1914 and returned to Germany. Vernon returned to Stoke. After the war, the brickworks and pottery re-opened, with the pottery now named Liverton Art Pottery. Joe Vernon returned around 1919 and immediately began

modeling wares for the firm, creating a large number of new designs. Success was not yet assured however, as Farrows Bank failed in December 1920, quickly followed by the demise of both Devon Ball Clay and Liverton Art Pottery. The pottery ceased production toward the end of 1921 and was liquidated on November 9, 1923. Joe Vernon returned to Stoke, not to come to Devon again, leaving his models and molds behind.

The Devonmoor Art Pottery rose out of these ashes. After the failure of the Liverton Art Pottery, Thomas H. Beare, the freeholder of the pottery, attempted to keep the factory working. He hired a manager, Mr. Sant, to assist him, but did not have much success. In the summer of 1922 Herford Hope and his wife Jennie appeared in Devon. Previously, Herford worked with his uncle, Mr. Mayer, at a pottery in the United States. Upon his uncle's death, Hope returned to England, and the couple began searching for a small pottery to own and operate. The Hopes founded Devonmoor Art Pottery in late 1922 through a lease of the

Mr. Pickwick Toby Jug

Miniature Standing Toby Jug

Tiny Judy and Highwayman Toby Jugs

Gay Old Bird Toby Jug

Newton Abbot site. They eventually purchased the pottery for 2,000 pounds. The lease and subsequent purchase included the existing assets of the factory and Joe Vernon's designs.

Herford Hope launched Devonmoor Pottery with the production of decorative giftware. The firm initially used readily available brown clay from the site, but by early 1923 Herford changed to a mixture of clays that fired to a hard white biscuit. Herford also experimented extensively with glazes. While the business was expanding using Vernon's molds, and Devonmoor's products were receiving industry recognition, there was a growing need to expand by adding new lines. This required the talents of a skilled modeler. Hope was not successful in trying to convince Joe Vernon to return yet again. Joe instead went on to work for Brannams of Barnstaple. The search for a modeler ended around Easter of 1924 when Bert Mellor joined the firm, moving to Devon from Stoke. Mellor designed a wide variety of wares for Devonmoor, including serving pieces, a wide range of quaint cottages, and a series of small animals in the mid 1940s.

The Second World War caused economic problems for the firm, but the telling blow was Herford Hope's death. On February 1, 1941, Hope was found dead near his treasured tennis court. Herford willed the company to the employees as a limited company, and Devonmoor Art Pottery became a limited company in 1941 with Bert Mellor the majority shareholder. Displeased with the will, Hope's family contested it and in May of 1949 the High Court ruled that Herford's wishes would last only for fourteen years; afterward the ownership of

the company would revert to the family.

Per the court order, on February 1, 1955, Roger Hope, Herford's son, became the Managing Director of the pottery, with Bert Mellor and the Directors all leaving the firm immediately. This change in management, plus changing public tastes, led to a drastic change in the pottery's offerings. Roger chose to produce more decorated utilitarian wares. Devonmoor's blue and white souvenir ware became a key creation at this time. However, in the 1960s and 1970s, sales began to decline. By 1977, few new wares were being introduced and production had sunk. The final high volume firing in 1977 consisted of a white mug commemorating the Silver Jubilee of Her Majesty the Queen. For the next several years there was little activity at the factory and no goods were produced after 1981. Under the Companies Act of 1985, the government closed Devonmoor Art Pottery in January of 1986.

As with many other potteries, it is common to find artist's initials handpainted on the base of an item. Since it is believed that decorators were paid by the item at Devonmoor, this sort of marking provided for an accurate accounting of work. Jennie Hope was the pottery's first paintress, and she likely trained many that joined the firm in the early years. Following is a list of artist's initials that may appear on Devonmoor pottery. Perhaps the most famous of Devonmoor's artists was Winifred Tapper, whose initials are WMT. Winifred was another of the early paintresses at Devonmoor, and was trained by Mrs. Hope herself. A table of the known artists and their initials follows.

Bacchus Character Jug in two colorways

BA	B. Andrews	IP	Isabel Proctor (also IB)
		JB	Jack Boucher
		JH	Jill Holcombe, later Jill Hope
BM	Barbara Morley	KS	Kathleen Sampson
BM	Betty Morrish (also BR)	LK	Louise Kropka later Kapaski
		LM	Leslie Manley
BR	Betty Rouse	MC	Marjorie Cornish
BT	Bernice Tarr	MT	Marjorie Tarr, later MC
DB	Doreen Butress	NG	Nesta Guest
DE	Daisy Emmett, later DRH	NP	Nora Ponsford (also NS)
		NS	Nora Slatterley
DID	Doris Davis	OG	unknown
DL	Dorothy Lloyd	PC	Phyllis Cann
DRH	Daisy Rees-Hill	PS	Phyllis Sanders
ES	Ethel Stick	RE	Rose Emmett
FW	Florrie Woolacott	SS	Sheila Sampson
GN	Gwen Norman	GP	Gladys Powlesland
HJL	Hazel J. Leaman	WM	Winifred Manley
HL	Hazel J. Leaman	WMT	Winifred M. Tapper
IB	Isabel Bloor	YS	Yvonne Street

Full and Empty reversible mug, showing upright and upside down positions

Character Jugs and Toby Jugs

Devonmoor produced several amusing and yet charming Character Jugs. During his prolific one year of designing for Liverton Art Pottery, Joe Vernon modeled a set of Character Jugs and related wares based on the seven travelers from the song *Widdecombe Fair*. The first verse of this well-known, and most popular, Devonshire song is:

"Tom Pearse, Tom Pearse, lend me your gray mare, All along, down along, out along lee, For I want to go to Widecombe Fair, Wi' Bill Brewer, Jan Stewer, Peter Gurney, Pety Davy, Dan'l Whiddon, Harry Hawk, old Uncle Tom Cobbleigh and all."

These jugs are very distinctive with pronounced facial features and a unique spout. They were produced in a variety of monochrome glazes, including yellow, green, blue and red. Uncle Tom Cobleigh also can be found in a rare full colorway. The character's name is impressed around the bottom of the jug, although this is often difficult to read due to heavy glazing and worn molds.

Vernon also created a Judy Toby in three sizes and the 6 1/2 inch Ordinary Toby Jug. Both of the taller Judy jugs came with a bonnet. However, over years of use most were either broken or lost, and so it is uncommon to find a Judy with her hat intact. Market values in the Price Guide are for Judy with her bonnet. The bird Toby Jug is titled A Gay Old Bird in painted letters around its base. This jug dates from early Devonmoor production and is a rare find today.

The most readily available Devonmoor Toby Jugs are the Ordinary Toby that comes in a wide variety of sizes and colors, ranging from a giant jug to some of the smallest tobies produced. Bert Mellor designed the majority of the Ordinary Toby jugs, perhaps one of the first tasks he undertook upon arriving at Devonmoor. Mellor added four smaller sizes to Vernon's Ordinary Toby, as well as a larger eight-inch Toby. An 8 1/2 inch Ordinary Toby that housed a music box in the base was added post World War II. The Ordinary Toby has a distinctive face with hand-painted crow's feet eyes and comes in a variety of colorways. The standard jacket colors are light green, maroon, dark blue and yellow; although other colors were used. Purple, dark green, light blue, and brown jackets are scarce. Early Toby Jugs have a horizontal line painted around the middle of the base, a brown pipe and brown handle. The line was dropped on later production, and the pipe and handle left white. Another unique characteristic that Devonmoor Ordinary Tobies share only with Watcombe Tobies is black painted jacket cuffs and pockets. This broad range of Toby Jugs was certainly one of Devonmoor's best selling lines.

Mellor's most ambitious undertaking was the giant version of the Ordinary Toby. This jug stands almost twenty-four inches tall and was designed as an eye-catcher to be used at Devonmoor's retail shops, enticing customers into the store. The giant Toby was made in a very limited quantity and handpainted by Daisy Rees-Hill. One such Toby was displayed at Marshall Field & Company's State Street store in Chicago for many years. From there it spent several more years adorning a hotel bar in Detroit. This particular jug now resides in the American Toby Jug Museum in Evanston, Illinois.

Following his Toby Jug success, Mellor created a broad selection of derivative Toby works including sugar shakers, cruet sets, and lamp bases. One such set was a Baron de Boeuf condiment set, which included a Baron creamer. Perhaps the most unique derivative item was a 6 3/4 inch tall Toby smoker piece that held the cigarettes in the body, with the hat serving as an ashtray, and with a place for the box of matches in the base. The Winker Character Jug also came with a matching shaving mug with Sweeney Todd painted around the top. The Highwayman Toby Jug is simply the tiny Standing Toby with a mask painted on his face.

Bert Mellor also designed the Simple Simon teaset in the style of Joe Vernon. The set consisted of an Old Mother Hubbard creamer, a Georgie Porgie sugar basin and jam pot, and a Simple Simon teapot. This teaset came in solid colors of green or blue, as well as in a basic cream finish with hand-painted accent colors around the face and collar. Mellor's range of Dickens Toby Jugs was produced post World War II and only in limited quantities, as very few have been seen. Each character's name is embossed on the front of the jug.

These jugs are most commonly stamped or impressed "Devonmoor Made in England", or "Devonmoor England". "Devonmoor Art Pottery" may also be found, as well as unmarked pieces. Toby Jugs also often carried the initials of the artist who hand painted the jug. More rarely, an incised "BM" for Bert Mellor can be found on ordinary tobies. Other initials found on Toby Jugs include A, B, DD, RS, ST, or X. Whose initials these are remain unknown. As much of Devonmoor's production was sold throughout England to tourist traffic, it is not uncommon to find jugs with town and village names painted on the front.

Most of the Devonmoor photos are from the collection of John Hobbs.

Character Jug Name	Height, Inches	Production Life
Bacchus	4	1923 - 1930s
Baron de Boeuf	3 3/8	1929 - 1930s
Bill Brewer	6 1/4	1922 - 1930s
Dan'l Whidden	6 1/4	1922 - 1930s
Harry Hawke	6 1/4	1922 - 1930s
Jan Stewert	6 1/4	1922 - 1930s
Old Mother Hubbard	3 1/4	1926 - 1930s
Old Uncle Tom Cobbleigh	6 1/4 1 1/4	1922 - 1930s 1922 - 1930s
Peter Davey	6 1/4	1922 - 1930s
Peter Gurney	6 1/4	1922 - 1930s
Winker	5	

Widecombe Fair Character Jugs; top row left to right - Dan'l Whiddon, Jan Stewert, Bill Brewer, and Harry Hawke; bottom row left to right - Peter Davey, Uncle Tom Cobleigh, and Peter Gurney

Toby Jug Name	Height, Inches	Production Life
A Gay Old Bird	8 1/2	1922 - 1932
Highwayman	1 1/2	1924 - 1955
Judy	10 1/4 7 3/4 1 1/2	1922 - 1960s 1922 - 1960s 1922 - 1960s
Mr. Micawber	3 3/4	1946 - 1950s
Mr. Pickwick	3 7/8	1946 - 1950s
Ordinary Toby	23 1/4 8 1/2 8 6 3/4 5 1/4 4 3 1/4 2 3/4 2 1/4	1930s 1946 - 1960s 1924 - 1955 1922 - 1955 1924 - 1955 1924 - 1955 1924 - 1955 1924 - 1955 1924 - 1955
Standing Toby	3 1/4 1 1/2	1924 - 1955 1924 - 1955
Tony Weller	6 1/2	1946 - 1950s

Three colorways of Uncle Tom Cobleigh Character Jug from Widdecombe Fair

Winker Character Jug and Sweeny Todd the Mad Barber shaving mug

Derivatives	Height, Inches
Cigarette and match holder - Ordinary Toby	
Music Box - Ordinary Toby	
Mustard Pot - Baron de Boeuf Judy Ordinary Toby	2 1/2 2 1/2
Pepper Shaker - Judy	2 1/2
Preserves Pot - Judy	
Salt Shaker - Ordinary Toby	2 1/2
Shaving Mug - Sweeney Todd	
Sugar Bowl - Georgie Porgie	3
Sugar Sifter - Ordinary Toby	5
Teapot - Simple Simon	

Ordinary Toby Jugs in rare colorways of dark green, lavender, and orange; the two tobies on the right are from the Joe Vernon mold

Three Judy Toby Jugs

Graduated set of six Ordinary Toby Jugs ranging from 8 1/2 inches tall to 2 3/4 inches tall (from the collection of Bill and Pam Foster)

Giant 23" tall Ordinary Toby surrounded by Ordinary Toby Jugs in various sizes and colorways, displayed at the American Toby Jug Museum

Ordinary Toby cigarette and match holder, the hat serves as an ashtray

Mother Goose teaset consisting of Georgie Porgie sugar, Simple Simon teapot, and Old Mother Hubbard creamer

Mother Goose teaset in blue colorway

Baron de Boeuf cruet set

Pair of Ordinary Toby Jugs with musical movements in their bases

Variety of cruet sets in various sizes and with lids on and off

Ebeling and Reuss
Devon, Pennsylvania

History

Ebeling and Reuss was an importer of high quality giftware and distributor to the North America market. The firm operated out of Philadelphia from 1886 and later relocated to Devon, Pennsylvania where it was still active in the late 1990s. Ebeling and Reuss was a major supplier of high-end porcelain figurines to jewelry shops in the northeastern United States. It imported a wide variety of goods in the first half of the twentieth century, including animal figures. Chintz dinnerware was imported from Czechoslovakia in large quantities after the end of World War I and into the 1930s. Chintz is highly collectible today, as are its Joan Walsh Anglund items. The company's import volume peaked in the 1940s and 1950s. George Ebeling was the long–time manager of the firm in the middle of the twentieth century.

The firm imported wares from many factories including the German firms of Furstenberg Porcelain in Furstenberg, E. Goebel Porcelain in Redental, Heinrich & Company in Selb, Jaeger and Company in Marktredwitz, and Carl Schumann Porcelain in Bavaria. Elsewhere in Europe, it also imported goods from Keramos in Vienna, Austria, Ditmar Urbach in Teplitz, Czechoslovakia, and Swarovski Crystal.

Carl Schumann supplied quality dinnerware from the 1960s through the 1980s. Before World War II the firm also imported goods from factories in Bohemia, Czechoslovakia. Pottery marked Czechoslovakia dates from 1918 to 1938, before the German occupation of the region in World War II. Production from this area became marked as Germany after 1938, perhaps by the same potter and with this same molds. Presently the names of these Bohemian potteries are unknown.

Many imported wares were sold using Ebeling and Reuss' tradename "Erphila." Erphila was derived from the E in Ebeling, R in Reuss, and phila from Philadelphia. Several marks appear on Ebeling and Reuss pottery. The most common mark is an ornate stamped E & R in script above "Est. 1886" with "Erphila" below. This mark appears on both Czechoslovakian and German wares. The Czech pieces are also stamped "Made in Czechoslovakia" in black. German pieces with this common mark are typically stamped in black ink with "Made in Germany" below, or the common mark may be enclosed within a circle with "Germany" underneath. Another mark on Czechoslovakian wares is an orange stamped "Made in Czechoslovakia by E R Erphila est 1886." This mark also appears on German goods with Germany substituted for Czechoslovakia.

In addition to importing goods for sale under its own tradename, Ebeling and Reuss also

Ebeling and Reuss Czechoslovakian backstamp

Ebeling & Reuss German Dickens Jugs backstamp

distributed goods for many other firms. In an agreement reached by George Ebeling and Gerald Wood, it distributed the ware of Price Brothers and later Price & Kensington for over twenty years.

Sailor Toby Jug

Character Jugs and Toby Jugs

Nicely modeled Character Jugs and Toby Jugs were produced for Ebeling and Reuss that were colorfully finished in underglaze paints. The majority of the Toby Jugs are Dickens characters with a round bulbous body and the character's name handpainted across the front of the jug's base. Besides the common Erphila mark, some pieces have been found stamped "Dickens Jugs Erphila Germany" or "Dutchy Jugs" in orange ink. The full range of Ebeling and Reuss' Toby Jug production has not yet been discovered.

The same Erphila Toby can be found with

either Czech or Germany marked on them. Often Erphila Toby Jugs were identified with only a foil label, which once removed makes conclusively identifying them more difficult. Jugs with the same bulbous body can also be found marked only "Germany;" perhaps these once had foil labels or were produced and distributed by the German potter after Ebeling and Reuss stopped importing from them.

It is highly likely, but yet unconfirmed, that Goebel produced some of the Ebeling and Reuss tobies. Certainly Erphila Dickens tobies and those of Goebel produced after World War II look virtually identical. More concretely, tobies have been found marked Erphila or Goebel, with both having the same model number impressed on the back of the jug. This tightly links the relationship between potter and importer. Ditmar Urbach designed the art deco animal jugs.

Character Jug Name	Height, Inches	Production Life
Goat "7038"	8 1/2	1918-1932
Mama Berenstain	3 3/4	1983

Toby Jug Name	Height, Inches	Production Life
Boy "S488 3/0"	4	1935-1949
Bumble	6 1/2	1932-1945
	4	1932-1945
Dog	6 1/2	
Dutch Boy "S486/2"	7	1935 - 1949
Dutch Girl "S484 3/0"	6	1918 - 1932
"S484 1/2"	5 3/4	1932-1945
	4 1/4	1932 - 1945
Hindu Boy "6185"	4 3/4	1932 - 1945
Mama Berenstain	8 1/4	1983
Mexican Boy	4 1/2	1918 - 1932
	3 3/4	1932 - 1945
Mexican Girl	4 1/2	1918 - 1932
Mr. Pickwick	6	1932 - 1945
	4	1932 - 1945
	3	1918 - 1945
Mrs. Gamp	4 3/4	1932 - 1945
	4	1932 - 1945
	3 1/8	1932 - 1945
"S28 3/0"	2 7/8	1932 - 1945
Quaker Man "S129 3/0"	3 1/2	
Rooster "921"	9 1/4	1918 - 1932
"1021"	6	1918 - 1932
Sailor	5 1/2	1918 - 1932
	4 1/4	1918 - 1932
Sam Weller	6 1/2	1932 - 1945
	4 3/4	1932 - 1945
	3 3/4	1932 - 1945
Standing Boy with pipe "6402"	5 7/8	1918 - 1945
Toucan "881"	9	1918 - 1932
"1796"	7 1/2	1918 - 1932
"3/8L"	6	1918 - 1932

Top row left to right - Mr. Bumble, Mr. Pickwick, and Sam Weller medium size jugs; bottom row left to right - Mrs. Gamp small and mini, mini Mr. Bumble, mini Mr. Pickwick, and Sam Weller in mini and small sizes

Left to right - Mexican Girl, Standing Boy with pipe, Hindu Boy, and Mexican Boy Toby Jugs

Two figural dog teapots of a Dachshund and a Terrier

History

Elijah Cotton founded the Lord Nelson Pottery of Hanley, England in 1758. Cotton located the pottery on a commercial road in Hanley that was on a major canal route. The canal provided the primary means of transportation for raw materials and finished goods. The pottery operated at this site for its entire existence. The street is now called Botteslow Street and a plaque commemorating the founding of the factory can be found on the corner.

The firm changed its name to Elijah Cotton, possibly shortly after Nelson's victory at Trafalgar because of the overwhelming popularity of Lord Nelson. However, it continued to use the tradenames Lord Nelson Ware and Lord Nelson Potteries on the majority of its production. During its history, the firm produced a wide range of pottery tableware.

During the 1930s, production was limited mainly to utilitarian everyday pottery and plain white hospital ware. After World War II, Elijah Cotton became world renown for its high quality breakfast ware, tea and coffee sets, and dinnerware. In the 1960s and 70s, Elijah Cotton formed a subsidiary named Contessa Giftware and used Contessa to market much of its decorative wares. Today the firm's chintz patterns are widely sought after and rising quickly in value.

Elijah Cotton remained in the Cotton family until 1975, when Emma Cotton converted the firm into a limited company and sold shares, many to the employees. At that time, Samuel Hodson, the Managing Director under Emma Cotton, took over as Chairman of the firm. He served in that capacity until 1979. Possibly precipitated by the lack of reinvestment in the firm, by 1979 the pottery was facing receivership. Rather than follow that path, the shareholders voted to sell the factory. The firm was taken over by Mr. Shemilt, who liquidated it one year later in 1980.

Character Jugs and Toby Jugs

Elijah Cotton produced Character and Toby Jugs from the late 1960s to the middle 1970s. These jugs are finished in an overall brown glaze with red, blue, black and metallic silver highlighting, creating a unique appearance. Derivative items were also made, including a Tub Boatman liquor container. Cotton used the tradename Royal Norfolk on this liquor container. Cotton's jugs did not sell well so were not produced in large volumes.

The 3 3/4 inch tall Ordinary Toby is incised "m/s", indicating medium size. This implies that there were larger and smaller versions produced, but these have not been found. Other jugs were probably produced which have not yet been identified. The stamped markings are "Lord Nelson Potteries" forming a semi-circle over an N with a sunburst above it. Other marks include a two-digit model number and a numeric code such as 9-74, which is possibly a production date code for September 1974. Jugs have also been found with incised marks or with no marks at all.

Character Jug Name	Height, Inches	Model Number
Beefeater	3 1/2	93
Fisherman	3 1/2	96
Old Gaffer	3 1/2	94
Tug Boatman	3 1/4	

Toby Jug Name	Height, Inches	Model Number
Ordinary Toby	3 3/4	91

Ordinary Toby Jug flanked by Character Jugs of Old Gaffer, Tug Boatman, Beefeater, and Fisherman

Enesco
See Jugs Marked by Country of Manufacture under Japan

Erphila
See Ebeling and Reuss

F. F. A. S.
See Jugs Marked by Country of Manufacture under France

Falcon Ware
See Shaw and Copestake, and J. H. Weatherby & Sons

Fancies Fayre
See Bairstow Manor

Fielding & Company Limited
Stoke, England

Chamberlain Character Jug with music box insert

Winston Churchill Character Jug

History

Fielding & Company had its beginnings in the 1870s when Simon Fielding, who previously worked for the Duke of Sutherland, invested his life's savings in the Railway Pottery Works at Sutherland Street in 1873. By 1878, Simon was on the verge of bankruptcy and his son Abraham bought the Railway Pottery outright, going into the business with his father. Abraham was instrumental in quickly growing the firm, so much so that operations were expanded in 1892 through new construction. Production volume increased by a factor of five by 1906. That year Simon passed away, and Abraham took over sole control of the firm. Fielding & Company became a limited company in 1905.

Fielding's initial wares included functional earthenware and several lines of majolica. By the beginning of the twentieth century, production of majolica ceased. The firm turned instead to vellum and red lusterware production, as well as musical novelties. The name Crown Devon came into use in the late 19th century and became Fielding's official tradename in 1905, after which most of its wares were marketed using the Crown Devon tradename and later Royal Crown Devon. To further reinforce the tradename's reputation, the Railway Works was renamed Devon Pottery in 1911.

Fielding & Company paid close attention to the demands of the public, attempting to capture the next fad or fancy to come along. More importantly, the firm also believed in continual modernization of its factory, adopting gas kilns as

early as 1913. This attention to customers' desires resulted in consistent growth through the 1920s and 1930s, with many new lines being added including fine examples of Art Deco products.

Ross Fielding, Abraham's son, took over the business in 1932 and led it through major reconstruction after World War II. Ross' son Reginald succeeded him in 1947. Reginald's largest challenge was a devastating fire in 1951 that destroyed most of the factory and a large amount of inventory. Production was completely halted for six months, and it took several years for the firm to match its pre-fire production volume. It was also Reginald who negotiated the purchase of Shorter and Son in 1964. Reginald retired in 1967, the last Fielding to manage the firm.

Fielding & Company was purchased by a Liverpool company in 1976, continuing operations under the Crown Devon name. The factory eventually closed in 1982 with the distinction of producing one of the widest ranges of wares by a family-owned pottery in over a century of operations. The firm's factory and manufacturing assets were sold to Caverswall China Company in May of 1983. Thomas Goode & Company, a London based retailer, acquired Caverswall one year later and soon sold the assets and molds at auction. The Fielding factory itself was demolished in 1987.

Older Fielding marks are "S. F. & Co England" with a lion on a crown, or crown on a shield. Between 1917 and 1930, the tradename Devon Ware was used. A "Crown Devon" mark is commonly found on production after 1905.

Character Jugs and Toby Jugs

Fielding & Company produced several Character Jugs and Toby Jugs throughout its active production life. One of the earliest known is Toby Sitting on a Barrel, which was done in a cream finish and marked with an impressed "Fieldings" on the base. A small sized Character Jug was imaged after Sarreguemines model number 3181, the Jolly Fellow. The Fielding version was sometimes issued with advertising. The firm also produced several advertising tobies. The musical Chamberlain Character Jug plays "Here's a Health unto His Majesty."

The Crown Devon Charrington Ale Toby comes with or without a Thorens music box in the base that plays the tune "Tavern in the Town". A yellow waistcoat on the Charrington jug is rare. The Burkes Whiskey jug has a continental look with a man sitting astride a barrel, and the Burkes name and slogan on it. The Ordinary Toby has a Devon Ware mark, which dates its production between 1917 and 1930.

Through its purchase of Shorter & Son in 1964, Fielding acquired the broad range of Shorter Toby and Character Jug molds. Driven by the popularity of the Shorter jugs, Fielding maintained the production of these jugs until going out of business. The Fielding-produced Shorter jugs initially carried the common Shorter & Son backstamp in green ink instead of black. Later, as the Shorter production was completely integrated into Fielding & Company, the Crown Devon mark was used on jugs from Shorter molds. One exception to this is the Winston Churchill Character Jug, which carries the Fieldings backstamp.

The following is a fairly comprehensive list of Fielding's jugs. New characters do occasionally surface though.

Charrington Toby Jug

Character Jug Name	Height, Inches	Production Life
Chamberlain with music box	6 1/4	
Dick Turpin	5	late 1960s
Hayseed	5 1/2	late 1960s
Jolly Fellow	4	1920s - 1930s
Pedro	5 1/2	late 1960s
Sheik	5 1/2	late 1960s
Winston Churchill	6 1/4	late 1960s

Toby Jug Name	Height, Inches	Production Life
Beefeater	8 3/4	late 1960s
Burkes Whiskey	11 1/4	1890 - 1910
Cavalier	9	late 1960s
Charrington Ale Toby yellow waistcoat	8 3/4 8 3/4	1913 - 1930 1913 - 1930
Chelsea Pensioner	6 1/2	late 1960s
Father Neptune	7	late 1960s
Guardsman	8 1/2	late 1960s
Long John Silver	9 3/4	late 1960s
Ordinary Toby	8 5/8 7 1/2 6 1/2	1917 - 1930
Scottie	8 3/4 4 3/8	late 1960s late 1960s
Toby sitting on barrel		1878 - 1905
Toby Phillpot	8 1/2	1920s - 1930s

Fieldings backstamp in black ink

Fitz and Floyd
Sri Lanka

History

Fitz and Floyd is a well-known distributor of ceramic giftware, with a large focus on holiday or special occasion items. The firm operates out of Sri Lanka, but much of the production is done in Taiwan and Japan. Tableware has been a mainstay for Fitz and Floyd. Early wares may be marked with a simple FF, a copyright symbol, and a year. More recent Fitz and Floyd products are marked OCI, which is Omnibus Collections International and operates as a division of the firm.

Character Jugs and Toby Jugs

As a part of its popular figural tableware offerings, Fitz and Floyd has produced a variety of Toby and Character Jugs over the past decade or two. Many of its jugs come as part of a set, such as creamers matched with sugars and teapots.

Witch Character Jug

Fitz and Floyd backstamp

Character Jug Name	Height, Inches	Production Life
Elsie	4 1/2	
Fancy Cat	7	1988
Gertrude Stein	4 3/4	1976
Hunting Fox	5	
Mad Hatter	4 3/4	1990 - 1992
Queen of Hearts	4	1992
Santa Clause	4	
Snowman		
Sherlock Hound	4 1/2	1993
Witch	3 1/2	1979

Frankenstein Toby Jug

Toby Jugs of Huntsman and Woman with basket

Toby Jug Name	Height, Inches	Production Life
Aunt Jemima		
Cat with fiddle	9	1986
Cockatoo	10 1/4	
Dracula	9	1987
Frankenstein	5 1/2	1978
Granny at tea	6 5/8	1992
Huntsman	9	
Leprechaun	5 1/4	1988
Owl	6 3	1978 1978
Parrot	6 1/8	1979 - 1980s
Santa Clause	10 5/8 9	1988 - 1994
Woman with basket	9	

Hunting Fox, Mad Hatter, and Fancy Cat Character Jugs

Leprechan and Granny at Tea Toby Jugs

Fives-Lille
Fives, France

Toby Jug Name	Height, Inches	Production Life
Automobilist Man		ca 1900
Automobilist Woman		ca 1900
Drunken Woman		
Frog		
Guard		
Je Sais Tout	9 3/4	
La Mere Michell		
Policeman		

History

Fives-Lille generally refers to pottery made in the general area of Lille, France, and its suburb Fives. Most notable among the potters of the area was the factory opened by Antoine Gustave De Bruyn in Lille, France in 1862. The site of the factory moved over the course of the first few years eventually ending up in Fives. Initial production was focused on stoneware and earthenware, then Antoine also began producing bricks and tiles. Beginning in 1887 and through 1938, the firm produced majolica.

De Bruyn left the company in 1891 and turned the firm over to his sons. The name was changed to De Bruyn & Sons and by World War I the pottery employed four hundred workers. In 1927 the name was simply De Bruyn Sons and the firm was experiencing internal struggles between the workers and the owners.

By 1950 the company was operating as three units. That year all three units were sold. Raymond Chevier purchased the Artistic Faience section. Raymond died in 1959 and Artistic Faience was closed on April 18, 1962. The De Bruyn mark is a D and B superimposed over an anchor.

Toby Jugs

The Artistic Faience unit of Fives-Lille is the group that produced the Fives-Lille Toby Jugs. Je Sais Tout means, "I know everything" and was a premium for purchasers of an entire encyclopedia set. La Mere Michelle depicts a French child's song about a woman who is crying because she lost her cat. Dating from just after the turn of the twentieth century, the Automobilist pair possibly depicts a husband and wife out for a Sunday drive in their new jalopy. All of these jugs are quite rare.

Foley
See Shelley Potteries

History

Thomas Forester entered the pottery business with a small pottery in 1877. Named the Church Street Majolica Works, the factory was located on High Street in Longton. Through much initial success and increasing demand, Thomas purchased nearby property and constructed a new factory, the Phoenix Works, in 1879. This was still not enough capacity to keep up with the demand, so he purchased a neighboring china factory shortly thereafter. By 1883, Forester employed approximately four hundred workers at the three sites. Around this time he brought his sons into the firm and changed the name of the company to Forester and Sons. In 1891, the pottery became a limited company.

With all three factories in full production, Forester was producing a wide variety of earthenware, bone china and majolica. Although not recognized for the same attention to detail as Minton, Forester built a widespread reputation for its majolica, and by the late 1800s, was producing a staggering twelve thousand pieces per week with new modern equipment. Forester's majolica production embodied many designs from other potters, such as Minton's storks and George Jones' birds and butterflies. Majolica production was cut back in 1888, but the firm continued producing other earthenware, including dinnerware. The pottery eventually closed in 1959.

Toby Jugs

Forester produced a three-quarter bodied majolica Monk Toby Jug in several sizes in the late 1800s and early 1900s. This Monk is quite content with a smile on his face and his hands caressing his belly. Although most Forester majolica was unmarked, the firm was known for the green and brown mottling of its majolica glazes. Forester was also known for its large range of gurgling fish jugs.

Toby Jug Name	Height, inches
Monk	11
	8
	6 1/2
	small

Monk Toby Jug

Frank Stoner
See Jugs Marked by Country of Manufacture under United Kingdom

Franklin Porcelain
Philadelphia, Pennsylvania

History

The Franklin Mint, headquartered in Philadelphia, has been the world's leading maker of limited edition collectibles for over three decades. In 1976 the firm launched a significant step in its corporate history by constructing a new porcelain production plant to expand its production capabilities.

On March 23, 1977 an open house was held at the new plant of Franklin Porcelain near Philadelphia. This 50,000 square foot, state-of-the-art plant was built in less than four months at a cost of two million dollars, and was the largest production house for collectible porcelain in the United States. Under the direction of Charles L. Andes as Chairman and CEO, and John Robinson as Vice President and General Manager, the plant started operations with one hundred employees, including sculptors, artisans, designers and production workers.

Production was centered on limited edition porcelain and bone china plates, figurines and sculptures. In spite of the plant's size and its talented workforce, Franklin Porcelain could not keep up with the demand for new products. By the end of 1977 another fifty employees had been hired and soon some production was moved to the Far East.

Character Jugs and Toby Jugs

Franklin Porcelain produced several series of limited edition Toby and Character Jugs, which were offered for sale on a subscription–only basis. Its first known venture into jug production was a series of high quality Toby Jugs produced in England by Wood and Sons. The Charles Dickens Toby Jug Collection was a series of twelve Dickens Toby Jugs released between 1978 and 1981. Peter Jackson, a famous English historical cartoonist, sculptor and artist, was selected to design the set. Please refer to Wood and Sons for detailed information on this collection.

Based on the success of the Dickens Toby Jug Collection, Franklin Porcelain next commissioned Jackson to design a second Toby Jug series called The Cries of Old London Toby Jugs. This authentic twelve jug collection depicted everyday folks from the streets of 19th century England.

Toby Jug Name	Height, inches
Baked Potato Vendor	6 3/4
Chimney Sweep	6 3/4
Coalman	6 1/4
Door Mat Maker	6 1/2
Flower Girl	6 1/2
Milk Maid	6 3/4
Old Clothes Man	6 3/4
Orange Girl	6 5/8
Organ Grinder	6 3/4
Oyster Woman	6 1/8
Street Doctor	6 1/2
Umbrella Man	6 3/4

Character Jug Name	Height, inches
Admiral Benbow	7
Admiral Jellicoe	7
Admiral Lord Cunningham	7
Admiral Lord Hood	7
Admiral Lord Howe	7
Admiral Lord Nelson	7
Admiral Lord St. Vincent	7
Admiral of the Fleet Lord Mountbaten of Burma	7
Admiral Robert Blake	7
Admiral Walter Raleigh	7
Alice	1 3/4
Artful Dodger	1 3/4
Captain Hook	1 3/4
Dick Turpin	1 3/4
Dr. Watson	1 3/4
Fagin	1 3/4
Friar Tuck	1 3/4
Henry V	1 3/4
Hornblower	1 3/4
Ivanhoe	1 1/2
King Arthur	1 3/4
Long John Silver	1 3/4
The Mad Hatter	1 3/4
Merlin	1 1/2
Mr. Micawber	1 3/4
Mr. Pickwick	1 3/4
Moll Flanders	1 3/4
Peter Pan	1 3/4
Richard III	1 1/2
Robin Hood	1 3/4
Robinson Crusoe	1 3/4
Scrooge	1 1/2
Sherlock Holmes	1 3/4
Sir Francis Drake	7
Sir John Falstaff	1 1/2
Sir Richard Grenville	7
Tom Jones	1 3/4

This collection was offered only by mail order subscription. Jugs were issued in a limited edition every other month beginning in late 1980 and running through 1982. The collection was originally priced at $55 each. Tobies from this series are more difficult to find than the Dickens tobies, possibly indicating that fewer were produced.

Franklin Porcelain followed these Toby Jug series with two Character Jug series. The first was a collection of twenty-five tiny sized Character Jugs called The English Heritage Miniature Toby Jug Collection. Note the misnomer of naming this a collection of Toby Jugs. Also designed by Peter Jackson, these jugs were issued by subscription in 1982 and 1983 through the Denver Mint, a Franklin subsidiary. Crafted in Malaysia, this is a high quality, hand painted porcelain Character Jug

collection with excellent modeling and design. The characters selected depict popular figures from many well-known works of literature, including those of Dickens, Shakespeare and Alice in Wonderland. Accompanying each jug was a card with a brief biography of the character. A Certificate of Authenticity was also provided with the set that was signed by Geoffrey Stroud, the Managing Director, and dated November 30, 1982.

The final series produced by Franklin Porcelain was the large sized Admiral Character Jug series. Depicting a collection of famous British Admirals, this series was modeled by Gerald Embleton and made in Malaysia for the Maritime Trust. The complete Admiral series numbered twelve and provides a spectacular collection when full.

Admiral Lord Cunningham and Admiral Lord Jellicoe Character Jugs

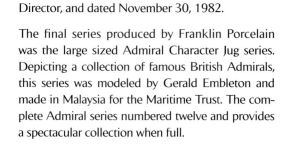

Group of tiny Character Jugs; top row left to right - Mr. Pickwick, Fagin, Scrooge, and Artful Dodger; bottom row left to right - Mr. Micawber, King Arthur, Merlin, and Long John Silver

Admiral Lord Hood and Admiral Lord St. Vincent Character Jugs

Group of tiny Character Jugs; top row left to right - Peter Pan, Captain Hook, Tom Jones, Alice, and Mad Hatter; bottom row left to right - Hornblower, Ivanhoe, Robinson Crusoe, and Dick Turpin

Admiral Lord Howe and Admiral of the Fleet Earl Mountbatten of Burma Character Jugs

Admiral Benbow Character Jug

Admiral Robert Blake Character Jug

Admiral Lord Nelson and Sir Richard Grenville Character Jugs

Group of tiny Character Jugs; top row left to right - Sir John Falstaff, Richard III, Henry V, and Moll Flanders; bottom row left to right - Sherlock Holmes, Dr. Watson, Robin Hood, and Friar Tuck

Cries of London Toby Jugs; left to right - Old Clothes Man, Door Mat Seller, and Chimney Sweep

Cries of London Toby Jugs; left to right - Orange Lady, Flower Girl, and Oyster Woman

Cries of London Toby Jugs; left to right - Street Doctor, Baked Potato Vendor, and Coalman

Sir Francis Drake and Sir Walter Raleigh Character Jugs

Franklin Porcelain Cries of London Series backstamp

Franklin Porcelain Admiral Series backstamp

Frankoma Pottery
Sapulpa, Oklahoma

History

John N. Frank founded Frankoma Pottery in 1933. After graduating from the Chicago Art Institute in 1927, Frank left Chicago and moved to Oklahoma. Before establishing his own pottery, John Frank formed a ceramic art department at the University of Oklahoma in Norman. He taught there as a ceramics professor for several years and also worked with the geological survey, identifying Oklahoma's clay deposits.

John Frank started a small pottery in Norman, Oklahoma in 1933 called Frank Potteries. Frank was equipped with one small kiln, a butter churn for mixing clay, and a few other simple tools. Three years later he left academic life and took up potting full-time. His wife Grace Lee joined him in this endeavor. Growth in demand and production exceeded the capacity of the studio and, in 1938, Frank relocated his firm to a larger facility in Sapulpa, Oklahoma, renaming it Frankoma.

Initial production used Oklahoma clay obtained near the small city of Ada. This clay resulted in a tan body after firing. In 1954 the firm switched to a local source of red clay from Sapulpa's Sugar Loaf Hill. This clay produced a terra-cotta looking body after firing. The firm uses a unique process of firing the clay and glaze together, fusing them at high temperatures. This process produces extremely rugged pottery.

Fire struck twice at the Sapulpa factory. The first fire happened shortly after opening during Frank's initial year at Sapulpa, a setback from which he simply rebuilt. This disaster was followed by many years of success and growth. The second fire occurred in 1983 and destroyed nearly the entire factory, including almost all of its molds. A new factory re-opened in the summer of 1984, but production was limited to only the molds created in 1983, plus any new designs. All of the old designs were lost.

The Frank's daughter, Joniece Frank, joined her parents at the firm, designing many new product lines for the pottery. Frankoma Pottery continues operating today and has the honor of being the only American pottery to be permanently exhibited at the International Ceramic Museum of Italy. The pottery produces dinnerware with serving pieces, mugs, commemorative pieces, novelties and souvenirs. Since 1993, it has skillfully combined local Native American Indian art and the Pioneer Spirit of over a century ago into collectible southwestern giftware.

Character Mugs

Frankoma made a series of Character Mugs that the firm referred to as six-ounce coffee mugs, all designed by Joniece Frank. These were issued annually beginning in 1976 with Uncle Sam commemorating the United States' bicentennial. After introduction, each mug was produced for a number of years; however, only mugs produced in the initial year carry the date of issue on the back of the mug, making them more desirable. During their introduction years, Uncle Sam was produced in a blue glaze, the Cowboy in prairie green, the Baseball Player and Irish in desert gold, and the Golfer in flame. A special red hued version of Uncle Sam was produced for the bicentennial year 1976. After the initial year of production, these mugs were glazed in a variety of colors. For example the Uncle Sam can also be found in vivid red, white and prairie green.

Character Mug Name	Height, Inches	Model Number	Production Life
Baseball Player	4 3/4	602	1978
Cowboy	4	601	1977
Golfer	4 1/2	603	1979
Irish	4	604	1980
Uncle Sam	4 4	600 600	1976 1977-1980s

Group of Character Mugs; top row left to right - Uncle Sam in bicentennial red, white, blue, and green colorways; bottom row left to right - Cowboy, Golfer, Irish, and Baseball Player

Frie Onnaing
See Onnaing

J. Fryer Limited
Tunstall, England

Oldcourt Pottery backstamp

NORTH AMERICAN HERITAGE
LIMITED EDITION
THE RT. HON. JOHN G. DIEFENBAKER
BY J. FRYER LTD. ENGLAND
FOR E. A. KEATE, VAN. B.C.

Gold underglaze backstamp of John Diefenbaker jug

History

James Fryer Senior founded his pottery in 1921 at Adam's on Furlong Road. The firm's initial production consisted of buying blank dinnerware from other potteries and decorating them. In 1931, James moved the pottery to the Oldcourt Pottery on Roundwell Street in Tunstall. This site dates back to the 15th century, and is an important part of the Tunstall area's history. For several centuries, one or more courts were located on the site, dispensing justice over a wide area. Records as early as the mid-18th century indicate that earthenware was produced on the site and a 19th century drawing shows a bottle kiln nearby. The offices and showroom of Fryer were located in a manor house built in the mid-19th century and referred to as Dr. Davenport's House.

Between 1939 and 1945, the British Ministry of Defense took over the J. Fryer factory, using it for storage during World War II. The plant was restarted in 1945 with government assistance. At this time James' son, James Junior joined the firm and the name of the pottery became J. Fryer & Son. The pottery began producing wares that were designed and modeled at the factory beginning in 1954. It built a coal-fired kiln for firing sugar bowls, figures, and hand painted giftware.

The name of the pottery was changed at this time to J. Fryer Limited, and it began using the tradename Oldcourt Ware.

James Fryer Junior's two sons joined the firm, John in 1961 and James III in 1968. James Senior died in 1970 and James Junior passed away in 1988, leaving the pottery under control of John and James III. The firm sold its wares through retail shops and had a distributor in Northern Ireland named Mahon.

A fire in the kiln area in 1986 destroyed most of the firm's records and production material. This setback caused J. Fryer to retrench back to production of basic transfer ware, reproduction flow blue, spongeware, and lamp bases. Fryer was also decorating pieces for Bridgewater Pottery and then Brixton Pottery in 1987.

By 1996, the firm had evolved to mainly lamp base production with a range of sponge tableware and giftware. The firm was now owned and operated by Managing Directors James Fryer III and his brother John Fryer, along with James' daughter Marianne Fryer. In 1998, it revived the early handpainted giftware tradition of the firm, using many of the old molds and creating new designs. To do this Fryer created a new company called Old Court Pottery on December 11, 1997 to market its new handpainted wares. In January of 1998, James and his daughter, Marianne, re-launched the firm's old pixie line at the Ceramic Showcase, an industry fair in Stoke. At the same time, under the direction of Marianne Fryer, the firm announced a Collector's Club for Old Court Pottery. The Collector's Club was oriented initially around the pixie ware, but also planned to promote new designs as they were introduced.

However, on November 22, 1998, J. Fryer ceased operating as an independent pottery due to financial difficulties. Cortman Limited purchased the Old Court Pottery portion of J. Fryer. James Fryer and Marianne Fryer joined Cortman at a new location across the street from Cortman's Crownford Works, and continued production of Fryer's art pottery, luster ware, and limited edition figurines and jugs using the Old Court Pottery name.

Character Jugs and Toby Jugs

Beginning around 1960, J. Fryer produced two series of medium sized Character Jugs using the Oldcourt Ware tradename, both well worth collecting. The first series was based on Robin Hood characters and the second was the Working Man's Series. The Sherwood series consisted of six jugs and was introduced in 1957 using on-glaze enamel colors. The series was produced for only a short time and then discontinued. In 1960, the Sherwood series was reintroduced using under glaze enamel colors, but again production stopped quickly. Therefore, there are relatively few jugs to be found.

Roy Smith, who worked at the firm from 1960 until 1964, modeled the Working Man's series. This series of six jugs was introduced in 1960 in on-glaze colors, which were changed to under glaze enamels a few years later. Production of the Working Man's series continued into the 1970s, making these jugs more plentiful today. All jugs from both series were very well modeled and finished in soft earth tones.

Jugs can be found with a gold backstamp, indicating that the jugs were finished in on-glaze enamels and are from earlier production around 1960. Jugs marked with a black ink stamp are more recent and decorated with under glaze enamel paint.

For a few years beginning in 1970, Fryer also produced a series of Character Jugs called the North American Heritage Limited Edition. These were on commission from Edward A. Keate of Vancouver, British Columbia. Included in this range were John Diefenbaker, the former Prime Minister of Canada, with the Canadian Bill of Rights as the jug's handle. Other jugs included W. C. Fields, Louis Armstrong, Lester B. Pearson, Talker - a Canadian who sailed a hand made canoe, and Bob Hope, complete with his trademark golf club as the handle. The factory estimates that perhaps as many as 500 Diefenbaker jugs were produced, but no more than 100 of any other character were completed.

Another group of Character Jugs was a limited edition series called the Faces of Contemporary History, Copper Series. A John F. Kennedy jug was a part of this series and all jugs were finished in a bright copper luster. No other jugs from this series have been identified. Around the late 1970s, Fryer was asked to reproduce the Allerton's Squat Toby Jug by a Swedish Antique dealer. Fryer's Squat Toby is identical to Allerton's in style and finish, complete with flow blue and gilding.

J. Fryer planned, but never released, Stan Laurel and Oliver Hardy jugs. The firm also modeled, but never produced, a group of Character Jugs including such characters as Uncle Tom Cobleigh, Black Dog, Bill Sykes, Fagin, Sairey Gamp, Mr. Pickwick, and Oliver Twist. Other jugs may have been planned as well. In 1999, *Collect It!* magazine commissioned a Robin Hood colorway jug in a limited edition of 500 to be sold only at its July 1999 Newcastle Fair. Under Cortman management, the firm is considering re-introducing the Sherwood and Working Man's Series jugs in a new colorway. Perhaps new jugs will be made as well now that the firm has begun producing hand painted wares again.

Most of the photos herein are from the collection of James Fryer III.

Sultan and Long John Silver figural bottles, possibly could be made into Toby Jugs in the future

Character Jug of John G. Diefenbaker, Prime Minister of Canada

James Fryer holding two figural bottles

Bob Hope and W. C. Fields Character Jugs, both with reconstructed handles

Character Jug Name	Height, Inches	Production Life
Alan a'Dale	4 1/2	1957 - 1964
Bob Hope	6	1970 Ltd Ed
Crossing Sweeper	4 1/2	1960 - 1970s
Fisherman	4 1/2	1960 - 1970s
Friar Tuck	4 1/2	1957 - 1964
Jester	5	1957 - 1959
John F. Kennedy (copper luster)	6 1/4	1970s Ltd Ed
John G. Diefenbaker	5 1/2	1970 Ltd Ed
Little John	4 1/2	1957 - 1964
Louis Armstrong	6	1970 Ltd Ed
Poacher	4 1/2	1960 - 1970s
Rat Catcher	4 1/4	1960 - 1970s
Robin Hood	4 1/2	1957 - 1964
Sheriff of Nottingham	4 1/2	1957 - 1964
Talker	6	1970 Ltd Ed
Tramp	4 1/2	1960 - 1970s
W. C. Fields	6	1970 Ltd Ed
Will Scarlett	4 3/4	1957 - 1964
Woodcutter	4 1/2	1960 - 1970s

Toby Jug Name	Height, Inches	Production Life
Ordinary Toby	large	1954-1968
Squat Toby	5 3/4	1980-1986

Working Man Series; top row-Fisherman, and Jester (not from series); bottom row-Tramp and Woodcutter.

Working Man Series; Rat Catcher on left and Crossing Sweeper on right

Sherwood Series Character Jugs from circa 1960; top row left to right - Little John, Robin Hood, and Sheriff of Nottingham; bottom row left to right - Alan a'Dale, Friar Tuck (new), and Will Scarlett

Sherwood Series colorway trial Character Jugs from 1998; top row left to right - Friar Tuck and Little John; bottom row left to right - Alan a'Dale, Robin Hood, and Will Scarlett

Gibson & Sons
See Jugs Marked by Country of Manufacture under United Kingdom

Gladding McBean
Los Angeles, California

Toby Jug Name	Height, inches
Monk	6

History

Gladding McBean was founded in 1875 in Los Angeles, California. Initially, the firm produced only sewer pipe. Terra-cotta production was added in 1884 and soon the factory was making a wide range of products including sanitary pottery, tiles, dinnerware, and art pottery. Fueled by the acquisition of a tile factory, by 1933 Gladding had become one of the largest tile makers in the United States. The firm's Franciscan Ware line was introduced in 1934 and included both dinnerware and art pottery. The dinnerware was of a china or earthenware body decorated with a variety of solid color glazes.

In 1962, Gladding McBean merged with Lock Joint Company and reincorporated in April of 1963 as Interpace Corporation. In 1979, Josiah Wedgwood purchased Interpace, and the factory was eventually closed in 1984.

Toby Jugs

So far only one Toby Jug produced by Gladding McBean has been identified. The firm produced a Monk Toby Jug as a part of its Franciscan line. Produced from 1934 into the 1940s, the Monk can be found in solid pastel glazes including cream, yellow, and pink. It is stamped with the firm's Franciscan mark.

History

W. Goebel Porzellanfabrik was founded on January 30, 1871, by Franz Detleff Goebel and his son, William Friedrich Goebel, in the village of Oeslau (now Rodental), located in the middle of Thuringa, Germany. This region was already well known for its high quality porcelain. Franz Detleff was an ambitious porcelain merchant with a strong desire to have his own manufacturing factory. The firm initially made slate blackboards, pencils and marbles because it lacked the money and means to begin porcelain production. However, after building a factory on the outskirts of town in 1876, Goebel quickly branched out into porcelain dinnerware and beer stein production. Figurines were introduced soon after, and one of the first designers of these was Carl Lysek. Carl became known for his children figurines, launching the firm into the direction it is so well known for today. Some of Lysek's figurines were modeled after William Friedrich's son, Max Louis Goebel, who was born in 1862, and later after Max's son Franz.

By the turn of the century Goebel employed around four hundred laborers and was one of the largest factories in the region. The Goebel family was very conscious of its workforce, providing health care and housing for workers and was adept at hiring and retaining top artistic talent. The firm had a good understanding of its customers' desires and tastes, including those of North America. Goebel offered variety, novelty and good value.

In 1911, the third and fourth generations of the Goebel family were operating the company, with Franz Detleff's grandson Max assuming the management of the company along with Max's son Franz E. Goebel. Max had grown up around the business and was sent to America at the age of sixteen to learn porcelain tastes, trends and production techniques. While in America, Max worked for Marshall Field and Company among other large firms. Upon returning to Germany Max purchased his own porcelain factory near Kronach. When William died in 1911, Max sold his factory and assumed control of Goebel.

By this time, Goebel was producing several thousand earthenware and porcelain products, to which Max and Franz added an internationally successful line of porcelain figurines. The early porcelain figures were done in a rococo style similar to Meissen. Otto Hohn was Goebel's pioneering artist in this style. Many new wares and designs were introduced in a very short time with the help of talented artists. The factory expanded to keep up with production, including adding a dedicated power station.

The First World War brought Goebel's expansion activities to a halt. Many workers were drafted into the armed services, including Max himself, who served from 1914 until 1916. Sales dropped off drastically and production followed this decline. Even after the war, things did not improve. Coal to fire the kilns was all but impossible to obtain, and inflation in Germany was out of control. Many companies were forced to close, but Goebel was able to manage through this difficult period.

Max died in 1929 at the age of 67, having driven the firm through sustained expansion and then managing through a period of great hardship. Upon Max's death, his son Franz took over at the helm of the firm, working with his brother-in-law Eugene Stock, who managed the financial aspects of the company. This pair, along with Max's widow Frida, who operated the factory while Max served his country in the First World War, carefully managed the firm into an economic climate worsened by the stock market crash. By 1930, the firm was reduced to half its size, with about the same production volume and number of employees as when Max took over eighteen years earlier. Success during the next several years was due to customer service, established high quality products, and limited new innovative designs.

1934 was a key year for the Goebel firm. This is the year that a young nun's sketches of children came to the attention of Franz Goebel. Goebel's Munich representative, Ernst Steiner, showed Franz art from a young Franciscan sister, Maria Innocentia Hummel. Shortly Franz, Sister Maria and the Convent of Siessen reached a satisfactory agreement with exclusive rights to the designs for Goebel. One year later, the first works of M. I. Hummel were introduced and became immediately loved by people around the world. Sculptors Arthur Moller and Reinhold Unger created figurines from the Sister's sketches. Sister Maria personally approved each model before it went into production, which Franz himself oversaw.

World War II brought new hardships to the region and the firm. The government attempted to convert all of Goebel's production capacity to dinnerware for the military. After some negotiation, the firm was allowed to continue with Hummel production as well. The

Spaniel and Boxer tiny Character Jugs

Three Tiny Character Jugs: Squire, Friar Tuck, and English Gentleman.

Mr. Pickwick tankard

workforce was cut in half again due to conscription into the German military, travel was restricted, and raw materials became difficult to obtain. Even after the war, resources were non-existent, and Goebel's workforce was reduced to around 100 people. The division of Germany into two countries almost resulted in Goebel being located in Eastern Germany, an event that would have probably closed the firm.

Once Thuringa became part of West Germany, things began to improve for the company. Goebel's tradition of warm, endearing figurines was broadened again in the late 1940s through the art of Charlot Byj. Charlot's paintings and the modeling of sculptor Gerhard Skrobek resulted in the popular line of red headed figurines, which was followed by a Blonde series, and then Byj Christmas plates. Goebel went on to offer figurines based on the art of Huldah Cherry Jeffe. These were in the form of turn of the century girls and young women. Also, Norman Rockwell's charming drawings of everyday life came to life in figurines produced by Goebel.

The firm modernized its factory, updated kilns and improved production techniques, all while maintaining its traditional handcrafting and handpainting, qualities that helped set Goebel apart. In 1969, Franz passed away, and control of the firm fell to his son Wilhelm, Eugene Stock, and Eugene's son Ulrich. Today Goebel is managed by the sixth generation of the family. Goebel Porzellanfabrik celebrated its 125th anniversary in 1996. At that time the firm consisted of seven operating companies employing some 1,800 people around the world.

Character Jugs and Toby Jugs

Goebel produced a variety of Character and Toby Jugs over quite a large time period, ranging from 1935 to the 1980s. The Friar Tuck line is probably the most familiar and easily found of all the Goebel jugs. Friar Tuck comes as a Character Jug, Toby Jug, and tankard. The Toby Jug depicts a standing monk with his hands on his belly and a pleased expression on his face. He is most commonly dressed in a brown robe. Some variations occur in modeling and painting, such as a black collar.

One key modeling variation was Friar Tuck's feet. Early production featured a Friar Tuck with sandals and his toes exposed. In later production the Friar wore black shoes. Friar Tuck with sandals is more valuable that one with shoes, and collectors are keenly interested in the examples with molded toes which are painted black. Perhaps the rarest Friar Tuck Toby is model number S141/II. This size jug was made for only a short time and the Friar Tuck Collector's Club knows of only nine in existence. This jug has made the Club's

Top Ten Most Wanted list. When the Friar is dressed in a red robe, he is called Cardinal Tuck.

Another early Friar Tuck design is the cross-eyed monk. The cross-eyed Tuck was produced from 1935 until 1955, when the mold was changed to give the eyes a more realistic and saintly appearance. Friar Tuck jugs with crossed-eyes painted over molded normal eyes have been documented. One story about these cross-eyed Tucks is that some decorators liked the cross-eyed monk better than the remodeled one, so painted the eyes crossed over the molded normal eyes. This might be true, or the eyes could have been repainted after leaving the factory. Another tale of the cross-eyed Tuck is that he was produced as a premium to reward Goebel dealers. Allegedly, one cross-eyed Friar Tuck was included in each wooden shipping crate. This special item was always placed in the same corner of the crate. While this is unlikely in general, it might have been true for a brief time after his better-sighted cousin replaced the cross-eyed monk. Regardless, the cross-eyed monks are more valuable because they are early Friar Tuck production items, and were produced in lower volumes than pieces from the 1960s.

Other characters were made in a large variety of sizes, such as the Chimney Sweep and Clown. The early Dickens Toby Jugs were dressed in matte brown clothes. Later production came in more brightly colored attire. Mr. Bumble was redesigned slightly from model S27 to S130. The Dickens tobies closely resemble those imported by Ebeling and Reuss under its Erphila tradename. Ebeling and Reuss did import from Goebel, so it is highly likely these jugs are from the same mold. Further evidence to support this are tobies found marked Erphila or Goebel, both with the same model number impressed on the back of the jug. This more tightly links the relationship between potter and importer. The Welsh Lady Character Jug has in Welsh "YOIYDIG O LADY" impressed on the front.

Gobel's most recent Toby Jug series was introduced in 1972 and produced for about ten years. It consisted of twelve five-inch tall tankards, all with round tops. The tankards are very colorful and whimsical, and make an interesting collection by themselves. Since discontinuing the Friar Tuck jugs and derivatives in 1972, Goebel has reproduced Archival versions of these products on commission from various companies. Such Archival commissions include Christmas ornaments, banks, and sugar shifters. To clearly distinguish these reproductions, the Friar is dressed in different colored robes, such as blue or green.

Several different marks were used on Goebel products during the time when jugs were produced. The Crown mark, or Crown WG as it is known, is a crown above an overlapping W and G and was used between 1935 and 1949. It can be found incised or stamped in blue ink, sometimes with "U. S. Zone". The Full Bee, a large flying bee above a V, which was stamped in blue in several forms between 1950 and 1955, followed this mark. From 1956 to 1972 variations of the Stylized Bee mark were used. Also stamped in blue, this mark was a smaller flying bee inside the V. "W Germany" was added to the Stylized Bee mark in 1960. In 1972, the mark was changed so that a large "Goebel" was dominant, above it the stylized bee and below "W. Germany". The bee was dropped in 1979 and W. Germany changed to simply Germany in 1991. A date is included in the marks on some jugs produced in the 1970s. Model numbers can be found impressed into the backs of jugs or marked on the base. Early

Goebel Dickens jugs in brown have also been found impressed with the Goebel model number and simply stamped with the character's name and "Western Germany". These date from just after the end of World War II.

Goebel also produced a variety of derivative products related to these jugs. Many of the Toby Jugs came as part of a creamer and sugar set. The Friar Tuck line also included a bank, ash tray, clock, cookie jar, mustard pot, cruet, salt and pepper set, thermometer with stand, several decanter variations, and numerous smoking related items. Friar Tuck Christmas ornaments were introduced in 1997. Similar Chimney Sweep and Clown derivatives were also produced. Other Goebel Toby and Character Jugs most certainly exist.

The majority of the Goebel jugs and derivatives pictured are from the collection of Andrea and Mike McNamara.

Character Jug Name	Model Number	Height, Inches	Production Life
Bear	S176	1 1/2	
Boxer	S168	1 1/2	
Cat	S169	1 5/8	1950 - 1955
Friar Tuck	LK94 S135	1 7/8 1 1/4	1956 - 1972
English Gentleman	S143	1 5/8	1950 - 1956
Santa Clause	T73D	2 1/4	1950 - 1955
Sneering Face Jug		5	1960s
Spaniel	S177	1 1/2	
Squire	S137	1 1/2	1950 - 1956
Welsh Lady			

Older Toby Jugs: Soldier, Dutch Girl in small and miniature sizes, and Chef

Five inch Toby Jugs; top row left to right - King, Bride, and Dwarf; bottom row left to right - Innkeeper, Clown with accordian, and Night Watchman

Five inch Toby Jugs; top row left to right - Bavarian Herr, Bavarian Frau, and Sailor; bottom row left to right - Vampire, Devil, and Chamber Maid

Toby Jug Name	Model Number	Height, Inches	Production Life
Bavarian Frau	74 016 12	5 1/4	1972 - 1980s
Bavarian Herr	74 015 12	5 1/4	1972 - 1980s
Boy with flowers	S788F	5 3/4	
	S485D 1/2	5 3/4	
Bride	74 024 13	5 1/8	1972 - 1980s
Cardinal Tuck	74 074 13	6	
	S141/1	5 1/2	1935 - 1949
	T74/1	5 1/2	1950 - 1972
	S141/0	4	1956 - 1972
	T74/0	4	1950 - 1972
	S141 2/0	2 1/2	1956 - 1972
	S141 3/0	1 5/8	1956 - 1972
Chamber Maid	74 023 13	5	1972 - 1980s
Chef	3788C	5 3/4	1935 - 1949
Chick	X730 G	5 3/4	1935 - 1949
	X730 D	2 3/4	
Chimney Sweep	74 342 14	5 1/2	1972 - 1980s
	74 342 11	4 1/4	1972 - 1980s
		3 1/2	1972 - 1980s
	74 342 07	2 5/8	1972 - 1980s
Clown	74 101 19	7 3/4	1956 - 1972
	S488	7	
	S198/I	6 1/2	1959
	74 316 14	6	
	74 315 14	5 1/2	
	74 101 12	5 1/4	1956 - 1972
	T77/I	5	1956 - 1972
	74 313 13	4 1/2	1960 - 1972
	S488 3/0	4	1935 - 1949
	74 605 10	4	
	74 604 11	4	
	S198/0	4	1959
	S198 2/0	2 1/2	1959 - 1972
Clown w/ accordion	74 011 12	5	1972 - 1980s
Devil	74 020 13	5 1/8	1972 - 1980s
Dutch Boy	S486/2	7	1935 - 1949
	S486 0 1/2	5 1/2	1935 - 1949
	S486/0	5	1935 - 1949
Dutch Girl	S492	9 1/4	1935 - 1949
	S484/2	7	1935 - 1949
	S484/0 1/2	5 3/4	1935 - 1949
	S484/0	5 1/4	1935 - 1949
	S484 3/0	4 1/4	1935 - 1949
		3 3/4	1935 - 1948
		2 1/2	
Dwarf	74 019 13	5	1972 - 1980s
Elephant	S487/2	6 1/2	1935 - 1949
	S487/0 1/2	5	1935 - 1949
Fish	VT764	5 1/2	1935 - 1949
Friar Tuck	S141 III	10	1950 - 1955
	S141/3	8 1/2	1950 - 1972
	T74/III	8	
	S141/II	6 1/2	1960 - 72, 79 - 91
	S141/I	5 1/2	1935 - 1955
	T74/I	5 1/2	1950 - 1972
with lid	T74/I	5 1/2	1956 - 1959
	T74/0	4	1960 - 1991
	S141/0	3 1/2	1950 - 1972
	S141 2/0	2 1/2	1950 - 1972
	S141 3/0	1 3/4	1950 - 1972
Girl Clown	S488	7	1935 - 1949
Groom	S491B	4 3/4	1935 - 1949
Innkeeper	74 014 12	5 1/8	1972 - 1980s
King	74 012 13	5	
Lady Golfer	S150	4 1/2	
Man	S788D	6	
Monkey	Hei 3A	4 3/4	1950 - 1955
Mr. Bumble	S130	6 3/4	
	S130 0	5 5/8	1935 - 1949
	S130 2/0	4 1/2	1935 - 1955
	S27	4	1950 - 1955
	S130 3/0	3 1/4	1935 - 1949
	S27 3/0	3	1945 - 1950
Mr. Pickwick	S25/1	6 1/8	1950 - 1954
	T75/0	4 1/4	1954 - 1970
	S25 3/0	3	1945 - 1950
Nightwatchman	74 012 12	4 7/8	1972 - 1980s
Owl	74 607	5	1979 - 1990
Parrot	S486/2	6	1935 - 1949
Quaker Man	S129/0	5	1935 - 1949
	S129		1935 - 1949
	S129 3/0	3 1/2	1935 - 1949
Sailor	S788E	6 1/4	
	74 013 12	5	1972 - 1980s
Sam Weller		3 1/2	
Santa Clause	S191	4	1956
Sarah Gamp		6	1950 - 1954
	S28/0	5	
	S28 3/0	2 7/8	1945 - 1950
Sea Captain	S17	6	1920s
	S17	5 1/4	1935 - 1949
Soldier	5130/0	5	
Vampire	74 022 13	5	1972 - 1980s

Collection of older Dickens Toby Jugs. top row: Mr. Pickwick Mini, Sarah Gamp small and mini; bottom row: Mr. Pickwick large, Mr Bumble small and mini, and Sarah Gamp large

Top row - Cardinal Tuck Toby Jugs in four sizes; bottom row - Cardinal Tuck tankards in two sizes

Top row - Clown Toby Jugs in two sizes; bottom row - Clown mugs in three sizes

Friar Tuck tankards; from left to right 7" 1 liter, 5" 1/2 liter, and 4" 1/4 liter sizes, note sandals instead of black shoes

Chimney Sweep Toby Jugs in medium, small, and miniature sizes

Friar Tuck; top row - Toby Jugs, 8", rare 6 1/2", 5 1/2", 4 1/4", 2 1/2", 1 3/4". and 1 1/2" Character Jug; bottom row - cross-eyed Friar Tuck Toby Jugs 5 1/2", 4 1/4", and 2 1/2"

Clown derivatives; top row - bank and three covered jars standing 5 1/2", 5", and 4 1/4" tall; bottom row creamer, egg cup, salt and pepper shaker

Friar Tuck steins; left to right - one liter, one-half liter, and one-quarter liter

Cardinal Tuck derivatives; top row left to right - cookie jar, napkin ring, pipe stuber, ash pot (rear), condiment set (salt, mustard and pepper), bank, egg cup, decanter, and shot glass; bottom row left to right - oil and vinegar bottles, cigarette holder, salt and pepper shakers on tray, match holder, and sugar and creamer on tray

Chimney Sweep derivatives; top row left to right - calendar, toothpick holder, egg timer, and liquor pourer; bottom row left to right - bank, egg cup, sugar and creamer, and rare perfume spender

Derivatives		Model Number	Height, Inches
Ash Pots	Friar Tuck	ZF43/II	large
	Friar Tuck	ZF43/I	medium
	Friar Tuck	ZF43/0	small
Ash Trays	Friar Tuck oval	RF104C	6
	Cardinal Tuck flat	RF142	3 3/4
	Friar Tuck flat	RF142	3 3/4
Banks	Single Friar Tuck	SD37	9
	Clown	50 012 17	6 1/2
	Chimney Sweep	50 002 14	5 1/2
	Cardinal Tuck	SD29	4 1/2
	Single Friar Tuck	SD29	4 1/2
	Archival Friar Tuck; blue or green robe	SD29	4 1/2
	3 seated Friar Tucks on keg	SD35	2 3/4
Bookends	Friar Tuck seated	XS184B	5 1/4
	Friar Tuck standing	XS184A	5 1/4
Calendars	Chimney Sweep	57 039 10	4
	Friar Tuck	KF55	
Christmas Ornaments-Archival Collection			
	Cardinal Tuck	73 153 348	3
	Friar Tuck in blue or green robe	73 153 348	3
Cigarette Boxes	Friar Tuck	RX104A	4 1/2
	Cardinal Tuck w/ open top	RX110	3
	Friar Tuck w/ open top	RX110	3
	Friar Tuck w/ closed top	RX99	
Cigarette Lighters			
	Friar Tuck	RX115	large
	Friar Tuck	RX109	2 1/2
Clocks	Friar Tuck	57 422 20	7 1/2
Cookie Jars	Cardinal Tuck	KL29	9
	Friar Tuck	KL29	9
Covered Jars	Clown	83 009 14	5 1/2
	Clown	83 432 13	5
	Clown	72 199 11	4 1/4
Creamers	Friar Tuck	M43A	4 1/4
Decanters	Cardinal Tuck	KL95	10 1/4
	Fat Friar Tuck	KL92	10 1/4
	Thin Friar Tuck	KL95	10 1/4
	Friar w/cigarette holder base	KL90	10 5/8
	Friar w/music box base	KL91	10 5/8
	Friar w/ 3 shot glasses in base	KL93	10 5/8
Display Plaques	Friar Tuck (5 varieties)	W22	
Egg Cups	Chimney Sweep	81 001 05	2 1/4
	Cardinal Tuck	E95A	2
	Clown	81 005	2
	Friar Tuck	E95A	2
Egg Timers	Chimney Sweep	81 501	3 1/2
	Two Friar Tucks	E96	3 1/4
	Friar Tuck	E104	3
Flasks	Friar Tuck	KJ97	4 1/2
Honey Pots	Friar Tuck	H9	4 1/2
Humidors	Friar Tuck	RX106/I	7 3/4
	Friar Tuck	RX106/II	7
	Friar Tuck	RX106	6 3/8
Liquor Bottle Pourers			
	Chimney Sweep	89 501 7	3 3/4
	Friar Tuck	XP78	3 1/2
Liquor Bottle Stoppers			
	Friar Tuck	XP75	3 1/2
	Friar Tuck head only	XP87	
Liquor Pourer & Stopper holder			
	Friar Tuck (yellow arch)	XP47	
Matchbox Stands			
	Cardinal Tuck	RX111	3 1/2
	Friar Tuck	RX111	3 1/2
Matchstick Holders			
	Friar Tuck	RX104B	2
Musicals	Friar Tuck with flute	KF60C	
	Friar Tuck with Hymnal	KF60A	
	Friar Tuck with violin	KF60B	
Mustard Jars	Cardinal Tuck	M42A/S183	3 3/4
	Friar Tuck	M42A/S183	3 3/4
Napkin Rings	Cardinal Tuck	X98	1 3/4
	Friar Tuck	X98	1 3/4
Oil & Vinegar Bottles			
	Cardinal Tuck	M80B&C	5 1/2
	Friar Tuck	M80B&C	5 1/2
Pepper Shakers	Cardinal Tuck w/ book	P176B	3
	Friar Tuck with book	P176B	3
	Friar Tuck musician	P189B	3
	Clown	73 182 07	2 3/4
	Friar Tuck	P153/0	2 3/8
Perfume Spenders with Night Lights			
	Chimney Sweep	EF55	6
	Friar Tuck	EF88	6
Pipe Stubbers	Cardinal Tuck	RX107	2 1/4
	Friar Tuck	RX107	2 1/4

Derivatives cont.		Model Number	Height, Inches
Place Cards – Archival Collection			
	Friar Tuck in blue robe	57 432	3
Razor Blade Holders			
	Friar Tuck	X103	4 1/2
Salt Shakers	Cardinal Tuck with book	P176A	3
	Friar Tuck with book	P176A	3
	Friar Tuck musician	P189A	3
	Friar Tuck	P153/I	2 7/8
	Clown	73 182 07	2 3/4
Signs – Archival Collection			
	Friar Tuck	59 002 10	3 5/8
	Cardinal Tuck	59 002 10	3 5/8
Sugar Bowls	Cardinal Tuck	Z37	4 1/2
	Friar Tuck	M43B	4 1/2
	Chimney Sweep	83 400 11	4 1/4
Sugar Shakers	Friar Tuck	Z50	
	Archival Friar Tuck in blue robe	73 054	4 1/2
Thermometers	Friar Tuck	KP56	4 1/4
Toast Racks	Friar Tuck	X128	
Toothpick Holders			
	Chimney Sweep	57 800 10	4
	Friar Tuck	X101	2
Tots (Shot Glasses)			
	Cardinal Tuck	KL94	2
	Friar Tuck	KL94	2
Trays	Cardinal Tuck sugar/creamer/tray	T69	7
	Friar Tuck sugar/creamer/tray	M436	7
	Cardinal Tuck condiment set	M43D	6
	Friar Tuck condiment set	M42D	6
	Cardinal Tuck salt/pepper/tray	T71	4 1/4
	Friar Tuck salt/pepper/tray	T71/1	4 1/4
	Friar Tuck egg cup tray	E95B	
Water Pitchers	Friar Tuck	S204	

Friar Tuck derivatives; top row left to right - liquor pourer and stopper in holder, razor blade holder, flask, honey pot, and thermometer; bottom row left to right - standing Friar bookend, one Friar egg timer, egg cup, two Friar egg timer, and seated Friar bookend

Friar Tuck smoking derivatives; top row left to right - three humidors (6 3/8", 7 3/4" and 7" tall) with rare cigarette lighter and pipe stubber; bottom row left to right - two ash trays, match holder, open top cigarette holder, and match holder and closed top cigarette holder on tray

Friar Tuck derivatives; top row left to right - clock, toothpick holder, very rare three Friar bank, napkin ring, and cookie jar; bottom row left to right - sugar and creamer, salt and pepper shaker on tray, oil and vinegar with third bottle marked H

Santa Clause Toby Jug, S191

Friar Tuck decanter derivatives; top row left to right - fat Friar decanter and thin Friar decanter (note sandals); bottom row left to right - decanters lift off bases to reveal a cigarette holder, music box, and shot glasses in holder

Three Friar Tuck liquor bottle stoppers with holder

Friar Tuck Archival Collection; top row left to right - Friar sign, Christmas ornaments in blue, red and green, Cardinal Tuck sign; bottom row left to right - blue and green robed Friar banks, place card holder in blue, and blue sugar shaker

Gold Medal China
See Owens China

W. H. Goss Limited
Stoke, England

History

W. H. Goss was a porcelain factory founded by William Henry Goss in 1858 at the Falcon Pottery Works in Stoke. Early in life, William Goss showed promise in literature, but chose to apply his creative talents to porcelain production. Before starting his own pottery, William honed his talents at Alderman with William Copeland, eventually becoming a chief designer and modeler with the firm. The initial production of W. H. Goss was centered on parian ware, busts in particular, and bone china. Not surprisingly, some of Goss' early production resembled that of Copeland.

One of the early results of Goss' creativity was the invention of a new process to insert enameled jewels into hollows in the body of porcelain. Goss' work was quickly recognized internationally when he was awarded a bronze medal at the 1862 International Exhibition for his exhibit of porcelains. Through Goss' skill and industry recognition, the business grew quickly. William's sons joined him in 1883.

W. H. Goss is probably most well known for creating the concept of, and building the market for, crested heraldic wares. Some argue that the bulk of the credit for this goes to William's eldest son, Adolphus, who strongly encouraged his father in the creation of crested ware. Crested ware is small and often humorous porcelain trinkets bearing local town, city, or district coat-of-arms, or crests. The pieces were originally inexpensive souvenirs for travelers to purchase and take home to remind them of their happy times at a locale. The interest in such souvenirs began in Victorian England in the 1860s and by the early 1900s had become a craze.

Goss started its production of crested ware in the 1880s and eventually dedicated most of its production capacity to crested ware. Over the years, Goss produced over 2,000 different crested ware shapes.

The Goss shapes attempted to be accurate representations of notable objects rather than the whimsical items produced by its competitors. In response to increasing competition, Goss strove to produce more detailed and higher quality mementos, the most intricate of which were its miniature cottages. The onset of World War I turned production of crested ware toward a more military theme, with war models of items such as tanks being produced.

Adolphus Goss employed a unique distribution method for crested ware. He selected a single local agent in each town who was responsible for selling souvenirs with only that town's crest. While many firms entered into the lucrative trade of crested ware, none could match Goss' quality. Today crested ware has become highly collectable around the world.

During World War I, the firm introduced parian statuary and busts, becoming widely known for these high quality products as well. The firm also produced porcelain doll heads at its Falcon pottery during this time, but these were of inferior quality compared to its other ware and

Character Jug Name	Height, inches
Welsh Lady	3 3/4

Toby Jug Name	Height, inches
British Sailor	2 3/8
Cross-legged Toby	4
Cross-legged Toby w/ arm handle	6 1/2 4 3/8 3 1/2
Female Toby standing standing standing, crested	3 1/8 2 3/4 2 3/4 1 5/8
Ordinary Toby inscription on front inscription on front crested crested on stool on stool	8 3/4 6 1/4 5 4 3 1/4 2 3/4 2 1/2 1 5/8
Standing Toby	3 1/2
Stratford on Avon Toby	2 1/4
Winston Churchill	6 1/2 2 3/4

that of other doll head manufacturers.

Unfortunately, increasing competition for the crested ware and the difficulties of the Great Depression caused serious business problems for the company. In 1929, the family sold the W. H. Goss business and assets to Cauldon Potteries for two thousand pounds. Cauldon renamed the firm Goss China Limited and continued using the Goss name for production of tea sets, cottage sets, and commemorative items. These wares were primarily done in brightly colored art deco designs. Harold T. Robinson, the owner of Cauldon Potteries, purchased Goss from Cauldon for twenty-five hundred pounds a few months later, and purchased the land and factory from the bank. Robinson had financial troubles in the early 1930s and stopped heraldic ware production in 1934. All production associated with the Goss name ended in 1940.

However, this was not the end of the Goss legacy. The Lawley Group purchased some original Goss production materials, the name and the trademark in 1956. Lawley was itself later purchased by Royal Doulton. At the same time, Portmeirion Potteries purchased the Falcon Pottery works. Doulton revived the Goss name and began using the trademark again in 1985, producing wares at the factory of Dunn Bennett and Company that it acquired in March of 1968.

Goss marked the majority of its ware with a stamped black ink goshawk over "W. H. Goss." "England" was added below the goshawk in 1929.

Character Jugs and Toby Jugs

W. H. Goss produced several china Character and Toby Jugs, some as crested ware jugs. Goss' Winston Churchill jug was the first Toby ever made of Churchill, who is now the most commonly found twentieth century subject of Toby Jugs. This Toby was made in 1927 when Churchill was Chancellor of the Exchequer and depicts a praying Churchill with the inscription "Any Odds - Bar one. That's me who Kissed the Blarney Stone" on his hat. As Chancellor, Churchill introduced the first betting tax to the UK in 1926. This was not a popular tax, and Churchill was quoted as saying he hoped he would have "the luck of the Irish," get acceptance of the tax as being in the national interest, and not pay too high a personal price in his political career. This satirical Toby Jug was produced for only a few years and can be found in either a blue or green jacket.

The Stratford on Avon Toby was made as a part of Goss' Historic Models series between 1900 and 1925 and came with a basin. The Stratford Toby was designed by Mr. W. Pearce and produced as a replica of the smallest known Toby of the time. Its mark includes "Stratford on Avon" with Goss' standard backstamp and was available only in Stratford on Avon, the birthplace of William Shakespeare. The inscription on the front of the Ordinary Toby's plinth reads "No tongue can tell No heart can think O how I love A drop to drink." The Welsh Lady has impressed "YCHYDIG O LAETH" around her base.

A comprehensive listing of the porcelain Character and Toby Jugs produced by W. H. Goss is provided. Other than noted above, all of Goss' jugs were made between 1900 and 1934.

Welsh Lady Character Jug and Stratford on Avon standing Toby Jug

Large Cross-legged Toby with arm handle

Small Cross-legged Toby with arm handle and small Ordinary Toby seated on a stool

Large Winston Churchill Toby Jug with inscription on hat

Grace S. Apgar
New Jersey

History

Grace Searls Apgar was a ceramics teacher and sculptor at the Big Brook Studio in Marlboro, New Jersey. She was also a skilled studio potter who experimented with different finishes. In 1952, Grace studied under Geza de Vegh, a well known sculptor and potter from Hungary.

Geza de Vegh immigrated to North America in

the early twentieth century and settled in the New Jersey area. He worked primarily with red clay bodies with underglaze finishes, but also designed high quality figural porcelains from the 1920s onward. de Vegh purchased the Old Mill, an iron factory in Tinton Falls, New Jersey, and established a studio pottery there. de Vegh taught pottery classes in the Old Mill in the 1950s.

The Old Mill site was rich in New England history, dating back to the 18th century. Some time after World War II, a flood in the lower level of de Vegh's pottery left much of his assets covered by mud and debris. This natural disaster was not enough to discourage de Vegh, who continued potting for some time at the site. Geza de Vegh signed his work with a bold, incised signature.

Character Jugs and Toby Jugs

In the late 1930s, de Vegh created a series of Toby Jugs based on early American settlers of the local area. These jugs were produced in small quantities at his studio in the Old Mill for only a short time. The disastrous flood at the pottery hid the blocks and cases of de Vegh's designs until he found them years later.

In 1958, Grace Apgar purchased the rights, blocks and cases for nine different Toby Jugs and one figurine of a Sultan from de Vegh. She restored a set of four piece molds for each item for use in her ceramic studio and introduced the jugs in 1961. Beginning in April 1962, Grace published a series of articles in *Popular Ceramics* discussing techniques for decorating the Toby Jugs. She applied for copyrights on the toby designs between May 1, 1962 and September 20, 1966. Most of the copyrights were approved by January 19, 1967.

A local mold maker initially approached Grace in the mid-1960s, offering to market the Toby Jug molds commercially. The two entered into business, but unfortunately he died a few years later and his business folded. Grace then had molds cast by the White Horse Company of Trenton and sold them through the Big Brook Studio. Again this lasted for only a short time. After these two false starts, Grace re-focused her efforts on teaching ceramics and traveling to national ceramic shows as a guest lecturer, demonstrator and judge. During this entire period, Grace estimates she sold only a few dozen sets of the Toby Jug molds. Each mold sold for between $13.75 and $16.25.

Production of the Toby Jugs soon took a new direction. A pair of partners had just launched Americraft Products, a distributor of giftware products located on W. Front Street in North Plainfield, New Jersey. Americraft wanted to purchase finished Toby Jugs from Grace in quantities too large for Grace to produce in her studio pottery. Grace and Harold E. Farber, the President of Americraft, entered into an agreement on June 7, 1967, and she turned to the Bay Ridge Pottery of Trenton, New Jersey for volume production of the Toby Jugs for Americraft. She placed two orders with Bay Ridge of 150 sets for each of the nine

jugs, the minimum quantity order the pottery would take.

Unfortunately, soon Bay Ridge was purchased by a large firm, and subsequently destroyed by a fire. With the help of Charles Jones, a local Trenton mold maker, Grace then moved production of the jugs to Pennsbury Pottery of Morristown, Pennsylvania. Pennsbury was a small family operated factory producing quality ceramics. Amazingly, Pennsbury's fate followed the same path as Bay Ridge's, first being purchased by a larger firm and then the factory destroyed by a fire.

Americraft initially had the jugs finished at a local firm in Plainfield, New Jersey. Around the same time as production moved to Pennsbury, the decorating firm went out of business and Americraft moved the decorating to Quacker Barrel. Quacker Barrel was a small decorating company in Colts Neck, New Jersey that was forced to relocate to make room for a new highway. The firm never fully recovered from the move. The jugs produced for Americraft are impressed on a flat base with the character's name and "Grace Apgar USA". Lamp bases were also made from the Toby Jug molds. Americraft did not renew the contract the following year, letting the relationship lapse on March 22, 1968. As a result of all of the fires and misfires, few Americraft jugs ever reached the market.

Grace recovered her blocks and cases from both Bay Ridge and Pennsbury. After several requests, Grace eventually sold the Toby Jug blocks and cases, copyrights, and other equipment to the Yozie Mold Company on June 7, 1976 for $2,000. Yozie Mold is a manufacturer of multiple part molds for a variety of products, including dolls, Christmas items, clocks, wedding pieces, animals, and customer molds for wholesale and retail. Audrey Yozie and her husband Mike founded Yozie Mold in the 1960s in the basement of their Pennsylvania home. In the late 1960s, they purchased the vacant Monarch school building in Dunbar, Pennsylvania to house the expanding business. Built in 1916, the school provides an historic locale for the mold firm. The couple's son Kent has been managing the company since 1994.

While the Toby molds were never large volume products for Yozie Mold, it carried the molds in its catalog until 1984, when they were priced at $38 each. As of 1998, the firm still offered the molds for $56 each. A complete set of molds were purchased in 1998 by Jim Hollock of Kingston, Pennsylvania who planned to reintroduce the line and promote it via articles in several ceramic magazines.

Jugs produced from the Yozie molds are impressed with "Yozie Mold", the character's name, the model number (T-1 for example), and "U.S.A." Stangl Pottery purchased the molds for

Grace Apgar Toby	Height, Inches	Production Life
Abraham Whipple	T-3	8 1/2
Betsy Ross	T-10	
Dr. Nicholas Bogardus	T-1	6 1/2
Governor on the Horse		
Innkeeper Hendrickson	T-7	8 3/4
Innkeeper's Wife	T-8	9
John Hays	T-6	
Long John Silver	T-4	9 1/2
Magistrate Cornbury	T-2	
Molly Pitcher	T-5	
Moses Butterworth	T-9	8

Abraham Whipple Toby Jug

Betsy Ross Toby Jug handpainted in a cold finish by Grace Apgar

Moses Butterworth Toby Jug hand painted by Grace Apgar in a cold finish

John Hays and Molly Pitcher, but it is not known if these jugs were ever produced. The New Geneva Stoneware Company of Masontown, Pennsylvania bought a set of molds and made a few prototypes in the late 1970s or early 1980s. Geneva Stoneware was founded in 1978 and featured hand turned pottery by artist Linn Newman.

Variations in modeling can be found when comparing versions of the same finished Toby Jug side-by-side. Given that Grace initially sold only molds, and later Americraft produced finished jugs, and with changes in body composition and decorating, it is no wonder that these tobies can be found in different variations. The modeling differences are slight, but easily seen. Immediately apparent is the height and weight differences; some are slightly taller and lighter than others are. The taller jugs also have a thinner, more angular handle. However, it is the base itself, and the lower portions of the jug that display the majority of the modeling differences.

While Grace originally purchased nine Toby Jug blocks and cases from Geza de Vegh, he later modeled the Betsy Ross and Governor on the Horse tobies for Grace, which she added to the line. The Governor on the Horse toby depicts Lewis Morris, New Jersey's Governor from 1738 to 1746. Grace presented one of these jugs to Mrs. Richard J. Hughes, the then current Governor's wife, in May 1963. She also kept one for herself, but never produced it commercially. Grace also gave the blocks and cases for the Governor to Yozie Mold, but the case was badly damaged. Kent Yozie was attempting to reconstruct this case in 1998.

The following characters comprise Apgar's Americraft Toby Jug set:

Betsy Ross was a prominent early American figure, famous for sewing the first flag of the United States.

Pearson Hendrickson and his wife were proprietors and innkeepers in Tinton Falls, New Jersey. The Hendrickson's inn was one of the first inns in New Jersey and served as a local gathering spot for politicians, businessmen and the local populace. Later, Hendrickson also managed Tinton Fall's first Post Office. Innkeeper Hendrickson sits on a keg of ale with pipe in hand. The Misses sits nearby contentedly knitting a sock.

Doctor Nicholas Bogardus was the first Dutch doctor providing medical services for the early settlers in the Northeast. He was one of the three founding doctors of the original Health Spa in Saratoga Springs, New York. Later he moved to Tinton Falls, New Jersey, where he negotiated water rights with the Lenape Indians. In his old age, Bogardus lived on the Old Mill Road in Tinton Falls and tended his plum orchard. He is

dressed in fine clothes of the time, clutching the stout cane he used to discourage young boys from raiding his orchard.

John Hays was a Revolutionary War hero of Valley Forge and the Battle of Monmouth. Hays enlisted in December of 1775 as a gunner in Proctor's Artillery. Two years later he re-enlisted in the infantry and served under General William Irvin, participating in the battle at Valley Forge. Later, at the Battle of Monmouth, Hays was wounded on June 28, 1778, ending his military career.

Molly "Pitcher" Hays was John's wife and the heroine of the Battle of Monmouth. Molly bravely carried water to refresh the wounded and dying soldiers, earning her nickname of Molly Pitcher. When her husband was wounded, Molly courageously donned Hay's army coat and continued firing his cannon. It is said that Molly fired the last volley of the battle. George Washington thanked Molly personally for her valor and made her a sergeant in the army. Later Congress voted her an annuity of $40 for her bravery. After the battle, Molly returned home with John Hays, caring for him until his death. John and Molly are both standing, bravely wearing the colors of the colonial army.

Magistrate Cornbury, Lord Edward Hyde the Third, was the first royal Governor of New York and New Jersey in 1702. The local population despised Cornbury for the turmoil he created with his bigotry and incompetence. After five years in office, the colonists, led by Louis Morris, forced Cornbury's removal from office. The ex-Magistrate was then jailed for nonpayment of his debts. Magistrate Cornbury is dressed in his official garb and holds a parchment in his right hand.

Captain Abraham Whipple became a Rhode Island hero for his involvement in what was known as the "Gaspee Affair." On June 9, 1772, a local packet, the Hanna, refused to follow British orders to lower its flags as a sign of respect. To punish the Hanna's insolence, the British sloop Gaspee set out after it. Hanna's crew skillfully maneuvered the ship around the bay in low tide, successfully grounding the Gaspee. When word of the incident reached Providence, Captain Whipple and sixty-four men rowed out to the Gaspee, sent its crew to shore and torched the sloop. The Gaspee's Captain was wounded in the following explosion and the British offered a $5,000 reward for capture of the rebels. Upon learning of Whipple's role in the incident, the British Admiral sent Whipple a note saying he would be hung. Whipple's reply was, "Sir, always catch a man before you hang him." Abraham Whipple wears a naval officer's jacket and is depicted holding cards close to his vest, as he is reputed to have done in real life. This jug was originally named Captain Huddy.

Pirates Long John Silver and Moses Butterworth represented the more notorious characters of the time. The fictional Long John Silver allegedly frequented the local ports of Sandy Hook and Delaware Bay. Upon being accused of piracy, Moses Butterworth confessed sailing with Captain William Kidd on Kidd's last voyage from the West Indies to Boston. When Butterworth appeared in court, a large mob stormed the courtroom and freed him, keeping the Governor, justices, sheriff and court officers under guard for several days while Butterworth made good his escape.

The photos herein are from Grace Apgar's own collection.

Magistrate Cornbury and Dr. Nicholas Bogardus Toby Jugs decorated in a cold finish by Grace Apgar

Innkeeper Hendrickson and the Innkeeper's Wife Toby Jugs

Governor on the Horse Toby Jug hand decorated by Grace Apgar

Long John Silver Toby Jug in an ironstone body and cold paint finish

John Hays and Molly Pitcher Toby Jugs decorated in underglaze paint

Grafton China
See A. B. Jones & Sons Limited

J. Green & Company
London, England

History

James Green opened a storefront in 1834 at St. Paul's Churchyard and was primarily a retailer for the local London area. James' sons entered the business in 1841 and the firm became J. Green & Sons. From 1842 onward, the firm was located at various addresses throughout London.

Toby Jugs

Around 1933 or 1934, Green distributed an advertising Toby Jug for the brewery of Hoare & Company. This Hoare Toby, and a similar one produced by Hancock & Corfield, was the predecessor to the more famous Charrington Toby Jug. Charrington Ales purchased Hoare & Company in 1934 and using the same Toby design commissioned production of Charrington advertising Toby Jugs from a number of other manufacturers.

Toby Jug Name	Height, inches
Ordinary Toby w/ Hoare advertising	9

Grimwades Limited
Stoke and Hanley, England

History

Leonard Lumsdem Grimwade, and his older brother Sidney Richard Grimwade, established Grimwade Brothers in 1886 at the Winton Pottery in Hanley. From the outset, the brothers drove the factory for high growth and expansion. To accommodate growing demand for its products, a new Winton Pottery was built in 1892, larger than the previous factory. By 1900, the firm had purchased the Elgin Potteries in Stoke-on-Trent and changed its name to Grimwades Limited. To further its expansion, the firm also acquired Stoke Pottery from James Plant in 1900. James Plant himself stayed on with Grimwades.

Character Jug Name	Height, inches
Canadian Mountie	5 1/4
	4
	3 1/2
	2 1/2
Cockatoo	
Franklin D. Roosevelt	4 1/2
	4
General Douglas MacArthur	7 1/2
	6
	5
	4 1/4
	3
General Sir Archibald Wavell	7
	6 1/4
	5
	4
	2 1/2
Indian Chief	6
	5
	4
	3 1/4
Jan Smuts	
John Bull	6
	5
	4 1/2
	3 1/2
	2 3/4
King George VI	6
	4 3/4
	3 3/4
	2 1/2
Old Jarvie	5
	3 1/4
Right Honorable Winston Churchill	6 3/4
	5
	3 3/4
	2 3/4
Scotsman	5 3/4
Uncle Sam	11 1/2
	7 1/2
	6
	4 3/4
	4
	3

Scotsman in cream finish 5 3/4" tall

Old Jarvie in two known sizes, from collection of Jay Hunzinger

From its beginnings and through the 1930s, Grimwades produced colorful tableware, decorative pieces for display, and ceramics for hotel and hospital use. In the early 1930s, the firm began producing chintz patterns in earnest, over time becoming perhaps the most prolific manufacturer of chintz. Grimwades used the tradename Royal Winton on much of its tableware.

During World War II, an effort was made to increase export sales by the Staffordshire Potteries as a whole. To that end, Grimwades established two dedicated studios for a small group of successful designers to focus on creating new designs. One of these designers was Mabel Leigh from Shorter & Son and another was Billy Grindy. These new designs proved very successful for Grimwades' Royal Winton lines in the post war years. After World War II, other key new lines were introduced to take advantage of the public's new tastes in ceramics. In the 1950s, Grimwades added a line of gold and silver luster products that also proved popular. Grimwades also sold bisque ware to other firms, so its designs may appear on the market from another manufacturer.

In 1964, Howard Potteries purchased Grimwades and the Winton factory was closed, ending seventy years of production. Pentagon Holdings bought Howard Potteries in the late 1960s and then in turn was purchased by Taunton Vale, one of its customers, in 1973. Staffordshire Potteries Limited bought Taunton Vale in 1979, which Coloroll Ceramics Division purchased in 1986. Coloroll went bankrupt around 1990 followed by a management buy-out of the Royal Winton assets and trademarks. In 1993 Spencer Hammer Association, which formed Burnan International Limited, bought the trademarks. The Royal Winton tradename was used throughout all of these corporate changes. Today Royal Winton continues to be produced in Longton by the Taylor Tunnicliffe Group. A variety of kitchenware, planters and vases are the primary products; however, the firm has reintroduced some of its old chintz patterns.

Character Jugs

Grimwades produced a variety of Character Jugs from the 1920s onward, many of which were based on wartime heroes of World War II. The Uncle Sam Character Jug dates from the 1920s and was one of the earliest produced. Uncle Sam can be found with either a dollar sign or ear of corn handle. The Indian Chief Character Jug was produced in the late 1930s through the early 1940s. Some of the Character Jugs were produced in a white cream colorway as well as a full colorway.

The wartime hero series was introduced in 1939 and marketed with the Royal Winton tradename. The designer of these jugs was Billy Grindy. Grindy was a creative talent who was exempt from active wartime service through his status as a reserve. Later in his career, Billy moved first to Thomas C. Wild & Sons to design under the Royal Albert tradename, and then on to Shaw and Copestake where he most likely modeled some of Shaw's SylvaC Character and Toby Jugs. With the possible exception of Franklin Roosevelt, the wartime hero jugs were each produced in at least four or possibly five sizes; those positively identified are included here. Winston Churchill can be found with either a gray or black hat and with either a navy or red tie.

Old Jarvie has been found in only two sizes, each with a different colored jacket, red and green; however other sizes may have been produced.

The Scotsman jug has been found only in one size and only in a white colorway. It also has been mistakenly identified as Henry VIII in one reference. No evidence of a Henry VIII jug has been found.

Derivative liquor containers were also produced after 1942, including Mr. Pickwick and Mr. Winkle. These stood four inches tall and had a stoppered hole on the top of the character's head. Interestingly, Mr. Pickwick has been found with the stopper at the front and at the back of his head. Identical liquor bottles have been found with Longton Pottery's Kelsboro mark, indicating that Billy Grindy most likely carried the molds with him from Grimwades to Longton or Shaw and Copestake. Grimwades also made an interesting series of at least eight relief molded tankards, all with Thoren's musical movements. The Phil the Fluter's Ball tankard plays "There's a Tavern in the Town."

Grimwades' jugs are typically marked with the character's name, and carry the common circular Royal Winton backstamp of a large "R" forming the left side of a circle with the remainder of Royal Winton completing it, and enclosing the words "Grimwades England". This mark was used starting in 1928. In 1934, the circular mark was modified with "Made in England" replacing "England". In 1942, the mark evolved again, with an "A" being added to comply with The ABC Pottery Firms manufacturer and supply order from the Board of Trade. Beginning in 1951, the circular mark was discontinued and replaced by "Royal Winton" in horizontal script and "Made In England" underneath.

Canadian Mountie in all four known sizes, a fifth size likely exists

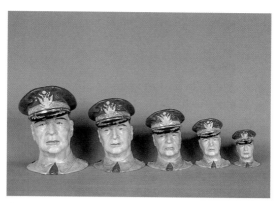

General Douglas MacArthur in the five known sizes

Royal Winton backstamp of Indian Chief jug

Liquor bottles derived from jugs: Mr. Pickwick with stopper in back, Mr. Winkle, and Mr. Pickwick with stopper in front

General Sir Archibald Wavell in the five known sizes produced

John Bull in five known sizes

Franklin D. Roosevelt in two known sizes

Indian Chief in three of four known sizes

Backside of Indian Chief jugs showing colorful headdress handle

King George VI in the four known sizes, a fifth size likely exists

Right Honorable Winston Churchill in four known sizes, a fifth likely exists; found with both black and tan hats in all sizes

Uncle Sam Character Jug in all five sizes (an 11 1/2" size has also been identified)

Backside of Uncle Sam jugs showing ornate corn cob and dollar sign handles

Grindley Artware Manufacturing Company
Sebring, Ohio

Character Jug Name	Height, inches
Uncle Sam	3 3/4

Toby Jug Name	Height, inches
Bird	4
Dutch Boy	4 3/4
Mrs. Gamp	4 7/8

History

Grindley Artware was founded in 1933 by Arthur Grindley and his sons, Arthur Junior and Dean. Prior to founding his own firm, Arthur had worked at other potteries. He became bored at these factories producing only dinnerware and wanted to express his creativity. He started Grindley Artware in the basement of his home in Sebring, Ohio, an area known as The Pottery Capital of the World. Growth of the firm precipitated a series of moves, first from the home into a barn on Arthur's property, and then into a small studio pottery across the alley.

The studio pottery was modernized over the next few years. At its peak in the 1940s, Grindley Artware employed one hundred and seventy-five people. The firm produced a wide variety of animal figurines, china, cooking ware, banks, teapots, pitchers, and salt and pepper sets. The pottery was probably best known for its large offering of horse figurines. Many of these figurines were done in an art deco style with brightly colored glazes.

Fire struck the factory in February of 1947, destroying most of the facility. After rebuilding, the firm's production never picked back up, and employment reached only twenty-five people. Not able to recover from the fire, the firm closed in 1952. Grindley Artware's products were marketed under the tradename Grindley Ware and typically marked only with a sticker.

Character Jugs and Toby Jugs

Grindley's known production of Character and Toby Jugs consists of only a few jugs. Uncle Sam is a very well modeled jug, stereotypical of what Uncle Sam should look like. It is almost an exact copy of the Grimwade's Uncle Sam jug, right down to the dollar sign handle. His hat comes in two colorways, a blue brim with either red stripes on a white background, or red stars on a white background. Uncle Sam was marked only with a Grindley Ware sticker. The Dutch Boy Toby is impressed "Grindley" and Mrs. Gamp is marked "Grindley Union Made Sebring O".

Dutch Boy Toby Jug and Uncle Sam Character Jug

H & K Tunstall
See Hollinshead & Kirkham

Hales, Hancock & Godwin Limited
London, England

Hales, Hancock & Godwin was a London retailer of glass, pottery and other gift items. The firm operated from 1922 until 1960. While there are no known Toby Jugs produced or commissioned by the firm, from 1930 onward it used a backstamp on commissioned pottery ware that was a Toby Jug above "H. H. & G. Ltd England".

Hall Brothers Limited
Longton, England

History

The Hall brothers opened a pottery at the Radnor Works in Longton in 1947. The firm produced china, figurines, and vases among other goods well into the 1960s. The majority of its production was marked with the Radnor tradename. The simple mark of "Radnor Bone China England" was used throughout the firm's production life. A circular banner mark with "Radnor Bone China" in the banner was used only from 1947 to 1951.

Character Jugs and Toby Jugs

Hall Brothers made very few Character and Toby Jugs. All were made in bone china and either of the Radnor trademarks can be found on these jugs. In general, the quality of these jugs is excellent, particularly Old King Cole. Additional jugs are sure to be found.

Hall's Radnor backstamp

Character Jug Name	Height, inches
Beefeater	5 1/4
	2 1/2
Bill Sykes	4 1/4
Bonnie Prince Charlie	2 7/8
Fat Boy	2 1/4
Friar Tuck	2 3/4
George Merrie (Pirate)	4 3/8
Irish Lass	2 1/2
Mr. Pickwick	3
	2
Robin Hood	5 3/4
	2 1/2
Sam Weller	4 1/2
	2 7/8

Toby Jug Name	Height, inches
Old King Cole	5 1/2
	2 1/2
Ordinary Toby	7
	3

Character Jugs; top row left to right - miniature Sam Weller, Friar Tuck, and Bonnie Prince Charlie; bottom row left to right - mid size Robin Hood, George Merrie, and Beefeater

Toby Jugs; large and miniature Ordinary Tobies with Old King Cole on right

Hancock & Corfield
London, England

History

Hancock & Corfield, also known as The Associated Potteries, was located in Mitcham, London.

Toby Jugs

During 1933 and 1934, Hancock & Corfield produced an advertising Toby Jug for the brewery of Hoare & Company. This Hoare Toby, and a similar one produced by J. Green & Company, were the predecessors to the better known Charrington Toby Jug. Charrington Ales purchased Hoare & Company in 1934 and commissioned production of Charrington advertising Toby Jugs using the same Toby design. See Charington Toby.

Original sketch for Hoare Toby

Toby Jug Name	Height, inches
Ordinary Toby w/ Hoare advertising	9

Hancock & Corfield backstamp

Harkers Pottery
Chester, West Virginia

History

Harkers Pottery was founded by Benjamin Harker Senior in 1840 in East Liverpool, Ohio. Before starting his own pottery, Benjamin mined and sold clay to local potters. Harker emigrated from the Stoke area of England and was experienced in the pottery industry. Because his youngest son George showed an interest in potting, Benjamin launched his own

Character Jug Name	Height, inches	Production Life
Daniel Boone	4 1/2	1960s
Jolly Roger	4 1/2	1960s

pottery. Early production included a wide variety of pottery using local clays. Products included were creamware, Rockingham glazes, and yellow ware.

Benjamin retired soon after starting Harkers Pottery. His two sons, George and Benjamin II, took over the business. In 1846, the firm built a new factory named Etruria where yellow ware and Rockingham goods were produced. The pottery operated as Harker, Taylor and Company for a time in the latter 1800s.

The firm relocated to Chester, West Virginia in 1931 where dinnerware became the focus of production. In the 1960s the small pottery was having financial difficulties. To re-energize the firm, Harkers produced a new line of Rockingham style products in the tradition of its successful goods from a century earlier. These goods were

marketed through gift shops and came in the traditional dark brown coloring, as well as a caramel or a green finish. The Jeanette Glass Company purchased Harkers in 1971 and operated the pottery as an independent subsidiary for a short time. Harkers closed in 1972.

Character Jugs

Harkers made two Character Jugs as a part of its gift shop line in the 1960s. Daniel Boone had an Indian on his handle. Both were produced in the three different finishes of the gift ware line. They are marked "Rockingham Harker 1840 USA." George Harker designed and produced a Standing Toby with hands in his pockets around 1877. This jug was finished in a Rockingham glaze.

A. G. Harley Jones
Fenton, England

History

Character Jug Name	Height, inches
Winston Churchill	
top hat	7 1/4
naval cap	7

A. G. Harley Jones operated a pottery at the Royal Vienna Art Pottery in Fenton from 1907 to 1934 under his own name. The firm produced both earthenware and china, using a variety of marks and tradenames, including Wilton Ware between 1923 and 1934. Potting must have continued at the Wilton factory after Jones ceased operations.

Character Jugs

The Wilton factory produced good quality Character Jugs of Winston Churchill in the 1940s, after Harley Jones closed. Winston Churchill in the top hat is a typical Churchill jug, depicting him in morning dress and smoking a cigar. It was issued in a full colorway, and a creamware version without the cigar. The naval Churchill is dressed in a blue jacket and wearing a yachting cap. These jugs were marked Wilton Ware and both had the inscription "Never was so much owed."

CHURCHILL

NEVER WAS SO MUCH OWED
BY SO MANY TO SO FEW
1940

WILTON POTTERY
UXBRIDGE
ENGLAND

Commemorative backstamp on the navel Churchill jug

Winston Churchill Character Jugs with Wilton backstamps, Naval jug on left and top hat jug on right

Harry Juniper
See Jugs Marked by Country of Manufacture under United Kingdom

Hart & Moist
See Jugs Marked by Country of Manufacture under United Kingdom

Heber & Company Porcelain Factory
Bavaria, Germany

History

Heber & Company was a maker of porcelain and bisque ware in Neustadt, Bavaria, Germany operating from 1900 to 1922. Its mark was an overlaid H and C inside a shield with a crown above and "Made in Germany" underneath.

Character Jugs and Toby Jugs

To date, only a very few jugs have been found with the Heber backstamp. These jugs are all well modeled porcelain, typical of German production and quality from the first quarter of the twentieth century. Certainly more jugs from Heber are likely to surface.

Character Jug Name	Height, inches
Indian Man Smoking Pipe	4 3/4
	4 3/4

Toby Jug Name	Height, inches
Standing Toby	5 3/4
	4 3/4

Standing Toby in medium and small sizes and Man Smoking Pipe Character Jug

Standing Toby derivative juice reamer

Heber backstamp

Heron & Son
Kirkcaldy, Scotland

History

Heron & Son grew out of the Fife Pottery that was founded in 1817 by partners John Methven and Robert Heron. Fife operated at the site of the Gallatoun Pottery of Gray and Company that dates back to 1790. By 1827, the firm was fully controlled by Robert Heron, and in 1850 the name changed to Heron & Son. It was Robert Heron and artist Karel Nekola of Bohemia who perfected a new brilliant style of earthenware pottery called Wemyss Ware.

From its introduction in 1882, the unique Wemyss Ware was the pottery's primary production focus. Wemyss was the family name of the local aristocrats who patronized the pottery. Wemyss pottery was made for decorative, not functional, purposes, and it is perhaps the most sought after Scottish pottery style. Wemyss Ware is known for its distinctive under glaze decora-tion of fauna and flora. The clay for Wemyss Ware was imported from Cornwall, Devon and Dorset.

Heron & Son marked its goods "R. H. & Son," and occasionally "R. H. F. P." The respected London firm of T. Goode & Company distrib-uted Heron's products throughout England. Heron & Son closed in 1929, and in 1930 the Bovey Pottery Company purchased the rights to Heron's Wemyss Ware designs and used them until 1952. The pottery was revived again in 1985. Today Wemyss Ware is extremely collectible and its value is rising.

Toby Jugs

Heron & Son produced a three-quarter bodied Sailor Toby in the early 20th century as a part of its Wemyss Ware production. This is the only known Toby Jug produced by Heron & Son.

Toby Jug Name	Height, inches
Sailor	11

Hewitt & Leadbeater
Longton, England

Toby Jug Name	Height, inches
Sailor Standing Toby	4

History

Hewitt & Leadbeater was a contemporary and competitor of W. H. Goss in the market for fine china and crested ware. Hewitt & Leadbeater began operations in 1907 at the Willow Pottery, producing bone china and parian ware under the trade names Willow Art and Willow China. By 1916 the pottery was producing over fourteen different porcelain doll heads and four sizes of arms and legs for doll manufacturers. In 1919, the firm changed its name to Hewitt Brothers and continued operating until 1926, when Cauldon Potteries purchased it.

Toby Jugs

Like Goss, Hewitt included Toby Jugs as a part of its production, both plain and crested. The factory used the tradename Willow China to market these. It is possible the firm might have produced these jugs on behalf of Goss. Other jugs may also exist.

Highmount
See Jugs Marked by Country of Manufacture under United Kingdom

Hoare Toby
See J. Green and Hancock & Corfield

Hoda
See Jugs Marked by Country of Manufacture under United States

Holkham Studio Pottery
See Jugs Marked by Country of Manufacture under United Kingdom

Hollinshead & Kirkham Limited
Tunstall, England

Toby Jug Name	Height, inches
Ordinary Toby	5 1/2

Hollinshead & Kirkham backstamp

History

Hollinshead & Kirkham Limited was established in 1870 in Burslem, England. Fueled in part by the purchase of Wedgwood & Company's Unicorn Pottery in Tunstall in 1876, the firm began a period of growth and prosperity. Hollinshead & Kirkham produced tableware, decorative bowls in art deco shapes, jugs, and other earthenware. Clarice Cliff joined the firm in 1915 from Lingard & Webster as a lithographer, but, after only a brief stay, she left to take a better offer at Wilkinsons' Royal Staffordshire Pottery, where she went on to achieve great fame.

Hollinshead & Kirkham went out of business in 1956, and the Unicorn factory was purchased by Johnson Brothers Limited of Hanley, which in turn was absorbed by Josiah Wedgwood.

Toby Jugs

From the 1920s through the 1940s, Hollinshead & Kirkham produced a range of Ordinary Toby Jugs, possibly in various sizes. Only one size has been identified to date. These jugs are marked "H&K Tunstall Made in England".

Ordinary Toby

L

History

A. Grant Holt and brothers Robert J. Howard and John Howard founded Holt-Howard in Stamford, Connecticut in 1948. The firm designed and sold whimsical ceramic giftware and kitchenware. Perhaps its most famous line was Pixieware, introduced in 1958 and produced into the early 1960s. Pixieware was a broad line of kitchen ceramics designed as expressive pixies.

Other designs included roosters, cats and even Santa Claus. Production of Holt-Howard designs was done primarily in Japan, so stickers with "Made in Japan" are commonly found.

Products were marked "Holt-Howard" or HH on smaller items. Kay Dee Designs purchased the pottery in 1990. Holt-Howard products became extremely collectible in the late 1990s.

Character Jugs

The Holt-Howard Santa Claus Character Jugs came as part of holiday beverage sets with Santa pitchers. These sets were produced in the late 1950s and early 1960s. The large jug is a winking Santa. Often a date can be found with the Holt-Howard mark. The years 1959 and 1960 are commonly found stamped on the Santa jugs.

Character Jug Name	Height, inches
Santa Claus	7 3/4
	6 1/4
	4 1/2
	2 5/8
	1 1/2

History

Homer Laughlin founded a small pottery in 1871 with the help of his brother, Shakespeare Laughlin. The brothers opened a two kiln studio pottery named Laughlin Pottery on the banks of the Ohio River in East Liverpool, Ohio. It was one of the first manufacturers of whiteware in the United States.

Louis I. Aaron and William Edwin Wells acquired the firm from Laughlin in 1897, renaming it Homer Laughlin. This pair focused on offering a broad range of attractive semi-vitrified dinnerware and everyday utilitarian pottery. The pottery experienced a period of high growth, and quickly three new factories replaced the original pair of kilns. In 1907, a modern thirty kiln plant, complete with company headquarters, was constructed across the Ohio River in Newell, West Virginia.

Soon after moving into the Newell facility, the pottery operated 62 high volume production kilns and 48 decorating kilns. Its capacity was 30,000 pieces of finished ware per day, accounting for roughly 10% of the dinnerware purchased in the United States. Frederick Hurton Rhead (1880 - 1942) joined the firm in 1927 and forever changed its place in history. Rhead created a variety of new patterns and styles that culminated in 1936 with the introduction of Fiesta. A rather plain design in attractive solid colors, Fiesta was an immediate hit with the American public and became Laughlin's best selling line of dinnerware. By 1939, the firm employed 3000 workers and produced approximately 360,000 pieces of dinnerware per day. Homer Laughlin was considered the largest supplier of dinnerware in the world.

Homer Laughlin was an exhibitor at the 1939 New York World's Fair in The American Potter Exhibit at the Home Furnishings Building. The American Potter Exhibit was jointly funded by the National Brotherhood of Operative Potters, an American Federation of Labor affiliate for the workers of the pottery industry, and five manufacturers: Cronin China, Hall China, Knowles China, Homer Laughlin China, and Paden City China. The exhibit consisted of a small-scale modern pottery factory that demonstrated the pottery production process to Fair visitors and encouraged them to purchase American made tableware. The huge mural produced for the Exhibit featured the two figures of Capital and Labor, flanked by life–sized figures depicting various phases of the pottery production process. Frederick Rhead was honored in the mural as the figure at the potter's wheel.

Homer Laughlin introduced new, fully vitrified china in 1959 and entered the hotel and restaurant marketplace. The firm was renamed Homer Laughlin China to reflect this new product emphasis. These initial designs were so successful that the firm added new shapes and patterns throughout the 1960s and 70s. Fiesta was reintroduced in 1986 in a fully vitrified body with lead-free glazes, redefining the standard of dinnerware for the food service industry.

Today Homer Laughlin China is one of the largest U.S. potteries. It is still operating at the site of the 1907 Newell plant and employs over 700 workers at its thirty-seven acre facility. The firm specializes in high-fired lead free glazes

Character Jug Name	Height, inches
George Washington	4 5/8
	2
Martha Washington	5
	2 3/8

and uses the latest modern technology to assure high quality production. Its Fiesta line is one of the most collected dinnerware patterns in the world.

Character Jugs

Since the primary production of Homer Laughlin has been dinnerware, it is surprising that the firm made any Toby or Character Jugs at all. However, the pottery designed two Character Jugs that were only produced during the 1939 New York World's Fair.

Seven World's Fair souvenirs are listed in The American Potter Exhibit's pamphlet, only three of which were actually produced at the exhibit; a George Washington Character Jug, a Potter's Wheel embossed plate, and hand thrown vases. Laughlin's George Washington Character Jug was cast and hand glazed at the exhibit for visitors to see, and then sold as a souvenir of the Fair. George Washington was produced to commemorate the 150th Anniversary of his Presidential Inauguration. Standing on the balcony of Federal Hall on Wall Street in New York City, George Washington took the oath of office as the first President of the United States of America on April 30, 1789. This jug was made in two sizes, the larger in pottery and the smaller in translucent bisque porcelain.

While not listed as an official Fair souvenir, a companion Martha Washington Character Jug was produced at the Fair in two sizes as well. Both jugs are marked "Joint Exhibit of Capital and Labor, The American Potter, New York World's Fair", and have a date of 1939 or 1940, depending on the year they were made. George may also have a model number of 1050. George can be found quite commonly, while Martha is more rare.

Left to right: George Washington Character Jugs in small and mini sizes, Martha Washington Character Jugs in mini and small sizes

Honiton Pottery
Honiton, England

Character Jug Name	Height, inches
Ordinary Toby shape 28	6
Toby with three spouts	4

History

Potting around the village of Honiton in Devon dates back before 1763, when records show Samuel Ford operating as a Master Potter in the area until the end of the 18th century. What is known today as the Honiton Pottery began operations in 1881 in Honiton under the ownership and management of James Webber. The firm produced brown utilitarian earthenware goods in a style similar to Brannam's. The pottery sold its ware predominately in Honiton and Exeter. In 1912, Webber sold the pottery to Foster and Hunt, which sold it to Charles Collard in 1918.

In 1886, a twelve year old Charles Collard began an apprenticeship with Aller Vale Pottery. While an apprentice, Collard also attended night Art School and developed his artistic talents under Domenico Marcucci, an artist and master designer from Italy. Collard remained with Aller Vale for a number of years, becoming its chief decorator by the mid-1890s. He left Aller Vale around 1905 to join the Crown Dorset Art Pottery factory in Poole, Dorset, but was driven to own his own pottery one day. In 1915, Collard sold his interest in Crown Dorset and moved to Honiton where he threw pots in a homemade kiln before purchasing Honiton Pottery.

After the purchase, Collard initially used only the local red clays from a clay deposit located behind the factory for his work. He introduced the now commonplace white slip décor on the red clay body. Later Collard began mixing the local clays with white china clays brought in from elsewhere, resulting in body colors from pink to beige. The red clay body can distinguish the earlier works of the firm. In addition to traditional torquay styles, he used many of the styles from Crown Dorset for his pottery. Collard became the first Honiton area potter to export products outside of the British Isles. In the 1920s, he changed to brighter colors and matte glazes, and later switched to a clay mix from Devon and Cornwall. During his ownership of the firm, Collard's name was often included in the pottery's marks.

The firm's production peaked in the 1930s when it employed twelve people. By 1934 the firm's catalogue listed one hundred and six pots and sixty animals. Honiton closed during World War II, reopening in October of 1945. Collard retired in 1947 and sold the company to Norman Hull, Harry Barratt, and the Chapplows. The pottery was renamed Honiton Art Pottery Limited. Norman Hull, who already owned the Norman Hull Pottery in Devon, served as both the Managing Director and Art Director. Nancy Hull, Norman's wife, and the Chapplows ran the daily activities of the pottery. Hull retired in 1951 and Barratt continued managing Honiton Art Pottery until 1956.

In December of 1960, Hull sold the factory to P. E. Cowell. Cowell sold it one year later, in January of 1961, to Paul Reevers, a former art and pottery teacher interested in operating a small pottery. Reevers continued production until 1991. At that time pottery production ceased, but the factory remained open as a retail outlet until 1996. Martin and Christine Wallis bought the site and rights to the Honiton Pottery name in October of 1996. The couple, along with their two sons, now operates a Pottery Shop Craft Centre and Tea Room at the site, promoting the Honiton Pottery name.

Character Jugs

Honiton Pottery produced rather featureless Character Jugs from the 1920s up to 1947. It must have produced very few as they rarely appear on the market. The jugs were not molded, but hand made by throwing the jug on a wheel, and then adding the facial details by rolling the jug into a flat mold. This production technique allowed the maker to easily change the face and other features, so jugs of the same basic shape may have very different appearances.

The marks found on Honiton jugs may include an impressed "Honiton England" which dates the jugs from 1920 to 1929. "Collard Honiton England" was impressed between 1927 and 1937. A larger impressed version of this same mark was used from 1935 to 1947. The shape number also commonly appears on the bottom of the jug. To date, only two different jugs have been identified. Others probably were produced.

Hornsea Pottery Company Limited
Hull, England

History

Two brothers, Colin and Desmon Rawson, founded the Hornsea Pottery in the resort community of Hornsea, England in 1949. Neither brother had any prior knowledge of potting, but both had keen artistic leanings. They started a studio pottery in a seafront house at 4 Victoria Avenue with a twelve cubic inch kiln. The brothers made only small items initially, including tiny Character Jugs, because they could get a good number of them fired in the kiln at one time. In addition to the Rawson brothers, one of the key designers for the firm was John Clappison. John designed for a number of years at Hornsea, eventually becoming the Design Director. In the 1990s he was a Chief Modeler with Royal Doulton.

To keep costs and production time down, Hornsea's early products were finished for the most part in soft pastel single colored glazes of brown, pink, green, yellow, or blue. Sometimes the inside would be finished in a white glaze and the outside in a pastel color, and occasionally an item would be finished in a full colorway. These early simple products sold well, and new wares were soon introduced. Hornsea's first major new product lines were Fauna and Fauna Royal, collections of animal figurines in natural settings. The firm's products quickly grew in popularity because of their innovation and design.

By 1953 the demand for Hornsea products outstripped the small kiln at home, and the pottery leased a larger facility in The Old Hall located in the center of Hornsea. As Hornsea was a seaside resort community, the Rawson brothers focused on souvenir pottery for the tourist and holiday traffic. Hornsea Pottery relocated again to the Edenfield Works in Hull, Yorkshire in 1954, and by the early 1960s, Hornsea Pottery became the largest employer in the community. The pottery grew from fifty-four employees in 1954 to roughly 180 in 1966 and 460 by 1979. To keep up with this high growth rate, the firm added another factory in Lancaster, Lancashire that operated from 1974 until 1984.

Hornsea encountered financial difficulties beginning in the late 1970s. Gordon Barker, a financial troubleshooter, was brought in as the Managing Director in 1982. However, Barker could not turn the pottery around. In 1984, Alexon, a clothing manufacturer which was part of the Steinberg Group of Companies, purchased the firm as a part of its diversification. Hornsea was re-launched in February of 1985 after an investment by Alexon. In May of 1987, Peter Black Holdings PLC, a Yorkshire based homeware group, purchased the Hornsea Pottery. Peter Black closed the Lancaster factory and continued production at Edenfield using the Hornsea trademark until March 1990. A notable product introduction during this time was the Ophelia tableware line designed by Pamela Greeves.

Hornsea Pottery has changed hands twice more in the 1990s, and today is still active at the Edenfield Works site under its fourth set of owners. Present production is strictly limited to tableware.

Character Jugs and Toby Jugs

For only a few years, from 1949 into the early 1950s, Hornsea Pottery produced a range of Toby and Character Jugs. Colin Rawson designed most of these jugs, which were among the firm's initial products. All of the jugs were discontinued after the move to The Old Hall in 1953. The tiny Toby and Character Jugs are more plentiful than the larger ones, although none were produced in large volumes. While most jugs are finished in Hornsea's distinctive pastel colors, rare jugs in full colorways can also be found.

As the jugs were the Rawson's early products, there was a large amount of experimentation going on both in the materials and processes used. Glazes were applied unevenly. Since the glaze formula was not perfected yet, crazing is common on these jugs. The molds were overused, so the modeling detail became fainter over time. The molds were also being perfected, so slight variations occur in the modeling of early jugs. In spite of these quality drawbacks, the early and limited production life of these jugs makes them very desirable, not only to jug collectors,

but also to Hornsea collectors for their historical significance.

The larger stern faced Character Jug was done as a prototype only and is therefore very rare. His handle comes to a point rather than being rounded like the other jugs. This jug is poorly modeled, finished in a pastel blue glaze, and unmarked. Colin designed the Nobleman Toby, a serious looking cross-legged Toby, in his own likeness.

Great humor can be found in the names of Hornsea's jugs. John Clappison designed one Character Jug as a gift to his mother, and named it Mrs. Clapp Soon. This jug is extremely rare. The Miss Happ Toby Jug depicts an old woman clutching a walking stick with a basket of flowers on her arm. The jug got its name when someone, while holding it and trying to think of an appropriate name, dropped it on the floor smashing it to pieces. This mishap became Miss Happ. Tommy Twaddle, an old man with crossed legs holding a walking stick, was named for the amount of sodium silicate deflocculant added to the slip, called twaddle in the trade.

Hornsea jugs can be found with several marks on them. The most common is an impressed "Hornsea" mark. Less often, a jug can be found with the incised horn over waves mark, but not the Hornsea name. Many were also unmarked, but are easily recognized by the distinctive character and coloring. Due to the limited distribution of its early wares, by far the best place to search for Hornsea jugs is in and around the Hornsea and Hull areas.

The following photos are from the collection of Brian Heckford.

Toby with pipe and walking stick handle

Toby with tankard in yellow pastel and full coloway

Smiling Toby Character Jug on left and Stern Face Character Jug on right (Coutesy of Brian Heckford)

Character Jug Name	Height, inches	Production Life
Mrs. Clapp Soon		1950 - 1951
Ordinary Toby	2 3/8	1950 - 1951
Sarah Thatcher	3 1/2	1951 - 1952
Sam Thatcher	3 3/4	1951 - 1952
Smiling Toby	1 5/8	1949 - 1950
Stern Toby	1 3/4	1949 - 1950

Toby Jug Name	Height, inches	Production Life
Miss Happ	4	1950 - 1951
Nobleman	5 3/4	1951 - 1952
Salt Peter	3 3/4	1950 - 1951
Toby with pipe & stick handle	3 3/4	1950 - 1951
Toby with tankard	6 1/2	1951 - 1952
	5 3/4	1951 - 1952
Tommy Twaddle	4	1950 - 1951

Toby with tankard Toby Jugs; left large in pastel blue finish, right small in pastel green finish (Coutesy of Brian Heckford)

Miss Happ Toby Jug in pastel yellow, blue, pink, and a rare full colorway

Group of Character Jugs; from left to right - Ordinary Toby, Stern Toby in two colors, and Smiling Toby

Sam Thatcher Character Jugs finished in the pink, cream, and blue pastel colors unique to Hornsea Pottery

Tommy Twaddle Toby Jug in cream, blue, and cream pastels

Salt Peter Toby Jug in yellow and pink pastels

Horton Ceramics
See Jugs Marked by Country of Manufacture under United States

International Artware Corporation
Cleveland, Ohio

History

In 1960, Irwin Garber founded the International Artware Corporation, or more commonly INARCO, in Cleveland, Ohio. INARCO was an importer of Far East ceramic goods and floral containers. Irwin learned the importing business through many years of service at the National Potteries Corporation (NAPCO), where he had worked since the mid-1940s. In 1986, NAPCO purchased INARCO and relocated it to Jacksonville, Florida, where NAPCO had moved in 1984.

Character Jugs

International Artware offered a range of Character Jugs dating most likely from the 1960s. INARCO Character Jugs were imported from Japan and are marked with "Cleve, Ohio", sometimes followed by a number and "INARCO".

Character Jug Name	Height, inches
Captain Bligh	4 1/2
Hungry Man	3 1/4
Robinson Crusoe	

John Humphries Pottery
See Jugs Marked by Country of Manufacture under United Kingdom

A. B. Jones & Sons Limited
Longton, England

History

Alfred B. Jones founded A. B. Jones in 1876 at the Grafton Works on Marlborough Road in Longton, Staffordshire. The firm produced china and earthenware. Production changed to primarily bone china around the turn of the century, with the firm becoming a significant competitor of W. H. Goss for crested ware. The pottery offered a wide range of badged and crested china, souvenirs, and tea sets by 1900.

In 1899 the factory at Marlborough Road was completely rebuilt due to its destruction caused by an underground fire. The company changed its name to A. B. Jones & Sons Limited in 1900, when Alfred's sons, Alfred Jones Jr. and W. B. Jones, joined him in the business. One of the first continuous coal fired kilns was installed just after the turn of the century. From the beginning of its china production, the firm used the tradenames Grafton and Grafton China, adding Royal Grafton in 1930 when the pottery received the Royal Warrant.

In the first third of the century, A. B. Jones & Sons' ivory glazes were among the best in the industry. However, because trace amounts of uranium were used to create the glazes, after the onset of World War II the firm could no longer obtain uranium to produce the glazes. In 1949 the coal fired kilns were converted to electric kilns, and in 1951 the factory itself was modernized when the region's first continuous gas fired tunnel kiln was constructed.

The pottery passed to the third generation of the family when Al Jones, Alfred B. Jones' grandson, joined the firm in 1956 as the Managing Director. Crown House Limited bought Jones & Sons in 1966. Then, in 1971, Crown House was purchased by Crown Lynn Potteries Limited of Auckland, New Zealand. The resulting firm was renamed Crown Lynn Ceramics Limited. In March 1985, Jones & Sons was sold off to a management group, RGC Limited, which continued producing goods under the tradename Royal Grafton China.

Toby Jug Name	Height, inches
Irishman	
John Bull	
Scotsman	
Welsh Lady	

Toby Jugs

A. B. Jones & Sons produced four known Toby Jugs in full colorways. Made from bone china, these jugs were produced from approximately 1900 through the 1930s and commonly carry the Grafton or Royal Grafton tradenames.

Joseph Bourne & Son
Denby, England

Toby Jug Name	Height, inches
Ordinary Toby	8 1/2

History

Joseph Bourne was born into a family of potters on July 11, 1788. His father, William Bourne, was a potter and Joseph apprenticed with his father from an early age.

During construction of a new road from Denby to neighboring Alfreton in 1806, workmen discovered a clay deposit along the road. Knowing that William Bourne was a local potter, the workmen brought this to his attention and William quickly leased the clay bed. Using clay from this bed, Joseph Bourne founded his own pottery in 1809 in the Derbyshire area. Operating as Joseph Bourne, the pottery began small and grew steadily. Initial production was centered on stoneware products with a focus on high standards of quality.

The firm's name was changed to Joseph Bourne & Son around 1850. Maintaining its commitment to high quality, the firm added other types of goods to its production over time.

By the 1960s, the firm was producing tableware, ovenware, and utilitarian earthenware. Coloroll, a large housewares company based in Manchester, England, took over the firm in 1987 and operated it for a few years. In 1990 the factory went into receivership and the assets were liquidated.

Toby Jugs

As an attempt to capitalize on the popularity of its Victorian English pottery, in the 1970s the firm re-issued the Ordinary Toby from its 1885 series of Toby Beer Jugs. The Ordinary Toby is marked with the firm's Denby tradename and carries model number 1809 on the bottom.

Joseph Strnact
See Jugs Marked by Country of Manufacture under Germany

Josiah Wedgwood & Sons, Limited
Stoke-on-Trent, England

Toby Jug Name	Height, inches	Production Life
Elihu Yale	6 3/4	1933 - 1939

History

One of the more famous factories in the Staffordshire region was that of Josiah Wedgwood. Josiah, born in Burslem on July 12, 1730, the youngest son of Thomas Wedgwood, entered into a family of potters dating back to the 1600s. Josiah's life as a potter began early when, after his father's death and at the young age of nine, he started working in his father's factory at the Churchyard Pottery. In 1744, Josiah was apprenticed to his older brother Thomas. After having a proposal for partnership rejected by his brother, Josiah entered into a brief partnership with John Harrison in Stoke in 1752. Another partnership followed this one with Thomas Whieldon in 1754. As Whieldon was considered one of the greatest English potters of his time, this partnership allowed Josiah to further develop his skills and begin experimenting with colored creamware.

Josiah Wedgwood ended his partnership with Whieldon and established his own pottery at the Ivy House factory in Burslem in 1759. From this small pottery would grow a viable, high quality corporation, which for almost two hundred years was managed by six generations of the Wedgwood family.

The early years were quite successful, as Josiah established a reputation for high quality products. Early production included red and black stoneware, Egyptian ware, pearlware and jasperware. Today Wedgwood is best known for its most popular line, jasperware, which was introduced in 1775. Perhaps Wedgwood's greatest contribution to the field of ceramics was his pearlware, a high quality creamware with a blue tint to the glaze, which Josiah had started developing during his partnership with Whieldon. Wedgwood's quality earthenware impressed Queen Charlotte so much that, in 1762, she appointed Wedgwood to make her a set of dinnerware. This cream colored earthenware became quite popular in England and abroad, becoming known as Queen's Ware. Wedgwood's creamware caught the eye of yet another noble in 1774, when Russia's Empress Catherine the Great ordered a creamware service consisting of 952 pieces.

Several years of negotiation beginning in 1762 finally resulted in a partnership with Thomas Bentley, established in 1769. The firm's reputation and success grew quickly after the Queen's commission, so Wedgwood built a factory and surrounding small village named Etruria, and moved into it in 1769. The factory was designed and outfitted to Wedgwood's specifications. Initially, only ornamental wares were produced in Etruria, but by 1773 Wedgwood consolidated all of its production there. In 1782, the Etruria factory was the first pottery to install a steam powered engine. Unfortunately, Bentley died in 1780 but he left with Josiah a legacy of good taste for the arts and important social connections. Josiah Wedgwood died in Etruria on January 3, 1795 as a well-respected potter, visionary, philanthropist, and political activist.

The early to mid-1800s brought hard times to the firm in the form of financial and management problems. Josiah's descendent Francis Wedgwood, who became a partner in the firm in 1817, and Francis' son Godfrey were able to turn the company around, but by then Wedgwood had tarnished its reputation and lost market opportunities for emerging products.

Majolica was introduced in 1860 to expand the firm's offering. Through modernization and the introduction of bone china, the company rebounded and exceeded the successes of the early years. In 1895, the firm was incorporated as Josiah Wedgwood and Sons Limited.

In the 1930s, beginning with the bicentenary of Josiah Wedgwood's birth, the firm set goals to enlarge its breadth and commissioned a number of leading designers to create new product lines for Wedgwood. This commitment to growth was led by the fifth Josiah Wedgwood and resulted in a new factory being constructed in 1938 at Barlaston Park, near Stoke-on-Trent. In 1940, the firm moved out of Etruria, the modern factory of the 18th century, and into Barlaston, one of the most modern factories of its time. This new electrified factory also included housing for the factory's employees. Production at Josiah's Etruria factory ended in the 1950s after almost 200 years of operation. Josiah's manor house in Etruria is now part of a hotel.

To celebrate the coronation of Queen Elizabeth II, Royal Blue Jasper ware was introduced in 1953. A second phase of growth for the firm occurred in the latter half of the 1960s and into the 1970s. This growth was spurred by purchases of other potteries rather than being driven internally with new product introductions. Beginning with

William Adams & Sons in 1966, this takeover frenzy included such factories as Susie Cooper and Coalport in 1967, Johnson Brothers in 1968, J. & G. Meakin and Midwinter in the early 1970s, and Crown Staffordshire in 1973. In the midst of this expansion, Wedgwood became a public company in 1967.

After the bulk of its acquisitions, Wedgwood reorganized as the Wedgwood Group, operating a Fine China Division and an Earthenware Division. Two glass companies were added, Kings Lynn Glass in 1969 and Dartington Glass in 1982. The Wedgwood Group resisted a hostile takeover bid by London International PLC in April of 1986, and instead was bought by the Waterford Glass Group in November 1986. In 1989, these combined Groups were renamed Waterford Wedgwood, and in March 1990, it received additional funding from Investco, a new investment company formed by Morgan Stanley Investment Bank.

Today Wedgwood continues its long tradition of producing high quality goods. Wedgwood, along with Royal Doulton, is one of the two giants of the British ceramic industry. It reached a joint marketing agreement with Rosenthal in 1997, of which it owns 25%, whereby each firm would market the other's products in its home nation.

Toby Jugs

Surprisingly, there is documentation of only one Toby Jug ever produced by Wedgwood. This Toby Jug is of Elihu Yale, the founder of Yale University, and was designed by Professor Robert G. Eberherd, head of the University's Department of Sculpture, from a 1717 portrait of Elihu Yale owned by the University. The Elihu Yale Toby was produced for the Yale Publishing Association and is mostly found in solid colors of blue, cream, tan and dark brown. There was also a polychrome version done, but this is extremely rare and therefore more valuable than any solid colorway jug. The jug is marked "The Elihu Yale Toby" and "Wedgwood" among other things. Two variations of the mark are known, one stating a patent has been applied for, and the other stating the patent number of 91059. Wedgwood verified that this is indeed the only Toby Jug it produced in modern times.

Elihu Yale Toby Jug in cream colorway

Elihu Yale Toby Jug in dark brown and blue colorways

Keele Street Pottery
Tunstall, England

Character Jug Name	Height, inches
Ordinary Toby	4 1/2
	3 1/4

Toby Jug Name	Height, inches
Ordinary Toby	6
	3 7/8
	3
Owl	3 1/2

Most common Keele Street Pottery backstamp

Another Keele Street Pottery backstamp

History

Keele Street Pottery was founded in 1913 on Keele Street in Tunstall, Staffordshire. The firm produced primarily earthenware goods for utilitarian use. Between 1945 and 1948, several companies merged to form the Keele Street Pottery Group, with each pottery continuing to operate independently. Beginning with the Keele Street Pottery, these other potteries included Paramount Pottery, Winterton Pottery, Thomas Cone, Collingwood Brothers, Conway Pottery, Lawton Pottery, and Piccadilly Pottery. SouthWestern Gas and Water purchased a 49% interest in the Group in 1949. One year later, the Group renamed itself Staffordshire Potteries Limited, and in 1951, it became a public company.

During the 1950s and 1960s, the more popular line from Keele Street was its Nurseryware, especially Andy Panda, the Lone Ranger, and Tom and Jerry. In 1955, the Keele Street Pottery began operating at the Meir Airport site in Longton, and by 1958 the firm had moved all production to this larger site, closing the original Keele Street factory. The pottery continued to use the Keele Street name until 1969.

In November 1979, Staffordshire Potteries amalgamated with the Howard Pottery Group and became the Staffordshire Pottery Group. The Howard Pottery Group consisted of Howard Pottery, Gibson and Sons, Norfolk Pottery, and Taunton Vale, which had purchased Grimwades and was operating as Royal Winton. Coloroll acquired the Staffordshire Pottery Group in July

1986 via a hostile takeover bid. This was one of the many potteries and pottery groups purchased by Coloroll.

Coloroll is a large housewares company based in Manchester, England. With the takeover of the Staffordshire Pottery Group, Coloroll reorganized its core business, becoming Coloroll Ceramics Division. The Staffordshire Pottery Group split and became kilnCraft by Coloroll and Coloroll Royal Winton. In 1990, kilnCraft was deleted and Coloroll absorbed the Group back into Coloroll Ceramics. With the acquisition of Denby in May 1987, Coloroll combined Denby with the Staffordshire Pottery Group and launched a new subsidiary named Coloroll Tableware Limited. Coloroll Tableware went into receivership in the early 1990s. At that time the Meir Airport factory was taken over in a management buyout and operated as Staffordshire Tableware Limited.

Most of the early production of Keele Street Pottery was unmarked. After World War II, the firm began stamping or incising its wares with "KSP" or "Keele St."

Character Jugs and Toby Jugs

Between 1945 and 1958, Keele Street Pottery produced nicely modeled, but commonplace, Ordinary Toby and Character Jugs, produced both in full colorway and in a cream glaze. The firm's marks of "KSP" or "Keele St." are found on the jugs, dating them to post World War II.

Pair of Keele Street Pottery Ordinary Toby Jugs flanking an Ordinary Toby Character Jug

Kelsboro Ware
See Longton New Art Pottery

Kenneth O. Speaks
See Jugs Marked by Country of Manufacture under United Kingdom

History

Kevin Pearson and Francis Salmon founded Kevin Francis Ceramics in 1988; however, this was not the first of their business ventures. Friends during college at Leeds in 1977, the pair was reunited in 1984 when Francis was searching for a flat and Kevin had just lost his roommate. Both had a budding interest in publishing, and after much discussion a price guide on Royal Doulton Character Jugs was in the works. The success of this book launched Kevin Francis Publishing in 1985. Three years later, six books were published including Vic Schuler's *Collecting British Toby Jugs*.

In 1988, Kevin Francis Cermics was launched, committed to producing the highest quality Toby and Character Jug designs in limited editions. The firm initially commissioned Royal Doulton to produce Character Jugs conceived by Kevin Francis and modeled by Geoff Blower. The result was Doulton's Collecting World series of three jugs: the Collector, Antique Dealer, and Auctioneer. Kevin Francis then went on to produce Toby Jugs under its own name, the first being a series of five jugs designed by the renowned Peggy Davies and produced by the pottery operated by her son, Rhodri Davies.

Business grew quickly, and in 1989 offices were opened in Tampa and Toronto to serve the North American market. While Kevin Francis began with Character and Toby Jug production, in 1992 the firm branched out into other high quality products such as wall masks, figurines, and vases. The firm also began receiving special commissions, the first being the Pavarotti Toby Jug for the Autistic Society.

From the outset Kevin Francis catered to its customers. Its publishing arm released topical books related to ceramics collecting. The Kevin Francis Collector's Guild began in 1993 including annual club member–only pieces, sometimes allowing members to select the colorway of their jug. The first Guild piece was the Prince of Clowns, a wonderful Toby Jug depicting Charlie Chaplin as the Tramp.

Kevin Francis utilized the talents of many well-respected designers and modelers. Initially the firm relied on the extensive talents of Geoff Blower, previously of Royal Doulton and Wedgwood, and the creative genius of Peggy Davies. Other notable designers who have worked for Kevin Francis include Andy Moss, who apprenticed with Peggy Davies;

Douglas Tootle, who had worked for Royal Doulton and Wood & Sons; and John Michael.

One modeler, Ray Noble, began working for the firm quite by accident and ultimately went on to form his own pottery. Ron Noble, a collector of Kevin Francis jugs, arranged an introduction of Kevin Pearson to his son Ray in 1992. Soon, Ray showed Kevin a sculpture of a political face mask he had modeled. Both Kevin and his partner Francis recognized Ray's natural talent and encouraged him to model other pieces. With this encouragement, Ray went to Peggy Davies Ceramics and learned more about sculpting from Andy Moss. He then began modeling jugs for Kevin Francis Ceramics. His first design for Kevin Francis was the Pershore Miller Toby Jug. Following the success of that jug, Ray modeled approximately six other jugs, including Napoleon, the Duke of Wellington, Stormin' Norman, and John Major.

Encouraged by expanding business in North America, Kevin Pearson moved to the United States in 1993 to develop further the business there. However, in 1994 Pearson and Salmon ended their partnership. Pearson retained the rights to the North American market for Kevin Francis Ceramics, Salmon took full control of the publishing business, and the Kevin Francis Ceramics business in the United Kingdom was sold to Rhodri Davies of Peggy Davies Studios. Kevin Pearson and Rhodri continued to operate Kevin Francis Ceramics in a new partnership. Kevin is also a partner in the American Toby Jug Museum in Evanston, Illinois.

Character Jugs and Toby Jugs

Claiming to produce the finest Toby Jugs in the world, and living up to that bold claim, Kevin Francis has designed and issued a large variety of finely detailed jugs in a little over a decade. These are arguably the highest quality Toby and Character Jugs of the late twentieth century. Overall, its jugs are produced with outstanding craftsmanship. The high degree of detail each piece communicates about its subject is beyond comparison.

More than any other firm, Kevin Francis has also embraced the development of the figural Toby Jug, a jug more human shaped and proportional than the traditional Toby. Also, more recent production has tended away from the traditional pouring spout, thereby raising the question of whether it is rightfully called a jug at all, although the decorative handles still provide the semblance of a pouring vessel. The

Designer Andy Moss in his studio with clay model of the Uncle Sam Toby Jug

Cavalier Character Jug

The Collector Character Jug, prototype of Royal Doulton's Collector Character Jug

George H. Dietz MD Character Jug designed by Peggy Davies on special commision from Dr. Dietz

John Major Character Jug

Leo Castelli Character Jug
designed by Meyer Vaisman

General Norman H.
Schwarzkopf Character Jug

President Clinton Character Jug

company has used this new Toby form to produce some very exceptional results. Another first for Kevin Francis was its Rocking Santa, the first rocking Toby Jug ever produced.

Peggy Davies designed Kevin Francis' initial Toby Jugs in 1988 and 1989. She first modeled the Vic Schuler jug as a traditional Toby, and then went on to design Winston Churchill, Postman, Shareholder, Cook, Gardener, and Doctor. Sadly, Peggy Davies died shortly after completing these designs. The last design Peggy did for the firm was a portrait character jug commissioned by Dr. George H. Dietz of Ohio. This jug was produced in a limited edition of 100, all of which were delivered to Dr. Dietz, and all but a few still remain in his possession.

Toby series produced by Kevin Francis include Great Generals, Political, Artists and Potters, Comical Animals, and historical characters. A whimsical series of cartoon characters was produced under the authorization of Warner Brothers. The Spitting Image Character Jug series takes a satirical look at English political figures, creating comical characatures with political messages. For example, the large nosed Neil Kinnock jug has a red rose handle making obvious his political biases. Ray Noble of Noble Ceramics designed the Charles & Di two-faced mug. The firm has also produced several jugs on private commissions that have never been offered to the market. Examples of these include George Dietz, Ed and Charley, and Leo Castelli, which was designed by Meyer Vaisman. Cleopatra, Isis and Zenobia comprise the Queens of the Nile series. The President Gorbachev Toby Jug has a piece of the Berlin wall incorporated into it. The first twenty Moe Wideman jugs have a slightly different colorway and were specially made for a Pittsburgh club. These are marked "ETC Society" on Moe's hat.

One of the more unusual topics for a Toby Jug is Kevin Francis' Star Trek series. Consisting of every Trekkie's favorites from the original Star Trek television show and *Star Trek: The Next Generation*, this was planned as a ten piece limited edition series beginning in 1995 with, of course, Captain Kirk as the first jug offered. Although fully authorized by Paramount Pictures, the Star Trek series encountered copyright and model approval problems which limited the series to five released characters, with an additional two prototype jugs sneaking out into the market in very limited quantities. As a cross collectible in a time when Star Trek's popularity continues to grow where no man has gone before, these jugs will certainly be hard to find in the future.

Kevin Francis sponsors a Collector's Guild for the many collectors of Kevin Francis products. Each year it develops a special Guild release with production quantities limited to the number of Guild members, so the exact number issued will vary. To further enhance the collectibility of its jugs, Kevin Francis destroys all molds at the completion of each limited edition issue.

Kevin Francis' jugs are very well marked, making identification easy for the collector. Some jugs carry special backstamps such as "North American Edition," which means that this particular colorway was released only in North America. Also, jugs marked "Kevin Francis USA" were only released to the North American market. Some jugs featured a special colorway available in small volumes. For example, out of the 750 piece limited edition of the Winston Churchill VE Day Toby, 200 were released for the International Churchill Society in a different colorway and with a different backstamp. Prototype jugs were marked "Kevin Francis Prototype." If the design proved a success and manufacturable and no changes were made to it, these became a part of the limited edition quantity. When prototype jugs appear on the market, they command significantly higher prices.

Since 1993, the introduction of new jugs has greatly diminished. Since that time, the company issued only a few new characters each year. Although some of the released jugs have not sold out their limited edition quantities, many have done so. The market value of Kevin Francis jugs could increase substantially in the years to come.

Spiting Image backstamp

Kevin Francis mark on early production pieces

Common Kevin Francis backstamp

More recent backstamp variation

Another recent backstamp variation

Margaret Thatcher large sized
Spitting Image Character Jug

The two sides of the Charles & Di Spitting Image Character Jug

Ed and Charley Character Jug, both front
and back shown. Likeness of Ed Pascoe
on the left and Charley Dombeck on the
right, produced for the annual Florida
Royal Doulton show in 1993

Left to right; John Major, Margaret Thatcher, and
Neil Kinnock Spitting Image Character Jugs

Character Jugs of Nigel Mansell on the left and
Ian Botham on the right

Queens of the Nile Character Jug Series;
left to right - Cleopatra, Xenobia, and Isis

Tetley Ale advertising Character
Jug

From left to right, famous artists and
designers Clarice Cliff, Susie Cooper , and
Peggy Davies Character Jugs

Art Deco Girls Character Jug Series: top row left
to right - Paradise and Masquerade; bottom row
left to right - Feathers, Starlight Champagne, and
Butterfly

Character Jug Name		Height, inches	Production Life
Butterfly	Art Deco Girl	5	1993 Ltd Ed of 200
Cavalier		6	1998 Ltd Ed of 75
Charles & Di	(Spitting Image)	7	1992 Ltd Ed of 350
Clarice Cliff		4	1994 Ltd Ed of 250
Cleopatra		6 1/4	1998 Ltd Ed of 350
Collector		6 1/2	Royal Doulton pilot
Ed and Charley		5 3/4	1993 Ltd Ed of 100
Feathers	Art Deco Girl	5	1994 Ltd Ed of 200
General Norman H. Schwarzkopf			1991 Ltd Ed of 1000
George H. Dietz, MD		7 1/2	1989 Ltd Ed of 100
Ian Botham		5	1990 Ltd Ed of 1000
Isis		6 1/4	1998 Ltd Ed of 350
John Major	(Spitting Image)	8	1991 Ltd Ed of 500
	(Spitting Image)	5	1992 Ltd Ed of 650
Leo Castelli		8	1993 Ltd Ed of 100
Margaret Thatcher	(Spitting Image)	large	
	(Spitting Image)	5	1991 Ltd Ed of 650
Masquerade	Art Deco Girl	5	Ltd Ed of 200
Neil Kinnock	(Spitting Image)	5	1992 Ltd Ed of 650
Nigel Mansell		6	1992 Ltd Ed 100
Paddy Hobkirk		6	
Paradise	Art Deco Girl	5	1994 Ltd Ed of 200
Peggy Davies		4	1994 Ltd Ed of 250
President Clinton		6 1/2	1993 Ltd Ed of 750
Starlight Champagne	Art Deco Girl	5	1994 Ltd Ed of 200
Susie Cooper		4	1994 Ltd Ed of 250
Tetley Ale		5	
Winston Churchill		5 1/2	1993 Ltd Ed of 750
Zenobia		6 1/4	1998 Ltd Ed of 350

Toby Jug Name		Height, inches	Production Life
Alligator Mini		4	1992 Ltd Ed of 1000
American Sailor		10	1998
Bernard Leach		9	1992 Ltd Ed of 200
Borg		10	1995 Ltd Ed of 350
Boris Yeltsin		8 3/4	1991 Ltd Ed of 250
British Bulldog		9	1990 Ltd Ed of 500
Bugs Bunny		8 3/4	1994 Ltd Ed of 750
Bulldog	Soccer	9	1994 Ltd Ed of 450
	Footballer	8 1/2	1994 Ltd Ed of 75
Bulldog Dinnertime (1992 Jug of the Year)		9	1992 Ltd Ed of 150
Captain Henry Morgan (1994 Jug of the Year)		9 1/2	1994 Ltd Ed of 250
Captain Kirk		8	1995 Ltd Ed of 750
Captain Picard	(Prototype)	8 3/4	1995
Cardassian modeled only			Ltd Ed of 400
Cat Mini		4	1992 Ltd Ed of 1000
Charlotte Rhead		9	1991 Ltd Ed of 350
Chicken Mini		3 3/4	1992 Ltd Ed of 1000
Christopher Columbus		9	1992 Ltd Ed of 750
Clarice Cliff	(Guild Issue)	8 3/4 4 1/4 2 1/2	1990 Ltd Ed of 350 1993 1993 Ltd Ed of 2500
Clown		9	1989 Ltd Ed of 1500
Cook		9	1989 Ltd Ed of 250

Toby Jug Name	Height, inches	Production Life
Councillor Troi not produced		Ltd Ed of 400
Daffy Duck	9	1994 Ltd Ed of 750
David Winter	8 3/4	1991 Ltd Ed of 950
Dick Turpin	9 1/2	1995 Ltd Ed of 250
Doctor	8 1/2	1989 Ltd Ed of 500
Doctor McCoy pilot	8	Ltd Ed of 450
Dog Mini	4	1992 Ltd Ed of 1000
Douglas Bader	8 3/4	1990 Ltd Ed of 750
Drunken Sal two colorways (Guild Issue)	10 4 1/4	1996 Ltd Ed of 100 1996
Duck Mini	4	1992 Ltd Ed of 1000
Duke of Wellington	9 1/2	1992 Ltd Ed of 750
Elephant Mini	4	1992 Ltd Ed of 1000
Elvis Presley (Prototype 1) (Prototype 2)	8	1992
Ferengi	8 1/2	Ltd Ed of 350
Field Marshall Montgomery	8 3/4	1990 Ltd Ed of 750
Field Marshall Rommel	8 1/2	1991 Ltd Ed of 750
Fisherman	8 1/4	1990 Ltd Ed of 500
Frog Mini	4	1992 Ltd Ed of 1000
Gardener	8 1/4	1989 Ltd Ed of 1500
General Eisenhower	8 3/4	1992 Ltd Ed of 750
General G. S. Patton	8 1/2	1991 Ltd Ed of 750
General Grant	9 1/4	1994 Ltd Ed of 750
General Lee	9 1/4	1994 Ltd Ed of 750
General Norman Schwarzkopf	8 1/2	1991 Ltd Ed of 750
Geordie (Prototype)		Ltd Ed of 400
George Tinworth	8 1/2	1993 Ltd Ed of 350
Gin Woman	10	
Golfer	9 5	1990 Ltd Ed of 1000 1991 Ltd Ed of 2500
Hannah Barlow	9	1991 Ltd Ed of 350
Hearty Good Fellow	8 1/2	1990 Ltd Ed of 750
Helmut Kohl	8	1991 Ltd Ed of 999
Henley Teddy	large	1990 Ltd Ed of 250
Henry Sandon green stripe colorway	9 9	1994 Ltd Ed of 750 1998
John F. Kennedy	9	1992 Ltd Ed of 750
Josiah Wedgwood	8 3/4	1991 Ltd Ed of 350
King Henry VIII	9	1991 Ltd Ed of 750
Kings of Comedy (Guild Issue)	9	1994
Lady Snufftaker 2 colorways	9 3/4	1998 Ltd Ed of 100
Lieutenant Worf	7 3/4	Ltd Ed of 400
Lion Cub Mini	4 1/4	1992 Ltd Ed of 1000
Little Clarice	6 1/4	1991 Ltd Ed of 2500
Little Gorby	4	1991 Ltd Ed of 2500
Little Teddy	5	1992 Ltd Ed of 2500
Little Vic	6 1/2	1989 Ltd Ed of 2500
Little Winston	5	1991 Ltd Ed of 2500
Lowell Davis	7	1994 Ltd Ed of 500
Lucie Rie	9	1993 Ltd Ed of 200
Margaret Thatcher red dress coloway	9 9	1989 Ltd Ed of 1000 1991
Mark Klause	9	1992 Ltd Ed of 750
Martha Gunn (Guild Issue)	10 4 3/8	1996 Ltd Ed of 100 1995
Marx Brothers (Guild Issue)	9	1996
Max Miller (Guild Issue)	9	1999
Midshipmite Fidel Castro	9 1/4	1999 Ltd Ed of 100
Midshipmite John Major	9 1/4	1993 Ltd Ed of 750
Midshipmite Kenneth Clarke	9 1/4	
Midshipmite Winston Churchill	9	1995 Ltd Ed of 100
Moe Wideman	9	1992 Ltd Ed of 350
Monkey Mini	3 1/2	1992 Ltd Ed of 1000

Clarice Cliff Toby Jug in large and small sizes, along with two colorways of Little Clarice Toby Jug

Christopher Columbus Toby Jug, showing both the front and back

Early Toby Jugs designed by Peggy Davies: left to right - Doctor, Gardener, Postman, Cook, and Shareholder

Clown Toby Jug

Backside of same group showing ornate handles, left to right - Doctor, Gardener, Postman, Cook, and Shareholder

Close up view of handle on Elvis second prototype

Two color versions of the first Elvis Presley prototype Toby Jug

Elvis second prototype Toby Jug

Douglas Bader Toby Jug on left and Lowell Davis on right

Drunken Sal Toby Jug in two colorways

Fisherman on left and Pershore Miller on right

Backside of Fisherman and Pershore Miller showing their ornate handles

Hearty Good Fellow Toby Jug in three colorways, produced in the image of Vic Schuler (from the collection of Vic Schuler)

Henry Sandon Toby Jug

Golfer Toby Jug in two sizes and two colorways

Left to right: Henley Teddy and Little Teddy Toby Jugs

Toby Jug Name	Height, inches	Production Life
Morecambe & Wise (Guild Issue)	9	1997
Napoleon Bonaparte	9 1/4	1992 Ltd Ed of 750
Nelson Mandela	9	1995 Ltd Ed of 250
Pablo Picasso	9	1992 Ltd Ed of 350
Pavarotti seated signed by Pavarotti (5 known)	9 9	1990 Ltd Ed of 2000
Peggy Davies (Guild Issue)	9 4	1993 Ltd Ed of 350 1994
Pepe Le Pew	8 1/2	1994 Ltd Ed of 750
Pershore Miller	9	1991 Ltd Ed of 1500
Pope John Paul II	8 1/2	1990 Ltd Ed of 350
Postman	9	1989 Ltd Ed of 1500
President Gorbachev	9	1990 Ltd Ed of 1000
Prince of Clowns (Guild Issue)	8 1/2	1993
Princess Diana	8 1/2	1992 Ltd Ed of 900
Puss in Boots (1993 Jug of Year)	8 1/2	1993 Ltd Ed of 250
Q (not produced)		Ltd Ed of 400
Queen Elizabeth II	9	1992 Ltd Ed of 400
Queen Mother two colorways	9	1990 Ltd Ed of 900
Rabbit Mini	3 3/4	1992 Ltd Ed of 1000
Ralph Wood (Guild Issue)	9 4 1/4	1992 Ltd Ed of 350 1993
Rocking Santa	6 1/2	Ltd Ed of 2500
Rule Britannia with detachable crown	9 1/2	1993 Ltd Ed of 350
Salvador Dali	9	1992 Ltd Ed of 350
Sandra Kuck	9	1992 Ltd Ed of 500
Santa Clause	8 1/2	1989 Ltd Ed of 1500
Shareholder	8 1/2	1989 Ltd Ed of 1500
Sherlock Holmes	8 1/4 4	1992 Ltd Ed of 750 1995 Ltd Ed of 2500
Sir Henry Doulton	9	1992 Ltd Ed of 350
Spock	9 1/4	1996 Ltd Ed of 750
Squire	8 1/2	1993 Ltd Ed of 750
Standing Pavarotti		Ltd Ed of 250
Stonewall Jackson	8 3/4	1993 Ltd Ed of 750
Susie Cooper	9	1991 Ltd Ed of 350
Sylvestor & Tweety	9	1994 Ltd Ed of 750
Tasmanian Devil	8 1/4	1994 Ltd Ed of 750
Teddy Mini	4	1993 Ltd Ed of 2500
Thin Man traditional color (1997 Jug of Year) new color (Guild Issue)	9 1/2 9 1/2 4 1/4	1997 Ltd Ed of 250 part of above edition 1997
Toby Fillpot (Guild Issue)	9 3 3/4	1992 Ltd Ed of 750 1993
Tommy Cooper (Guild Issue)	9 1/2	1997 - 1998
Uncle Sam		1999
Vic Schuler blue jacket yellow jacket colorway (Guild Issue)	8 1/2 8 1/2 4 1/4	1988 Ltd Ed of 1000 1998
Vincent Van Gogh	9	1993 Ltd Ed of 350
William Moorcroft	9	1991 Ltd Ed of 350
William Shakespeare	9	1990 Ltd Ed of 1000
Winston Churchill Naval VE Day D Day Political Seated Standing Seated Standing	9 1/4 9 9 9 8 3/4 8 3/4 4 1/2 4 1/2	1992 Ltd Ed of 750 1992 Ltd Ed of 750 1992 Ltd Ed of 750 1992 Ltd Ed of 750 1989 Ltd Ed of 5000 1992 Ltd Ed of 750 1993 Ltd Ed of 2000 1993 Ltd Ed of 2000

John F. Kennedy Toby Jug

King Henry VIII Toby Jug

Kings of Comedy Toby Jug depicting Laurel and Hardy

Mark Klause Toby Jug

Lady Snufftaker Toby Jug in two colorways

Lady Snufftaker Toby Jug, U. S. version

Margaret Thatcher Toby Jug in blue dress and red dress colorways

Large size Martha Gunn Toby Jug

Two views of Marx Brothers Toby Jug featuring Groucho with Harpo and Zeppo looking on

Left to right - Midshipmites Winston Churchill ,John Major, Kenneth Clarke

Max Miller 1999 Guild Issue Toby Jug

Morecambe & Wise 1997 Guild Issue Toby Jug

Pavarotti seated Toby Jug

Standing Pavarotti Toby Jug

Moe Wideman Toby Jug, both front and back views

Large President Gorbachev Toby Jug alongside Little Gorby Toby Jug

Prince of Clowns depicting Charlie Chaplin, both front and back views

Rocking Santa jug on left and Santa Clause jug on right

Rule Britannia Toby Jug with a detachable crown

American Sailor Toby Jug on left and 19th century original jug on right

Kevin Francis Squire Toby Jug on left and 18th century Squire on right

18th century Thin Man Toby Jug on left with Kevin Francis Thin Man in two sizes

Large Toby Fillpot and tiny Toby Fillpot Toby Jugs

Tommy Cooper Toby Jug

Vic Schuler Toby Jug in large and small sizes, Little Vic Toby Jug

Three trial colorways of the Vic Schuler Toby Jug (from the collection of Vic Schuler)

Set of graduated Winston Churchill Seated Toby Jugs in large, small and miniature sizes

Collection of Winston Churchill jugs; top row left to right - large and small Seated Toby, Character Jug, Political, and D-Day Toby Jugs; bottom row left to right - two Naval colorways, V-E Day, and two Standing colorways

Winston Churchill Standing Toby Jugs, two large jugs in blue and gray colorways flanking a miniature jug

Clay model of Uncle Sam Toby Jug slated for 1999 production

From left to right - Peggy Davies large and miniature sizes, and Susie Cooper miniature and large sizes

From left to right - backside of Clarice Cliff large and miniature, Susie Cooper large and miniature, and Peggy Davies large and miniature

Pottery Artists from left to right - Hanna Barlow, Charlotte Rhead, Lucie Rie, and Sandra Kuck

Backside of Barlow, Rhead, Rie, and Kuck jugs showing decorative handles

Josiah Wedgwood Toby Jug on left and William Moorcroft jug on right

Artists from left to right - Vincent Van Gogh, Pablo Picasso, and Salvador Dali

Backside of Van Gogh, Picasso, and Dali jugs showing decorative handles

Ralph Wood Toby Jug on right and David Winter jug on left

Potters from left to right - Bernard Leach, Sir Henry Doulton, and George Tinworth

Backside of Leach, Doulton and Tinworth jugs showing decorative handles

Duke of Wellington Toby Jug on left and Napoleon Bonaparte on right

U.S. Civil War Generals; from left to right - General Lee, General Grant and Stonewall Jackson

Backside of Generals Lee, Grant and Jackson showing patriotic handles

World War II Generals Field Marshall Montgomery on left and Field Marshall Rommel on right

Famous 20th century United States Generals; left to right - General Eisenhower, General G. S. Patton, and General Norman Schwartzkopf

Decorative handles of Generals Eisenhower, Patton and Schwartzkopf jugs

Detailed handles of Montgomery Toby Jug on left and Rommel on right

Political jugs of Boris Yeltsin on left and Helmut Kohl on right

Female British Royalty from left to right - Queen Mother in blue colorway, Queen Elizabeth II, Princess Diana, and Queen Mother in red colorway

Statesmen Nelson Mandela on left and Pope John Paul II on right

Sherlock Holmes on left and William Shakespeare on right

Handles of Sherlock Holmes jug on left and William Shakespeare on right

Handles on the back of the Mandela and Pope John Paul II jugs

Dick Turpin Toby Jug on left and Captain Henry Morgan on right

Handles on Dick Turpin and Captain Morgan Toby Jugs

Related Bulldog figurines; left to right - Squire, Boxer, and Chef

Looney Toons Toby Jugs; from left to right - Bugs Bunny, Pepe Le Pew, Tasmanian Devil, Daffy Duck, and Sylvester & Tweety

Backside of Looney Toons jugs; Bugs Bunny, Pepe Le Pew, Tasmanian Devil, Daffy Duck, and Sylvester & Tweety

Star Trek Series Toby Jugs; left to right - Lieutenant Worf, Borg, and Ferengi

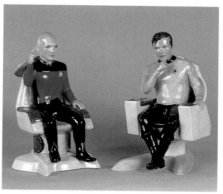

Star Trek Series Toby Jugs; Captain Picard on left and Captain Kirk on right

Star Trek's Spock Toby Jug in two different color-ways

Prototype Dr. McCoy Toby Jug from the Star Trek series

Bulldog Dinnertime Toby Jug on left, Puss in Boots center, British Bulldogs on right

Backside of Bulldog Dinnertime, Puss in Boots and British Bulldog jugs

Animal miniature Toby Jugs; left to right - Lion Cub, Duck, Frog, and Chicken

Animal miniature Toby Jugs; left to right - Rabbit, Dog, Monkey, and Alligator

Miniature Elephant and Teddy Toby Jugs

Kingston Pottery
Hull, England

History

Two brothers, John and Herbert Love, started the Kingston Pottery in the mid-1970s. Beginning in 1962, the brothers became business partners, operating a series of five Love Brothers retail pottery stores throughout the Hull area, and regularly setting up stalls at outdoor markets and fairs. As a part of its regular inventory, the Love Brothers' shops carried a large volume of products from Shorter & Son.

When Shorter & Son went out of business in 1964, and the availability of its products dwindled, the brothers decided to enter into the pottery business themselves. They began Kingston Pottery on a small scale and with little knowledge of the pottery business. Colin Rawson of nearby Hornsea Pottery, who had become recognized as a leader in ceramic design, consulted with the Love brothers as they launched Kingston Pottery. The brothers learned the pottery business quickly and grew production at an astonishing rate during the

Mark on Charles
Dickens Series Jugs

English Royalty Series backstamp

roughly fifteen years of its existence. The Kingston Pottery factory was built on Scarborough Street in Hull with state of the art technology and large capacity kilns. The company introduced broad lines of earthenware and china products, including figurines, large animal figural groups, Toby Jugs, and Character Jugs. Its china cats have become quite collectible today.

At its peak, Kingston Pottery was producing six to eight tons of pots each week. The pottery exported quite a bit of its products to the United States, and some products were created primarily for export to North America. A firm in San Diego headed by Bill Younger eagerly purchased all the figural elephant pieces that the pottery could make. A prominent gift shop at the head of Niagara Falls carried a large selection of Kingston Pottery jugs.

To expand into bone china production, Kingston Pottery purchased Royal Cauldon from Mr. Tim Brown. At the time, the Royal Cauldon factory was making a large amount of bone china pudding ware and other fine porcelain items, with annual revenues of around eight million pounds. In 1984, John Love bought a third large factory in Hull, Ferrybridge Pottery, to keep up with growing demands. Then disaster struck.

The UK coal miner's strike in December of 1984 became the downfall of the Kingston pottery. The strike forced Kingston to buy continental coal rather than local coal. The imported coal was coarser and came in slabs as opposed to small evenly sized pieces, making it more difficult to manage. This coal also cost more and burned less efficiently. The recent purchase of the third factory left Kingston Pottery in a cash depleted state, and the strike used up its remaining resources. To complicate matters, orders fell off beginning in December as well.

In June of 1985, the Kingston Pottery went into receivership, and for several months Spicer and Pegler and Partners, one of the joint receivers, managed the firm. At the time the firm employed fifty-four people. After several months of searching for a buyer, John Love finally sold the three factories. Royal Cauldon was sold to the Perks Ceramic Group of Yorkshire, which renamed it Cauldon Potteries Limited and added it to a group of factories. Mason Cash purchased the original Kingston factory. He had no interest in Kingston's wares, but wanted the high capacity kilns and production capabilities of the factory for production of his own high volume products. John Love stayed on with Mason Cash for three months to transfer the business. Some of the molds for the large animal groups were sold to Masterpiece Sculpture Limited, also of Hull, which continued to produce and market them. Unfortunately, many of the molds were

destroyed when the business changed hands, some by disgruntled mold makers.

The retail shops were also affected by the financial hardships. John sold three shops, and gave the other two stores to his daughter. She ran them for three more years before going out of business herself. Several years later, John Love attempted to start up a pottery again. However, the high costs of starting over forced him to give up on these plans. John and Herbert's Kingston factory still stands, now owned by a plastics company.

Character Jugs and Toby Jugs

Kingston Pottery made three different series of Character and Toby Jugs. These jugs were produced over a relatively short period of time, with all jug production ending in 1982. Kingston used a hand spraying process to apply the paint, making it possible to produce them cheaply and quickly.

Introduced in 1978, the first series was a limited edition set of twelve nicely modeled, large sized Character Jugs called the English Royalty series. Kingston fully researched the background and activities of many monarchs, selecting the most notorious of those as subjects for its Character Jugs. The first jug in the series was King John. After completing three of these jugs, the modeler, Frank Garbutt of Stoke, wanted to retire. John Love cajoled him into creating nine additional jugs, rounding out the set to an even twelve. These Royalty jugs were extremely popular, with Henry VIII being the biggest seller, and Kingston Pottery attempted to expand the series further. Unfortunately, Frank Garbutt died shortly after designing the twelfth character. Other modelers were asked to design additional jugs; however, no one could quite capture the same look as Frank's designs. Therefore, no additional jugs in this series were ever produced. Based on the research of each monarch, a detailed biography of the individual, with a summary of his or her deeds, was published by J&H Love Production and shipped with each jug. This biography also included the edition number of the jug.

The Elizabeth I jug was the only one of the English Royalty series produced without a spout. This caused export problems with New Zealand because the piece became classified as a decorative item and carried a 100% import tariff. The firm simply modified Elizabeth jugs that were destined for New Zealand by hand forming a spout with the thumb before firing. This allowed for classification as a water pitcher and avoided the stiff import tariff. These hand-modified jugs are rare and have a much higher market value than the standard Elizabeth I jug.

The firm's second series of Character Jugs was

called Charles Dickens Characters and consisted of sixteen well-known characters from the works of Dickens. The Dickens series was modeled at the end of the 1970s by Peter Dunn, a talented freelance sculptor and designer in the Hull area, and was introduced in 1979. John Love estimates that around five hundred of each Dickens jug was produced. Dickens jugs have been found without the company marks, possibly indicating these were pirated copies.

Based on the success of the Dickens Character Jugs, Kingston Pottery again retained Peter Dunn to design several different Irish Water Jugs, more commonly known as Toby Jugs. These jugs depicted colorful characters familiar to the common man and were sold in large volumes at three pounds each to New York pubs and taverns. John Love is especially proud of the detail and workmanship of the Phil the Fluter Toby; however, Molly Malone also makes a very attractive Toby Jug. Kingston was approached about making smaller sized versions of the Water Jugs for the U.S. Air Force and Army bases, but the idea never took off. Peter Dunn still does freelance work at Studio Tortus in Hull, now joined by his daughter, Yvonne, who is honing her creative design talents by his side.

The list of monarchs and Dickens jugs below is complete. There may be a few Irish Water Jugs yet to be identified.

The photographs of the English Royalty Character Jugs are courtesy of John Love.

Mrs. Micawber Character Jug

English Royalty Character Jugs from left to right - Charles I, Edward I, Richard I, and Charles II

English Royalty Character Jugs from left to right -William I, George II, Henry VIII, and Richard III

English Royalty Character Jugs from left to right - Edward III, Victoria, Elizabeth I, and King John

Character Jug Name	Height, inches	Production Life
Artful Dodger	7	1979 - 1982
Betsy Trotwood	7	1979 - 1982
Bill Sykes	7	1979 - 1982
Charles I	7	1978 - 1982
Charles II	7	1978 - 1982
Convict (Provis)	7	1979 - 1982
Edward I	6 1/2	1978 - 1982
Edward III	6 7/8	1978 - 1982
Elizabeth I	7	1978 - 1982
Fagin	6 5/8	1979 - 1982
George II	7	1978 - 1982
Henry VIII	7	1978 - 1982
King John		1978 - 1982
Miss Havisham		1979 - 1982
Mr. Bumble	5 3/4	1979 - 1982
Mr. Dick		1979 - 1982
Mr. Micawber		1979 - 1982
Mr. Peggoty	6 3/4	1979 - 1982
Mrs. Bumble	6 3/4	1979 - 1982
Mrs. Micawber	7	1979 - 1982
Oliver Twist	6 5/8	1979 - 1982
Pickwick	5 3/4	1979 - 1982
Pip		1979 - 1982
Richard I	6 1/2	1978 - 1982
Richard III		1978 - 1982
Sam Weller		1979 - 1982
Victoria	6 1/2	1978 - 1982
William I	7	1978 - 1982

Toby Jug Name	Height, inches	Production Life
Danny Boy	9 3/4	1980 - 1982
Molly Malone	10 1/4	1980 - 1982
Mother Machree	10	1980 - 1982
Phil the Fluter		1980 - 1982

Dickens Character Jugs; top row - Betsy Trotwood and Mr. Pickwick; bottom row - left to right - Mr. Bumble, Mrs. Bumble, and Peggoty

Dickens Character Jugs; top row - Oliver Twist and Fagin; bottom row left to right - Artful Dodger, Bill Sykes, and The Convict (Provis)

Irish Water Toby Jugs from left to right - Molly Malone, Danny Boy, and Mother Macree

Kirkland & Company
Etruria, England

Character Jug Name	Height, inches
Winston Churchill	7 3/4

Toby Jug Name	Height, inches
Winston Churchill	10 1/2

Backstamp on Winston Churchill Character Jug

History

Kirkland and Company was founded in Etruria, Staffordshire in 1892 and began producing a wide range of earthenware goods. In 1938, the firm was renamed Kirklands Limited of Etruria, and in 1947, renamed again to Kirklands Limited of Staffordshire. The firm ceased operations around 1969.

Character Jugs and Toby Jugs

Kirkland produced only two known jugs, both during the 1940s. These were a Character Jug and a Toby Jug of Winston Churchill. Both jugs are a tribute to Churchill as the First Lord of the Admiralty, a position he was appointed to for the second time in 1939. The Character Jug was introduced in 1941 and offered in creamware, green glaze, and full colorway finishes. The jug has a nautical look to it with Churchill looking like a ship's masthead. This jug is marked "Kirkland Etruria."

Introduced in 1943, the Churchill Toby Jug depicts the Statesman in formal dress with a detachable top hat, and has a ship's figural head as its handle. It was produced in both a cream colorway and full colorway.

Kirkland Winston Churchill Character Jug

Kirkland Winston Churchill Toby Jug

Konigliche Porzellan Manufactur (KPM)
See Jugs Marked by Country of Manufacture under Germany

KSP
See Keele Street Pottery

History

Ron Smith is the owner of the Personalities and Events shop in Camden Passage, Islington, London. He is also the author of books on Winston Churchill and Margaret Thatcher memorabilia; *Churchill, Images of Greatness* and *The Premier Years of Margaret Thatcher*, respectively. Ron uses the tradename Lady Grace China for ceramics he commissions. Most of his designs are coffee mugs celebrating key events, political and otherwise, in the English scene. Examples include coronations and royal weddings.

Toby Jugs

In 1997, Ron commissioned an exciting new limited edition Toby Jug titled "The King's Dilemma" from Peggy Davies Ceramics. Designed by Andy Moss, the jug depicts a seated Edward VIII with Wallis Simpson looking over his shoulder as the handle. This jug commemorates the sixtieth anniversary of the abdication of the English throne on December 10, 1936 by Edward VIII in favor of the woman he loved. This high quality political commemorative sold out quickly and will most likely rise in value over the next several years.

Toby Jug Name	Height, inches	Production
The King's Dilemma	9 1/4	1997 Ltd Ed of 350

Ornate mark found on The King's Dilemma limited edition Toby Jug

Edward VIII and Wallis Simpson in The King's Dilemma Toby Jug

Lancaster and Sandland Limited
Hanley, England

History

Mr. Lancaster founded Lancaster Pottery in 1901 at the Dresden Works in Hanley, England. The pottery first operated as Lancasters, and then changed its name in 1906 to Lancaster and Son, Edwin Lancaster being the son who joined the firm. Lancaster & Son became a limited partnership in 1920. Having been an employee with the firm for a number of years, Thomas Henry (TH) Sandland invested in Lancaster and Sons Limited in the mid-1930s, and co-managed the firm with Edwin Lancaster.

Thomas Sandland attended school at the Burslem College of Art, where he won prestigious awards for his designs. At Lancaster and Sons, TH, as he was commonly known, immediately demonstrated his skills as an excellent modeler. He was also a storyteller and full of fun, liked by fellow employees and loved by his family. TH often went out after hours and sold the firm's wares himself. By 1940, Sandland purchased full control of the company, and in 1944 he renamed the pottery Lancaster

and Sandland Limited. The last active Lancaster family member at the pottery died in the Spring of 1946.

Throughout its production history the firm strove to modernize facilities, improving production techniques and the quality of goods produced. In 1905, Lancaster installed one of the first pieces of pressure slip casting equipment, a process that soon became widely adopted. It also converted from steam engines to electric motors sooner than most, and was the second Staffordshire pottery to install large static vacuum machinery to clean the factory.

The firm enjoyed much success and growth through expanding upon old favorite products and developing new lines to meet the public's changing tastes. To keep up with demand, Lancaster and Sandland purchased additional land in 1948 and began construction of a new 12,000 square foot factory in 1953. This new, modern factory included electric kilns and an air conditioning plant to reduce dust and regulate humidity.

Three backstamps used between 1920 and 1944

Two marks used from
1949 through the 1950's

Backstamp used from the 1950's
through 1968

Two marks used in the 1950's and
1960's

Miniature Charles I Character Jug
(courtesy of John Sanderson)

Lancaster and Sandland was a family run business whose motto was "We will make anything for anybody anywhere." Lancaster and Sandland typically exported a large percentage of its production. Exports rose to as much as sixty percent of the total output in the 1950s and 1960s, a large portion of which was destined for North America. During this period the firm employed over one hundred people.

TH Sandland retired in the early 1950s. Lancaster and Sandland was then operated by Edwin Henry Sandland, Thomas's son, who served as Chairman until the firm closed in 1968. The last Managing Director of the pottery working with Edwin was Sam Talbot, who joined the firm as Art Director in 1959. Thomas Sandland died in 1956, leaving the business to Edwin and Edwin's three sisters; Phyllis, May and Joyce. Some of the original figurine molds are still in the family's possession, currently held by Chris Slater, May Sandland's son. Chris remembers his grandfather selling Lancaster and Sandland pieces at the local pub in Stone. Joyce became a WW II bride and moved to America, where she now lives in the Washington D. C. area. She also has fond memories of her father.

The word Sandland may be found marked on some items beginning as early as 1949. Marks from the early 1960s indicate that the firm added bone china production around that time. Sandland Ware was the last mark used by the firm, which closed in the late 1960s. Through its entire history, Lancaster and Sandland produced a wide range of ceramics from fancy goods to decorative art pottery to utilitarian wares.

Character Jugs and Toby Jugs

In the 1930s, Lancaster and Sandland began capitalizing on the success of Royal Doulton's introduction of Character Jugs with its own line of jugs based on many of the same characters as Royal Doulton's. TH Sandland himself modeled the initial line of Dickens figures. Royal Doulton sued Lancaster and Sandland for copying its Dickens jugs. However, when TH calmly pointed

out to Doulton executives that there was no copyright on the works of Charles Dickens, the lawsuit was dropped.

Lancaster and Sandland also introduced new and creative collections of Character Jugs based on Gods, Composers, Royalty, politicians, literary figures, and even canines. Some of the larger jugs were produced to accommodate music boxes in their bases. The firm also expanded the idea of the Character Jug into a series of character tankards that were slightly larger and slimmer than a jug, had no spout, and were finished with a silver rim. Today, many tankards are found without the silver rim. It is possible they were sold that way at a lower price. Tankards are denoted in the jug listing with a "T" in the name column. As a result of the pottery's innovations, there exists quite a large variety of Character Jugs. Many Lancaster and Sandland Character Jugs are regularly available at reasonable prices. Others are quite rare, and command a much higher price.

Lancaster and Sandland also produced at least two Toby Jugs to honor the leaders of the British Forces of World War II, those being of Neville Chamberlain and Winston Churchill. Both tobies were designed by Thomas Sandland and are rare and difficult to find. It is possible that tobies of other war leaders were also produced. The Charrington Toby was produced as an advertising premium for Charrington Ale. The Mr. Brandyman half-body jug was produced on commission for Martell Liquors in 1957. The John Peel jugs can also be found named Tally O, while the Henry VIII jugs are sometimes called King Hal or Bluff King Hal.

Dickens derivative works in the form of relief molded pitchers and tankards, vases, ashtrays, teasets, and figurines were also produced. The relief portrait molded tankards and jugs came in several sizes and included Henry VIII, Mine Host, Uncle Tom Cobbleigh, Oliver Twist, Nancy, King Hal and Six Wives.

Eight different backstamps have been verified on Lancaster and Sandland Character Jugs. A few of these marks date from the 1930s, before the firm became Lancaster and Sandland, with the majority dating after 1944. The tradename English Ware is also found with several of these marks.

Miniature David Copperfield
Character Jug (courtesy of John
Sanderson)

Falstaff large silver rim tankard on left and
miniature sized Character Jug on right

Fisherman Character Jug in large, miniature
and small sizes

Henry VIII grouping, left to right - large tankard, medium jug, miniature jug, large jug, and wall pocket

Medium size John Bull Character Jug

Highwayman large tankard, miniature jug and large jug

Left to right, Pickwick large jug, miniature tankard and miniature jug

Large and miniature sized Jolly Boy Character Jugs

Long John Silver grouping, left to right - large jug, large tankard, small tankard, miniature jug, and tiny jug

Rare extra large Micawber Character Jug on left, miniature jug in center and large tankard on right (from the collection of Chris Slater)

Micawber large tankard with silver rim, plus miniature and tiny sized Character Jugs

Puck group, left to right - large tankard with silver rim, miniature tankard, miniature jug, and large jug

Medium sized Policeman Character Jug (from the collection of Chris Slater)

Character Jug Name		Height, inches	Production Life
Bacchus		4	1950s
Beethoven		2 1/2	1950s
Before and After		3 3/4	
Bizet		2 1/2	1950s
Bloodhound		2 1/2	1938 - 1944
Bluff King Hal	T	5 1/2 4 2 3/4	1940s - 1950s
Boxer		2 3/4	1938 - 1944
Bulldog		2 1/2	1938 - 1944
Burns		2 1/2	1950s
Chamberlain		2 3/4	1950s
Charles I		2 3/4	1940s - 1950s
Chopin		2 1/2	1950s
Chow Dog		2 3/4	1938 - 1944
Collie		2 1/2	1938 - 1944
Dalmation		2 3/4	1938 - 1944
David Copperfield		3	1930s - 1950s
Dickens		5 2 3/4	1930s - 1950s 1930s - 1950s
Disraeli		2 1/2	1950s
Drake		3	1930s - 1950s
E. A. Poe		3	1930s - 1950s
Edward VII		3	1940s - 1950s
Emerson		2 1/2	1950s
Falstaff	T	5 1/2 2 1/2	1940s - 1950s 1940s - 1950s
Fisherman		5 1/4 4 2 3/4	1950s 1950s 1950s
Grave & Joy two faced jug		5 3/4	
Grieg		2 1/2	1950s
Handel		2 3/4	1950s
Hayden		2 3/4	1950s
Henry VIII	T	5 1/2 5 1/4 4 1/4 2 1/2	1940s - 1950s
Highwayman	T Reg # 813213	5 1/4 5 2 3/4	1940s - 1950s
Indian Chief		2 1/2	1930s - 1950s
Jester			
Jock		3 1/2	1950s - 1960s
John Bull	T "172"	5 1/2 5 1/2	1944 - 1960s 1944 - 1960s
John Peel	T T	5 1/2 4 2 1/2	1940s - 1950s 1940s - 1950s
Jolly Boy		5 2 1/2	1940s - 1960s
Jupiter		3 1/2	1950s
King Charles Spaniel		2 1/2	1938 - 1944
Lincoln		2 1/2	1950s
Liszt		2 1/2	1950s
Longfellow		2 1/2	1950s
Long John Silver	T T Reg # 813218	5 1/4 5 4 1/4 3 1/2 2 1/2 1 1/4	1944 - 1950s 1944 - 1950s 1944 - 1950s 1944 - 1950s 1944 - 1950s 1944 - 1950s
Lowell		2 1/2	1950s
Micawber	T	8 1/4 5 3/4 3 1 1/2	1930s - 1950s 1930s - 1950s 1930s - 1950s
Mozart		2 1/2	1950s
Oliver Cromwell		2 1/2	1940s - 1950s
Othello			
Otter Hound		2 1/2	1938 - 1944
Pan		3 3/4	1950s

Character Jug Name		Height, inches	Production Life
Perseus		3 3/4	1950s
Pickwick	T	4 3/4	1930s - 1950s
	T	2 3/4	1930s - 1950s
	T	2 3/4	1930s - 1950s
Pluto		3 3/4	1950s
Policeman		4 1/2	
Poodle		2 1/2	1938 - 1944
Puck	T	5 1/2	1940s - 1950s
		5	
		3	1940s - 1950s
	T	2 3/4	
Queen Bess		2 3/4	1940s - 1950s
Raleigh		3	1940s - 1950s
Robin Hood		5 3/4	1944 - 1950s
	T	5 1/2	1940s - 1950s
		2 3/4	1944 - 1950s
	T	2 3/4	1944 - 1950s
Roosevelt, Franklin D.		2 3/4	1940s
Sarah Gamp	Reg # 828018	5 1/2	1930s - 1950s
	T	5 1/2	1930s - 1950s
		4	1930s - 1950s
	T	3 1/2	1930s - 1950s
		2 1/2	
		1 1/4	
Schubert		2 1/2	1950s
Scottie	T	5 1/2	1944 - 1950s
	version 1	4 3/4	1944 - 1950s
		2 3/4	1944 - 1950s
		1 1/4	1944 - 1950s
	version 2	2 1/2	1944 - 1950s
Sherlock Holmes		3 3/4	1950s
Sheik		5 1/2	1920s - 1930s
Sibelius		2 3/4	1950s
Spaniel		2 1/2	1938 - 1944
St. Bernard		2 1/2	1938 - 1944
Tally O		4	1940s - 1950s
		2 1/2	
Tchaikowsky		2 1/2	1950s
Tennyson		2 1/2	1950s
Thackery		2 1/2	1950s
Uncle Tom Cobleigh		5 1/2	1930s - 1950s
	T	5	1930s - 1950s
	Reg # 813217	4	1930s - 1950s
	T	3 1/2	1930s - 1950s
		3 1/2	1930s - 1950s
		2 3/4	1930s - 1950s
		1 1/4	1930s - 1950s
Verdi		2 1/2	1950s
Victoria		2 3/4	1940s - 1950s
Wagner		2 1/2	1950s
Water Spaniel		2 1/2	1938 - 1944
Weller		8 1/4	1930s - 1950s
	T	5 1/4	1930s - 1950s
		3	1930s - 1950s
		1 1/2	1930s - 1950s
Welsh Lady		5	1950s
		3	
William Shakespeare		5 1/4	
	T	5 1/4	1940s - 1950s
		3 1/2	
		2 3/4	
Winston Churchill		3	1940s
Yeoman of the Guard	T	5 1/2	1944 - 1950s

T - indicates Tankard

Toby Jug Name	Height, inches	Production Life
Chamberlain	6 3/8	1944 - 1950s
Charrington Toby	7 1/4	1950s
Mr. Brandyman	6 1/4	1957
Squat Toby	5	1920 - 1944
Winston Churchill		1944 - 1950s

Robin Hood, left to right - large Tankard, mini Character Jug, and mini Tankard

Top row left to right - Sarah Gamp small jug, small tankard, mini and tiny jugs; bottom row left to right - large jug and large tankard

Group of five tiny sized Scottie Character Jugs in different colorways

Left to right Scottie large tankard, miniature jug, tiny jug, and large jug

Weller large silver rim tankard, miniature jug, tiny jug, rare extra large jug, and large jug (courtesy of John Sanderson)

Large sized Sheik Character Jug

William Shakespeare large silver rim tankard, medium tankard, miniature jug, and wall pocket

Uncle Tom Cobleigh large silver rim tankard, tiny jug, miniature jug, and large jug

Drake miniature sized Character Jug on left and Raleigh miniature sized jug on right

From left to right Welsh Lady Character Jug in small and miniature sizes

From left to right, small sized tankards of Jock, Sherlock Holmes, and Yeoman of the Guard with silver rim

Collection of tiny Character Jugs; from left to right - Tony Weller, Long John Silver, Sarah Gamp, Mr. Micawber, Scottie, and Uncle Tom Cobleigh

Collection of large sized silver rim tankards; top row from left to right - Mr. Micawber, Tony Weller, Yeoman of the Guard, and Puck; bottom row left to right - Robin Hood, Falstaff, Uncle Tom Cobleigh, and William Shakespeare

Collection of miniature Composer Character Jugs; top row from left to right - Beethoven, Bizet, Chopin, Grieg, Handel, and Liszt; bottom row left to right - Mozart, Sibelius, Tchaikowsky, Verdi, and Wagner

Collection of miniature sized Literary Character Jugs; top row left to right - Burns, Emerson, Dickens, Longfellow, and Lowell; bottom row left to right - E.A. Poe, Shakespeare, Stevenson, and Tennyson

Collection of small sized God Character Jugs, left to right - Bacchus, Jupiter, Pan, Perseus, and Pluto

Before and after two-faced Character Jug showing both sides

Group of miniature Royalty and Statesmen Character Jugs; top row left to right - Oliver Cromwell, Henry VIII, Queen Bess, Victoria, and Edward VII; bottom row left to right - Disraeli, Lincoln, Chamberlain, Winston Churchill, and Roosevelt

Collection of Dog miniature sized Character Jugs; top row left to right - Water Spaniel, Otter Hound, Collie, Bloodhound, and Poodle; bottom row left to right - Bulldog, King Charles Spaniel, Boxer, Spaniel, and Chow Dog

Ashtrays with Matchstand	Height, inches
Drake	
Mr. Pickwick	

Biscuit Boxes	Height, inches
Fagin	
Fat Boy	
Mr. Micawber	
Sarah Gamp	

Bottle Stoppers	Height, inches
Falstaff	2 3/4
John Bull	2 3/4
Long John Silver	2 3/4
Sarah Gamp	2 3/4
Scottie	2 3/4
Uncle Tom Cobleigh	2 3/4

Busts	Height, inches
Fat Boy	
Ben Franklin	
Mr. Micawber	
Mr. Pecksniff	
Raleigh	
Sarah Gamp	

Cigarette Lighters	Height, inches
Mr. Pickwick	2 3/4

Creamers	Height, inches
Nancy	

Liquor Bottles	Height, inches
Falstaff	10

Musical Jugs	Height, inches
John Peel	5 1/2

Relief Portrait Jugs & Tankards	Height, inches
Henry VIII	
King Hal and Six Wives	8 3/4
Nancy	4
	2 3/4
Oliver Twist	5
Pickwick Papers	
Uncle Tom Cobleigh	5
Village Blacksmith	2 1/2

Shaving Mugs	Height, inches
Before & After	3 3/4

Sugars	Height, inches
Drake	3
Nancy	
Tige	2 1/4
Weller	3

Teapots	Height, inches
Oliver Twist	
Sarah Gamp	

Tobacco Jars	Height, inches
Sheik	5 1/2

Wall Pockets	Height, inches
Henry VIII	5 1/4
William Shakespeare	5 1/4

Indian Chief on left and Scottie 2nd version on right Character Jugs

Charrington advertising Ordinary Toby Jug on left and Mr. Brandyman half-body advertising Toby Jug on right

Falstaff Liquor Bottle with detachable head (from the collection of Chris Slater)

Chamberlain Toby Jug

Winston Churchill Toby Jug (courtesy of Ron Smith)

Group of figural bottle stoppers, from left to right - Long John Silver, Falstaff, John Bull, Uncle Tom Cobleigh, Scottie, and Sarah Gamp

Three Scottie bottle stoppers in different colorways (from the collection of Chris Slater)

Group of Charles Dickens Character Busts from left to right - Mr. Pecksniff, Fat Boy, Mr. Micawber, and Sarah Gamp (from the collection of Chris Slater)

Group of political busts, from left to right - Sir Walter Raleigh, Benjamin Franklin in two colorways, and Abraham Lincoln (from the collection of Chris Slater)

Before and After two-sided Shaving Mug, showing both sides of Mug

Group of cream colored miniature Character Jugs produced for the Australian market; left to right - Raleigh, Falstaff, Uncle Tom Cobleigh, Mr. Pickwick, Highwayman, Robin Hood, and Mr. Micawber (courtesy of John Sanderson)

Pickwick Relief Tankard (from the collection of Chris Slater)

Reverse side of Pickwick Relief Tankard (from the collection of Chris Slater)

Relief Mug of Henry VIII and his Wives (from the collection of Chris Slater)

Group of Pickwick Papers Relief Jugs and Tankards, left to right - large and small Gamp/Weller jug, Oliver pitcher, miniature Gamp/Weller jug, and large Pickwick/Weller tankard

Reverse side of same group of Relief Jugs and tankards

Henry VIII Relief Mug with axe handle (from the collection of Chris Slater)

Oliver relief teapot and pitcher (from the collection of Chris Slater)

Reverse side of Oliver teapot and pitcher (from the collection of Chris Slater)

Nancy relief set; left to right - creamer, sugar, and large pitcher (from the collection of Chris Slater)

Sheik tobacco jar (from the collection of Joyce Mc Gowan)

Mr. Pickwick Cigaretter Lighter

John Peel Musical Tankard

Sarah Gamp teapot (from the collection of Chris Slater)

Sugar bowls, left to right - Tony Weller, Tige, and Drake

Drake and Mr. Pickwick Ashtray and Matchstands (courtesy of John Sanderson)

Biscuit Boxes, from left to right - Fagin, Mr. Micawber, Sarah Gamp, Fat Boy, and Fagin in second colorway (courtesy of John Sanderson)

Lancasters
See Lancaster and Sandland

Lefton China
Chicago, Illinois

Lefton China backstamp

History

George Z. Lefton, a Hungarian sportswear designer and manufacturer, founded Lefton China in 1940. While George's profession didn't lend itself to founding a ceramic firm, his hobby as a porcelain collector did. Lefton emigrated from Hungary to Chicago in 1939. His enthusiasm for ceramics led George to start his own ceramics business the next year.

The conclusion of World War II presented George with the opportunity to import oriental porcelain from the Far East to address the growing demand for these products in North America. Lefton China began as a marketing firm, importing fine china and porcelain for sale in the United States. The firm remained strictly a marketing company into the 1960s. Unlike other marketing companies however, George participated in the design of many of the pieces that he imported. He also insisted on high quality products, so he instituted a quality control process to assure only the highest quality imported goods.

Lefton's business enjoyed much success and George became known as "The China King." The breadth of Lefton's offering includes vases, figurines, birds, salt and peppers, and Hummel look-alikes produced in bisque, china and porcelain finishes. George Lefton died on May 29, 1996. Today, Lefton China is a leading producer and importer of ceramic giftware.

Character and Toby Jugs

Lefton China produced a series of well-modeled, high quality Character Jugs of American patriots in the late 1970s. These are extensively collected and widely sought after today. The Santa Claus mug was produced as part of a beverage set with a pitcher and six mugs for drinking your favorite holiday refreshment. Mr. & Mrs. Claus is a two sided mug also made for the holidays. Lefton produced a series of Miss Priss wares, including a teapot, sugar and creamer. All of these items depict the cute kitty in different forms. A similar Mr. Toodles dog line was also produced. Both series are highly desired today.

Toby Jug Name	Height, inches	Model Number
Betsy Ross	6 1/4	
Blue Bird	4	435
Elf Boy	3	
Kitty	3 5/8	
Mr. Toodles	4 1/2 3 1/2	292 3235
Uncle Sam	6 1/2	

Character Jug Name	Height, inches	Model Number
Abraham Lincoln	5 1/2 4 1/2	KW2364 KW1113
Andrew Jackson	5 4 1/4	KW2332 KW1112
Benjamin Franklin	4 1/2	KW2525
Dainty Miss		322
Elf Girl	3 1/2	1708
George Washington	6 4 1/2	KW2326 KW1110
Grandpa	4	
John Adams	4 1/2	
Little Miss	4 1/2	6820
Miss Priss	5 1/4 4 1/4	1504 1503
Mr. and Mrs. Claus	4	868
Pixie	4 1/2	6977
Robert E. Lee	5 1/4 4 1/8	KW2365 KW1111
Santa Claus	1 5/8	1383
Snowman	4	
Theodore Roosevelt	5 1/4 4 1/2	KW2379 KW2191
Thomas Jefferson	5 4 1/2	KW2352 KW2195
Ulysses S. Grant	4 1/4	KW2517

U.S.A. Political Character Jugs: top row left to right - Benjamin Franklin small, George Washington large and small, and Thomas Jefferson large and small; bottom row left to right - Abraham Lincoln large and small and Theodore Roosevelt large and small

U.S. Civil War Character Jugs: left to right - Robert E. Lee large and small, Ulysses S. Grant small, and Stonewall Jackson small and large

History

Lenox China grew out of the Ceramic Art Company, which was founded in 1889 by Jonathan Coxon and Walter Scott Lenox. Both men left the firm of Otto & Brewer together to start their own pottery with the dream of creating high quality American fine china, equal to or surpassing that of Europe. Lenox had apprenticed and designed for Otto & Brewer as early as the 1850s. In 1894, Walter Lenox bought out Coxon's interest in Ceramic Art, and in 1906 he changed the company's name to Lenox, Incorporated. Unfortunately Walter Lenox died in 1920.

From the start, Ceramic Art's production focused mainly on decorative pieces, as the partners tried to create a high quality Belleek-like product, going so far as to hire talented designers from Ireland. Production of this ware continued up to 1920, when dinnerware, which Lenox first introduced in 1917, became the primary product of the firm. Around this time Lenox became the first American firm to be exhibited at the National Museum of Ceramics in Sevres, France. President Woodrow Wilson selected Lenox China to produce the official state table service for the White House in 1918. Lenox was the first American company to be selected for this honor, and it has been chosen by many Presidents since.

By the 1930s, Lenox was the major manufacturer of dinnerware in North America. The firm was able to greatly expand its markets and production during World War II, due mainly to limited exports coming from Britain. The 1960s was another period of great expansion for the company, as it branched out through acquisitions into new product areas including silver and crystal.

Today Lenox remains a thriving diversified company. It is the only major producer of fine china in the United States. The firm takes pride in its tradition of uncompromising quality standards and dedication to handcrafted skills. It has earned its worldwide reputation for high quality, durable china. Production still follows the handcrafted process and high standards set by the founders. The firm employs around 275 workers at its Oxford plant, which is the flagship factory owned by Lenox.

Toby Jugs

In the first third of the twentieth century, Lenox produced fine china Toby Jugs of George Washington, Theodore Roosevelt, and William Penn. These jugs are quite scarce, especially those of Washington and Roosevelt. Lenox collectors seek these jugs as passionately as Toby collectors. The William Penn and Theodore Roosevelt jugs are three-quarter body jugs.

Isaac Broome designed the George Washington Toby in 1896, although W. Gallimore has also been credited with its design. It was offered in six different sizes through the early 1900s. So far only four of these sizes have been identified. Lenox sold only creamware Washington Toby Jugs under its own name. More commonly, a decorating firms would purchase blanks from Lenox and finish the jugs, distributing them under its labels. One such firm was Higgins & Seiter, whose lavender mark can be found on many Washington tobies.

The Theodore Roosevelt jug was produced during his Presidency and depicts "Roughrider" Teddy on a big game safari, complete with an elephant head handle. The jug was designed by Edward Penfield and modeled by Isaac Broome. It is also marked "The Toby Potteries New York."

The William Penn Toby was designed by W. Gallimore in 1930 and celebrated the signing of the William Penn Treaty with the Leni Lenape tribe of the Delaware Indians roughly 250 years earlier. The jug was produced in the 1930s with a variety of pastel body colors; white, coral, blue and yellow. It was generally done in a white body with a colored handle, or a colored body with a white handle. A limited number were produced in over-glaze colors with handpainted details. These would command a premium price. The jug features an American Indian as the handle and the Treaty as the back of the jug. Lenox reissued the Penn Toby in 1950 in a solid cream color only. Jugs from the original 1930s issue have a "B" impressed underneath and behind William's left hand.

Backstamp found on William Penn Toby Jug

Backstamp found on George Washington Toby Jug

DESIGN OF EDWARD PENFIELD

THE TOBY POTTERIES NEW YORK
A

Backstamp found on Theodore Roosevelt Toby Jug

Toby Jug Name	Height, inches	Production Life
George Washington	10 1/4	1896-ca 1910
	7 1/4	1896-ca 1910
	6	1896-ca 1910
	4 3/4	1896-ca 1910
Theodore Roosevelt	7 1/2	1912 - 1920
William Penn	12	1930 - 1939
	12	1950
	6 3/4	1930 - 1939
	6 3/4	1950

Theodore Roosevelt Toby Jug on left and early William Penn Toby Jug on right

Graduated set of George Washington Toby Jugs in the 10 1/4 inch, 6 inch, and 4 3/4 inch sizes

Leonard Jarvis
England

Toby Jug Name	Height, inches
Lord Mackintosh	7 1/2
Winston Churchill	7

Mark on Winston Churchill Toby Jug

History

Leonard Jarvis, although known primarily as a restorer, did model and produce some high quality pottery pieces in a studio pottery. He was actively potting for many years from the 1930s through the 1950s.

Toby Jugs

Although little is known of Leonard Jarvis, he produced two of the most highly regarded and desired Toby Jugs of the twentieth century.

The Winston Churchill jug was a limited edition of perhaps 250 jugs produced in 1948. The Toby depicts a victorious Churchill holding an artist's palette and brushes in his left hand. A book, inkwell and quill sit by his right foot and a trowel by his left foot. Churchill is raising his right hand in his signature victory sign. This jug captures the diverse talents of the man: author, bricklayer, painter, and statesman. The jug comes in versions with a brown, yellow or blue coat. It is signed "L. Jarvis" and numbered. The highest numbered jug verified to date is 173. This probably indicates a limited edition of less than 250, or even less than 200 jugs.

The Lord Mackintosh jug was designed to honor a well-respected English figure. Lord Mackintosh of Halifax owned the Halifax Confectionery company and was a long time and renowned collector of Toby Jugs. Mackintosh was instrumental in encouraging Jarvis to create the Churchill Toby. Around twelve Mackintosh jugs were made in 1953. At this time, most are still in the possession of the Mackintosh family; however, one resides in an American collection.

Lord Mackintosh Toby Jug

Side view of Lord Mackintosh Toby Jug

Winston Churchill Toby Jug in two colorways

L

144

**H. G. Lesser & R. F. Pavey Limited
London, England**

History

H. G. Lesser & R. F. Pavey is a London based importing firm specializing in giftware and ceramics. In the 1990s, it imported a wide variety of giftware, most notably animal figurines in large volumes. The firm uses the tradename Leonardo Collection for much of its ware, a tradename appropriately reflecting the country of manufacture, Italy.

Character and Toby Jugs

From the early 1990s until 1996, a series of Toby and Character Jugs were imported by Lesser & Pavey as part of its Leonardo Collection. Leonardo Toby Jugs are made of lightweight porcelain and all have a distinctive rolled rim. The marks on the jugs vary, some saying "The Leonardo Collection Fine Porcelain Italy", others marked "Leonardo Foreign", or some simply "Leonardo Collection". Others were sold with identifying stickers only, which may have been removed from the jug. These can still be easily identified as Leonardo by their distinctive rolled rims.

The Toby Jug listing comes from a Lesser & Pavey flyer and therefore is comprehensive. More Character Jugs are waiting to be discovered however.

Character Jug Name	Height, inches
Bill Sykes	5
Falstaff	
Farmer	2 1/2
Farmer's Wife	2 1/2
Huntsman	2 1/2
Inn Keeper	
Leprechaun	
Lord Mayor	2 1/2
Mrs. Bardell	
Mrs. Bumble	4 1/2
Old Salt	2 1/2
Pip	5
Tipsy Man	2 1/2

Toby Jug Name	Height, inches
Beggarman	5 1/4
Coachman	
Fisherman	6
Friar Tuck	5 1/4
Inn Keeper	4 3/4
Jester	
Judge	
Little John	5 1/4
Lord Mayor	4 3/4
Maid Marion	
Mayor	5
Minstrel	
Organ Grinder	6
Pirate	
{5 different varieties}	
Poorman	5 1/4
Professor	2 1/4
Richman	5 1/2
Robin Hood	
Sailor	
Sheik	6
Smuggler	
Soldier	5 7/8
	4
Squire	
Tailor	4
Thief	5 1/4
Tinker	5 1/2
Town Crier	6
{5 different varieties}	5 1/2
	4
Turk	5 7/8

Charles Dickens Mark

Generic Leonardo mark

Ornate Leonardo Mark

Group of three Character Jugs, left to right - Pip, Mrs. Bumble, and Bill Sykes

Toby Jugs; top row left to right- Town Crier, Lord Mayor, and Town Crier (second version); bottom row left to right - Fisherman, Turk, and Organ Grinder

Toby Jugs; top row left to right - Tinker, Soldier, and Sailor; bottom row left to right - Richman, Poorman, Beggarman, and Thief

Second version of Soldier and Tailor Toby Jugs in Squat Toby style

Lingard, Webster & Company Limited
Tunstall, England

Character Jug Name	Height, inches
Humpty Dumpty	
Mr. Pickwick	2 3/4
Sairey Gamp	4 3/4

Sugars	Height, inches
Mr. Pickwick	
Sairey Gamp	

Teapots	Height, inches
Mr. Pickwick	
Sairey Gamp	

History

Founded in 1900, Lingard, Webster & Company operated at the Swan Pottery in Tunstall, producing everyday tea service products and associated ware for local consumption. In 1960 the pottery became recognized as a leading supplier of tea services throughout England. In 1967 it ventured outside of teaware and added floral containers to its offerings. Thomas Hill created this floral line from a prototype model designed by Managing Director Jack Webster for demonstration purposes. Still operating today, the firm promotes itself as the "teapot specialists of England since 1867."

Character Jugs

Lingard produced a variety of ceramic tea services, some based on characters from the works of Charles Dickens. The creamers from the sets can be classified as Character Jugs. The Mr. Pickwick tea service was titled "Mr. Pickwick Proposes a Toast" and consisted of a sugar, creamer and teapot. Part of a Sairey Gamp tea service, the Gamp creamer is marked with "Lingard" in a banner and "Made In England" below. Impressed is "Sairey Gamp from Dickens Martin Chuzzlewit."

Mr. Pickwick teapot set, left to right sugar, teapot, and creamer; also Sairey Gamp teapot

LJB Ceramics
See Cortman Limited

LVNH
See Melwood Pottery and Truscott Pottery

Lomonosov Porcelain Factory
St. Petersburg, Russia

History

Dancing Girl Character Jug

The Lomonosov Porcelain Factory dates back to the Royal St. Petersburg Factory, which was established in St. Petersburg in 1744. This factory was the first high quality, commercial porcelain factory in Russia. In the 1830s, potters from the Staffordshire area of England immigrated to St. Petersburg to join the factory, having an immediate and profound impact on the pottery's ware.

D. I. Vinogradov invented the firm's porcelain formula, which is still used today. Up to 1917, the majority of the firm's porcelain ware was produced for the Czar and his Court. Only a small amount was sold to the general population, and that was very expensive and affordable only by the wealthy. The pieces based on national themes were the most popular. In 1920, the factory began participating in international exhibitions, where it received high praise. International demand for products grew dramatically after the New York World's Fair of 1939.

Today Lomonosov is a leading producer of high quality, artistic porcelain wares. Since the 1950s, the factory has used modern processes in conjunction with techniques that are over one hundred years old. The firm retains the top

Character Jugs and Toby Jugs

artistic talent from St. Petersburg and Moscow to produce high quality, hand crafted giftware, tea and coffee services, animal figurines, and crockery. In today's Russia, the factory operates as a joint-stock company.

Character Jugs and Toby Jugs

Only two Lomonosov jugs have been found: the Dancing Girl Character Jug and Lady with Soup Bowl Toby Jug.

Character Jug Name	Height, inches	Production Life
Dancing Girl	5 1/2	1948-1960

Toby Jug Name	Height, inches	Production Life
Lady w/ Soup Bowl		

Longton New Art Pottery
Longton, England

History

Longton New Art Pottery Company Limited operated at the Gordon Pottery in Longton, England from 1932 to 1966, producing a variety of earthenware products. For its entire production life, the firm used the tradenames Kelsboro Ware or Kelsboro.

Character Jugs and Toby Jugs

Longton New Art Pottery created a series of Character and Toby Jugs in the 1950s, marking the jugs with its tradename Kelsboro Ware forming an oval. From 1962 to 1965, the mark was Kelsboro Ware on an artist's palette. Longton designed and issued The Pickwick Series, a series of Character Jugs based on popular Dickens' characters. Billy Grindy quite possibly designed this series. The Mr. Pickwick liquor container is identical to that of Grimwades'. Most likely Billy Grindy brought the design with him to Longton from Grimwades.

Five characters have been identified from the Shakespeare series. More likely exist. The Santa Clause and King Neptune Character Jugs are from the same mold with a different color-way and handle.

Shaw and Copestake bought the molds for Longton's jugs in the 1960s, so identical jugs may be found marked Kelsboro Ware, SylvaC, or Crown Winsor, which owned the molds after Shaw and Copestake. For photographs of other Longton New Art Pottery jugs, please refer to Shaw and Copestake, which used the same Character and Toby Jug molds.

Character Jug Name	Height, inches
Anne Hathaway	5
Auld Mac	4 3/4
	2 1/2
The Colonel	3 1/2
Georgie	3
Jolly Roger	4 1/4
	2 3/4
King Neptune	4 1/8
	3
Mr. Pickwick	3 1/4
Mr. Winkle	4 3/4
Mr. Wolfe	3 1/4
Mrs. Bardell	5
	4 1/4
	3 1/4
	2
Nellie	2 1/4
Old Gaffer	4 1/4
	3 3/4
Sam Weller	5
	2
Santa Clause	3
Scrooge	3 1/4
Silas Sly	3 1/4
Simon	3 3/4
	2 1/4
Squire	4 1/4
	2 1/2
Tony Weller	5 1/4
	4 3/4
	3 1/4
	2
The Watchman	4 1/2
William Shakespeare	4 3/4
Winston Churchill	4 1/2

Toby Jug Name	Height, inches
Cavalier	7 1/2
	5 1/2
Coachman	5 1/2
	4
Falstaff	6
Hamlet	7
Juliet	7
Mandolin Player	6 1/2
	4
Shylock	6 1/2
Toby Jug	8 1/4
	7 1/2
	5 1/2
	4
	2 3/4
Touchstone	6 1/4

Liquor Container	Height, inches
Mr. Pickwick	

Left to right - Auld Mac medium and small sizes, Jolly Roger medium and small sizes

Georgie miniature size Character Jug (from the collection of Emmett Mathews)

Older Kesboroware mark

PICKWICK SERIES
HAND PAINTED
Kelsboro Ware
MADE IN ENGLAND
MR. BARDELL

Newer Kesboroware mark

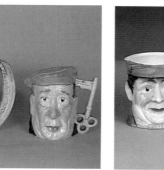

Large Sam Weller and medium Watchman Character Jugs

Mr. Winkle in large and mini sizes

Mrs. Bardell in large, medium and small sizes

147

Tony Weller in large, medium, small, and tiny sizes

Medium size Santa Clause Character Jug

From left to right - Coachman Toby Jug in medium and small sizes, small Ordinary Toby, and Squire Toby

William Shakespeare and Anne Hathaway Character Jugs

From left to right - Mandolin Player Toby Jug, Silas Sly, Simon, and Colonel Character Jugs

Group of Shakespearean Toby Jugs; left to right - Hamlet, Touchstone, Juliet, Shylock, and Falstaff

Lord Nelson Potteries
See Elijah Cotton Limited

Lurdes
See Jugs Marked by Country of Manufacture under Portugal

Mafra and Son
Caldas, Portugal

Standing Man Toby Jug

History

Opening a factory in 1853, Manuel Cypriano Gomez Mafra began making pottery in Caldas de Rainha, Portugal. Caldas de Rainha, or the Queen's bath, is located about seventy miles north of Lisbon and is known as the center of Portuguese pottery. Eduardo Mafra, Manuel's son, took over the firm in 1897. The firm made majolica and other ware. Zoomorphic vessels were a specialty of the firm.

Products were marked with "M. Mafra" over an anchor and "Caldas Portugal" underneath. After 1890, the name of the county was added to the mark.

Character Jugs and Toby Jugs

Several jugs were catalogued as a part of Mafra's majolica production; however, few have been positively identified as yet. These jugs were produced from the late 19th century and into the early 20th century. The following jugs have been identified thus far, more remain to be discovered.

Character Jug Name	Height, inches
Bust Character Jug	9

Toby Jug Name	Height, inches
Lizard	13 1/4
Standing Toby	12 1/2
	11 1/4

Magrou
See Jugs Marked by Country of Manufacture under Portugal

Manor
See Bairstow Manor Pottery

Manor Ware
See Truscott Pottery

Margardt Unlimited
See Jugs Marked by Country of Manufacture under United States

R. W. Martin & Brothers
Fulham & Southall, England

History

The Martin Brothers pottery was founded in 1873 by Robert Wallace Martin (he preferred Wallace) at Pomona House, a small studio pottery in Fulham near London. Robert Wallace Martin (1843 - 1923) had learned carving at a young age and attended night classes at the Lambeth School of Art. He experimented with terra-cotta sculptures beginning in the 1860s, operating out of a small studio on Devonshire Street. Martin did a variety of ceramic freelance work until opening his own pottery.

The firm operated as R. W. Martin, and initial production was strictly salt glazed stoneware, but soon excellent art pottery was also produced. Ware was modeled at Pomona House and fired at the nearby Fulham Pottery. Through early success from the patronage of local prominent citizens, the firm's business grew. No longer being allowed to fire its ware at the Fulham Pottery, Martin expanded its operations to an old soap works site in rural Southall, England in 1878.

Wallace's brothers Walter, Edwin and Charles joined the firm in the late 1870s and early 1880s. Walter and Edwin both previously worked for Doulton, providing valuable experience for the upstart pottery. Although each brother performed all aspects of creating pottery, it was generally acknowledged that Wallace was the chief modeler, Walter was the primary thrower, and Edwin the principal decorator. Charles provided the financial management of the firm and marketed the products through a London retail outlet. Through his regular contact with customers, Charles guided much of the pottery's decorative styles.

In 1882, the company changed its name to R. W. Martin & Brothers, today more commonly known as Martin Brothers. The 1880s and early 1890s were the most prosperous for the pottery. During the 1880s, the grotesques, for which the firm is so famous today, evolved. The latter 1890s saw demand for Martin's art pottery decline, and the firm filled the void with common stoneware bottles and jars and earthenware. Business declined steadily from 1900 onward. Friction and discontent grew rapidly between the brothers after years of working so closely together. Wallace withdrew from everyday activities to sculpt and pot non-commercial items that interested him. Little ware was produced in the early 1900s as each brother occupied himself with his own affairs. After Charles died in 1910 and Walter in 1912, the remaining two brothers worked little together. Edwin died of cancer on April 2, 1915, effectively closing the pottery. The firm remained a small studio pottery throughout its active life, so its products are almost completely handcrafted with no two being exactly alike. Even after the closure of Martin Brothers, Wallace continued modeling with the aid of his son Clement until his death on July 10, 1923.

Today, Martin Brothers' products are highly desired and valued. Perhaps the brothers are best known for their grotesque bird tobacco jars, or Wally-birds, monsters, figures and jugs. The pottery's products are typically incised with a variation of R. W. Martin, the town of production, and a month and year of production.

Character Jugs and Toby Jugs

Martin Brothers made a variety of jugs in the

Toby Jug Name	Height, inches	Production Life
Dog	4 1/2	1885 - 1900
Monk		1900 - 1914
Ordinary Toby		1900 - 1914

shape of human heads. Inspired by the two-faced Roman God Janus, these jugs were first modeled by Robert around 1885. Martin Brothers Character Jugs are similar to head jugs of earlier time, and not created in the vane of the Character Jugs of today. Nonetheless, they are Character Jugs and generally grotesque ones at that. Most of these jugs have a different face on the two sides of the jug, generally a smiling face on one side and a frowning face on the other. Early jugs have a satyr appearance and have been found with one to four faces. The two-sided jug of Joseph Chamberlain and Arthur Balfour was made during this pair's political confrontation over tariff reform. Face jugs with female features are very rare.

Experts attribute only three Toby Jugs to the Martin Brothers: a Dog, a Monk, and an Ordinary Toby. Even though the Dog pours from his mouth, it is included here. Other figural animal spoon warmers are very similar in appearance to a Toby jug. Another Toby derivative was Martin's Eskimo jugs, produced from the late 1880s to early 1900s. These were tall jugs with the face of an Eskimo wrapped in furs, possibly inspired by the polar expeditions of the time. These jugs are marked "Martin Ware London and Southall 11-1903".

Character Jug Name	Height, inches	Production Life
Barrister	6 1/2	ca 1910
Brother Jonathan & John Bull		
Female Jug		
Head Jug	9	1885 - 1914
four satyr faces	8 1/4	1892
	8 1/4	
	8	1885 - 1914
	6 1/4	1885 - 1914
	4 3/4	1885 - 1914
Joseph Chamberlain & Arthur Balfour		1902 - 1906
Mr. Pickwick & The Farmer		1912

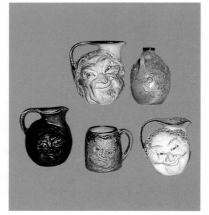

Collection of Martin Brothers jugs and mugs

Backside of same collection

Marutomoware
See Jugs Marked by Country of Manufacture under Japan

Mason's Ironstone
Hanley, England

Good Companions back-stamp

Modern Mason's mark

History

The firm known today as Mason's Ironstone, or simply Mason's, has a history that dates back 200 years. Miles Mason founded the company in 1796 in Liverpool. Partners in the firm were Thomas Wolfe, an experienced potter, and John Lucock, a talented modeler. Miles started the porcelain business because of the heavy taxation levied on his china and glass importing business to fund the early years of the Napoleonic wars. Soon Miles left the Liverpool partnership and formed a new partnership with George Wolfe, Thomas' brother, at the Victoria Works in Stoke-on-Trent. Operating as Wolfe & Mason, this partnership was also short lived, ending in July of 1800.

Miles continued to operate the Victoria Works until 1806, when he moved to the Minerva Works in Fenton, which was previously managed by his former partner, John Lucock. Miles' oldest son, William, joined the firm as a partner in 1806. The business flourished, and in 1813 Miles' other sons, George Miles Mason and Charles James Mason, took over operation of the factory under the name of G. M. and C. J. Mason, by which time William had left the family pottery. The firm patented its production of ironstone china in July of 1813. Ware was impressed with the firm's first ironstone mark, "Mason's Ironstone China." The common stamped form of this mark came into use in the 1820s.

Miles Mason died at the age of seventy on April 26, 1822. In 1826, George Mason retired and Charles Mason took over full control of the firm, renaming it Charles James Mason & Company in 1829. Charles continued ironstone production until 1848, when the firm went bankrupt and was taken over by Francis Morley & Company.

Ironstone production between 1813 and 1848 is considered the finest in Mason's two hundred year existence. Charles later resumed potting for a brief period from 1851 until 1854.

Francis Morley moved the operations to the Broad Street Works in Shelton, Hanley. Morley continued Charles Mason's ironstone production, marking ware with the Mason's Ironstone mark. Morley entered into a partnership in 1859 with his son-in-law, Taylor Ashworth, and Taylor's father, George Leech Ashworth, producing both earthenware and ironstone. Only three years later Morley retired and the Ashworths took over full control of the pottery, renaming it G. L. Ashworth & Brothers.

Ashworth & Brothers became a Limited company in January of 1884. The pottery continued operations on Broad Street until 1968, producing both earthenware and ironstone wares, and using the Mason's Ironstone mark throughout this time. The firm also began including Ashworth in the mark.

From 1968 onward, the firm operated as Mason's Ironstone China Limited and began reissuing many of its most popular patterns. In April of 1973, Mason's joined the Wedgwood Group, retaining its individual style and changing its name again to Mason's Ironstone.

Mason's built a long-standing reputation for the creation of large, highly decorated ironstone wares. The latest mark of the firm is "Mason's Made in England". Wedgwood closed the Mason's factory in early 1998.

Character Jugs

Surprisingly, jug production by Mason's has not been plentiful. In the 1970s, the Good Companions series of large sized Character Jugs was introduced. This is a nicely modeled series depicting occupational figures from everyday life. In the early 1980s, a miniature set of Character Jugs was produced, but only for a short time due to lack of demand. These are nicely modeled in the tradition of Royal Doulton. They bear the modern Mason's backstamp. Following is a complete list of Mason's Character Jugs. The photographs of the miniature Character Jugs are from the collection of Edna Wilkinson.

Character Jug Name	Height, inches
Chef	2 3/4
Doctor	5 1/2
Farmer	5 7/8
Farmer's Wife	5 1/4
Flower Seller	2 1/4
Gentleman	2 3/4
Grandmother with Child	2 1/4
Huntsman	2 1/4
Jolly Jack Tar	2 1/4
Lady Equestrian	2 1/4
Lady with Muff	2 1/4
Little Girl	2 1/4
Maid of All Work	2 1/4
Old Lady	2 1/4
Policeman	5 1/2
Policewoman	5 1/2
Postman	2 1/4
School Master	5 1/2
Scotsman	2 1/4
Secretary	5 1/2
Squire	2 1/4
Undergraduate	2 3/4
Vicar	2 1/4

From left to right: Lady Equestrian, Gentleman and Vicar miniature Character Jugs

From left to right: Flower Seller, Lady with Muff and Old Lady miniature Character Jugs

From left to right: Maid of All Work, Grandmother with Child, Little Girl and Undergraduate miniature Character Jugs

Left to right: Postman, Squire and Jolly Jack Tar miniature Character Jugs

Good Companions Character Jug series; top row left to right - Doctor, Secretary, Policewoman and Policeman; bottom row left to right - Farmer, Farmer's Wife and Schoolmaster

McCoy Pottery
See Nelson McCoy Pottery

J. & G. Meakin Limited
Hanley, England

Character Jug Name	Height, inches	Production Life
Winston Churchill	6 3/8	1941 - 1943

History

J. & G. Meakin was founded as a partnership in 1851 in Hanley, Staffordshire. The partners produced everyday earthenware and ironstone goods for sale locally. The firm completed construction of its Eagle Pottery in Hanley in 1859. Expansion due to increased demand and production volume resulted in the acquisition of the nearby Eastwood Works in 1887. By 1912, the firm had expanded into china production.

Meakin sold the Eastwood Works in 1958 to Johnson Brothers, and then enlarged and modernized the Eagle Pottery. In September 1968, W. R. Midwinter and J. & G. Meakin merged to form a new holding company under which both firms operated independently, but had the joint goal of obtaining a quotation on the stock exchange. The Wedgwood Group bought this amalgamated firm in January 1970.

Character Jugs

The Winston Churchill jug was designed by Frank A. Potts in 1941 and comes in a creamware glaze. Churchill has a stern demeanor, probably reflecting the difficulties of the time. The jug was produced in two sizes and available in a creamware finish or other solid colors. Frank Potts also designed the Beswick Churchill Toby Jug around the same time.

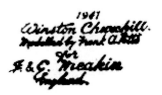

Winston Churchill backstamp

Creamware Winston Churchill Character Jug

Medalta Potteries Limited
Medicine Hat, Canada

Character Jug Name	Height, inches
Franklin D. Roosevelt	
Paul Revere	
Winston Churchill	5

History

Medalta Potteries operated at Medicine Hat in Alberta, Canada from 1915 until 1954. The Medicine Hat area had plentiful supplies of clay and gas, two ingredients essential to pottery production. As a result, many pottery, brick, and tile companies operated in the area over the past one hundred years, dominating the local economy in the first half of the twentieth century. Medalta Potteries was the most significant of these firms. Medalta manufactured a wide variety of clay products including pipes, tiles, stoneware, crockery, houseware, and hotel ware. During the lifetime of the firm, it produced over 700 different designs, ranging in size from a small cup to a fifty-gallon crock. At its peak, the art department employed thirty artists and designers who created high quality stoneware products.

Several men were key to the growth and development of the Medalta Potteries. Tom Hulme was Medalta's Art Director and led the firm's breadth of development. He is considered by some to be the first true industrial designer of Alberta, Canada. Carl Baumler was a German potter from the Bavaria area, who joined the firm in the early 1930s and was responsible for diversifying the product line with new shapes and colors. In 1937, Ed Phillipson, a ceramic engineer just out of school, became the Superintendent of the pottery with the agreement that a quarter of a million dollars would be spent to upgrade and modernize the plant. Ed directed the introduction of the firm's hotel china line, produced using Saskatchewan white clay.

Today the Medalta Potteries Museum preserves the history of the firm and displays the largest known collection of Medalta pottery. The Museum is open to the public and located in Medicine Hat.

Character Jugs

Included in Medalta Potteries' production were several Character Jugs made between 1937 and 1954. Winston Churchill and Franklin Roosevelt were most likely produced in 1940. All jugs came in mono-color glazes with Churchill available in solid colors of cobalt, brown cane or yellow coloring. Churchill's hat has "We shall not flag or fail" in relief and has the date "June 1940" on the side of the jug. It is impressed Carter Scott on the base (possibly the name of the designer) and was distributed through Period Arts Limited of Victoria, British Columbia.

Melwood Pottery
England

Character Jugs and Toby Jugs

Melwood's Tibby Brittain Toby Jug was a limited edition advertising jug produced for Arthur Bell distillers in 1976. Sergeant Major Brittain served in the Coldstream Guards for many years, training over 4000 officers. He was renowned for having the loudest voice in the British Army. With such a reputation, he was a good choice for a Town Crier style jug, Tibby being depicted ringing a bell. Allen Sly designed Tibby Brittain.

The Arnold Elliott jug was produced on commission in 1978 to raise funds for the Licensed Victuallers National Homes (LVNH). Elliott was the publican of The Bell at Hillmorton.

Melwood was also involved in an earlier series commissioned by the Licensed Victuallers National Homes organization in the 1970s. This set of six Character Jugs, called the Royal Toby Year series, depicted Prince Philip and a group of five English pub owners. The set was produced by Truscott Pottery, with the exception of Prince Philip, who was produced by Melwood. This is the only known Character Jug of Prince Philip. The backstamp on this set includes the character's name and "Created by Ted Elkins and sculpted by John Armstrong London".

Charcter Jug Name	Height, inches	Production Life
Prince Philip	6 3/4	1970s

Toby Jug Name	Height, inches	Production Life
Arnold Elliott	6	1978 Ltd Ed of 500
Tibby Brittain	8	1976 Ltd Ed of 300

Lester Piggott LVNH Character Jug

Lester Piggott LVNH backstamp

Meredith
See Jugs Marked by Country of Manufacture under United Kingdom

Merit
See Jugs Marked by Country of Manufacture under Japan

Metlox
Los Angeles, California

History

T. C. Prouty, and his son Willis O. Prouty, founded Metlox in 1927. Metlox was actually the re-creation of the Prouty's earlier endeavor called Proutyline Products Company. Proutyline Products began as a development firm for the marketing of new inventions. T. C. and Willis Prouty moved from Michigan to Southern California in 1919 to further pursue their inventive ideas. Willis began experimenting with local clays for ceramic production. He found what he was looking for in Death Valley. In 1920, he patented a clay formula for use in making tiles. The Proutys built a two-story factory at Hermosa Beach in 1922, launching Proutyline's tile production under the tradename Hermosa Tile. Willis devised and patented a new high efficiency

Character Jug Name	Height, inches
Colonial Man	4 1/4 3 1/2

kiln for the factory in 1923. The Hermosa factory was sold to American Encaustic Tiling Company of Ohio in 1926.

One year later, in 1927, the Proutys opened Metlox at a new ultra-modern four-story facility in Manhattan Beach. The name Metlox was created by contracting metal oxide. The firm's initial production consisted of outdoor ceramic signs for use with electrified advertising. This was a good business until the beginning of the Great Depression, when sales began to falter. After T. C. Prouty's death in 1931, Willis reorganized the firm and branched out into new areas, including dinnerware. The first line of Metlox dishes was introduced in 1932. Called California Pottery, this was a plain table service design finished in bright colors in the Bauer style.

This popular line of dinnerware was followed up with the Poppytrail table and kitchenware line in 1934. Poppytrail dishes were very basic in shape and design, and offered in fifteen different solid colors over a production life of eight years. Poppytrail dinnerware was so successful that Metlox adopted "Poppytrail" as the corporate tradename in 1936. Other plain dinnerware shapes followed. In the late 1930s, Carl Romanelli, a talented sculptor, became the first artware designer hired by the firm. Somewhat later Romanelli introduced the Metlox miniature figurines, which have become so popular with collectors today.

World War II effectively closed the firm, reducing capacity by 90% while the pottery was converted to primarily defense work. After the war, production was ramped back up, and the firm's first decorated dinnerware was introduced. Evan K. Shaw, who previously owned the American Pottery of Los Angeles, purchased Metlox from Willis in 1946 and was responsible for reenergizing the firm. Shaw grew the business at a rapid pace into the 1950s, employing well over 500 workers. He manufactured a line of Disney figurines that was licensed to his by now closed American Pottery. Metlox purchased Vernon Kilns in 1958 and added many lines of artware in the 1950s and 60s. Poppets by Poppytrail, a collection of stoneware doll-like flower holders, were designed by Helen Slater and introduced in the 1960s.

Evan Shaw died in 1980, and the firm was taken over by Kenneth Avery. In 1988, Melinda Avery took over management of the pottery. Only one year later, in 1989, Metlox closed.

Character Jugs

Metlox made a Colonial Man Character Jug with a red jacket and black hat. This jug is impressed "Poppytrail 117" and was produced in the 1940s.

W. R. Midwinter Limited
Burslem, England

Character Jug Name	Height, inches
Ben Gunn	4 1/4
Black Dog	5 1/4
Dr. Livesey	4 3/4
Jim Hawkins	4 1/4
Squire Trelawney	5

Treasure Island mark

History

In the 1890s, an enterprising young William Robinson Midwinter entered the pottery business right out of school as an assistant to the head of Doulton in Burslem. He worked at Doulton for eighteen years, saving enough money to eventually leave and start a pottery of his own. W. R. Midwinter Limited was established in 1910 by William Midwinter at the Bournes Bank Pottery in Burslem. By 1914, the primary focus of the firm was traditional teaware and toiletware.

William Midwinter quickly made two acquisitions, first the Albion Pottery in Burslem, and then, after a brief service in the Royal Navy in World War I, he bought a factory owned by Stewart Maddock Limited in 1918. These two acquisitions allowed Midwinter to increase its production of teaware and add an offering of dinnerware. One of its well-known lines was called Fairyland with nursery rhyme characters as the principle decoration. In the 1930s, a line of small pottery animal figures became quite popular. One of the better known artists who worked

for the firm was Jessie Tate-Hazelhurst, who was both a modeler and a designer.

Roy Midwinter, William's son, went to work at the pottery in 1945, became Works Director in 1948, and eventually assumed control of the firm. He had no formal training, but was a self-taught designer who created pots that he liked. Roy spent time in America in the early 1950s. When the British Board of Trade lifted the ban on decorated domestic ware, Midwinter was prepared. The firm was a leader in producing new contemporary designs throughout the remainder of the decade. Artists such as Jessie Tate, Terence Conran, Colin Melbourne, and Sir Hugh Casson created these new captivating designs. W. R. Midwinter made another significant acquisition when it purchased A. J. Wilkinson and the Newport Pottery in 1965, operating it as a subsidiary. Lack of demand for new styles and shapes placed Midwinter in a financial bind only a short time after taking over the Newport Pottery. In September 1968, W.R. Midwinter and J. & G. Meakin merged to form a new holding company under which both firms operated independently, but had the joint goal of obtaining a quotation on the stock exchange.

It is believed that for a time in the late 1960s and 1970s, Midwinter had access to old William Kent molds through John Kent. In January 1970, the Wedgwood Group merged a now fully amalgamated W. R. Midwinter into its organization, operating Midwinter as an independent unit with Roy becoming a Design Coordinator for the Wedgwood Group. Eve Midwinter, Roy's wife, joined him at Midwinter that same year. She had trained in fine art, painting and sculpture and, although not an employee, had been contributing designs to the firm for many years. The pottery started the trend of coordinated tableware and linen with Tate's Spanish Garden line introduced in 1971.

Jessica Tate left the firm for Johnson Brothers in 1974. Roy retired in 1981 to become a design consultant, but the family business continued under the guidance of Eve Midwinter as Design Studio Manager. Eve brought out new and interesting products, including Clarice Cliff replicas in 1985, which were called the Bizarre Collection. In December of 1986, Waterford took over Wedgwood and Eve retired. Then, on Good Friday of 1987, the W. R. Midwinter factory and Newport Pottery were closed. However, three popular dinnerware patterns remained in production under Wedgwood until the end of 1991. Today W. R. Midwinter is best known for its fashionable tableware from the 1950s, 60s and 70s.

Character Jugs

W. R. Midwinter produced a series of six Character Jugs in the 1960s based on *Treasure Island*. These jugs are of good quality and carry ornate backstamps with a palm tree and sailing ship. So far, only five of a suspected six jugs have been identified.

Treasure Island Character Jugs, top row left to right - Ben Gunn, Jim Hawkins, Dr. Livesey; bottom row left to right - Black Dog and Squire Trelawney

Minton
Stoke-on-Trent, England

History

In 1793, Thomas Minton left his engraver's apprenticeship to Josiah Spode to form his own pottery. He purchased property in Stoke-on-Trent that was rich in clay and tin, and eventually built a factory at this site. To accomplish his dream, Thomas formed a partnership with William Pownal and Joseph Poulson, opening a factory in 1796 that was known as Minton, Poulson, and Pownal. Early wares were mainly parian, with which Minton faced fierce competition from Spode and Copeland, and a cream colored earthenware with blue print which became known as Minton ware. Minton also popularized the Willow pattern.

From the outset, Minton was a family run business.

Samuel Poulson acted as the firm's modeler and mold-maker. Arthur Minton, Thomas' brother, was the company's trade agent. Thomas' sons, Thomas and Herbert, became partners by 1817, and Herbert was instrumental in building the business to become one of the leading potteries in England. At this time, the pottery changed its name to Minton and Sons. Bone china rivaling that of Sevres was introduced in the 1820s, using the Sevres process of pate-sur-pate. When Herbert took full control of the company in 1836, Minton and Sons was the largest potter in the area. It was also the most popular supplier of dinnerware in the 19th century to foreign embassies and heads of state.

From the mid-1800s, Minton hired talented artists

Character Jug Name	Height, inches
Franklin D. Roosevelt	6 1/2
Winston Churchill	6
	5 1/4
	4 1/2

Toby Jug Name	Height, inches	Model Number
Jack		
King		
OBL Whiskey		
Quaker Man (Barrister)	12	1140
Quaker Woman (Lady w/Fan)	11 1/2	1139
Queen		

from across Europe. These artists developed a series of new techniques and produced a wide range of high quality products. One of the first of these was the French designer Emile Jeannest. Thanks to personal and professional ties to continental Europe, and through the employment of key developers, Minton entered into majolica production, creating high quality pieces of exceptional design. Minton quickly became famous for its majolica patterns and colors. After seeing the Minton display at the 1851 Great International Exhibition, Queen Victoria called Minton's "the world's most beautiful china." Herbert Minton died in 1858, and since that time no Minton family member has been associated with the firm.

Minton became a limited company in 1892 and was renamed Minton Limited. In spite of Minton's huge success with majolica and growth through the 19th century, the firm remained fairly traditional up to the 1920s, keeping to the old designs, styles and production methods. Reginald Haggar became Art Director in 1930 and led the firm to the production of more modern tableware. Minton was purchased by Royal Doulton in September of 1968 in a three for one stock trade valued at over five hundred and fifty thousand pounds.

Character Jugs and Toby Jugs

This is an exhaustive summary of the limited number of jugs offered by Minton. Only two

Character Jugs were produced, a pair of porcelain jugs in 1941 featuring the two key heroic Statesmen from the Second World War, Winston Churchill and Franklin Roosevelt. These jugs were modeled by Eric Owen and produced in a white creamware or solid slate blue finish. Churchill came in two versions, one with a hat and one without.

Modeled around 1862, Minton produced a male and female Toby Jug as companion pieces. These jugs are listed in Minton's shape book as Quaker Man and Quaker Woman, but today they are better known as the Barrister and Lady with a Fan, respectively. Both jugs are most desired when finished in the vivid majolica colors that were a trademark of the firm. Other known finishes for the Barrister include a green/yellow running majolica glaze, and an all over green glaze. These jugs optionally came with silver mounts. This pair of tobies was produced from 1865 into the twentieth century. In 1923 they were remodeled and reissued.

An advertising water jug for OBL Whiskey was modeled in 1927 and produced in limited quantities. The Minton archives also hold the designs for Toby Jugs based on the playing card designs of Augustus Jannsen, similar in style to his playing card plates for Royal Doulton and Wedgwood. The drawings show a King, Queen, and Jack. There is no evidence that these jugs were ever produced.

Winston Churchill jug on left and Franklin Roosevelt on right

Quaker Man Toby Jug in an all over green majolica finish

Quaker Man ("Barrister") and Quaker Woman ("Lady with Fan") Toby Jugs in majolica finish

Quaker Man and Quaker Woman Toby Jugs in white stoneware (from the collection of Robert Keylock)

Nanco
See Jugs Marked by Country of Manufacture under Japan

National Potteries Corporation (NAPCO)
See Jugs Marked by Country of Manufacture under United States

Nelson McCoy Pottery
Roseville, Ohio

History

McCoy Pottery traces it beginnings back to the J. W. McCoy Pottery Company that was established in September of 1899 by J. W. McCoy. The firm was located in Roseville, Ohio and produced mostly stoneware with a few art pottery lines. In October of 1911, the firm merged with two others and in December formed the Brush-McCoy Pottery Company. This pottery continued with the earlier McCoy wares and added many new art pottery products. Much of the pottery by Brush-McCoy is unmarked.

A separate firm, The Nelson McCoy Sanitary Stoneware Company, was founded in April of 1910 by Nelson McCoy and his father J. W. McCoy. On land donated by the city of Roseville, Ohio, the firm constructed a new factory and began production immediately. It took advantage of available resources such as local clays and a trained workforce that consisted of many immigrants from Europe. Nelson McCoy's early production consisted of primarily utilitarian and decorative stoneware including jugs, poultry fountains, foot warmers, crockery, and other vessels for storing food and beverages. As other potteries started near the Roseville area, McCoy also began selling raw clay to other potters, becoming a profitable part of its overall business. J. W. McCoy died on December 11, 1914.

In 1915, Nelson McCoy began a period of expansion both in the amount and variety of products produced. In 1925, the McCoy family sold its interest in the Brush-McCoy Pottery and focused fully on Nelson McCoy. Nelson McCoy built new and more modern production facilities, and more artists and designers were hired. A new three hundred foot tunnel kiln was installed which dramatically increased production capacity, and allowed the firm to add more decorative art pottery products to its offering. These new goods included jardinieres, pedestals, umbrella stands, and vases, for which the firm is well known today.

During the 1920s and 1930s, the firm produced large quantities of art pottery in designs of leaves and flowers, all with blended glazes. Sydney Cope, who in 1936 became the firm's Lead Designer, was the driving force behind McCoy's art pottery expansion. The Depression brought hardship to the pottery, and to survive it formed a co-operative with many other potteries called the American Clay Products Company. This co-op provided a single marketing entity for all member potteries. An unfortunate side effect was that ware from the different companies soon began to look alike. To change the image of the firm and reflect its emphasis on art pottery, the name of the company was changed to The Nelson McCoy Pottery Company in the mid-1930s.

In the 1940s, more modern equipment was installed which increased throughput and reduced the risk of fire. Included in this new equipment were circular kilns with a fifty foot diameter and could fire five thousand pieces of pottery at one time in a 24-hour firing. During World War II, McCoy received a contract from the government for production of clay body land mines, reducing the amount of clay available for pottery production. McCoy developed and introduced a line of dinnerware in the 1940s, which became a best seller for many years.

During the post-war period and into the 1960s, McCoy continued its production of both functional and decorative wares. Its most significant new product line introduced during this period was cookie jars, items that have become extremely collectible today. A large fire in the 1950s destroyed the entire factory; however, the company rebuilt new, larger facilities and continued operations. At its peak, McCoy employed around 450 workers, some being descendants of original employees. Four generations of the McCoy family managed the pottery for over one hundred years.

The McCoy pottery was sold to The Mount Clemens Pottery Company in 1967. Then the Lancaster Colony Corporation bought the factory from Mount Clemens in 1974. The factory was closed in 1990 after several years of falling demand and dwindling profits.

Character Jugs and Toby Jugs

The Nelson McCoy Pottery produced only a few Character and Toby Jugs in the 1960s and 70s. The Dwight Eisenhower jug comes in a matte yellow finish. The W. C. Fields jug was a promotional item for the Turtle Bay Distilling Company and has "W. C. Fields" in raised lettering on the front

Character Jug Name	Height, inches
Buccaneer	
Cavalier	
Dwight D. Eisenhower	5
King Kong "9235"	
Parrot	7 1/4
W. C. Fields	7 5/8

Toby Jug Name	Height, inches
Chicken	6

and "Kentucky 86 Proof Whiskey" around his shoulders. There is a matching W. C. Fields decanter. A hard to find Cavalier Character Jug was also produced. King Kong was introduced in 1978. The Buccaneer is not marked and is quite rare.

In 1971, McCoy produced two relief-molded tankards, a derivative of the Character Jug, depicting Richard Nixon and Louis Armstrong. These were produced for Rumph and are not considered Character Jugs, but mentioned here as highly collectible derivative items.

New Devon Pottery
See Jugs Marked by Country of Manufacture under United Kingdom

Newport Pottery
See A. J. Wilkinson

Nimy
See Onnaing

Noble Ceramics
Hayling Island, England

History

In 1993, Ron Noble and his son, Ray, started a ceramics company named Noble Ceramics. The events leading up to Noble Ceramics were based on common interests held by both father and son. Since childhood Ray displayed a keen interest in ceramics. As a youngster, Ray started making decorative items out of plasticine. At the height of the race for Prime Minister between Major, Heard and Hessintine, Ray modeled a bust of each of these men.

By the early 1990s, Ron Noble had amassed a large collection of Kevin Francis Toby Jugs. Ron arranged to introduce Ray to Kevin Pearson of Kevin Francis in 1990, and shortly thereafter, Ray showed Kevin a sculpture of a political face-mask he had modeled. Kevin and his partner, Francis Salmon, recognized Ray's natural talent and encouraged him to do other modeling.

Shortly, Ray visited Peggy Davies Ceramics, the manufacturer of Kevin Francis' designs, and soon began modeling for Kevin Francis Ceramics. His first design for Kevin Francis was the Pershore Miller Toby Jug. Following the success of that jug, Ray modeled approximately six other jugs for Kevin Francis, including Napoleon, the Duke of Wellington, Stormin' Norman, the Charles and Di Spitting Image jug, and John Major.

Ray modeled for Kevin Francis until 1993, when the partners of Kevin Francis split and there was uncertainty about the future direction of the

pottery. At that time, Ray and Ron decided to form their own pottery based on the talent and promise of Ray's skills. With Ray as the designer and modeler, Noble Ceramics was born. Ron negotiated the rights to many of the characters and worked through the approval processes. The production of the majority of ware was done at Peggy Davies Studios on behalf of Noble Ceramics. Primary distribution was done through three well-known English collectible dealers.

In 1998, the firm launched a new limited edition series of quality porcelain busts, called Porcelain Portraits. Princess Diana was the first of this series and other subjects included Winston Churchill and Prince Charles. A bust of Harold MacMillan was produced on commission. These busts were issued in white porcelain or in a bronze finished resin and were produced by a small local pottery on Hayling Island. Ray plans to continue introducing new, quality pieces, including jugs.

Character Jugs

Starting in 1993, Noble Ceramics produced several series of high quality, well-modeled Character Jugs in an extra large size. Ray Noble has an extraordinary ability to capture the facial expression of his subjects, adding to the quality and desirability of these fine pieces. The first jug produced by Noble Ceramics was of Nick Faldo, the famous European golf professional. That jug launched The Managers series of famous British soccer managers. Ron Atkinson was the first in the series and Kevin Keegan the second. The Keegan jug was not approved and so only one or two dozen were made. The West Bromwich Albion Football Club commissioned the Jeff Astle jug. Noble Ceramics then moved on to other series including Historical Legends, Royal Family and Sporting Legends, with Jack Charlton as the first issue. The Historical Legends Series proved to be the most popular.

The George Washington Character Jug was produced in a 1997 limited edition of 100 to celebrate the centenary of George Washington's birth. John H. Keck commissioned the jug for the Las Caballeros De La Republica Del Rio Grande of Laredo, Texas. This well modeled characterization of George Washington includes Martha

Washington and Pocahontas on the handle. The first jug of the edition was presented to George W. Bush, the Governor of Texas. John Keck has the second jug, which was done in a gray colorway.

All of the jugs were produced at Peggy Davies Studios with the exception of The Queen Mother jug, which was produced at Bairstow Manor Pottery. The Queen Mother edition was split into three colorways of 250 pieces each, and collectors could select the color of dress they preferred. All jugs were produced in limited editions with the molds destroyed after the edition was complete. The jugs did not sell well, perhaps because of their extra large size, so most of the editions were not fully completed.

The photos herein are from Ray Noble's personal collection.

An example of the Noble Ceramics backstamp

Alex Ferguson Character Jug

Jack Charlton Character Jug

Jackie Bouvier Kennedy Character Jug

George Washington Character Jug

Jeff Astle Character Jug

John F. Kennedy Character Jug

Character Jug Name	Series Name	Height, inches	Production Life
Alex Ferguson	The Managers	7 1/8	Ltd Ed of 1500
George Washington	Historical Legends	8 1/2	1997 Ltd Ed of 100
Jack Charlton	Sporting Legends	8 1/2	Ltd Ed of 1500
Jackie Bouvier Kennedy	Historical Legends	8	Ltd Ed of 1500
Jeff Astle	The Managers	7 1/2	Ltd Ed of 1500
John F. Kennedy	Historical Legends	8	Ltd Ed of 1500
Kevin Keegan	The Managers	7	1994 Ltd Ed of 1000
Margaret Thatcher	Historical Legends	8	Ltd Ed of 1500
Nick Faldo		6 1/2	1993 Ltd Ed of 500
Princess Diana	Royal Family	8	1994 Ltd Ed of 500
The Queen Mother	Royal Family	6 1/4	Ltd Ed of 750
Richard Branson	Historical Legends	8	Ltd Ed of 500
Ron Atkinson	The Managers	7	1994 Ltd Ed of 1000
Winston Churchill VE Day	Historical Legends	8	Ltd Ed of 1000

The Queen Mother Character Jug in three colorways; blue, rose and lime green

Kevin Keegan Character Jug

Margaret Thatcher Character Jug

Nick Faldo Character Jug

Princess Diana Character Jug

Richard Branson Character Jug

Ron Atkinson Character Jug

Winston Churchill Character Jug

Old Castle
See Jugs Marked by Country of Manufacture under United Kingdom

Old Staffordshire Ware
See William Kent

Old Staffs Toby
See Shorter and Son

Onnaing
Onnaing, France

History

The history and relationship of the firms Onnaing, located in Onnaing, France, and Nimy, located twenty miles away in Belgium, are intertwined. Charles, Knight of De Boursies, and Frederick, Baron of Secus, founded Nimy in 1798. In February of 1821, these two partners, along with Charles' two brothers, founded a pottery in Onnaing, France. Around this time, Charles and Frederick brought the Mayor of Nimy, Jean-Pierre Mouzin, into the Nimy firm as director. In 1858, Jean-Pierre and his brother, Jean-Baptiste, became the administrators at Onnaing, they or their family serving in this capacity until 1894.

Both potteries built their fame around production of majolica figures and jugs. As they shared the same deposits of clay and were managed by the same people, the products of both factories look very similar in style, body and finish. Onnaing produced rustic faience between 1821 and 1838 and majolica between 1870 and 1920.

In March of 1894, the two potteries were formally combined into one firm called the Onnaing Society. The Mouzin family controlled the Onnaing Society. Onnaing's production quality sagged in the early twentieth century, its ware appearing mass produced. At the outbreak of World War I, demand for Onnaing majolica dried up and the firm struggled to survive by importing German porcelain. After the war, the firm began producing majolica again, but had to create new molds as the originals were destroyed during the war. These new pieces had little success, and in 1938 Onnaing went out of business. Over the course of its majolica production, it has been estimated that Onnaing produced over one million pieces.

Nimy marked its products "Mouzin Freres" or "Mouzin-Lecat" in a circle. The most common Onnaing mark is "Frie O" with a crest and model number, or sometimes written out "Frie Onnaing" for Faiencerie d'Onnaing. Older pieces have only a circle with three whisker-like lines and the model number.

Character Jugs and Toby Jugs

Both potteries fame with majolica production included a reputation for comical and colorful Toby Jugs. Nimy and Onnaing both characterized famous, and not so famous, people of the time in jug form. Some jugs were political statements, such as Onnaing's Deputy Toby Jug satirizing Auguste Baudon, a deputy of accounting, who was asked to investigate pay raises for deputies, and of course, reported that a raise was indeed justified. The La Madelon Toby honored Mde. Madelon, who served food and entertained troops during World War I.

The people depicted in other Onnaing jugs included Raymond Poincare, who was the President of France from 1913 to 1920, and Francisco Ferrer, a Spanish anarchist. Paul Deroulede was the President of the Patriotic League in 1882 and wrote patriotic songs and poems before World War I. As with the Deputy Toby, Onnaing used contemporary events as inspiration for its jugs. For example, the Railroader wears a turn of the century uniform of one of the ten French railroads. L'entente Cordiale was produced in recognition of the French-Russian Treaty of 1894. The jug depicts a Russian bear atop a French woman's head. Victor Alglave modeled Jupe Coulotte.

Even before turning a jug upside down to examine the mark, most Onnaing Toby Jugs are easily identified by the deep burgundy interior glaze.

For a fuller description of the Onnaing and Nimy history and factories, as well as additional photos, please refer to *Majolica Figures* by Helen Cunningham. The listings herein are comprehensive.

Nimy Products

Toby Jug Name	Height, inches
Dranem	13
Owl	
Sailor	10 1/2

Nimy Dranem Toby Jug

Nimy three-quarter body Sailor Toby Jug

Onnaning Products

Character Jug Name	Model Number	Height, inches	Production Life
Alsatian Woman with Braids	808	9 1/2	
Francisco Ferre	762		
King's Jester (Puck)	451	7 1/2	
L'Entente Cordiale	789	9 1/2	
Marianne	763	10 1/4	1900 - 1910
Paul Deroulede	826		
Poincare	816		
Railroader	775	10 1/4	

Toby Jug Name	Model Number	Height, inches	Production Life
Bear with Drum	123	9 1/4	1900 - 1910
Bear with Stick	126	8 1/2	1900 - 1910
Bulldog	36		
Chinaman		10	
Comique Troupier	329	11	
Deputy	741	10 3/4	1904
Dolphin	778	9	
Drunken Army Reservist	752	10 3/4	
Duck	712	9 1/4	
Hotel Manager	737	10 1/2	
Joan of Arc (3/4 body)	791		
Jupe Coulotte	784	12	1904
La Madelon			
Miner (3/4 body)	797	8 1/2	
Monk	706	9	
Pig with ham	755		
Rooster	758		1912 - 1917

Onnaing Marianne patriotic Character Jug (courtesy of Helen Cunningham)

Onnaing Deputy Toby Jug

Onnaing jugs, left to right: L'Entente Cordiale Character Jug (also called "Peau d'ane"), and Drunken Army Reservist and Monk Toby Jugs

Toby Jugs attributed to Onnaing; left to right - Comique Troupier, Bear with Drum, and Chinaman

Onondaga Pottery
See Syracuse China Company

Orchies
France

History

In 1879, Emile Lhermine founded a pottery in Rimbaud, Belgium at a long famous pottery site. Early success and high demand required an expansion of the facilities, so in 1886 he and his brothers bought a nearby textile factory and installed three new kilns. Growth continued and soon the firm expanded again and opened a new pottery near the Belgium border in Orchies, France.

At the turn of the twentieth century Orchies produced a line of around twenty majolica figures and jugs. In the early 1900s Orchies spe-cialized primarily in tableware, but with the added capacity it added lines of hand-painted luxury items. By 1910 the factory in Orchies employed 175 workers. In 1923, Orchies purchased the Moulin des Loups & Hamage factories located in St. Amand-les-Eaux. The firm continued to enjoy success through the middle of the twentieth century, employing over five hundred people during this time. The factory closed in 1988, after over one hundred years of operation. The building was destroyed in 1992 to make way for new development.

The common Orchies mark is from post 1923 and includes a windmill with "Orchies, Moulin des Loups, Hamage". Most Orchies pieces are also marked with two letters that represent the French word for the name of the piece.

Toby Jugs

As a part of its majolica production, Orchies produced four known Toby Jugs of people, and a large number of animal tobies. The vast majority of these jugs were made between 1900 and 1920. As these were produced for only a short time, these jugs are fairly hard to find. Beware, some are being reproduced today.

Orchies predominantly marked its jugs with a single or pair of letters; sometime a number also appears. For example, the Zouave is marked "ZV," and depicts the French soldiers stationed in North Africa. The Fireman is marked "SP" for "sapeur-pompier." The Student can be found with Foubert, the artists' name, incised on the back near the base.

Toby Jug Name	Model Number	Height, inches
Automobilist		
Badger		8 3/4
Bear "Coree"	RJ	
Cat	KL	
Cat playing mandolin	Z	
Donkey		
Duck	CR	
Fireman (3/4 body)	SP	
Fox	RF	
Frog	AG	10 9
Hen	AD	
Pelican	PL	
Pig "C2"		
Policeman	PC	
Rabbit	LP	9 1/4
Rooster	EB	12 9
Squirrel	AE	large medium small
Student (3/4 body)		
Swan	CY	
Zouave	ZV	10 1/4

Owens China Company
Minerva, Ohio

History

Ted Owens founded the Owens China Company in Minerva, Ohio in 1906. Mr. Owens used local clay to produce semi-porcelain hotel china, tea and dinnerware. Introduced in 1906, Swastika Keramos was not only its first line of dinnerware, but also its most successful. The firm also produced well made metallic lusters in copper, brass and bronze. Owens China closed in 1932 due to financial difficulties caused during the depression.

Toby Jugs

At the request of the Patriotic Products Association of Philadelphia, the Owens China Company designed a pair of presidential creamware pottery Toby Jugs in the mid-1920s.

These jugs were designed in a style similar to Ashtead's, with oversized heads and small bodies. The Syracuse China Company of Syracuse, New York produced similar jugs in china, also for the Patriotic Products Association. The size difference between the earthenware jugs produced by Owens China and those in china by Syracuse is noteworthy. Please refer to Syracuse China.

These jugs can be found with an elaborate mark of Patriotic Products Association in a shield and "Gold Medal China O. C. Co., Made in U. S. A. Patent Applied For". They were produced in a limited quantity of 7000, making them less common than the Syracuse china versions. These jugs are very desirable today, both by Toby collectors and political collectors, with the Owens China jugs commanding a higher market value than the Syracuse China versions.

Toby Jug Name	Model Number	Production Life
Al Smith	7	1927 - 1930
Herbert Hoover	7	1927 - 1930

Pacific Clay Products Pottery
See Jugs Marked by Country of Manufacture under United States

Padre
See Jugs Marked by Country of Manufacture under United States

Papel
See Jugs Marked by Country of Manufacture under Japan

Paragon Fine China
See Royal Paragon China

Paramount Pottery
See Jugs Marked by Country of Manufacture under United Kingdom

Pearl China
See Jugs Marked by Country of Manufacture under United States

Peasant Village
See Jugs Marked by Country of Manufacture under United Kingdom

Peggy Davies Ceramics
Stoke, England

Prestige Jugs backstamp

Rhodri Davies at the pottery with Toby Jug of Toby authority Vic Schuler

History

Peggy Davies founded a studio pottery in 1982 in northern Staffordshire with her son Rhodri. Peggy was born Margaret May Gibbons in 1921. At the age of 12 she won a scholarship to the Burslem College of Art and went there to study ceramics. After graduating in 1935, Peggy joined Wilkinson's Newport Pottery as an assistant designer to Clarice Cliff. She also continued her education in the evenings and in her spare time. When her two-year contract with Newport expired, Peggy joined W. R. Midwinter as a full-time designer. Peggy then joined Royal Doulton in Burslem in 1939. Between 1945 and 1982, Peggy was a freelance designer under contract to Royal Doulton. During this time she modeled over 240 figurines for Doulton, some of which were not introduced until after her contract ended. Peggy's first design for Royal Doulton, introduced in 1947, was Christmas Morn. She went on to design the Fair Ladies series of bone china figurines.

For many years Peggy wanted to explore her own creative ideas independently. She eventually ended her contract with Doulton in 1982 to venture out and fully develop and manufacture designs uniquely her own. She started a small studio pottery with her son, Rhodri, who was in charge of production, and four assistants. Rhodri obviously grew up in a pottery-oriented family and first entered the ceramics business himself in 1967 with the Wedgwood Group. Due to high market acceptance of Peggy's designs and growth in production, the firm moved out of the small studio and into a factory in Stoke-on-Trent. Once on her own, Peggy not only created designs for her Studio, but also developed designs for other firms, including Kevin Francis. Peggy was also an accomplished portrait painter and especially enjoyed painting children.

In the late 1980s, Peggy was introduced to Kevin Pearson of Kevin Francis Ceramics and the pair quickly recognized the potential of working together. The result had Peggy modeling several of Kevin Francis Ceramics' first Toby Jugs. Sadly, Peggy Davies died in 1989 at the age of 68. However, Rhodri Davies continues in the tradition of producing high quality ceramic art, both under Prestige Jugs, the Peggy Davies trade-name, and for other companies such as Noble Ceramics. Rhodri's son Rhys joined the firm and has taken the lead with the marketing and promotional activities of the business, thus adding the third generation to a young company of only sixteen years.

Peggy Davies Ceramics purchased Kevin Francis Ceramics in 1996 and continues to operate it as a separate concern. Co-founder Kevin Pearson remains involved, managing the North American aspects of Kevin Francis.

Peggy Davies Ceramics doubled the size of its facilities in early 1998 to keep up with its rapidly growing business. It strictly enforces its policy of destroying limited edition molds once the edition is complete.

Character Jugs and Toby Jugs

Peggy Davies' first experience modeling jugs was The American Patriot Series, a set of limited edition historical Character Jugs she created on commission from Pascoe & Company of Miami. This series included Abraham Lincoln, Betsy Ross, Thomas Jefferson, and John F. Kennedy. From there she went on to design Toby Jugs for Kevin Francis in 1988 and 1989, creating seven of the first jugs which Kevin Francis introduced.

Peggy Davies Ceramics created a number of jugs on commission. The Grant and Lee jugs were done at the request of Joe Boulton. The Huntsman was an advertising item for Tetley's

Ale. The Collector, a London retail firm, specially commissioned the Louise Irvine Character Jug in a limited edition of 350. Compo and Nora Batty are characters from "Last of the Summer Wine," a British television comedy. A retailer in Holmefirth, England, where the show is filmed, commissioned the pair.

The Leprechaun jug was made in two styles. The first version has a pot of gold handle. The handle on the second version was a shoe and hammer. Commissioned by her family, the Mary Davis jug was presented to Mary upon her retirement after many years as a headmistress.

Peggy Davies Ceramics also continues to produce jugs for other firms, such as Noble Ceramics and Lady Grace China. Peggy Davies produced a promotional Sherlock Holmes Toby Jug for the Sherlock Holmes Memorabilia Company, which is located on Baker Street in London. Some early jugs produced by the firm carry the Prestige label.

Large George Washington Character Jug (from the collection of Irene and Vern Rauf)

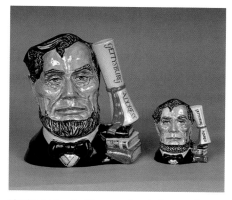

Abraham Lincoln Character Jugs in large and small sizes

Compo Character Jug on left and Nora Batty on right

American Patriot Series backstamp

Betsy Ross Character Jugs in large and small sizes

Sir Francis Drake Character Jug on the left and Elizabeth I on the right (from the collection of Irene and Vern Rauf)

Character Jug Name	Height, inches	Production Life
Abraham Lincoln	7 1/4 3 1/2	1987 Ltd Ed of 250 1987
Betsy Ross	7 3/4 3 3/4	1987 Ltd Ed of 250 1987
Compo	4	1988
Elizabeth I	8	
George Washington	8	
Huntsman Tetley's Ale	6 1/2	1997 Ltd Ed of 300
John F. Kennedy	7	1988 Ltd Ed of 50
King Phillip		
Leprechaun version 1 version 2	4 4	1986 1986
Louise Irvine	6	1995 Ltd Ed of 350
Mary Davis	5 1/2	1998
Nora Batty	4	1988
Old Father Time	8	
Robert E. Lee	7 1/4	1987
Santa Clause	7 1/2	
Sir Francis Drake	8	
Thomas Jefferson	7 3 3/4	1988 Ltd Ed of 250 1987
Ulysses S. Grant	7 1/4	1987

Toby Jug Name	Height, inches	Production Life
Sherlock Holmes	4 1/4	1996 - 1998

John F. Kennedy large sized Character Jug

Louise Irvine Character Jug

Mary Davis Character Jug, prototype creamware jug, one of only two made

Thomas Jefferson Character Jug in large and small sizes (from the collection of Irene and Vern Rauf)

Old Father Time Character Jug (from the collection of Irene and Vern Rauf)

Large Santa Clause Character Jug

Sherlock Holmes Toby Jug

Winston Churchill Character Jug (Prestige label)

Ulysses S. Grant Character Jug on left and Robert E. Lee Character Jug on right

Pair of Leprechaun Character Jugs, version 1 on left and version 2 on right

Samurai Warrior porcelain figurines, one glazed and one unglazed, designed by Peggy Davies

Pfaltzgraf Company
York, Pennsylvania

Pfaltzgraf embossed mark

History

The Pfaltzgraf family, immigrant potters from Germany, founded the Pfaltzgraf pottery in York, Pennsylvania in 1811. Salt glazed stoneware was the pottery's initial product and was manufactured in a small factory. Pfaltzgraf was built upon family traditions of craftsmanship and quality.

Between 1932 and 1937, the firm produced art pottery, and then again in the early 1950s. The pottery remained in the hands of the Pfaltzgraf family, with five generations growing the firm from its modest beginnings into one of America's leading producers of casual dinnerware and accessories. Today the firm continues producing dinnerware, but has also expanded into stainless steel flatware, glassware and giftware. Pfaltzgraf's goal is to provide a complete line of accessories to complement its dinnerware patterns. The firm is also reaching out to markets beyond North America, providing tableware to the world. Today it claims the honor of being the oldest active pottery in the United States.

Character Jugs and Toby Jugs

Pfaltzgraf made several Toby and Character Jugs. Jessop, a noted designer at the firm, modeled the Cross-legged Toby. The Pluto Character Jug was made for Disney and distributed by Treasure Craft.

A derivative series is the Muggsy coffee mugs, also designed by Jessop. These have facial features in relief on one side of the mug. Different Muggsy characters were created such as Sleepy Sam, Cockeyed Charlie, Pickled Pete, Jerry the Jerk, Flirty Gertie, Nick, and Handsome Herman. These mugs stand approximately 2 3/4 inches tall and are marked "Pfaltzgraf" with sometimes "USA" plus a model number.

Ordinary Toby on left and Colonial Man Character Jug on right

Character Jug Name	Height, inches
Colonial Man Mouse	4 1/2
Pluto	5 5/8

Toby Jug Name	Height, inches
Cross-legged Toby Ordinary Toby	6 1/2

Poppytrail
See Metlox

Prestige
See Peggy Davies Ceramics

Price & Kensington Potteries Limited
Longport, England

History

The firm of Price & Kensington Potteries started as two separate companies. Two brothers founded Price Brothers in 1896 at the Crown Works in Burslem. The pottery operated there until 1961, producing a variety of earthenware goods. The firm became a limited partnership in 1903. In the 1930s, Price Brothers went into liquidation and was bought out by Gerald Wood. In the early 1950s, Gerald merged the Price factory into the Arthur Wood Group of potteries, which he took over from his father, Arthur Wood.

Kensington Pottery Limited opened in 1922 at the Kensington Works on Robson Street in Hanley. It moved from the Kensington Works in 1937 to the Trubsham Cross factory in Burslem. Kensington's primary production also was everyday pottery goods. With the move to Trubsham Cross, Gerald Wood took over as Managing Director of Kensington Pottery as well, although Price Brothers and Kensington continued to operate independently. In an agreement reached by Gerald Wood and George Ebeling, Ebeling and Reuss was Price Brothers' and Price & Kensington's primary distributor in the United States for twenty years. In 1962, the two factories merged and reorganized. Price & Kensington Potteries was the resulting firm's name. The merged firm located all of its activities at the Price Brothers factory in Longport. This is the site where it continues to operate today.

The firm was owned and managed for many years by Gerald Wood, who was succeeded by his son Anthony Wood, the current Chairman. After graduating from college, Anthony Wood went to work for both Price Brothers and Arthur Wood & Sons. Around 1970, when Gerald became the Chairman of the Arthur Wood Group, Anthony succeeded him as the Managing Director of Arthur Wood & Son, while continuing with his position at Price & Kensington.

Another prominent figure at the firm was long time Managing Director Albert E. Arrowsmith, who joined Price Brothers as an Assistant Warehouse Manager in 1947 after serving six years in the Royal Air Force. Arrowsmith retired thirty-six years later in 1983. He was named a Director in the early 1960s, and soon became a Joint Managing Director along with

Price & Kensington wreath mark

John William Wood. When John Wood retired in 1972, Arrowsmith and Arthur Wood became the Joint Managing Directors of Price & Kensington. With Arrowsmith's retirement in 1983, Anthony Wood took over as the Managing Director.

Since its inception, Price & Kensington's core product line was teapots. Today, the pottery also offers novelty and decorative items, dinnerware and functional ceramics. It is currently producing about 20,000 pieces per week. The pottery marked its products underglaze with "Price Kensington" in a laurel wreath. The factory has one of the few remaining bottle kilns still standing in the Potteries. It is under historic preservation

Toby Jugs

Introduced sometime after the merger in early 1962, Price & Kensington produced a tableware set called Toby ware. Toby ware had pattern number 4321. The set consisted of pitchers, a teapot, creamer, sugar, and tankard. Toby ware was marked with the firm's standard mark and "Made In England" incised. The Toby ware set was still in the firm's 1986 catalog. The pottery also made a two-faced character mug named Mustache Man, which is impressed around the bottom of the mug. Mustache Man was finished in an all over brown glaze and was

produced in small volume over a period of five or six years. The Ordinary Toby and Charrington Toby were produced in a full colorway and a Rockingham brown glaze. The Rockingham finish was the better seller.

Price and Kensington also made an excellent pair of satirical three-quarter bodied gurgling Toby Jugs around 1973. Prime Ministers Edward Heath and Harold Wilson were the subjects of these jugs. Harold Wilson was a member of the Labor Party and elected Prime Minister in 1964. Heath defeated Wilson in the 1970 election. Edward Heath was the Conservative Party's Prime Minister from 1970 until 1973. However, due to inflated wage controls and a strike in Northern Ireland, Heath resigned in 1973. Wilson was once again elected Prime Minister in the following 1974 election. Wilson remained Prime Minister until 1976. The Heath jug is numbered 3900 and features a portion of his boat, Morning Cloud, for its handle. Heath won England's Admiral's Cup race with the Morning Cloud. The Wilson jug is number 3901 with a pipe handle. Both jugs say "Gurgling Jug" across the front. These gurgling tobies proved not popular and were made for a short time in a small volume. They certainly are difficult to find.

Character Jug Name	Height, inches	Production Life
Mustache Man	5	1970s

Toby Jug Name	Height, inches	Production Life
Charrington Toby		
Edward Heath	7 1/4	1973 - 1975
Harold Wilson	7 1/4	1973 - 1975
Ordinary Toby	8 1/4	1962 - 1986
	6 1/4	1962 - 1986
	3 7/8	1962 - 1986

Gurgling Jugs: Harold Wilson on the left and Edward Heath on the right

Two sizes of the Ordinary Toby

Ordinary Toby Creamer and Sugar

History

Quimper pottery refers generally to pottery produced in or near the town of Quimper, located in the Brittany region on the westernmost side of France. Beginning in the 1600s, with the making of tin glazed enamel pottery, production of faience pottery in Quimper has been continuous over the past three hundred years. Over this time many factories were founded, flourished and closed in the region. Several of the potteries formed the foundation of today's pottery industry in the area. In the late 1700s, three potteries were the mainstay of production in the area; the Grand Maison de HB, the Eloury Pottery, and the Dumaine factory.

The Grand Maison de HB (Hubaudiere and Bousquet) pottery had its beginnings around 1690, when Jean Baptiste Bousquet moved northward and founded a pottery in Locmaire. He chose the site due to its plentiful sources of local clay and wood for firing, plus the nearby Odet river for transportation. Bousquet and other local potters produced mainly simple, plain earthenware faience for use by the local population. Upon Jean Bousquet's death in 1708, the firm passed along to his son Pierre. Pierre's granddaughter and her husband, Pierre Clement Caussy, took control of the pottery in 1749. In 1792, Pierre Caussy died and his son-in-law Antoine de la Hubaudiere assumed control of the firm. Under Antoine's direction, the firm expanded production to more decorative wares, importing clays more suitable to these delicate designs. By the last decade of the 18th century, the firm employed approximately one hundred people. Although more decorative faience was being produced, the quality of the work remained more like folk art.

This changed in the late 19th century under the guidance of new owners Felix la Hubaudiere and M. Fougeray, the latter who became the art director of the factory in 1872. This pair raised the level of the faience decoration to more of an art, and perhaps also was responsible for the beginning of the Breton man and woman, for whom Quimper faience is so well known today. Beginning after Felix's death in 1882, the HB factory was owned and operated by his widow and son, Guy de la Hubaudiere. The pottery suffered through many years of financial hardship, selling assets and shares in the company simply to keep production going. After Guy was killed in World War I, the family pottery was sold to Jules Verlingue, a maker of faience from Boulogne-sur Mer.

The Eloury Pottery operated under the direction of Charles Porquier in the first half of the 19th century. Charles' son assumed control of the firm in 1850. It is not known exactly whether HB or Eloury created the first Breton people designs in the latter part of the 19th century, designs that have become so famous on Quimper faience. Noted designer Jules Henriot joined Eloury in 1886 and launched the firm into enamel glazed earthenware. In 1926, he assumed control of the firm and began marking his designs "Henriot Quimper".

The period between World War I and World War II was an important one for Quimper. During this period, Quimper faience became known more broadly throughout the world, and many new designs were introduced, including dinnerware. In the United States, several department stores began carrying the Breton designs, including Macy's and Bloomingdale's. In 1968, Jules Henriot merged his pottery and The Grande Maison together, naming the resulting firm Les Faenceries de Quimper. The pottery is still operating today.

Character Jugs and Toby Jugs

Quimper is known to have made only a few jugs, which are all difficult to find. Perhaps the most interesting is the graduated set of female Character Jugs. These jugs were designed by Maillard and produced in the 1940s. They have nice modeling and good facial expressions. The mark found on the jugs is "Henriot Quimper" with an overlapping C and M, dating them to post 1926. The sitting man Toby is marked "Henriot Quimper France."

Character Jug Name	Height, inches
Man lighting pipe	5 3/4
Pierrot Woman	8
Woman eating	2 3/4

Toby Jug Name	Height, inches
Lady Toby	2 1/2
Man sitting on book	2 1/2
Ordinary Toby	2 1/2

Character Jug of Woman Eating

Small Woman Character Jug

Pierrot Character Jug

Man lighting pipe on left and large Woman Character Jug on right

R. S. Germany
See Jugs Marked by Country of Manufacture under Germany

Radnor
See Hall Brothers

Regal Pottery
See Jugs Marked by Country of Manufacture under United Kingdom

Ridgways Limited
Hanley, England

Character Jug Name	Height, inches	Production Life
Drake	2 7/8	1950 - 1964
Uncle Sam	11 1/4	1909 - 1920
	3 1/4	1909 - 1920

History

The Ridgway name in Staffordshire pottery has a long and fine tradition. Job and George Ridgway started a pottery together in Cauldon Place, Hanley in the late 1700s. Job became the sole owner, and in 1802 the firm was named Job Ridgway. In 1808, Job's sons, John and William, joined the family business and the name of the pottery became Job Ridgway & Sons. The family continued potting at Cauldon Place for many years, with the name of the firm changing to reflect new ownership and partnerships. Chronologically these were J. & W. Ridgway (1814 - 1830), John Ridgway & Company (1830 - 1855), and Ridgway Bates & Company (1856 - 1858). The name Ridgway appears in the name of many other potteries throughout the late 19th and 20th centuries.

The Ridgway pottery of interest here is Ridgways Limited. This pottery traces its lineage back to the Ridgway, Sparks & Ridgway Pottery that operated at the Bedford Works in Shelton in the mid-1800s. This factory became Ridgways Pottery in 1879 and registered the name Ridgways as a trademark in 1880. The firm became a limited partnership in 1916 and changed its name to Ridgways Limited by 1920.

Ridgways Limited was purchased by Cauldon Potteries in 1929, but continued to operate as a separate entity. The Globe Pottery bought Ridgways from Cauldon in 1932. Lawleys Limited purchased an interest in the Globe Pottery in 1941, and used Ridgways for the production of bone china. In 1948, Globe and Ridgways became wholly owned subsidiaries of the Lawley Group, which in turned was acquired by S. Pearson & Son Limited in 1952. Pearson was a diverse conglomerate with interests in entertainment, publishing and industry. Beginning in 1964, it operated as the Allied English Potteries. The Doulton Group acquired Allied English in 1972.

Throughout all of these corporate changes, Ridgways Limited continued to operate independently. Pearson renamed the pottery Ridgway & Adderley on October 21, 1952. The firm became Ridgway, Adderley, Booths & Colcloughs for a brief period in 1955 from January 1 until February 28. Thereafter it operated as Ridgway Potteries Limited until closing in 1964.

Character Jugs

Ridgways is known to have produced only a few Character Jugs. These jugs are well modeled and very detailed, a nice addition to any collection. The Uncle Sam jug was made in the first quarter of the 20th century and offered in several sizes. The Ridgways name does reappear on more recent Toby and Character Jugs produced by Sterling Pottery, which likely had rights to use the name through its merger with Allied English Potteries. See also Sterling Pottery.

Ridgway by Sterling
See Sterling Pottery

L

History

Roy Kirkham grew up in the pottery business and formally trained as an engraver with William Adams. Roy then worked for Josiah Wedgwood, until he struck out on his own and started a business designing and hand engraving ceramic transfers in a home studio. As his business grew, Roy's studio became cramped, and he needed more space. This drove his purchase of a factory in Tunstall and the formalization of Roy Kirkham Pottery.

Initially Roy simply moved his ceramic transfer business to the Tunstall site, but after a while he investigated the status of an old kiln in the lower level of the factory. Finding it serviceable, Roy entered into the complete production of his own ceramics around 1980. About this time, Enoch Wedgwood Limited, formerly Wedgwood & Company, was being sold to Josiah Wedgwood, Roy's old employer. For 200 pounds, Kirkham was able to purchase several hundred different Wedgwood & Company molds of figurines, jugs and animals, with which he launched his own product lines. Initially, Kirkham's produced only items from these purchased molds. As the business grew, Kirkham sought to diversify to compensate for the peaks and valleys in the demand for any one type of product. One successful area of diversification was into tableware.

Roy Kirkham Pottery remains a family pottery. All three of Roy's sons participate in the business. Steven Kirkham, Roy's oldest son, is the Production Manager. Ian Kirkham works in sales for the pottery as well as with a firm that produces transfers for the factory. Andrew Kirkham, the youngest son, works at the factory as well. In the late 1990s, the pottery was the United Kingdom's largest maker of fine china coffee cups and mugs, producing approximately 190,000 pieces every five days.

Character Jugs and Toby Jugs

Roy Kirkham produced exciting, high quality Toby Jugs for a relatively brief time. Kirkham's first production of tobies in 1973 consisted of seven small tobies and two Character Jugs done in a black basalt Wedgwood-like finish. In fact, there was no finish on these jugs, the black material was the actual bisque itself. These basalt jugs were produced for only a short time and sold exclusively through an UK distributor. Therefore they are rare with only around 500 pieces of each basalt jug made. The jugs were also produced in polychrome versions. At the same time, a short-lived group of five small Character Jugs was offered, consisting of the King, Knight, Earl, Bishop, and Judge.

Included in Roy's purchase of Wedgwood & Company molds were all the original Toby Jug molds. The molds were in terrible condition. To produce the jugs, Kirkham had to remodel some of the features. For example, the Kirkham's Nightwatchman has his lantern attached by a metal ring. The Wedgwood & Company version had the lantern and arm molded as one piece. Roy even thought of adding a light to the lantern. Therefore the Wedgwood & Company tobies and the Kirkham versions may differ. Roy launched these Toby Jugs in 1980. The model numbers on the bottom of these Kirkham jugs correspond to the model numbers used by Wedgwood & Company.

This series was so successful that Kirkham began producing Toby Jugs of original design. Several series of Toby Jugs were issued over the following years. These included a ten-jug Charles Dickens Series, a Towncrier Series consisting of twelve jugs, and a Sherwood Forest series. Kirkham used several freelance artists to develop many of its jugs. Mary Malone was one of these. She was hired as a modeler to create tobies and began work on the Dickens series. Another freelance modeler, Alan Malinowski, later of Royal Doulton fame, also created some new Toby designs for the firm. The Mad Hatter Character Jug has "M. Naylor" painted on the bottom. The Miner Toby was introduced towards the end of the British miner's strike in the early 1980s. This jug came with a removable pick and attached lantern. The tiny sized Sherwood Forest Toby collection was made in the early 1980s, near the end of Kirkham's Toby production. Three of these jugs also were prototyped at roughly half their height.

During his production of tobies, Roy Kirkham made exciting contributions to the legacy of the Toby Jug. One of these contributions was the black basalt Wedgwood-like material that Roy invented. The value of these basalt jugs is considerably more than their polychrome counterparts. The 1979 limited edition Margaret Thatcher Toby Jug was done in bone china and depicts the Prime Minister seated in a blue dress with a briefcase at her feet and a sheaf of papers in her left hand. The factory presented jug number one to Margaret Thatcher on the day she took office. Today this jug is on display at 10 Downing Street in

Roy Kirkham backstamp

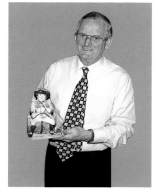

Roy Kirkham with a favorite single edition Toby Jug of Toby Philpot on a Barrell

Toby Philpott seated on a barrel Toby Jug, the only one produced (from Roy Kirkham's personal collection)

Mad Hatter Character Jug (from Roy Kirkham's personal collection)

Limited edition Margaret Thatcher Toby Jug (from Roy Kirkham's personal collection)

Miner Toby Jug

London. Thatcher jugs have been found on the market in an undecorated white finish. These were most likely excess jugs that somehow escaped the factory.

Kirkham's most impressive endeavor however was his creation of what was then the world's largest Toby Jug, standing thirty-one and one-half inches tall and weighing over eighty pounds! This giant jug of Toby Philpott was created as a promotional item and only three copies of the jug were made. One was completed without a handle and sold. The second cracked during the firing process and remains unfinished at the pottery. The third was wonderfully hand painted, including a willow transfer pattern on Toby's ale mug, but never glazed. It is also stored at the Roy Kirkham Pottery. In 1998, Cortman Limited eclipsed Kirkham's honor of potting the world's largest Toby Jug with its giant Toby Philpot jug standing over three feet tall. In 1981, Kirkham created another unique Toby Philpott jug. This Toby is sitting on a barrel with a dog at his feet. The barrel itself is functional, complete with a tap for dispensing a beverage of choice and Toby's hat serving as a cup. Three of these jugs were produced. Two remain at the factory, one in bisque and undecorated, and the other rests prominently on Roy's desk.

Roy Kirkham Pottery's early backstamps were incised, followed by a rubber stamped "Roy Kirkham Pottery," and then a transfer lithographed version of the rubber stamp. At one time, the factory was producing Toby Jugs almost exclu-

sively. However, the demand did not keep the kiln busy, and the profit margins on Tobies were not as high as on other products, due mainly to the large amount of handwork required in Toby production. As the demand for his more profitable products grew, Roy could no longer financially justify the labor intensive production of Toby Jugs, and with some regret, he sadly discontinued general production of Toby Jugs in 1983.

At the time he had plans in place to produce an Australian series of three or four tobies to be distributed through Warrenbrook, an Australian distributor. Kirkham made prototypes of Swaggie, Sheep Shearer and Digger for this series. The Sheep Shearer was based on Jackie Howe, a famous Australian shearer. A very few of the Australian series were produced and made their way into the secondary market. They would be considered a valuable rarity today.

Ian Kirkham has expressed interest in reviving Toby Jug production at the pottery. Roy has also been approached by another pottery interested in purchasing the molds for production. Perhaps one day Roy Kirkham Pottery will again produce Toby Jugs. In the meantime, we expect Roy Kirkham Toby and Character Jugs to become highly collectible with corresponding increased values in the 21st century.

"Nobody really makes any money making Tobies - especially compared to alternative ceramics."

Roy Kirkham, 1997

Character Jug Name	Height, inches	Production Life
Bishop	3 3/8	1973 - 1975
also in basalt	3 3/8	1973 - 1977
Earl		1973 - 1977
King		1973 - 1977
Knight		
Judge	2 7/8	1973 - 1975
also in basalt	2 7/8	1973 - 1977
Mad Hatter	5	1988

Left to right - Fagin, Oliver Twist, Artful Dodger, and Bill Sykes Toby Jugs

Left to right: Mr. bumble, Scrooge, and Mrs. Bumble Toby Jugs

Left to right - Mr. Pickwick, Sairey Gamp, and Sam Weller Toby Jugs

From left to right: Towncrier, Nightwatchman, and Beadle large sized Toby Jugs

Character Jugs clockwise from top: Prince, Knight, Judge, and Bishop.

Lord Chief Justice Toby Jug

Giant Toby Philpott jug, standing over 31 inches tall, hand painted but not glazed

From left to right: Lord Mayor, Vicar, Squire, and Sweep large sized Toby Jugs

From left to right: Innkeeper, Schoolmaster, Town Clerk, and Shepherd large Toby Jugs

Australiian Series Toby Jugs, left to right: Swaggie, Sheep Shearer, and Digger

Toby Jug Name	Height, inches	Model Number	Production Life
Allan a'Dale	7 1/4 2 1/8		1981 1983
Artful Dodger	7 1/2		1983
Beadle	7	756/1	1980 - 1983
Beggarman	7 5 3/8	795	1980 - 1983 1980 - 1983
Bill Sykes	7		1983
Digger	9 1/2		1983 Prototype
Fagin	7 1/2		1983
Friar Tuck	7 2 1/4		1981 - 1983 1983
Innkeeper also found in basalt	7 4 5/8	762/1	1980 - 1983 1973 - 1975
King John	7 1 3/4		1981 1983
Little John	7 1/2 2 1/4		1981 1983
Lord Chief Justice	7 1/4	777	1980 - 1979
Lord Mayor	7 1/4	753	1982 - 1983
Margaret Thatcher	6 1/2		1979 Ltd Ed of 500
Miner	7		1980 - 1983
Mr. Bumble	7		1983
Mr. Pickwick	7		1983
Mrs. Bumble	7		1983
Nightwatchman also found in basalt	6 3/8 4 3/8	754/1	1980 - 1983 1973 - 1975
Oliver Twist	7		1983
Pedlar also found in basalt	5 4 1/2		1980 - 1983 1973 - 1975
Poorman	5 1/8	798	1980 - 1983
Richman	5 1/4	796	1980 - 1983
Robin Hood	6 1/2 2		1981 - 1983 1983
Sailor	5	733	1980 - 1983
Sarah Gamp	7 1/4		1983
Sam Weller	7 1/4		1982
Schoolmaster also found in basalt	7 4 1/4		1982 - 1983 1973 - 1983
Scrooge	7		1983
Sheep Shearer	8		1983 Prototype
Shepherd also found in basalt	7 4 3/4	766/1	1979 - 1983 1973 - 1975
Sheriff of Nottingham	7 2		1981 1983
Soldier	5 1/4	782	1980 - 1983
Squire	6 3/4	763/1	1980 - 1983
Swaggie	9		1983 Prototype
Sweep	6 7/8		1982 - 1983
Tailor	5 1/4	781	1980 - 1983
Thief	5 1/4	784	1980 - 1983
Tinker	5 1/4	780	1980 - 1983
Toby Philpott sitting on barrel	31 1/2 11		1980 1981
Town Clerk also found in basalt	6 1/2 3 5/8		1982 - 1983 1973 - 1975
Towncrier	7 1/4 4 1/4	750/1 750/3	1980 - 1983
Vicar also found in basalt	7 4 1/4	764/1	1980 - 1983 1973 - 1975

From left to right: Tinker, Tailor, Soldier, and Sailor Toby Jugs

From left to right: Richman, Poorman, Beggarman, and Thief Toby Jugs

Large and small sized Towncrier Toby Jugs; note the modeling differences

Left to right Sherwood Forest series Toby Jugs: Allan a'Dale, King John, and Little John

Left to right Sherwood Forest series Toby Jugs: Friar Tuck, Robin Hood, and Sheriff of Nottingham

Left to right Sherwood Forest series Toby Jugs in the tiny size, handpainted but not yet glazed: Robin Hood, Friar Tuck, Allan a'Dale, Sheriff of Nottingham, Little John, and King John (from Roy Kirkham's personal collection)

From left to right: Innkeeper, Nightwatchman, Vicar, and Pedlar small sized Toby Jugs

Collection of Basalt jugs; top row left to right - Pedlar, Nightwatchman, Schoolmaster, and Towncrier; bottom row left to right - Bishop, Shepherd, Innkeeper, Vicar, and Judge (from Roy Kirkham's personal collection)

Royal Albert
See Beswick

Royal Aller Vale & Watcombe Pottery Company
Devon, England

Character Jug Name	Height, inches
Character Jug like Sarreguemines	6
Grand Old Man	
Monk	5 3/4
Unknown Man	

History

Royal Aller Vale and Watcombe Pottery began as two independent potteries before merging in 1901 and becoming the Royal Aller Vale and Watcombe Pottery Company.

Royal Aller Vale's history began as John Phillips & Company. John Phillips founded a pottery in 1868 at the Aller Pottery factory, halfway between Torquay and Newton Abbott in Devon. Phillips was born in 1835 in southern Dartmoor and followed his father into the pot business. Phillips produced mainly architectural earthenware goods. After a devastating fire in 1881, Phillips re-opened the firm as Aller Vale Art Pottery and began producing everyday earthenware products. The clay was dug at the site of the pottery, and all the glazes and paints were made at the factory. Phillips was keenly interested in the style of the Arts and Crafts movement, so he concentrated on slipware with ornate scroll designs and detailed flowers, birds or other animals. He was also very interested in handcraftsmanship and developing local talent, so he taught evening courses at the local art school he helped found in 1881, and opened his pottery up for interested students to experiment during the day.

Aller Vale produced its first mottoware pieces in the early 1880s, possibly creating the genre of mottoware pottery. By the turn of the century, mottoware had become so popular that the other Devon potteries were copying the style. In 1886, a twelve year old Charles Collard began an apprenticeship with the firm. The pottery was further bolstered when it attracted Domenico Marcucci from Italy to join it in 1889. Domenico was one of the firm's chief designers and shared Phillips belief in developing local artistic talent, also teaching at local schools. Two of his most notable students were Bill Howard, who joined the Longpark facility as a designer, and Charles Collard, who became Aller Vale's chief decorator by the mid 1890s and then went on to operate his own potteries. Aller Vale attracted royal attention in the form of Princess Louise, who liked its products. Aller Vale leveraged this into its marketing, increasing demand for its products into the 1890s. John Phillips died in 1897, after which Hexter Humpherson and Company, local clay merchants in Kingsteignton, acquired the firm. Its products were incised "Aller Vale".

George Allen founded Watcombe Pottery in September of 1869 at St. Mary Church in South Devon. Allen was a retired barrister who moved to the Devon area in the 1860s. He took up residence at the Watcombe House near St. Mary Church. During construction at his home, Allen took note of the reddish, fine textured clay being unearthed and shortly had several pieces of pottery fired from this clay. He decided to take advantage of his unexpected natural resource and opened a pottery. Originally called the Watcombe Terracotta Clay Company, for the next thirty years the pottery produced earthenware busts, urns, vases and figures, as well as terra-cotta ornamental and architectural ware. Much of this production was left unglazed.

By the 1880s, terra-cotta products were becoming less popular and the demand for handpainted glazed pottery was becoming substantial. In response to this change in public taste, Watcombe hired new artists who produced mottoware and artware, including colorful, decorative pottery of fauna and flora. The firm's most popular line of this type of pottery was Royal Devon Ware, which featured primarily apple or prune blossoms on a sage green background. Terra-cotta production was phased out by the end of the 19th century. The firm incised its wares with "Watcombe Torquay" or "Watcombe Pottery".

In 1901, Hexter Humpherson took over the Watcombe Pottery as well. The Watcombe and

Aller Vale potteries merged and re-located the combined company at the St. Mary Church site. This new amalgamated pottery operated as Royal Aller Vale and Watcombe Pottery Company, producing wares of both firms. The pottery continued making existing products and introduced many new lines. However, shortly after the merger, key members of Aller Vale, including Charles Collard left the firm. Production focused mainly on mottoware after 1904, but quality began to decline steadily until Royal Aller Vale ceased production in 1924.

Meanwhile at the Watcombe facility, mottowares had become the mainstay of the firm. Because it was the largest pottery in the area, Watcombe was the only local pottery to remain open during World War II, producing undecorated wares to comply with the Board of Trade regulations. After World War II, Watcombe tried to recapture its old markets, but high production costs and slipping quality caused demand for its products to fall. Production at the factory halted on September 30, 1962. Ware can be found with any of the following incised or printed marks: "Royal Aller Vale", "Devon Motto Ware", "Royal Torquay Pottery", or "Royal Watcombe Torquay England" in a circle after 1957. However not all pieces are marked.

Character Jugs and Toby Jugs

As with most Devon area potters, Watcombe and Royal Aller Vale jugs are made from the red clay native to that region of England. Albert Edward Clements credited his older brother, Fred Clements, a modeler, as being the first at Watcombe to make Toby Jugs. Watcombe's Monk Character Jug was introduced around 1901 and produced throughout the life of the pottery. A matte green glaze color indicates an early production period; whereas, lime green and blue glazes date from the late 1950s. The Monk is incised "Many have told of the monks of old What a saintly face."

The Grand Old Man Character Jug depicts Mr. Gladstone, featuring an axe handle poised at his head. Aller Vale produced it between 1887 and 1901. The name Grand Old Man is found in relief around the rim of the jug. Aller Vale produced the Sarreguemines-like jug around 1900, marked "Aller Vale Devon England".

The Watcombe Toby Jug is very similar in appearance to that of Devonmoor, but not quite as well modeled. As with other Devon potters, the Ordinary Toby was decorated in a wide variety of colorways. The Watcombe jug can be found with teal, red, purple, dark green, ochre, blue, and pale green jackets. A unique characteristic of Watcombe and Devonmoor

Toby Jug Name	Height, inches
Farmer	5 1/2
Old Salt	6
Ordinary Toby	6 1/2
	5 1/2
	4 1/2
	3 1/2
	2 3/4

Monk Character Jug in solid green colorway (from the collection of Virginia Brisco)

Character jug like Sarreguemines Jolly Fellow Jug (courtesy of Torquay Collectors Society)

Old Man Character Jug ca. 1900 (courtesy of Torquay Collectors Society)

Ordinary Toby Jugs is the distinctive black painted jacket cuffs and pockets.

In the 1950s, Watcombe reintroduced some of its character jugs finished in a black semi-matte glaze. These did not sell well, so are difficult to find today. The Farmer and Old Salt Toby Jugs are finished in a caramel glaze and carry a mark consisting of an overlapped "PW" above "Torquay," which has been attributed to Watcombe Pottery.

Old Salt on left and Farmer on right; Toby Jugs attributed to Watcombe

Royal Aller Vale and Watcombe Ordinary Toby Jugs in a variety of sizes and jacket colors; the teal and dark green jackets are less common (from the collection of John Hobbs)

Royal Art Pottery
See Clough's Royal Art Pottery

Royal Bayreuth
See Royal Tettau Porcelain Factory

Royal Carlton
See Arnart Imports

Royal Cauldon
See Cauldon Potteries

Royal Crown
See Arnart

Royal Crown Derby Porcelain Company
Derby, England

History

Potting in the town of Derby goes well back into history, with good quality Derby porcelain figurines dating from 1750. Perhaps the first truly commercial factory in the town was the Nottingham Road factory, established by Andrew Planche in 1756. Planche produced china figurines there in the French style. This factory flourished for many years under the guidance of several Directors.

The first of these Directors was William Duesbury, who initially went into partnership with Planche, and eventually assumed control of the factory. By 1770, Duesbury had also acquired the Chelsea China Works and transferred many skilled artisans to the Derby factory from Chelsea. He also opened a London retail shop in 1773, broadening the availability and reputation of Derby's china. King George III often patronized the firm, and he granted the factory the rare honor of incorporating a crown into its backstamp in 1775.

William Duesbury died in 1786, and the factory was taken over by his son, William Duesbury II. With a team of highly skilled artists, William II embarked on a program of further improving quality, broadening product offerings, and widely distributing ware. Products from this era are perhaps the most desired Derby pieces. Unexpectedly, William died in 1797 at the young age of 34. Upon his death many of the talented artists left. Without this creative force, the factory began a period of decline.

In 1811, the firm came under control of Robert Bloor. Immediately Bloor began rebuilding the reputation of Derby by hiring a team of talented painters. Soon this team began introducing new lines of exciting bone china. Several of these lines had a Japanese influence, such as the Imari line. Robert Bloor suffered through a long illness and died in 1846. The Bloor family operated the factory during and after his illness, finally closing it in 1848.

After the 1848 closure of the Nottingham factory, Sampson Hancock and five key Nottingham employees transplanted many of the workers and remaining assets of the company to a new Derby factory, known as the King Street factory. This factory operated from 1848 until 1935 under a series of partnerships, producing traditional ware from Crown Derby molds. First among these partnerships was Locker & Company, then Courtney, which was followed quickly by Stevenson Sharp & Co.

The most lasting partnership operating the King Street factory was Stevenson & Hancock, managing it from 1859 until 1935. Between 1861 and 1935, Stevenson & Hancock marked its ware with one adapted from the standard Derby mark used between 1782 and 1825. This old Derby mark had traditional crossed swords with dots, above it a crown, and below a script D. Stevenson & Hancock added an S and H to the left and right of the crossed swords respectively.

Edward Phillips and William Litherland purchased land on Osmaston Road in Derby in 1875 with the intent of building a potting factory. A new pottery, Derby Crown Porcelain, commenced production there in 1877. Shortly thereafter the firm employed 400 workers and was producing china, parian ware and stoneware. Queen Victoria granted the factory the royal warrant in 1890, and

the firm became the Royal Crown Derby Porcelain Company. The pottery remained in control of the Phillips and Litherland families until 1929, when Harold T. Robinson purchased a large stake in the company and assumed control of the firm. Harold was named chairman of Royal Crown Derby and served in that capacity until 1953, at which time his son Phillip succeeded him.

Royal Crown Derby continued successful production of quality goods for many years. Figurine production grew tremendously in the 1920s and 1930s. Royal Crown Derby purchased the King Street factory in 1935, uniting the history of Derby pottery into one firm. During the Second World War, production continued but was focused mostly on utilitarian goods. The mid-1950s brought the firm fame from its production of serving sets for Middle Eastern royalty and heads of state, increasing exports dramatically. The firm's success culminated with an impressive showing of its products at the 1956 British Industries Fair.

Phillip Robinson resigned as Chairman in 1961, turning over control of the firm to A. T. Smith and ending the Robinson family's involvement in the firm. In January of 1964, Royal Crown Derby became part of Allied English Potteries Limited, formerly the Lawley Group. Allied continued operating Royal Crown Derby as an independent unit until it was merged into Royal Doulton Tableware Limited in 1973.

Under Doulton's control, Royal Crown Derby continues producing high quality fine bone china products today. The early figurines and other decorative wares are highly sought after by collectors around the world.

Toby Jugs

According to company records, Derby Crown produced an Ordinary Toby around the turn of the twentieth century as shape 744 and described in a marketing brochure as "Toby Jugs, plain shape, eight sizes". The 1934 Price List from the King Street factory contained a standing Toby Jug, numbered 42 and priced at 4 shillings and 6 pence. This standing Toby is the Snufftaker, which has the Stevenson & Hancock mark on it, and has been found in both a red or green jacket. Doris Pacey was one of the decorators at the King Street factory who hand painted the Snufftaker.

Toby Jug Name	Height, inches	Production Life
Ordinary Toby	ex large	1900 - 1920s
	large	1900 - 1920s
	medium	1900 - 1920s
	intermediate	1900 - 1920s
	small	1900 - 1920s
	ex small	1900 - 1920s
	mini	1900 - 1920s
	tiny	1900 - 1920s
Snufftaker	1 1/2	1920 - 1935

Pair of tiny Snufftaker Toby Jugs

Royal Doulton & Company Limited
Lambeth & Burslem, England

History

Royal Doulton was founded by John Doulton (1793 - 1873), who received his training in pottery production at the Fulham Pottery, becoming a thrower. With his life's savings, Doulton purchased a one hundred pound share of a small non-descript pottery on the River Thames in Vauxhall Walk, Lambeth in 1815. Martha Jones, a recent widow, was the new and inexperienced owner of her late husband's pottery there. John Watts, the former foreman of the pottery, was made a partner with Doulton. This firm was named Jones, Watts and Doulton, and the principle output of the pottery was salt-glazed stoneware. Over the next few years, five of John's sons would join him at the factory, including Henry and James. Quickly the pottery became a success, with stoneware drain pipes and bottles the primary products. By 1826, Doulton & Watts, as it became known, was one of the more important Lambeth potteries.

In the late 1820s, Henry Doulton (1820 - 1897), John's second oldest son, joined the firm. He quickly learned all aspects of the pottery business, such that he soon was key in the operations of the firm. In the late 1830s and into the 1840s, Henry led a growth phase for Doulton & Watts, during which Doulton purchased many of its local competitors. The pottery had now branched out into terra-cotta products and garden ornaments. Foreseeing the public outcry for more sanitary living conditions, Henry exquisitely timed Doulton & Watts' entry into the production of stoneware piping and conduits. The firm was so successful that by 1846 the Lambeth factory was leading the sanitary revolution in England as one of the few suppliers of stoneware drainpipes. Doulton's success in this mundane business laid the foundation for the sterling reputation the firm still maintains today.

Through the urging of John Sparkes, the Principal of the Lambeth School of Art, Henry hired some of Sparkes' students on a trial basis and put them to work in the Lambeth factory. The initial pieces from these students were so well received at the 1867 Paris Exposition that Henry established a studio for art pottery within the Lambeth factory. By the 1880s, this studio had over two hundred designers and artists.

In 1877, Doulton & Watts invested in Pinder, Bourne and Company, a Staffordshire potter with a Burslem factory. Thomas Shadford Pinder retired in 1882, and Doulton purchased the firm outright. Henry faced stern opposition from the local merchants, who viewed Doulton as an outsider who would quickly depart. Henry

instead created new styles and designs at the Burslem factory, including production of bone china. Art Director John Slater directed the Burslem factory with plant manager John C. Bailey. Both the Lambeth and Burslem factories grew, producing a wide variety of products. So broad was Doulton's offering that the firm displayed over 1,500 different items at the 1893 Chicago International Exhibition.

Charles C. Noke joined Doulton and Company in 1889 as a modeler at the Burslem factory. Later he would become Art Director at Burslem. Noke was responsible for the introduction of many new lines, designs and styles. One of the most significant of these was a range of transmutation glazed ware to rival Sevres and Dresden.

The Queen knighted Henry Doulton in 1887 for his contribution to the British ceramics industry. Ten years later, in 1897, Henry died, leaving behind one of the most amazing pottery legacies of all time. The successful operation and expansion of the firm continued under the guidance of Henry's son, Henry Lewis Doulton (1853 - 1930), John C. Bailey, Charles Noke and John Slater, becoming a limited company in 1898. In 1901, Doulton was granted the Royal Warrant by Edward VII, becoming Royal Doulton. Harry Fenton joined Doulton in 1903, and, except for a fifteen-year stint in the United States between 1912 and 1927, was a key modeler with the firm until 1953.

Royal Doulton continued to grow through World War I and the Great Depression. Henry Lewis Doulton took great interest in new developments such as flambé glazes like Sung and Chang, the secret ingredients of which are still a closely guarded corporate trade secret. Figurines were introduced in 1913, and today Royal Doulton dominates this category of ceramics. Peggy Davies, who joined Royal Doulton in 1939 from Newport Pottery, was the artist most responsible for Doulton emerging as the leader in figurine production. She designed more that 240 figurines over forty years, some of which were not introduced until many years after she stopped designing for the firm. Peggy's first figurine, introduced in 1947, was Christmas Morn. She also designed the Fair Ladies series of figurines, and Royal Doulton won the Grand Prix award at the 1958 Brussels Exposition for her Marriage of Art and Industry figure.

By the 1930s, Royal Doulton was known worldwide as a leading producer of fine china. Post World War II, public tastes turned toward simpler, more affordable dinnerware, and Royal Doulton kept pace. New manufacturing and decorating techniques were employed to make fine china affordable by everyone. Driven by the ongoing need for sanitary piping, the Lambeth factory maintained its role in the Doulton empire of producing utilitarian and functional stoneware until it closed its doors in 1956. With Lambeth closed, the Burslem factory became the core of the Doulton company. For more efficient operations, it was reorganized into four subsidiaries, plus various overseas companies.

In 1953, Orrok Sherwood Doulton (1916 - 1977) became Director of the firm. In the mid-1950s, Jo Ledger joined the firm as Art Director. Doulton continued to expand and diversify in the 1950s and beyond through the purchase of other firms, notably Minton, Beswick, Royal Albert, Paragon, Ridgway and a host of others. In 1966, Royal Doulton won its first Queen's Award for Technical Innovation for its development of translucent china, a new china product it invented and introduced in 1960. It won a second Queen's Award in 1970 for Outstanding Export Performance. In 1972, Eric Griffiths was the Art Director of Sculpture, responsible for the firm's figurine designs and production. Today Phil Holland serves as Royal Doulton's Art Director.

Michael Doulton began working with the company in 1970 under an assumed name so that he could learn all aspects of production from the ground up. In July of 1972, Royal Doulton and Allied English Potteries merged and reorganized the new, larger amalgamated firm into four operating divisions. Eventually Michael Doulton became a Director of the family firm, the fourth generation to do so.

Today Royal Doulton, along with the Wedgwood Group, is perhaps one of the two largest ceramic conglomerates in the world. Royal Doulton celebrated the 100th anniversary of Henry Doulton's death in 1997 with a three month long celebration honoring his life and work. The celebration included a major exhibit of Doulton ware covering 120 years of production at the Burslem factory. A 1997 management change named thirty-seven year Doulton veteran Patrick Wenger as Chief Executive. He is preparing Royal Doulton to boldly enter the next century. From John Doulton's humble beginnings, fed by Henry's broad vision, Royal Doulton has most likely exceeded everyone's expectations.

For a more detailed history of Royal Doulton and Co., refer to the Shine publication, *"Royal Doulton"* by Julie McKeown.

Character Jugs and Toby Jugs

When most people think of Character Jugs or Toby Jugs, they immediately think of Royal Doulton. The company undoubtedly has produced more jugs than any other single company, probably more than any other ever will. While most collectors are acquainted with the broad variety of Character and Toby Jugs that Royal Doulton has been making since the 1930s, Doulton's production of these jugs began much earlier with an extremely well designed offering of stoneware jugs.

Although the Lambeth factory was primarily dedicated to the manufacture of utilitarian stoneware products, the financial stability that Henry Doulton brought to the factory allowed it to experiment with other designs and decorator ware. This experimentation led to the production of salt-glazed stoneware jugs as early as the 1820s. John Doulton's fascination with Lord Nelson inspired the first stoneware Character Jugs and busts made by Doulton at that time. Later in the 19th century, large stoneware Double XX, or Man on a Barrel, jugs were created.

During the early years of the 20th century, noted Doulton sculptor Leslie Harradine designed several stoneware Character Jugs. These include Theodore Roosevelt, a pair of Veteran Motorist jugs, an ugly Highwayman, a beaming Old King Cole, and a humorous Mr. Pecksniff, that was produced in both cream and brown treacle glaze finishes. Beginning in 1924, Doulton produced an exceptional line of stoneware Toby Jugs and derivatives designed by Harry Simeon. These are excellently crafted and difficult to find today. These jugs were produced at the Lambeth factory until about 1929; the exact discontinuance date is not known. The Double XX jug can be found in several colors, both with and without a handle. The standing stoneware Toby came in a brown or orange vest. The Armchair Toby came in various colors, and when he appears with a hole in the back, he is considered an ashpot.

The Charlie Chaplin Toby is rare indeed, with less than fifty jugs known. Charlie was made in 1918 and has a removable bowler hat. His name is incised on the front of the base. Produced around 1925, the George Robey Toby is similar to Chaplin's, complete with removable hat and incised name. The Robey jug was designed by Charles Noke, and, given the similarity in modeling, it is probable that Noke also designed the earlier Charlie Chaplin jug. Both Charlie and George came from music hall backgrounds in England and were entertainers. They were also probably at least acquaintances. Folklore suggests that the George Robey Toby Jug was made exclusively for Robey himself, which he used as gifts for his friends and associates.

Even though Face Jugs were produced as early as the 18th century, Charles Noke is commonly thought of as the father of the Character Jug. It was his genius and creativity that produced the first Royal Doulton Character Jug in 1934, John Barleycorn, which was followed that same year by Old Charlie. In subsequent years, a host of others followed with subjects taken from legend, history and literature, such as the popular Charles Dickens' characters. One of Noke's more significant and unique designs was his Winston Churchill Character Jug. Issued in 1940, this was a large two-handled creamware jug that had a limited production life, rumored so because Churchill was not fond of his likeness. At this same time Derivatives, or remodellings of Character Jugs, were produced in the form of ash bowls, cigarette lighters, and teapots. In 1939 Toby Jugs also were introduced, with the early examples being similar to Simeon's Lambeth Toby ware. Charles Noke launched a product line that has lasted for over sixty-five years, and been widely copied by potters around the world.

1960 brought a significant change to the line of Character and Toby Jugs. That year Royal Doulton withdrew seven Toby Jugs and seventy-four Character Jugs of all sizes. All together thirty different characters were retired, including John Barleycorn. This sudden reduction in Doulton's active jugs sparked an even larger number of new introductions in the following decade. It also sparked the collecting craze for discontinued Doulton jugs that continues today.

The breadth and variety of Doulton's Character Jugs has grown to a staggering level, now consisting of well over four hundred retired and current characters in as many as five different sizes, plus over seventy Toby Jugs. Many noteworthy designers have created Character Jugs for Doulton. These include Harry Fenton, Max Henk, David Biggs, Eric Griffiths, William Harper, Michael Abberley, Peter Gee, Alan Maslankowski, Gerry Sharpe, Robert Tabbenor, Stan Taylor, and Douglas Tootle. The Miller of Bath and his wife, two Canturbury Tales Pilgrim jugs that were prototyped and never released, were both designed by William Harper.

Royal Doulton has honored many famous and heroic people, immortalized characters out of legend and fantasy, and depicted respected trades and avocations. The result is a large number of jugs to satisfy the most selective collector. There is literally something for everyone!

Following is a complete list of Royal Doulton Character Jugs, Toby Jugs, and derivatives as of the publication date of this book. The Royal Doulton International Collector's Club magazine, *Gallery*, and the Francis Joseph publication *Collecting Doulton* will keep the collector abreast of new introductions and discontinuances as they occur.

Doulton & Watts and Royal Doulton Lambeth Stoneware Character Jugs

Character Jug Name	Height, inches	Production Life	Other Information
Admiral Lord Nelson	7 1/2	1821 - 1830	
	6	1821 - 1830	
	6	1905 - 1910	Reproduction of 1821 jug
	5	1821 - 1830	
	2 1/2	1821 - 1830	
bust	11 3/4	1845 - ca 1890	
bust	11 3/4	1905 - 1910	Reproduction of 1845 bust
Arthur Wellesley	7 1/2	1821 - 1830	First Duke of Wellington
Highwayman	unknown	1912 - 19??	
Marriage Day / After Marriage	4 3/4	1924 - ca 1929	Smiling face on marriage day
	3 1/2	1924 - ca 1929	that frowns when turned
	1 7/8	1924 - ca 1929	upside down
Mr. Pecksniff	7 1/2	1912 - 19??	Ivory or brown treacle glaze
Napoleon	large	ca 1850 - 1870	Light or dark brown glaze
Old King Cole	large	1910 - 19??	
Theodore Roosevelt	large	1910 - 19??	
Veteran Motorist	large	1905 - 19??	Goggles up or down
Wee Mac	unknown	1908 - 19??	

Doulton & Watts and Royal Doulton Lambeth Stoneware Toby Jugs

Toby Jug Name	Height, inches	Production Life	Other Information
Armchair Toby	6	1924 - ca 1929	Many color variations exist
	4	1924 - ca 1929	
The Best is Not Too Good	4 1/4	1924 - ca 1929	Smiling or somber face.
	3 3/4	1924 - ca 1929	Left hand either holding a pipe or grasping his lapel
	2 3/4	1924 - ca 1929	
Double XX	14 1/2	1863 - ca 1890	Light and dark brown glazes
	12 1/2	1863 - ca 1890	Light and dark brown glazes
	10 1/2	1863 - ca 1890	Light and dark brown glazes
	9		
	8	1924 - ca 1929	Orange/brown, orange/blue or olive/blue waistcoat/jacket
	6 3/4	1924 - ca 1929	Orange/brown, orange/blue or olive/blue waistcoat/jacket
handleless	6	1924 - ca 1929	Light brown, dark brown, or white/brown waistcoat/jacket
handleless	5 1/2	1924 - ca 1929	Olive/blue or orange/blue waistcoat/jacket
Ordinary Toby	3 1/8	1924 - ca 1929	
Squat Toby	2 1/2	1924 - ca 1929	
Soldier	10	ca 1910	
Soldier Boy	10	ca 1910	
Standing Toby	8 1/2	1924 - ca 1929	Smiling or somber face; orange, brown or green waistcoat;
	7	1924 - ca 1929	some jugs have silver rims; also found in light and dark
	6 1/4	1924 - ca 1929	brown glazes
"8572"	4 3/4	1924 - ca 1929	
	2 3/4	1924 - ca 1929	
Three sided Standing Toby	10	1924 - ca 1929	

Doulton & Watts and Royal Doulton Lambeth Stoneware Derivatives

Stoneware Item	Height, inches	Production Life	Other Information
Angel Pepper shaker	3 1/4	1924 - ca 1929	
Armchair Toby Bottle	7 1/2	1924 - ca 1929	
Best is Not Too Good Bottle	8 1/4	1924 - ca 1929	Moon faced bottle
Tobacco jar	4 1/2	1924 - ca 1929	
Double XX Liquor Bottle	7 1/2	1924 - ca 1929	Orange waistcoat
Liquor bottle on stand	10 1/4	1924 - ca 1929	Metal stand and hanging basket, orange waistcoat
Drummer Boy Matchstand	5	1924 - ca 1929	
Honest Measure Tea caddy	4	1924 - ca 1929	Detachable hat
Ink well	2 3/4	1924 - ca 1929	Detachable head
Matchstand	2 3/4	1924 - ca 1929	
Mephistopheles Candleholder	3	ca 1910	Double faced
Mephistopheles/Marguerite Match holder	3	ca 1910	Double faced
Ordinary Toby Candleholder	3 3/4	1924 - ca 1929	Various colorways known
Sailor Tobacco jar	7 1/2	1924 - ca 1929	Lid separates at shoulders
Smoker Toby Matchstand	2 3/4	1924 - ca 1929	
Votes for Women Salt shaker	3 1/4	1924 - ca 1929	

Photographs of Doulton & Watts and Royal Douton Lambeth Stoneware Jugs and Derivitives

Admiral Lord Nelson bust, and Admiral Lord Nelson Character Jugs, 6" and 5" tall respectively (from the collection of Emmertt Mathews)

Stoneware Double XX Toby Jugs in three sizes; 14 1/2", 10", and 9"

Stoneware Standing Man in two color variations (from the collection of Emmertt Mathews)

Napoleon stoneware Character Jug on the left and Arthur Wellesley Character Jug on the right (from the Royal Doulton archival collection)

Highwayman stoneware Character Jug

Old King Cole stoneware Character Jug

Theodore Roosevelt stoneware Character Jug

Mr. Pecksniff stoneware Character Jugs in both ivory and brown treacle glaze

Two versions of Veteran Motorist Stoneware Character Jug

Soldier Boy stoneware Toby Jug (from the collection of Joan and Charles Dombeck)

Soldier stoneware Toby Jug

Sailor stoneware tobacco jar; the top separates at the shoulders

Three sided Standing Toby stoneware jug (from the collection of Tony D'Agostino)

Double XX 8" and 6" Toby Jugs with blue jackets and brown waistcoats; 8" with blue jacket and orange waistcoat

Double XX stoneware bottle with blue jacket and orange waistcoat, 8" tall

Double XX liquor bottle on metal stand and with hanging bucket

Group of stoneware Double XX handleless Toby Jugs in a variety of colorways

Stoneware Standing Toby with blue jacket and brown waistcoat shown in four graduated sizes

Graduated group of four stoneware Standing Toby jugs with blue jacket and orange waistcoats

The Best is Not Too Good stoneware Toby Jug in two sizes

Armchair stoneware Toby Jug, two 4" tall and one 6" tall; with hole in back sometimes referred to as ashpots, armchair toby bottle with stopper on right

Left to right Marriage Day/After Marriage stoneware Character Jugs in three sizes; Marriage Day facing up (except small jug)

Same grouping of Marriage Day/After Marriage stoneware Character Jugs only turned upside down showing After Marriage

Stoneware Honest Measure 4" tea caddy and 2 3/4" ink well

Same Honest Measure tea caddy and ink well, now with tops removed

The Best is Not Too Good stoneware moon faced bottle on left, 8 1/4" tall, and tobacco jar on right, 4 1/2" tall

Stoneware Ordinary Toby Jug

Two Honest Measure matchstands flanking an Ordinary Toby candleholder

Stoneware Drummer Boy, 5" tall, and Smoker, 3 3/4" tall, matchstands

Votes for Women and Angel stoneware salt and pepper shakers

Mephistopheles two-faced candle holder, good side

Mephistopheles 3" tall candle holder, evil side

Royal Douton Burslem Character Jugs

Character Jug Name	Model Number	Height, Inches	Production Life	Other Information
Abraham Lincoln	D6936	large	1992	Limited Edition of 2500, Presidents Series
Airman	D6870	small	1991 - 1996	Comrades in Arms Set
	D6903	small	1991	Limited Edition of 250, "On Guard for Thee" Canadian Set
	D6982	small	1994	National Service Special Edition, oxygen mask handle
Aladdin's Genie	D6971	large	1994	Limited Edition of 1500, Flambé Series
Albert Einstein	D7023	large	1996 - 1997	
Alfred Hitchcock	D6987	large	1995 - 1997	No MCA backstamp increases value
	D6987	large	1995	Colorway: pink curtain instead of white
Angel	D7051	mini	1996	Christmas Miniatures Series, US RDICC distribution only
Angler version 1	D6866	small	1990 - 1995	Characters from Life Series
version 2	D7065	small	1997 - current	Early pieces carry D6866 backstamp, new larger small size
Ankhesenamun		small	1999	Ltd Ed of 1500 for Lawleys, Paired with Tutankhamen
Anne Boleyn version 1	D6644	large	1975 - 1990	Henry VIII and Six Wives Series
	D6650	small	1980 - 1990	
	D6651	mini	1980 - 1990	
version 2	D7042	tiny	1994	Limited Edition of 2500 for Lawleys By Post, Six Wives of Henry VIII Set
Anne of Cleves version 1	D6653	large	1980 - 1990	Henry VIII and Six Wives Series
	D6653	large	1980 - 1981	Horse handle with ears up
	D6753	small	1987 - 1990	
	D6754	mini	1987 - 1990	
version 2	D7044	tiny	1994	Limited Edition of 2500 for Lawleys By Post, Six Wives of Henry VIII Set
Annie Oakley	D6732	mid	1985 - 1989	Wild West Collection
Antique Dealer	D6807	large	1988	Limited Edition of 5000 for Kevin Francis Ceramics, Collecting World Series
Antony & Cleopatra	D6728	large	1985	Limited Edition of 9500, Star Crossed Lovers Collection; two faced jug; proto with brown hair and pudgy Anthony face known
Apothecary	D6567	large	1963 - 1983	Characters from Williamsburg Collection
	D6574	small	1963 - 1983	
	D6581	mini	1963 - 1983	
Aramis	D6441	large	1956 - 1991	Characters from Literature Collection
	D6829	large	1988	Limited Edition of 1000 for Peter Jones China
	D6454	small	1956 - 1991	
	D6508	mini	1960 - 1991	
'Ard of Earing	D6588	large	1964 - 1967	
	D6591	small	1964 - 1967	
	D6594	mini	1964 - 1967	
ARP Warden	D6872	small	1991	Ltd Ed of 9500 for Lawleys By Post, Heroes of the Blitz Set
'Arriet	D6208	large	1947 - 1960	
	D6236	small	1947 - 1960	
see also "Pearly Girl"	D6250	mini	1947 - 1960	
	D6256	tiny	1947 - 1960	
'Arry	D6207	large	1947 - 1960	
	D6235	small	1947 - 1960	
see also "Pearly Boy"	D6249	mini	1947 - 1960	
	D6255	tiny	1947 - 1960	
Arsenal FC	D6927	mid	1992 - current	Football Supporters Series
Artful Dodger	D6678	tiny	1982 - 1989	Charles Dickens Commemorative Tinies Set for Lawleys By Post
Aston Villa FC	D6931	mid	1992 - current	Football Supporters Series
Athos	D6439	large	1956 - 1991	Characters from Literature Collection
	D6827	large	1988	Limited Edition of 1000 for Peter Jones China
	prototype	large	1988	Prototype colorway for Peter Jones China
	D6452	small	1956 - 1991	
	D6509	mini	1956 - 1991	
Auctioneer	D6838	large	1988	Special Edition of 5000 for Kevin Francis Ceramics, Collecting World Series
	prototype	large	1987	
Auld Mac	D5823	large	1938 - 1986	See also Owd Mac; Owd Mac backstamp with Auld Mac
	D5824	small	1938 - 1985	impressed on back continued until 1940
	D6253	mini	1946 - 1985	
	D6257	tiny	1946 - 1960	
Auxiliary Fireman	D6887	small	1991	Ltd Ed of 9500 for Lawleys By Post, Heroes of the Blitz Set
Bacchus	D6499	large	1959 - 1991	
	D6499	large	1960	Stoke-on-Trent Jubilee Issue
	D6505	small	1959 - 1991	
	D6521	mini	1960 - 1991	
Baden-Powell	D7144	small	1999	Limited Edition of 2500 for Travers Stanley Collections
Bahamas Policeman	D6912	large	1992	Special Edition of 1000, same D number as Snake Charmer
Baseball Player	D6624	large	1970	Pilot jug; two colorways known: red/green and blue/black
	D6878	small	1991 - current	Characters from Life Series
	D6878	small	1991	Limited Edition of 500 for Britannia Limited, special backstamp
	D6957	small	1993	Philadelphia Phillies issue. Ltd Ed 2500 for Strawbridge
	D6973	small	1994	Toronto Blue Jays issue. Limited Edition of 2500
Beefeater (GR handle)	D6206	large	1947 - 1953	
	D6206	large	1947	Yellow and gold handles
	D6233	small	1947 - 1953	
	D6233	small	1947	Yellow and gold handles
	D6251	mini	1947 - 1953	
	D6251	mini	1947	Yellow and gold handles

Character Jug Name	Model Number	Height, Inches	Production Life	Other Information
Beefeater (ER handle)	D6206	large	1953 - 1986	The London Collection, pink tunic
	D6206	large	1987 - 1996	Red tunic
	D6206	large	1978	Commemorative of last firing in bottle oven
	proto	large	1988	Keys for handle, has neither GR or ER
	D6233	small	1953 - 1986	Pink tunic
	D6233	small	1987 - 1996	Red tunic
	D6251	mini	1953 - 1986	Pink tunic
	D6251	mini	1987 - 1996	Red tunic
	D6806	tiny	1988	Red tunic, RDICC issue
Beethoven	D7021	large	1996 - current	Great Composers Series
Benjamin Franklin	D6695	small	1982 - 1989	
Betsy Trotwood	D6685	tiny	1982 - 1989	Charles Dickens Commemorative Tinies Set for Lawleys
Bill Shankley see Liverpool Centenary Jug				
Bill Sykes	D6981	large	1995	Limited Edition of 2500, Dickens Characters Collection
	D6684	tiny	1982 - 1989	Charles Dickens Commemorative Tinies Set for Lawleys
Blacksmith	D6571	large	1963 - 1983	Characters from Williamsburg Collection
	prototype	large	1963	Different hat and hairstyle
	D6578	small	1963 - 1983	
	D6585	mini	1963 - 1983	
Bonnie Prince Charlie	D6858	large	1990 - 1994	
Bootmaker	D6572	large	1963 - 1983	Characters from Williamsburg Collection
	prototype	large	1963	Different hairstyle and hat
	D6579	small	1963 - 1983	
	D6586	mini	1963 - 1983	
Bowls Player	D6896	small	1991 - 1995	Characters from Life Series
Brian Johnston see "Johnners"				
Britannia	D7107	small	1997	Special Edition of 1997 for Travers Stanley Collections
Buddy Holly	D7100	large	1998	Limited Edition of 2500
Buffalo Bill version 1	pilot	large	unknown	only 3 known
version 2	D6735	mid	1985 - 1989	Wild West Collection
Busker	D6775	large	1988 - 1991	London Collection
	prototype	large	1988	One man band handle
Buz Fuz	D5838	mid	1938 - 1948	Charles Dickens Characters Collection
	D5838	small	1948 - 1960	
		small	1982	Limited Edition of 2000 with Pickwick advertising
Cabinet Maker	D7010	large	1995	RDICC Spl Ed 1500, Char. from Williamsburg Collection
	D6659	large	1979	Prototype, same mold as Special Edition jug
Captain Ahab	D6500	large	1959 - 1984	
	D6506	small	1959 - 1984	
	D6522	mini	1960 - 1984	
Captain Bligh version 1	D6967	large	1995	1995 Jug of the Year
version 2	D7074	small	1997	Ltd Ed of 2500 for Lawleys, paired with Fletcher Christian
Captain James Cook version 1	D7077	large	1997 - current	
version 2	D7086	tiny	1997	Limited Edition of 2500 for Lawleys, Great Explorers Tinies Set
Cap'n Cuttle	D5842	mid	1938 - 1948	Two versions: green or brown hat
	D5842	small	1948 - 1960	Charles Dickens Characters Collection
Captain Henry Morgan	D6467	large	1958 - 1981	
	D6467	large	1959 - 1960	Commemorative of Stoke-on-Trent Jubilee Year
	D6469	small	1958 - 1981	
	D6510	mini	1960 - 1981	
Captain Hook version 1	D6597	large	1965 - 1971	
	D6601	small	1965 - 1971	
	D6605	mini	1965 - 1971	
version 2	D6947	large	1994	1994 Jug of the Year
Captain Scott	D7116	large	1998	
	D7082	tiny	1997	Limited Edition of 2500, Great Explorers Tinies Set
Cardinal	D5614	large	1936 - 1960	
	D6033	small	1939 - 1960	
	D6129	mini	1940 - 1960	
	D6258	tiny	1940 - 1960	
Caroler	D7007	mini	1995	Christmas Miniatures Series, USA RDICC distribution only
Catherine of Aragon version 1	D6643	large	1975 - 1989	Henry VIII and Six Wives Series
	proto	large	1974	Found with scroll or trumpet prototype handle
	D6657	small	1981 - 1989	
	D6658	mini	1981 - 1989	
version 2	D7041	tiny	1997	Limited Edition of 2500 for Lawleys, Six Wives of Henry VIII Set
Catherine Howard version 1	D6645	large	1978 - 1989	Henry VIII and Six Wives Series
	D6692	small	1984 - 1989	
	D6693	mini	1984 - 1989	
version 2	D7045	tiny	1997	Limited Edition of 2500 for Lawleys, Six Wives of Henry VIII Set
Catherine Parr version 1	D6664	large	1981 - 1989	Henry VIII and Six Wives Series
	D6751	small	1987 - 1989	
	D6752	mini	1987 - 1989	
version 2	D7046	tiny	1997	Limited Edition of 2500 for Lawleys, Six Wives of Henry VIII Set
Cavalier	D6114	large	1950 - 1960	
	D6114	large	1940 - 1950	With goatee
	D6173	small	1941 - 1960	

Character Jug Name	Model Number	Height, Inches	Production Life	Other Information
Celtic FC	D6925	mid	1992 - current	Football Supporters Series
Charles I version 1 version 2 see also "King Charles I"	D6995 D6985	tiny small	1994 1995	Ltd Ed of 2500 for Lawleys, Kings & Queens of Realm Set Ltd Ed of 2500 for Lawleys By Post, Paired with Oliver Cromwell
Charles Dickens version 1 version 2 version 3	D6676 D6901 D6939	tiny small large	1982 - 1989 1991 1995	Charles Dickens Commemorative Tinies Set for Lawleys Limited Edition of 7500 for RDICC Limited Ed of 2500, left handle: OliverTwist/Sairey Gamp/ Scrooge; right handle: Little Nell /Pickwick/Little Dorritt
Charlie Chaplin	D6949	large	1993	Limited Edition of 5000 for Lawleys By Post
Chef	D7103	small	1998 - current	New larger small size
Chelsea Pensioner	D6817 D6830 D6831 D6832 D6833	large large large large large	1989 - 1991 1988 1988 1988 1988	London Collection Limited Edition of 250 for Joseph Homes Limited Edition of 250 for D. H. Holmes Limited Edition of 250 for Higbee Co. Limited Edition of 250 for Strawbridge & Clothier
Chief Sitting Bull and George Armstrong Custer	D6712	large	1984	Limited Edition of 9500, The Antagonists Collection; Two Faced jug; found with both gray and brown eyed Sitting Bull
Chopin	D7030	large	1996 - current	Great Composers Series
Christopher Columbus version1 version 2 version 3	D6891 D6911 D7081	large small tiny	1991 - 1997 1992 1997	 RDICC issue, Limited Edition of 7500 Ltd Ed of 2500 for Lawleys, Great Explorers Tiny Set
Churchill - version1 version2 see also "Sir Winston Churchill" & "Winston Churchill"	D6170 D6170 D6170	large large large	1940 - 1941 unknown unknown	Older Churchill, white jug with two handles Younger Churchill, partially decorated, only three known Younger Churchill, full colorway, only three known
City Gent	D6815	large	1988 - 1991	London Collection
Clark Gable	D6709	large	1984	Celebrity Collection. Thought less than 100 made. Black haired colorway is known
Clown version 1 version 2	D5610 D6322 prototype D6834	large large large large	1937 - 1942 1951 - 1955 unknown 1989 - 1995	Red or brown hair White hair Black hair, authenticity has been questioned With hat, Circus Performers Series
Collector	D6796 D6906	large small	1988 - 1991 1991	Spl Ed of 5000 for Kevin Francis, Collecting World Series Special Edition of 1500
Confucius	D7003	large	1995	Limited Edition of 1750, Flambe Series
Cook & Cheshire Cat	D6842	large	1990 - 1991	Alice in Wonderland Series
Count Dracula	D7053	large	1997	1997 Jug of the Year, Monster Series
Cyrano De Bergerac	D7004	large	1995 - 1997	Characters from Literature Collection
D'Artagnan	D6691 D6764 D6765	large small mini	1982 - 1995 1987 - 1995 1987 - 1991	Characters from Literature Collection
David Copperfield	D6680	tiny	1982 - 1989	Charles Dickens Commemorative Tinies Set for Lawleys
Davy Crockett & Antonio Lopez de Santa Anna	D6729	large	1985	Limited Edition of 9500, Antagonists Series, Two Faced Jug
Dennis & Gnasher	D7005 D7033	large small	1995 - 1999 1996 - 1999	British Cartoon Series
Dennis Compton	D7076	small	1996	Ltd Ed of 9500 for Lawleys By Post, Sporting Heroes Series
Desperate Dan	D7006 D7034	large small	1995 - 1999 1996 - 1999	British Cartoon Series
Dick Turpin version 1 with mask up version 2 with mask down	D5485 D5618 D5618 D6128 D6951 D6528 D6535 D6542	large small small mini tiny large small mini	1935 - 1960 1936 - 1960 1936 1940 - 1960 1994 1960 - 1980 1960 - 1980 1960 - 1980	Early versions have RT on the butt of the pistol handle Marked "Souvenir from Bentalls 1936" Diamond Anniversary Set Horse handle
Dick Whittington	D6375 D6846	large large	1953 - 1960 1989	 Ltd Ed of 5000 for Guild of Specialist China and Glass
"Dickie" Bird (Harold Dennis) M.B.E.	D7068	small	1996	Ltd Ed of 9500 for Lawleys By Post, Sporting Heroes Series
Doc Holliday	D6731	mid	1985 - 1989	Wild West Collection
Don Quixote	D6455 D6460 D6511	large small mini	1957 - 1991 1957 - 1991 1960 - 1991	Characters from Literature Collection
Dr. Livingstone	D7085	tiny	1997	Ltd Ed of 2500 for Lawleys, Great Explorers Tinies Set
Dr. Watson	D7011	tiny	1996	Ltd Ed of 2500 for Lawleys, Sherlock Holmes Tinies Set
Drake version 1 see also "Sir Francis Drake" version 2	D6115 D6115 D6115 D6174	large large large small	1940 1940 1940 - 1960 1941 - 1960	Hatless with red tunic Hatless with green tunic

Character Jug Name	Model Number	Height, Inches	Production Life	Other Information
Duke of Wellington see also "Wellington"	D6848	large	1989	Limited Edition of 5000 (only 2500 produced) for UK International Ceramics, Great Generals Series
Earl Mountbatten of Burma version 1 version 2	D6851 D6944	small large	1989 1993	Ltd Ed of 9500 for Lawleys By Post, Heroic Leaders Set Limited Edition of 5000 for RDICC
Edward VII see also "King Edward VII"	D6993	tiny	1994	Ltd Ed of 2500 for Lawleys By Post, Kings & Queens of the Realm Set
Elephant Trainer	D6841 D6856 D6857	large large large	1989 - 1993 1989 1989	Circus Performers Series Limited Edition of 250 for Higbee Co. Limited Edition of 250 for Strawbridge & Clothier
Elf	D6942	mini	1993	Christmas Miniatures Series, USA RDICC distribution only
Elgar	D7118	large	1998 - current	Great Composer Series
Elizabeth I see also "Queen Elizabeth I"	D6992	tiny	1994	Ltd Ed of 2500 for Lawleys By Post, Kings & Queens of the Realm Set
Elvis Presley	pilot	large	1987	Proposed for Celebrity Collection, only two known
Engine Driver	D6823	small	1988	Limited Edition of 5000 for Lawleys, Journey Through Britain Series
Equestrian see Master				
Eric Knowles	D7130	small	1999	Limited Edition of 1500 for Lawleys By Post
Everton FC	D6926	mid	1992 - current	Football Supporters Series
Fagin	D6679	tiny	1982 - 1989	Charles Dickens Commemorative Tinies Set for Lawleys By Post
Falconer	D6533 D6798 D6800 D6540 D6547	large large large small mini	1960 - 1991 1987 1987 1960 - 1991 1960 - 1991	Limited Edition of 250 for Joseph Horne Limited Edition of 1000 for Peter Jones China
Falstaff	D6287 D6797 pilot D6385 prototype D6519	large large large small small mini	1950 - 1995 1988 1943 1950 - 1995 1998 1960 - 1981	Characters from Literature Collection Ltd Ed colorway of 1500 for UK Fairs with yellow tunic Pilot with green hat and red-orange tunic Prototype colorway for UK Fairs with yellow tunic
Farmer John	D5788 D5788 D5789	large large small	1938 1938 - 1960 1938 - 1960	Backstamp "Coleman's Compliments" Handle can be attached inside or outside of the large or small jugs
Fat Boy	D5840 D5840 D6139 D6142	mid small mini tiny	1938 - 1948 1948 - 1960 1940 - 1960 1940 - 1960	Charles Dickens Characters Collection
Field Marshall Montgomery see also "Monty" & "Viscount Montgomery of Alamein"	D6908	large	1992	Limited Edition of 2500, commemorating the 50th anniversary of the North African victory over Rommel
Fireman version 1 version 2	D6697 D6697 D6839	large large small	1983 1984 - 1991 1988	Designed for Griffiths Pottery House Ltd Ed of 5000 for Lawleys By Post, Journey Through Britain Set
Fisherman	pilot	large	unknown	
Fletcher Christian	D7075	small	1997	Ltd Ed of 2500 for Lawleys By Post; Paired with Captain Bligh , version2
Fortune Teller version 1 version 2	D6497 D6503 D6523 D6874	large small mini large	1959 - 1967 1959 - 1967 1960 - 1967 1991	 1991 Jug of the Year
Francis Rossi (Status Quo)	D6961 prototype	small small	1993 1993	Limited Edition of 2500, Paired with Rick Parfitt Prototype with red vest
Frankenstein's Monster	D7052	large	1996	Limited Edition of 2500, Monster Series
Freddie Truman	D7090	small	1997	Ltd Ed of 9500 for Lawleys By Post, Sporting Heroes Collection
Friar Tuck	D6321	large	1951 - 1960	
Gaoler	D6570 D6577 D6584	large small mini	1963 - 1983 1963 - 1983 1963 - 1983	Characters from Williamsburg Collection
Gardener version 1 version 2	D6630 D6630 D6634 D6638 D6867 D6868	large large small mini large small	1973 - 1980 1972 1973 - 1980 1973 - 1980 1990 - 1991 1990 - 1995	 Prototype colorway with red neckerchief Younger face Older face, Characters from Life Series,
General Custer	D7079	large	1997 - current	
General Eisenhower	D6937	large	1993	Special Edition of 1000 for UK International Ceramics, Great Generals Series
General Gordon	D6869	large	1991	Special Edition of 1500 for UK Intn'l Ceramics, Great Generals Series
General Patton	D7026	large	1996	Special Edition of 1000 for UK Int'l Ceramics, Great Generals Series
Genie	D6892 pilot	large large	1991 1990	Mythical Characters Series Flambe' pilot
Geoffrey Chaucer	D7029	large	1996	Limited Edition 1500, left handle: Friar, Wife of Bath, Squire, right handle: Knight, Princess, Miller. All on horseback.

Character Jug Name	Model Number	Height, Inches	Production Life	Other Information
George Harrison	D6727	mid	1984 - 1991	Beatles Set, distributed only in the UK
George Stephenson	D7093	large	1997	Limited Edition of 1848 for Lawleys By Post
George Tinworth	D7000	small	1995	RDICC issue
George Washington version 1	D6669	large	1982 - 1994	Issued for 250th anniversary of Washington's birth
	pilot	large	1981	Washington Monument handle
see also next listing	D6824	small	1989 - 1994	Issued for 200th anniversary of election as President
	D6825	mini	1989 - 1991	Issued for 200th anniversary of election as President
version 2	D6965	large	1995	Limited Edition of 2500, President's Collection
George III & George Washington	D6749	large	1986	Limited Edition of 9500, The Antagonists Collection, Two Faced Jug
Geronimo	D6733	mid	1985 - 1989	Wild West Collection
Gladiator	D6550	large	1961 - 1967	
	D6553	small	1961 - 1967	
	D6556	mini	1961 - 1967	
Glenn Miller	D6970	large	1994 - 1998	Jugs issued in 1994 include years of birth and death in mark
Golfer version 1	D6623	large	1971 - 1995	
	D6787	large	1987	Limited Edition colorway of 1000 for John Sinclair
	D6756	small	1987 - 1990	
	D6757	mini	1987 - 1992	
version 2	D6865	small	1990 - 1995	Characters from Life Series, found without #18
version 3	D7064	small	1997 - 1999	New larger small size
Gondolier	D6589	large	1964 - 1969	
	D6592	small	1964 - 1969	
	D6595	mini	1964 - 1969	
Gone Away	D6531	large	1960 - 1981	
	D6538	small	1960 - 1981	
	D6545	mini	1960 - 1981	
Graduate (male)	D6916	small	1991 - 1995	
Granny	D5521	large	1934 - 1940	Early toothless version
	D5521	large	1941 - 1983	Also with musical movement
	D6384	small	1953 - 1983	
	D6520	mini	1960 - 1983	
	D6954	tiny	1994	Diamond Anniversary Set
Groucho Marx	D6710	large	1984 - 1988	Celebrity Collection
	D6710	large	1984	Prototype with two Marx Brothers on handle
Guardsman version 1	D6568	large	1963 - 1983	Characters from Williamsburg Collection
	D6575	small	1963 - 1983	
	D6582	mini	1963 - 1983	
version 2	D6755	large	1986 - current	London Collection
	D6755	large	1986	Prototype with sword handle draped with Union Jack
	D6771	small	1987 - 1999	
	D6772	minl	1987 - 1991	
Gulliver	D6560	large	1962 - 1967	
	D6563	small	1962 - 1967	
	D6566	mini	1962 - 1967	
Gunsmith	D6573	large	1963 - 1983	Characters from Williamsburg Collection
	prototype	large	1963	Prototype with different hairstyle and handle
	D6580	small	1963 - 1983	
	D6587	mini	1963 - 1983	
Guy Fawkes	D6861	large	1990 - 1996	
	D6861	large	1990	Limited Edition of 750 for Canadian Art Show
Hamlet	D6672	large	1982 - 1989	Shakespearean Collection
Hampshire Cricketer	D6739	mid	1985	Limited Edition of 5000 for Hampshire Cricket Club
Handel	D7080	large	1997 - current	Great Composers Collection
Herold Dennis Bird see "Dickie" Bird				
Henry V version 1	D6671	large	1982 - 1989	Shakespearean Collection
	D6671	large	1982	With embossed handle
	D6671	large	1982	Yellow crown, gold & red colors missing
version 2	D6994	tiny	1994	Ltd Ed of 2500 for Lawleys, Kings & Queens of Realm Set
Henry VIII version 1	D6642	large	1975 - current	Henvry VIII and Six Wives Series
	D6642	large	1975	Prototype colorway, green jacket with yellow tunic
see also "King Henry VIII"	D6647	small	1979 - 1999	
	D6648	mini	1979 - 1991	
version 2	D6990	tiny	1994	Ltd Ed of 2500 for Lawleys, Kings & Queens of Realm Set
Henry Cooper	D7050	small	1996	Ltd Ed of 9500 for Lawleys, Sporting Heroes Collection
H. G. Wells	D7095	large	1998	Limited Edition of 1998
Home Guard	D6886	small	1991	Ltd Ed of 9500 for Lawleys, Heroes of the Blitz Collection
Humphrey Bogart	pilot	large	1985	Pilot for Celebrity Collection
Ian Botham	D7091	small	1998	Ltd Ed of 9500 for Lawley's, Sporting Heroes Series
Inspector Lestrade	D7012	tiny	1996	Ltd Ed of 2500 for Lawleys, Sherlock Holmes Tinies Set
Izaak Walton	D6404	large	1953 - 1982	
	D6404	large	1959 - 1960	Stoke-on-Trent Jubilee Year backstamp
Jack Hobbs	D7131	small	1999	Limited Edition of 5000, for Lawleys By Post
Jane Eyre & Mr. Rochester	D7115	small	1998	Limited Edition of 1500, double Character Jug

Character Jug Name	Model Number	Height, Inches	Production Life	Other Information
Jane Seymour version 1 version 2	D6646 D6746 D6747 D7043	large small mini tiny	1979 - 1990 1986 - 1990 1986 - 1990 1997	Henry VIII and Six Wives Collection Limited Ed. of 2500 For Lawleys By Post, Six Wives of Henry VIII Set
Jarge	D6288 D6295	large small	1950 - 1960 1950 - 1960	
Jefferson Hope	D7013	tiny	1996	Ltd. Ed. of 2500 for Lawleys By Post, Sherlock Holmes Tinies Set
Jesse Owens	D7019	large	1996	Character Jug of the Year
Jester	D5556 D5556 D6953 pilot	small small tiny XLarge	1936 - 1960 1936 1994	Green and yellow tassels may be reversed "Bentalls" backstamp Diamond Anniversary Set Two handled, two faced with smiling and frowning faces
Jimmy Durante	D6708	large	1985 - 1986	Celebrity Collection
Jockey version 1 version 2	D6625 D6629 D6877	large mid small	1971 - 1975 1974 1991 - 1995	Unique pilot Characters from Life Series
Johann Strauss II	D7097	large	1998 - current	Great Composers Series
John Barleycorn version 1 version 2	D5327 D5327 D5327 D5327 D5735 D6041 D6952 D6780	large large large large small mini tiny mid	1934 - 1960 1938 - 1939 ca 1930s 1978 1937 - 1960 1939 - 1960 1994 1988	First modern Character Jug, handle into jug rarer Coleman's Compliments backstamp Salt River Cement Works backstamp Limited Reproduction Edition of 7500 Diamond Anniversary Set Limited Edition of 600 for American Express
John Bull	pilot	large	unknown	Pilot in white finish or full colorway
John Doulton	D6656 D6656	small small	1980 - 1981 1981 - 1994	RDICC charter member issue, clock shows 8 o'clock RDICC new member issue, clock shows 2 o'clock
John Gilpin	pilot	large	1968	Only two known
John Lennon	D6725 D6797	mid mid	1984 - 1991 1987	Beatles Set, turquois jacket, distributed only in the UK Ltd Ed of 1000 for John Sinclair with red jacket
John Peel	D5612 D5612 D5731 D6130 D6259	large large small mini tiny	1936 - 1960 1950s 1937 - 1960 1940 - 1960 1947 - 1960	Found with both grey and black/orange handles Golden horn handle; base inscribed "Good Hunting Jocko"
John Shorter	D6880	small	1991	Limited Edition of 1500 for Australia Collectors Club
Johnners (Brian Johnston)	D7018	small	1995	Ltd Ed of 9500 for Lawleys By Post, Sporting Heroes Series
Johnny Appleseed	D6372	large	1953 - 1969	
Juggler	D6835 prototype	large large	1989 - 1991 1989	Circus Performers Series Prototype colorway with red shirt
King Arthur	D7055	large	1998	Ltd Ed of 1500 for Lawleys By Post, Paired with Merlin 2nd version
King Arthur & Guinevere	D6836	large	1989	Limited Edition of 9500, Star Crossed Lovers Collection; two faced jug
King Charles I see also "Charles I"	D6917	large	1992	Limited Edition of 2500, three handles: left Queen Henrietta, right Cromwell , plume in back
King Edward VII see also "Edward VII"	D6923	small	1992	RDICC issue
King Henry VIII see also "Henry VIII"	D6888	large	1991	Limited Edition of 1991; left handle: Anne Boleyn, Catherine of Aragorn, Jane Seymour; right handle : Anne of Cleves, Catherine Howard, Catherine Parr
King John	D7125	large	1999	Ltd Ed of 1500, RDICC issue, Paired with Richard III
King Philip of Spain	D6822	small	1988	Ltd Ed of 9500 for Lawleys, Paired with Queen Elizabeth I
Lawyer	D6498 D6504 D6524	large small mini	1959 - 1996 1959 - 1996 1960 - 1991	
Leeds United FC	D6928	mid	1992 - current	Football Supporters Series
Len Hutton	D6945	small	1993	Ltd Ed of 9500 for Lawleys By Post, Sporting Heroes Series
Leprechaun	D6847 D6847 D6899 D6899	large large small small	1991 - 1996 1990 1992 - 1996 1991	Special Edition of 500 for Site of the Green Special Edition of 500 for Site of the Green
Lewis Carrol	D7096	large	1998	1998 Character Jug of the Year
Little Mester Museum Piece	D6819	large	1988	Special Edition of 3500 for John Sinclair
Little Nell	D6681	tiny	1982 - 1989	Charles Dickens Commemorative Tinies Set
Liverpool Centenary Jug (Bill Shankley)	D6914	mid	1992	Limited Edition of 5500, for 100th Anniversary of Liverpool Football Club
Liverpool FC	D6930	mid	1992 - current	Football Supporters Collection
Lobster Man	D6617 D6783 D6620 D6652	large large small mini	1968 - 1991 1987 - 1989 1968 - 1991 1980 - 1991	Special colorway with blue-grey jersey Small with light blue jacket also found
London Bobby	D6744 D6762 D6763	large small mini	1986 - current 1986 - current 1987 - 1991	London Collection Hat embossed with badge increases value

Character Jug Name	Model Number	Height, Inches	Production Life	Other Information
Long John Silver	D6335	large	1952 - current	Characters from Literature Collection
	D6799	large	1987	Limited Edition colorway of 250 for D. H. Holmes
	D6386	small	1952 - current	
	D7138	small	1999	Colorway for Michael Doulton Treasure Chest events
	D6512	mini	1960 - 1991	
Lord Mayor of London	D6864	large	1990 - 1991	London Collection
Lord Nelson see also "Nelson" and "Vice-Admiral Lord Nelson"	D6336	large	1952 - 1969	Special backstamp "Battle of Trafalgar"
	D6336	large	1955	Three exist with unique backstamp "First Lord",
	D6336	large	1955	"First Sea Lord", or "Secretary"
Lord Nelson and Lady Hamilton	D7092	small	1997	Limited Edition of 1500. First double headed jug.
Louis Armstrong	D6707	large	1984 - 1988	Celebrity Collection
Lumberjack	D6610	large	1967 - 1982	Canadian Centenial Collection
	D6610	large	1967	Canadian Centennial Backstamp
	D6613	small	1967 - 1982	
	pilot	mini	unknown	Small number issued, 5 to 10 known to exist
Macbeth	D6667	large	1982 - 1989	Shakespearean Collection
	D6667	large	1981	Witches on handle face outward
Mad Hatter	D6598	large	1965 - 1983	Alice in Wonderland Collection
	D6748	large	1985	Limited Edition of 250 for Higbee
	D6598	large	unknown	Rare with 5 on hat
	D6598	large	1960s	Rare with red hat
	D6602	small	1965 - 1983	
	D6790	small	1987	Limited Edition of 500 for Higbee
	D6606	mini	1965 - 1983	
Mae West	D6688	large	1983 - 1985	Celebrity Collection
	D6688	large	1983	Limited Edition of 500 for American Express
Manchester United FC	D6924	small	1992 - current	Football Supporters Collection
Maori	pilot	large	1939	Two versions, serious and friendly faces
March Hare	D6776	large	1989 - 1991	Alice in Wonderland Collection
Marco Polo	D7084	tiny	1997	Produced for Lawleys By Post; Great Explorers Tinies Set
Marilyn Monroe	D6719	large	1983	Celebrity Collection, only two known to exist
Mark Twain	D6654	large	1980 - 1990	
	D6694	small	1983 - 1990	
	D6758	mini	1986 - 1990	
Master–known as "Equestrian" in the U.S.	D6898	small	1991 - 1995	Characters from Life Series
McCallum	D269	large	1930	Ivory glaze, 1000 pieces made
	D270	large	1930	Brown coloring, 1000 to 1500 pieces made
		large	unknown	Full colorway, blonde hair and beard
Mephistopheles	D5757	large	1937 - 1948	Two Faced Jug
	D5757	large	1937 - 1948	With rhyme verse
	D5758	small	1937 - 1948	With or without rhyme verse
Merlin version 1	D6529	large	1960 - 1998	Characters from Literature Collection
	D6536	small	1960 - 1998	
	D6543	mini	1960 - 1991	
version 2	D7117	large	1999	Ltd Ed 1500 for Lawleys By Post, Paired with King Arthur
Michael Doulton see also "Sir Henry Doulton and Michael Doulton"	D6808	small	1988 - 1990	Limited Edition of 9500, sold only at Michael Doulton events
Mikado	D6501	large	1959 - 1969	
	D6507	small	1959 - 1969	
	D6525	mini	1960 - 1969	
Miller of Bath Canterbury Tales Pilgrim	pilot	large	1987	Two pilots: one with wagon wheel handle, other with bagpipes handle
Mine Host	D6468	large	1958 - 1982	
	D6470	small	1958 - 1982	
	D6513	mini	1960 - 1982	
Minnie the Minx	D7036	small	1996 - 1999	British Cartoon Collection
Monty see also "Field Marshall Mongomery" & Viscount Montgomery of Alamein"	D6202	large	1946 - 1991	Yellow accents to badge on cap discontinued 1954
Mozart	D7031	large	1996 - current	Great Composers Collection
Mr. Bumble	D6686	tiny	1982 - 1989	Charles Dickens Commemortive Tinies Set for Lawleys By Post
Mr. Micawber version 1	D5843	mid	1938 - 1948	Charles Dickens Characters Series
	D6138	mini	1940 - 1960	
	D5843	small	1948 - 1960	
	D6143	tiny	1940 - 1960	
version 2		small	1985	Limited Edition of 100 with PickKwick advertising
version 3	D7040	large	1996	Limited Edition of 2500 for Australian market
Mr. Pickwick version 1 one of two jugs made in five different sizes	D6060	large	1940 - 1960	Charles Dickens Characters Series
	D5839	mid	1938 - 1948	
	D5839	small	1948 - 1960	
	D6254	mini	1947 - 1960	
	D6260	tiny	1947 - 1960	
version 2		small	1982	PickKwick Ltd Ed of 2000, plain whiskey bottle handle
		small	1984	PickKwick Ltd Ed of 2000, Jim Beam bottle handle
version 3	D6959	large	1994	Limited Edition of 2500 for Lawleys By Post
	D7025	small	1996	Limited Edition of 2500 for RDICC
Mr. Quaker	D6738	large	1985	Limited Edition of 3500 for Quaker Oats

Character Jug Name	Model Number	Height, Inches	Production Life	Other Information
Mrs. Bardell	D6687	tiny	1982 - 1989	Charles Dickens Commemorative Tinies Set for Lawleys
Mrs. Claus	D6922	mini	1992	Christmas Miniatures Series; USA RDICC distribution only
Mrs. Hudson	D7014	tiny	1996	Ltd Ed of 2500 for Lawleys By Post, Sherlock Holmes Tinies Set
Murray Walker	D7094	small	1997	Ltd Ed of 2500 for Lawleys By Post, Sporting Heroes Series
Napoleon version 1 version 2	D6941 D7001	large small	1993 1995	Limited Edition of 2000 Ltd Ed of 2500 for Lawleys By Post, Paired with Wellington
Napoleon & Josephine	D6750	large	1986	Limited Edition of 9500, Star Crossed Lovers Collection; two faced jug
Nelson see also "Lord Nelson" & "Vice-Admiral Lord Nelson"	D6963	small	1994 - 1995	RDICC issue
Neptune	D6548 D6552 D6555	large small mini	1961 - 1991 1961 - 1991 1961 - 1991	
Night Watchman	D6569 D6576 D6583	large small mini	1963 - 1983 1963 - 1983 1963 - 1983	Characters from Williamsburg Collection Known colorway with blue coat lapels
North American Indian	D6611 D6611 D6611 D6786 D6614 D6665	large large large large small mini	1967 - 1991 1967 1973 1987 1967 - 1991 1981 - 1991	Canadian Centenial Series Canadian Centennial backstamp Limited Edition of 180 for Okoboji Anniversary Limited Edition colorway of 1000 for John Sinclair Small Colorway with war paint and headress variation known Small and mini Sinclair colorways also known
Old Charley	D5420 D6761 D5527 D6791 D5527 D6046 D6144	large large small small small mini tiny	1934 - 1984 1986 1935 - 1984 1987 1935 - 1936 1939 - 1984 1940 - 1960	Limited Edition colorway of 250 for Higbee Limited Edition colorway of 500 for Higbee Bentalls backstamp
Old King Cole	D6036 D6036 D6037 D6037 D6871	large large small small tiny	1938 - 1939 1939 - 1960 1938 - 1939 1939 - 1960 1990	With yellow crown With yellow crown RDICC issue
Old Salt	D6551 D6782 D6554 D6557 D6557	large large small mini mini	1961 - current 1987 - 1990 1961 - current 1984 - 1991 1984	Special colorway, light and dark blue jersey Mermaid with open arm
Oliver Cromwell version 1 version 2	D6968 D6986	large small	1994 1995	Limited Edition of 2500, 2 handles: Fairfax & Charles I Ltd Ed of 2500 for Lawleys By Post, Paired with Charles I, version 2
Oliver Hardy	D7009	small	1996	Ltd Ed of 3500 for Lawleys By Post, Paired with Stan Laurel
Oliver Twist	D6677	tiny	1982 - 1989	Charles Dickens Commemorative Tinies Set for Lawleys By Post
Ornothologist	pilot	small	ca 1990	Developed but not released
Othello	D6673 D6673	large large	1982 - 1990	Shakespearean Collection Wearing white earing
Owd Mac see also "Auld Mac"	D5823 D5824	large small	1937 1937	Backstamp continued on Auld Mac incised jugs until 1940.
Paddy	D5753 D5768 D6042 D6145	large small mini tiny	1937 - 1960 1937 - 1960 1939 - 1960 1940 - 1960	Grey haired small prototype found
Parson Brown	D5486 D5529 D5529 D6955	large small small tiny	1935 - 1960 1935 - 1960 1935 - 1936 1994	Bentalls mark 1935 and 1936; Darley & Son mark 1936 Diamond Anniversary Tinies Set
Paul McCartney	D6724	mid	1984 - 1991	Beatles Set
Pearly Boy original version of "Arry", all marked as "Arry"	D6207 D6207 D6207 D6235 D6235 D6235 D6249 D6249 D6249	large large large small small small mini mini mini	1947 1947 1947 1947 1947 1947 1947 1947 1947	Blue coat with white buttons on hat Brown coat with white buttons on hat Brown coat with brown buttons on hat Blue coat with white buttons on hat Brown coat with white buttons on hat Brown coat with brown buttons on hat Blue coat with white buttons on hat Brown coat with white buttons on hat Brown coat with brown buttons on hat
Pearly Girl original version of "Arriette", all marked as "Arriette"	D6208 D6236 D6250	large small mini	1947 1947 1947	Version with brown coat found in large and small sizes
Pearly King	D6760 D6844	large small	1987 - 1991 1990 - 1991	London Collection
Pearly Queen	D6759 D6843	large small	1987 - 1991 1990 - 1991	London Collection
Pendle Witch	D6826	large	1989	Special Edition of 5000 for Kevin Francis Ceramics
Phantom of the Opera	D7017	large	1995	Limited Edition of 2500 for Lawley By Post, Monster Series
Pharaoh	D7028	large	1996	Limited Edition of 1500, Flambe Series

Character Jug Name	Model Number	Height, Inches	Production Life	Other Information
Pied Piper	D6403 D6403 D6462 D6514	large large small mini	1954 - 1980 1954 1957 - 1980 1960 - 1980	Prototype with white rat on handle
Pierre Trudeau	pilot	large	unknown	Only one known
Pilgrim Father	pilot	large	1969	Only one known
Piper	D6918	large	1992	Limited Edition of 2500
Plug (of the Bashstreet Kids)	D7035	small	1996 - 1999	British Cartoon Series
Poacher	D6429 D6781 D6464 D6515	large large small mini	1955 - 1995 1987 - 1989 1957 - 1995 1960 - 1991	Colorway with maroon coat and black hat
Policeman	D6852	small	1989	Ltd Ed of 5000 for Lawleys By Post, Journey Through Britain Set
Porthos	D6440 D6828 D6453 D6516	large large small mini	1956 - 1991 1988 1956 - 1991 1960 - 1991	Characters from Literature Collection Limited Edition colorway of 1000 for Peter Jones China
Postman	D6801	small	1988	Ltd Ed of 5000 for Lawleys By Post, Journey Through Britain Set
Prince Albert	D7073	small	1996	Ltd Ed of 2500 for Lawleys By Post, Paired with Queen Victoria, version 2
Professor Moriarty	D7015	tiny	1996	Ltd Ed of 2500 for Lawleys By Post, Sherlock Holmes Tinies Set
Punch & Judy	D6946	large	1993	Limited Edition of 2500, RDICC issue, two faced jug
Punch & Judy Man	D6590 D6593 D6596	large small mini	1964 - 1969 1964 - 1969 1964 - 1969	
Quasimodo	D7108	large	1998	Limited Edition of 2500 for Lawleys By Post, Monster Series
Queen Elizabeth I see also "Elizabeth I"	D6821	small	1988	Ltd Ed of 9500 for Lawleys By Post, Paired with King Philip of Spain
Queen Victoria version 1 see also "Victoria" version 2	D6816 D6788 D6913 D7072	large large small small	1989 - 1992 1988 1992 1996	Limited Edition colorway of 3000 for Specialist Guild Limited Edition of 1500 for Pascoe & Company Ltd Ed of 2500 for Lawleys By Post, Paired with Prince Albert
Rangers FC	D6929	mid	1992 - current	Football Supporters Series
Red Queen	D6777 D6859 D6860	large small mini	1987 - 1991 1990 - 1991 1990 - 1991	Alice in Wonderland Collection
Regency Beau	D6559 D6562 D6565	large small mini	1962 - 1967 1962 - 1967 1962 - 1967	
Richard III	D7099	large	1998	Ltd Edition of 1500, RDICC issue, Paired with King John
Rick Parfitt (Status Quo)	D6962	small	1993	Limited Edition of 2500, Paired with Francis Rossi
Ringmaster	D6863 D6863	large large	1990 - 1993 1990	Circus Performers Series Ltd Ed of 750 for 1990 Toronto Royal Doulton Weekend
Ringo Starr	D6726	mid	1984 - 1991	Beatles Set, distributed only in the UK
Rip Van Winkle	D6438 D6785 D6463 D6517	large large small mini	1955 - 1995 1987 1957 - 1995 1960 - 1991	Limited Edition colorway of 1000 for John Sinclair
Robin Hood version 1 version 2 version 3 version 4	D6205 D6234 D6252 D6527 D6534 D6541 pilot D6998	large small mini large small mini large large	1947 - 1960 1947 - 1960 1947 - 1960 1960 - 1992 1960 - 1992 1960 - 1992 1987 1996	Feather handle Bow and quiver handle; Characters from Literature Collection Only one known, handle on left Limited Edition of 2500, left handle: Friar Tuck & Sheriff of Nottingham; right handle: Maid Marian & Little John
Robinson Crusoe	D6532 prototype D6539 D6546	large large small mini	1960 - 1982 1960 1960 - 1982 1960 - 1982	Prototype with black beard
Romeo	D6670 prototype prototype	large large large	1983 - 1989 1982 1982	Shakespearean Collection Juliette on balcony handle Vial of poison over dagger handle
Ronald Reagan	D6718 D6718	large large	1984 1984	Ltd Ed of 5000 for Republican National Committee, only 2000 made Prototype with grey coat, green cord handle exists
Ronnie Barker	D7114	small	1998	Ltd Ed of 5000 for Lawley's By Post, Paired with Ronnie Corbett
Ronnie Corbett	D7113	small	1998	Ltd Ed of 5000 for Lawley's By Post, Paired with Ronnie Barker
Sailor	D6875 D6904 D6984	small small small	1991 - 1996 1991 1994	Comrades in Arms Set Limited Edition of 250, "On Guard for Thee" Canadian Set Special National Service Edition, rope handle
Sairey Gamp	D5451 D6770 D5528 D5528 D6789 D6045 D6146	large large small small small mini tiny	1935 - 1987 1986 1935 - 1987 1935 - 1936 1987 1939 - 1987 1940 - 1960	Charles Dickens Characters Series Limited Edition of 250 for Strawbridge & Clothier Known colorway with black hat Bentalls backstamp, Darley in 1936 Limited Edition of 500 for Strawbridge & Clothier

Character Jug Name	Model Number	Height, Inches	Production Life	Other Information
Sam Johnson	D6289	large	1950 - 1960	
	D6296	small	1950 - 1960	
Sam Weller one of two jugs made in five different sizes	D6064	large	1940 - 1960	Charles Dickens Characters Series
	D5841	mid	1938 - 1948	
	D5841	small	1948 - 1960	
	D6140	mini	1940 - 1960	
	D6147	tiny	1940 - 1960	
Samson & Delilah	D6787	large	1988 - 1991	Limited Edition of 9500, Star Crossed Lovers Collection; two faced jug
Sancho Panca	D6456	large	1957 - 1982	Different backstamps made with no change in value
	D6461	small	1957 - 1982	
	D6518	mini	1957 - 1982	
Santa Claus version 1	D6668	large	1981	Doll handle
	D6675	large	1982	Reindeer handle
	D6690	large	1983	Stocking with toys handle
version 2	D6704	large	1984 - current	Plain handle
	D6793	large	1988	Special Edition of 1000 for CVN, red candy cane handle
	D6794	large	1988	Special Edition of 5000 for HSN, wreath handle
	D6840	large	1989	Special Edition of 1000 for ACS, red/grn candy cane handle
	prototype	large		Candy cane handle colorway: roses and vine
	prototype	large		Candy cane handle colorway: rose blossoms
	prototype	large		Candy cane colorway: light green & dark green stripes
	prototype	large		Candy cane colorway: light green stripes
	pilot	large		Christmas cracker handle pilot
	D6705	small	1984 - current	Plain handle
	D6964	small	1996	Special Edition of 1000 for HSN, bell handle
	D6706	mini	1984 - 1991	Plain handle
	D6900	mini	1991	Limited Ed 5000, Christmas Mini Series, wreath handle
	D6950	tiny	1993	Special Edition of 2500 for Seaway, plain handle
	D6980	tiny	1994	Special Edition of 2500 for Seaway, candy cane handle
	D7020	tiny	1995	Special Edition of 2500 for Seaway, gift box handle
	D7060	tiny	1996	Special Edition of 2500 for Seaway, teddy bear handle
version 3	D7123	large	1998	Special Edition of 1500 for Pascoe & Co, tree handle
Scaramouche version 1	D6558	large	1962 - 1967	
	D6561	small	1962 - 1967	
	D6564	mini	1962 - 1967	
	D6814	large	1988 - 1991	Characters from Literature Collection
version 2	D6774	large	1987	Special Ed colorway of 1500 for Specialists Guild
Scarlet Pimpernel	pilot	large	unique	Only one known
Schubert	D7056	large	1997 - current	Great Composers Series
Scrooge	D6683	tiny	1982 - 1989	Charles Dickens Commemorative Tinies Set for Lawleys By Post
Shakespeare see also "William Shakespeare"	D6938	small	1993 - 1999	
Sheffield Wednesday FC	D6958	mid	1993 - current	Football Supporters Series
Sherlock Holmes	D7016	tiny	1996	Ltd Ed of 2500 for Lawleys By Post, Sherlock Holmes Tinies Set
Simon the Cellarer	D5504	large	1935 - 1960	
	D5616	small	1935 - 1960	
	D5616	small	1936	Souveir Edition of for Bentalls
	D6956	tiny	1994	Diamond Anniversary Set
Simple Simon	D6374	large	1953 - 1960	
Sir Francis Drake see also "Drake"	D6805	large	1988	Special Edition of 6000 for Specialists Guild
Sir Henry Doulton version 1	D6703	small	1984	RDICC issue depicting younger Henry Doulton
version 2	D7054	large	1996	Limited Edition of 1977 with two handles, left: Lambeth vase, right: Hannah Barlow with Lambeth rabbit
version 3	D7057	small	1997	Ltd Ed of 1997 for RDICC, depicting older Henry Doulton
Sir Henry Doulton & Michael Doulton	D6921	small	1992	Special Edition for Michael Doulton appearances; two faced jug
Sir Thomas More	D6792	large	1988 - 1991	Henvry VIII and Six Wives Series
Sir Winston Churchill see also "Churchill" & "Winston Churchill"	D6849	small	1989	Ltd Ed of 9500 for Lawleys By Post, Heroic Leaders Set
Sleuth	D6631	large	1973 - 1996	
	D6635	small	1973 - 1996	
	D6773	small	1987	Limited Edition colorway of 5000 for Lawleys By Post
	D6639	mini	1973 - 1991	
Smuggler	D6616	large	1968 - 1980	
	D6619	small	1968 - 1980	
	pilot	mini	unknown	
Smuts	D6198	large	1946 - 1948	
	prototype	large	1946	Prototype colorway with red tie
Snake Charmer	D6912	large	1992	Limited Edition of 2500 Bahamas Policeman has same D number
Snooker Player	D6879	small	1991 - 1995	Characters from Life Series
Snowman version 1	D6972	mini	1994 - current	Christmas Miniatures Series, US and RDICC distribution only
version 2	D7062	mini	1997	Limited Edition of 2000 for John Sinclair, scarf handle
	D7124	mini	1998	Limited Edition of 2000 for John Sinclair, stocking and gifts handle
		mini	1999	Limited Edition of 2000 for John Sinclair, handle to be determined
Soldier	D6876	small	1991 - 1996	Comrades In Arms Set
	D6816	small	1991	Limited Edition of 250, "On Guard For Thee" Canadian Set
	D6983	small	1994	National Service Edition, Jerry Can and haversack handle

Character Jug Name	Model Number	Height, Inches	Production Life	Other Information
St. George version 1	D6618	large	1968 - 1975	
	D7129	large	1998	Limited Edition of 2500 for Lawleys By Post
version 2	D6621	small	1968 - 1975	
Stan Laurel	D7008	small	1996	Ltd Ed of 3500 for Lawleys By Post, Paired with Oliver Hardy
Tam O'Shanter	D6632	large	1973 - 1979	
	prototype	large	1973	Colorway with red cloak is known
	D6636	small	1973 - 1979	
	D6640	mini	1973 - 1979	
Tchaikovsky	D7022	large	1996 - current	Great Composers Series
Terry Fox	D6881	large	1990	Limited Edition of 3
Thomas Jefferson	D6943	large	1994	Limited Edition of 2500, Presidential Series, only in US
Toby Gillette	D6717	large	1984	Limited Edition of 3
Toby Philpots	D5736	large	1937 - 1969	Early backstamps say "Toby Philpotts"
	D5737	small	1937 - 1969	
	D6043	mini	1939 - 1969	
	pilot	tiny	1994	Pilot for Diamond Anniversary Set
Tony Weller	D5531	xlarge	1936 - 1942	Only extra large jug ever issued by Royal Doulton
	D5531	large	1936 - 1960	
	D5530	small	1936 - 1960	
	D5530	small	1935 - 1966	Darley & Son or Bentalls backstamp
	D6044	mini	1939 - 1960	
Tottenham Hotspur FC	D	mid	1995 - current	Football Supporters Series
Touchstone	D5613	large	1936 - 1960	
Town Crier version 1	D6530	large	1960 - 1973	
	D6537	small	1960 - 1973	
	D6544	mini	1960 - 1973	
version 2	D6895	large	1991 - 1994	
Trapper	D6609	large	1967 - 1982	Canadian Centennial Series
	D6609	large	1967	Canadian Centennial backstamp
	D6612	small	1967 - 1982	
	pilot	mini	1983	Small number issued, 5 - 10 known to exist
Tutankhamen	D7127	small	1998	Ltd Ed of 1500 for Lawleys, Paired with Ankhesenamun
Ugly Duchess	D6599	large	1965 - 1973	Alice in Wonderland Series
	D6603	small	1965 - 1973	
	D6607	mini	1965 - 1973	
Ulysses S. Grant & Robert E. Lee	D6698	large	1983	Limited Edition of 9500, Antagonists Series
	Prototype	large	1983	Prototype with Washington Monument handle
	prototype	large	1983	Prototype with 4 stripe handpainted flag, not 7 stripe
Uncle Sam		small	1986	Limited Edition of 500 for Pickwick Wines & Spirits
	pilot	large	unknown	Pilot, white and full colored versions thought to exist
Uncle Tom Cobbleigh	D6337	large	1952 - 1960	
	pilot	unknown	1975	Never put into production
Uriah Heap	D6682	tiny	1982 - 1989	Charles Dickens Commemorative Tinies Set for Lawleys
Vasco de Gama	D7083	tiny	1997	Ltd Ed of 2500 for Lawleys, Great Explorers Tinies Set
Veteran Motorist	D6633	large	1973 - 1983	
	D6637	small	1973 - 1983	
	D6641	mini	1973 - 1983	
Vicar of Bray	D5615	large	1936 - 1960	
Vice-Admiral Lord Nelson see also "Lord Nelson" and "Nelson"	D6932	large	1993	1993 Character Jug of the Year
Victoria see also "Queen Victoria"	D6991	tiny	1994	Limited Edition of 2500, Kings & Queens of the Realm Set
Viking	D6496	large	1959 - 1975	
	D6502	small	1959 - 1975	
	D6526	mini	1960 - 1975	
Village Blacksmith	D6549	large	1991	Prototype, never put into production
Viscount Montgomery of Alamein see also "Monty" & "Field Marshall Montgomery"	D6850	small	1989	Limited Edition of 9500 for Lawleys By Post, Heroic Leaders Set
W.C. Fields	D6674	large	1983 - 1986	Celebrity Collection
	D6674	large	1983	Special Edition of 1500 for American Express
W.G. Grace	D7032	large	1996 - current	
	D6845	small	1989	Limited Edition of 9500
Walrus & Carpenter	D6600	large	1965 - 1979	Alice in Wonderland Series
	D6604	small	1965 - 1979	
	D6608	mini	1965 - 1979	
Wellington see also "Duke of Wellington"	D7002	small	1995	Limited Edition of 2500 for Lawleys By Post, Paired with Napoleon, version 2
Wife of Bath Canterbury Tales Pilgrim	pilot	large	1987	Only one known
Wild Bill Hickock	D6736	mid	1985 - 1989	Wild West Collection

Character Jug Name	Model Number	Height, Inches	Production Life	Other Information
William Shakespeare version 1 see also "Shakespeare" version 2	D6689 D6933	large large	1983 - 1991 1992	Shakespearean Collection Limited Edition of 2500; left handle: Romeo, Falstaff, and Titania; right handle: Juliette, Hamlet, and Touchstone
version 3	D7136	large	1999	1999 Character Jug of the Year
Willie Carson	D7111	small	1998	Ltd Ed of 2500 for Lawleys, Sporting Heroes Series
Winston Churchill see also "Churchill" and "Sir Winston Churchill"	D6907 D6934 D6934	large small small	1992 1992 - current 1992	1992 Character Jug of the Year Prototype with Union Jack shield handle
Witch	D6893	large	1991	Mystical Series
Wizard	D6862 D6909	large small	1990 - 1996 1992 - 1998	Mystical Series
Wyatt Earp	D6711	mid	1985 - 1989	Wild West Series
Yachtsman version 1	D6626 pilot	large small	1971 - 1979	Only two known
version 2	D6820 D6820	large large	1988 - 1991 1988	Limited Edition of 750 for Canadian Doulton Show
Yeoman of Guard	D6873 D6883 D6882 D6885 D6884	large large large large large	1991 - current 1990 1990 1990 1900	London Collection Limited Edition of 50 for Dillards Limited Edition of 75 for Horne Limited Edition of 75 for Strawbridge & Clothier Limited Edition of 250 for Higbee

Photographs of Royal Doulton Burslem Character Jugs

The character jug photos following are principally from the collections of Tony D'Agostino, Irene and Vern Rouf and Neil Galatz, supplemented by and with the cooperation of Royal Doulton specialist dealers and Royal Doulton and Co, Ltd.

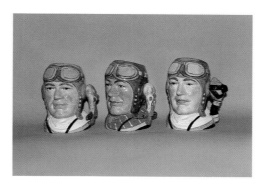

Airman Character Jugs; left to right – from the Comrades in Arms D6870, On Guard for Thee D6903, and National Service D6982 sets

Abraham Lincoln large Character Jug D6936

Ankhesenamun small Character Jug D7128 (Courtesy of Royal Doulton)

Aladdin's Genie flambé large Character Jug D6971

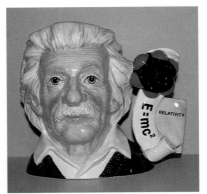

Albert Einstein Character Jug D7023

Alfred Hitchcock Character Jugs D6987 with white and pink shower curtain color-ways

Angler Character Jugs; small size D6866 1st version on left and mid size D7065 2nd version on right

Anne Boleyn character jugs. Clockwise: version 1, large D6644, miniature D6651,small D6650,and version 2, tiny D7042 sizes

Anne of Cleves character jugs. Clockwise: version 1, large with ears up D6653, miniature D6754 and small D6753 with ears down, and version 2 tiny D7044 sizes

Angel Character Jug D7051

Antique Dealer Character Jug D6807

Annie Oakley Character Jug D6732

Anthony and Cleopatra two sided Character Jug D6728, showing both sides

Apothecary Character Jugs in large D6567, small D6574, and miniature D6581sizes

Aramis Character Jug in large D6441,miniature D6508 and small D6454 sizes

Limited Edition colorway Aramis jug produced for Peter Jones China D6829

'Ard of Earing Character Jug in large D6588, miniature D6594 and small D6591 sizes

'ARP Warden small Character Jug D6872

Large size Auctioneer Limited Edition Character Jug D6838

Set of 'Arriette Character Jugs in large D6208, tiny D6256 ,miniature D6250 and small D6236 sizes

Artful Dodger tiny Character Jug D6678

Set of 'Arry Character Jugs in large D6207, tiny D6255 ,miniature D6249 and small D6235 sizes

Athos Character Jug in large D6439, small D6452, and miniature D6509 sizes

Limited edition colorway Athos jug produced for Peter Jones China D6827

Large regular issue Athos Character Jug alongside the only known prototype colorway

Group of Auld Mac Character Jugs in large D5823, miniature D6253, tiny D6257, and small D5824 sizes

Rear view of Owd Mac jug on left and Auld Mac on right, note incised names

Small size Auxiliary Fireman Character Jug D6887

Bacchus Character Jug in large D6499, miniature D6521, and small D6506 sizes

Baden - Powell small Character Jug D7144, Founder of The Scout Association of the U.K. (courtesy of Travers Stanley Collections)

Bahamas Policeman large Character Jug D6912

Large Baseball Player 1st version with blue cap D6624, only known pilot jug

Large Baseball Player 1st version with red cap D6624, only known pilot jug (courtesy of Princess and Barry Weiss)

Baseball Player small D6878, Philadelphia Phillies edition D6957, and Toronto Blue Jays edition D6973

Beefeater Character Jug in small D6233, large D6206, tiny D6806 and miniature D6251 sizes

Beefeater large prototype jug with keys handle (courtesy of Francis Salmon)

Backside of Beefeater jugs showing variety handle colors; pink, yellow, gold, and red

Large Beethoven Character Jug D7021

Benjamin Franklin small Characater Jug D6695

Betsy Trotwood tiny Character Jug D6685

Bill Shankley Character Jug D6914, also known as the Liverpool Centenary Jug

Large Bill Sykes Character Jug D6981 with tiny Character Jug D6684

Large Bonnie Prince Charlie Character Jug D6858

Small Bowls Player Character Jug D6896

Set of Blacksmith Character Jugs, from left to right large D6571, miniature D6585, and small D6578

Blacksmith large prototype jug on left and regular production version on right

Backside of Blacksmith and Bootmaker jugs with prototype versions on right

Small Britannia Character Jug D7107

Group of Bootmaker Character Jugs, left to right Large D6572, miniature D6586, and small D6579

Bootmaker large prototype jug on right and regular production version on left

Buffalo Bill 2nd version Character Jug in mid size D6735

Buddy Holly large Character Jug D7100

Buffalo Bill 1st version pilot Character Jug in large size (From the collection of Ann and Joe Nemes)

Left to rigth: mid size Buz Fuz D5838, small Buz Fuz D5838, and small Buz Fuz advertising jug

199

Large size Busker jug D6775

Large Cabinet Maker jug D7010

Captain Hook in large D6597, miniature D6605, and small D6601 sizes; large sized second version D6947 on right

Captain Ahab Character Jugs in large D6500, miniature D6522, and small D6506

Large D6967 and small D7074 sized Captain Bligh jugs

Set of Cardinal Character Jugs in large D5614, small D6033, miniature D6129, and tiny D6258 sizes

Large D7077 and tiny D7086 sized Captain James Cook Character Jugs; liquor container on right

Captain Henry Morgan in large D6467, small D6469, and miniature D6510 sizes

Clockwise from left, a group of Catherine of Aragon jugs in large D6643, miniature D6658, small D6657, and tiny D7041 sizes

Large D7116 and tiny D7082 sizes of Captain Scott Character Jug

Cap'n Cuttle mid sized D5842 and small D5842 Character Jugs

Catherine of Aragon jugs with prototype handles, one with scroll and one with bugle (courtesy of Francis Salmon)

Miniature Caroler Character Jug
D7007

Clockwise from left, Catherine Howard Character
Jugs in large D6645, miniature D6693, small
D6692, and tiny D7045 sizes

Clockwise from left, Catherine Parr Character Jugs in
large D6664, miniature D6752, small D6751, and
tiny D7046 sizes

Cavalier Character Jug in large D6114 and
small D6173 sizes; large Cavalier with goatee
jug D6114

Large size Cavalier Protoype Colorway
with Scarlett Plume (Courtesy of Ron
Smith)

Charles Dickens Character Jugs in large D6676, tiny
D6939, and small D6901 sizes

Charlie Chaplin Character Jug
in large size D6949

Mid size Chef Character Jug
D7013

Chelsea Pensioner large jug
D6817, the three limited edition
jugs are identical in appearance
but with different backstamps

City Gent Character Jug in large
size D6815

Charles I - see King
Charles I

Chief Sitting Bull and George Armstrong Custer
large two-sided Character Jug D6712 showing
both sides

Large Chopin Character Jug D7030

Christopher Columbus in large D6891, tiny D7081,
and small D6911 sizes

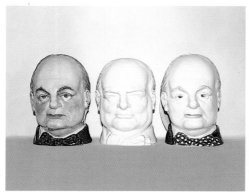

Group of large Churchill two-handled Character Jugs D6170; full colorway on left, partial colorway on right, cream colorway in center

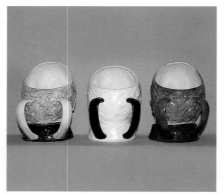

Rear view of the three Churchill jugs showing the loving cup handles

Large Clark Gable Character Jug D6709

Three colorways of the 1st version Clown Character Jug D5610: brown hair, white hair and red hair

Backside of three Clown jugs showing the handles (Courtesy of Princess and Barry Weiss)

Large sized 2nd version Clown Character Jug D6834

Confucius large sized Character Jug in flambe' finish D7003

Cook and Cheshire Cat large Character Jug D6842

Count Dracula large Character Jug D7053

David Copperfield tiny Character Jug D6680

Collector Character Jug in small D6906 and large D6796 sizes

Cyrano De Bergerac large sized Character Jug D7004

Three D'Artagnan Character Jugs in large D6691, miniature D6765, and small D6764 sizes

Davy Crockett and Antonio Lopez de Santa Anna two-sided Character Jug D6729, showing both sides

Character Jugs based on an English cartoon; Dennis and Gnasher in large D7005 and small D7033 sizes

Desperate Dan, another British cartoon based Character Jug, in both large D7006 and small D7034 sizes

Small Dennis Compton Character Jug D7076

Small "Dickie" Bird M. B. E. Character Jug D7068

Doc Holliday mid-size Character Jug D6731

Limited Edition Dick Whittington jug D6846 on left and the original version D6375 on the right

Clockwise from left, Dick Turpin Character jugs in large D5485, small D5618, miniature D6128, and tiny D6951 sizes; first version with the face mask up

Second version Dick Turpin with the face mask down; large D6528, miniature D6542, and small D6535 sizes

Don Quixote Character Jug in large D6455, small D6460, and miniature D6511 sizes

Hatless Drake Character Jug D6115 in both red and green colorway

Backside of the same pair of hatless Drake jugs

Left to right: Drake second version in large D6115 and small D6174 sizes, and large Sir Francis Drake jug D6805

Dr. Livingstone tiny Character Jug D7085

Dr. Watson tiny Character Jug D7011

Large Duke of Wellington Character Jug D6848 on left and small Wellington D7002 on right

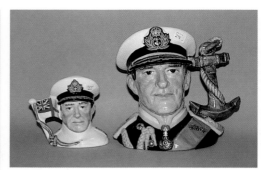

Earl Mountbatten of Burma Character Jugs; small D6851 and large D6944

Large Elephant Trainer Character Jug, D6841. Ltd Ed for Higbee D6856, and Ltd Ed for Strawbridge D6857 same size and colorway

Small sized Engine Driver Character Jug D6823

Large Elgar Character Jug D7118

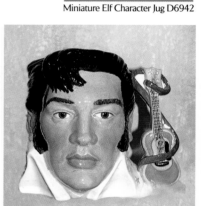

Miniature Elf Character Jug D6942

Small sized Eric Knowles Character Jug D7130 (courtesy of Royal Doulton)

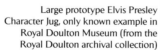

Edward VII - see King Edward VII
Elizabeth I - see Queen Elizabeth I
Equestrian - see Master

Large prototype Elvis Presley Character Jug, only known example in Royal Doulton Museum (from the Royal Doulton archival collection)

Fagin tiny Character Jug D6679

Falconer Character Jugs - left to right large Horne Ltd Ed D6798, miniature D6547, small D6540, and large D6533

Large Falconer Character Jug D6533 on left and Peter Jones colorway D6800 on right

Falstaff Character Jugs; large D6287, miniature D6519, and small D6385

Falstaff Character Jugs; left to right - regular issue in large D6287 and small D6385, UK Fairs colorways in small prototype and large D6797

Falstaff large 1943 pilot colorway (courtesy of Ron Smith)

Farmer John large D5788 with handle on the outside of jug; Farmer John small D5789 and large with handle inside of jug

Pilot Fisherman Character Jug, believed unique

Set of Fat Boy Character Jugs; mid-size D5840, small D5840, miniature D6139, and tiny D6142 sizes

Field Marshall Montgomery - see Monty

Large Fireman Character Jug D6697, first version

Second version of the Fireman small size Character Jug D6839

Small sized Fletcher Christian Character Jug D7075

Arsenal FS Character Jug D6927

Aston Villa FS Character Jug D6931

Celtic FS Character Jug D6925

Everton FS Character Jug D6926

Leeds United FS Character Jug D6928

Liverpool FS Character Jug D6930

Manchester United FS Character Jug D6924

Rangers FS Character Jug D6929

Sheffield Wednesday FS Character Jug D6958

Tottenham Hotspur FS Character Jug

Clockwise from left, Fortune Teller 1st version Character Jug in large D6497, small D6503, and miniature D6523 sizes; large 2nd version D6874

Francis Rossi small Character Jug D6961

Francis Rossi colorway trial jug with red vest

Frankenstein's Monster Character Jug in large size D7052

Freddie Truman small Character Jug D7090

Friar Tuck large size Character Jug D6321

Gaoler Character Jug in three sizes; large D6570, miniature D6584, and small D6577

1st version Gardener Character Jug in large D6630, miniature D6638, and small D6634 sizes

1st version large size Gardener with red scarf colorway (courtesy of Francis Salmon)

2nd version Gardener jug in large D6867 and small D6868 sizes

Large size General Eisenhower Character Jug D6937

General Gordon large Character Jug D6869

General Patton large size Character Jug D7026

General Custer Character Jug in large size D7079

Large Genie Character Jug, in normal colorway D6892 on left and flambe prototype on right

Geoffrey Chaucer two-handled Character Jug D7029

Mid size George Harrison Character Jug D6727, part of the Beetles set

George Stephenson large Character Jug D7093

Small George Tinworth Character Jug D7000

George Washington 1st version jug in large D6669, small D6824, and miniature D6825 sizes; large size second version D6965 ; above shows reverse of George III &George Washington two-faced jug

George Washington prototype jug with Washington monument handle

George III & George Washington two-faced Character Jug D6749

Geronimo mid sized Character Jug D6733

Gladiator Character Jug in large D6550, small D6553, and miniature D6556 sizes

Glenn Miller Character Jug in large size D6970

1st version Golfer Character Jug in large D6623, miniature D6757, and small D6756 sizes

1st version large size Golfer in color-way for John Sinclair limited edition D6787

2nd version Golfer in small D6865 size on left and 3rd version Golfer in mid size D7064 on right

Gondolier Character Jug in large D6589, miniature D6595, and small D6592 sizes

Gone Away Character Jug in large D6531, miniature D6545, and small D6538 sizes

Small Graduate Character Jug D6916

Clockwise from left, Group of Granny Character Jugs in large D5521, small D6384, tiny D6954, and miniature D6520, plus a large toothless Granny jug on the right

Groucho Marx Character Jugs, prototype handle on left and regular issue D6710 on right

Close up of handle on Groucho Marx Jug, copyright problems halted production (courtesy of Princess and Barry Weiss)

Three 1st version Guardsman Character Jugs from the Williamsburg collection in large D6568, small D6575, and miniature D6582 sizes

2nd version of the Guardsman Character Jug, in large D6755, miniature D6772, and small D6771 sizes

Gulliver Character Jug in large D6560, miniature D6566, and small D6563 sizes

Gunsmith Character Jug in large D6573, miniature D6587, and small D6580 sizes

Large Guy Fawkes Character Jug D6861

Large Hamlet Character Jug D6672

Hampshire Cricketer mid sized Character Jug D6739

Large Handel Character Jug D7080

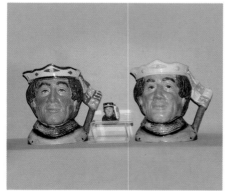

Henry V large jug D6671 with embossed handle on left, tiny D6994 Character Jug in center and yellow crown on right

Clockwise from left, Group of Henry VIII Character Jugs in large D6642, small D6647, tiny D6990 and miniature D6648 sizes; King Henry VIII large two-handled jug D6888 on the right

Small size Henry Cooper
Character Jug D7050

Harold Dennis Bird –
see "Dickie" Bird

Large H. G. Wells Character Jug
D7095

Small Home Guard Character Jug
D6886

Humphrey Bogart pilot jug; located in
Royal Doulton Museum, only one
known to exist (from the Royal
Doulton archival collection)

Small Ian Botham Character Jug
D7091

Tiny Inspector Lestrade
Character Jug D7012

Izaak Walton Character Jug in large
size D6404

Jarge Character Jug in large D6288 and small
D6295 sizes

Jack Hobbs, D7131, photo not available at time of publication.

Tiny Jefferson Hope
Character Jug D7013

Jane Eyre and Mr. Rochester double
headed jug D7115

Clockwise from left: Jane Seymour Character Jug
grouping in large D6646, miniature D6747, small
D6746 and tiny D7043 sizes

Large size Jesse Owens Character
Jug D7019

Pair of small Jester Character Jugs D5556 showing
reversed tassle colorways; tiny Jester Character Jug
D6953 in center

Pilot Jester two sided Character Jug; extra large
size with two handles (from the Royal Doulton
archival collection)

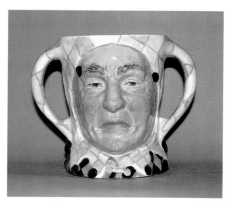

Reverse side of two sided, two handled pilot
Jester Character Jug

Large Jimmy Durante Character Jug D6708

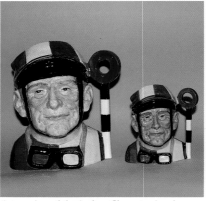

1st version of the Jockey Character Jug; large D6625 size on left, mid-size pilot that was not put into production on right

Large Johann Strauss II Character Jug D7097

2nd version of the Jockey Character Jug in the small size D6877

John Barleycorn 2nd version jug in mid-size D6780 produced as a limited edition for American Express

John Barleycorn Character Jug in large D5327, small D5735, miniature D6041, and tiny D6952 sizes; an early production large size with handle inside the jug on the right

Left pilot Character Jug of John Bull in large size; right John Bull liquor container

Small size John Doulton Character Jug D6656 with clock showing 8 o'clock

Mid size D6725 John Lennon Character Jug, John Sinclair colorway on right D6797

John Peel Character Jug group in large D5612, miniature D6130, tiny D6259, and small D5731 sizes

Large pilot Character Jug of John Gilpin; not produced, only two jugs known (courtesy of Princess and Barry Weiss)

Small Johnners (Brian Johnston) Character Jug D7018

Large John Peel jug with golden horn handle, only one known (courtesy of Francis Salmon)

Large Johnny Appleseed Character Jug D6372

Small John Shorter Character Jug D6880

Large Juggler Character Jugs; prototype color-way on left and regular issue D6825 on right

Large King Arthur Character Jug D7055

Large King Arthur & Guinevere two-sided Character Jug D6836, both sides shown

King Edward VII small Character Jug D6923 on the left and Edward VII tiny Character Jug D6993 on the right

Left to right: King Charles I large Character Jug D6917, Charles I 1st version jug in tiny size D6995, Charles I 2nd version small sized jug D6985

Large King John Character Jug D7125

Leprechaun Character Jug in large D6847 and small D6899 sizes

King Henry VIII - see Henry VIII

Small size King Phillip of Spain Character Jug D6822

Lawyer Character Jug in large D6498, miniature D6524, and small D6504 sizes

Large Lewis Carroll Character Jug D7096

Large Little Mester Museum Piece Character Jug D6819

Small size Len Hutton Character Jug D6945

Liverpool Centenary jug - see Bill Shankley

Tiny Little Nell Character Jug D6681

Lobster Man Character Jug grouping; left to right - large D6617, small D6620, and miniature D6652 sizes

London Bobby Character Jugs in small D6762, large D6744, and miniature D6763 sizes; early versions had embossed badge on hat rather than decals

Long John Silver Character Jug in large D6335, miniature D6512, and small D6386 sizes

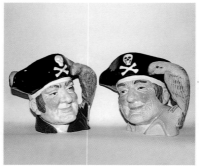

Large Long John Silver D6799 colorway for D. H. Holmes Company with standard version

Small Long John Silver D7138, available only at Michael Doulton Treasure Chest events in the UK

Lord Mayor large Character Jug, D6864

Lord Nelson Trafalger backstamp

From left to right: Lord Nelson large Character Jug D6336; small Nelson jug D6963; and large Vice-Admiral Lord Nelson jug D6932

Lord Nelson and Lady Hamilton double jug D7092 in small size

Louis Armstrong Character Jug in large size D6707

Lumberjack Character Jug in large D6610, pilot miniature, and small D6613 sizes

Large MacBeth Character Jug D6667

Early version of large MacBeth Character Jug with witches facing out on handle (courtesy of Francis Salmon)

Large size Mae West Character Jug D6688

Left to right: Mad Hatter jug in large D6598, small D6602, and miniature D6606 sizes; Mad Hatter Higbee colorways small D6790 and large D6748; top is a prototype colorway

Large Mad Hatter red hat prototype colorway (courtesy of Francis Salmon)

Large March Hare Character Jug D6776

Marco Polo tiny Character Jug D7084

Front view of the large size Maori Character Jug

Side view of Maori jug

Marilyn Monroe large Character Jug D6719, only two copies known (from the Royal Doulton archival collection)

The Master Small Character Jug D6898, known as Equestrian in the United States

Mark Twain Character Jug in small D6694, large D6654, and miniature D6758 sizes

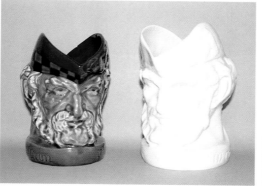

McCallum promotional Character Jug in kingsware and cream glazes

McCallum promotional Character Jug in full coloway (courtesy of Princess and Barry Weiss)

Mephistopheles two-sided Character Jug; large smiling face D5757, small frowning face D5758

Reverse side of Mephistopheles two-sided Character Jug; large frowning face D5757, small smiling face D5758

Merlin Character Jug 1st version in large D6529, miniature D6543, and small D6536 sizes

Merlin large Character Jug 2nd version D7117

Mikado Character Jug in large D6501, small D6507, and miniature D6525 sizes

Two Miller of Bath prototype jugs in large size, note different handles on the jugs (from the Royal Doulton archival collection)

Mine Host Character Jug in large D6468, small D6470, and miniature D6513 sizes

Small Michael Doulton D6808 and reverse of Sir Henry Doulton and Michael Doulton two sided jug D6921

Minnie the Minx small Character Jug D7036

Large Mozart Character Jug D7031

Left to right: large Monty D6202, small Viscount Montgomery of Alamein D6850, and large Field Marshall Montgomery D6908

Mr. Micawber 2nd version advertising jug

Mr. Micawber Character Jugs, counter clockwise left to right large 3rd version D7040, 1st version tiny D6143, miniature D6138, mid size D5843, and small D5843 sizes

Mr. Pickwick character jug in five sizes, clockwise: large D6060, small D5839, mid D5839, tiny D6260 and miniature D6254

Mr. Pickwick 3rd version jug in large D6959 and small D7025 sizes

Mr. Pickwick small 2nd version advertising jugs with plain and Jim Beam handles

Large Mr. Quaker Character Jug D6738

Tiny Mrs. Bardell Character Jug D6687

Mrs. Claus miniature Character Jug D6922

Tiny Mrs. Hudson Character Jug D7014

Small Murray Walker Character Jug D7094

Front side of Napoleon & Josephine large Character Jug D6750; small D7001 and large D6941 size Napoleon jugs

Napoleon & Josephine two-sided Character Jug showing both sides

Neptune Character Jug in large D6548, miniature D6555, and small D6552 sizes

Night Watchman Character Jug in large D6569, miniature D6583, and small D6576 sizes

North American Indian Character Jug in large D6611, small D6614, miniature D6665, and large Sinclair colorway D6786

Old Charley Character Jug large D6761 and small D6791 Higbee colorways, regular issue tiny D6144, miniature D6046, large D5420, and small D5527 sizes

Old King Cole Character Jug original issue with yellow crown in large D6036 and small D6037; regular issue with gold crown large D6036, and tiny D6871; small D6037 above

Old Salt Character Jug in large size D6554, early miniature with open arm, miniature D6557, and small D6554 sizes

Large Old Salt jug regular issue on left and colorway on right D6782

Oliver Cromwell Character Jug; left and right: 2nd version small size D6986, 1st version two handled large jug D6968

Small Oliver Hardy Character Jug D7009

Nelson
-- see Lord Nelson

Tiny Oliver Twist Character Jug D6677

Small prototype Character Jug of Ornothologist

Large size Othello Character Jug D6673

Paddy Character Jug in large D5753, small D5768, miniature D6042, and tiny D6145 sizes

Paddy comparison of small sized gray hair prototype on left and regular issue on right

Parson Brown Character Jug in large D5486, miniature D6955, and small D5429 sizes

Mid sized Paul McCartney Character Jug D6724, one of four Beatles jugs

Pearly Boy jugs; large D6207 with brown coat and white buttons, miniature D6249 blue coat and brown coat, small D6235 brown coat, large blue coat; top small blue coat

Pearly Girl Character Jugs in large D6208, miniature D6250, and small D6250 sizes

Pearly Girl small colorways in blue coat and brown coat

Pearly King Character Jug in large D6760 and small D6844 sizes

Pearly Queen Character Jug in large D6759 and small D6843 sizes

Large Pendle Witch Character Jug D6826

Large Phantom of the Opera Character Jug D7017

Large Pharaoh Character Jug in flambé finish D7028

Group of Pied Piper Character Jugs; large D6403, small D6462 and miniature D6514sizes

Large prototype Pied Piper jug with one white rat handle on right and regular issue three rats on left (courtesy of Francis Salmon)

Large Pierre Trudeau pilot Character Jug (courtesy of Jocelyn Lukins)

Large Pilgrim Father pilot Character Jug (courtesy of Francis Salmon)

Large Piper Character Jug D6918

Small Plug of the Bashstreet Kids Character Jug ,D7035

Poacher Character Jug group, left to right large D6429, miniature D6515, and small D6464 sizes

Large size regular issue Poacher jug on left and large 1980s colorway on right D6781

Porthos Character Jug group, left to right large D6440, miniature D6516, small D6453, and large Peter Jones China colorway D6828

Small Policeman Character Jug D6852

Small Postman Character Jug D6801

Small Prince Albert Character Jug D7073

Professor Moriarty tiny Character Jug D7015

Large Punch and Judy two-sided Character Jug D6946 showing both sides

Punch and Judy Man Character Jug in small D6593, large D6590, and miniature D6596 sizes

Large Quasimodo Character Jug D7108

Small Queen Elizabeth I D6821 on left, tiny Elizabeth I D6992 on right

From left to right: Queen Victoria 1st version Character Jug left in large D6816 and right in small D6913; 2nd version small D7072 above; and Victoria tiny jug D6991 below

Red Queen Character Jug in large D6777, small D6859, and miniature sizes D6860

Regency Beau Character Jugs in large D6559, small D6562, and miniature D6565 sizes

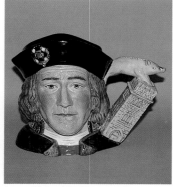

Large Richard III Character Jug D7099

Clockwise from left Rip Van Winkle Character Jugs in large D6438, small D6463, large John Sinclair colorway D6785, and miniature D6517

Small Rick Parfitt Character Jug D6962

Large Ring Master Character Jug D6863

Mid size Ringo Starr Character Jug D6726, one of the four Beatles

Robin Hood 1st verion Character Jug in large D6205, miniature D6252, and small D6234 sizes

Robin Hood 2nd verion in large D6527, miniature D6541, and small D6534 sizes

Robin Hood 3rd version large pilot jug

Robin Hood 4th version large two-handled jug D6998

Robinson Crusoe Character Jugs in large D6532, small D6539, and miniature D6546

Robinson Crusoe large color trial with black beard on right with standard version on left

Prototype Romeo jug with Juliet on balcony handle

Large Romeo Character Jug D6670

Small Sailor left to right; Comrads in Arms D6875, On Guard for Thee D6904, and National Service Edition D6984

Ronnie Barker & Ronnie Corbett - see Two Ronnies

Ronald Reagan large Character Jugs, on left regular issue D6718, on right color trial with pale blue coat

Prototype Romeo jug with daggar and vial of poison handle (courtesy of Francis Salmon)

Sam Johnson Character Jug in large D6289 and small D6296 sizes

Samson & Delilah two-faced large Character Jug D6787 showing both sides

Sam Weller Character jugs in large D6064, miniature D6140, small D5841, tiny D6147, and intermediate D5841

Clockwise from left Sairey Gamp Character Jugs large D5451, small D5528, large Strawbridge & Clothier colorway D6770, miniature D6045, tiny D6146, and small Strawbridge & Clothier colorway D6789

Sancho Panca Character Jug in large D6456, small D6461, and miniature D6518 sizes

Large Santa Claus Character Jug with doll handle D6668

Large Santa Claus Character Jug with reindeer handle D6675

Large Santa Claus Character Jug with stocking handle D6690 on left and prototype stocking handle on right

Clockwise from left Santa Claus Character Jugs all with plain handles; large D6704, small D6705, tiny D6950, and miniature D6706

Large Santa Claus jugs with candy cane handles; red stripe for CVN D6793, red and green stripe for ACS D6840

Santa Claus Character Jugs with wreath handles; large D6794 for HSN and limited edition miniature D6900

Tiny Santa Claus jugs commissioned by Seaway China; plain handle D6950, candy cane handle D6980, teddy bear handle D7060, and gift boxes handle D7020

Pair of large, unreleased Santa Claus Character Jugs with prototype handles; rose vine on left and roses on right (from the Royal Doulton archival collection)

Small Santa Claus Character Jug with bell handle D6964 for HSN

Pair of large, unreleased Santa Claus Character Jugs with prototype candy cane handles; green and black stripe on left and green and white stripe on right (from the Royal Doulton archival collection)

Large pilot Santa Claus Character Jug with Christmas cracker handle (from the Royal Doulton archival collection)

Close up view of the Christmas cracker handle

Large Santa Claus Character Jug with tree handle for Pascoe D7123

1st version Scaramouche Character Jug in large D6558, small D6561, and miniature D6564 sizes

2nd version Scaramouche Character Jug; large colorway D6774 for Specialist China and large standard version D6814

Large pilot Scarlet Pimpernel Character Jug (courtesy of Princess and Barry Weiss)

Shakespeare - see William Shakespeare

Large Schubert Character Jug D7056

Tiny Scrooge Character Jug D6683

Tiny Sherlock Holmes Character Jug D7016

Sir Henry Doulton Character Jugs; left to right - reverse side of jug, small D6703, and small D7057

Simon the Cellarer Character Jug in large D5504, small D5616, and tiny D6956 sizes

Large size Simple Simon Character Jug D6374

Sir Henry Doulton and Michael Doulton small two-sided Character Jug D6921 showing both sides

Sir Francis Drake - see Drake
Sir Winston Churchill - see Winston Churchill

Large Sir Henry Doulton two handled Character Jug D7054

Large Sir Thomas Moore Character Jug D6792

Sleuth Character Jug in large D6631, miniature D6639, small D6635, and small Lawley's By Post commission D6773

Smuggler Character Jug in large D6616 and small D6619 sizes

221

Large Smuts Character Jug D6198, regular issue on left and color trial prototype on right

Large Snake Charmer Character Jug D6912

Small Snooker Player Character Jug D6879

Miniature Snowman Character Jugs; top row 1st version D6972 and 1997 John Sinclair issue D7062; bottom 1998 John Sinclair issue

St. George Character Jug 1st version in large D6618 and small D6621

Large St. George Character Jug 2nd version D7129

Small Soldier Character Jugs; Comrades in Arms jug D6876, National Service edition D6983, and On Guard for Thee Canadian issue D6816

Tam O'Shanter Character Jug in large D6632, small D6636, and miniature D6640 sizes

Tam O'Shanter red cloak color trial large Character Jug

Tchaikovsky large Character Jug D7022

Small Stan Laurel Character Jug D7008

Large Terry Fox Character Jug D688(from the Royal Doulton archival collection)

Large Thomas Jefferson Character Jug D6943

Large Toby Gillette Character Jug D6717

Toby Philpots Character Jug in large D5736, miniature D6043, and small D5737 sizes

Tiny pilot Toby Philpots Character Jug

Tony Weller Character Jug in extra large D5531, large D5531 above, small D5530, and miniature D6044 sizes

Touchstone large Character Jug D5613

Town Crier Character Jugs; 1st version large D6530, small D6537, and miniature D6544; large 2nd version D6895

Trapper Character Jugs in large D6609 size, miniature size pilot, and small D6612 size

Tutankhamen small size Character Jug D7127

Two Ronnies small Character Jugs; Ronnie Barker D7114 on left and Ronnie Corbett D7113 on right

Ugly Duchess Character Jugs in large D6599, small D6603, and miniature D6607 sizes

Ulysses S. Grant & Robert E. Lee two-sided large Character Jug D6698 showing both sides

Ulysses S. Grant & Robert E. Lee two-sided large prototype Character Jug with Washington Monument handle

Uncle Sam large uncolored pilot Character Jug

Small Uncle Sam advertising character jug

Large Uncle Tom Cobleigh Character Jug D6337

Large Uncle Tom Cobleigh pilot Character Jug (courtesy of Francis Salmon)

Uriah Heep tiny Character
Jug D6682

Vasco de Gama tiny
Character Jug D7083

Vice-Admiral Lord Nelson - see Lord Nelson
Victoria - see Queen Victoria
Viscount Montgomery of Alamein - see Monty

Veteran Motorist Character Jug in large D6633, small
D6637, and miniature D6641 sizes

Large Vicar of Bray Character
Jug D5615

Village Blacksmith extra large pilot
Character Jug

Viking Character Jug in small D6502, large D6496, and
miniature D6526 sizes

Large W. C. Fields Character Jug
D6674

W. G. Grace Character Jug in large D7032,
and small D6845

Walrus and Carpenter Character Jug in small D6604, large
D6600, and miniature D6608 sizes

Wellington - see Duke of Wellington

Large Wife of Bath pilot Character Jug
(from the Royal Doulton archival
collection)

Wild Bill Hickock mid size Character
Jug D6736

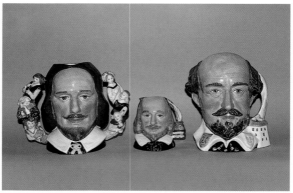

William Shakespeare Character Jugs; left large 2nd version two-
handled jug D6933, center small size Shakespeare jug D6938,
right 1st version large size jug D6938

Large William Shakespeare 3rd
version character jug D7136

Small Willie Carson Character
Jug D7111

Mid-sized Wyatt Earp Character
Jug D6711

Winston Churchill small prototype with Union Jack handle

Winston Churchill Character Jugs; left small
D6934, center large D6907; right Sir Winston
Churchill small jug D6849

Large Witch Character Jug D6893

Wizard Character Jug in large D6892 and small
D6909 sizes

Yachtsman Character Jugs; 1st version large D6626 and
small pilot; 2nd version large D6820

Yeoman of the Guard Character Jug
D6873; all limited edition jugs are
same size and colorway

Three Musketeers Peter Jones colorway large Character
Jugs; Aramis D6829, Athos D6827, and Porthos D6828

Christmas Series of miniature Character Jugs; top
row - Elf, Angel, and Caroler; bottom row - Mrs.
Claus, Snowman, and Santa Claus

Charles Dickens tiny Character Jug set; top row left to
right - Charles Dickens, Artful Dodger, Bill Sykes,
Betsy Trotwood, David Copperfield, and Fagin; bottom
row left to right - Little Nell, Mr. Bumble, Mrs. Bardell,
Oliver Twist, Scrooge, and Uriah Heep

Diamond Anniversary tiny Character Jug set;
top to bottom - John Barleycorn, Dick
Turpin, Jester, Granny, Parson Brown, and
Simon the Cellerar

Kings and Queens of the Realm tiny Character
Jug set; top row left to right - Charles I, Victoria,
and Edward VII; bottom row left to right - Henry
V, Henry VIII, and Elizabeth I

Queens of Henry VIII tiny Character Jug set; top row left to right - Anne of Cleves, Catherine Howard, and Catherine Parr; bottom row left to right - Cahterine of Aragon, Anne Boleyn, and Jane Seymour

Sherlock Holmes tiny Character Jug set; top row left to right - Inspector Lestrade, Professor Moriarty, and Jefferson Hope; bottom row left to right - Dr. Watson, Sherlock Holmes, and Mrs. Hudson

Great Explorers tiny Character Jug set; top to bottom - Marco Polo, Columbus, Vasco de Gama, Captain Cook, Dr. Livingstone, and Captain Scott

Royal Doulton Burslem Toby Jugs

Toby Jug Name	Model Number	Height, Inches	Production Life	Other Information
Albert Saggar, potter	D6745	4	1986	Doultonville Collection, RDICC issue
Alderman Mace, mayor	D6766	4	1987 - 1991	Doultonville Collection
Bearded Spook	D7133	5 1/4	1998	Ltd Ed of 1500 for Lawleys, Paired with Spook
Best is Not Too Good	D6107 D6977	4 1/2 1 1/2	1939 - 1960 1994	Limited Edition of 2500 By Post, Tiny Tobies Set
Betty Bitters, barmaid	D6716	4	1984 - 1990	Doultonville Collection
Cap'n Cuttle	D6266	4 1/2	1948 - 1960	Charles Dickens Toby Set
Captain Prop, pilot	D6812	4	1989 - 1991	Doultonville Collection
Captain Salt, sea captain	D6721	4	1985 - 1991	Doultonville Collection
Charles Dickens	D6997	5	1995	Limited Edition of 2500 for Lawleys By Post
Charlie Chaplin		11	1918	removable bowler hat
Charlie Cheer, clown	D6768	4	1987 - 1991	Doultonville Collection
Charrington Toby	D8074 D8074 D8074	9 1/4 9 1/4 9 1/4	1937 - 1938 1938 - 1939 1934 - 1938	inscribed on base "One Toby Leads to Another" inscribed on base "Charrington's" inscribed on base "Toby Ale"
Cliff Cornell		9 1/4 9 1/4 9 1/4 5 1/2 5 1/2 5 1/2	1956 1956 1956 1956 1956 1956	blue suit, approximately 500 made dark brown suit, approximately 500 made light brown suit, approximately 250 made blue suit, approximately 375 made dark brown suit, approximately 375 made light brown suit, less than 100 made
Clown	D6935	5 1/2	1992	Limited Edition of 3000
Dr. Jeckel and Mr. Hyde	D7024	5	1996 - 1998	two sided jug
Dr. Pulse, physician	D6723	4	1985 - 1991	Doultonville Collection
Falstaff	D6062 D6063	8 1/2 5 1/4	1939 - 1991 1939 - 1991	
Fat Boy	D6264	4 1/2	1948 - 1960	Charles Dickens Toby Set
Father Christmas	D6940	5	1993	Limited Edition of 3500
Fire King	D7070	5	1997	Limited Edition of 1500, Paired with Ice Queen
Flora Fuchsia, florist	D6767	4	1987 - 1990	Doultonville Collection
Fred Fearless, fireman	D6809	4	1989 - 1991	Doultonville Collection
Fred Fly, fisherman	D6742	4	1986 - 1991	Doultonville Collection
George Robey		10 1/2	ca 1925	detachable hat as a cover
Happy John	D6031 D6070 D6979	9 5 1/2 2 1/2	1939 - 1991 1939 - 1991 1994	Limited Edition of 2500, Tiny Tobies Set
Henry VIII	D7047	3 1/2	1996	Limited Ed of 2500, Set with Character Jugs of his six wives
Honest Measure	D6108 D6974	4 1/4 2 1/2	1939 - 1991 1994	Limited Edition of 2500, Tiny Tobies Set
Huntsman	 H090 D6320	7 3/4 8 7	ca 1910 - 1927 ca 1919 - 1930 1950 - 1991	Kingsware colorway in browns Red or orange coat, with or without silver rim
Ice Queen	D7071	5	1997	Limited Edition of 1500, Paired with Fire King
Jester version 1 version 2 version 3	pilot D6910 D7109	9 5 5	ca 1981 1992 1998	Only one known Limited Edition of 2500 Limited Edition of 1500, Paired with Lady Jester
John Wesley		11+	ca 1925	only two known, inscribed base
Jolly Toby	D6109 D6109 D6976	6 1/2 6 1/2 2	1939 - 1991 1994	Colorway with blue breeches Limited Edition of 2500, Tiny Tobies Set
Judge and Thief	D6988	5	1995 - 1998	Two sided jug
King & Queen of Clubs	D6999	5 1/4	1995	Limited Edition of 2500, two sided jug

Toby Jug Name	Model Number	Height, Inches	Production Life	Other Information
King & Queen of Diamonds	D6969	5 1/4	1994	Limited Edition of 2500, two sided jug
King & Queen of Hearts	D7037	5 1/4	1996	Limited Edition of 2500, two sided jug
King & Queen of Spades	D7087	5 1/4	1997	Limited Edition of 2500, two sided jug
Lady Jester	D7110	5	1998	Limited Edition of 1500, Paired with D7109 Jester
Len Lifebelt, lifeboatman	D6811	4	1989 - 1991	Doultonville Collection
Leprechaun	D6948	5 1/4	1994	Limited Edition of 2500
Lewis Carroll	D7078	6 1/2	1997	Limited Edition of 1500 for Lawleys By Post, on centenary of his death
Madam Crystal, clairvoyant	D6714	4	1984 - 1989	Doultonville Collection
Major Green, golfer	D6740	4	1986 - 1991	Doultonville Collection
Mansion House Dwarf	D7135	4 3/4	1998	Limited Edition of 1500 for Lawleys By Post
Mike Mineral, miner	D6741	4	1986 - 1989	Doultonville Collection
Miss Nostram, nurse	D6700	4	1983 - 1991	Doultonville Collection
Miss Studious, schoolmistress	D6722	4	1985 - 1989	Doultonville Collection
Monsieur Chasseur, chef	D6769	4	1987 - 1991	Doultonville Collection
Mr. Brisket, butcher	D6743	4	1986 - 1991	Doultonville Collection
Mr. Furrow, farmer	D6701	4	1983- 1989	Doultonville Collection
Mr. Litigate, lawyer	D6699	4	1983 - 1991	Doultonville Collection
Mr. Micawber	D6262	4 1/2	1948 - 1960	Charles Dickens Toby Set
Mr. Pickwick	D6261	4 1/2	1948 - 1960	Charles Dickens Toby Set
Mr. Tonsil, towncrier	D6713	4	1984 - 1991	Doultonville Collection
Mrs. Loan, librarian	D6715	4	1984 - 1989	Doultonville Collection
Old Charley	D6030 D6069 D6978	8 3/4 5 1/2 2 1/2	1939 - 1960 1939 - 1960 1994	Limited Edition of 2500, Tiny Tobies Set
Old Father Time	D7069	6 1/2	1996	Limited Edition of 2500 for Lawleys By Post
Pat Parcel, postman	D6813	4	1989 - 1991	Doultonville Collection
Rev. Cassock, clergyman	D6702	4	1983 - 1990	Doultonville Collection
Sairey Gamp	D6263	4 1/2	1948 - 1960	Charles Dickens Toby Set
Sam Weller	D6265	4 1/2	1948 - 1960	Charles Dickens Toby Set
Sgt. Peeler, policeman	D6720	4	1985 - 1991	Doultonville Collection
Sherlock Holmes	D6661	8 3/4	1981 - 1991	Inscribed "50th Anniv. Death of Doyle"
Sir Francis Drake	D6660	9	1981 - 1991	Inscribed "400th Anniversary of Circumnavigation of the World"
Spook	D7132	6 1/4	1998	Ltd Ed of 1500 for Lawleys By Post, Paired with Bearded Spook
Squire	D6319	6 5 3/4	1910 - 1917 1950 - 1969	Kingsware finish with silver rim Modification of Simeon stoneware Standing Man
Toby XX (Double XX)	D6088 D6975	7 2	1939 - 1969 1994	Modification of Harry Simeon design Limited Edition of 2500, Tiny Tobies Set
Tom Bowling		11 1/2		by Charles Vyse, Chelsea
Town Crier	D6920	5	1992	Limited Edition of 2500
Winston Churchill	D6171 D6171 D6172 D6172 D6175 D6175	9 9 5 1/2 5 1/2 4 4	1940 1941 - 1991 1940 1941 - 1991 1940 1941 -1991	Backstamp: Prime Minister of Britain - 1940 Backstamp: Prime Minister of Britain - 1940 Backstamp: Prime Minister of Britain - 1940

Photographs of Royal Doulton Burslem Toby Jugs

The Best is Not Too Good Toby Jug; 4 1/2 inches tall D6107, and 1 1/2" tall D6977

Falstaff Toby Jug 8 1/2" tall D6062 and 4 1/4" tall D6063

Fire King Toby Jug 5" tall D7070 on left and Ice Queen Toby Jug 5" tall D7071 on right

Charles Dickens Toby Jug, 5' tall, D6997

Charlie Chaplin Toby Jug on left and George Robey Toby Jug on right

Charlie Chaplin and George Robey Toby Jugs with their hats removed

Charrington 9 1/4" tall Toby Jugs D8074; left to right - Toby Ale, One Toby Leads to Another, and Charringtons

Cliff Cornell Toby Jugs in 9 1/4" and 5 1/2 sizes and three colorways; brown, blue and tan suit; small tan jug is very rare.

Albert Sagger, the Doultonville potter, 4" tall D6745, RDICC issue

Set of 25 Doultonville Tobies; top row left to right - Fred Fly, Mr. Brisket, Mike Mineral, Major Green, Alderman Mace, Charlie Cheer, Flora Fuchsia, Monsieur Chasseur, Pat Parcel, Capt. Prop, Len Lifebelt, Fred Fearless, and Albert Sagger; bottom row left to right - Rev. Cassock, Miss Nostrum, Mr. Furrow, Mr. Litigate, Mr. Tonsil, Betty Bitters, Madame Crystal, Mrs. Loan, Dr. Pulse, Miss Studious, Sgt. Peeler, and Capt. Salt

1983 Doultonville Toby Jug introductions - Rev. Cossack D6702, Miss Nostrum D6700, Mr. Furrow D6701, and Mr. Litigate D6699

1984 Doultonville Toby Jug introductions - Mr. Tonsil D6713, Betty Bitters D6716, Madame Crystal D6714, and Mrs. Loan D6715

1985 Doultonville Toby Jug introductions - Dr. Pulse D6723, Miss Studious D6722, Sgt. Peeler D6720, and Capt. Salt D6721

1986 Doultonville Toby Jug introductions - Fred Fly D6742, Mr. Brisket D6743, Mike Mineral D6741, and Major Green D6740

1987 Doultonville Toby Jug introductions - Alderman Mace D6766, Charlie Cheer D6768, Flora Fuchsia D6767, Monsieur Chasseur D6769

1989 Doultonville Toby Jug introductions - Fred Fearless D6809, Len Lifebelt D6811, Capt. Prop D6812, and Pat Parcel D6813

Dr. Jekyl and Mr. Hyde two-sided Toby Jug, 5" tall, D7024 showing both sides

Henry VIII 3 1/2" tall Toby Jug D7047

Honest Measure Toby Jug, 4 1/4" tall D6108 and 2 1/2" tall D6974

Happy John Toby Jug 9" tall D6031, 5 1/2" tall D6070, and 2 1/2" tall D6979

Huntsman Toby Jug; 1910 Kingsware version on left 7 3/4" tall, 1920s red coat version in center 8" tall, and modern issue 7" tall D6320

Pilot Jester Toby Jug 9" tall (from the Royal Doulton archival collection)

Jester Toby Jug 5" tall D7109 on left , Lady Jester Toby Jug 5" tall D7110 on right

Jolly Toby 6 1/2" tall D6109 and 2" tall D6976

Judge and Thief two-sided Toby Jug 5" tall D7024 showing both sides

King and Queen of Clubs two-sided Toby Jug 5 1/4" tall D6999 showing both sides

King and Queen of Diamonds two-sided Toby Jug 5 1/4" tall D6969 showing both sides

King and Queen of Hearts two-sided Toby Jug 5 1/4" tall D7037 showing both sides

King and Queen of Spades two-sided Toby Jug 5 1/4" tall D7087 showing both sides

Lewis Carroll Toby Jug 6 1/2" tall D7078

Mansion House Dwarf Toby Jug 4 3/4" tall D7135

Limited edition 5" tall Toby Jugs; left to right - Jester D6910, Town Crier D6920, Clown D6935, Leprechaun D6948, and Father Christmas D6940

Old Father Time Toby Jug 6 1/2" tall D7069

Old Charley Toby Jug 8 3/4" tall D6030, 5 1/2" tall D6069, and 2 1/2" tall D6978

Sherlock Holmes Toby Jug 8 3/4" tall D6661 on the left, Sir Francis Drake Toby Jug 9" tall D6660 on the right

John Wesley Toby Jug over 11" tall

Seated Dickens Toby Jugs, all 4 1/2" tall; from left to right - Mr. Pickwick D6261, Mr. Micawber D6262, Sam Weller D6265, Sairey Gamp D6263, Fat Boy D6264, and Cap'n Cuttle D6266

Spook Toby Jug 5 3/4" tall D7132 on left and Bearded Spook 5 1/4" tall D7133 on right

Squire Toby Jug; 1910 Kingsware version 6" tall on left and modern version 5 3/4" tall D6319 on right

Winston Churchill Toby Jug 9"tall D6171, china version 8 1/2" tall D6171, 5 1/2" tall D6172, and 4" tall D6175

Toby XX 7" tall D6088 and 2" tall D6975

Due to the popularity of Royal Doulton Character and Toby Jugs, several fake jugs have appeared on the market; fake meaning created with the intention to deceive. These jugs are clearly of inferior quality and bear improper Doulton marks. For the experienced collector, these jugs pose no problem. However, less experienced folks can be fooled, including antiques and collectibles dealers. In addition, numerous makers, particularly the Japanese, have copied Royal Doulton jugs. These are not meant to be fakes, but only copies. In most instances the maker has applied its own maker's mark to the jug so it is not difficult to identify it as a copy.

Photographs of Royal Doulton Fakes and Copies are from the Collection of Bill Cumming.

Fake Royal Doulton Character and Toby Jugs

Character and Toby Jug Name	Height, Inches	Other Information
John Barleycorn Character Jug	7	Standard crown and lion mark with Manchester England. Doulton has no Manchester factory
Ordinary Toby Jug	8	Fake Doulton Lambeth mark of 1891 - 1902, the outer wheel is the wrong shape.
	5	Incomplete or damaged mark, misproportioned crown and lion

Auld Mac Royal Doulton small jug on left and miniature copy on right

Cardinal Royal Doulton small jug on left, copy sugar bowl on right

Jester small Royal Doulton jug on left with two small copies and a mid-sized copy

John Barleycorn large Royal Doulton jug on left and large fake with incorrect Royal Doulton backstamp on right

John Barleycorn small Royal Doulton jug on left and small copy on right

John Peel and Fat Boy miniature Royal Doulton jugs on left and copies on right

Johnny Appleseed large Royal Doulton jug on left and large copy on right

John Barleycorn Royal Doulton backstamp on left and fake Doulton backstamp on right

Old Charley large and small Royal Doulton jugs on left and copies on right

Paddy large plaster of Paris copy on left and small Royal Doulton jug on right

Mr. Pickwick small Royal Doulton jug on left and copy on right

Parson Brown large Royal Doulton jug on left and shrunken copy on right

Old King Cole, two copies flanking the Royal Doulton small jug in the center

Sairey Gamp large Royal Doulton jug on left and large plaster of Paris copy on right

Lumberjack small Royal Doulton jug on the left and a copy on the right

For further details on Royal Doulton Character and Toby Jugs, refer to *The Character Jug Collector's Handbook*, Francis Joseph Publishing; *The Charlton Standard Catalogue of Royal Doulton Beswick Jugs*, Charlton Press; and *Collecting Royal Doulton Character and Toby Jugs*, self-published by Jocelyn Lukins.

The following tables include the various derivative items produced based on the Character Jug designs. As it was prolific in its production of Character Jugs, Royal Doulton also offered a wide range of derivative wares.

Royal Doulton Burslem Derivative Products

Ashpots or Ash Bowls	Model Number	Height, Inches	Production Life
Auld Mac	D6006	3	1938 - 1960
Farmer John	D6007	3	1938 - 1960
Old Charley	D5925	3	1938 - 1960
Paddy	D5926	3	1938 - 1960
Parson Brown	D6008	3	1938 - 1960
Sairey Gamp	D6009	3	1938 - 1960

Ash Trays	Model Number	Height, Inches	Production Life
Dick Turpin	D5601	3 1/4	1936 - 1960
John Barleycorn	D5602	3 1/2	1936 - 1960
Old Charley	D5599	3 1/4	1936 - 1960
Parson Brown	D5600	3 1/2	1936 - 1960

Bookends	Model Number	Height, Inches	Production Life	Other Information
Dr. Watson	D7039	7 3/4	1996 - 1997	*Adventures of Sherlock Holmes* on spine
	D7039	7 3/4	1997 - current	*The Memoirs of Sherlock Holmes* on spine
Falstaff	D7089	7 3/4	1997 - current	
Henry V	D7088	7 3/4	1997 - current	
Mr. Micawber	HN1615	4	1934- 193	
Mr. Pickwick	HN1623	4	1934- 1939	
Oliver Hardy	D7120	7 3/4	1998	Limited Edition of 2500
Sairey Gamp	HN1625	4	1934- 1939	
Sherlock Holmes	D7038	7 3/4	1996 - 1997	*Adventures of Sherlock Holmes* on spine
	D7038	7 3/4	1997 - current	*The Hound of the Baskerfields* on spine
Stan Laurel	D7119	7 3/4	1998	Limited Edition of 2500
Tony Weller	HN1616	4	1934 - 1939	

Busts		Model Number	Height, Inches	Production Life
Buz Fuz		D6048	3	1939 - 1960
Mr. Micawber		D6050	2 3/4	1939 - 1960
Mr. Pickwick		D6049	3 1/4	1939 - 1960
Mountie	- 1873 model	HN2555	8	1973 Ltd Ed of 1500
	- 1973 model	HN2547	8	1973 Ltd Ed of 1500
Sairey Gamp		D6047	2 3/4	1939 - 1960
Sam Weller		D6052	3	1939 - 1960
Tony Weller		D6051	3 1/4	1939 - 1960

Lighters	Model Number	Height, Inches	Production Life
Bacchus	D6505	4	1964 - 1974
Beefeater	D6233	3 1/2	1958 - 1974
Buz Fuz	D5838	4	1958 - 1959
Captain Ahab	D6506	4	1964 - 1974
Captain Cuttle	D5842	4	1958 - 1959
Falstaff	D6385	3 1/2	1958 - 1974
Granny pilot only	D6384	3 1/2	unknown
Lawyer	D6504	4	1962 - 1974
Long John Silver	D6386	4	1958 - 1973
Mr. Micawber	D5843	3 1/2	1958 - 1959
Mr. Pickwick	D5839	3 1/2	1958 - 1962
Old Charley	D5527	3 1/2	1958 - 1974
Poacher	D6464	4	1958 - 1974
Porthos (Musketeer)	D6453	4	1958 - 1959
Rip Van Winkle	D6463	4	1958

Photographs of Royal Doulton Burslem Derivative Products

Left: Ashpots; left to right - top row Auld Mac D6006, Farmer John D6007, and Paddy D5926; bottom row - Sairey Gamp D6009, Old Charley D5925, and Parson Brown D6008

Ash Trays; left to right - Old Charley D5599, Parson Brown D5600, Dick Turpin D5601, and John Barleycorn D5602

Bookends; Sherlock Holmes D7038 on left and Dr. Watson D7039 on right

Bookends; Falstaff D7084 on left and Henry V D7088 on right

Bookends; Stan Laurel D7119 on left and Oliver Hardy D7120 on right

Bookends; left to right - Mr. Pickwick D1623, Tony Weller D1616, Sairey Gamp D1625, and Mr. Micawber D1615

Miniature Busts; left to right; top row - Buz Fuz D6048, Mr. Micawber D6050, and Mr. Pickwick D6049; bottom row - Sairey Gamp D6047, Sam Weller D6052, and Tony Weller D6051

Mounties Busts, 1873 Mountie HN2555 on left and 1973 Mountie HN2547 on right

Granny pilot lighter

Lighters; top row left to right - Mr. Pickwick D5839, Cap'n Cuttle D5842, Beefeater D6233, Buz Fuz D5838, and Mr. Micawber D5843; middle row left to right - Poacher D6464, Old Charley D5527, Porthos D6453, Bacchus D6505, and Lawyer D6504; bottom row left to right - Rip Van Winkle D6463, Falstaff D6385, Long John Silver D6386, and Cap't Ahab D6506

Liquor Containers	Model Number	Height, Inches	Production Life	Other Information
Captain Cook	none	4 3/4	1985	Ltd Ed of 2000, International Collection for Pickwick Wines and Spirits
Falstaff	D6385	4	1960s	Commissioned by W. Walklate Limited
John Bull	none	4	1985	Ltd Ed of 2000, International Collection for Pickwick Wines and Spirits
Mr. Micawber	none	5	1983	Ltd Ed of 2000, Pickwick Collection for Pickwick Wines and Spirits
Mr. Pickwick and Sam Weller	none	5	1985	Ltd Ed of 2000, Pickwick Collection for Pickwick Wines and Spirits, two faced
Old Mr. Turveydrop	none	5	1985	Ltd Ed of 2000 for Pickwick Wines and Spirits
Poacher	D6464	4	1960s	Commissioned by W. Walklate Limited
Rip Van Winkle	D6463	4	1960s	Commissioned by W. Walklate Limited
Samurai Warrior	none	5	1986	Ltd Ed of 2000, International Collection for Pickwick Wines and Spirits
Town Crier of Eatonswill	none	5	1986	Ltd Ed of 2000 Pickwick Collection for Pickwick Wines and Spirits
Uncle Sam	none	5 1/4	1984	Ltd Ed of 2000, International Collection for Pickwick Wines and Spirits; eagle and Jim Beam handles
William Grant	none	7	1986	Ltd Ed of 5000, oak casks handle, has been found with red beard, 100th anniversary of William Grant & Sons
	none	7	1987	Ltd Ed of 2500, oak casks handle, 100th anniversary of when first whiskey flowed at William Grant & Sons
	none	7	1988	Ltd Ed of 5000 for William Grant & Sons, sword handle

Musical Jugs	Model Number	Height, Inches	Production Life	Other Information
Auld Mac	D5889	6 1/4	ca 1939	Tune "The Campbells are Coming"
Granny	pilot	6 1/4	ca 1939	
Old Charley	D5858	5 1/2	ca 1939	Tune "Have a Health unto His Majesty"
Old King Cole yellow crown	D6014	5 3/4	ca 1939	Tune "Old King Cole was a Merry Old Soul"
gold crown	D6014	5 3/4	ca 1939	Tune "Old King Cole was a Merry Old Soul"
Paddy	D5887	6	ca 1939	Tune "An Irish Jig"
Tony Weller	D5833	6 1/2	ca 1939	Tune "Come Landlord, Fill the Foaming Bowl"

Napkin Ring Boxed Set	Model Number	Height, Inches	Production Life
Fat Boy	M59	3 1/2	1935 - 1960
Mr. Micawber	M58	3 1/2	1935 - 1960
Mr. Pickwick	M57	3 1/2	1935 - 1960
Sairey Gamp	M62	3 1/2	1935 - 1960
Sam Weller	M61	3 1/2	1935 - 1960
Tony Weller	M60	3 1/2	1935 - 1960

Salt & Pepper Shakers	Model Number	Height, Inches	Production Life
Toil for Man	D7067	3	1996 - current
Tweedledee (pepper)	D7122	3 1/4	1998 - current
Tweedledum (salt)	D7121	3 1/4	1998 - current
Votes for Women	D7066	3	1996 - current

Square Jugs & Tankards	Model Number	Height, Inches	Production Life	Other Information
Old Curiosity Shop	D5584	5 1/2	1935 - 1960	Jug depicting Little Nell and her Grandfather, on reverse is the Marchioness
Old London	D6291	5 1/2	1949 - 1960	Jug depicting Old Charley on front & Sairey Gamp on back
Oliver Asks for More	D6285	5 1/2	1949 - 1960	Jug depicting Oliver asking for more food
Oliver Twist	D6286	6 1/4	1949 - 1960	Tankard, Oliver watching Artful Dodger pick a pocket
	D5617	5 1/2	1949 - 1960	Jug depicting Oliver, Fagin, Artful Dodger, & Bumble
Peggoty	D6292	5 1/2	1949 - 1960	Jug depicting scene from David Copperfield
Pickwick Papers	D5756	5 1/2	1937 - 1960	Jug depicting Mr. Pickwick, Sam Weller, Tony Weller, and Fat Boy outside the White Hart Inn

Sugar Bowls	Model Number	Height, Inches	Production Life
Old Charley	D6012	2 1/2	1939 - 1960
Sairey Gamp	D6011	2 1/2	1939 - 1960
Tony Weller	D6103	2 1/2	1939 - 1960

Liquor Containers; left to right - Poacher D6464, Falstaff D6385, and Rip Van Winkle D6463

Liquor Containers; William Grant with barrels handle; regular issue on left, William Grant red bearded prototype on right

William Grant Liquor Container with sword handle

Pickwick Collection of Pickwick Wines and Spirits Liquor Containers; top row left to right - Mr Micawber and Old Mr. Turveydrop; bottom row Town Crier of Eastenwil flanked by the two sides of the Sam Weller/Mr. Pickwick container

International Collection of Liquor Containers; top row left to right - Uncle Sam with eagle handle and John Bull; bottom row left to right - Cap't Cook and Samurai Warrior

Prototype Granny Musical Jug

Napkin Ring Boxed Set; left to right - Fat Boy M59, Sam Weller M61, Tony Weller M60, Sairey Gamp M62, Mr. Micawber M58, and Mr. Pickwick M57

Salt and Pepper Shakers; Toil for Men D7067 on left and Votes for Women D7066 on right

Salt and Pepper Shakers; Tweedledee D7122 on left and Tweedledum D7127 on right

Dickens Square Jugs - Peggoty D6292 on left and Oliver Asks for More D6285 on right

Dickens Square Jugs and Tankards; top row left to right - Oliver Twist tankard D6286, Old Curiosity Shop D5584, and Pickwick Papers D5756; bottom row Old London D6291, Old Curiosity Shop backside, and Oliver Twist jug D5617

Teapots	Model Number	Height, Inches	Production Life	Other Information
Falstaff	D6854	6 1/2	1989 - 1991	
Long John Silver	D6853	6 1/2	1989 - 1991	
Minton Chinaman		5 1/2	1997	
Minton Fish		5 1/2	1997	
Minton Monkey		5 1/2	1993	Limited Edition of 1993
Old Balloon Seller	D6855	6 1/2	1989 - 1991	
Old Charley	D6017	7	1939	
Old Salt	D6818	6 1/2	1988	RDICC issue
Sairey Gamp	D6015	7	1939	
Tony Weller	D6016	7	1939	

Tobacco Jars	Model Number	Height, Inches	Production Life	Other Information
Old Charley	D5844	5 1/2	1937 - 1960	
Paddy	D5854	5 1/2	1939 - 1942	Two backstamps found

Toothpick Holders (mini Sugars)	Model Number	Height, Inches	Production Life
Old Charley	D6152	2 1/4	1940 - 1960
Paddy	D6151	2 1/4	1940 - 1960
Sairey Gamp	D6150	2 3/4	1940 - 1960

Wall Masks	Model Number	Height, Inches	Production Life
Friar of Orders Gray (Friar Tuck)		12	
Jester		12	

Wall Pockets	Model Number	Height, Inches	Production Life
Jester	D6111	7 1/4	1939 - 1941
Old Charley	D6110	7 1/4	1939 - 1941

Whiskey Decanters	Model Number	Height, Inches	Production Life	Other Information
Irishman	D6152	7	ca 1930s	Commissioned by Asprey & Company; pair in locking tantalus
Scotsman	D6151	7	ca 1930s	

Teapots, Creamers, Sugar Bowls, and Toothpick Holders; top left to bottom right - Tony Weller teapot D6016, sugar bowl D6012, and creamer D5330; Sairey Gamp teapot D6015; Paddy toothpick D6151; Old Charley teapot D6017; Sairey Gamp sugar D6011, toothpick D6150, and creamer D5528; Old Charley creamer D5527, toothpick D6152, and sugar D6103

Teapots; top row Long John Silver D6853 and Old Balloon Seller D6855; bottom row Falstaff D6854 and Old Salt D6818

Top - Minton Monkey teapot, reproduction of Minton 1893 production; bottom - Fish and Chinaman teapots, also Minton reproductions by Royal Doulton

Tobacco Jars; left to right - Old Charley D5844 and Paddy D5854 (courtesy of David and Sheila Bearman)

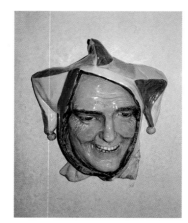

Jester Wall Mask

Friar of Orders Gray Wall Mask

Old Charley Wall Pocket D6110

Jester Wall Pocket D6111

Whiskey Decanters in locking tantalus commissioned by Asprey and Company; Scotsman on left and Irishman on right (courtesy of David and Sheila Bearman)

History

Royal Dux Porcelain traces its roots back to 1853 as one of the first ceramic factories founded in the small town of Duchcov in Bohemia of the Austrian Empire. After a brief period of general purpose ceramics production, Eduard Eichler, an experienced modeler, purchased the factory and renamed it E. Eichler Thonwaren-Fabrik. Eduard transformed the company into an award winning pottery and expanded production into majolica, terra cotta and faience. In 1898, the firm went public, selling shares as the Duxer Porzellan-Manufaktur. Duxer Porzellan introduced new lines of porcelain goods, including figurines, vases and other Art Nouveau decorative accessories. This is the porcelain for which Royal Dux is world famous today.

Immediately before the outbreak of World War I, the firm had established satellite offices throughout Europe, and employment peaked at over 500 workers. From 1918 until 1932, Bohemia was a part of Czechoslovakia. During this time, the firm had difficulties returning to the production levels enjoyed before the First World War, due in large part to a lack of funds and lost distribution channels. In 1932, the area was overrun and became a part of Germany.

After World War II, Bohemia returned to Czechoslovakian control. The communist Czechoslovakian government nationalized the factory in 1948, naming it Royal Dux. Unfortunately, when the firm was nationalized,

most of the experienced workforce moved back to Germany, and the factory's records, as well as many of its' molds, were destroyed. The pottery persevered, however, opening an apprentice training center and relationships with other art schools. Two prominent artists, Professor Jaroslav Jezek and Vladimir David, were key to new, exciting designs in the 1950s and 60s.

With the fall of the Czechoslovakian government in 1992, the firm became privatized again and is now located in the Czech Republic. Royal Dux Porcelain is still producing fine, high quality products today. Since 1900, Royal Dux has been marking its porcelain products with an easily recognized pink porcelain triangular piece fired to the bottom of the ware. A pink triangle with "E" in the center dates from 1900 through 1918. When Duchcov became part of Czechoslovakia in 1918, the "E" in the pink triangle was replaced with a "D". Other impressed marks are commonly found, including a model number.

Character Jugs and Toby Jugs

Due in large part to the destruction of the firm's records, very little is known about Royal Dux's production of Character Jugs and Toby Jugs. Only four examples have been identified so far. All of these jugs are well modeled, high quality porcelain pieces in keeping with Royal Dux's well-earned reputation.

Royal Dux pink porcelain triangle

Character Jug Name	Height, Inches	Production Life
Cyrano "301 12"	6	1900 - 1918
Falstaff	7	1900 - 1918
Old Man with bow tie	6	1900 - 1918

Toby Jug Name	Height, Inches	Incised Marks	Production Life
Wiseman	8 1/4	804 11/57 333	1900 - 1918

Falstaff Character Jug on left, Wiseman Toby Jug center and Cyrano Character Jug on right

Royal Grafton China
See A. B. Jones & Sons

Royal Paragon China Limited
Longton, England

Paragon backstamp

History

Paragon China has its roots in the Star China Company, which was founded by H. J. Aynsley in 1897. Star China was located at the Atlas Works, formerly Sutherland Works, in Longton and produced bone china. In 1904, the firm began using Paragon China as its tradename, paragon meaning model of excellence. In 1920, Paragon China became the official name of the firm. Paragon became a limited company in 1930. In 1933 the firm was renamed Royal Paragon China Limited after receiving the first of its three Royal Warrants.

During the first third of the twentieth century, Paragon China produced some of the finest dinnerware and teaware in England. The firm built a strong tradition of producing high quality, distinctive designs. After World War II, Paragon began exporting extensively. It also introduced a limited line of lifelike bone china figurines that rivaled those of Royal Doulton. To address this competition, Doulton began pressuring its retailers not to carry Paragon by threatening to limit the number of Doulton products the retailer would be allowed to carry. The strategy was effective. As a result, Paragon's figurine market and production was limited, making these highly collectible figurines difficult to find today.

Royal Paragon modernized its factory in the late 1940s and early 1950s, converting to gas and electric tunnel kilns. The firm continued to retain its commitment to the fine handcraftsmanship required to produce high quality ware. Under the management of Leslie Irving, Royal Paragon China continued to sell dinnerware and fine china into the 1950s. T. C. Wild & Sons Limited purchased Paragon China in 1960, absorbing Paragon into its Royal Albert production. The Lawley Group purchased T. C. Wild in 1964. Ironically, after working so hard to curtail Paragon China as a figurine competitor, Royal Doulton acquired Paragon China as part of its buyout of Wild's Royal Albert production in 1972. The Atlas works was eventually closed in July of 1987.

Toby Jugs

From the 1920s through the 1940s, Paragon China produced very desirable china Punch and Judy jugs. While not exceptionally well modeled or decorated, Punch always seems to brighten one's day. Judy is much rarer than Punch, a fact reflected in her market value. These jugs are typically marked "Paragon Fine China England". However, one example has been found marked "Star China Co.", dating it to between 1900 and 1919, before the firm became Paragon China.

Punch and Judy Toby Jug pair

Royal Tettau Porcelain Factory
Bavaria, Germany

History

The Royal Tettau Porcelain Factory was founded by decree of King Friedrich Wilhelm II in 1794 in Tettau, Bavaria. Before becoming Royal Tettau, the factory in Bayreuth was owned and operated by a variety of individuals. The factory first opened in 1714 under Adolf Fraenkel and Johann Georg Knoeller. Two key artists worked for the factory during its early years, Johann Kaspar Rib from 1714 to 1717 and Joseph Philipp Dannhoeffer from 1737 to 1744. Between 1745 and 1747, the factory was owned by Johann Georg Phiffer and Adolf

Fraenkel's widow. In 1747, Georg Phiffer became the sole owner, and the factory was passed on to his heirs and operated by them until 1788.

In 1793, George Christian Friedemann Greiner and Johann Friedrich Paul Schmidt set out to establish a high quality porcelain factory. The pair purchased the Bayreuth factory and received King Wilhelm's decree in 1794, forming the Royal Tettau Porcelain Factory. The company was the first to mass-produce porcelain affordable by the public. Initial production consisted of primarily tableware. Doll heads and figurines were added in the 1800s.

In 1817, Balthasar Greiner took over the business from his father George and the Greiner family operated Royal Tettau until 1852. Production peaked for the porcelain factory in the 1820s and 1830s. After the Greiner family sold the factory to Otto Hausler of Breslan in 1852, it went through a series of owners over the next sixty years. Hausler added a partner, Ferdinand Klaus, in 1857. From 1866 until 1879, Wilhelm Sontag and Karl Birkner operated the factory. Birkner and L. Marsel were partners in the firm from 1879 to 1902, during which time the original factory was destroyed by fire and a larger facility was built to replace it. Between 1902 and 1915 the factory was operated by Sontag and Sons.

In 1915, the Royal Tettau factory, or Royal Bayreuth as it was commonly known, became a public company. New management was appointed in 1918 to aggressively grow the business, and by 1920 the firm acquired two nearby factories. Royal Tettau employed over 600 laborers by the beginning of the First World War. WW I caused the workforce to be reduced to around 480 by the early 1920s. World War II created problems for the firm as well, with demand for goods decreasing and raw materials difficult to obtain. Even after WW II, Royal Tettau's location near the East German border made transportation of materials and goods difficult, as well as providing challenges in retaining employees.

Over its many years of production, the firm produced a wide range of tableware and souvenir items under the "Royal Bayreuth" tradename. It is perhaps best known for its porcelains shaped as flowers, animals, people, fruits and vegetables. Today the firm operates as Royal Tettau Company. Royal Tettau acquired three figurine factories in 1989 to expand its business. Today it employs around two hundred workers and produces mostly fine china dinnerware. The firm's marks vary but typically include "Royal Bayreuth" over a stylized crest. Items marked Bavaria date between 1870 and 1919.

Character Jugs and Toby Jugs

Royal Tettau made a variety of Toby and Character Jugs, all marked with the common Royal Bayreuth tradename. A large number of these are animal pitchers and creamers, including birds, fish, dogs, and wild animals.

The Man of the Mountain Character Jug was finished all in black or dark gray. Royal Tettau Toby Jugs based on people are mainly three-quarter bodied jugs, with the exceptions being the Standing Toby, Devil, Milkmaid, and Santa Clause. Santa was produced in three colorways with a brown, red or green coat. From tallest to shortest, the four Toby Jug sizes are referred to by the firm as a lemonade pitcher, water pitcher, milk pitcher and creamer respectively. Because Royal Bayreuth china is so highly collectible, these jugs are very expensive when found.

Character Jug Name	Height, inches
Bull	3 1/2
Chamois	5 1/2
all stirrup jugs	5 1/4
	5
Cow	5
	4
	3 1/2
Elk	7
beer mug	6
stirrup pitcher	5 1/2
	5 1/4
shaving mug	4 1/2
stirrup creamer	4 1/2
	4 1/4
stirrup cup	4
	3 1/4
Fish	7 1/2
	6
	5
	4
Fox stirrup jug	4
Horse	
Hound	3
Ibex stirrup jug	4
Man of the Mountain	3 1/2
Mountain Goat	3 1/2
Saint Bernard	5
	3 3/4
	3
Water Buffalo	4 1/4
	3 3/4

Toby Jug Name	Height, inches
Alligator	7
	5
	4 1/2
Bear	5 1/2
	4 1/4
Beetle	6
Bellringer	7 1/2
	5
	4 1/2
Bird of Paradise	3 3/4
	3 1/4
Butterfly (closed wing)	6 1/2
	4
	3 1/4
Butterfly (open wing)	6 1/2
	4 1/4
	3 1/2
Calico Cat	4 3/4
Cat	5 1/2
	4 3/4
Chick	7
	4
Chimpanzee	4
Clown yellow jacket	6 1/2
	6 1/2
	4 1/2
green jacket	3 3/4
	3 1/2
Coachman	7
	4 3/4
	4 1/4
Cockatoo	4 3/4
	4
Crow	5 1/2
	4 3/4
Dachshund	6
	5
	4
Duck	6 3/4
	4 1/2
	3 3/4
Eagle	6
	4 1/4
	3 1/2

Royal Bayreuth blue ink mark

Character Jugs of Bull on left and Cow on right

Elk Character Jug

Toby Jug Name	Height, inches
Falcon	5 1/2
Flounder	4 1/4 4
Frog	4 3/4 3 2 1/2
Girl with basket	4 1/4
Girl with pitcher	5 4
Gorilla	5 1/4
Kangaroo	4 3/4
Lady Bug	6 4 3/4 3 3/4
Lamplighter	7 3/4 5 3/4 4 3/4
Leopard	3
Lion	
Lobster purple colorway purple colorway	6 3/4 6 3/4 4 1/2 3 3/4 3 3/4 1 3/4
Milkmaid	4 3/4
Monk	4 1/4
Monkey	6 1/2 5 4 3/4 4
Mouse	7 1/2 5 4 1/2
Owl	7 4 3/4 3 3/4
Parakeet	6 1/4 4 1/2 3 1/2
Pelican	6 3 1/2
Penguin	7 3/4 4 3/4
Perch	7 1/4 4
Pig	4 1/4
Platypus	4
Poodle	5 1/4 4 1/2
Rabbit	7 1/2 4
Red Devil	4 1/4 3 1/2
Robin	7 4 3/4 3 3/4
Rooster	7 1/4 5 4 1/4
Santa Clause	6 1/4 5 1/4 4 1/4
Seal ad for Old Ben	6 3/4 4 3/4 4 3/4 4
Snake	6 1/4 4 3/4 3 3/4
Standing Toby	5
Squirrel	8 5 1/2 4 3/4
Tiger	4
Trout	8 6 1/4 4 1/2
Turtle	4 1/2 3 1/4 2 1/2 2

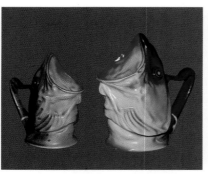

Fish Character Jugs in five and six inch sizes

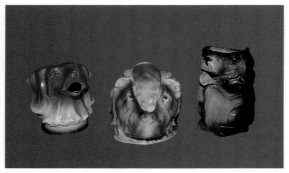

Hound Character Jug left, St. Bernard Character Jug center, and Dachshund Toby Jug right

Three Cat Toby Jugs in black and white colorways

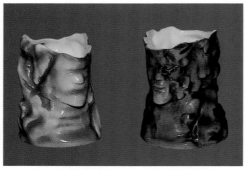

Man of the Mountain Character Jug in two shades of gray

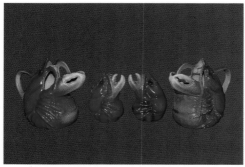

Two Lobster Toby Jugs flanking a Lobster salt and pepper shaker set

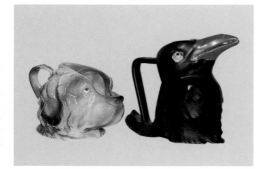

St. Bernard Character Jug on the left and Crow Toby Jug on the right

Three-quarter bodied Toby Jugs; from left to right - Coachman, Bellringer, and Lamplighter

Robin Toby Jug on left and Duck Toby Jug on right

Royal Worcester Porcelain Company
Worcester, England

History

The Royal Worcester Porcelain Company traces its founding back to 1751, when the Worcester Porcelain Company, led by physician Dr. John Wall and William Davis, acquired the Bristol pottery of Benjamin Lund and Mr. Miller, moving it to the banks of the Severn River in Worcester, England. Wall's and Davis' purchase included the rights to the Bristol soaprock formula, plus continued participation by Lund for one year, both of which got the factory off to a rapid start. Its first ware was porcelains done in blue underglaze paint, soon followed by lines of products using enamel overglaze paints. From the outset and to this day, the firm uses 50% calcium phosphate derived from bone and 22k gold gilding in its ware. Worcester developed transfer print decoration in the 1760s.

The firm created such a widespread reputation for fine ware, that King George III granted Worcester Porcelain a Royal Warrant in 1789. After William Davis' death in 1783, a series of partnerships, changes and moves took place until 1852, when W. H. Kerr and Richard William Binns assumed the reigns of the company and began forging a new direction. Some of these interim owners were Flight and Barr, Chamberlain, and Hadley. In 1862, Kerr retired and Binns created a limited partnership that began trading as Royal Worcester Porcelain Company Limited. Beside Binns, who served as Art Director, the other two principals of the firm were Edward Phillips, in charge of production, and William Litherland, a London retailer.

One of the less than successful developments of Royal Worcester was a type of pottery trade-named Crownware. Crownware was a high fired earthenware body, a form of semi-porcelain containing a large proportion of clay. The body, which was heavy and opaque, was then decorated with overglaze colors and lightly fired. One result of this process is that the overglaze paint quickly wore off, so the process was used sparingly. However, Crownware items were produced from 1870 to 1930. Items produced using this method often carried a "CW" as a part of their backstamp.

After World War II, the company was among the first to produce ware utilizing the concept of serving with porcelain direct from the oven to the table. The popularity of this product line was huge, precipitating construction of a new, modern factory for its production. Always popular were Worcester's porcelain figurines. Limited edition horse figurines sculpted by Doris Lindner were produced in the 1960s and 70s. Today these are scarce and very expensive.

Royal Worcester purchased Spode Limited in 1974, and the two fully merged two years later, becoming Royal Worcester Spode. Between 1983 and 1988, Royal Worcester Spode was owned by Crystalate Company, then London International PLC, and finally Derby International, a North American investment group. In December of 1988, Derby reorganized its British operations, renaming it The Porcelain & Fine China Companies Limited and operating Spode Limited and Royal Worcester Limited as independent companies. Today Royal Worcester is one of the largest manufacturers of fine bone china and porcelain in England.

From the Kerr and Binns period forward, the basic mark of the firm was a circular figure with four script "Ws" inside and a crown on top. "Royal Worcester England" was added to the mark in 1891. Use of dots above the "d" in "England" to date production began with one dot in 1892 and ended with twenty-four dots in 1915.

Toby Jugs

Royal Worcester produced several well-modeled, high quality porcelain Toby Jugs in the

Mephistopheles Toby Jug

Royal Worcester mark

first half of the twentieth century. Some of these were made using its unique Crownware process. All of these jugs are highly desirable. Some, like Paddy, Jester and the Irishman were only produced in a large size. Mephistopheles, Punch, and Judy were produced in multiple sizes. Toby model number 2832 is documented in the company records, but has not been yet identified. It is most certainly Paddy, Jester or the Irishman. All of these are exceptionally detailed and rarely appear on the market.

The Standing Toby and Mrs. Toby are the most commonly found Royal Worcester jugs. They came as a pair in three sizes, and are found with orange-red or blue coats. A less common medium sized Standing Toby has been found in a black coat priced significantly higher. Standing tobies with green coats are the most rare of the colorways. The Standing Toby, model numbers 2831 and 2832, came with or without a cover and were also offered as a salt and pepper set with Mrs. Toby. While not found yet, a Crownware version of Mrs. Toby most likely exists as a companion to the Crownware Standing Toby. The smallest size is the most scarce and difficult to find, while the larger sizes are more available. The tallest Standing and Mrs. Toby Jugs appear as if they are standing on top of wooden pedestals. This is all a part of their molds.

Royal Worcester also created a set of four animal and bird jugs around 1930. These jugs were produced both in white porcelain and polychrome versions. The full colorway is very uncommon and commands prices at the high end of the market value.

Graduated sets of Standing Toby and Mrs. Toby jugs in all three sizes

Toby Jug Name	Model Number	Height, Inches	Production Life
Cockatoo			1930 - 1940
Elephant			1930 - 1940
Irishman			
Jester			
Judy		2	
Mephistopheles	2850	7	1929 - 1940
	2850	medium	1929 - 1940
	2850	3 3/8	1929 - 1940
Mrs. Toby	2841	6	1927 - 1955
	2841	3 1/2	1927 - 1955
	2841	1 3/4	1927 - 1955
Paddy			
Pelican	2853		1930 - 1940
Punch	2856	6 1/2	1931 - 1940
	2856	2	1931 - 1940
Standing Toby	2831	5 3/4	1927 - 1955
	2831	3 1/2	1927 - 1955
	2831	1 3/4	1927 - 1955
Crownware	2840		1927 - 1955
Squirrel			1930 - 1940

Royce Wood
Derby, England

Royce Wood backstamp

History

Artist Royce Wood operated a small studio pottery out of her home in Derby, England. Royce's entire family was involved in the pottery enterprise. Today she does freelance modelling for various potteries.

Character Jugs

Over a brief period of time in the 1980s, Royce Wood designed a range of over twenty Character Jugs. The firm's literature promoted these jugs as follows. "The Pageantry and History of England is the inspiration for our range of lifelike sculptured Character Jugs of lustrous quality handcrafted and handpainted with artistry and skill by Royce Wood."

The Henry VII and Richard III jugs were produced as a pair to commemorate the 500th anniversary of the Battle of Bosworth in 1485.

All of the jugs were produced and hand painted at the Pageant Pottery. These jugs are very well modeled and of very high quality. They are marked "Pageant Royce Wood" or just "Royce Wood". Following is a comprehensive list of all the known Royce Wood jugs.

The photographs are from the collection of Emmett Mathews.

Large Charles Dickens Character Jug

Character Jugs from left to right - young Henry VIII large size, and older Henry VIII in medium and large sizes

Character Jugs from left to right - large and medium size King Charles I, and large size Charles I

Large King Henry VII Character Jug on left, and medium Henry VII jug on right

Character Jugs from left to right - medium and large size King Richard III, and medium size Richard III

Large Queen Henrietta Maria, wife of Charles I, on the left, and medium Queen Elizabeth I of England on the right

Character Jug Name	Height, inches
Charles I	7
Charles Dickens	8
Diana, Princess of Wales	7 1/2
Henry VII	6
Henry VIII - young older older	8 8 6
King Charles I	7 3/4 6
King Henry VII	7 1/2 6
King Richard III	8 6
Miss Marple	7 1/2
Oliver Cromwell	7
Queen Elizabeth I	5 1/2
Queen Henrietta Maria	7 1/2
Richard III	6 1/4
Rob Roy	5 1/2
Robin Hood	7 1/2
Sir Thomas Moore	7 1/2
Sherlock Holmes	8 6 1/2
Town Crier	5 3/4
Viking	4
William Shakespeare	8 6
Winston Churchill	7 3/4
Yeoman Warder	7 3/4 6

Large Robin Hood on left, and large Miss Marple on right

Sherlock Holmes Character Jugs in large and medium sizes

Large Sir Thomas Moore on left, and large Oliver Cromwell on right

William Shakespeare Character Jugs in large and medium sizes

Large Character Jugs of Winston Churchill and Diana, Princess of Wales

Large and medium sized Yeoman Warder Character Jugs

Rumph
See Jugs Marked by Country of Manufacture under United States

Samson Smith
See Jugs Marked by Country of Manufacture under United Kingdom

Sanchia Wood
See Tony Wood Limited

Sandizell Porcelain Factory
Bavaria, Germany

Toby Jug Name	Height, inches
Fat Boy	3
Ordinary Toby	3
Standing Lady	3
Standing Man	5 3/8
	3
Sydney Carton	3
Tony Weller	2 7/8

Sandizell blue ink mark

History

The Sandizell Porcelain Factory began operating in 1951 in the village of Sandizell, Bavaira, which is now a part of Schrobenhausen. Sandizell made high quality porcelain ware, primarily figurines and other decorative items. The Firm was still operating in the early 1990s. Sandizell typically stamped its items in blue underglaze ink with a crown above an N and sometimes the word "Dresden" underneath. "Germany" also can be found stamped.

Toby Jugs

Sandizell Porcelain made several well-modeled porcelain Toby Jugs beginning in 1951 and into the 1960s. The standing tobies appear holding a variety of items. The woman may be holding a basket of flowers or a dead rabbit. The man appears with his hands in his pockets or holding a bouquet of flowers, of course for the woman. The Dickens characters have the character name incised across the front of the base and are similar to those produced by other factories, including Sitzendorfer and Crown Staffordshire.

Dickens Toby Jugs, left to right: Sydney Carton, Fat Boy, and Tony Weller

Standing Man, three inches tall

Sandyford Pottery
See Jugs Marked by Country of Manufacture under United Kingdom

Sarreguemines
Sarre, France

History

Sarreguemines refers generically to pottery produced in and around the Sarreguemines region of northeastern France, being situated just across the Sarre River from Saarbrucken, Germany. The town of Sarreguemines, France was ideally suited for the production of pottery, with the river providing transportation for distribution of finished products and the nearby Vosges Forest providing wood for the kilns. Clay for the pottery was imported. Today one of the old "bottle" kilns still stands at the Regional Museum.

In roughly 1778, two Strasbourg tobacconists, brothers Nicolas Henri Jacobi and Paul Augustin Jacobi, founded a ceramic factory in Sarreguemines. The brothers were soon joined by Francois Paul Utzschneider and began by producing cream-colored earthenware in the style of Wedgwood. In the 19th century, tableware was produced with printed decoration. In the 1860s, Sarreguemines launched its famous majolica range. Extremely popular, these items ranged from monumental pieces, such as grandiose fountains, to novelty Character Jugs. They were of high quality, distinguished by bold and often humorous molded shapes and bright colors. Production peaked between the 1890s and 1914, when Sarreguemines was one of the most important potteries of its kind in Europe.

Not much is know about the Sarreguemines factory during World War I when that region was under German control, but there apparently were ties to Mettlach. After the war, the area returned to French control and the factory began making ceramics for ships. Majolica was manufactured until the 1930s. The factory continued with successful production of other goods throughout this time. During World War II Villeroy and Boch ran the factory.

The factory itself is no longer in production, having closed in 1983. St. Clement bought the old molds and reproduced the most popular of the Sarreguemines patterns at its location in a nearby city. Examples are shipped to Sarreguemines to what is now an outlet store, but was once the production area of the factory.

The Sarreguemines Regional Museum proudly displays not only magnificent examples of majolica produced by the famed pottery, but also examples of the tremendous variety of other wares produced there. As Sarreguemines was once the largest pottery manufacturing center in Europe, the variety of ware is most impressive. Technically skilled, the designers and craftsmen were constantly testing their capabilities. Besides majolica, Sarreguemines manufactured stoneware, lusterware, parian, and table services. Examples of this production inspire awe in the museum visitor.

Sarreguemines marked its products fairly well and sometimes included the country of manufacture on its ware after passage of the McKinley Tariff Act of 1891. A black ink mark sometimes seen on old Sarreguemines products is the Lorraine crest with the words "Made in Germany" underneath. After Lorraine was ceded to Germany in 1871 following the Franco-Prussian War, the ware of that period carried a German mark such as "Saargemund/Fayence". Since the province of Lorraine was returned to France after World War I, ware thus marked are easy to date. The letter occasionally found on the base of some jugs is not the initial of the designer as one might imagine, but the initial of the decorator. As decorators were paid by the piece, it was necessary to identify their labor.

Sarreguemines pottery is among some of the finest ever produced, and its expressive tobies are capturing the attention of discerning collectors on both sides of the Atlantic.

Character Jugs and Toby Jugs

Included in Sarreguemines' early production were several Toby and Character Jug designs, including jugs in animal form. All the factory's Toby and Character Jugs were marked with either the name of the factory impressed into the clay before firing, or later, a black ink mark. The black ink marks often included the factory name with the letters "U&C" for Utzschneider and Company, or after 1920, "DV" for Digoin and Vitry overwritten. Along with the impressed or ink mark, the words "Majolica" or "depose'" might also be stamped, meaning the piece was a registered pattern. The large three or four digit numbers on the bottom of all Character Jugs are the number of the mold, 227 means majolica production, and the smaller numbers are the date of product.

Since all the Toby and Character Jugs were individually painted, no two are exactly alike. It is quite appealing to see several examples of the same jug side by side. Some collectors want duplicates for just this reason. In all, Sarreguemines produced approximately fifty different Toby and Character Jugs.

There were no copyright laws in existence at the end of the 19th century, so imitation was common. Copies of the more popular Sarreguemines Character Jugs exist, but the coloring is unmistakably not Sarreguemines. Though appealing in their own right, these copies lack the wonderful subtlety of the originals.

Sarreguemines-like majolica jugs were manufactured by other French, German and English potters. In addition to differences in coloring, these jugs are not marked in the same manner. However, while these are often mistaken for Sarreguemines jugs, they do command significant market value in their own right and make nice additions to any Sarreguemines collection.

Most of the Sarreguemines Character Jugs were manufactured in two sizes, though some models appeared in three sizes and one mold came in five sizes. Several patterns were made in only one size, as is the case with the full figured tobies.

Condition, coloring, detail, size, rarity, and, above all, collectability affect prices for these jugs. The solid colored examples, though uncommon because fewer were produced, do not bring as much as other examples. They are simply not as collectable. The female examples generally cost significantly more than the male jugs. The smaller pieces often bring as much as, or more than, large ones because fewer of them seem to have survived. Since some of the Sarreguemines

Character Jug Name	Model Number	Height, Inches	Production Life
Bartolome Mitre	3726		1920s
Big Nose	3264	4 3/4	1906
Blackamoor	5055 3884	6 3/4	1925 1905 - 1925
Blackamoor Woman	4885		1905 - 1925
Boozer	3323 3323	large medium	1925 1925
Bulldog	4024	7	1902 - 1925
Chairman Michelsen	3733	6	
Chamberlain	3466	6	1903
Chamois	4023		1925
Clown	4638	6 1/2	1925
Danish Woman	3319	7	1903
Deer	4027	9	
English	3210	7 3/4	1903 - 1925
Francis Joseph			
French Soldier	4305		1925
General Ferdinand Foch			
Gnome	1197		1880s
High Collar	3297	8 1/2	1925
Horse	4021		
John Bull	3257 3257	7 1/4 6 3/8	1925 1925
Jolly Fellow with advertising	3181 3181 3181 3181 3181	8 1/2 6 3/4 6 5 4	1904 - 1925 1904 - 1925 1904 - 1925 1904 - 1925 1904 - 1925
Judge	4502 4502	7 1/2 6 1/2	1925
Jug	3611 3612		1925 1905
Lion	4020	6 1/2	1920 - 1925
Mustache Man	3450		1905
Napoleon	4610		1925
Normandy Jug	1752	9	1880 - 1920
Norwegian Lady	3331		1925
Paul Kruger	3185	8	
Puck	652 653	7 1/2 7	1880 - 1925 1880 - 1925
Ram	4022	6 1/2	1925
Red Beard	3323	large small	
Russian Head	3300	7	1902 - 1925
Sad Clown	4639	6 1/2	1920s
Sailor	4317	7 1/2	
Suspicious Eyes	3320	7	1925
Toothache	3321 3321	7 medium	1903 - 1925
Two Superimposed Heads	2313	8 3/4	1901 - 1905
Uncle Sam	4316		1925
Upward Eyes	3258	8	1902 - 1925
Woman with Blonde Hair	3358		1925

Toby Jug Name	Model Number	Height, Inches	Production Life
Cat	3675		
Dog	3677		
Griffin	903		
John Bull	3429	13	1904 - 1925
Judy	3430	12 1/2	1904 - 1905
Parakeet	3566		1925
Pig	3318	9 3/4	1904 - 1920
Punch	3431	12 3/4	1904 - 1925
Raven	3567		1925

Character Jugs were created for export to particular countries, for example Armenia and Argentina, these examples are rare and hard to find in the United States. When a collector indeed does stumble across one, the price is usually noteworthy.

Though the mold number on the Character Jugs may indicate that the pattern is one of the oldest ones, such as Puck, the piece may not be as costly as a more recent mold. Because the older piece may have been manufactured for a longer time, more examples exist, so the price is not as high. Some of the latest molds were manufactured for only a short time before the factory ceased production of majolica, thus making some of these newer pieces rather valuable. Often jugs carried advertising on them, which can raise the value slightly. Some jugs can be found with pewter lids. These are rarer and more valuable as well.

For a fuller description of Sarreguemines' factory and production, as well as additional photos, please refer to *Majolica Figures* by Helen Cunningham. The listing herein is a comprehensive one of Sarreguemines jugs.

Sarreguemines impressed mark

Blackamoor Character Jug, very rare

Bulldog Character Jug (coutesy of Helen Cunningham)

Clown Character Jug, very rare (coutesy of Helen Cunningham)

The English Character Jug

John Bull Character Jug in 7 and 6 1/2 inch sizes

Judge Character Jug

Red Beard Character Jug, rare (coutesy of Helen Cunningham)

Jolly Fellow Character Jugs in large, medium and small sizes

Napoleon Character Jug

Puck Character Jug in two colorways

Two Superimposed Heads Character Jug; happy face showing, sad face when inverted

Danish Woman jug on left and Normandy Jug on right

Three Animal Character Jugs: Deer stirrup on left, Lion in center, and Ram on the right

Character Jugs of Paul Kruger on the left and Chamberlain on the right

Suspicious Eyes Character Jug on the left and Upward Eyes on the right

John Bull Toby Jug on the left, Punch in the center, and Judy on the right

Sarreguemines-like Jugs Manufactured in France, Germany, or England

These are reproduction jugs of the popular Sarreguemines jugs from roughly the same time period. They are jugs with the same appearance as Sarreguemines, but are not recorded in the factory's records, and have different marks. Some are the same character as Sarreguemines, and others are different. There are several different theories as to the purpose of the small bottles that were made from the same molds as the three inch jugs. They could have been used as ink wells or perfume bottles, or as small sample liquor bottles. Marks found on jugs are in quotes.

Character Jug Name	Model Number	Height, Inches
Aly Sloper		6
Barrister		
Black Bill Hat	7891	7 1/4
	7891	5 3/4
	8025	3 1/2
smiling or frowning bottle		3 1/2
Floral Hat	8716	
Green Hat, Black Bill		3
Hat with Bow	7890	large
impressed "13"	7890	3 1/2
Huntsman		
L'entente Cordial		
Matelot	7892	XLarge
	7892	8 1/2
Ad for "Hallmeuer"	7892	6
	7892	6
Impressed "25"	7892	5 1/2
	7892	small
bottle	8344	3
Pelican	8529	8
Popeye	8715	6
Puck		5 3/4
Scotsman	7889	8 1/4
	7889	7 1/4
	7889	6 1/4
	7889	5 1/2
Sleepy	8714	large
	8714	small
Smoker double handled	7208	2 1/2
Station Master	7850	8 1/2
	8024	3 1/2
Vicar		

Graduated set of three Black Bill Hat majolica Character Jugs

English majolica Aly Sloper Character Jug (coutesy of Helen Cunningham)

Graduated set of four Scotsman majolica Character Jugs

Graduated set of four Matelot Character Jugs and a Matelot bottle

Collection of mini jugs and bottles; left to right - Black Bill with green hat and pink bow, two Black Bill jugs with green hat (smiling and frowning); two Black Bill bottles (smiling and frowning) and a Matelot bottle

Savoy China
See Birks, Rawlins & Company Limited

L

250

History

Schafer & Vater was a high quality porcelain manufacturer located in Volkstedt Rudolstadt, Thuringa, Germany. Gustav Schafer and Gunther Vater founded the firm in 1890. Success and a growing business led to the 1896 purchase of the List porcelain factory in Neuhaus. As early as 1910, Sears Roebuck & Company distributed Schafer & Vater ware in the United States. Throughout its operation, Schafer & Vater produced a wide range of hard paste porcelain ware, including luxury items, figurines, and doll heads. The firm also produced soft paste porcelain, bisque items as decorative blanks, and majolica. Jasperware was a major product line for the firm. Between 1890 and the 1920s, Schafer & Vater produced a wide range of porcelain figural liquor bottles for export. These bottles were often used as giveaways by pubs for their loyal customers.

By 1913, Paul Schafer had taken over his father's interest in the firm, working alongside Vater. At this time, the firm had three kilns and employed two hundred workers. It advertised porcelain doll heads and knick-knacks among other ware. The original factory was destroyed by fire in 1918, but a new factory was located and production soon resumed there. Production of doll heads ceased sometime after 1941, and the firm closed in 1962. In 1972, the East German government assumed control of the dormant Schafer & Vater factory. All remaining records, molds and other evidence of the pottery were destroyed.

Crown and star mark

Schafer & Vater is perhaps best known for its detailed and comical figural items. These include pitchers, creamers, bottles, matchstrikers, and planters. Schafer & Vater's products were impressed with a crown above an R in a starburst. Sometimes "Made in Germany" is stamped in black. Many of the pieces were not marked. Schafer & Vater figural items are quite desirable today.

Character Jugs and Toby Jugs

Schafer & Vater produced many Character and Toby Jugs, which it referred to as creamers or pitchers. Schafer and Vater referred to creamers that were produced in three specific sizes as master creamers. These were made both in a full colorway and a blue glaze. The full colorways have a higher market value than the blue glazed jugs. Other jugs were made in only one size and are not referred to as master creamers. Schafer & Vater produced some jugs on commission or with advertising. For example, a Maid with keys has been found with "Hotel Martinque" stamped on the bottom. The Apple Character Jug is the creamer from a teaset, which includes the sugar, creamer, teapot, and liquor bottle.

Many of these jugs pour from the character's mouth and, although technically not a Toby Jug, merit inclusion. The following list includes the complete set of master creamers, plus other known jugs. Still more remain to be found.

Top - Blackamoor; bottom from left to right - Boy with Umbrella, Oriental with bird, and Maid with keys

Character Jug Name	Height, inches
Apple	4
Child in hat	4 1/2
	3 1/4
Toby	5
Welsh Lady "8838"	4 3/4

Toby Jug Name	Height, inches
American Indian	5 1/4
Blackamoor	5
	4
	3 1/2
Bear with muff	6 1/8
	5 1/4
"6493"	4 1/2
	3 5/8
Boy with umbrella	5 1/2
	4
	3 1/2
Bull in hat and pants	5
	4
	3 1/2
Cat	5 7/8
Cow in coat	5 1/2
	4
"6517"	3 1/2
Devil with wings	5
	4
	3 1/2
Elf on pig	4 5/8
Goat wearing coat	6 7/8
	5 3/4
	4
	3 1/2
Goose in bonnet "6452"	5 1/2
	4
Gorilla wearing hat	6
	5
	4 1/4
Maid with fan	5
	4 1/4
	3 1/2
Maid with keys	5 1/4
	4
	3 1/2
Maid with purse	4 3/4
	3 1/2
Minstrel with mandolin	5
	4
	3 1/2
Monkey in derby	5 3/4
	4
	3 1/2
Mothergoose in hat	5
	4 3/4
	3 1/2
Oriental with baby	6
	5 1/4
	4
	3 3/4
Oriental with bird	6 1/2
	5 1/4
	4 1/2
	3 7/8
Oriental grinning	5
	4
	3 1/2
Oriental with monkey	5 1/2
	4 1/2
	3 3/4
Pig in Monk's habit	6 1/2
	5 1/2
	4 1/4
	3 1/2

Sebastian Studios
Hudson, Massachusetts

History

Prescott W. Baston was born in 1909 in Massachusetts. His father was a miniature modeler and woodcarver for Olmstead Brothers in Brookline, Massachusetts. Olmstead was the landscape architectural firm that designed New York City's Central Park, among other famous landmarks. Baston followed his artistic desires and heritage and entered the Vesper George School of Art. At school he specialized in mural painting, while also working with his father modeling miniatures. During the Depression, Baston created large abstract sculptures via the Federal Art Project.

While still with the Federal Art Project, Prescott Baston was propelled into his own business in 1938 by the owner of the Shaker Glen House in Woburn, Massachusetts, who asked him to make a miniature Shaker man and woman for her. Working in the basement of his Arlington, Massachusetts home at night, Baston created this pair, which led to other miniatures. Soon Baston's miniature figures were being carried at a nearby retail store, Olsens, in Cambridge. The demand by collectors for his miniatures quickly grew, and Baston's hobby became Sebastian Studios.

With the bombing of Pearl Harbor in December of 1941, Prescott Baston went to work for MIT's Radiation Labs where his technical skills in miniaturization were put to good use. Meanwhile his wife, Marjorie, managed production at Sebastian Studios. Baston returned to the Studios in 1945. The next year the business had outgrown the basement, and a new, larger studio was built in Marblehead, where creation and production of miniature figurines continued.

In January of 1976, Sebastian Studios merged with Lance, America's leading fine art metal foundry. The Studios moved forty miles to Hudson, Massachusetts. The merger expanded the distribution of Sebastian Miniatures from primarily the New England area to nationwide. This relationship also resulted in Prescott Baston Jr. working for Lance as the Manufacturing Manager.

Prescott Baston created a legacy of excellence in sculpted miniature scenes. He has been quoted as saying, "Two goals have guided my work through the years. First, to do the most honest portrayals I can. Second, to create scenes so appealing that other people immediately experience a sense of pleasure from them." To date, two hundred and eighty-three different models have been developed, two hundred and thirty for public consumption and fifty-three that were privately commissioned.

Toby Jugs

Sebastian made a small number of Toby Jugs in 1963 as a part of its expanding line of products. These depicted famous Americans and were of limited production, so they are valued by both Sebastian and Toby collectors.

Toby Jug Name	Height, Inches	Production Life
Abraham Lincoln	large	1963 - 1965
Ben Franklin	large	1963 - 1965
George Washington	large	1963 - 1965
Jackie Kennedy	mini	1963 - 1965
John F. Kennedy	large	1963 - 1965
	mini	1963 - 1965

Shaw & Sons Limited
Tunstall, England

Character Jug Name	Height, inches
Algy	2 1/4
Billy	3 1/2
Henry VIII	4 1/4
Sandy	6 1/2

History

Shaw & Sons Limited of Tunstall was founded at the Willow Pottery by John Shaw in 1931. The firm operated there until 1963, producing a wide range of earthenware and bone china products. Burlington and Burlington Ware were the firm's tradenames. Early products might be marked "J. S. S." and "Burlington Art Pottery". Dr. Paul Singh of Staffordshire Fine Ceramics purchased Shaw & Sons' factory and equipment in 1963, and still operates at that location today.

Character Jugs and Toby Jugs

Shaw & Sons made a series of Toby and Character Jugs from the late 1950s through the end of its active production life in 1963. The look of the jugs is distinctive such that one can recognize them at first glance. Some of the larger jugs can be found with music box inserts in their base; these would be more valuable. The common mark found on Shaw's jugs is a script "Burlington Ware" within a square.

Staffordshire Fine Ceramics re-issued some of Shaw's jugs as a part of its Traditional Tobies series. The Billy Character Jug looks like a young Old Bill, with the same wild-eyed look, but missing the monocle. Billy was produced in a Rockingham glaze. Most curious are Shaw's Henry VIII and Sandy Character Jugs, which are identical to the porcelain jugs produced by Arthur Bowker. Shaw most likely purchased the Bowker molds when Bowker went out of business.

Toby Jug Name	Height, inches
Boozer	9 1/4
Bo Peep	4 1/2
Capt. Hook	6 3/4
Cavalier seated	8 1/4
standing	6 7/8
standing	4
Cross-legged Toby	9
'Erbert 'Appyday	9 1/2
Humpty Dumpty	4 1/2
Huntsman	3 3/4
Jack Horner	4 7/8
John Bull	
Judge	3 3/4
Lawyer	6 1/4
	4 3/4
Long John Silver	10 1/2
with music box	10 1/2
Old King Cole	3 3/8
Olde Ale	6
Ordinary Toby	9
with raised mug	8 1/2
	4 1/2
	3 1/4
Oyez	6 1/4
Pirate	6
Poacher seated	3 1/2
standing	3 1/2
Porgy	5
Sailor	
Singer	6 1/4
Sleeper	6
Sneaker	5 1/8
Snuffer	3 1/2
Spud	6 1/4
Squat Toby	3 3/4
Squeaker	6 1/4
Town Crier	6 1/2
Winker	6 1/4

Burlington Ware mark

Small Henry VIII and tiny Algy Character Jugs

Medium size Sandy Character Jug

Group of miniature Toby Jugs; left to right - Squat Toby, Judge, Huntsman, Old King Cole, and Poacher

Two large size Musical Toby Jugs - Long John Silver and Cavalier

Six small sized Toby Jugs; top-Singer, Spud and Oyez, bottom - Winker, Sleeper, and Squeaker

Large Toby Jugs, left to right - Cross-legged, Ordinary Toby with raised mug, 'Erbert 'Appyday, and Ordinary Toby

Small size Nursery Rhyme Toby Jugs - Humpty Dumpty, Bo Peep, Jack Horner, and (Georgy) Porgy

Small Toby Jugs; Sneaker flanked by two Ordinary Tobies

Two medium size Toby Jugs, Pirate on left and standing Cavalier on right

Shaw and Copestake
Longton, England

History

Shaw and Copestake was founded in 1894 by William Shaw and William Copestake. Copestake left the firm shortly after its founding, and his interests were taken over by Richard Hull by the turn of the century. Shaw and Copestake situated itself on Normacot Road in Longton, first at the Drury Works and then the Sylvan Works. Shaw and Copestake's SylvaC tradename was derived by Richard Hull Jr. from the Sylvan Works. The capital "S" stood for Shaw and capital "C" for Copestake. An interesting aspect of the firm is that the bulk of the actual designs were contracted from outside the factory, or existing molds were purchased from other firms.

Early Shaw and Copestake products included vases, jugs, flower pots, toiletware and fancy earthenware. Many of these designs were very ornate and heavily decorated with gold. One of the many designers who worked for the firm was Reginald Thompson, who joined Thomas Lawrence in 1917 at the young age of 14 as a painter. After completing his art education through scholarship at the Hanley School of Art, he joined Shaw and Copestake, becoming the youngest Decorating Manager in Staffordshire at the age of 19. Reginald remained with the firm for an amazing sixty-two years, retiring in 1978.

Attractive clock sets were produced after World War I and into the 1920s. In the late 1920s, the first animal figurines were introduced. Low-fired matte glazes were developed in the 1930s by Shaw and Copestake and were a unique contribution to Staffordshire ceramics. These glazes eventually came out in many colors, including cream, blue and green, and were used into the 1980s. As no other pottery could replicate this popular glaze, Shaw and Copestake's matte glazed products became quite successful and today are very much coveted by collectors.

Shaw and Copestake became a limited company in 1936 with William Shaw as Director. At this time Richard Hull Jr., who had joined the firm in 1924, took over as Shaw's partner in the business. Shaw and Copestake and Thomas Lawrence Limited of Longton merged in 1938 through family connections via Richard Hull. Thomas Lawrence, which was founded in 1892 at the Trent Bridge Pottery, operated the Falcon Pottery from 1897. This brought Lawrence's Falcon Pottery, which was established in 1887, and its tradename "Falcon Ware," into use by Shaw and Copestake.

By the 1950s, both firms were at full capacity, and while operating independently, they shared designs from one to the other and co-marketed products. Construction of a new modern factory began in 1955 on Barford Street, near the Sylvan Works. This new factory combined the production of Shaw and Copestake and Thomas Lawrence into one facility, with the first piece being produced on January 22, 1957. The office buildings were finished and the new site completed in 1962. Weinstock's Department Store distributed the firm's ware in North America during this time.

Thomas Lawrence ceased trading under its own name and fully merged with Shaw and Copestake by 1964. The Falcon Ware tradename was also discontinued at this time. Beswick purchased the old Thomas Lawrence facility at Longton in 1957. Today this is the site where Royal Doulton's Character and Toby Jugs are produced at the Beswick Studio.

Another key designer was George Matthews, who joined the firm in 1966. He was educated at the Newcastle School of Art and received broad experience in the daily activities of a pottery at the Boston Pottery in Sandiford, a small facility where all employees helped in every aspect of the business. After proving to be an exceptional talent, George became

Reginald's key associate in modeling new designs.

The 1970s brought a steady decline in business to Shaw and Copestake due to recession and fierce competition from the Far East. In May of 1982, Shaw and Copestake went into voluntary liquidation and all production halted. The factory and assets were purchased by the North Midland Co-operative Society. The Society leased the land, buildings and the rights to the SylvaC and Falcon Ware tradenames to Longton Ceramics, a worker's co-operative. Longton Ceramics also purchased the remaining stock on hand. Longton Ceramics survived only eighteen months.

North Midland became the United Co-Operative Society, which took over the Shaw and Copestake factory in 1984 and ran it under the name of Crown Winsor. Crown Winsor re-produced the original SylvaC and Falcon Ware designs. The Co-Operative Society went out of business in 1989, and the factory and assets were sold to Frank Heath in June of that year. By November 1989, the pottery was in receivership. Heath was hoping to sell the pottery as a going concern. However, this did not come to pass, and in December of 1989 the pottery closed. One month later, Portmeiroin Potteries purchased the property and machinery. In 1998, a Longton studio potter began reproducing Shaw and Copestake ware, marking them SylvaCeramics, so one can expect to see a number of old SylvaC designs coming onto the market with the new SylvaCeramics mark.

Character Jugs and Toby Jugs

Shaw and Copestake's offering of Character Jugs and Toby Jugs proved to be quite popular. The majority of the SylvaC jugs produced were actually designed by another firm, Longton New Art Pottery Company Limited, which was active from 1932 to 1966. Shaw and Copestake bought the molds for these jugs in the 1960s. Longton New Art Pottery also used these molds, producing the same jugs under its Kelsboro Ware tradename. Shaw and Copestake created some of its own designs including Punch, Henry VIII, Cavalier, Yeoman of the Guard, William Shakespeare, and the highly collectible Sherwood Forest Character Jug series.

Between Longton and Shaw, three designers were responsible for almost all of the jugs. Reginald Thompson designed model numbers 4486 through 4492, and 5206. George Matthews created model numbers 4493 through 4497, 5113 through 5118, and 5198 through 5203. An artist with the initials O. M. modeled numbers 4400 through 4485.

Shaw and Copestake jugs are most commonly decorated in vivid hand painted colors; however, older production can be found in its popular matte glazes. Shaw and Copestake began impressing the tradename SylvaC into pieces in 1937, but was using the SylvaC tradename before that. In the following listing of Shaw and Copestake jugs, there is no distinction between those marked SylvaC and Falcon Ware. In the 1940s and 1950s, a line of novelty animal jugs was offered under the Falcon Ware tradename. These jugs are quite rare today. The Benskins advertising tankard was commissioned in 1981 in a limited edition of 500.

Falcon Ware mark   Common SylvaC tradename mark   Older SylvaC back-stamp

The most common SylvaC mark on Character and Toby Jugs says "SylvaC Staffordshire Hand Painted Made in England" with the name of the jug underneath. This mark was used from the 1960s through 80s. A more basic mark with just "SylvaC England" or "SylvaC Made in England" was used from 1936 to the 1950s. A new SylvaC mark, with a distinctive "SylvaCeramics", appeared in 1998. These are reproductions from a Longton studio potter. The script Falcon Ware mark and its few variations were used in the 1950s and 60s. The Harrod's Doorman jug was created on commission in 1981 for Harrod's Department Store as a promotional item.

The possibility of finding the same Toby with a SylvaC, Kelsboro Ware, Falcon Ware or Crown Winsor mark, all with the same incised model number, is noteworthy. Perhaps a more curious relationship exists between Shaw and Copestake and Grimwades as indicated by the existence of the same SylvaC jug with a Royal Winton backstamp. It seems likely that Billy Grindy, one of Grimwades chief jug designers, took some designs with him upon leaving Grimwades, and eventually these ended up at Shaw and Copestake. The following list is very comprehensive. Please also refer to photos in the Longton New Art Pottery and Crown Winsor references, as these firms produced jugs from SylvaC molds.

Character Jug Name	Model Number	Height, Inches	Production Life
Abraham Lincoln	2892		1960s
Allan a'Dale	5118	6 3/4	1973 - 1981
Ann Hathaway	4470	5 1/4	1960s - 1975
	4471	3 1/4	1960s - 1982
	4472	small	1960s
Auld Mac	4409	4 1/2	1960s - 1982
	4410	2 1/2	1960s - 1975
Benskins	5222	5 3/4	1981
Bricklayer	5202	6	1974
Cabby	4467	2 3/4	1960s - 1982
Cavalier	306	4 3/4	1945 - 1965
	4453	medium	1960s
	4454	small	1960s
	4487	4 3/4	1965 - 1982
Charles	4466	2 3/4	1960s - 1982
Chelsea Pensioner	4493	4 1/4	1978 - 1982
Churchill	4476	4 1/4	1980 - 1982
Clerk	5199	6	1974
Coachman	4408	4	960s - 1975
Colonel	4420	3 1/4	1960s - 1982
Cook	5203	6	1974
Dick Turpin	un-numbered	4 3/4	1950s
	4486	4 3/4	1960s - 1975
Duffy the Pixie	4484	medium	1960s
Fisherman	5198	6	1974
	4496	5	1980 - 1982
	4417	2 1/4	1980 - 1982
Friar Tuck	5113	6 1/4	1973 - 1981
Gaffer	4415	3 3/4	1960s - 1982
	4416	2 1/2	1960s - 1982
George	4455	medium	1960s
	4456	small	1960s
George Bernard Shaw		6 1/4	
	3279	5 1/2	1950s
	4492	5 1/2	1960s - 1975
Grenadier Guardsman	4494	5	1978 - 1982
Hamlet	4485		1960s
Harrod's Doorman	4497	4 1/4	1981
Henry VIII	un-numbered	4	1950s
	4488	4	1960s - 1982
Horse Dealer	5200	6	1974
Irish Leprechaun	4483	medium	1960s
James	4419	small	1960s
John Bull	un-numbered	5	1960s
John F. Kennedy	2899	6	1960s
	5206	6	1974
Jolly Roger	4413	med	1960s - 1970s
	4414	small	1960s - 1970s
Juliet	4482	large	1960s
King Neptune	4425	x large	1960s
	4422	4 1/4	1960s - 1975
	4423	3 1/4	1960s - 1982
	4424	2	1960s - 1975
Lifeboatman, Seaman Jones	3799		1960s
Lifeguard	4490	5	1978 - 1982
Little John	5116	6 3/4	1973 - 1981
Louis	4464	small	1960s
Madame Marie Pompadour	4465		1960s
Maid Marian	5117	6 1/4	1973 - 1981
Milady	4468	medium	1960s
Miner	5201	6	1974
Mr. Micawber	1453	6 1/8	1938 - 1960s
Mr. Pickwick	1452	5 7/8	1938 - 1960s
	4430	5 3/4	1960s
	4431	4 1/4	1960s - 1982
	4432	3 1/4	1960s - 1982
	4433	2 1/4	1960s - 1982
Mr. Winkle	4446	extra lg	1960s
	4447	4 1/2	1960s - 1975
	4448	3 1/4	1960s - 1982
	4449	2 1/4	1960s - 1975
Mr. Wolfe	4459	3 1/2	1960s - 1982
	4460	2 1/4	1960s - 1982

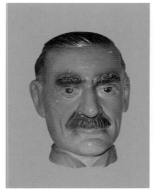

Neville Chamberlain Character Jug

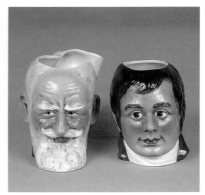

Character Jugs depicting George Bernard Shaw on the left and Robert Burns on the right

John Bull Character Jug in brown glaze with old Falconware mark and in color with modern Sylvac mark

Older models of Mr. Pickwick, model number 1452, on the left and Mr. Micawber, number 1453 on the right

Punch Character Jug in brown glaze

Graduated set of the second version of Mr. Pickwick Character Jugs in large, small and miniature sizes

Henry VIII Falconware Character Jug in brown glaze

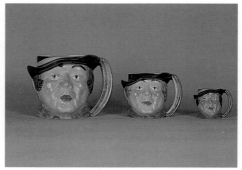

Graduated set of Sam Weller Character Jugs in large, small and miniature sizes

Selection of Character Jugs; top row left to right - Gaffer small and miniature, and small Mr. Wolfe; bottom row left to right - Cabby, King Neptune, Charles I, and Welsh Lady, all miniature size

Mr. Pickwick Falconware Bud Vase from T. Lawrence

Small size Character Jugs, from left to right; top row - Dick Turpin, Yeoman of the Guard, Cavalier; bottom row - Henry VIII, Skull, and Punch

Sherwood Forest Character Jug series: top row left to right - Allan a'Dale, Maid Marian, and Sheriff of Nottingham; bottom row left to right - Robin Hood, Little John, and Friar Tuck

William Shakespeare and Ann Hathaway miniature sized Character Jugs

Large and small Squire Toby Jugs, and large and small size Squire Character Jugs

Musketeer Toby Jug with new SylviaCeramics backstamp

Character Jug Name	Model Number	Height, Inches	Production Life
Mrs. Bardell	4442	extra lg	1960s
	4443	large	1960s
	4444	medium	1960s
	4445	small	1960s
Nellie	4418	2 1/4	1960s
Neptune	4423	3	
Neville Chamberlain	1463	6 1/4	1938 - 1940s
Punch	un-numbered	5	1940s - 1960s
Robert Burns	2815	5 5/8	1960s
	3106	5 5/8	1960s
Robin Hood	5114	6 1/4	1973 - 1981
Romeo	4481	large	1960s
Sam Weller	4438	extra lg	1960s
	4439	4 1/4	1960s - 1975
	4440	3 1/4	1960s - 1982
	4441	2	1960s - 1975
Santa Clause	4426	extra lg	1980 - 1982
	4427	4 1/2	1980 - 1982
	4428	3 1/4	1960s - 1982
	4429	small	1960s
Sheriff of Nottingham	5115	6 1/4	1973 - 1981
Silas Sly	4421	3 1/4	1960s - 1975
Simon	4457	3 3/4	1960s - 1975
	4458	2 1/2	1960s - 1975
Skull	4570	4	
Squire	4411	4	1960s - 1982
	4412	2 1/2	1960s - 1975
Tony Weller	4434	extra lg	1960s
	4435	4 3/4	1960s - 1975
	4436	3 1/4	1960s - 1982
	4437	2 1/4	1960s - 1975
Touchstone	4480	large	1960s
Uncle Sam	2888	6 1/2	1960s
Watchman	4450	4 1/2	1960s - 1975
	4451	3 1/2	1960s - 1975
	4452	2 1/4	1960s - 1982
Welsh Lady	4477	2 3/4	1960s - 1982
William Shakespeare	2815	5	1950s - 1960s
	4491	5	1969 - 1982
	4473	4 3/4	1960s - 1975
	4474	3	1960s - 1982
	4475	small	1960s
Yeoman of the Guard	312	4 1/2	1950s - 1960s
	4489	4 1/4	1960s - 1982

Toby Jug Name	Model Number	Height, Inches	Production Life
Bulldog	47	5	1940s - 1950s
Cat	42	5	1940s - 1950s
Coachman		6 7/8	
	4407	5 1/2	1960s - 1982
Dog	45	5	1940s - 1950s
	46	5	1940s - 1950s
Duck	43	4 3/4	1940s - 1950s
Elephant	41	5	1940s - 1950s
Falstaff	4479	6 1/4	1960s - 1982
Leprechaun	4495	4 1/2	1980 - 1982
Mandolin Player music box	4462	8	1960s
	4461	4	1960s - 1982
	4463	small	1960s
Mine Host	4400		1960s - 1970s
Musketeer	4469	5 7/8	1980 - 1982
Ordinary or New Toby	4401	7 1/4	1960s - 1982
	4402	5 1/4	1960s - 1982
	4403	3 3/4	1960s - 1982
Old Toby	4404	7 7/8	1960s - 1982
	4405	4	1960s - 1982
	4406	3	1960s - 1982
Rabbit	44	5	1940s - 1950s
Rhino	40	5	1940s - 1950s
Sarah Gamp		9	1936 - 1940s
	1230	6 1/2	1936 - 1940s
Sam Weller	813	8 3/4	1936 - 1940s
	1231	6 1/2	1936 - 1940s
Shylock	4478	6 1/2	1960s - 1982

Derivative	Height, inches
Mr. Pickwick bud vase	4 3/8

Old Toby in large and small size

Large size Sarah Gamp and Sam Weller Toby Jugs in solid color glazes of green and blue respectively

A full colorway Sam Weller Toby Jug in the large size

Shawnee Pottery
Zanesville, Ohio

Character Jug Name	Height, inches
Ram	4

Toby Jug Name	Height, inches
Little Bo Peep "USA"	9 1/4
"USA 47"	7 1/2
	7
Little Boy Blue "USA 46"	7 1/2
Ordinary Toby "USA"	5 3/4
	4

History

Unlike most other potteries of its time, Shawnee Pottery was a large public corporation focused on returning profits to its shareholders. The pottery was incorporated in Delaware on December 9, 1936. Two days later the firm agreed to lease the Ohio Encaustic Company's facility in Zanesville, Ohio. Residing on thirty-five acres, this fifty-seven building facility had been constructed by American Encaustic Tile beginning in 1874. Ohio Encaustic was forced to sell due to financial hardships caused by the Depression. The first President of Shawnee Pottery was Addis Emmett Hull Junior, the former President and General Manager of Hull Pottery.

Shawnee re-opened the Zanesville plant in the summer of 1937, much to the delight of the local townspeople. The first designer hired by the firm in 1937 was Louise Elizabeth Bauer, who created the Shawnee Indian arrowhead logo. Before the outbreak of World War II, and for a few years into the war, the pottery produced primarily dinnerware, console sets, tea and coffee sets, planters, figurines and other utilitarian wares. The goods were typically produced in solid color glazes with minimal cold painted decorative highlights. For less than one year beginning in 1938, the firm also potted products for George Rumrill of Little Rock after his falling out with Red Wing Pottery.

The government took over most of the factory from May of 1943 until October 1945, greatly reducing Shawnee's output. After regaining full use of the facility, Shawnee's post war production ramped up quickly, and from that time until 1954, the firm produced its more collectible wares, including cookie jars, Corn King dinnerware, teapots, vases and figurines. Shawnee also began fully decorating its wares with hand painting or spraying under glaze.

Arthur Grindley served briefly as Shawnee's President from July 1, 1953, until resigning on January 11, 1954. Grindley was the former owner of Grindley Artware from nearby Sebring, Ohio, whose pottery could not rebound from a devastating fire. In 1954, John F. Bonistall became President and General Manager of the pottery. He drastically changed the firm's operations and products to become more competitive. Gone were the labor intensive, decorative designs of the previous decade. The factory focused on mass production of the new Corn Queen dinnerware and floral items.

In 1963, the stockholders voted to liquidate Shawnee. Production ceased and the pottery closed on June 20, 1963. United Technologies' Automotive Group currently inhabits the site. Shawnee is perhaps best known today for its cookie jars.

Character Jugs and Toby Jugs

Shawnee introduced Toby Jugs in 1944, although Shawnee collectors refer to them as pitchers. The designs for Little Bo Peep and Little Boy Blue were filed by Rudolph V. Ganz in June of 1944; however, the jugs were probably in production before the filing. Little Bo Peep was design patent number 139093 and was impressed "Patented Bo Peep USA." Bo Peep and Boy Blue came in a variety of handpainted colorways and carry the mark "Shawnee U.S.A." and the numbers 47 and 46, respectively. Only a few heavily gilded Bo Peep jugs were made. These would command a much higher value. Little Bo Peep was redesigned a few years later. The two versions are slightly different in height and easy to tell apart.

The Shawnee Ordinary Toby was produced before World War II. It was produced in the solid color glazes of the time; Dusty Rose,

Burgundy, Turquoise, and Old English Ivory. Ivory jugs have been found with black cold paint accents to the eyes and face. These jugs are impressed "U.S.A." It is common to find what appear to be hand potted and painted Shawnee Ordinary Toby jugs. It is unknown whether the Shawnee mold became available to studio potters, or many individuals simply hand decorated the rather plainly finished Shawnee jug.

Little Bo Peep on the left and Little Boy Blue on the right

Ordinary Toby in creamware glaze

Shelley Potteries Limited
Longton, England

History

The Shelley Potteries traces its roots back to the beginning of the Foley Pottery, which was established by John Smith of Fenton Hall. The Foley Pottery was built between Longton and Fenton on land owned by the Foley family. Under a series of names, most notably Elkin Knight & Company, the Foley Pottery operated from 1822 until 1846, producing a variety of dinnerware and utilitarian products.

John Knight took over the factory in 1846 and continued operations. In 1853, Knight took in Henry Wileman, a London based pottery and glass retailer, as a partner. Knight retired three years later, and Wileman renamed the firm after himself. To expand into china production, Henry immediately built a second factory next to the Foley factory and named it Foley China Works. Henry decided to operate the two potteries independently. While he retained control of the Foley Pottery, management of the Foley China Works was entrusted to James F. Wileman and Charles J. Wileman. This pair traded under the names James & Charles Wileman between 1864 and 1869, then as James F. Wileman until 1892.

Meanwhile, at the original Foley Pottery, Henry Wileman hired Joseph Ball Shelley as a traveling salesman. Joseph was from a strong family of potters dating back to Randle Shelley in 1748. Joseph Shelley became Wileman's partner in 1872. When Henry later retired, Joseph assumed control of the firm. Joseph's son Percy Shelley joined the Foley Pottery in 1881 with a strong desire to expand exports and improve the quality of the firm's products, which up to this point were of good quality, but no better in any way than that of other factories.

James Wileman and Joseph Shelley consolidated control of the Foley Pottery and Foley China Works in 1892. The combined pottery became known as Wileman & Company. The enterprise underwent a significant expansion starting in 1893 under the direction of Joseph's son, Percy Shelley. After visiting the Chicago Columbian Exhibition earlier that year, Percy decided the means to achieve his goals of increasing quality and expanding the firm could be reached through fine bone china production. Percy hired artists to design new patterns, and overseas agents were appointed who successfully sold these new china designs, primarily to North America and the British colonies. Joseph Shelley died in 1896 and Percy assumed full control of the pottery. In spite of the economic difficulties following the Boer War, Percy continued producing new wares.

The first notable artist hired by Percy was Rowland Morris. Rowland focused on redesigning the firm's bone china products and remained with the firm until his death in 1896. Frederick H. Rhead joined the firm in 1897 as Art Director. Frederick and Percy were primarily responsible for raising the quality and artistic beauty of the firm's products. Frederick created

Shelley Foley mark, Intarsio used instead of faience when appropriate

Victorian Baby Toby Jug in Intarsio finish (courtesy of Les and Enid Foley)

Friar Tuck Toby Jug in Intarsio finish

259

John Bull Toby Jug in Intarsio finish

Irishman Toby Jug in Intarsio finish

Scotsman Toby Jug in Intarsio finish

Unkel Sam Toby Jug in creamware finish, marked Wardle

Elf Toby Jug (from the collection of John Hobbs)

Intarsio Lloyd George teapot (from the collection of John Hobbs)

the Intarsio line in 1898 that combined Dutch coloring methods and designs. The name Intarsio was derived from the Italian form of inlay pottery intarsia. This line was characterized by hand painting on under glaze transfer prints with designs of bold, bright colors, often over a green or brown background. Rhead's Intarsio line carried pattern numbers between 3000 and 3388. Rhead left the firm in 1905.

Wileman and Company used the trade name Foley China from 1892 into the 1910s. Due to conflicts with another Foley label, the firm began using the tradename Shelley China in 1910. Between 1920 and 1925 another tradename, Foley Art China, was used. In 1925, the firm's name was changed to Shelley, and then in 1929 changed again to Shelley Potteries Limited. One constant throughout these changes was the firm's consistent concern with maintaining a positive market image. At one point, Shelly marketed itself as "Potters to the World."

Walter Slater was hired from Doulton as the new Art Director in 1905. Beginning in 1911, Walter created a new Intarsio series that had an Art Nouveau flair, floral designs and brighter colors than Rhead's. Walter's son Eric Slater joined the firm in 1919 as a designer. Eric served as the Art Director for Shelley from 1928 until the firm was sold in 1966. Eric led the development of new lines and designs of dinnerware. Percy's three sons, Bob, Norman and Jack all joined the firm full-time after the end of World War I.

The firm's popularity peaked in the 1930s, when its most famous bone china dinnerware patterns were introduced. Shelley Potteries remained in active production until 1966, when it was taken over by Allied English Potteries and the Shelley factory was renamed Shelley China Limited. Allied English was later merged into the Doulton Group in 1971, which still uses the Shelley name.

Character Jugs and Toby Jugs

As a part of Frederick Rhead's Intarsio line, Shelley developed six high quality Toby Jugs at the Foley factory in the early twentieth century. These jugs came in the Intarsio finish, a creamware finish, or a full faience colorway. The Intarsio tobies are characterized by their dark brown and green coloring. So far, only five have been positively identified. Four of these jugs were named Jonbuljug, Paddijug, Sandyjug, and Unkelsamjug in a Foley sketch book. The Intarsio Unkle Sam exists so far only in this factory design book; a potted example has not been found. However, a speciman identical to the Unkle Sam design in the sketch book has been found with an impressed "Wardle" mark.

Shelley issued a small Character Jug under the Foley name imaged after Sarreguemines' Jolly Fellow, model number 3181. The Shelley version was sometimes commissioned with advertising and as such would be valued at the higher end of the range. Shelley also produced crested china tobies similar to those of Goss. In 1926, Mabel Lucie Attwell introduced a nursery tea set with an Elf motif. The creamer from this set makes a very nice Toby Jug. Attwell designed a similar animal teaset in 1930 with a chick sugar, rabbit creamer, and duck teapot. The Ordinary Toby was an advertising piece produced for Hoare & Company. Written around the base of the jug is "Hoare & Co Toby Ale in Bottle".

Common marks found on Shelley products include the name "Shelley" in block letters inside a shield and "England" underneath. This was used between 1912 and 1925 with the words "Late Foley" sometimes included up to 1916. The later mark, used between 1925 and 1945, was a flowing script "Shelley", also inside a shield with the block "England" underneath. The most desirable Shelley tobies are the Foley Intarsio jugs that are very difficult to find.

Character Jug Name	Height, Inches	Production Life
Jolly Fellow	5	1920s

Toby Jug Name		Model Number	Height, Inches	Production Life
Elf	Reg # 724421		6 1/8	1926 - 1930s
Friar Tuck	Intarsio	3138	8 1/2	1911 - 1920s
Irishman	Intarsio	3460	8 1/2	1898 - 1920s
	faience	7623	8 1/2	1910 - 1916
John Bull	Intarsio	3105	7 1/2	1898 - 1920s
	faience		7 1/2	1910 - 1920s
Ordinary Toby for Hoare		8040	9	1920s - 1934
Rabbit			5	
Scotsman	Intarsio	3459	7 3/8	1898 - 1920s
Standing Toby crested				1900 - 1920s
Unkel Sam	Intarsio		7 3/4	1898 - 1920s
Victorian Baby	Intarsio	3134	6 1/2	1898 - 1920s

History

Arthur Shorter founded the Shorter & Son family pottery business in 1874. Before founding his own firm, Arthur worked as an apprentice at Hope and Carter in Burslem, the renowned Minton factory in Stoke-on-Trent, and Bodley's China in Burslem.

Arthur's first venture was a pottery located in Hanley, but he soon sold that site to Albert Wenger, a Swiss ceramic maker. A firm known as Shorter and Company, consisting of a partnership of Shorter, Bethelley and Millward, followed this. Documentation shows that this partnership was dissolved on November 9, 1878. However, out of this came a partnership of Arthur Shorter and James Boulton, recently from Wedgwood, which operated under the name of Shorter and Boulton, and began producing earthenware and majolica. Around this time, Arthur married Henrietta Wilkinson, a woman slightly his senior, who also happened to be the sister of Arthur J. Wilkinson. In 1878, Shorter and Boulton began operating on Copeland Street in Stoke-on-Trent, the location at which Shorter & Son would remain until 1964.

Arthur Wilkinson started his pottery in Burslem in 1885, completely independently from that of his brother-in-law's. However, Wilkinson's life ended too early in a tragic accident in 1891, and Arthur Shorter took over the operation of Wilkinson's factory, while Boulton continued to run Shorter and Boulton. In 1894, Shorter purchased the Wilkinson factory, consolidating the two factories into one enterprise, each operating under its own name. By the turn of the century, both of Shorter's sons, Colley and Guy, along with Boulton's son, had joined the firm and James Boulton had retired.

In 1906, the firm changed its name to Shorter and Son, and by World War I the business had grown significantly. The end of World War I brought Arthur's retirement from the business, and the reigns of the company were passed to his sons. A boom in business occurred after World War I, enhanced by a huge demand for functional earthenware. As a part of its expansion, Shorter and Son purchased the Newport factory in Burslem in 1920 and operated it in association with the Wilkinson factory. Colley Shorter remained the driving force behind all three of the factories.

By 1925, Clarice Cliff was associated with Shorter and Son through Wilkinsons, being taken under Colley's wing as a budding artistic talent. Initially, Clarice began by decorating blanks from the Newport factory. She produced bold, colorful designs in what probably can be called the beginnings of her famous Bizarre Ware. Clarice eventually became the second wife of Colley Shorter in 1940. This marriage was not fully welcomed by the family.

Shorter and Son became a limited company in 1933 with three partners, Colley Shorter, Guy Shorter and Harry Steele. Harry Steele was named the manager of the Shorter factory at this time. With his public flair, Harry became key to the successful marketing of the firm and its products. It was also this year that Harry hired Mabel Leigh. From this point forward, designs, styles and production expanded greatly.

Business continued strongly through World War II and into the 1950s, with a series of new product lines and bold publicity campaigns. By 1960, foreign competition, older facilities, and changes in consumer's tastes were taking their toll on the success of the company. Colley Shorter retired in 1961 due to worsening health and died in 1963. He bequeathed the bulk of his estate to his wife, Clarice Cliff. Clarice sold the Wilkinson and Newport factories to Midwinter in 1963. The remainder of the Shorter and Son firm merged with Fieldings & Company in 1964, and the Shorter factory was shut down.

After Fieldings closed in 1982, various potteries obtained Shorter molds and began reproducing its ware. Many of these pieces carry new Shorter marks, so are easily distinguished from original production. By 1997, the Newport factory was abandoned and beyond renovation and was demolished in March of that year to make way for apartments and houses.

For a more detailed history of Shorter and Son, please refer to *The Shorter Connection* by Irene and Gordon Hopwood.

Character Jugs and Toby Jugs

The first reference to Shorter & Son production of Toby Jugs occurred in 1917, when they were described as a sideline to the firm's regular trade. From the introduction of its first "quaint Toby's and Tubby figures" in 1917, as described by the *Pottery Gazette*, Shorter and Son produced a wide range of Character and Toby Jugs for the next forty-five years. During it reign, only Royal Doulton out produced Shorter & Son in the number of different character designs. The first documented Toby was a twelve inch tall Ordinary Toby designed after a 19th century jug produced

Shorter mark used by Sherwood

GENUINE
STAFFORDSHIRE
HAND PAINTED
SHORTER & SON LTD.
ENGLAND.

Most common Shorter &Son
backstamp

by Hollins of Hanley. This jug has become known as the Shorter Hollins Toby. Other early tobies include the Coachman, Punch, Judy, a twelve inch tall Standing Toby with grape vines decorating his hat, and a standing Female Toby.

Many new Toby and Character Jugs were introduced in the 1930s and 1940s. Themes and sets were produced, one of the more interesting being "The Queen's Men Series," which consisted of the Outrider, Royal Volunteer and Trumpeter, all standing on parade in full military dress. Factory design notes mention that Betty Silvester designed some of these jugs. The large Winston Churchill Character Jug was introduced in 1939, when Churchill was appointed the First Lord of the Admiralty for the second time. After World War II, jugs became one of the firm's most successful product lines.

Shorter & Son produced several advertising jugs. The Totem Mug, complete with menacing face and hatchet handle, was a promotional piece for Butlin's Holiday Camp. It can be found with the slogan "Butlins Beachcomber Souvenir" and impressed S912. The Tudor Court Character Jug, listed as the Tasmanian Tudor in *The Shorter Connection*, was a promotional jug to be sold at the Tudor Court in Hobart, which is the capital of Tasmania, Australia. Tudor Court is a tourist attraction in Sandy Bay, a district of Hobart south of the city proper. It is a highly detailed, large-scale model of a medieval English village built by John Palotta, a polio victim. The jug depicts an 18th century gentleman in a tricorn hat. Around the brim of the hat is lettering in relief that reads "Hobart Tasmania Tudor Court." The Butler Character Jug has the word Butler's on both sides of its handle. Of course, the Nut Brown Ale Toby promotes his favorite brand of beverage. He is often incised 402 and can be found in a full colorway or Rockingham-brown finish and in two sizes.

One can become confused between the Sailor, Old Salt and H.M.S. Cheerio Toby Jugs. All three names have been used, and all the jugs are identical. However, the incised names on the base of the jugs are either Sailor or Old Salt. H.M.S. Cheerio is the lettering around his hat, not the jug's name. The Admiral Character Jug has been found as a Cortman reproduction with Cortman's Shorter backstamp. It is assumed this jug is identical to Shorter's original mold. Also Cortman produces a 3 1/4 inch Pirate Character Jug attributed to Shorter. However, this has not been correlated with any known Shorter jug.

In 1949, Shorter & Son issued a new set of figural Toby Jugs based on the actors and costumes in several Gilbert and Sullivan operas. This series of Toby Jugs was different than any other jugs issued by Shorter and are among the finest and most sought after 20th century jugs produced by any maker. Shorter had negotiated permission from D'Oyly Carte to model and produce fourteen jugs from five different Gilbert and Sullivan operas. The characters were depicted posing from a scene in their respective operas, and wearing their authentic D'Oyly Carte Opera Company stage costumes. The characters produced from each of these operas were:

The Gondoliers	*H. M. S. Pinafore*
Duke of Plaza Toro	Dick Dead-Eye
Duchess of Plaza Toro	Buttercup
Don Alhambra	Sir Joseph Porter

Pirates of Penzance	*The Mikado*
Pirate King	Mikado
Pirate Maid	Katisha
Major General	Ko Ko
	Pooh Bah

The Yeoman of the Guard
Jack Point

Clarice Cliff was the Art Director of Shorter & Son at the time, and was responsible in large part for the design of this series, being personally involved in creating some of the original drawings of the D'Oyly Carte actors. It is also known that Betty Silvester modeled the Duchess of Plaza Toro, the Pirate King and the Pirate Maid.

These jugs were made in two sizes: ten inches tall and approximately five inches tall. Most jugs had a backstamp with the name of the character incised, "Shorter & Son Ltd." in a scroll, plus the words "REPRODUCED BY PERMISSION OF THE D'OYLY CARTE OPERA CO." Some have been found with only the character's name incised and no backstamp.

A few jugs of a slightly smaller size than the Shorter small jugs may be found with no backstamp, only the character's name impressed into the base. These were produced in 1985 by Rockingham and have a considerably lower market value than Shorter originals. Each Rockingham jug originally came with a Certificate of Authenticity that was signed by T. M. M. Rate, the Managing Director.

In the 1980s, Larry Ewing of Sherwood China reissued the entire set of D'Oyly Carte tobies in an even smaller size, just over four inches tall. Around two hundred sets were issued via a numbered limited edition mail-order subscription through Scotland Direct. The backstamp on this reissue includes a unique Shorter & Son Limited mark, the name of the character, and the name of the opera. The quality of the Sherwood jugs is not as good as the Shorter originals or even the earlier Rockingham reproductions. The market value for the set is also considerably lower than that of this original Shorter jugs and somewhat lower than the Rockingham set. It is also likely that Artone Pottery was asked by Scotland Direct to fill in missing pieces of Sherwood's limited edition sets after Sherwood went out of business.

Cortman Limited now owns the Sherwood D'Oyly Carte molds and is re-producing new sets of these small tobies. It is important to be aware of the various re-productions of these jugs. The originals are worth far more than the re-productions. A few examples of large sized D'Oyly Carte re-productions have been seen at Staffordshire Fine Ceramics; however, these were only put into limited production.

Another reissued jug of note is the 1993 edition of the small Father Neptune Toby. This was commissioned to celebrate the release of *The Shorter Connection* by Irene and Gordon Hopwood. This special release has a different colorway than the original, with a black lobster instead of red, and was produced by Staffordshire Fine Ceramics for the Hopwoods.

Marks on older Shorter jugs include the phrase "Old Staffs Toby". The most common original Shorter mark, however, is "Genuine Staffordshire Hand Painted Shorter & Son Ltd England" stamped in black. Two other derivative items were produced by Shorter that are quite at home in a collection of Toby and Character Jugs. These are the Daisy Bell and Mother Goose spill vases. Both were made around the 1950s in a large and small size.

With its purchase of Shorter and Son in 1964, Fielding & Company assumed ownership of the firm's assets including inventory, molds and trademarks. This included the molds of the

Toby and Character Jugs. Many Shorter jugs appear with the common Shorter backstamp in green ink. This is most likely the first mark used on jugs produced by Fieldings. Shorter jugs are also found with a green ink Crown Devon mark, the Fieldings tradename. In the late 1980s, Wood Potters of Burslem began issuing jugs from Shorter molds using a mark with "Shorter" inside a loop formed by a ribbon. Today several firms are using Shorter Toby molds, including Staffordshire Fine Ceramics and Cortman Limited. In 1996, Cortman used a black ink mark with "Shorter" in large block letters. It changed to an oval with the words "Shorter Hand Painted" inside in 1997. Beginning in 1997, Cortman re-issued the set of small sized D'Oyly Carte jugs with this mark, priced at roughly $15 each. In 1998 a Longton studio potter started reproducing Shorter & Son jugs using a modern looking version of the old mark.

Today, Shorter and Son jug molds are owned by many firms and may continue to appear on the market with new and different backstamps. Of course, more recent jugs produced by others from Shorter molds have a considerably lower market value than the equivalent Shorter jug. The collector should be aware of these differences, although the newer jugs will most likely become collectible in their own right over time. Please refer to the sections for these other potters elsewhere in this book.

Original Shorter and Son Character and Toby Jugs likely will become some of the most collectible jugs during the next century. The following listings are complete in terms of the characters produced by Shorter. Jugs with specific sizes and market values are those positively identified and catalogued. A separate list includes those jugs from company records and literature, but which have not yet been identified, even as to whether they are Character or Toby Jugs.

Shorter & Son D'Oyly Carte backstamp

Sherwood China D'Oyly Carte backstamp

Block letter Shorter & Son mark used by Cortman Ltd

More ornate Shorter mark used by Cortman Ltd

Character Jug Name	Height, Inches	Production Life
Beefeater	2	1949 - 1964
Beefeater Gin Jug	6 1/2	1960 - 1964
Butler	5	
Captain Ahab	4 1/2	1950s - 1964
Cavalier	4 1/4	1940 - 1950s
Clown	5	
Coachman	7 1/2 4 3/4 4	1920s - 1950s 1920s - 1950s 1920s - 1950s
Covent Garden Bill	3 1/2	1949 - 1964
Dick Turpin	5	1950s - 1960s
Father Neptune	3 3/4	1949 - 1964
Fisherman	3 3/4	1949 - 1964
Friar Tuck	7	
Guardsman	2 1/4	
Hayseed	5 1/2	1950s - 1960s

Character Jug Name	Height, Inches	Production Life
Highwayman	3 1/4	1949 - 1964
Huntsman	3 3/4	1949 - 1964
Irish Mike	3 3/4	1949 - 1964
Mountaineer	4 1/2	
Old Bill	4 3 1/2	
Pedro	5 1/2	1950s - 1960s
Pirate Head incised S908	4 1/2	1950s - 1960s
Robert Burns	4 1/4	
Robin Hood	8	
Sheikh incised 836	5 1/2	1950s - 1960s
Sinbad	4 3/4	1950s - 1960s
Totem Mug	4 3 3/4	
Tudor Court (Tasmanian Tudor)	3 1/2	
Winston Churchill	6 4 1/2	1939 - 1940s 1939 - 1940s

Clown Character Jug (from the collection of Lionel Bailey)

Mountaineer Character Jug on left and Captain Ahab on right

Old Bill Character Jug in large and small sizes

Robert Burns Character Jug (from the collection of Lionel Bailey)

Robin Hood and Friar Tuck large sized Character Jugs

Totem advertising mug

Tudor Court jug advertising for the Tudor Court in Hobart, Tasmania (from the collection of Paul Singh)

Set of medium size Character Jugs from the 1950s; top row left to right - Dick Turpin, Sinbad, and Pirate; bottom row left to right - Pedro, Sheik, and Hayseed

Toby Jug Name	Height, Inches	Production Life
Beefeater	8 3/4	1930s - 1964
	7 1/4	1930s - 1964
	4 3/4	1930s - 1964
Buttercup	10	1949 - 1955
	5	1949 - 1955
(Sherwood)	4 1/2	1980s - current
Cavalier	6 1/2	
Chelsea Pensioner	9	1930s - 1964
	6 1/2	1930s - 1964
	4 1/4	1930s - 1964
	2	
Coachman	8 1/2	1920s - 1950s
	4 1/2	1920s - 1950s
Covent Garden Bill	8	1940 - 1950s
Dick Dead-Eye	10	1949 - 1955
	4 3/4	1949 - 1955
(Sherwood)	4 1/4	1980s - current
Dick Whittington	4 1/2	1935 - 1950s
Don Alhambra	10 1/4	1949 - 1955
	4 1/2	1949 - 1955
(Sherwood)	4 1/4	1980s - current
Duchess of Plaza Toro	9	1949 - 1955
	4 3/4	1949 - 1955
(Sherwood)	4 1/2	1980s - current
Duke of Plaza Toro	10 1/4	1949 - 1955
	4 3/4	1949 - 1955
(Sherwood)	4 1/4	1980s - current
Father Neptune	10 1/4	1950s
	7	1950s
1993 reissue	7	1993
Female Toby	9	1920s - 1950s
Fisherman	7	1940 - 1950s
Flower Seller	9 1/4	1930s - 1964
	7	1930s - 1964
	5 1/4	1930s - 1964
	3 1/4	1930s - 1964
Gardener	8 1/2	1930s - 1964
	6 1/2	1930s - 1964
	4 1/2	1930s - 1964

Toby Jug Name	Height, Inches	Production Life
Guardsman	8 1/2	1930s - 1964
	6 1/2	1930s - 1964
	4 3/4	1930s - 1964
Henry VIII	10	1935 - 1950s
	5	1935 - 1950s
Highwayman	6	1939 - 1950s
	2 1/4	1939 - 1950s
H.M.S. Cheerio see Sailor or Old Salt		
Huntsman	6 7/8	1949 - 1964
Irish Mike	7	1949 - 1964
Jack Point	10	1949 - 1955
	5	1949 - 1955
(Sherwood)	4 3/4	1980s - current
John Bull	5 1/4	1940s - 1950s
Judge	7	1950s
Judy	6	1920s - 1950s
Katisha	10	1949 - 1955
	4 3/4	1949 - 1955
(Sherwood)	4 1/4	1980s - current
Ko Ko	9 3/4	1949 - 1955
	4 1/4	1949 - 1955
(Sherwood)	4	1980s - current
Long John Silver	9 3/4	1935 - 1950s
	5 3/4	1935 - 1950s
Lord Mayor	6 7/8	1950s
Major General	10 1/2	1949 - 1955
	5	1949 - 1955
(Sherwood)	4 1/2	1980s - current
Mikado	10 1/4	1949 - 1955
	5	1949 - 1955
(Sherwood)	4 1/2	1980s - current
Mr. Farmer	7 1/2	1933 - 1950s
	4 3/4	1933 - 1950s
Mrs. Farmer	7 1/4	1933 - 1950s
	4 3/4	1933 - 1950s
Nut Brown Ale	7 1/4	1933 - 1940s
	5	1933 - 1940s

Jugs referred to in Shorter & Son records, but not confirmed

Abraham Lincoln
Admiral
George Washington
Guy of Gisborne
Innkeeper
King of Hearts
Mac
Queens of Hearts
Red Indian
Santa Claus
Sheriff of Nottingham
Sir Walter Scott

Toby Jug Name	Height, Inches	Production Life
Old King Cole	10 1/4 5 1/2	1935 - 1950s 1935 - 1950s
Old Salt (see also Sailor)	8 1/2 6 1/2 4 1/4	1930s - 1964 1930s - 1964 1930s - 1964
Old Toby	11 1/4	
Ordinary "Hollins" Toby	12 1/2	1917 - 1930s
Outrider	7 1/8 4 5/8	1950s - 1964 1950s - 1964
Parakeet	8 7/8	1950s - 1964
Parson John Brown	8 1/4 6 3/4	1935 - 1950s 1935 - 1950s
P.C. 49 (Policeman)	7 5	1930s - 1964 1930s - 1964
Pearly King	7	
Pearly Queen	7 1/2	
Pirate King (Sherwood)	10 5 4 1/2	1949 - 1955 1949 - 1955 1980s - current
Pirate Maid (Sherwood)	9 3/4 4 3/4 4 1/4	1949 - 1955 1949 - 1955 1980s - current
Pooh Bah (Sherwood)	9 1/2 4 3/4 4 1/4	1949 - 1955 1949 - 1955 1980s - current
Punch		1920s - 1950s
Robin Hood	7	1950s - 1964
Royal Volunteer	7 1/2 4 3/4	1950s - 1960s 1950s - 1960s
Sailor (see also Old Salt)	8 1/2 6 1/2 4 1/4	1930s - 1964 1930s - 1964 1930s - 1964
Scottie	8 3/4 6 3/4 4 3/4	1930s - 1964 1930s - 1964 1930s - 1964
Sir Joseph Porter (Sherwood)	10 5 4 1/2	1949 - 1955 1949 - 1955 1980s - current
Soldier	2 1/4	1939 - 1950s
South American Joe	9 3/4 5 1/2	1935 - 1950s 1935 - 1950s
Squire	4	
Standing Toby	12 8 1/4 5 4	1933 - 1950s 1933 - 1950s
Toby "491" impressed	12 11 1/4 8 5 1/2 4 3 1/4 3 2 1/4 2	1927 - 1930s 1927 - 1930s 1927 - 1930s
Toby (No. 2)	5 1/2	
Town Crier	3 3/4 3 1/4 2 1/2	
Trumpeter	7 1/4 4 3/4	1950s - 1960s 1950s - 1960s
Uncle Sam	5 3/4	

Two different Winston Churchill Character Jugs

Cavalier Toby Jug and Character Jug set

Beefeater collection: large, medium, and small Toby Jugs followed by a salt shaker, tiny Character Jug, and the Beefeater Gin Jug

Covent Garden Bill Toby Jug and Character Jug set

Chelsea Pensioner Toby Jug in large, medium, small and tiny sizes

Fisherman Toby Jug and Character Jug set

From left to right: Coachman Toby Jug, bust, small Character Jug, and large Character Jug

Flower Seller Toby Jug in large, medium, small and tiny sizes

Gardener Toby Jug in large, medium and small sizes

From left to right: large and medium Guardsman Toby Jug, Guardsman tiny Character Jug, small Guardsman Toby Jug

Large Henry VIII Toby Jug (from the collection of Ann and Joe Nemes)

Highwayman Toby Jug and Character Jug set

Huntsman Toby Jug and Character Jug set

Irish Mike Toby Jug and Character Jug set

Judge Toby Jug (from the collection of Mike Doyle)

Left to right: Long John Silver lamp base, small and large Long John Silver Toby Jugs (from the collection of Mrs. John Hobbs)

Large and small Mr. Farmer on the left; small and large Mrs. Farmer on the right

Large Nut Brown Ale Toby Jug, small Nut Brown Ale Toby Jug, and large Nut Brown Ale Toby Jug in Rockingham glaze

Old King Cole large teapot on top, small teapot on bottom left side, small Toby Jug center, large Toby Jug on right side; teapots are two-faced reversible

Left and center – large and small Parson John Brown Toby Jugs; right – comparable Mr. Pickwick Toby by Samson Smith ca 1890

Graduated set of Old Salt or Sailor Toby Jugs in large, medium, and small sizes, along with Old Salt pepper shaker; also known as H. M. S. Cheerio

Parakeet Toby Jug

Scottie Toby Jug in large, medium, and small size

South American Joe Toby Jug in medium and large sizes (coutesy of Bill and Pam Foster)

Standing Toby Jug in full colorway, red glaze, and brown glaze

John Bull and Uncle Sam patriotic Toby Jugs

Queen's Men Series Royal Volunteer Toby Jug in large and small sizes

Queen's Men Series Trumpeter Toby Jug in large and small sizes

Queen's Men Series small Outrider Toby Jug

Left to right: Lord Mayor, Robin Hood, Pearly King, and Pearly Queen medium size Toby Jugs

Left to right: Henry VIII, P.C. 49, and Dick Whittington small Toby Jugs

Ordinary "Hollins" Toby on left and Standing Toby with floral hat on right

Collection of small toby items: top row left to right - Preserves Jar, Tobacco Jar, and Toby No. 2; bottom row three Ordinary Tobies

Collection of tiny and miniature Toby Jugs; top row left to right - Highwayman, Soldier Flanked by two Ordinary Tobies, and Chelsea Pensioner; bottom row left to right - two Town Criers, Flower Seller, and two Ordinary Tobies

D'Oyly Carte Buttercup Toby Jug from *H.M.S. Pinafore* in large and small size

D'Oyly Carte Dick Dead-Eye Toby Jug from *H. M. S. Pinafore* in large and small size

D'Oyly Carte Don Alhambra Toby Jug from *The Gondoliers* in large and small size

D'Oyly Carte Duchess of Plaza Toro Toby Jug from *The Gondoliers* in large and small size

D'Oyly Carte Duke of Plaza Toro Toby Jug from *The Gondoliers* in large and small size

D'Oyly Carte Jack Point Toby Jug from *The Yeoman of the Guard* in large and small size

D'Oyly Carte Katisha Toby Jug from *The Mikado* in large and small size

D'Oyly Carte Ko-Ko Toby Jug from *The Mikado* in small and large size

D'Oyly Carte Major General Toby Jug from *The Pirates of Penzance* in large and small size

L

D'Oyly Carte Mikado Toby Jug from *The Mikado* in large and small size

D'Oyly Carte Pirate King Toby Jug from *The Pirates of Penzance* in large and small size

D'Oyly Carte Pirate Maid Toby Jug from *The Pirates of Penzance* in large and small size

D'Oyly Carte Pooh Bah Toby Jug from *The Mikado* in large and small size

D'Oyly Carte Sir Joseph Porter Toby Jug from *H. M. S. Pinafore* in large and small size

D'Oyly Carte cigarette boxes featuring Dick Dead-Eye and Pirate King

Selection of small sized D'Oyly Carte Toby Jugs showing difference in sizes of reproductions from originals; three on left by Shorter, three on right reproductions by Sherwood China

Backside of several large size D'Oyly Carte Toby Jugs showing their intricate and decorative handles; from left to right - Major General, Pirate King, Dick Deadeye, Sir Joseph Porter, and Jack Point

Ashtrays	Size, inches
Chelsea Pensioner	4 X 2 3/4
Fisherman	4 X 2 3/4
Guardsman	4 X 2 3/4
Highwayman	4 X 2 3/4

Candy Boxes	Size, inches
Chelsea Pensioner	5 X 3 3/4
Dick Dead-Eye	5 X 3 3/4
Pirate King	5 X 3 3/4
Ordinary Toby	5 X 3 3/4

Creamer	Height, inches
Standing Toby	

Cups	Height, inches
Ordinary Toby	2 1/4

Humidors	Height, inches
Ordinary Toby	5

Lamp Bases	Height, inches
Beefeater	9
Father Neptune	9
Long John Silver	9
Mother Goose	9
Old King Cole	9
Pirate King	9
Scottie	9

Plates	Dia, inches
Daisy Bell	10
Long John Silver	4 5/8
Ordinary Toby	10
Squat Toby	3 3/4

Preserves	Height, inches
Ordinary Toby	5

Salt & Pepper Shakers	Height, inches
Beefeater	
Old Salt	

Saucers	Height, inches
Ordinary Toby	4 3/4

Spill Vases	Height, inches
Daisy Bell	10
	5 1/4
Mother Goose	10 3/4
	5 1/4

Sugar	Height, inches
Ordinary Toby	2 1/2
	2
	1 7/8

Teapots	Height, inches
Old King Cole	7
	5
Squat Toby	5 3/4
	4 3/4
	3 5/8

Wall Pockets	Height, inches
Daisy Bell	
Mother Goose	

Derivative ash trays of Chelsea Pensioner, Long John Silver, Ordinary Toby, and Fisherman

Mother Goose derivative spill vase in large and small sizes

Left to right, large Daisy Bell derivative spill vase, Daisy Bell 10 inch plate, small Daisy Bell spill vase

Collection of Squat Toby teapots

Variety of Toby derivative items including a large plate, large and small sugar and creamer sets, cup and saucer, salt and pepper, and humidor

Half-body Standing Toby set consisting of teapot, sugar, preserves jar, and six mugs; reproduced in the 1980s from Shorter & Son molds by Staffordshire Fine Ceramics

Sigma Giftware
See Jugs Marked by Country of Manufacture under Japan

History

Mr. Leibermann founded the Sitzendorfer porcelain factory in Thuringa, Germany in 1845. The Thuringa area had a long history of quality porcelain production due to an abundance of local natural resources. Only a few years later, in 1850, the factory was taken over by the Voight brothers and operated as Gebruder Voight. The Voight brothers operated the factory until 1900, producing fine quality decorated porcelain ware and figures in the Meissen style. From 1900 to 1902, the factory was owned solely by Alfred Voight and operated as Alfred Voight AG. In 1902, the firm was sold to new owners and the name changed to Sitzendorfer Porzellanmanufaktur.

Under the Voight brother's guidance, production peaked between 1870 and 1910. High quality porcelain, both decorative and everyday ware, continued until 1972. Earthenware production was added in 1923 to expand the variety of goods produced at the factory. In 1957, the firm was partially nationalized. Sitzendorfer was fully nationalized in 1972, and VEB was added to the firm's name. The firm is still active today and offers tours of its porcelain production process to visitors.

Early Sitzendorfer marks include two parallel diagonal lines crossed by a third line in blue underglaze ink. This third line was angled between 1887 until 1900. A horizontal crossing line was also used from 1887, but for a longer period of time. Twentieth century marks include an underglaze blue crown over a blue S, with one line through the S horizontally crossed by two small diagonal lines. A crown with a small cross on top was used between 1902 and 1972. A more modern crown has been used from 1954. Other ware is marked with a gold anchor on the back of the jug, sometimes occurring with a gold stamped "Germany" in a circle on the base.

Toby Jugs

Sitzendorfer produced high quality, porcelain Toby Jugs in the 1930s and 1940s. As with many other makers, Sitzendorfer offered a line of Dickens characters, marking its ware with the gold anchor on the back. These Dickens tobies are similar in style to other German Dickens tobies, such as the plump-bodied jugs marked Erphila, the figural tobies by Sandizell with the character's name incised on the base, or others simply marked "Germany". They are also virtually identical to English tobies by Crown Staffordshire. The apparent intertwining of the molds for these jugs remains a mystery.

The Town Crier comes in two different versions. The first Town Crier version holds his bell high in his right hand. Mouth open wide, he is reading from a piece of paper in his left hand. This Town Crier has been found with blue, green, or red jackets. Town Crier version 2 holds his bell in the left hand, reading from the paper in his right. He also has a lantern hanging from the crook of his right arm.

The Ordinary Toby, Snufftaker, and Town Crier are very desirable and typically found with the blue crown and S mark. The tiny tobies, less than two inches tall, typically have the gold anchor mark on the back of the jug and are unmarked on the base. It is commonly believed that this gold anchor mark was the mark of Samson of Paris or Chelsea of England; however, for toby jugs this is not the case.

Sitzendorfer gold anchor mark

Blue ink mark used by Sitzendorfer

Toby Jug Name	Height, inches
Betsy Prigg	3
Captain Cuttle	3 1/2 3 1/8
Hunchback Toby	7 4 1/2
Huntsman	
John Bull	5 1/4 4 1/4
Judy	5 1/2 4
Little Dorrit	3 1/4 3
Mr. Pickwick	3 3/4 3
Mrs. Gamp	3 3/4 3
Ordinary Toby	8 1/2 5 1/2 4 1/2 4 2 1/2
with mug raised	1 1/2
Punch	4
Snufftaker	8 1/2 7 5 3/4
Squire	
Standing Lady hands on hips	3 1 5/8
Standing Toby hands in pockets	5 3/4 3 1/4 3 1 1/2
Tony Weller	3 1/4
Town Crier version 1	8 3/4 7 1/2 5 1/4 3 3/4 2 1/2
version 2	2 5/8 2
Woman Toby hands on ears hands in lap	1 1/2 1 1/2

Sitzendorfer Derivatives

Derivative Product	Height, inches
Tweedle Dee creamer	5 1/2
Tweedle Dum sugar shaker	5 1/2

Pair of Hunchback Toby Jugs, large and small sizes

John Bull Toby Jug in medium and small sizes

From left to right: medium Judy, small Judy, and medium Standing Toby

Punch Toby Jug with removable hat

Ordinary Toby Jugs in large and small sizes and two color-ways

Large and medium Snufftaker Toby Jugs

Collection of Town Crier Toby Jugs; note two different versions; five sizes shown

Squire Toby Jug on left and Huntsman on right

Group of tiny Toby Jugs, left to right - Lady hands on hips, Woman hands on ears, Lady hands on hips, Toby with mug raised, Standing Toby, Woman with hands in lap

Tweedle Dee and Tweedle Dum creamer and sugar shaker condiment set

Group of Dickens Toby Jugs; top row left to right – small size Mrs. Gamp, Little Dorrit, Cap'n Cuttle, and Mr. Pickwick; bottom row left to right – miniature Little Dorrit, Cap'n Cuttle, and Mr. Pickwick

Snel Ware
See Jugs Marked by Country of Manufacture under United Kingdom

Southern Potteries Incorporated
Erwin, Texas

Earthenware Betsy Toby Jug

History

Southern Potteries was established in Erwin, Texas in 1916. Erwin was a young and booming railroad town, established by the Carolina, Clinchfield and Ohio Railroad. In 1916 the railroad formed the Southern Pottery along its line in Erwin as a commercial enterprise to provide an additional source of revenue for the railroad. The firm soon became one of the largest local employers. The pottery produced a wide variety of china dinnerware and other earthenware products. These products included vases, decorative plates, and pitchers.

Southern was the original producer of Blue Ridge china. Due to its popularity, this pattern was widely copied. The firm used several Blue Ridge marks on its products, including one with a mountain and pine tree. Many pieces left the factory unmarked, however. Unmarked greenware was also sold to jobbers, agents or distributors, who used their own marks. The pottery closed in 1957, finding it difficult to keep pace with low cost Japanese imports. Southern Potteries' products are widely collected today with the original Blue Ridge china highly sought after.

Character Jugs and Toby Jugs

Southern Potteries made a small number of Character Jugs and Toby Jugs. All the Character Jugs were made in china and produced in small quantities, making them very scarce. Reproductions of the Character Jugs were made after Southern Potteries closed. These were not done in a china body and were unmarked. They of course would be less valuable as well.

Southern's Betsy Toby comes in both china and earthenware. She is dressed in a variety of dinnerware patterns, including floral patterns, such as tulip, and one called brick. The china Betsy is marked "Blue Ridge China Hand Painted Underglazed Southern Potteries Inc. Made in U.S.A." The earthenware versions are commonly found unmarked. A 5 1/2 inch tall china Chick pitcher was also produced, but is not included here as a Toby because it pours from the mouth.

Character Jug Name	Height, inches
Daniel Boone	6
Indian	6 3/4
Paul Revere	8 1/2
	6
Pioneer Woman	6 3/4

Toby Jug Name	Height, inches
Betsy china	8 1/2
earthenware	8 1/2

Spencer Stevenson & Company
See Jugs Marked by Country of Manufacture under United Kingdom

Spode
See W. T. Copeland & Sons

St. Clement
St. Clement, France

History

The factory at St. Clement, France was established in 1758 as an expansion of Jacques Chambrette's Luneville pottery, which was founded in 1731. The region certainly was selected for its resources, but also because it offered Chambrette an exemption from French import taxes. Chambrette's son-in-law, Charles Loyal, with partners Richard Mique and Paul Louis Cyffle, a master sculptor from Luneville, operated the factory. Chambrette's son Gabriel soon joined these three. After Chambrette's death in 1758, the two factories encountered financial troubles. Cyffle left St. Clement in 1766, and in 1788 the Luneville factory was sold to Sebastian Keller.

In 1824, St. Clement was sold to Germain Thomas, who, along with his sons, operated the factory until 1892. It was Thomas and his family who produced majolica at St. Clement over a forty-year period. In 1892, the St. Clement factory was sold to the then current owners of the original Chambrette Luneville factory, Sebastian Keller and Messr. Guerin. The St. Clement factory was purchased by the Fenal family in 1922.

St. Clement is known for its distinctive majolica with detailed, subtle coloring. The factory specialized in figural pieces that had soft, blended coloring. Many of the figural pieces are animal jugs.

Toby Jugs

St. Clement is known to have made only a few Toby Jugs of people, including Mirelle, Henry IV, Napoleon, Joan of Arc, and a Monk, along with many animal tobies. The first four people jugs were produced as three-quarter body Toby Jugs with a grayish majolica finish and pink or white monotone faces. The animal jugs usually came in several sizes and are typically, but not always, embossed with St. Clement's superimposed K and G for Keller and Guerin. The factory used this mark from 1892 until 1922. Sometimes the mark includes an S and C, also superimposed. Items produced after World War I were marked with St. Clement in script. Even if unmarked, the majolica finish of these jugs allows for positive identification as St. Clement.

The Man on a Barrel jug was produced in the 1950s and was a reproduction of the jug made earlier by Tessier. St. Clement's version is an inferior jug, being more poorly modeled and decorated with sprayed paint. The animal jugs served as liquor containers and can be found with paper labels from the distillery still affixed.

Toby Jug Name	Height, inches
Cat	12 1/4
Cockatoo	15 1/2
	14
"468"	12 1/2
Duck	17
Elephant	10
Gypp - whippet dog	
Henry IV	
Joan of Arc	
Leopard	
Man on a barrel	
Monk	
Monkey	9 1/2
Mirelle	
Napoleon	
Parrot	
Pig seated	
Poodle "579"	11 3/4
Rooster	14
	12

Poodle Toby Jug

Staffordshire Figure Company Limited
Cheshire, England

Toby Jug Name	Height, inches
Nelson	11 1/2
Squat Toby	5 1/2

History

The Staffordshire Figure Company operates on Hospital Street in Nantwich, Cheshire. It has been active since 1971, producing a wide range of ceramic figurines. Director Mr. M. Rowan manages the firm.

Toby Jugs

Staffordshire Figure's 1996 catalog listed two Toby Jugs: a squat Toby in the Allerton's style, and a large Lord Nelson.

Staffordshire Fine Ceramics Limited
Tunstall, England

Dr. Paul Singh in the Staffordshire Fine Ceramics Showroom

Early Staffordshire Fine Ceramics backstamp

Typical Staffordshire Fine Ceramics backstamp

Shakespeare Collection backstamp

History

Staffordshire Fine Ceramics is a specialist manufacturer of earthenware and fine bone china. Dr. Paul Singh founded the firm as a hobby in 1963. Dr. Singh purchased the Shaw & Sons factory on Williamson Street in Tunstall. Paul, his wife, and a factory manager began by making ceramic cameos and two figures. The business struggled for five years, and then it began production of popular blue and white china wall plaques. From this line of successful wall plaques, the firm was able to expand into a wide variety of ceramics production, including earthenware and bone china teapots, jugs, and figurines.

Singh modeled many of his own designs and also hired artists to work for the pottery. One of the young talented designers employed by the firm was Anthony Cartlidge. Anthony designed and modeled many of the firm's figural teapots and other products. Lionel Goldsmith was hired as Staffordshire Fine's representative in the United States. Goldsmith was also the US representative for Artone Pottery.

The goal of the firm is to target the high quality markets for ceramics. Great emphasis is placed on quality, the result of which can be seen in the detailed modeling of its products. Staffordshire Fine has been successful in catering to this market and expanding production.

Today much of the firm's high volume production, primarily teapots and cup and saucer sets, has been outsourced to a 100,000 square foot factory in the Far East. Design, modeling and production still continue at the Williamson Street factory. The firm currently produces cottageware, teaware, china miniatures, a wide range of giftware, and reproductions of antique Staffordshire dinnerware and figures from original molds. Arguably, today Staffordshire Fine is England's largest producer of figural teapots, offering over 280 different designs in 1999. It also produces specially commissioned ceramics as limited editions or advertising promotions.

Character Jugs and Toby Jugs

Staffordshire Fine produced a wide variety of Character and Toby Jugs. It was one of the most prolific producers of Toby Jugs in the latter 20th century, offering nearly two hundred different characters and sizes since 1963, and producing three to four hundred jugs per week at its peak. Due to the decreasing demand for Toby and Character Jugs, the firm stopped producing jugs in volume in 1985, redirecting its production capacity toward high volume items. Production of some jugs continued after 1985 in low volume; however, only very few new characters were added to the range. Today there remains stock on hand of finished and bisque jugs, but with no marketing emphasis.

Of the many Toby and Character Jugs designed by Staffordshire Fine, the majority were grouped into different series, such as Alice in Wonderland, Country Folk, Pirates and Lawmen, Sea Farers, Days of Olde, and Woodland. Through the purchase of the Shaw & Sons factory, Staffordshire Fine obtained all of Shaw's Burlington Toby Jug molds, and immediately began producing tobies with a Staffordshire Fine mark, in essence continuing the production of Burlington tobies. This series is called Traditional Tobies. Staffordshire Fine also produced tobies from Wood & Sons and Shorter molds it purchased, often renaming the characters. For example, Shorter's Mrs. Farmer is renamed Martha. Using molds acquired from Wedgwood & Company, Staffordshire Fine Ceramics also produced some of Wedgwood's excellent Toby Jugs. The Days Gone By series has the same characters, but with different names, as the Just So Series produced by Westminster, the Co-operative Wholesale Society, and Anton Potters.

Two of Staffordshire Fine's many original designs are its most exciting offerings. These are the large Abraham Lincoln Toby and the oversized Sir Toby Belch Toby, which stands 21 1/2 inches tall. Both of these are well modeled, highly detailed, and expertly painted jugs, as demonstrated by the large eagle handle on the Lincoln jug. Sir Toby Belch was handpainted by world-renowned artist John Kay. Both jugs were produced in very limited quantities with only about sixty of the Lincoln Toby Jug being made for the American Embassy. Sir Toby Belch was intended to be a limited edition of fifty jugs. However, only twenty-two were actually made, two of which are still in possession of the pottery. The firm modeled another extra large jug of Toby Fillpot. Unfortunately the molds were destroyed in a 1994 fire, and no jugs were ever produced.

Two of the firm's Toby Jugs were produced in a prestige finish. These jugs were King Henry VIII and John Peel. The prestige finish was more than just a different, limited edition colorway. It also included much extra hand painting and gilding. These jugs are truly exceptional and a welcome addition to any collection.

The Woodland Series is based on the children's story "The Woodland Children." The story is about an orphanage deep in an enchanted forest where twenty children are cared for by the forest animals and a fairy queen. These caring forest animals are the subjects of Staffordshire Fine's Woodland Toby Jug series.

Among other wonderful characters, the firm produced a Newsboy Toby Jug under its teaware tradename, Crown Dorsett, and a comical set of Leprechaun tobies. Anthony Cartlidge designed many of these Toby Jugs, including the Leprechaun set, Pirate, Judge, Lamplighter, Paddy Hopkirk as a special commission from the Hopkirk driving team, Gary Linaker of soccer fame, and Anthony's namesake jug, Toby Cartlidge. WR Racewear commissioned the Nigel Mansell Toby for Nigel Mansell. The jug included Nigel's signature on the jug. It was introduced in 1992, the year after he won the Formula 1 title, but unfortunately the same year he switched to Indy car racing. Although the limited edition size was 5000 jugs, only around 600 or 700 were made due to Mansell's drop in popularity in England upon changing to Indy racing.

The marks on the firm's jugs tend to vary slightly, but all are well identified. All jugs have a stamped mark with the firm's name that often includes the name of the jug. Older jugs have "Staffordshire Fine Ceramics" in raised lettering on the bottom. This raised lettering was discontinued in 1985. Although almost all jug production ended in 1985, finished jugs were still available for purchase at the factory for at least another fourteen years. The list of Staffordshire Fine's jugs is comprehensive, as the factory provided it.

A considerable portion of the following photos were taken at the Staffordshire Fine Ceramics' showroom, courtesy of Paul Singh.

Blue Danube Character Jug

Unfinished Butlers Character Jug, likely from the Shorter & Son Butler jug

Captain Ahab Character Jug from the Shorter and Son mold

Miniature Alice in Wonderland Character Jugs, left to right: Alice, Cheshire Cat, White Rabbit, and Queen of Hearts

Tiny Alice in Wonderland Character Jugs, top row left to right - Cheshire Cat, Mad Hatter, King of Hearts, and Queen of Hearts; bottom row left to right - Doormouse, Alice, White Rabbit, and Mock Turtle

Sherwood Character Jug Collection, top left to bottom right: Friar Tuck, Little John, Will Scarlet, Maid Marian, Robin Hood, Sheriff of Nottingham, Alan a'Dale, and Prince John

Large Robin Hood Character Jug, most likely from a Shorter & Son mold

Olde Timers Series, left to right - Jolly, Say Again, Whiskers, and Beaky

Days Gone By Series, top row left to right - Paddy, Mother Riley, Jenny Jones, and Whiskers; bottom row left to right - Rob Roy, Dick Turpin, and Hiawatha

War Heroes Series, tiny character jugs; top left to bottom right: Churchill, Ike, MacArthur, Rommel, DeGaulle, Monty, Mountbatten, and Smuts

Sir Winston Churchill Character Jugs, two models one without tophat and one with tophat, both from Shorter & Son molds

Character Jug Name	Series Name	Height, Inches
Allan a'Dale	Sherwood	2
Alice in Wonderland	Alice	1 3/4 / 1 1/4
Beaky	Olde Timers	3
Blue Danube # 711		5 3/4
Cheshire Cat	Alice	1 1/2 / 1 1/4
Churchill	War Heroes	2 1/4
DeGaulle	War Heroes	2 1/4
Dick Turpin	Days Gone By	3 3/4
Doormouse	Alice	mini 1 1/4
Fagin		4
Friar Tuck	Sherwood	2
Gary Linaker		
Hiawatha	Days Gone By	4 1/4
Ike	War Heroes	2 1/4
Jenny Jones	Days Gone By	4
Jolly	Olde Timers	3
King Neptune		6 1/4
King of Hearts	Alice	1 1/4
Little John	Sherwood	2
MacArthur	War Heroes	1 3/4
Mad Hatter	Alice	mini 1 1/4
Maid Marian	Sherwood	2
Mock Turtle	Alice	1 1/4
Monty	War Heroes	2
Mother Riley	Days Gone By	4
Mountbatten	War Heroes	1 3/4
Mutton Chops		3 3/4
Paddy	Days Gone By	4
Prince John	Sherwood	2
Queen Elizabeth I model # 652	Ltd Ed of 1000	7 1/2
Queen of Hearts	Alice	2 / 1 1/4
Rob Roy	Days Gone By	4
Robin Hood	Sherwood	7 1/4 / 2
Rommel	War Heroes	2
Say Again?	Olde Timers	3
Sheriff	Sherwood	2
Sir Winston Churchill	Ltd Ed of 1000	9 / 5 3/4
Smuts	War Heroes	2
Tudor Court		3 1/2
Whiskers	Days Gone By / Olde Timers	4 / 3
White Rabbit	Alice	2 / 1 1/4
Will Scarlet	Sherwood	2

Toby Jug Name	Series Name	Height, Inches	Model Number
Abraham Lincoln	1975 Limited Edition	11 3/4	
Angus with hat / without hat	Last Orders	9	
Aramis	Musketeers	7 1/4	722
Archbishop	Royalty & Dignitaries	8	771
'Arry	Last Orders	9	
Arthos	Musketeers	7 3/4	723
Barrister		8	
Beef Eater	London / London	7 1/4 / 4 3/4	
Beggar Man	Tinker, Tailor	7 1/4	
Benjamin Toby			
Captain M. B. Silvester	Pirates & Lawmen	large / small	
Charrington Jug	Last Orders	8 1/2	
Chelsea Pensioner	London / London	9 / 6 1/2	
Coachman	Days of Olde	4 1/4	
Customs Man	Pirates & Lawmen / Jack of All Trades	8 / 4 3/4	
D'Artagnan	Musketeers	7 1/2	720
Dart Player	Last Orders	8 1/2	
Dr. Swamp	Woodland	4	
Earl, Order of St. Patrick	Royalty & Dignitaries	8	775
Fagin	Charles Dickens	5 1/2	
Falstaff	Shakespeare	7 3/4	651
Farmer Giles	Country Folk		
Farmer Nut Brown Ale	Country Folk	7 1/2 / 4 5/8	
Festival Mouse - Hasty		5 3/4	
Festival Rabbit - Hoppy		6	
Fisherman holding net	Jack of All Trades	4 3/4 / 4 1/4	
Game Keeper	Country Folk / Jack of All Trades	4 3/4	
Grenadier Guard	London / London	6 1/2 / 4 3/4	
Hamlet	Shakespeare	8	653
Han			
Happy John	Last Orders	8	
Hettie		5 1/2	
Highwayman	Country Folk		
Hornblower	Jack of All Trades	4 3/4	
Huntsman	Country Folk	7 1/2	
Inn Keeper	Days of Olde	4 1/2	
Jailor	Days of Olde	4 3/4	
Jock	Last Orders	9	
John Bull	London	5 1/4	
John Peel / prestige finish		10 / 10	709
Jolly Fred	Little Brown Jug	7 1/4	
Jolly Jack	Little Brown Jug		
Judge	Pirates & Lawmen / Traditional Toby	7 3/4 / 6	
King	Royalty & Dignitaries	7 1/4	725
King Collier	Jack of All Trades	4 1/2	
King Henry VIII / prestige finish	Ltd Edition of 1000	8 3/4 / 8 3/4	724 / 724
King Lear	Shakespeare	8	
Knight, Order of the Garter	Royalty & Dignitaries	8	744
Lamp Lighter	Days of Olde	4 1/2	
Leprechaun / in barrel / pot of gold at feet / with crossed legs		7 1/2 / 4 / 4 / 3 1/2	
Long John Silver	Pirates & Lawmen	9 3/4	
Lord Mayor	Royalty & Dignitaries	8	
MacBeth	Shakespeare	8	Sfc60
Martha	Country Folk	6	4 5/8
Mary Queen of Scots	Ltd Edition of 1000	9 1/4	

Abraham Lincoln limited edition Toby Jug

Back side of Abraham Lincoln Toby Jug showing ornate handle

Barrister and Vicar Toby Jugs from Wedgwood & Company molds

Toby Cartlidge Toby Jug, named after designer Anthony Cartlidge

Days of Olde Series, top left to bottom right - Innkeeper, Pedlar, Jailor, Coachman, Sweep, and Lamplighter

Country Folk Series, top row left to right - Huntsman, Martha, and Highwayman; bottom row left to right - Nut Brown Ale, Poacher, and Robin Hood; all but Poacher from Shorter and Son molds

Country Folk Series left to right: Huntsman, Squire, and Gamekeeper

Fagin Character Jug and Toby Jug

Toby Jug Name	Series Name	Height, Inches	Model Number
Mr. Chips	Woodland	4	
Mr. Diddy	Diddies		
Mr. Hawthorne		5 1/2	
Mr. Micawber	Charles Dickens		
Mr. Peggotty	Charles Dickens		
Mr. Pickles	Woodland	4	
Mr. Pickwick	Dickens		
Mrs. Diddy	Diddies		
Mrs. Hawthorne		6	
Ned (the Snufftaker)	Last Orders	8 1/2	
Neptune	Sea Farers	6 3/4	
Newsboy		5 1/4	
Nick	Yarns	3 1/2	
Nigel Mansell	1992 Ltd Ed of 5000	9	
Oberon	Shakespeare	8	
Old King Cole			
Olde Brown Jug			Sfc48
Othello	Shakespeare	8	
'Owd Jack	Little Brown Jug		
P. C. Brock	Woodland	4 1/2	
Paddy Hopkirk			
Pearly King	London	7	
Pearly Queen	London	6 3/4	
Pedlar	Days of Olde	4 3/4	
Peter Post	Woodland	4	
Pirate	Pirates & Lawmen	7 3/4	
Poacher	Country Folk	6 3/4	
Poor Man	Tinker, Tailor	7 1/4	
Porthos	Musketeers	7 3/4	701
Publican	Traditional Toby	6	
Pub Orator	Traditional Toby	6	
Queen	Royalty & Dignitaries	7	726
Queen Ann Boleyn	Ltd Edition of 1000	9	
Queen Elizabeth I			
Queen Victoria	Ltd Edition of 1000	9 7	
Reverend Pew	Woodland	4	
Rich Man	Tinker, Tailor	7 1/2	705
Robin Hood	Country Folk	7	
Sailor	Tinker, Tailor	7 1/4	
Sam Toby	Little Brown Jug	7 1/2	
Santa		5	
Scrooge	Charles Dickens		
Sea Fisherman	Sea Farers	6 3/4	
Shylock	Shakespeare	8	654
Sir Francis Drake	Sea Farers	7 3/4	
Sir Toby Belch		21 1/2	
Sir Winston Churchill	Ltd Edition of 1000 London	9 3/4 small	
Sleepy	Traditional Toby	6	
Smithy	Jack of All Trades	4 3/4	
Smuggler	Pirates & Lawmen	7 3/4	
Snuffy	Yarns	3 1/2	
Soldier	Tinker, Tailor	7 1/2	703
Squire	Country Folk Jack of All Trades	7 4 3/4	763/1
Sweep	Days of Olde	4 3/4	
Tailor	Tinker, Tailor	7 1/4	702
Tall Story	Yarns	3 1/2	
Thief	Tinker, Tailor	7 1/2	708
Tinker	Tinker, Tailor	7 1/4	701
Toby	Last Orders Traditional Toby Yarns	9 6 3 1/2	
Toby Cartlidge	Country Folk	7	
Town Crier	Traditional Toby Diddies	6 3 1/2	
Touchstone	Shakespeare	8	
Vicar		7 1/4	
Widecombe		4	
Will Toby	Little Brown Jug	7	
William Shakespeare	Shakespeare	8	650

Festival Rabbit on the left and Festival Mouse on the right

Fisherman with net Toby Jug

Henry VIII Toby Jug in regular finish on the left and prestige finish on the right

Hettie Toby Jug on left and Newsboy Toby Jug on right

Jack of All Trades Series; top left to bottom right - Gamekeeper, Fisherman, Hornblower, Customs Man, King Collier, Squire, and Smithy

John Peel Toby Jug in regular finish on the left and prestige finish on the right

Last Orders Series: left to right - Dart Player, Ned, Happy John, and Toby

From Shorter and Son mold, Angus of Last Orders Series; Toby Jug on the right, same mold modified to produce an Angus humidor on left

Charrington Toby from the Last Orders Series

Leprechaun Toby Jug set; left to right - with pot of gold, in barrel, large seated, and with crossed legs

Martha Toby Jug in two sizes, produced from Shorter & Son Mrs. Farmer molds

Mr. and Mrs. Hawthorne Toby Jug pair

Nigel Mansell Toby Jug

Little Brown Jugs Series: left to right - Jolly Jack, Will Toby, and Jolly Fred

Musketeer Series: left to right - Aramis, Athos, Porthos, and D'Artagnan

Pearly King and Pearly Queen Toby Jug pair

Pirates and Lawmen large Toby Jug series; top left to bottom right - Customs Man, Judge, Smuggler, Long John Silver, and Pirate

Limited Edition large queen Toby Jugs; left to right - Queen Anne Boleyn, Mary Queen of Scots, and Queen Victoria

Queen Elizabeth I Character Jug on left and Queen Victoria medium size Toby Jug on the

Royalty and Dignitaries Toby Jug series from Wedgwood molds; from left to right - Lord Mayor, Knight Order of the Garter, Archbishop, Earl Order of St. Patrick

King and Queen from the Royalty and Dignitaries Series

Santa Toby Jug

Fisherman, Neptune, and Raleigh from the Sea Farers Series; first two from Shorter and Son molds

Sir Winston Churchill limited edition Toby Jug

William Shakespeare Toby Jug

Characters from Shakespearean Comedies; left to right - Falstaff, Touchstone, Oberon, Shylock

Characters from Shakespearean Tragedies; left to right - King Lear, Othello, Hamlet, and MacBeth

Sir Toby Belch giant Toby Jug, 21" tall

Tinker, Tailor, Soldier, and Sailor Toby Jugs from the Tinker, Tailor Series

Rich Man, Poor Man, Beggar Man, and Thief from the Tinker, Tailor Series

Traditional Tobies Series from left to right - Pub Orator, Sleepy, Toby, and Town Crier; produced from Shaw & Sons molds

Woodland Collection, top left to bottom right - Mr. Chips, Dr. Swamp, Mr. Pickles, Peter Post, P. C. Brock, and Reverend Pew

Yarns Series from left to right - Nick, Snuffy, Tall Story, and Toby

John Bull teapot

Pirate bell and Town Crier wall pocket

Santa teapot in center flanked by Mr. and Mrs. Clause creamer and sugar

Winston Churchill teapot produced from a modified Shorter & Son Character Jug mold

Staffordshire Ware
See William Kent

Stangl Pottery
Flemington, New Jersey

History

The history of Stangl Pottery is intertwined with that of Fulper Pottery. Both firms' heritages date back to Samuel Hill, who started a pottery business producing primarily drain tiles in Flemington, New Jersey around 1805. Operating as the American Pottery Company, Hill used the deposits of red clay in the surrounding county to produce his tiles. Hill died in 1858, and the factory was purchased by one of his workers, Abraham Fulper. Fulper broadened the firm's production by adding stoneware and earthenware products, such as

jugs, jars, bottles and other utilitarian kitchen items. Out of this small beginning, the Fulper Pottery Company was incorporated in 1899 under the direction of William Fulper II.

Fulper was one of the driving forces behind the art pottery movement in the United States, introducing its first line, Vasekraft, in 1909. Most of the firm's art pottery was done in the Arts and Crafts genre, with deco lines and a wide variety of glazes. In 1910, a young Johann Martin Stangl joined the Fulper pottery as a ceramic engineer. Stangl became proficient with the firm's many production techniques, and invented many of the firm's glazes. In 1914, Stangl left Fulper Pottery to work for Haeger Pottery.

Stangl returned to Fulper in 1926 as the President of the company. A devastating fire destroyed the Fulper plant in 1929. Rather than rebuild, William Fulper sold the business to Johann Stangl, who wanted to operate his own pottery. Stangl rebuilt the Flemington factory and continued operating as the Fulper Pottery, but he also began a separate operation in Trenton, which he named Stangl Pottery. In 1940, the first realistic, detailed Stangl bird figurines were introduced. These birds were very successful and were produced until Stangl closed. As the firm expanded, production of these birds was moved to the Trenton factory, but they were returned to the Flemington plant to be handpainted. During World War II, fifty decorators could not keep up with the demand for Stangl birds, so local individuals were recruited to paint as well.

Stangl introduced its famous hand-carved, handpainted, red body dinnerware in 1942. A large number of other dinnerware patterns were introduced during the 1940s and 1950s. One of the key designers of these patterns was Kay Kastner Hackett, who created Blueberry, Fruit and Thistle, among others. Hackett also prototyped some ceramic jewelry, which Stangl never put into production. Rose Herbeck designed many of the later dinnerware patterns but is probably best known for her Gingerbread decorations.

Stangl produced a variety of other wares in addition to dinnerware, including lamp bases and Art Deco art pottery. In 1955, the operation of both potteries was officially renamed Stangl Pottery, and the Fulper name was no longer used. Sales of the factory's products decreased continually in the 1960s and into the 1970s. The firm was dealt a major setback when Johann Stangl passed away in 1972. Demand for the popular red body dinnerware dropped off drastically, such that the dinnerware was discontinued in 1974. Four years later the Stangl Pottery closed on November 1, 1978. The last piece to go through the kiln was a twenty-two inch tall duck, owned for many years by Stangl designer Irene Sarnecki. Today one of Stangl's oldest buildings, dating to 1814, is used as a showroom by the Pfaltzgraff Pottery.

1970s reissue of the Parson Character Jug, shown without hat

Character Mugs

Stangl produced a set of nine Character Mugs in 1936 that were designed by Tony Sarg. Six of the mugs came with removable hats that could be used as an ashtray. It is rare to find the hat still with the mug. Two, Batch and Grand, came with attached hats. All these characters had comical expressions and were colorfully handpainted. They are marked with the model number and "Stangl U.S.A.". A Stangl Character Mug is affectionately known as a "stoby" to Stangl collectors. A prototype of Smoke has been found, but it is not clear whether this stoby ever went into production.

In the 1970s, Stangl reissued six of the mugs, three of which are noted below. The colors for the reissue were brown with black trim, a solid yellow, or solid chartreuse. The brown versions were produced in a smaller quantity and therefore are valued at the high end of the market. As times had changed since the initial release, Depression was renamed Crybaby for the 1970s reissue. The heights listed below are for mugs with the hat. Without the hat, the mugs are approximately five inches tall. The market values for the original issue do not include the hat; expect to pay a hefty premium for that. The values for the reissued mugs include the hat, although it is still common to find the hats missing on these. Not a part of the stoby set, a Cossack Character Jug has also been identified.

Character Mug Name	Model Number	Height, Inches
Archie	1681	6 1/2
Batch	1679	6
Chief	1676	6
Cossack		6 3/4
Crybaby	1677	6
Depression	1677	6
Grand	1673	6
Henpeck	1680	6 1/4
Parson	1675	6 1/2
	1675	6 1/2
Smoke	1674	
Sport	1678	5 1/2
	1678	5 1/2

All Jugs Production Life 1936 - 1940s – Crybaby, Parson, and Sport amoung those reissued in 1970s

Star China
See Royal Paragon China

Sterling Pottery Limited
Fenton, England

History

Sterling Pottery began operating in Fenton in 1947, producing a wide range of products. Lawley's Limited, a retailer, purchased Sterling Pottery in 1948 and continued to run the pottery independently. Lawley's was acquired by S. Pearson & Son Limited in 1952 and amalgamated into a group of potteries that were later known as the Allied English Potteries. The Sterling factory closed in 1953. In 1972, the Doulton Group acquired Allied English. Rights to the Ridgway name were possibly available through the merger with Allied English Potteries.

Character Jugs and Toby Jugs

Sterling Pottery produced a variety of high quality and well-modeled Character and Toby Jugs. Many jugs were produced from molds purchased from Cooper Clayton Pottery. These are all marked with the tradename "Cooper Clayton Characters," and

Sterling backstamp for products from Cooper Clayton molds

Sterling urn backstamp

Sterling backstamp with Ridgway tradename

RIDGWAY

Another Sterling mark using the Ridgway tradename

originally came with attached labels.

The Annie Character Jug was the creamer in a very nice sugar/creamer/teapot set which carried the Ridgways backstamp. Mac was the sugar and Jock the teapot. Uncle Sam also likely was produced from old Ridgway's molds. The Winston Churchill Character Jugs depict the Prime Minister with a trilby hat and the ever-present cigar clenched firmly between his lips. The handle of the Churchill jug is an umbrella.

Perhaps the most common mark found on Sterling jugs is "Sterling English Characters" within an urn. This mark was used from 1947 to 1953. From 1952 to 1953, Sterling sometimes included the tradename "Ridgway" on its jugs, using a mark very similar to a

contemporary one in use by Ridgways.

Character Jug Name	Height, Inches	Production Life
Annie	3	1952 - 1953
Bill Sykes	4 1/2	1947 - 1953
	3 1/2	1950 - 1953
	1 3/4	1952 - 1953
Cap'n Patch	3 1/2	1952 - 1953
	1 3/4	1947 - 1953
Drake	4 1/2	1952 - 1953
Farmer Giles	4 1/4	1947 - 1953
	2 1/2	1952 - 1953
Farmer's Wife	3 1/4	1952 - 1953
	1 3/4	1947 - 1953
Fortune Teller	4	
	3 1/4	1947 - 1953
	1 3/4	
Gaffer	4 1/2	1947 - 1953
	2	
Granny	4 1/4	1947 - 1953
	3 1/4	1947 - 1953
	2 3/4	
Jock	2 3/4	1952 - 1953
John Bull	4 3/8	
Queen Elizabeth I	4 1/2	
Uncle Sam	5	1952 - 1953
	4 1/4	1952 - 1953
	3 1/4	
Winston Churchill	3 1/2	1941 - 1945
	1 3/4	1941 - 1945

Toby Jug Name	Height, Inches	Production Life
Coachman	7 1/4	
	6 7/8	1947 - 1953
	5 1/2	
Davy Jones	9	1952 - 1953
	7 3/4	1952 - 1953
	5 1/2	1952 - 1953
Huntsman	large	
Ordinary Toby	8 1/2	1952 - 1953
	7 1/4	1952 - 1953
	6	
Town Crier	9 1/2	1947 - 1953
	7 1/4	1952 - 1953

Bill Sykes Character Jug in three sizes

Cap'n Patch Character Jug in small and tiny sizes

Granny Character Jug in three sizes

Elizabeth I Character Jug on left and Drake on right

Farmer Giles Character Jug in small and mini sizes

Farmer's Wife Character Jug in small and tiny sizes

Fortune Teller Characer Jug in small and miniature sizes

John Bull Character Jug

Pair of Uncle Sam Character Jugs

Three sizes of the Coachman Toby Jug

Left to right: Davy Jones Toby Jug in two sizes, large Town Crier Toby Jug, and Ordinary Toby in two sizes

Davy Jones Toby Jug colorway

Teaset: Annie creamer or Character Jug, Jock teapot, and Mac sugar

Extra large Huntsman Toby Jug attributed to Sterling; prototype found in the Royal Doulton Archival Collection

Side view of Huntsman Toby Jug

Studio D
See Audley Pottery

Studio Szeiler
See Jugs Marked by Country of Manufacture under United Kingdom

SylvaC
See Shaw & Copestake

Sylvan Pottery Limited
Hanley, England

Character Jug Name	Height, inches
General Eisenhower	6 3/4
General MacArthur	7
George Washington	1 3/4
Robin Hood	1 3/4
Scottie	1 3/4
Welsh Lady	3 3/4

Toby Jug Name	Height, inches
Aramis	7 1/8
Athos	7 1/8
Mandolin Player	8
Ordinary Toby	7 3/4
	4 1/2
Porthos	7 1/4

GENUINE HARD PAINTED
SYLVAN POTTERY LTD.
STAFFORDSHIRE, ENGLAND

Sylvan backstamp

History

Sylvan Pottery began operating in 1946 at the Sylvan Works in Hanley, Staffordshire. The Sylvan Works factory was formerly operated from 1921 until 1941 by the Podmore China Company, which made primarily china. The factory stood idle until 1946 when Sylvan Pottery took over the site and produced earthenware there until 1985.

Character Jugs and Toby Jugs

Sylvan made a well modeled series of tiny Character Jugs of famous historical personages. These jugs are similar to those made by Longton New Art Pottery and Shaw and Copestake. Perhaps the most significant Toby Jug produced by Sylvan was a creamware jug of General MacArthur in a style similar to Ashtead's, with MacArthur having an oversized head and smaller body features. The large Mandolin Player and Porthos tobies can be found with music boxes in their bases. Following are the Sylvan jugs identified to date. More certainly exist.

General Eisenhower Character Jug

Robin Hood and George Washington tiny Character Jugs, flanking small Welsh Lady Character Jug

Athos Toby Jug   Porthos Toby Jug

Mandolin Player and Aramis Toby Jug with musical box in base

Syracuse China Company
Syracuse, New York

History

The history of the Syracuse China Company dates back to 1841 and a small pottery started in Syracuse, New York by W. H. Farrar. In 1855, this small pottery became the Empire Pottery, which in turn was incorporated as the Onondaga Pottery Company on July 20, 1871.

By 1890, Onondaga Pottery developed a vitrified white, translucent china. Using this body, the firm introduced new dinnerware at the 1893 World Exhibition in Chicago. This china was tradenamed "Syracuse China" and won a medal at the Exhibition. Thereafter, much of the pottery's ware used this tradename. In 1896, the firm introduced another new concept, its rolled edge china, which became the standard in the commercial food industry. R. Guy Cowan worked at Onondaga before leaving to start his own pottery. His most successful design was Shelledge.

For the next sixty years, Onondaga Pottery continued its success and growth. The name of the firm was officially changed to Syracuse China in 1966. Syracuse China closed its consumer division in 1970 in the face of strong Japanese competition. The firm is still operating today and is one of the largest commercial pottery producers in the world. The firm is probably best known for its high quality dinnerware and restaurant china.

Toby Jugs

Onondaga Pottery produced presidential white china Toby Jugs in a style similar to Ashtead's, with oversized heads and small bodies. Using the Syracuse China tradename, these were produced for the Patriotic Products Association of Philadelphia, beginning with Al Smith and Herbert Hoover for the 1928 Presidential convention and campaign, and adding Franklin Roosevelt in 1932. The Owens China Company of Minerva, Ohio produced similar earthenware jugs, also for the Patriotic Products Association.

These jugs can be found with an elaborate mark of the Patriotic Products Association in a shield, the tradename "Syracuse China", and Onondaga's "O. P. CO." mark. The Smith and Hoover jugs were produced in a limited edition of 25,000 with each jug being numbered. A facsimile signature of the candidate appears on the side of the jugs. Instead of the candidate's signature, the Roosevelt jug had his name in relief block letters. A few jugs have been reported in a full colorway. The production quantity of the Roosevelt jug remains unknown. These jugs are very desirable today, both by Toby collectors and political collectors. Unmarked versions can be found, but Onondaga China may not have produced these.

Syracuse China mark

Large Herbert Hoover on left, small Franklin Roosevelt in center, and large Al Smith on right

Toby Jug Name	Height, Inches	Production Life
Al Smith	6 1/2	1928 - 1930
	4 1/2	1928 - 1930
Franklin D. Roosevelt	7	1930 - 1932
	4 1/2	1930 - 1932
Herbert Hoover	6 3/4	1928 - 1930

Tessier
France

History

Emile Tessier trained in the production of pottery with Leon Pouplard at Malicorne. In 1924, he opened his own factory. The pottery employed ninety-nine workers by 1940 and was producing faience, with a reputation as one of the more important makers of faience in the area. The factory remained in family hands, being managed by Emile's grandson until 1984, when Victor Deschang purchased it.

Financial difficulties plagued the firm in recent times. Today the factory is small, reduced to only a handful of employees, although products are still produced, primarily for export to the United States. Tessier marked his products with a connected T and E.

Toby Jugs

Emile Tessier made several entertaining Toby Jugs in the late 1930s and the early 1940s. These jugs represent French stereotypes and each has a green plinth base. The Man on the Barrel delivers an interesting message when the numbers on his barrel are read in French: "Oh, wine without water." The Gendarme is the classical French law enforcement official from the turn of the century. The Tenue Garance is a French soldier dressed in the brightly colored uniform used in the first few years of World War I, before the French learned that bright colors made an easy target.

Toby Jug Name	Height, inches
Gendarme	
Man on Barrel	
Tenue Garance	

Thomas Cone
See Jugs Marked by Country of Manufacture under United Kingdom

Thomas Goode & Company
London, England

Character Jug Name	Height, inches
Paul Kruger	6 1/4

History

Thomas Goode founded the retail firm of Thomas Goode & Company in the 1840s, located on South Audley Street in London. Shortly after starting operations, Minton selected Thomas Goode as its London retailer, a key driver behind Goode's success. The two companies built a very close working relationship, and over time Goode became Minton's primary supplier to all of England. Goode also distributed ware of Robert Heron's Fife Pottery in Scotland, including its famous Wemyss ware.

In 1984, Thomas Goode purchased the Caverswall China Company, which owned the assets of Fielding & Company, forming a manufacturing arm for the retailer. Thomas Goode &

Company was offered for sale in 1991, but no buyer stepped forward.

Today Goode, under its Caverswall China manufacturing name, still produces giftware and teaware, both of old Caverswall designs as well as new designs.

Character Jugs

At the turn of the twentieth century, Thomas Goode & Company sold the Paul Krueger Character Jug under its own label. The jug has "1900" embossed at the bottom of the jug and has an ornate crown handle. While the maker of the jug remains unknown, the mark on the bottom is "Vulliamy Regd".

Thomas Goode backstamp

Paul Kruger Character Jug

Thorley China Limited
Longton, England

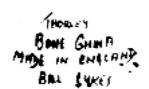

Hand painted mark

THORLEY BONE CHINA
HAND MADE
AND HAND PAINTED
AT STOKE-ON-TRENT
ENGLAND
Long Fina Hand

Thorley stamped ink mark

History

Thorley China Limited operated at the Wellington Works in Longton, Staffordshire from 1940 until 1970. The founder of Thorley China worked for a time at Wedgwood, leaving after World War II to found his own company and produce floral fancies. During its production life, the firm produced a variety of fine china, china jewelry, and bone china products. At one point, Thorley China allegedly produced fake Wedgwood ware.

Character Jugs and Toby Jugs

Thorley China made a large number of bone china Character and Toby Jugs using a variety of themes and common jug characters. Although of mid-range quality, a grouping of Thorley jugs makes an interesting display. The Winston Churchill Character Jug shows

Churchill smoking a cigar and wearing a Homburg hat. The handle is a flagpole and the Union Jack. Sairy Gamp has been found in a creamer and sugar set, the creamer qualifying as a Character Jug.

Thorley's Toby Jugs are of somewhat better quality than its Character Jugs and appear less often on the market. The Winston Churchill Toby is nicely modeled and depicts the Statesman in a traditional Toby pose. It has a unique rampant lion handle and is marked "The Captain."

Thorley jugs carry a handpainted mark of "Thorley Bone China Made in England." Identical earthenware Character Jugs have also been found marked with the Highmont and Snel Ware backstamps. One Character Jug has been found which carries the marks of both Thorley and Highmont. The connection between these three firms remains unknown.

Left to right: Captain Flint, Robbie Burns, Jock, and Old Mac small Character Jugs

Left to right: Walter Raleigh, Beefeater, and Town Crier miniature Character Jugs

Left to right: Paddy, Fat Boy, and Bill Sykes miniature Character Jugs

Tiny Character Jugs, top left to bottom right: Henry VIII, Ann Boleyn, Queen Elizabeth I, Drake, Walter Raleigh, Abraham Lincoln, Winston Churchill, Florence Nightengale, Pirate, Pirate's Wife, Robin Hood, Friar Tuck, Mr. Micawber, and Peggoty

Left to right: Abraham Lincoln, Winston Churchill, Franklin Roosevelt and Eisenhower small Character Jugs

Jolly Miller and Miller's Wife miniature Character Jugs

Sairey Gamp creamer and sugar set

Left to right: Beefeater, Long John Silver and Hookey Toby Jugs

Character Jug Name	Height, inches
Abraham Lincoln	3 1/4 1 1/2
Ann Boleyn	1 1/2
Beefeater	3 1/4
Bill Sykes	2 3/4
Captain Flint	5
Drake	1 1/2
Eisenhower	3 1/4 2 1/4
Fat Boy	2 1/2
Florence Nightengale	1 1/2
Franklin D. Roosevelt	3 1/4
Friar Tuck	1 1/2
Henry VIII	1 1/2
Jock	4 1/2
Jolly Miller	1 3/4
Miller's Wife	1 3/4
Mr. Micawber	1 3/4
Old Mac	4 1/4
Paddy	2 3/4
Peggoty	1 3/4
Pirate	1 1/2
Pirate's Wife	1 1/2
Queen Elizabeth I	1 1/2
Robbie Burns	4
Robin Hood	1 1/2
Sairey Gamp	2 1/4
Town Crier	2 3/4
Walter Raleigh	2 1/4 1 1/2
Winston Churchill	3 1/2 1 1/2

Toby Jug Name	Height, inches
Beefeater	4
Hookey	3 3/4
Long John Silver	7 1/2
Winston Churchill	
The Captain	5

Tony Wood Limited
Fenton, England

History

After the closing of Wood and Sons in 1980, Tony Wood, the eighth generation of Wood potters, formed his own pottery. Tony Wood Studio 82 was founded in 1982 with Elizabeth Capper, who served as partner and business manager. Elizabeth Capper and Tony had worked together for many years, she having been the Director's secretary at Wood and Sons Ellgreave factory when Tony first joined the family pottery. Later, Elizabeth was in charge of sales for first Wood and Sons, and later for H. J. Wood. Sadly, Elizabeth Capper died in 1997 at

Character Jug Name	Height, inches
Clown	5
Hearty Good Fellow	3 1/4
Judge	5 1/2
Monty	5 3/4
Mr. Holly	5 1/4
Oliver Hardy	5 1/2
Ralph Wood	4
Sailor	3
Stan Laurel	5 1/2
Winston Churchill	5 3/4

Character Jug Name	Height, inches
Alice	3 1/2
Betsy	6
Black Knight	3 1/2
Carpenter	3 1/2
Cat	5
Caterpillar	3 1/2
Charrington Toby	7 1/2
Drunken Parson	
Hearty Good Fellow	
Jabberwocky	3 1/2
Jabez	7 3/4
King of Hearts	3 1/2
Lion	3 1/2
Little Old Lady	4
Lord Mayor	
Mad Hatter	3 1/2
March Hare	3 1/2
Martha Gunn	7 1/2
Moses	6
Ordinary Toby	5 1/2 / 3 1/2
Piper	7 1/2
Punch (w/o hat)	7
Queen of Hearts	3 1/2
Toby Philpot	5 / 3 1/2
Tweddle Dee & Tweedle Dum	3 1/2
Ugly Duchess	3 1/2
Unicorn	3 1/2
Walrus	3 1/2
White Knight	3 1/2
White Rabbit	3 1/2

the age of 69. Tony was able to bring with him many of the assets and molds from the Wood and Sons factory. Wilf Blanford joined Tony from Wood and Sons and did almost all of the modeling for the firm.

Unfortunately the factory was destroyed by fire in 1984, and for about six months, a limited amount of ware was produced in a Wade factory. The firm then purchased a new factory in Cobridge and began ramping up production again. However, the pottery never fully recovered, and in 1991 it was forced into liquidation. In 1992, the assets of the firm were purchased from receivers by Scotland Direct, a Scottish mail order house that had been distributing products made by Tony Wood Studio. Production of the same basic wares continued by Scotland Direct under the name Wood Potters of Burslem.

This was not the end of potting for Tony Wood, however. Tony soon started anew, this time as Tony Wood Limited. This pottery operated for a few years before also going into liquidation. In 1996, Tony again began producing pottery on a much smaller scale with a kiln at his home. Using existing molds, blocks and cases, he started making and selling familiar ware that were marked by hand "Tony Wood Family Pottery". This ware was hand decorated by Sanchia Wood, Tony's daughter and the ninth generation of Wood potters. Sanchia is a talented freelance modeler and paintress in her own right. She created limited edition figurines and jugs under the Tony Wood Family Pottery label and her own name.

Character Jugs and Toby Jugs

Tony Wood Studio continued production of many of the Wood and Sons Toby and Character Jugs. The pottery also created its own jugs. The Alice in Wonderland Series was produced for Perennis between 1982 and 1983. This highly collectible series was extensively marketed in Australia and later introduced to England and the United States. The Mr. Holly Character Jug was a creamer from a holiday set commissioned by Marshall Field's department store in Chicago. Along with the Mr. Holly Character Jug/creamer came a seven inch Mr. Holly coffee pot, and a 6 1/2" tall Mrs. Mistletoe teapot with matching five inch sugar bowl. Tony Wood had permission to produce this set under his own label as well.

The Ralph Wood Collection of Character Jugs included the Sailor and Hearty Good Fellow. The Drunken Parson Toby was modeled by Roy Simpson and issued in a limited edition of 2000. This jug was the first in a new series of limited edition traditional Toby Jugs under The Wood Family Collection.

Sanchia Wood created a few unique Toby Jugs in the 1990s, including traditional Toby Jugs of a Sailor, Hearty Good Fellow, and Mr. Micawber. All these jugs stand around 4 1/2 inches tall. She also created a limited edition Equestrian Toby.

From his experience at Wood and Sons and with his own pottery, Tony concludes that quality Toby Jugs are too expensive to produce, due in large part to the extensive handpainting, and retailers just don't want to pay the price.

Stan Laurel and Oliver Hardy Character Jug pair

A variety of marks found on Tony Wood jugs.

Left to right: Hearty Good Fellow, Ralph Wood, and Sailor Character Jugs

Perennis Alice In Wonderland Toby Jugs; left to right - Alice, March Hare, Carpenter, White Rabbit, Caterpillar, and Tweedle Dee & Dum

Christmas teaset: Mrs. Mistletoe teapot and sugar, Mr. Holly creamer and coffee pot

Jester and Cross-legged Toby teapots

Torquay Pottery Company
Torquay, England

History

The Torquay Pottery Company has its history rooted in the Torquay Terra Cotta Company (TTC). TTC operated from 1875 to 1909 at the Hele Cross factory in Torquay, Devon. Under owner and Chief Director Dr. Gillow, the firm produced terra-cotta products, figures, plaques, vases, statuary, and other earthenware. Other key members of the firm were head potter Thomas Bentley and head of the artistic department, Alexander Fisher Sr. The firm's marks include "Torquay" impressed, "Torquay Terracotta Co. Limited" impressed or stamped, an overlapped TTC impressed or printed, and sometimes "Royal Torquay". Between 1900 and 1909, a more ornate circular mark was incised or stamped with the overlapped TTC trademark surrounded by "Torquay Terra Cotta Co. Limited". Torquay Terracotta closed by 1910.

The Torquay Pottery Company opened at the TTC site and operated there from the 1910s to the early 1920s. The firm imitated the mottoware and other production of fellow Devon potteries. Around this time, Enoch Staddon became the owner of Torquay Pottery and the firm began trading as Royal Torquay Pottery.

Within a few years, the Torquay Pottery Company built a reputation for undercutting its rivals, even to the point of purchasing seconds and using only one firing for both biscuit and glaze. These short-cuts resulted in poor quality goods. On the other hand, the firm also produced much high quality art pottery during this time, some of it from designer Sam Shufflebotham. The Great Depression placed the firm in such a serious financial situation that a Winding-up Petition was presented by the pottery. The firm went into receivership for eighteen months, and on June 20, 1933, the liquidation was completed and creditors paid. This was not the end of potting for Torquay, however.

In early 1932, even before the final accounting of Torquay Pottery Company was completed, several of the Directors started a new firm called Torquay Pottery Limited. The stated goal of this firm was "to carry on the business of manufacturers of pottery, earthenware, china, terra-cotta, etc". The first Directors of this new firm were Enoch Staddon, F. E. Bowen and M. R. Staddon. This firm simply carried on with production as before. Small animal figures were introduced in 1938, quickly becoming popular. As with most Devon potters, Torquay Pottery closed for some period during World War II and reopened after the war. Enoch Staddon sold his interest in the pottery sometime in the 1940s. Rising labor costs in the 1950s made it economically difficult for Torquay to continue production using its traditional methods of hand casting each piece. Precisely when the firm closed is unknown, but the laundry next door bought the site.

Character Jugs and Toby Jugs

Character and Toby Jugs produced by Torquay have the distinctive red clay bodies common to all Devon area potters. A graduated set of five Toby Jugs was exhibited at the 1931 British Industries Fair and mentioned in company literature through 1938. The Character Jugs were produced in the 1920s and came in several single colored glazes, including green, black, and blue. The Winker jug has a companion shaving mug with "Sweeney Todd" painted around its top.

As with many of the Devon area potters, Torquay Pottery produced a set of Character Jugs based on the popular folk song "Widdecombe Fair," featuring the seven men traveling to the fair. Torquay appears to have produced this set in three sizes. The Uncle Tom Cobleigh jug has his name and Widdecombe Fair painted around the back of the jug. Torquay made an Ordinary Toby Jug similar in appearance to ones produced by Devonmoor. In fact, the 5 3/4 inch Ordinary appears to be the same as the Joe Vernon Toby created for Devonmoor. They could be from the same mold. Torquay produced a second Ordinary Toby with a different appearance or style.

Torquay Pottery also used the tradename "Devonia Pottery", and some jugs have been found with this mark, such as the Long John Silver and small Uncle Tom Cobleigh. The small Ordinary Toby has been found marked only "Made In England". Derivative Toby condiment sets and liquor containers were also produced.

Most of the Following photos are from the collection of John Hobbs.

Character Jug Name	Height, inches
'Arry 'Awke	6 3 1/4
Barnacle Bill	3
Bill Brewer	6
Dan'l Whiddon	4 3 1/4
Duchess of Devonshire	3 1/2
Jan Stewart	
Long John Silver	3 1/2
Peter Davey "B-4"	5 3/4
Peter Gurney	4
Punch	3 1/2
Tom Pearce	
Uncle Tom Cobleigh "B-5"	6 3 1/2

Toby Jug Name	Height, inches
Ordinary Toby style 1	11 8 5 3/4 4 1/2 3 1/4 1 3/4
Ordinary Toby style 2	6 1/2 4 3/4 2 1/2 2 1/4
Squat Toby	5 3 1/2 3 2

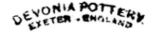

Devonia backstamp

Peter Davey Character Jug on the left and Uncle Tom Cobleigh on the right

More Widecombe Fair Character Jugs: Peter Davey on the left, medium and small Dan'l Whiddon in the center, and small 'Arry 'Awk on the right

Uncle Tom Cobleigh and Long John Silver Character Jugs marked Devonia

'Arry 'Awke Character Jug (courtesy of Torquay Collectiors Society)

Barnacle Bill Character Jug (courtesy of Torquay Collectiors Society)

Grouping of graduated Ordinary Toby jugs measuring 8, 5 3/4, 4 1/2, and 2 3/4 inches tall

Group of Ordinary Tobies of slightly different modeling, measuring 6 1/4, 4 3/4, 2 3/4, and 2 1/4 inches tall

Peter Gurney Character Jug

Uncommon Ordinary Toby with an odd facial expression

Comparison of Devonmoor Joe Vernon Ordinary Toby on left and Torquay Ordinary Toby from a Joe Vernon mold on right

Graduated group of Squat Toby Jugs, measuring 5, 3 1/2, 3, and 2 inches tall

Truscott Pottery
Newton Abbot, England

History

Truscott Pottery was another in a long line of potteries that have potted in the Devon area of England. Truscott operated from at least the 1950s until the early 1980s.

From its inception, the firm produced a wide range of inexpensive souvenir and gift items that peaked in the 1960s and 1970s with its Manor Ware tradename. These wares were made from white clay with an unglazed bottom and typically carried the name of the resort or tourist attraction where the item could be purchased. These souvenirs have been found with transfer decorations of ships, cottages and pixies, often with an upbeat slogan or saying as well.

Around 1960 the firm opened a new, modern factory at the Newton Abbot Industrial Estate, presumably to keep up with demand for its souvenir ware. In a 1960 advertisement the firm promoted its wide range of souvenirs hand decorated by a team of twenty-five skilled lady decorators. In addition to its own production ware, Truscott also undertook a variety of commissions from around the world.

Character Jugs and Toby Jugs

In the 1970s, and in conjunction with Melwood Pottery, Truscott produced the Royal Toby Year

Character Jug series commissioned by the Licensed Victuallers National Homes (LVNH) organization. This set of six Character Jugs depicted Prince Phillip and a group of English pub owners. Truscott produced the five pub owners and Melwood made the Prince Phillip jug. The backstamp on the jugs includes the character's name and "Created by Ted Elkins and sculpted by John Armstrong London".

Truscott also made Ordinary Toby Jugs and Toby comdiment sets marked with its Manor Ware tradename.

Character Jug Name	Height, inches
Bram Nicholson	7 1/2
Henry Porter	7 1/2
John Mulligan	6 1/2
Paul Smith	6 1/2
Robert McNeile	6 3/4

Toby Jug Name	Height, inches
Ordinary Toby	

Derivatives	Height, inches
Long John Silver salt shaker	2 1/2
Pirate pepper	2 1/2

Truscott LNVH backstamp

Manor Ware Pirate and Long John Silver salt and pepper shakers

LNVH Character Jugs; top row left to right - Robert McNeile, Lester Piggott by Melwood, and Paul Smith; bottom row left to right - Henry Porter, John Mulligan, and Bram Nicholson

Ubag China
See Jugs Marked by Country of Manufacture under Japan

Viking Pottery Company
Cobridge, England

History

The Viking Pottery Company started as the Viking Tile Company. Founded in Cobridge, Staffordshire, the firm initially made only earthenware tiles. In 1950, as part of expanding into new product areas, the firm renamed itself Viking Pottery and began making a broader range of earthenware and porcelain products. The pottery closed in 1964.

The mark found on Viking's ware is a double circle

with "Viking Cobridge" inside and a winged Viking helmet at the top of the circle. This mark was used throughout Viking Pottery's short existence.

Character Jugs and Toby Jugs

The Knave Character Jug and Highwayman Toby Jug are the only jugs identified so far. They are well made and stamped "bone china." Given its high quality, surely Viking produced additional jugs.

Character Jug Name	Height, inches
Knave	2 1/2

Toby Jug Name	Height, inches
Highwayman	4 7/8

Viking Pottery backstamp

Highwayman Toby Jug on left and Knave Character Jug on right

Vincent Kane
See Jugs Marked by Country of Manufacture under United Kingdom

Wade Ceramics Limited
Burslem, England

Wade Highwayman backstamp

Toby Jim Jug

Highwayman Toby Jug

McCallum Character Jug in three sizes

History

In 1810, Henry Hallen founded a small pottery at the site of the Manchester Pottery to produce pottery fittings for machinery. In the middle of the 19th century the firm moved to Burslem, then in 1922 it was purchased by George Wade and operated under several different names until 1927, when it was renamed Wade, Heath and Company Limited. In the mid-thirties, the firm of A. J. Wade Limited was spun off.

In the 1950s, several of the Wade factories amalgamated and formed the public company Wade Potteries Limited. The Beauford Group purchased Wade Potteries in 1989 and renamed it Wade Ceramics Limited. Today Wade is the UK's leading contract manufacturer of promotional and industrial ceramics. Wade currently has three factories in Burslem and several others scattered throughout the isle. Wade has become famous worldwide for its nursery rhyme characters and other whimsical figurines, novelty teapots and promotional items.

Character Jugs and Toby Jugs

Wade made a variety of Character and Toby Jugs over many years. Some, like the Charrington and Toby Ale jugs, were commissioned for promotional or advertising purposes. The Highwayman and Pirate were produced in gold and copper luster versions, as well as a full colorway. The Toby Jim Jug characterized a famous British radio and television comedian, Jimmy Edwards. The large McCallum Character Jug is similar to that of Royal Doulton. It was offered in three sizes and was produced in a Kingsware glaze limited production run, making it very desirable to Wade collectors. The prototype Mr. Pickwick Character Jug was produced on commission for Bass Breweries, but never went into production; only two samples are known to exist, one selling at a UK auction in April of 1997.

Charater Jug Name	Model Number	Height, Inches	Production Life
Coachman		2 7/8	
Fisherman		3	1948 - 1953
Horse	150	4 1/4	
Indian Chief			1958 - 1962
McCallum	447	8	
	448	6 3/8	1950 - 1959
	449	4 1/2	1950 - 1959
	790	2 3/4	1950 - 1959
Mr. Pickwick	Prototype		late 1960s
Old Charlie		3	
Ordinary Toby		2 7/8	
RCMP Officer			1958 - 1962
Sailor		3	1948
Toby Jim Jug		4 3/8	1968

Toby Jug Name	Model Number	Height, Inches	Production Life
Bunny			
Charrington Toby	1221	7 1/4	1958 - 1990
		6 1/2	
Highwayman Limited Edition 1000	1042	6	1948 - 1955
North American Indian			prototype
Pirate Limited Edition 750	1041	6	1948 - 1955
Toby Ale		7 1/4	1958
Toby Philpot		7 1/4	1953 - 1958
		4 3/4	1953 - 1958
		3	1953 - 1958

History

Horace Wain founded H. Wain & Sons in 1946 at the Melba Works in Longton. Horace grew up around the pottery business, his father serving as the Director of Carlton Ware at one time. Beginning in 1951, Wain produced wares using the tradename Melba Ware. This tradename was previously used by Harlows Limited of Longton. Among other products, the company produced dinnerware of similar fashion to Carlton Ware and lifelike bird and animal figurines.

The pottery experienced difficult financial times in the early 1960s, due to the cost of producing new ware, such as the animal figurines and increasing competition in the giftware market. However, business prospered in the 1970s such that Wain & Sons opened a new factory in 1977 and doubled production through improved exports in a matter of years.

During the late 1970s and early 1980s the firm was introducing about twenty new designs per year. Elizabeth Wain, Horace's daughter-in-law, served as the Sales Manager during this time and helped establish a sales arm in New York City. In 1985, Elizabeth took over the pottery and renamed it Melba-Wain. Melba-Wain went into receivership in November 1997 and was liquidated.

Toby Jugs

H. Wain & Sons produced several Toby Jugs between 1946 and 1956. The Wain Toby Jugs are excellent in modeling and color. Its hallmark is the pinkish coloring of the glaze that provides the jugs with an eye-catching yet soft overall appearance. This glaze is called Vanilla glaze and was created by Horace to provide a more lifelike effect on the skin coloring. The largest sizes of tobies sometimes contained music boxes in the base.

All but the Cardinal Wolsey were modeled outside of the factory, then produced and finished by Wain & Sons. Horace Wain modeled the Cardinal Wolsey jug, basing it on his father. The Winston Churchill Toby was a prototype, at least one of which was produced. It left the firm and was last known to be in a Staffordshire pub. Horace's family would very much like to recover this jug.

Wain & Sons Toby Jugs did not prove to be too popular, so only small quantities were produced. In the mid-1950s, the remaining stock of the jugs was sold off inexpensively or destroyed, quite a shame for tobies that have such a unique appearance and artistry. These jugs are rapidly becoming collector's favorites.

Toby Jug Name	Height, inches
Cardinal Wolsey	11 3/4
Henry VIII	9
	7 3/4
	6 1/4
	6
Punch	7 1/2
	6 1/4
	5
Shylock	9
	8
Tale Teller	8 1/2
	7 3/4
	small
Winston Churchill	

Melba Ware backstamp

Cardinal Wolsey Toby Jug

Henry VIII Toby Jug in large, medium and small sizes

Medium and small size Punch Toby Jugs

Tale Teller Toby Jug in three sizes

Large Shylock Toby Jug

Wales China
See Jugs Marked by Country of Manufacture under Japan

Wardle & Company
See Jugs Marked by Country of Manufacture under United Kingdom

Watcombe Pottery
See Royal Aller Vale & Watcombe Pottery

J. H. Weatherby & Sons Limited
Hanley, England

Character Jug Name	Height, inches
Fat Boy Henry VIII	4 1/2

Toby Jug Name	Height, inches
Dog "45"	5

History

John Henry Weatherby founded J. H. Weatherby & Sons in 1891, potting at the Falcon Pottery in Hanley, Staffordshire beginning in 1891. John Weatherby was born in 1843 and apprenticed as a thrower and turner with his uncle, William Wood, at Wood and Company. Weatherby produced pottery tableware with attractive designs for everyday use, as well as lines of novelties and giftware. The firm built its reputation around the durability of its products.

Beginning in the 1920s, Weatherby adopted the tradename "Falcon Ware" and used the Union Jack in many of its marks from 1925 onward. The tradename Weatherby Ware was also used from 1936. The Falcon Ware tradename used by Weatherby & Sons can easily be confused with that of Thomas Lawrence Limited of Longton. However, even when using its Falcon Ware tradename, Weatherby always included the firm's name as well.

Character Jugs and Toby Jugs

Weatherby & Sons range of Dickens' Character Jugs was produced in the 1950s. Only a few jugs have been identified, but certainly more exist.

Wedgwood
See Josiah Wedgwood & Sons

Wedgwood & Company Limited
Tunstall, England

Wedgwood & Co. backstamp

History

Wedgwood & Company had its beginnings in the Podmore, Walker & Company pottery of Tunstall, Staffordshire. Podmore, Walker was founded in 1834 at the Well Street Works. In 1850, the firm moved to a factory on Amicable Street. Six years later, in 1856, the firm added another partner, Enoch Wedgwood, and changed the pottery's name to Podmore, Walker & Wedgwood.

Enoch assumed control of the company by 1860, and renamed it Wedgwood & Company, operating at the Unicorn and Pinnox factories in Tunstall. The firm sold its Unicorn Pottery to Hollinshead & Kirkham in 1876. In 1900, the firm became a limited partnership and added "Limited" to its name and backstamp.

The pottery continued operating successfully for almost a century, producing a variety of high quality pottery and porcelain products throughout its operation. In 1964, the company was taken over by Semart Importing Company, later known as Automatic Retailers of America. One year later, Wedgwood & Company was renamed Enoch Wedgwood Limited. A. G. Richardson & Company bought Enoch Wedgwood in March of 1974. Don Brooks was the Managing Director of Enoch Wedgwood during this time and until 1980.

In 1980, Josiah Wedgwood & Sons, now the Wedgwood Group, purchased Enoch Wedgwood. The pottery was renamed the Unicorn Pottery and began using the tradename "Bull in a China Shop".

Toby Jugs

Wedgwood & Company produced a large range

of high quality, brightly decorated Toby Jugs in the early part of the twentieth century. Colley Shugglebottom was the modeler who created the majority of these fine, well-detailed jugs. Many have features that required a large amount of hand modeling, such as the Lord Mayor's scepter and the Coachman's whip. The jugs were marked "Wedgwood & Co. Ltd." with a unicorn head symbol and a raised or incised model number. Often the name of the character was incised. The jugs are handpainted in part with overglaze paint, which unfortunately may flake. An Alice in Wonderland series and Snow White series of Toby Jugs are rumored to exist, but no jugs have been positively identified.

Wedgwood & Company made and sold jugs until the 1950s, at which time they were taken out of production. When the Wedgwood Group acquired the pottery in 1980, the firm sold its Toby molds to Roy Kirkham. However, some molds ended up at Staffordshire Fine Ceramics. Both potteries produced jugs from these molds. Also, in the 1950s and 60s, Japanese reproductions of these jugs were made and are commonly found. These Japanese reproductions are of lesser quality and are marked "Japan" or unmarked, see photos in the Japan section under Jugs Marked by Country of Manufacture.

From left to right: Beadle, Schoolmaster, and Pedlar Toby Jugs

Lord Mayor group, lamp base on left, large Toby Jug in center, and small Toby Jug on right

From left to right: Prince Order of Thistle, Lord Chief Justice, Knight Order of the Garter, and Earl Order of St. Patrick

Coachman large and small Toby Jug

Innkeeper large and small Toby Jug

Nightwatchman large and small Toby Jug

Toby Jug Name	Height, Inches	Model Number
Archbishop		778
Beadle	7 1/4	756
Beggarman	5 3/8	795
Coachman	5 1/2 3 3/4	757 757/3
Earl, Order of St. Patrick	7 1/2	775
Innkeeper	7 5	762/1 762/3
Knight, Order of the Garter	7	774 II
Lord Chief Justice	7 1/2	777
Lord Mayor	7 1/4 6 4 7/8	753 753/3
Nightwatchman	6 1/2 4 1/4	754 754/3
Pedlar	6 3/4 5 1/4	761/1
Poorman	5 1/8	798
Prince, Order of Thistle	7 1/2	776 II
Richman	5 1/4	796
Sailor	5 1/4	783
Schoolmaster	7 4 1/2	765/1 765/3
Shepherd	7 4 7/8	766/1 766/3
Squire	7 1/4 5 1/4	763/1 763/3
Tailor	5 1/4	781
Thief	5 1/4	784
Tinker	5 1/4	780
Town Clerk	5 3/4 4	755 755/3
Town Crier	6 1/4	750
Town Crier II	7 1/4 4 7/8	760
Vicar	7 1/2 4 1/4	764/1 764/3

Derivitive	Height, Inches
Lord Mayor lamp base	8 1/4

Shepherd large and small Toby Jug

Large and small Squire Toby Jug

Left to right: Tinker, Soldier, Sailor, and Beggarman from the Tinker, Tailor series of Toby Jugs

Large and small Town Clerk Toby Jug

Large, medium and small Town Crier Toby Jug

Small Vicar Toby Jug

Weetman Figures
Tunstall, England

Character Jug Name	Height, inches
Clown	2 5/8
Friar Tuck	4 1/2
	2 5/8
Mouse	2 3/4
Woman	2 1/2
Woman with bonnet	3 3/4

Toby Jug Name	Height, inches
Dick Whittington	5

History

Weetman Figures has been potting in Sandyford, Tunstall since 1952. The firm specializes in china and earthenware figures and giftware, using the tradename "Weetman Giftware".

Character Jugs and Toby Jugs

Several Character and Toby Jugs of average quality have been found with the Weetman Giftware mark. In addition to a cream finish, these jugs come in a variety of pastel colors including yellow and blue. The Mouse is a half-bodied jug and looks like he stepped off the pages of Cinderella.

Friar Tuck and Clown Character Jugs flanking Dick Whittington Toby Jug

Weetman Giftware backstamp

Wemyss Ware
See Heron & Son

History

Westminster Pottery operated in Hanley, Staffordshire from 1948 until 1956, producing a variety of earthenware goods. After Westminster closed, many of its molds were obtained by the Co-operative Wholesale Society, which produced wares from these molds under its Crown Clarence tradename.

Character Jugs and Toby Jugs

During the firm's brief production life, Westminster produced a series of Toby Jugs called the Tavern Collection. Only a few of that series have been identified and certainly more exist. The firm also produced Character Jugs in a series called the "Just So Series." Four jugs have been found so far in this series, which likely numbers six.

The Co-operative Wholesale Society also produced a Just So Series and the jugs from the Tavern Series with its Crown Clarence tradename. Although the connection between these two firms is not known, most likely Westminster's molds were purchased by the Co-operative Wholesale Society after 1956. The Character Jug molds continued to move around Staffordshire, as the same jugs also appear marked "Jon Anton," and Staffordshire Fine reproduced the Just So Series as its "Days Gone By" series. For other jugs in the Just So Series. Please see Co-operative Wholesale Society, Anton Potteries, and Staffordshire Fine Ceramics.

The mark found on Westminster jugs is a stylized crown above "Westminster Made in Staffs England".

Character Jug Name	Height, inches
Big Chief	4 1/2
Gramp	3 3/4
Gran	3 3/4
Jock	4 1/2
Outlaw	3 7/8
Paddy	
Sheik	

Toby Jug Name	Height, inches
Gaffer Jarge	7 1/4
Mine Host John	8 7/8
Mine Hostess	8 3/8
Watchman Jeremy	8

Character Jugs from the Just So Series; top - Gramp and Gran; bottom - Jock and Outlaw

Mine Host and Mine Hostess large Toby Jugs from the Tavern Series

Watchman Jeremy and Gaffer Jarge Toby Jugs from the Tavern Series

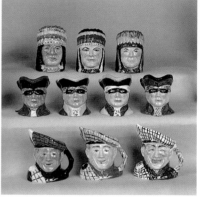
Grouping of Just So Series Jugs from Westminster, Anton Potteries, Crown Clarence, and Staffordshire Fine Ceramics (See page 338 for more photo comparisons)

R. C. White
See Jugs Marked by Country of Manufacture under United Kingdom

A. J. Wilkinson Limited
Burslem, England

History

Arthur J. Wilkinson was potting for several years in the partnership Wilkinson & Hulme. In 1885, the partnership dissolved and he founded A. J. Wilkinson. That same year, he purchased the Burslem Churchyard Works Pottery, one of the oldest active potteries in Staffordshire, and incor-

porated it into his Central Pottery and Bodley Works. This amalgamated factory became known as the Royal Staffordshire Pottery. Arthur Wilkinson died unexpectedly in an accident in 1891. Arthur Shorter, the founder of Shorter & Son and Arthur Wilkinson's brother-in-law, took over operation of the factory.

Newport Pottery Clarice Cliff
backstamp

John Peel Toby Jug

Admiral John Jellicoe prototype
Toby Jug, note positioning of jug

Old Bill Character Jug

Wilkinson's Royal Staffordshire Pottery continued to be run as an independent pottery under Arthur Shorter until 1894, when Shorter purchased the Wilkinson factory outright and consolidated his Shorter & Son factory and Wilkinson into one enterprise. The activities of the Wilkinson pottery were moved to Middleport in 1898. However, only a few of the Royal Staffordshire designs and trademarks were used after the consolidation of the factories. Wilkinson's became a limited partnership in 1896.

In 1916, a young designer and artist named Clarice Cliff joined the Wilkinson factory after studying handpainting and lithography at several schools and one year of service at Hollinshead & Kirkham Limited. Born in Tunstall in 1899, Clarice was one of eight children of an ironmonger. When Clarice was thirteen years old, she left school and began her training in the arts. After her apprenticeship with Hollinshead & Kirkham, Clarice worked as a gilder for Wilkinson. However, because she demonstrated skills as a ceramic artist, the firm sent Clarice to the Royal College of Art in London to study and develop her talents. In 1920, Shorter & Son purchased the Newport factory, which stood on the banks of the Trent and Mersey Canal in Longport, and operated it under the Wilkinson name. Shortly thereafter, Clarice Cliff returned to Shorter & Son at the Newport factory. It was here that Clarice Cliff created her Bizarre range.

Wilkinsons continued active production until 1963 as a part of Shorter & Son. Colley Shorter, the director of Shorter & Son and Arthur Shorter's son, died that year and bequeathed the bulk of his estate to Clarice Cliff, whom he had married in 1940. Cliff sold the Wilkinson and Newport factories to W. R. Midwinter that year. Upon taking control of A. J. Wilkinson, Midwinter allegedly found unfinished stock in storage and sold it off inexpensively. Please also refer to Shorter and Son and for more a more detailed history of A. J. Wilkinson, refer to *The Shorter Connection* by Gordon and Irene Hopwood.

Character Jugs and Toby Jugs

Between 1915 and 1919, the Wilkinson factory produced one of the most significant series of twentieth century Toby Jugs depicting World War I Allied Commanders. There were eleven Commanders produced in this set, all designed by F. Carruthers Gould, a famous British political cartoonist. These jugs were distributed exclusively through Soane & Smith of London and originally sold for between two and four pounds apiece, or roughly $5 to $10. The jugs were introduced over a four year period in the following order: Kitchener, French, Joffre, Jellicoe, Lloyd George, Haig, Beatty, Foch, Wilson, Botha, and King George. An Old Bill Character Jug based on Bruce Barnsfather was produced and advertised along with the Allied Commander series.

A letter from the London retailer of Soane & Smith dated December 19, 1931 outlines the sales status of these jugs. It states that all but Foch, Wilson, Botha and King George were sold out. These four were still in stock with the first three priced at 3.3 pounds and King George at 7.7 pounds, or about $20. Soane & Smith quoted prices on the secondary market for Kitchener of about $80 and Jellicoe for around $40. The letter states that King George was "intended to be a fitting conclusion to the series." The letter also ends with "General Allenby was not modeled in one of these jugs."

The King George V jug was approved by His Majesty himself and came in a partial colorway, as well as full color. The creamware version has a market value of one-third that of the full colorway. A unique version of the Admiral John Jellicoe jug has been found with Jellicoe's mug held in his lap, not on his knee, and with different writing on the jug. This is most likely a one-of-a-kind prototype. Other Wilkinson World War I tobies have appeared on the market in an unfinished state. It is possible these were part of the unfinished stock, which Midwinter found and sold off when they purchased the Royal Staffordshire factory, making these unfinished tobies a part of the limited edition number.

A commonly held belief is that a Winston Churchill Toby was intended to round this set out to twelve jugs, but was dropped due to adverse public opinion over the Dardenelles affair. Some speculate that a toby designed by Clarice Cliff at the beginning of World War II, with Churchill in the uniform of the Lord Warden of the Cinque Ports, was issued to rectify this earlier omission. However the uniform Churchill wears dates from World War II, not World War I, so it is more likely that this jug was produced as a result of Churchill's rebound in popularity in the 1930s. The Soane & Smith letter also disputes the World War I theory.

The Churchill jug was the first of a new set of World War II Toby Jugs, capitalizing on the success of its previous World War I series. Prototype jugs of Wavell, Chamberlain, Mitchell, and Franklin D. Roosevelt were created, but never put into production. Most likely the curtailment of non-military ceramic production during the war, coupled with a shortage of skilled artists, aborted this series.

Under the Newport Pottery name, Clarice Cliff also designed several Toby Jugs for Wilkinson, including Toby Fillpot in several sizes, a Standing Toby, and Don Quixote.

Backstamp on WW I Allied
Commander Toby Jugs

Left to right: Lord Kitchener, Admiral David Beatty,
Field Marshal Douglas Haig, and Admiral John Jellicoe

Character Jug Name	Height, Inches	Production Life	Edition Size
Old Bill	5	1915 - 1918	

Toby Jug Name	Height, Inches	Production Life	Edition Size
Admiral David Beatty	10 1/4	1917	350
Admiral John Jellicoe	10 1/4	1915	350
Balfor			ca 1940
Don Quixote (Newport)			
Field Marshal Douglas Haig	10	1917	350
Franklin D. Roosevelt			ca 1940
General Archibald Wavell	12	ca 1940	proto
General Louis Botha	10 1/2	1919	250
John Peel	14 1/2	1915	
King George V	12 1/4	1919	1000
Lord John French	9 3/4	1915 - 1916	350
Lord Kitchener	10	1919	250
Marshal Ferdinand Foch	11 3/4	1914 - 1918	500
Marshal Joseph Joffre	10	1915	350
Neville Chamberlain	12	ca 1940	
Reginald J. Mitchell	11 3/4	ca 1940	
Rt. Hon. David Lloyd George	10	1916	350
Scholar	2 1/4	1939 - 1940s	
Squat Toby	6 3/4	1939 - 1940s	
Toby Fillpot #859	11	1939 - 1940s	
(Newport Pottery)	9 1/2	1939 - 1940s	
(Newport Pottery) #862	8 1/4	1939 - 1940s	
(Newport Pottery) #860	6 1/2	1939 - 1940s	
(Newport Pottery)	4	1939 - 1940s	
(Newport Pottery) #869	2 1/2	1939 - 1940s	
Winston Churchill	11 1/2	1941	200
Woodrow Wilson	10 1/2	1918	500

King George V Toby Jug in a full and
partial colorway

Left to right: Marshal Joseph Joffre, Lord John
French, and Rt. Hon. David Lloyd George

Left to right: Woodrow Wilson, Marshal Ferdinand Foch,
King George V, and General Louis Botha

Three Toby Fillpot Toby Jugs in 9 1/2, 8 1/4, and
6 1/2 inch sizes; designed by Clarice Cliff

Tiny Standing Toby, 6 1/2" Toby Fillpot Toby Jug,
and Toby Fillpot creamer and sugar by Clarice
Cliff

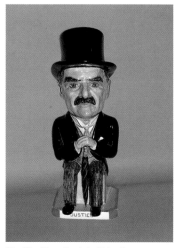

General Archibald Wavell Toby
Jug

Neville Chamberlain Toby Jug

Reginald J. Mitchell Toby Jug;
designer of the Spitfire

Winston Churchill Toby Jug

William Kent Limited
Burslem, England

History

William Kent, who came from a family of potters, established a small factory on Auckland Street in Burslem in 1878, where the pottery remained throughout its entire life. He dedicated himself to following traditional methods in the production of ware, primarily figures and ornamental items. In 1880, Kent formed a partnership with John Parr that lasted until 1894, when he again went on his own, this time with his sons, E. J. Kent, S. H. Kent and W. F. Kent. In 1944, the firm was renamed Kent Porcelains Limited, possibly following William Kent's death, after which it was managed by William's three sons. John S. Kent, W. F. Kent's son, became the third generation to own and operate the family pottery, managing the firm until 1962, when the factory was sold to Blakeney Art Pottery.

The firm took pride in its production of a wide variety of traditional Staffordshire earthenware products, including busts, figurines, animals, cottageware, boxes, and figural groups. William Kent used original 19th century molds, many likely obtained from Machin & Potts Waterloo Pottery in Burslem after that firm closed in 1877. Traditional handcrafted methods were maintained, and the pottery operated under the slogan "Let Craftmanship Prevail." Master craftsmen produced ware by hand pressing plastic clay into the molds. After firing, artists then meticulously handpainted each piece. Although a good portion of its production was unmarked, the firm used the tradenames "Old Staffordshire Ware" and "Staffordshire Ware". Its later mark had the tradename above a Staffordshire knot and "Kent Made in England" underneath.

After the pottery closed, John Kent regularly consigned the molds and designs to other potters under the condition that all ware produced would be marked with the Kent name. Among the firms that produced Kent's ware were Blakeney Art Pottery, Lancaster and Sandland, Midwinter and currently Bairstow Manor Pottery. Experience, an eye for the details of an item, and its apparent age should help the collector determine which ware the Kent factory produced, and which was produced more recently.

Character Jugs and Toby Jugs

Throughout its entire history, William Kent produced a variety of Character and Toby Jugs in traditional forms. Many of Kent's initial Toby molds were purchased from William Machin in the late 1870s. Kent produced these tobies regularly from the late 1890s through 1962. The comprehensive listing below comes directly from a 1960 Kent brochure titled *The Story of "Olde Staffordshire" Pottery by Kent of Burslem* edited by Douglas C. Hall. Names in parenthesis are the jug's more common name today.

A pair of Punch and Judy Toby Jugs have been found with "Mr. A. Hind" handpainted on their bases. It is not known if Mr. Hind was a factory employee, or possibly the jugs were custom made for him. Souter Johnnie and Tam O'Shanter are similar in form to the classic 19th century George Whitfield Toby, without handle and complete with their names around the front of the bases. The Squat Toby can be found with a blue willow pattern decorating his jacket. This is more desirable that a plain blue jacket. The small Snufftaker Toby is free standing, meaning he stands on his own two feet not a base. Similarly, the Kneeling Toby has no base. These two tobies are marked only with "England" handpainted in black between their legs. Kent also produced Toby Jug derivatives in the form of teapots, figures, creamers, mugs, and cruets.

While much of Kent's jug production was unmarked, its more recent production carries the backstamp "Old Staffordshire Ware England". When marked, older production jugs have on their base an orange-red stamped "Made in England" inside a square with a black model number handpainted, or just the handpainted black model number. In the late 1990s, Kent's Toby molds were being used by Bairstow Manor Pottery, which produced excellent reproduction jugs marked with "Staffordshire Ware", "Kent", and a Staffordshire knot per the terms of the agreement.

Punch and Judy Toby Jug and Character Jug pairs

John Bull and Cromwell Toby Jugs

Nelson, Joan, and Snufftaker Toby Jugs

Toby Jugs without bases, Standing Toby on left and Kneeling Toby on right

Tam O' Shanter and Souter Johnnie handleless Toby Jugs

Jug and Glass, Pickwick, and Jolly Miller Toby Jugs

Character Jug Name	Height, Inches	Model Number
Face, Mug - special	5 3/4	524
Face, Frog Mug (Bacchus)	4 3/4	511
Judy	4 3/4	315
Punch	4 3/4	315

Toby Jug Name	Height, Inches	Model Number
A Broth of a Boy	7 3/4	529
Cromwell (Cavalier)	9 3/4	384
Darby	10	376
Falstaff	8 1/2	383
Father Christmas	8	378
Hearty Good Fellow	11 1/4	373
Joan	9	377
John Bull	11 10	374 375
Jolly Miller (Cross-legged Toby)	9	370
Judy	11	382
Jug & Glass (Hunchback Toby)	9 1/2	389
Large	10	385
Men (Standing Toby) (Kneeling Toby)	3 3/4 3	481 483
Mermaid Handle	10	371
Nelson	11 1/2	372
Ordinary Toby	10 1/2 9	387 386
Pickwick	7 1/2	391
Punch	12 1/2	381
Sailor	11	465
Snufftaker	8 1/4 3 3/4	390
Souter Johnnie	9	470
Squire	11	380
Tam O'Shanter	9	471
Toby Mug (Squat Toby)	5 3/4	368
Watchman	8 3/4	464
Women	3 3/4 3	481 483

William MacLean
United States

Character Jugs

William MacLean was an American artist and designer. In the mid to late 1950s, he designed a Great Americans Series of Character Jugs celebrating historical and fictional figures from United States' history. This is a high quality series of jugs and was produced in Japan. Some characters were produced in two sizes. Jugs can be found both in a cream finish and full colorway.

Impressed William MacLean mark

Character Jug Name	Height, inches
Abraham Lincoln	5 1/4
American Indian	5 1/4 3 1/2
Beckey Thatcher	
Benjamin Franklin	5 1/4
Captain Ahab	5 1/4 3 1/2
Daniel Boone	5 1/4 3 1/2
Dwight Eisenhower	5 1/2 3 1/2
General George Custer	5 3/4
George Washington	5
Huckleberry Finn	5 1/4
Ichabod Crane	5 1/4
Robert E. Lee	5 1/4
Thomas Jefferson	6 1/4
Ulysses S. Grant	

Benjamin Franklin, Thomas Jefferson, and Abraham
Lincoln Character Jugs in full color

Creamware Character Jugs from top left to bottom
right - Dwight Eisenhower large and small, Daniel
Boone, American Indian, and Captain Ahab

Willow Art and Willow China
See Hewitt & Leadbeater

Wilton Ware
See A. G. Harley Jones

Windy Ridge Studios
See Jugs Marked by Country of Manufacture under United Kingdom

H. J. Wood Limited
Burslem, England

Character Jug Name	Height, inches
King of Hearts	3 3/8
Quaker Man	3 1/2

Toby Jug Name	Height, inches
Batsman Cricketer	7 1/2
Bowler Cricketer	7 1/2
Goalkeeper Cricketer	7 1/2
Golfer	7 1/2
Jack of Hearts	7
Joan	4 1/2
King of Hearts	7
Lady Tennis Player	7 1/2
Martha Gunn	7 1/2
Ordinary Toby	6
Queen of Hearts	7
Standing Toby	5 1/2
Wicketkeeper Cricketer	7 1/2
Woman Toby	5 1/2
	4 1/2

Pack of Cards Series
BY
H.J. WOOD
ENGLAND

Pack of Cards Series backstamp

History

Harry J. Wood founded H. J. Wood Limited in 1884 at the Alexandra Pottery in Burslem, producing pottery for everyday and ornamental use. In 1899, a strong and long lasting relationship was formed between H. J. Wood and Wood and Sons when Harry Wood also began working with the Directors of Wood and Sons. It was through his efforts at Wood and Sons that Harry became very influential in the ceramic industry by encouraging young talented artists like Charlotte Rhead and Susie Cooper. Charlotte Rhead went to work at Wood and Sons in 1913, leaving there for Burgess & Leigh in 1926. She then worked for a time for Crown Ducal and eventually joined H. J. Wood in 1942 as Art Director. While at H. J. Wood, Charlotte designed over one hundred new patterns.

Eventually, Harry assumed control of Wood and Sons, and in the 1960s merged the two firms together. Harry turned control of the consolidated company over to H. Francis Wood and Paul Wood. Other members of the Wood family also worked at the firm, including Tony Wood and E. Kenneth Wood, the H. J. Wood Production Manager. The pottery eventually closed and was sold in 1980.

Character Jugs and Toby Jugs

H. J. Wood produced nicely modeled and hand-painted jugs. The Quaker Man was a promotional item for Quaker Oats. In the 1970s, it introduced an excellent series of Character and Toby Jugs call the Pack of Cards Series, featuring face cards of hearts. The Joan toby was the creamer to a Darby and Joan teaset that included a 2 3/4" tall Darby and Joan sugar and 5" teapot.

Most of these molds were used by Wood and Sons and then moved on to Tony Wood.

Golfer Toby Jug

Martha Gunn Toby Jug

Left to right: King of Hearts, Queen of Hearts, and Jack of Hearts Toby Jugs, with King of Hearts Character Jug overviewing

Standing Toby on left and Female Toby on right

Teaset; left to right - Joan creamer, Ordinary Toby teapot, Darby and Joan sugar

Wood and Sons
Burslem, England

History

The success of the Staffordshire potteries is due in large part to the Wood family, which was a major force in the development of small peasant potteries into an organized and widely respected industry. The Wood family can trace its legacy of potters back to brothers Ralph and Aaron, who were potters in the middle of the 18th century. They were followed by the next generation, namely Ralph Jr., John, William and Enoch Wood. The family also had ties to John Astbury, Thomas Whieldon, and the Wedgwood family, with William and Enoch both working for a time at Wedgwood's factory.

The firm of Wood and Sons had its beginning more recently. Thomas Francis Wood, the great-great-great-grandson of Ralph Wood the Miller, founded the pottery in 1865. Operating at the Trent and New Wharf Potteries, Wood and Sons carried on this fine family tradition. Thomas's son, Harry, was also a potter, owning H. J. Wood Limited. In 1899 Harry joined Wood and Sons and the firm of H. J. Wood became associated with Wood and Sons. Harry Wood became very influential in the ceramic industry by encouraging young talented artists like Charlotte Rhead and Susie Cooper. Eventually Harry took complete control of Wood and Sons and directed both firms independently.

Primarily a maker of low cost earthenware, Wood and Sons expanded into art pottery production. To achieve this goal, it hired Frederick Rhead as the Art Director in 1912. Rhead's daughter Charlotte joined the firm the following year. Charlotte Rhead left in 1926 to join Burgess & Leigh, only to return again in 1942 with H. J. Wood, where she designed over one hundred new patterns.

Success and growth required expansion, so the firm purchased the Crown Works factory in 1920 to expand its art pottery line, and then the Ellgreave Pottery in Burslem in 1921 to produce Lottie Rhead Ware designed by Charlotte Rhead.

In 1930, Harry Wood also provided Susie Cooper with the freedom to design her whiteware shapes at the Ellgreave factory. In the 1940s, Tony Wood, an eighth generation member of the Wood family, joined Wood and Sons, initially selling for the firm out of the Ellgreave pottery, which was run by Director Ben Capper. At this time, the Ellgreave factory was producing a large volume of teapots. The Ellgreave factory was leased to Artone Pottery in 1946 when Wood and Sons moved to its new site at Newport Lane. Cortman Limited later occupied this factory from 1996 through 1997.

In the 1960s, Harry fully integrated H. J. Wood into Wood and Sons and began operating the result as a single company. When he retired, Harry turned over control of the firm to H. Francis Wood and Paul Wood. Other members of the Wood family were also active participants at H. J. Wood and Wood and Sons, including E. Kenneth Wood, the Production Manager at H. J. Wood. A key employee at the pottery was Wilf Blanford. Wilf had worked with molds for many years, becoming the head mold maker. He also became quite an accomplished modeler.

Tony Wood was Chairman and Managing Director of the firm when it went into receivership and was liquidated in 1980. The firm employed about 1000 people at the time of its closure. The York family purchased Wood and Sons' Stanley factory in March of 1982. During its last twenty years of operation, Wood and Sons operated as a public company managed by a Board of Directors. Subsequently, Tony Wood started a new pottery under his own name, see Tony Wood Studio.

Character Jugs and Toby Jugs

An exciting series of Character Jugs produced in the early 1980s by Wood and Sons' was its Pride of Britain Portrait Jug series, honoring famous people from British history. This series, in the form of bust jugs, includes Admiral Lord Nelson, Anne Boleyn, the Duke of Wellington, Henry VIII, Lord Montgomery, and Winston Churchill. The

Pride of Britain backstamp

Backstamp on limited edition traditional Toby Jugs

WOOD & SONS ENGLAND

*THE CHARLES DICKENS
TOBY JUG COLLECTION
FAGIN*

CREATED EXCLUSIVELY FOR
FRANKLIN PORCELAIN LONDON
© FRANKLIN PORCELAIN 79

Charles Dickens Toby Jug
Collection backstamp

Wood and Son common backstamp

Montgomery and Churchill jugs have been found in a slightly larger, matte glazed version. The pair has "Jayne D" hand incised on the bottom. These two items are likely one-of-a-kind prototypes or colorway trials. Jayne could have been the modeler or the artist who painted the trials.

In the mid 1970s, Wood and Sons made an excellent limited edition series of six traditional Toby Jugs that were carefully designed to capture the look of 18th century tobies. The Ralph Wood Toby was modeled by Ernest Sambrooks and the remaining five jugs were all designed by Wilf Blandford. Without the Wood and Sons backstamp on the Ralph Wood Toby, it would be difficult for the inexperienced eye to tell the difference between Wood and Sons' Ralph Wood Toby and the 18th century original.

Wood and Sons also produced "The Charles Dickens Toby Jug Collection" on commission from Franklin Porcelain between 1978 and 1981. Peter Jackson, a famed historical cartoonist, depicted Dickens' most loved characters in his design of these twelve tobies. On some of these jugs, most likely those produced early in the production run before the mold became worn, the impressed initials PJ can be found.

Several Wood and Son jugs came from H. J. Wood molds, while many reappeared subsequently under the Tony Wood label. The Quaker Man was a promotional item originally produced for Quaker Oats by H. J. Wood. In 1999 several characters from the same molds were produced by Cortman Limited under the Wood of Burslem label. See also Tony Wood and Wood Potters of Burslem.

Character Jug Name	Height, Inches	Production Life
Admiral Lord Nelson	4	1980s
Anne Boleyn	5	1980s
Ben Franklin	3 1/2	1980s
Duke of Wellington	6 3/8	1980s
Henry VIII	5 5/8	1980s
King of Hearts	7	
Lord Montgomery matte glazed prototype	5 3/4 6	1980s 1980
Mr. Quaker	3 1/2	
Napoleon Bonaparte	5 5/8	1980s
Winston Churchill matte glazed prototype	5 3/4 6	1980s 1980

Toby Jug Name	Height, Inches	Production Life
Benjamin Toby	10 7 1/2	1973 Ltd Ed of 500
Betsy	6 1/2 5	1990s 1990s
Bob Cratchit & Tiny Tim	5 3/4	1980
Charrington Toby	7 1/4	1980 - 1981
David Copperfield	6	1981
Fagin	6	1979
Jack of Hearts	7	
Little Nell	5 7/8	1979
Lord Howe	9 3/4 6 1/8 4 1/2	1973 Ltd Ed of 500
Martha Gunn	11	1973 Ltd Ed of 1000
Miss Havisham	6	1981
Mr. Micawber	6	1979
Mr. Pickwick	5 1/2	1978
Mrs. Gamp	5 1/4	1980
Oliver Twist	5 3/4	1979
Ordinary Toby	7 1/4 6 1/2 5 4 3 1/2 3 1/4	1970s
Peggoty	6	1979
Ralph Wood Toby	10	1973 Ltd Ed of 1000
Sailor	11	1975 Ltd Ed of 500
Scrooge	5	1980
Squire	11	1975 Ltd Ed of 500
Uriah Heep	6 1/8	1980

Group of Ordinary tobies in a variety of sizes; note the facial expressions; the four jugs on the left have narrow faces with stern expressions, the three on the right have rounder faces with happier expressions

Pride of Britain Jugs, top left to bottom right: Admiral Lord Nelson, Duke of Wellington, Lord Montgomery, Henry VIII, Anne Boleyn, and Winston Churchill

Production versions of Winston Churchill and Lord Montgomery flanking matte glazed prototypes of each

Mr. Quaker large and miniature Character Jug

Comparison of Ralph Wood Toby replica on the left alongside an original Toby Jug by Ralph Wood ca 1770

Franklin Porcelain Dickens Toby Jug set, top left to bottom right: Uriah Heep, Fagin, Oliver Twist, Little Nell, David Copperfield, Miss Havisham, Mr. Pickwick, Mrs. Gamp, Mr. Micawber, Peggoty, Scrooge, and Bob Cratchit with Tiny Tim

18th century replica Toby Jugs; left to right - Squire, Ralph Wood Toby, Martha Gunn, Lord Howe, Benjamin Toby, and Sailor

Comparison of Wood & Son replica Toby Jugs on the bottom row with their 18th century counterpart above; left to right - Ralph Wood Toby, Squire, Martha Gunn, Lord Howe, Sailor, and Benjamin Toby

Wood Potters of Burslem
Burslem, England

History

Wood Potters of Burslem was started in 1992 by Scotland Direct, a Scottish mail order house for a wide variety of giftware. One of Scotland Direct's early lines was figural thimbles. Scotland Direct purchased the assets of Tony Wood Studio from receivers in 1992. Previously, Scotland Direct carried ware produced by Tony Wood, and, by starting Wood Potters, continued production of those ware under this new name. The leadership behind this purchase was Arthur Bell, Scotland Direct's Director, and Mark Bolton, a long time employee of Tony Wood who became an agent for Scotland Direct. Wood Potters of Burslem ceased production in 1996 and the firm's assets were auctioned off.

Character Jugs and Toby Jugs

Wood Potters of Burslem produced essentially the same range of jugs that Tony Wood produced. Wood Potters also introduced a very nice line of miniature Toby Jugs of its own design. These jugs stand just over three inches tall and include the Clerk, Drunken Parson, Gamekeeper, Haymaker, Lover, Martha Gunn, Musician, Ralph Wood, Sailor, Shepherd, Shepherdess, and Toby Philpot. The Mr. Holly Character Jug was a creamer from a holiday set commissioned by Marshall Field's Department store in Chicago. Along with Mr. Holly came a teapot and Mrs. Mistletoe sugar bowl.

The firm also purchased Shorter & Son molds from Larry Ewing of Sherwood China in the latter 1980s. Wood Potters used a mark with "Shorter" inside a loop formed by a ribbon on its production from these molds. With the closure of Wood Potters, some of the Shorter molds then moved on to Cortman Limited. See also Tony Wood Studio and Wood and Sons.

Character Jug Name	Height, inches
Beefeater	5 1/4
Dick Turpin	5 1/4
Long John Silver	5 1/2
Mad Hatter	8
Mr. Holly	5 1/4
Winston Churchill	5 1/4

Toby Jug Name	Height, inches
Aaron	7
Benjamin	7 1/2
Betsy	6
Clerk	3 1/2
Coachman	8 1/4
Drunken Parson	3 1/2
Gamekeeper	3 1/2
Haymaker	3 1/2
Hearty Good Fellow	
Highlander	8
Jabez	7 1/4
Jester	6 1/4
Lord Howe	6 1/4
Lover	3 1/4
Mad Hatter	8 1/2
Martha Gunn	6 3 1/2
Moses	5 3/4
Musician	3 1/2
Ordinary Toby	5 1/2 4
Piper	7 3/4
Ralph Wood	3 1/2
Robert Burns	
Sailor	6 3 1/2
Shepherd	3 1/2
Shepherdess	3 1/2
Squire	
Toby Philpot	7 6 3 1/2 3
Tubby Toby	6 1/2

Teapots	Height, inches
Darby & Joan	5
Joshua	6 1/2
Mad Hatter	
Sherlock Holmes	7 1/4

Thimbles	Height, inches
Benjamin	1 1/2
Squire	1 1/2
Toby Philpot	1 1/2

MARTHA GUNN

Wood Potters of Burslem mark

Beefeater Character Jug

Winston Churchill Character Jug

Left to right: Benjamin, Jabez, and Aaron Toby Jugs

Left to right: Betsy, Jester, and Moses Toby Jugs

Lord Howe Toby Jug on left and Martha Gunn Toby Jug on right

Left to right: Highlander, Piper, and Coachman Toby Jugs

Mini Toby Jugs from top left to bottom right: Ralph Wood, Martha Gunn, Drunken Parson, Shepherdess, Shepherd, Gamekeeper, and Sailor

Group of Ordinary Toby Jugs, three stern faced jugs on the left and two round smiling faces on the right

Teapots from upper left to lower right: Mad Hatter, Jester, Sherlock Holmes, Joshua, Mad Hatter, and Darby & Joan

Three figural thimbles

Yozie Mold
See Grace S. Apgar

Jugs Marked by Country of Manufacture

Austria Character Jugs

One Austrian Character Jug has been identified thus far. The American Indian has a makers mark of an overlapped H and J, plus "Vienne Austria."

Character Jug Name	Height, inches
American Indian "HJ Vienne"	6

Canada Character Jugs and Toby Jugs

An advertising Ordinary Toby has been found which has "Toby's Trounce Alley" on the front of its base. In relief on the bottom is "Green Thumb Victoria". This jug is finished in a brown Rockingham glaze and has no handle. There is an area known as Trounce Alley in Victoria, Canada. It is a shopping district geared toward tourist traffic. Records do show a Green Thumb Gardening operating in that area in the 1990s, and possibly earlier, but no one knows if it was this firm that commissioned the jug to promote the shopping district. The jug dates from within the past twenty years.

Character Jug Name	Height, inches
Don Bradman "Ltd Ed of 3000 Bendigo Pottery, Victoria"	

Toby Jug Name	Height, inches
Cat "CWI Brooklyn NY"	
Dog "CWI Brooklyn NY"	
Indian Chief	4 1/2
Lion "CWI Brooklyn NY"	
Pig "CWI Brooklyn NY"	
Trounce Alley Toby "Green Thumb Victoria"	5 3/4

Czechoslovakia Character Jugs and Toby Jugs

Several Toby and Character Jugs were produced by Czechoslovakian firms and simply marked with their country of origin. Markings in addition to Czechoslovakia are indicated in quotation marks. Some of these jugs appear to be modeled after real people, but who they might be remains a mystery, perhaps political figures of the time. The art deco looking duck impressed with "926" is attributed to designer Ditmar Urbach. Many Czech jugs also carry an Erphila backstamp. For more information see Ebeling and Reuss.

Left to right: Squat Toby, Guardsman Character Jug, and Standing Woman Toby Jug

Character Jug Name	Height, inches
Bearded Man "83/3056 CN/95"	6 1/4
Colonial Man "7347"	7
Guardsman	5
	3 3/4
Ordinary Toby	5 5/8
	2
Ordinary Toby	6
	5
	4 3/4
	4
	3 3/4
incised "8299"	3 3/4
incised "8300"	3 3/4
	2 1/2
Owl	6
Parrot	4 5/8

Toby Jug Name	Height, inches
Charlie Chaplin "461"	8 3/4
Duck "926"	6 1/2
	4 3/4
Dutch Girl (like Erphila)	4 1/2
Felix the Cat "5026/1/2"	6
Mexican Boy "8168"	4 1/2
with serape	2
Mexican Girl	4 3/4
Mr. Bumble	3 1/2
Pickwick (like Goebel)	3 1/4
Priest (3/4 body)	4 1/2
Rooster	7
Seated Toby	5 3/4
Squat Toby "421/3"	5 1/2
	4
	2 1/4
Standing Toby "5013"	4 3/4
	4
	2
Standing Woman "425/1"	5 1/2
"425/3"	4
Woman	1 1/2

France Character Jugs and Toby Jugs

Character Jug Name	Height, inches	Production Life
Charlie Chaplin	8 5/8	1950s
Jules Ferry majolica	8 1/2	
King Charles Spaniel majolica	7 3/4	ca 1900
Lion, lizard in mouth majolica	8	
Pierrot "Imperial Decormain"	3 1/4	
Railroader "F.F.A.S."		1980s - 1990s
Soldier with mustache	7	1980s - 1990s

Toby Jug Name	Height, inches	Production Life
Bacchus	5 1/4	
Badger with umbrella "F.F.A.S."		1980s - 1990s
Bear with drum		
Bird "Sevres"	7 1/2 5	
Cat "Edeve" majolica	12	ca 1900
Cat with mandolin "F.F.A.S."		1980s - 1990s
Chinaman 3/4 body	10	
Cross-legged Toby "Rouen"	6 1/2 6	
Frog with pipe "F.F.A.S."		1980s - 1990s
Fu Man Chu	3 1/2	ca 1925
Lady Toby	13	
Ordinary Toby	large	
Parakeet "F.F.A.S."		1980s - 1990s
Pierrot with hat	12 3/4 medium	
Pig Waiter "F.F.A.S."		1980s - 1990s
Snufftaker	large 7	1880 - 1910
Standing Lady		
Standing Toby faience	13 9 5 1/2 4 1/4	1930s
Town Crier	7	1880 - 1910

Toby and Character Jugs marked simply France, or unmarked but attributed to a French manufacturer, are available in the marketplace. Markings in addition to France are indicated in quotation marks.

Some of these are French porcelain jugs from the early twentieth century, for example the Town Crier and Snufftaker. Fu Man Chu is a finely detailed porcelain jug finished in matte bisque with bright colors.

Commercial production of china in the **Rouen** region of France dates back to 1673 when Louis Poterat received patent letters providing an exclusive monopoly of china production for thirty years. Early production was soft paste porcelain dinnerware.

In the latter part of the 20th century, the Faiencerie d'Art de la Sorgue of France produced popular majolica of earlier French factories. These reproductions include more than a dozen Toby Jugs. Although reproductions, these jugs are clearly marked with "F.F.A.S. Made in France" and have become collectible in their own right.

Soldier with mustache 7" Character Jug

Charlie Chaplin 8 5/8" Character Jug

Jules Ferry majolica Character Jug

Majolica Character Jugs of King Charles Spaniel on the left and a Lion with salamander in mouth on the right

Chinaman majolica Toby Jug

Bisque porcelain Toby Jugs; left to right - Bacchus, Fu Man Chu, and Standing Toby

Two Standing Toby Jugs

Two Cross-legged Toby Jugs by Rouen

Large Pierrot Toby Jug

Dutch Man and Lady Toby pair, both 13" tall

Four large Toby Jugs in a delft finish; left to right - Standing Man, Snufftaker, Pierrot, and Ordinary Toby

Germany Character Jugs and Toby Jugs

A number of Toby Jugs marked simply Germany or Western Germany are regularly available on the market. Typically those marked Germany are from before the beginning of World War II and those marked Western Germany are post World War II. Occasionally a German Toby will be marked U.S. Zone. This dates production to the ten year post war occupation period of 1945 to 1955.

Albert Stahl Company of Germany reproduced many of the old Ernst Bohne Soehe steins, some from original molds and others from recreated molds. Some of these steins are figural and can be classified as lidded Toby or Character Jugs. The Sherlock Holmes jug is a Stahl original and is a three-quartered body jug with Holmes' hat as the lid. As figural steins are well covered in other texts, they are not included here.

Joseph Strnact Company produced a Character Jug in the shape of Sarreguemines' Jolly Fellow, model

number 3181. The Strnact mark is a J and S in a shield.

The **Konigliche Porzellan Manufactur (KPM)** dates back to Meissen's production in Berlin in the 1720s. Since then KPM has become associated with high quality German porcelain, and more specifically Berlin area porcelain, from the 18th century onward. One of the products the firm is famous for is porcelain dolls heads, which it began producing in the 1830s.

The **R. S. Germany** mark is found on products made at Reinhold Schlegelmilch's porcelain factory in Tilowitz, Germany, an area abundant with the natural ingredients necessary for porcelain production. The factory operated from 1869 until 1956, when it came under control of the Polish socialist government and was closed. The Puck Character Jug can be found signed V. Whitner and is identical to the one produced by Sarreguemines.

Character Jug Name	Height, inches	Production Life
American Indian	1 1/2	
Jolly Fellow Strnact mark		1930s
King George V	5 7/8	ca 1910
Pig "4610"	4	
Puck "R. S. Germany"	6 5 3/4	1910 - 1930s 1910 - 1920s
Queen Mary	5 3/4	ca 1910
TV Hopfingen "Kossinger KG"	6	1985
TV Karlsbrunn "Kossinger KG"	6 1/4	1987
Witch Albert Stahl Co. 6753		
Wood Nymph "Musterschutz"	5	

Toby Jug Name	Height, inches
Bird	5
Bumble	6 1/2 2
Cross-legged Boy with flowers	3 1/2
Dog	2
Eagle "6868/II"	4 3/4
Friar "155"	7 7/8 5 1/4
Gentleman (3/4 body) , incised "77 Germany" on back	4 3/4
Golfer	3 1/2
Hunchback Toby	4 1/2
Indian Chief	4 3/4
King of Hearts (3/4 body)	
Lady Toby	2 1/8 1 1/2
Little Dorrit	3 1/2
Lloyd George	
Lord Asquith	
Monk "Lagrein Kretzer Stiftkellerei Muri Gries" on handle	7 1/4
Monkey	3 3/4
Mr. Pickwick	6 1/4 4 1/2 2
Mrs. Gamp incised "65282"	5 1/2 4 1/2
Napoleon -3/4 body, arm handle	6
Old Lady	5

King George V and Queen Mary porcelain bust Character Jugs

Monk Toby Jug

Toby Jug Name	Height, inches
Ordinary Toby - treacle glaze	8 14
- treacle glaze	5
	3 3/4
"Royal Crown Germany"	2
	2
	1 1/2
Oriental Man "KPM"	5
	3 7/8
sitting cross-legged	3
Owl	5 3/4
Parakeet	4 3/4
Rabbit	5 1/4
Rooster "Ditmar Umbal"	7
Sam Weller incised "2672 37"	3 1/2
	2
Scotsman "G & C Germany"	6
Seated Man holding plant "459"	7
Sherlock Holmes - model 6736 Albert Stahl Co.	
Standing Boy - like Sandizell	3
Standing Girl - like Sandizell	3
Standing Lady - hands on ears	1 5/8
Standing Toby	5 1/2
"Grandenthal 3421"	3 1/2
Toucan "1796"	7 1/2
Town Crier	3 1/2
	3
Winnie the Pooh "Stephen Slesinger Inc. Richard G. Krueger"	3
Witch with cards "MV Co"	4

An unknown German maker produced an exciting series of fine quality, thin porcelain Toby Jugs in the early twentieth century. Although the mystery of who made these jugs remains today, the quality of the porcelain, plus the detail of the hand decorating, suggest these were produced by a high quality firm.

The William Howard Taft and Admiral Perry jugs make a nice commemorative set, Taft being President of the United States when Perry's nine month long expedition reached the North Pole on April 6, 1909. Many of the tobies produced were three-quarter bodied jugs including Perry, Taft, Benjamin Franklin, the Farmer and Sea Captain, all in full color matte finish. The Clown, Jester and Sea Captain are finished in a mottled blue and white glazing.

These jugs are impressed with a model number, and some or all of the following impressed marks on the base or the back of the jug: "ges gesch", "Germany", "Depose'". Depose' is short for modele depose' and indicates the design is registered or trademarked in France. Ges gesch, short for gesetzlich geschuzt, indicates a German registered design protected by law. Sometimes "Germany" is replaced with "Made in Germany". Some jugs have the character's name impressed on the front. Some collectors refer to these jugs generically as Ges Gesch jugs.

While all of these jugs are difficult to find today, perhaps the most scare is Theodore Roosevelt. Certainly other characters exist as well.

Four blue and white Ges Gesch Toby Jugs; left to right Clown, Jester, Old Salt, and Squire

3/4 bodied Ges Gesch Toby Jug pair of William Howard Taft and Admiral Perry

"Ges Gech" Toby Jug Name	Model Number	Height, inches
Admiral Robert Perry	5569	4 3/8
Benjamin Franklin	5091	
Bird with fish	5828	5
Captain Cook	5568	5
Cat	5790	5 1/4
Clown	6087	4 3/4
Dutch Boy	5080	5 1/4
Dutch Girl	5080	5 1/4
Farmer	5191	5
Gardener	5061	5
Gentleman	5337	5
Jester	6086	4 3/4
Man in robe	5060	5
Old Salt	5059	5
Sea Captain		4 3/4
Shepherd	5335	5
Squire		5
Squirrel	5789	5 1/2
Theodore Roosevelt		
Veteran Motorist	5332	5 1/4
William Howard Taft	5440	5

3/4 and full bodied Ges Gesch Toby Jugs; from top to bottom; left to right – Veteran Motorist, Sea Captain, Farmer, Shepherd, and Gardener

Ges Gesch Toby Jugs of Dutch Boy and Dutch Girl in full colorway. and blue and white finish

So far only one unattributed Irish Character Jug has been identified.

Character Jug Name	Height, inches
Leprechaun "MZ Ireland"	5

Leprechaun Character Jug

Italy Character Jugs

Several Character Jugs marked "Made in Italy" have been found. Additional markings are provided in quotes.

A series of Character Jugs were produced using the familiar **Capo-di-Monte** crown over N mark. Capo-di-Monte primarily refers to a style of porcelain produced in Italy. Creation of this style is attributed to a soft paste porcelain factory founded in 1743 by King Charles of Naples. In 1760, this factory moved to Buen Retiro, Spain, but in 1771, a new factory opened in Naples that produced both soft and hard paste porcelain. Doccia of Florence purchased the molds from this factory in 1834 and continued production, marking its wares with the familiar crown over N mark. Capo-di-Monte style ware was widely produced by factories in Italy, Germany, and France. **Societe Richard Ceramica** uses the crown over N mark today on Capo-di-Monte ware and produced these modern Character Jugs around 1970, marking them with a crown over an N.

Group of Capo-di-Monte Character Jugs; top - small Barrister, Woodsman, and Friar; bottom - large Woodsman, Angler, and Yeoman of the Guard

Capo-di-Monte Drake Character Jug

Copy of Capo-di-Monte Character Jug, 8" tall

Character Jug Name	Height, inches
Angler "Capo-di-Monte"	6 1/2
Bacchus "Farnesiana Parma"	7 1/2
Barrister "Capo-di-Monte"	4 7/8
Beefeater "Capo-di-Monte"	7 5/8
Christopher Columbus "480 GCI Italy"	2 1/4
Drake "Capo-di-Monte"	
Fisherman "Made in Italy"	4 1/2
Friar "Capo-di-Monte"	4 7/8
Huntsman "Suvesco Foreign"	6 1/2
Innkeeper "Capo-di-Monte"	9
Sea Captain "A1 N 1970"	5
Woodsman "Capo-di-Monte"	7 5/8 5 1/2

Toby Jug Name	Height, inches
Monk "Societe Ceramica Richard" ca 1900	9
Ordinary Toby "Italy 3060"	10
Standing Woman "Italy 1035"	7

Modern Japanese ceramics started with the fall of the Tokugawa shongunate in 1868, which launched the country on a path of industrialization, mass production and westernization. Along with forms and designs drawn from Japan's heritage, outside influences began to have an impact. Probably the most recognized was Englishman Bernard Leach, who worked in Japan with perhaps the most influential artists in early twentieth century Japan, including Shoji Hamada, Kawai Kanjiro and Yomimoto Kankichi. Hamada-San even spent four years in

Character Jug Name	Height, inches
Abraham Lincoln "Papel"	5 1/4
American Eagle "Quon - Quon MCMLXXX"	6
American Indian	3
Artful Dodger "Nanco"	4 1/2
Auld Mac	3 1/2
Barbie "Mattel Enesco Corp"	4 7/8
Bear in tophat "Quon - Quon MCMLXXX"	6
Bearded Man "Castle Brand" Squirrel handle	5 5 2 1/2
Benjamin Franklin "Papel"	5 1/4
Biker Scout "Sigma"	
Bill Sikes "Nanco"	5
Blackbeard "Swank Japan 1960"	
Boy with bow tie	4 1/4
C3PO "Sigma"	4 1/2
Calico Kitty "Enesco 203995"	4
Cathy "Papel 1995"	
Chef "PY UCAGCO Ceramics"	3 3/4
Chewbacca "Sigma"	4 1/4
Chinaman impressed "KKS 669"	5
Collie	4 1/4
Colonial Man	4 3 2 2/4 2
Cross-eyed Man	3 1/2
Darth Vader "Sigma"	7 4
Dick Turpin "Florart" "OVG" superimposed (like Doulton)	3 1/4 2 1/2 2 1/2 2 1 3/4
Dog in tophat "Quon - Quon MCMLXXX"	5 1/2
Don Bradman "Marutomoware"	
Elsie the Cow	4 1/4
Falstaff "Har-Bell"	5
Fat Boy "py UGAGCO"	4
Fozie Bear "Sigma"	3 7/8
Francis Drake shamrock in wreath mark	3 7/8
Frankenstein "Erneli 1981 Universal Studios"	5 3/4
Gamorrean Guard "Sigma"	4
General MacArthur "Merit"	4 1/2
George Washington "Papel" eagle mark	5 1/4 5 4
Golfer	5
Guardsman w/ music box	8
Han Solo "Sigma"	4 1/2
Harlequin "Sigma"	5
High Hat	
Humpty Dumpty	4 1/2
Huntsman	3 2 1/4
Irishman "ARDCO"	5 1/2
Jester "Wales"	3 1/4 3
John Adams	5 1/4
John Barleycorn	3

Cornwall between 1920 and 1924. While these artists and others were exploring new designs and individual expression, the Japanese pottery industry also began mass-producing replicas of popular products. The widespread success of Noke's Character Jugs at Royal Doulton did not go unnoticed.

Production of Character and Toby Jugs from Japan has been plentiful from the 1930s through today, peaking in the 1940s and 50s. Japanese makers commonly reproduced the popular products from other firms such as Royal Doulton, Wedgwood & Company, Lancaster and Sandland, Shorter & Son, Clarice Cliff's designs for Newport Pottery, German style jugs, and others. The quality of most Japanese jugs is noticeably poorer than that of other makers, making identifying even the unmarked Japanese jugs relatively easy with only a little experience.

Since many U. S. firms imported ware produced in Japan, a number of Character and Toby Jugs from Japan are commonly available on the market. These might be marked simply "Japan", "Made in Japan", or be unmarked. These jugs come in full colorway and brown Rockingham-like finishes. The Character Jugs with animal handles were probably made by the same factory and make a comical set. Many Japanese jugs do carry a makers mark, although little is known of the manufacturer. Partial information is provided.

Jugs marked **Enesco** were produced in Japan for Enesco Corporation, a giftware distributor located in Itasca, Illinois. Enesco was founded in 1958 as a division of N. Sure Company. Today Enesco is managed by Founding Chairman Eugene Freedman and offers over 10,000 gift and collectible items. The company has a workforce of over 1,500 throughout eighteen counties worldwide, including a 500 person sales force. The firm's mission statement is "Touching People's Lives with Beauty and Emotion."

Marutomoware Character Jugs are very good quality jugs for this period of Japanese production. Several are made in the image of Royal Doulton jugs and are faithful reproductions of the Doulton originals. These jugs are marked "Marutomoware" with a circled T trademark symbol and "Handpainted Japan".

Merit produced Character Jugs from the 1940s onward; some of its jugs also include an Occupied Japan mark.

Nanco made a series of good quality Character Jugs called Charles Dickens Toby Jugs. Each jug is marked with this series name, the name of the character, and "Nanco".

Papel made a Great American series of famous historical figures. These are high quality jugs reminiscent of Lefton's similar series. The Cathy jug by Papel is part of a tea service set that included teapot, sugar, creamer, and sugar pack holder.

Chenson Associate's **Sigma** Giftware produced a series of Character Jugs based on popular characters of the 1970s through 1990s. The Star Wars mugs were similar to those sold by Applause and made in the early 1980s, primarily in 1983. A Sesame Street series consisting of Kermit, Miss Piggy, Oscar, Big Bird, Bert, and Ernie was made in the 1990s. Sigma's promoted itself as "Sigma the Tastesetter."

The **Ubag China** Company started as the United China and Glass Company. It is still operating, now as the United China and Gift Company. The firm produced some Dickens Toby jugs of better than average quality for a Japanese firm during the late 1940s and early 1950s. Its mark is the company name, or sometimes the letters U, G, and C all superimposed on each other.

Wales' products generally had a foil label with "Wales Japan" or were stamped "**Wales China** Japan". The firm of Nanri Boeki and Company, which closed in 1978, used the Wales tradename. After 1978, Mogi Shoji and Company used the tradename. This firm is still active and often includes "Reg. U.S. Pat Off." in its mark. The Ordinary Toby is the creamer from a tea set.

A comprehensive list of Japanese Character and Toby Jugs would be an exhausting undertaking. The lists provided here are a representative compilation of easily found jugs; see also the Occupied Japan section.

L

Patriotic American Character Jugs; left to right -
Benjamin Franklin, George Washington, John Adams,
and Thomas Jefferson

Uncle Sam Character Jug

Colonial Man and Guardsman Character
Jugs with music box inserts

Shriner Character Jug

High Hat Character Jug

Sigma Yoda, Wicked Warrick, and Gamorrean Guard
Character Jugs

Left to right: Robin Hood, Jester, John Bull, and Golfer
Character Jugs

Ordinary Toby Jug creamer and sugar set

Japanese reproductions of Wedgwood & Co Toby Jugs;
left to right - Vicar, Beadle, Pedlar in two sizes, and
Squire

Character Jug Name		Height, inches
King	sword handle	5 3/4
		4 3/4
	"Nasco"	4
Klaatu	"Sigma"	
Knight in Armor	"Nasco"	4
Lady	"Sigma"	4 1/2
Lando Calrissian	"Sigma" 1983	4 1/4
Lion in tophat	"Quon Quon MCMLXXV"	5 1/2
Long John Silver	"Lego 1960 469"	4 1/2
Longshoreman	"Tilso"	5 1/2
Luke Skywalker	"Sigma"	4 1/4
Man	glasses, squirrel hndl	5 1/4
	stern face, "West Pac"	1 5/8
Mickey Mouse	"Disney Japan"	5
Miss Piggy	"Sigma"	4 1/2
		3 7/8
Mr. Micawber	(like Lancasters)	3
Mr. Peggotty	"Nanco"	4 1/2
Mr. Pickwick	"Wales"	4 1/4
		3 1/2
	"Hal-Sey Fifth ave"	3
Mrs. Bumble	"Nanco"	4 3/4
Mrs. Micawber	"Nanco"	5 1/4
Musketeer		4
Old Bill		1 5/8
Old Charlie		6 1/4
	"Hal-Sey Fifth ave"	4 1/2
	"py UCAGCO"	3 3/4
	"Marutomoware"	3 1/2
		3 1/2
	"Pico China"	3
	"Wales China"	3
	"Takiya"	2 3/.4
		2
Oliver Twist	"Nanco"	4 1/2
Oriental Man		1 7/8
Parson Brown	"Marutomoware"	2 3/4
Pink Panther	"Royal Orleans 1981"	4
Pip	"Nanco"	4 1/2
Pirate	"Japan - Art Mark"	4 1/2
	"Nasco"	4
	"Trader Vic"	
Ponce de Leon		5 1/4
Princess Leia	"Sigma"	
Queen	"Nasco"	4
		3 1/8
Robin Hood		6
		5
Rowlf	"Sigma"	3 3/4
Sailor	diamond shaped "G"	4 1/2
	pipe in mouth	4
Sairy Gamp	"Hal-Sey fifth ave"	4 1/2
		3 1/4
	"Marutomoware"	2 1/2
		2 1/2
Santa Claus	"Jamar"	7
	upside down Y in circle	3
		3
		1 3/4
Sea Captain		5
Sheik		
Shocked Man	hand to mouth, dog hndl	5 1/4
Sir John Falstaff		5 1/2
Smiling Man with cigar		5 3/4
		2 1/4
Soldier	with music box insert	8
	"Enesco"	5
	"Nasco"	4 1/2
Sultan	"Tilso"	5 1/4
Thomas Jefferson	"Papel"	5 1/4
Toby Philpot		4
	"Wales China"	2 1/2
Touchstone	"Wales China"	3
	"Marutomoware"	2 1/2

Character Jug Name	Height, inches
Town Crier	5 1/2
Uncle Sam	4
	3 1/2
"Marutomoware"	2 7/8
Uncle Tom Cobbleigh	3 1/4
Wicket W. Warrick "Sigma"	4 1/4
Winker "UCAGCO"	4 1/2
Wolfman "Erneli 1981 Universal City Studios"	6
Woodsman "Royal Seal"	6 1/4
Yoda "Sigma"	4 1/2

Japanese reproductions of Wedgwood & Co Toby Jugs; left to right - Coachman in three sizes, Innkeeper in two sizes, and Schoolmaster in two sizes

Toby Jug Name	Height, inches
Balloon Woman	2
	1 1/2
Beer Man	5
	3 1/4
Beadle	7 1/2
Black Chef	3 1/2
Black Mammy	3 1/2
Black Man	3 1/2
Coachman (like Wedgwood & Co)	5 1/4
(like Wedgwood & Co)	3 3/8
	3 1/4
Cook	2
Dutch Girl	5 1/4
Fred Roberts	5 1/4
Huntsman (like Wedgwood & Co)	7 3/4
	6
3/4 body	5 1/2
Girl	4
George Washington "Royal Cornwall"	3 1/4
Huntsman	
Innkeeper (like Wedgwood & Co)	3 3/4
King	2 1/2
Lady Toby	5 1/2
	5
	4 1/2
	3 1/4
	2 1/2
	2
	1 3/4
	1 1/2
hands on ears	1 1/4
Lord Mayor (like Wedgwood & Co)	3 1/2
Mandolin Player	
Mickey Mouse	7
Midshipman	
Mr. Pickwick (like Doulton)	3 1/2
	1 3/4
Mrs. Gamp (like Erphila)	3 1/4
Nightwatchman	
Ordinary Toby clover in laurel wreath	6 1/4
	5
(like Devonmoor)	4 7/8
"B Japan"	4 3/4
	4
3/4 body, gazelle handle	3
"Wales" with arm handle	3
"Royal Cornwall"	3
3/4 body, rabbit handle	2 7/8
3/4 body, gazelle handle	2 3/4
	2 1/2
"Orion" like Clarice Cliff	2 1/4
"M	K"	2
	1 1/2

Toby Jug Name	Height, inches
Owl "Otagiri OMC"	3 1/2
Pedlar (like Wedgwood & Co)	7 1/2
	5
	3 1/2
Pig Waiter "Sigma" (like Onnaing)	10 3/8
	8
	3
Pirate	
Preacher	7 1/2
Queen	2 1/2
Sailor "Enesco"	6 1/2
Sairey Gamp (like Doulton)	5 1/4
"Ubag China"	5
(like Ebeling & Reuss)	4 1/2
Sam Weller	1 3/4
Schoolmaster (like Wedgwood & Co)	4 3/4
(like Wedgwood & Co)	3 1/2
Senor Siesta	5 1/2
Sinbad	9 1/4
Snowman "Enesco 1979"	4 1/2
Soldier	4 1/2
Squat Toby	2 1/2
Squire	7 1/4
Standing Lady	4
	3 1/4
	3
	2
Standing Toby "Moriyama"	5 1/2
	4
hands in pockets	3 1/4
	3
hands in pockets	2
	1 3/4
Taxman	4
Vicar (like Wedgwood & Co)	

Benjamin Franklin and Thomas Jefferson Character Jugs from the American Patriot Series by Papel

Group of tiny Standing Toby and Standing Lady Toby Jugs, all under two inches tall

Mandolin Player, Standing Lady, and Huntsman Toby Jugs

Mr. Pickwick and Sam Weller Toby Jugs, 1 3/4 inches tall

Nightwatchman on left and Midshipman on right

Korea Character Jugs

A series of Jetson jugs was made in Korea under license from Hanna Barbera in 1990. These are marked **Vandor.** The licensing fell through and few jugs were produced. The Charlie Chaplin jug is marked "Exclusively Distributed by Presents P3788. A Division of Hamilton Gifts. Bubbles Inc. S. A. 1990. Represented by Bliss House Inc. Springfield MA. 01103 Made in Korea". Also made in Korea was a set of Care Bear Character Jugs commissioned in 1984 by American Greetings.

Character Jug Name	Height, inches
Care Bear "53034"	
Charlie Chaplin	
Cheer Bear	
Elroy Jetson	4
Friend Bear "53031"	
Funshine Bear	
George Jetson	4
Jane Jetson	4
Judy Jetson	3 7/8

Mexico Character Jugs and Toby Jugs

An unknown number of Character and Toby Jugs were made in Mexico.

Character Jug Name	Height, inches
Pirate	5

Toby Jug Name	Height, inches
Dapper Man "Shields"	6
Mayan Idol "Mexico (B. L)"	6 3/4

Mayan Idol Toby Jug

Occupied Japan Character Jugs and Toby Jugs

In spite of the physical and economic devastation of Japan resulting from years of war and culminating in the dropping of two nuclear bombs on the country, pottery production continued after the country's surrender at the end of World War II. Items marked "Made in Occupied Japan" or just "Occupied Japan" were produced during the brief period of the United Nations' directed occupation of Japan immediately after the war, from Japan's unconditional surrender on August 15, 1945 to the restoration of Japanese sovereignty on April 28, 1952. Per the McKinley Tariff Act, goods destined for export to the United States were marked in one form or another as being made in Occupied Japan. Jugs marked Occupied Japan tend to command a higher price than similar jugs marked only Japan. Any company marks also found are noted in parenthesis.

Left to right: American GI and General MacArthur

Character Jug Name	Height, inches
American GI	
American Indian	3
'Arriet "Mocco"	1 3/4
'Arry "Mocco" (like Doulton)	2 1/4
"Mocco"	1 3/4
Auld Mac (like Doulton)	2
"Mocco"	1 3/4
Bearded Man squirrel handle	5
Black Man	5
Bluff King	2 3/4
Bulldog	
Cardinal	3
"Mocco"	1 3/4
Colonial Man	4
	3
	2 1/4
David "Seiloff"	4
Devil	2 1/2
Dick Turpin (like Doulton)	4
	3 1/4
	2 1/2
General MacArthur	4 1/4
Granny (like Sterling)	4 1/2
Huntsman	4
John Peel "Mocco" (like Doulton)	2 1/4
"Mocco"	1 3/4
King	5
Man with Fez	2 1/2
Mr. Pickwick	5
"03 500"	3
Old Charlie	5 1/4
	3 1/2
Sairy Gamp (like Doulton)	3 3/8
Touchstone (like Doulton)	4 1/2
Winker	
Woman	4
xshield & leaves "MS"	2 1/2
"Pico"	2 1/2
	2 1/4

Toby Jug Name	Height, inches
Beadle (like Wedgwood & Co)	7 1/2
Buttercup	5 1/2
Coachman (like Wedgwood & Co)	4 1/2
Colonial Man	2
Devil	
Dutch Boy	2
Female Toby	3
	2 1/4
	2
General MacArthur	
Girl with flowers (like Sitzendorfer)	3
Innkeeper (like Wedgwood & Co)	5
Jailor	6
Lord Mayor (like Wedgwood & Co)	5
Nightwatchman (like Wedgwood & Co) "Klamkin"	5
Ordinary Toby	5
	3
	2 3/4
	2 1/4
	2 1/2
(like Newport Pottery)	2
	2
	1 3/4

Toby Jug Name	Height, inches
Parrot	2 3/4
Parson (like Wedgwood & Co)	
Pedlar (like Wedgwood & Co)	7
	5
Professor (like Wedgwood & Co)	5
Robin Hood	3
Soldier	5 1/4
Squat Toby	2 3/4
Standing Lady	4
	3
	2
Standing Toby	3 1/4
	3
	2 1/2
	2
	1 1/2
Tax Man (like Wedgwood & Co)	5
Toby on barrel	2 1/2
Town Crier (like Wedgwood & Co)	5

Portugal Character Jugs and Toby Jugs

Character Jug Name	Height, inches
Friar Tuck	2
Perriot "Estrella de Conimbriga"	6
Ratcatcher	4 3/4
Sea Captain "Artmark"	5 1/2
Winston Churchill	
Working Man	9 1/2
"Magrou Artmark"	6 1/2

Toby Jug Name	Height, inches
Budha with children	
Cat "Mottahedeh"	12
Cross-legged Toby	9
"A. C. Pereira"	8
Hearty Good Fellow	
Ordinary Toby	12
	11 1/4
"LURDES"	9
	8 1/2
Pig Waiter	
Salamander "Martan"	11 1/2
Standing Toby	5 3/4

A number of Character and Toby Jugs marked simply Portugal are regularly available on the market.

The **Lurdes** Toby Jug is better modeled than many jugs from Portugal and is decorated in lively colors. Toby is signed on the base "CFO ViAnnDo Castelo 359-501 HAnd PAiNtED By LURDES MADE in PORtUGAl".

The Working Man Character Jug looks like it comes from a series. Attached to this jug is a paper flyer that says "Certificado de Garantia, Artigo totalmente fabricado e pintado a mao" on one side and "**Magrou**, Made in Portugal" on the other. A sticker also came affixed to the jug that said "Imported by ArtMark, Made in Portugal."

The Standing Toby has his hands behind his back, an unusual position for this jug.

Ordinary Toby and Hearty Good Fellow Toby Jug

Russia Character and Toby Jugs

Character Jug Name	Height, inches
Queen	

Toby Jug Name	Height, inches
Lion	6 1/4
Lady with Soup Bowl	6

So far very few Russian Character and Toby Jugs have been identified, other than those from Lomonosov. The Lion was produced in the 1970s.

Queen Character Jug

One Toby Jug marked simply "Switzerland" has been identified. This is a well modeled, standing Long John Silver Toby with a music box included in the base.

Toby Jug Name	Height, inches
Long John Silver	11

United Kingdom Character Jugs and Toby Jugs

Following are brief histories of several less known U.K. makers of Character and Toby Jugs, followed by a list of jugs produced in the United Kingdom, some being marked as such and others only suspected to have been produced there, but with no indication of the specific manufacturer.

The markings found on the base of the jug are indicated in quotations after the jug name. The bold marks are names found on the front of the jug's base. These jugs with bold names typically have a chalky body with overglazed paint and were probably produced as a souvenir from that town or city.

Adams & Sons Limited was founded in Staffordshire in 1769 by William Adams, although the opening of the factory dates back to 1657. The pottery operated as Adams & Company until 1800, and then as William Adams & Sons. The firm operated factories in Tunstall and Stoke. The mark found on the Standing Toby was used by the firm on earthenware and stoneware from 1896 into the 20th Century.

Anton Potteries Limited was founded by Jon Anton in 1968 in Longton, Staffordshire. Anton Potteries operated at the Crown Clarence factory, formerly of the Co-Operative Wholesale Society. Although it only operated until 1975, the firm produced a variety of both earthenware and bone china. The firm apparently purchased some of Westminister's molds when that company ceased to exist, as the jugs pictured are identical to Westminster's Just So Series.

Barina Potteries had a short life and therefore little is known about the pottery. Barina operated in Luton, Bedfordshire. The tradename Barina was registered in 1949 and the pottery went out of business around 1955. A second tradename used by the firm was St. Alban Ware. Ordinary Toby Jugs have been found marked with "St. Alban Ware" above a building with other words below.

The **Barrington** Dwight D. Eisenhower Character Jug depicts Ike as a Five Star General. He held this position for the period between 1945, right after the Battle of the Bulge of World War II, and 1953, when he was sworn in as the 34th President of the United States of America. This dates the jug to the late 1940s. The jug was issued in a limited edition of 2,000 and is commonly found. However, its high quality maintains a decent market for the jug.

Pair of Anton Potteries marks

Barrington backstamp

Barrington Dwight D. Eisenhower Character Jug

Anton Potteries Character Jugs: Indian Chief, Highwayman, and Tam O'Shanter

Goldscheider miniature Character Jugs: Blue Boy (from Gainsborough painting) and unidentified character (presumably from another painting)

Frank Stoner Midshipman Toby Jug depicting F. S. Hooker (from the collection of Vic Schuler)

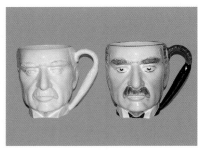

Neville Chamberlain Character Jug by Gibson & Sons, creamware version on left and full colorway on right

Exeter Punch Character Jug by Hart and Moist (from the collection of John Hobbs)

Highmount backstamp   Snel Ware backstamp

In the 1930s, **Frank Stoner**, a London antique dealer with a shop on King Street, had six traditional 18th century style Midshipman Toby Jugs completely hand cast to his specifications. The first was modeled after his friend and fellow collector, F. S. Hooker, as a gift and was incised with the initials FSH.

Gibson & Sons was founded in 1885 when the partnership of Gibson, Sudlow & Company was ended. The firm produced earthenware at the Albany and Harvey Potteries in Burslem often using the tradenames Albany & Harvey or Royal Harvey. Howard Pottery purchased the company in 1965 and then sold it on to Coloroll Ceramics in 1986.

Marcel Goldscheider operated **Goldscheider Pottery** Limited in Hanley between 1946 and 1959. The firm produced both earthenware and bone china products.

Harry Juniper is a contemporary studio potter located in North Devon, England. He primarily produces puzzle jugs, but in the 1990s he created on commission eight unique Ordinary Toby Jugs from an old Devonmoor mold. John Hobbs, a collector and expert on Devonmoor Pottery, had eight Ordinary Toby Jugs created for himself and his seven grandchildren. Standing eight inches tall, each jug bears the individual's name and birthdate. None are likely to appear on the market; however, Mr. Hobbs presented an unfinished bisque jug to the authors.

Hart and Moist of Exeter, Devon produced a wide range of mottoware and high quality art pottery from the late 1890s until forced to close in 1932 by the Depression. William Hart and Mr. Moist founded the firm. Hart had previously been employed at Aller Vale Pottery, and thereafter by the short lived but prolific Exeter Art Pottery, which operated in Exeter from the late 1880s until 1896. Hart and Moist generally impressed its ware "H.M. Exeter" or "Exeter".

Identical **Highmont, Snel Ware** and Thorley Character Jugs can be found, indicating there is a connection between these two firms. One jug has been found with the backstamp of both Highmont and Thorley on it.

Holkham Studio Pottery was founded in Holkham Hall, Holkham, Norfolk in 1951. In 1961 the firm reorganized and operated as Holkam Pottery. The Elizabeth and Duke of Edinburgh Character Jug pair was designed by E. Leicester and produced in a limited edition for the 1953 coronation of Elizabeth. These jugs are extremely rare.

John Humphries Pottery of Staffordshire produced the Santa Clause Character Jug as an advertising piece for Dewars. There are at least two different editions of Humphries' Santa. Another interesting set produced by Humphries is the Beam Boozers Collection, a special commission for Pickwick Wine and Spirits of Derby in a limited edition of 1000. This was a set of six jugs issued in the 1980s, with each jug having a Jim Beam bottle for its handle.

Group of tiny Snel Ware Character Jugs; from top left to bottom right: Florence Nightengale, Friar Tuck, and Maid Marian, Winston Churchill and Abraham Lincoln flanking a miniature Town Crier

Holkham Studio Pottery backstamp

Santa Clause advertising Character Jugs for Dewars, produced by John Humphries (from the collection of Neil Galatz)

John Humphries Beam Boozers Collection; from top left to bottom right in order of issue: Aly Sloper, Mr. Micawber, Toby Philpot, Hunting Fox, Cowboy, and Hobo (from the collection of Emmett Mathews)

Bust Character Jugs of the Duke of Edinburgh and Queen Elizabeth II by Holkham

Rev "Tubby" Clayton holding dog Toby Jug by K. O. Speaks (from the collection of Vic Schuler)

Group of Marshall Taplow Advertising chalkware Toby Jugs, left to right: Bagpiper, Queen, Long John Silver, and Old Salt

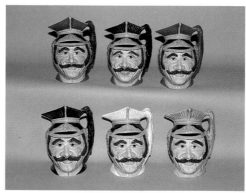

Michael Sutty Royal Lancers Series, from top left to bottom right - 5th (Royal Irish), 9th (Queen's Royal), 12th (Prince of Wales), 16th (The Queens), 17th (The Duke of Cambridge's Own), and 21st (Empress of India's) (from the collection of Emmett Mathews)

Michael Sutty Royal Artillery Series, from top left to bottom right - Royal Artillery I, Royal Horse Artillery, and Royal Artillery II (from the collection of Emmett Mathews)

NE British Miniature backstamp

NE British miniature Character Jugs from top left to bottom right - Gaffer, Squire, Charles I, Sam Weller, Fisherman, and Watchman, all from Sylvac Molds

Kenneth O. Speaks modeled the Reverend P. B. "Tubby" Clayton Toby Jug in 1969. Tubby Clayton was the founder of Toc H, an organization formed after World War I that provided fellowship for war veterans. Only six jugs were made, each hand modeled out of red clay and fired. Some were painted and glazed while others were not. As each jug was hand modeled, there are differences among the six. For example, only five show Tubby holding his dog, from which he was never separated. The one jug seen by the authors was an unfinished red bisque body incised "The Padre" and "K O Speaks".

Langdale Pottery operated for a short time at the Belgrave Works in Hanley, England between 1947 and 1958.

Several Toby Jugs are listed that have stickers on the bottom from **Marshall Taplow Whitehall Distillery** of London. These are heavy, cold painted chalkware tobies. The cavity of each jug is square in shape to accommodate a miniature whiskey bottle.

Pauline and John **Meredith** of Berkshire produced a range of tiny ordinary tobies. They were done in porcelain for use in miniature dollhouses.

Michael Sutty, another British studio potter, produced two very high quality series of Character Jugs in the 1980s; the Royal Lancers Series of six jugs in 1989

and the Royal Artillery Series of three jugs in the late 1980s. All of these jugs were produced in a limited edition of 250.

A number of miniature Character Jugs have recently surfaced which were produced from the molds of Shaw and Copestake. These jugs are marked "**NE British Miniature** Toby Jug Collection Handmade in England," plus the character's name. The Shaw and Copestake impressed model numbers can barely be seen. These jugs were likely produced in the 1990s after Crown Winsor ceased production.

The **New Devon Pottery** was founded on September 30, 1957 at the Newton Abbot in Devon, England. The principal founder of the pottery was Bert Mellor, the long time designer and modeler at Devonmoor Pottery, along with Philip Harold Carter and Mary Elizabeth Carter. After leaving Devonmoor, Bert Mellor was determined to continue designing and making quality art pottery. After a brief partnership with George Burnside Wright, he financed this new venture from his stake in Devonmoor. The firm is still operating today, producing a variety of earthenware products.

Old Castle Squat Toby Toby Jug flanked by creamer on left and sugar on right

Old Castle mark

Royal Stuart backstamp

Peasant Village Lord Howe, Standing Woman, and Standing Man Toby Jugs

Royal Stuart Fagin Character Jug by Spencer Stevenson

Old Castle's Toby Jugs were produced in china and done in a style very similar to Allertons with a gilded flow blue finish.

Paramount Pottery opened in Longton, Staffordshire in 1946, producing earthenware goods. The mold for the Falstaff Toby Jug may have come from another pottery as an older majolica version of the same jug has been found.

Peasant Village produced jugs marked with "PV" in a circle or "made for PV" in the 1940s and 1950s. Peasant Village reissued primarily railway earthenware goods targeted for the North American market; however, many were sold in the UK. These jugs are of fair to average quality.

The Regal Ware RPC ordinary Toby was produced by **Regal Pottery** Company Limited. Regal Pottery operated a factory on Elder Road in Cobridge between 1925 and 1931.

The Landlord Toby depicts Toby sitting astride a barrel of ale. **Samson Smith** produced this twentieth century Landlord as an advertising piece from its 1860 molds. In raised letters on the front of the ale cask is "Bass & Co Ale" or "Homes Brewery". The bottom of these jugs is marked "**Wetley China** Made in England", a tradename used by Samson Smith between 1923 and 1941, with the mark dating the pieces between 1925 to 1930.

Royal Stuart was the tradename used by the pottery **Spencer Stevenson & Company**. Spencer Stevenson produced both earthenware and china at the Dresden Works in Longton from 1948 until 1960, after which time the firm stopped potting and became a distributor only. The Royal Stuart tradename was used primarily during the 1950s. The firm's few Toby Jugs were made in bone china.

Studio Szeiler produced earthenware novelties, figurines and souvenirs. The pottery opened in Hanley in 1951 and moved to Burslem in 1955, where it continued production until 1989. The pottery is perhaps best known for its figurines.

Thomas Cone founded his pottery in 1892 at the **Alma Works** in Longton and began producing earthenware goods. The firm used Alma Ware as its tradename from 1935 to 1946. The tradename Royal Alma dates from 1946 to 1950. After this the words "Est. 1856" were also included in the backstamp. Around 1945 Coloroll Ceramics acquired Thomas Cone and continued producing Royal Alma labeled products. The only known Toby Jug produced by the pottery is Owd Bill. He is impressed on the bottom "Cone".

Another studio potter, **Vincent Kane**, produced a series of Ordinary Tobies in the 1940s from Torquay Pottery molds. Kane's tobies came in three heights, 4 1/2 inches, 3 1/2 inches and 2 3/4 inches, and are found with a variety of different jacket colors. The 4 1/2 inch tall Toby is incised 485.

Vincent Kane Ordinary Toby Jugs produced from Torquay molds; 4 1/2, 3 1/2, and 2 3/4 inches tall

Thomas Cone Owd Bill Toby Jug

Owain Glyndwr Character Jug by Regal

Santa Claus Character Jug by Regal

L

Formerly known as James Wardle, **Wardle & Company** operated at the Washington Works in Hanley from 1871 until 1935, producing earthenware, parian and majolica. A. J. Robinson & Sons took over Wardle in 1910 and operated the pottery independently as Wardle Art Pottery. In 1935 **Cauldon Potteries** purchased the pottery.

Perhaps the rarest of all the Winston Churchill Toby Jugs produced was by **R. C. White** of England. This jug is excellent in all regards and depicts a seated Winston dressed primarily in blue with a cigar in his mouth, his left hand raised with thumb up. On the right side of his chair is a flag. This jug is unmarked and extremely rare. It can be found in both a full colorway and creamware version.

Another recently produced Character Jug is that of Terry Pratchett, a noted British science fiction and fantasy author. The Terry Pratchett jug was produced at **Windy Ridge Studios** in Suffolk, England. Bernard and Isobel Pearson founded Windy Ridge around 1973 and produce art objects in clay, plaster and resin. Having been friends with Terry Pratchett for over eight years, the couple honored Pratchett for his fiftieth birthday with this fine porcelain jug.

Character Jug Name		Height, inches	Production Life
5th (Royal Irish)	Michael Sutty	6	1989
9th (Queen's Royal)	Michael Sutty	6	1989
12th (Prince of Wales)	Michael Sutty	6	1989
16th (The Queens	Michael Sutty	6	1989
17th (The Duke of Cambridge's Own) Michael Sutty		6	1989
21st (Empress of India's) Michael Sutty		6	1989
Abraham Lincoln	"Highmont" "Snel Ware"	3 1/2 1 3/4	
Aly Sloper	"John Humphries" stoneware	6 1/4 5 1/2	
Anne Boleyn	"Snel Ware"	1 3/4	
Aristocrat	"Goldscheider"	3	1946 - 1959
Blue Boy	"Goldscheider"	2 3/4	1946 - 1959
Buccaneer "Buccaneer of Britain" David Sharp		5	
Cabby "London Horse Carry Richton Studios"		5	
Catherine of Aragon script "F" in circle		1 1/4	1980s
Chelsea Pensioner "Johnson Ceramic"		2 7/8	
Coachman	Devon area jug		
Cowboy	"John Humphries"	6 1/4	
Dick Turpin	"Jon Anton"	3 1/2	
Duke of Edinburgh "Holkham Studio Pottery"		7	1953
Dwight D. Eisenhower "Barrington"		7 1/4	late 1940s
Edward VIII (music box) "Salopian" "G. Priest"		8 1/4 7	ca 1937 ca 1937
Fagin	"Royal Stuart"	2 3/4	
Falstaff	"Morlor Staffordshire"	4 3/4	
Fisherman	"NE British Miniatures"	2 1/4	
Florence Nightingale "Snel Ware"		1 3/4	
French Military Officer with music box		7	
Friar Tuck	"Taylor" "Snel Ware"	2 1 1/2	
Gaffer	"NE British Miniatures"	2 1/2	
George VI	"England"	4 1/4	
Henry VIII	"Highmont" "Snel Ware"	1 3/4 1 1/2	
Highwayman	"Jon Anton"		
Hobo	"John Humphries"	5 1/2	
Hod Carrier	"Elliott" on hat	6	1987
Hunting Fox	"John Humphries"	6 1/4	
Hutch	"Token Pottery"	4 1/4	
Indian Chief	"Jon Anton"	4 1/2	
Judy	Devon area jug		
King	"Newburgh Engle Studio"	6	
King Charles	"NE British Miniatures"		
Lord Kitchner	"#105", brown uniform	6 1/4	
Mad Hatter	"Johnson Ceramic"	2 5/8	
Maid Marian	"Taylor" "Snel Ware"	2 1 1/2	
Miner		4	
Mr. Micawber	"John Humphries" "Friar Ware Devon"	6 1/4 3	
Neville Chamberlain Gibson & Sons		5 1/2	ca 1930s
Old King Cole "Ricard Studio Products"		4 1/4	
Old Salt	"England"	4 1/4	
Owain Gylndwr	"Studio Szeiler"	3 7/8	
Pan "Montrose, Scotland", brown glaze		3 1/2	
Pirate	"Bournemouth Pottery" "PAL Ware"	6 1/4 3	
Pirate's Wife	"Snel Ware"	1 1/2	
Puck	"1786 Wardle"	7 1/4	1891 1910
Punch	majolica Hart and Moist "H. M. Exeter"	6 3 3/4	early 1900s 1900 - 1932

Wardle Uncle Sam Toby Jug, believed to be produced from the Shelley mold

Winston Churchill Toby Jug by R. C. White

Cabby Character Jug by Richton Studios

Johnson Ceramics backstamp

Morlor backstamp

Ricard Studio backstamp

Coronet Squat Toby Jug

Coachman and Judy Character Jugs produced in the Devon region

Character Jug Name		Height, inches	Production Life
Queen Elizabeth II	"Holkham Studio Pottery"	6 7/8	
	"Snel Ware"	1 1/2	
Robin Hood	"Taylor"	2	
	"Snel Ware"	1 1/2	
Royal Artillery I	Michael Sutty	6 1/2	late 1980s
Royal Horse Artillery	Michael Sutty	6 1/4	late 1980s
Royal Artillery II	Michael Sutty	7	late 1980s
Sam Weller	"NE British Miniatures"	2	
Santa Clause	"John Humphreys Pottery"	4	
Santa Clause	"Regal"	5	
Sir Francis Drake	"Snel Ware"	1 3/4	
Skipper		2 3/4	
	"Devon?? Pottery"	2	
Squire	"NE British Miniatures"	2 1/2	
Tam O'Shanter	"Jon Anton"	4 3/8	
Terry Pratchett	"Windy Ridge" Ltd Ed 1500	7 7/8	1998
Toby	smoking pipe, "PV" in circle	2 1/4	
	"1904 - 1927 ENGLAND Wild Brothers" "Morlor Staffordshire"		1904 - 1927
Toby Philpot	"John Humphries"	6 1/2	
Touchstone		3	
Town Crier	"Snel Ware"	2 3/4	
Two Superimposed Heads (like Sarreguemines, motto in English)		8 3/4	1980s -1990s
Viking	"Studio Szeiler"	5	
Watchman	"NE British Miniatures"	2 1/4	
Welsh Lady	"Brakenlea Pottery"	3 3/4	
Winston Churchill	incised 126/2	7 1/4	1940s
	"United Kingdom"	3 1/4	
	"Norton China"		
	"Snel Ware"	1 3/4	
Vicar	"Morlor"	4 3/4	
Young Girl	"Rd No 16188 1265 I"	6	1890 - 1910

Toby Jug Name		Height, inches	Production Life
Bagpiper	"Marshall Taplow Whitehall Distillery"	5 3/8	
Barrister	majolica	11 1/2	
Convertible Chair Toby	"Compliments of Toby Convertible Chair Co."	6 1/4	1930s
Cross-legged Toby	"3003/2"	4 1/2	1940s - 1950s
Dick Whittington	"Sandyford Pottery"	4 1/2	
Doormouse	"Royal Fenton Fenton Ware"	4	
Falstaff	"Paramount Pottery"	7 1/2	1946 - 1958
Flower Seller	"Sandyford Pottery"	5 1/4	
Flute Player	"England"	5 1/4	
Henry VIII	"Devon Pottery"	3 7/8	
Huntsman on saddle, fox handle Ridgway? with rabbit, 3/4 body		8 3/4	1930s
I'm on the Black List	"RD 476210"	11	1906 - 1910
John Bull	like Shelley, 3/4 body	6 3/8	
Judy		1 3/4	
Landlord	"Wetley China"	9	1925 - 1930
Long John Silver	"Marshall Taplow Whitehall Distillery"	5 3/8	
Lord Howe	"PV" in circle	4 1/4	1940s - 1950s
	"PV" in circle	2 3/4	1940s - 1950s
Lord Makintosh Midshipmite	"Frank Stoner"	6 1/2	1930s
Motorist	raised anchor and "4305"	8 1/2	1920s
Mr. Pickwick	"Staffordshire"	3 1/2	
Old Bill (Gamekeeper)		9 3/8	1917 - 20s
Old Roof Thatcher	"Sandyford Pottery"	6	
	"Sandyford Pottery"	4 7/8	
	"Sandyford Pottery"	4 3/8	
Old Salt	"Marshall Taplow Whitehall Distillery"	5 3/8	

Edward VIII Character Jug marked "G. Priest"

Old King Cole Character Jug by Ricard

Hod Carrier limited edition produced in 1987 for HE Elliott, a construction company, as a gift for employees as it closed, one of several varieties

Johnson Ceramics Mad Hatter and Chelsea Pensioner Character Jugs

English majolica Aly Sloper Character Jug from early 20th century

Aly Sloper stoneware Character Jug

Morlor Falstaff and Vicar Character Jugs

Bill the Burglar by P. Mock

Standing Man Toby Jug with music box insert

Convertible Chair Toby Jug in two majolica colorways (from the collection of Cliff Adkins)

Three English majolica 3/4 body Toby Jugs; Parson, John Bull, and Huntsman

English majolica Barrister Toby Jug

I'm On The Blacklist Toby Jug on left and Old Bill Toby Jug on right

Two sizes of Old Roof Thatcher Toby Jugs from Sandyford Pottery

Pastel finished Sandyford Toby Jugs of Old Roof Thatcher, Dick Whittington, and Flower Seller

English majolica Pug Dog Toby Jugs in two sizes

Large Snufftaker Toby Jug flanked by miniature Standing Woman on left and Standing Man on right

Devon area Standing Man and Town Crier Toby Jugs

Henry VIII Toby Jug marked "Devon"

Majolica Standing Man, large Standing Toby, and Snufftaker (from the collection of Robert Keylock)

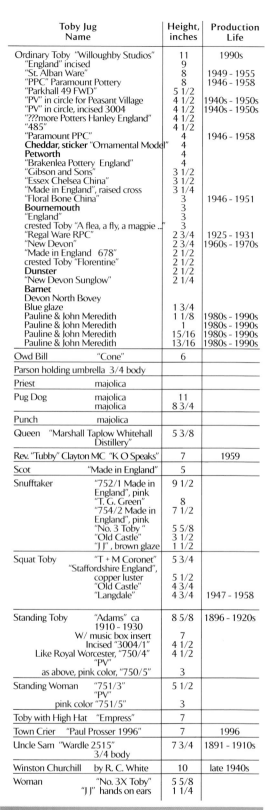

Toby Jug Name		Height, inches	Production Life
Ordinary Toby	"Willoughby Studios"	11	1990s
	"England" incised	9	
	"St. Alban Ware"	8	1949 - 1955
	"PPC" Paramount Pottery	8	1946 - 1958
	"Parkhall 49 FWD"	5 1/2	
	"PV" in circle for Peasant Village	4 1/2	1940s - 1950s
	"PV" in circle, incised 3004	4 1/2	1940s - 1950s
	"???more Potters Hanley England"	4 1/2	
	"485"	4 1/2	
	"Paramount PPC"	4	1946 - 1958
	Cheddar, sticker "Ornamental Model"	4	
	Petworth	4	
	"Brakenlea Pottery England"	4	
	"Gibson and Sons"	3 1/2	
	"Essex Chelsea China"	3 1/2	
	"Made in England", raised cross	3 1/4	
	"Floral Bone China"	3	1946 - 1951
	Bournemouth	3	
	"England"	3	
	crested Toby "A flea, a fly, a magpie ..."	3	
	"Regal Ware RPC"	2 3/4	1925 - 1931
	"New Devon"	2 3/4	1960s - 1970s
	"Made in England 678"	2 1/2	
	crested Toby "Florentine"	2 1/2	
	Dunster	2 1/2	
	"New Devon Sunglow"	2 1/4	
	Barnet		
	Devon North Bovey		
	Blue glaze	1 3/4	
	Pauline & John Meredith	1 1/8	1980s - 1990s
	Pauline & John Meredith	1	1980s - 1990s
	Pauline & John Meredith	15/16	1980s - 1990s
	Pauline & John Meredith	13/16	1980s - 1990s
Owd Bill	"Cone"	6	
Parson holding umbrella	3/4 body		
Priest	majolica		
Pug Dog	majolica	11	
	majolica	8 3/4	
Punch	majolica		
Queen	"Marshall Taplow Whitehall Distillery"	5 3/8	
Rev. "Tubby" Clayton MC	"K O Speaks"	7	1959
Scot	"Made in England"	5	
Snufftaker	"752/1 Made in England", pink	9 1/2	
	"T. G. Green"	8	
	"754/2 Made in England", pink	7 1/2	
	"No. 3 Toby "	5 5/8	
	"Old Castle"	3 1/2	
	"JJ" , brown glaze	1 1/2	
Squat Toby	"T + M Coronet" "Staffordshire England", copper luster	5 3/4	
		5 1/2	
	"Old Castle"	4 3/4	
	"Langdale"	4 3/4	1947 - 1958
Standing Toby	"Adams" ca 1910 - 1930	8 5/8	1896 - 1920s
	W/ music box insert	7	
	Incised "3004/1"	4 1/2	
	Like Royal Worcester, "750/4"	4 1/2	
	"PV"		
	as above, pink color, "750/5"	3	
Standing Woman	"751/3"	5 1/2	
	"PV"		
	pink color "751/5"	3	
Toby with High Hat	"Empress"	7	
Town Crier	"Paul Prosser 1996"	7	1996
Uncle Sam	"Wardle 2515" 3/4 body	7 3/4	1891 - 1910s
Winston Churchill	by R. C. White	10	late 1940s
Woman	"No. 3X Toby"	5 5/8	
	"JJ" hands on ears	1 1/4	

Tiny jugs of Standing Man, Woman with hands on ears, Devonmoor Judy, and Ordinary Toby

United States Character Jugs and Toby Jugs

Character Jug Name	Height, inches
Abraham Lincoln "Jane Holland"	5
American Indian "Byron Mold 1973" 1867 Peace Treaty "Rosemeade"	4 3/4
Benjamin Franklin "Byron Mold 1974"	5
Betty Boop "King Features 1995"	
Blackamoor "USA"	3 1/2
Buffalo Bill "Byron Mold"	5
Captain "1947 Jane Holland Calif"	7 1/4
Chewie "Rumph! Califoriginals"	7
Colonel Sanders "M", dark brown glaze	4 5/8
Colonial Man"Pacific Pottery Coralitos"; on hat: "A genial smile be his who drinks from Toby's jug"	4
Cowardly Lion "Star Jars and Leeber, Ltd."	5
Daisey Mae "Pearce Pottery"	3 1/2
Darth Vader "Rumph! Califoriginals 1977"	7 1/2
Davy Crocket "Horton Ceramics"	6
Dick Tracy "Disney"	5 1/4
Dorothy "Star Jars and Leeber, Ltd."	5
Dwight D. Eisenhower "Standford Ware Sebring, Ohio"	4 3/4
Falstaff "Hoda 1972"	5 1/2
Fisherman "Channel Is Ca."	5
Franklin Roosevelt	
Frontiersman "??amar Mallory Studio 75"	4 1/8
George Washington "Dwight Morris China"	4 3/8
High Hat "Hoda"	7
Horse	6
Johnny Walker "Somerset Importers, NY"	5 1/4
Lamplighter "Napcoware C-5592"	3 1/2
Li'l Abner "UFS Inc. 1952 Al Capp. Pearce"	4
Long John Silver "Byron Mold 1974"	5
Mamie Eisenhower "Standford Ware Sebring, Ohio"	4 3/4
Mammy Yokum "UFS Inc. 1952 Al Capp. Pearce"	3 1/2
Master Toby "68 Jane Holland Calif"	4
Mark Twain "Byron Mold 1976"	6 1/2
Miss Cutie Pie "Napcoware"	4
Mr. Pickwick "Atlantic Mold Sally Bush"	5
New England Whaler "Patty 95"	8 1/2
Obi-Wan Kenobi "Rumph Califoriginals 1977"	6 1/2
Oil Driller "Oil Centennial Titusville, PA 1859 - 1959"	2 7/8
Oliver Hardy "Duncan Ceramics 1973"	
Pirate "Joys of California" "Joys of California"	7 4
Queen of Hearts "Kliene Co. HM"	3 1/2
Santa Clause "Napcoware" "Napcoware" "Johanna Calif."	6 1/2 3 1/4 3 1/4
Scarecrow "Star Jars and Leeber, Ltd."	5
Scotsman "Erna Cuman 1951"	4 3/4
Stan Laurel "Duncan Ceramics 1973"	
Tin Man "Star Jars and Leeber, Ltd."	5
Uncle Tom Cobleigh "Greyson Potteries California"	5 3/4
Victor Moore "James Warren CA" ca 1940s	5
William Bendix "James Warren CA" ca 1940s	5

This section lists miscellaneous Toby and Character Jugs marked simply "USA" or otherwise attributed to an USA manufacturer which most likely had little Toby production. Most probably some are unique and were possibly produced as a part of a ceramics course.

Horton Ceramics operated in Eastland, Texas from 1949 to 1962. Horton produced a Davy Crocket Character Jug, probably in the 1950s to 1960s. Davy wears his signature raccoon hat, the tail of which forms the handle of the jug.

Maggie Sanders, the daughter of Harland "Colonel" Sanders (1890 - 1980), had a lifelong interest in sculpting. Eventually this led to her forming a studio pottery, **Margardt Unlimited**, in Los Angeles, California. In the 1970s, Margardt produced items honoring Colonel Sanders, including a ceramic bank and Character Jug. The story on the tag attached to the jug reads, "Daughter if you can't eat it, forget it. Quit playing with that clay. Can't you see the romance in food?' The Colonel used to tell Maggie. Responding to her father's advice, Maggie Sanders did get interested in food and was involved in the world's first Kentucky Fried Chicken store with take out service only. But her first love was art and she continued to sculpt. Today the Colonel is glad she did. Her bronze portrait sculptures are in art collections the world over. Now she has ventured into creating a variety of artistic products which allow her to share her unique talents with everyone."

The National Potteries Corporation (NAPCO) was established in Bedford,

Ohio in 1938 and was a large importer of Japanese giftware. Irwin Garber joined NAPCO in the mid-1940s, leaving in 1960 to form his own competitive firm, INARCO. In 1986, NAPCO purchased INARCO and relocated it to Jacksonville, Florida, where NAPCO had moved in 1984.

The Oil Driller was a commemorative Character Jug produced for the Ethyl Corporation in 1959. That year Ethyl celebrated the centennial of the Drake Well, its first successful oil well in Pennsylvania, near the town of Titusville.

William Lacy founded the **Pacific Clay Products Pottery** by consolidating several southern California potteries together, operating primarily out of the Lincoln Heights Plant in Los Angeles. The pottery initially produced only stoneware and prospered during the boom of the 1920s. Through the guidance of ceramic engineer Frank McCann in the early 1930s, the firm expanded into earthenware production, including imitations of the popular Bauer tableware. Designed in 1937 by Matthew J. Lattie, Coralitos ware was lightweight, pastel colored tableware for daily use. The Lincoln Heights plant was converted to full-time defense work in World War II and never returned to ceramic production. Today Pacific Pottery produces roof tiles in its Corona plant.

Padre operated from the 1930s into the 1950s in Los Angeles, California. Jane Holland designed the Padre Ordinary Toby Jugs.

Pair of Pacific Clay Coloniel Man Coralitos ware Character Jugs

Pearce China Li'l Abner and Daisey Mae Character Jugs

Character jugs from the Al Capp comic strip "Li'l Abner", including Li'l Abner himself, Daisey Mae, and Mammy Yokum, were produced by the **Pearce China Company** under license by United Features Syndicate.

Rosemeade Pottery operated in Wahpeton, North Dakota between 1940 and 1961. Laura Taylor and her husband, R. Hughes, founded the pottery, which also was known as the Wahpeton Pottery. The pottery's principle products were art pottery and utilitarian ware. Today its figural items are highly collected.

The **Rumph** Chewbacca mug was produced in 1977 with the approval of 20th Century Fox to coincide with the release of Star Wars. It was produced only for a limited time.

The **Star Jars and Leeber, Ltd.** Character Mugs from the movie *The Wizard of Oz* were produced under approval from Turner Entertainment Co., owner of the rights to the film.

Toby Jug Name	Height, inches
Bear all three registered and trademarked in 1907 and done in a majolica finish	9 3/4 7 5 1/2
Blackamoor Lady "Mr Jenkins USA 94"	7 3/4
Dauchshund	6
Donald Duck "Walt Disney USA" made by Leeds Pottery ca 1940s	6 1/4
Dumbo "Walt Disney USA" made by Leeds Pottery ca 1941	6 5
King of Hearts "Walt Disney" Regal China	7
Lion "Lionstone 1973"	8 1/2
Monk "Calif. 179 USA"	8 1/2
Ordinary Toby "Padre California 545" "Padre California 546" "8/25/68 SPC"	11 6 5 1/2
Owl "Morley & Co. Wellsville O." "Dwight C. Holmes"	8 1/2 5 1/2
Pig "S. C. Co. Patriot China Disney"	4 1/4
Pillsbury Doughboy "The Pillsbury Company, Copyright 1985"	5
Robin "Artistic Potteries California 709"	5
Toby on barrel brown/orange glaze, by Camark?	9
Toucan "Artistic Potteries 3570"	7
Woman holding rum barrel "Paul Finholdt USA " ca 1979 "Maison"	11 8 1/2

Falstaff Character Jug by Hoda for The Falstaff Brewing Company of St. Louis, Missouri

Byron Molds Character Jugs; top - Benjamin Franklin; bottom - Long John Silver and Buffalo Bill

Majolica Bear Toby Jugs

Blackamoor Lady Toby Jug

Lion advertising Toby Jug for Lionstone Whiskey

"Wizard of Oz" Character Mugs by Star Jars and Leeber, Ltd.; left to right – Judy Garland as Dorothy, Ray Bolger as The Scarecrow, Jack Haley as The Tin Man, and Bert Lahr as the Cowardly Lion

Unattributed Character and Toby Jugs

Character Jug Name	Height, inches
Abraham Lincoln cojoined "WF"	5
Admiral John Jellicoe	7
	6 1/2
African	
American Indian "Casanis C-87"	6 1/4
"Roberts Ceramics Barn Wapato"	4 1/2
	2 1/2
Andy Panda	4
Bear "Strawberry Hill 1984"	
Beefeater "Windsor Canadian Whiskey"	8
Benjamin Franklin "Dorchester Pottery 1976"	7
	5
Blackbeard	4 3/4
Bob Hope plaster of Paris, ca 1940s	2 1/2
"Puck"5	5
Bootmaker	6 1/2
Brutus "MGM"	3 1/2
Calico Kitten	
Cap'n Patch	2 1/4
Captain Richard Hennessy "Schieffelin	
& Co New York H1011"	8
Carmen Miranda plaster of Paris, ca 1940s	5
Charlie McCarthy	10 1/2
Chef	
Chef Pierre the Pig "Figi"	8 1/8
Coalminer "C.B. Madpotters"	4 1/8
Colonial Man "T-6"	4 1/4
Cure All Pills "The Shafford Co. 5963Y"	3
Crying Baby "Helen Ware"	7
Daffy Duck "The Good Co. Disney 1989"	4 1/2
Dalmation	4
Davy Crockett	3 1/2
Dick Turpin "E-8210"	5
Dopey "Little Pitchers" on front	
Elf - winking	
Elmer Fudd "The Good Co Disney 1989"	4 1/2
Evil Witch ca 1900	
Falstaff "1982 FP"	1 1/2
Field Marshal Douglas Haig	7
Fireman "Alexander Hotel"	
Fortune Teller	2 1/4
Franklin Roosevelt "Roosevelt"	3 5/8
Fred Flintstone "Vandor 1990"	4 1/4
Friar Tuck	
Frog Boy "R. Tallin Majolica"	3 1/2
Frog Girl "R. Tallin Majolica"	3 1/2
General Pershing	7
Genie - from Disney's Aladdin	6
George Washington ca 1932	
Girl "Vandor"	5
"Workman Studios"	
"Kleine Co. Lillian"	
Golfer "Vandor 1993"	
Groucho Marx "Expressive Designs"	5
Granny "Anfora" (like Royal Doulton)6	
Guardsman "Windsor Canadian Whiskey"	8 1/2
Hessian Soldier "Gilbey's Vodka"	6
Highwayman "Embassy NSP"	7
Huntsman	5
Indian Chief "Vandor"	6 1/2
Irishman	5
"APCO"	4 1/2
Jailor with handle of keys	5 3/4

The following Character and Toby Jugs have been documented, but there is no indication as to which pottery manufactured the jugs, or even in which country they were produced. Any markings found on the base of the jug are indicated in quotations after the jug name.

One very interesting tiny Character Jug series is the Presidents of the United States. The quality of the jugs is poor to fair, being not well modeled, sloppily painted and produced from overused molds. However, a large collection of these jugs is impressive and historically significant. Typically stamped on the bottom of each jug is information about the President, for example "32nd F. D. Roosevelt 1933." Incised across the front of each jug is the President's name. On some jugs remnants of paper labels can be found. One jug has been found stamped on the base with "Severo E Soria" in a box. This could indicate an Italian manufacturer. Below are those jugs positively identified to date. Given that Franklin Roosevelt is the most recent President found so far, it is most likely that a full set of Presidents was produced just before, and up to, World War II, but did not continue afterward.

Presidential Character Jug Series

Character Jug Name	Height, inches
J. Adams	1 7/8
Arthur	1 7/8
Cleveland	1 7/8
Coolidge	1 7/8
Fillmore	1 7/8
Garfield	1 7/8
Grant	1 7/8
Harding	1 7/8
B. Harrison	1 7/8
Hayes	1 7/8
Hoover	1 7/8
Jackson	1 7/8
Jefferson	1 7/8
Lincoln	1 7/8
Madison	1 7/8
McKinley	1 7/8
Monroe	1 7/8
Polk	1 7/8
F. D. Roosevelt	1 7/8
T. Roosevelt	1 7/8
Taylor	1 7/8
Tyler	1 7/8
Van Buren	1 7/8
Washington	2
Wilson	1 7/8

Presidential Character Jug Series arranged in ascending order from top left to bottom right: Washington, J. Adams, Madison, Monroe, Jefferson, Jackson, Van Buren, Tyler, Taylor, Filmore, Lincoln, Grant, Hayes, Garfield, Arthur, Cleveland, B. Harrison, McKinley, T. Roosevelt, Wilson, Harding, Hoover, F. D. Roosevelt

African Character Jug

Two Whaler Character Jugs

Abraham Lincoln Character Jug

Beefeater Character Jug

Friar Tuck Character Jug, likely English

Guardsman advertising jug for Windsor Canadian Whiskey

Frankenstein Character Jug

Dwight D. Eisenhower and Mamie Eisenhower marked "Standford Ware"

Left to right: William Shakespeare, Leonardo DaVinci, and Nicholaus Copernicus Character Jugs

Majolica John Bull and Uncle Sam Character Jugs

Large Winston Churchill Character Jug

Excellently molded WW1 military leaders, left to right: General Pershing, Field Marshal Douglas Haig, Admiral John Jellicoe, and Lord John French

World's smallest Character Jugs; Long John Silver on left and Squire on right, 1/2" tall

Miscellaneous grouping of unattributed Character Jugs and Toby Jugs

John Barleycorn Character Jug

Character Jug Name	Height, inches
Jiggs Clown ""Puck KSS"	5 1/4
Jimmy Durante plaster of Paris, ca 1940s	5
John Alden "by Ynez 1943"	7 1/2
John Barleycorn	4 1/4
like Doulton, brown glaze	3
In white porcelain	2 3/4
John Bull	
John Major "Patricia Parson 1993"	6
John Paul Jones "A.S. C W"	5 5/8
John Wayne "1985"	5 5/8
Johnny Appleseed	6 3/4
Judy red clay, blue/white glaze	4 3/8
King Kong "Hamilton Gifts"	5
Leonardo DaVinci	7
Long John Silver raised "T-5"	5
	1/2
Lord John French	7
Lord Kitchner ca 1900	7
	6 1/4
	4 1/2
Mammy	3
Man smoking pipe "0-667"	6
"6363 73"	4
Moses Butterworth raised "T-6"	4 3/4
Mr. Cobbler "Hoffman 1978"	6
Mr. Doctor "Hoffman 1978"	6
Mr. Lucky "Hoffman 1978"	6
Mr. Micawber "Netta 12-50"	3 1/2
Mr. Pecksniff "Meggie"	6
Nicholaus Copurnicus	7
Old King Cole "Pats Hobby Korral"	3 5/8
Old Mat	2 1/4
Olive Oil "Vandor" ca 1980 - 1990	4
"MGM"	3 1/2
Oliver Hardy "JMM 75"	6 1/2
"Expressive Designs Inc."	5 3/4
"P B 2"	4
Ordinary Toby "From Miniatures by Marjo"	1/2
Pig with hat	5 3/4
Pink Panther "Dakin" 1994	4
Pioneer Woman "Cc 392" like Southern's	
"Claire Potar"	6 3/4
Pirate	4 1/4
Popeye "Vandor King Features" ca 1980s	4 1/4
"MGM"	3 1/2
Porky Pig "The Good Co Disney 1989"	3 3/4
Portia Porcupine	4
Puck "Handel Ware"	5 1/2
Punch red clay, blue/white glaze	4 3/8
Queen of Spades "MX"	6 1/2
Santa	4
	3 1/4
"Brinns TX-747"	2 3/4
	2 3/4
Scottie "Irene"	
Sheik "2993"	5 1/8
Shriner "Kosair 1974"	7
	5 1/4
Snowman	6 1/2
Squire	1/2
Stan Laurel "S. Newman '75"	6 1/2
"Expressive Designs Inc."	5 3/4
"P B 2"	4
Taz "The Good Co Disney 1989"	3 1/2
Theodore Roosevelt with rifle handle	
Uncle Sam	5 1/2
W. C. Fields	5 1/2
Whaler version 1	10
version 2	10
Wicked Witch	4 1/2
William Shakespeare	7
Wimpy "MGM"	3 1/2
Winston Churchill	7
Woman with black hat, white collar	5

General Kitchner and Admiral Jellcoe Character Jugs

Arab Character Jug on left and French Trapper Character Jug on right

A group of Toby Jugs based on British political figures from early this century included Douglas Hogg, the first Viscount of Hailsham, Earl Stanley Baldwin, Sir Harry Lauder, Lord Asquith, David Lloyd George, and Ramsey MacDonald. Lloyd George was a Welsh Liberal politician who became Prime Minister of a coalition government in 1916 and remained in office until 1922. MacDonald was the leader of the British Labor Party in 1911 and became Prime Minister of England in 1930. They make a very attractive set. These jugs were well modeled and finished in soft colorways and were marked with only the model number in relief one-half inch tall numbers. An unknown manufacturer produced the jugs shortly after World War I ended

and into the 1930s.

A very interesting Toby Jug line of historical political leaders has been identified. This line was allegedly prototyped in the early 1970s, but not released. It has been attributed to Masons but this has not been confirmed. These tobies are around four inches tall and are very well modeled and detailed. Some characters are seated, like Churchill and Wilson, while others are standing. The handle on Wilson is of his famous mackintosh. Occasionally some of these jugs come to market, usually in a creamware finish, with rare full colorways known to exist. Nine seems like an odd number to produce, so perhaps there were more characters prototyped, or at least intended for the group.

Political Leader Series

Toby Jug Name	Height, inches
Abraham Lincoln	4 1/4
Field Marshal Montgomery	
Franklin D. Roosevelt	
General Eisenhower	3 3/4
George Washington	
Harold Wilson	
John F. Kennedy	
Lord Kitchener	4 1/4
Stanley Matthews	
Winston Churchill	

Political Leaders Series: Lord Kitchner on the left and General Eisenhower on the right

King of Clubs and Clown Toby Jugs

Huntsman on saddle (cork stopper in hat) and Town Clerk Toby Jugs

Toby Jug Name	Height, inches
Betty Boop "1981 KFS Vandor"	
Bunny	6
Cat	7 1/2
Chef "CWK"	4
Chinaman impressed "6552"	5
Clown	
Douglas Hogg	6
Dumbo	6
Dutch Girl	5 1/2
Earl Stanley Baldwin "451"	7
Elephant "1537"	10 / 5 1/2 / 4 1/2
Falstaff "30"	5
Girl lifting skirt	3 1/2
Golfer	6
Harry Lauder "460"	7
Highlander 3/4 body, probably Continental	5 3/4
Huntsman 3/4 body majolica	7 3/4
Huntsman on saddle	7 1/2
Indian	4 1/2
John Bull 3/4 body majolica / 3/4 body "J. Bull" in relief	7 1/2 / 4 3/4
King of Clubs	

Toby Jug Name	Height, inches
Likker Pikker	5
Little Red Riding Hood "Pat. Des. No. 135889"	7 3/4
Mad O'Rourke "Little Pub Co."	9 1/2
Monk "A25E Viera SM"	9 1/4
	7 1/4
"18" same as five inch jug below	7
"L-225"	5
"33"	5
drinking "GR & Argott"	4
hands on belly "GR & Argott"	4
Monkey "S4331"	12
"3187"	4 1/2
"5527 2/0"	3 3/4
	3 1/4
Mr. Bumble probably German	3
Napoleon – half body	
Old Salt	
Ordinary Toby "Faragna Santander"	7 1/2
	6 1/2
Rockingham glaze	6
brown glaze, 3/4 body, kick-up bottom	6
"Royal China 22kt Gold"	6
Ardica-Florence, pot on right knee	4
Haldon Group 1981	
"From Miniatures by Marjo"	1/2

Large Napoleon Toby Jug and small half body jug

Toby Jug Name	Height, inches
Owl	6 1/4
Parrot contemporary majolica	9
Parson 3/4 body majolica	8
Pig porcelain	7
Pig Chef	3 1/2
Piper	6
Popeye	6
Prince Charming	3 1/2
Queen Victoria	
Ram	8 1/4
majolica	6 3/8
Ramsey MacDonald "452"	6 1/2
Sairey Gamp	2 1/8
Santa Clause "Avon 1983" 3/4 body	3 1/4
School Boy "Kreiss"	
Scotsman	
Soldier (from Le Pere Pottery of Ohio?)	5 1/2
Spaniel	9 1/2
Squat Toby	6 3/8
Squire	
Standing Man majolica ca 1900	13 1/2
large head, hands at sides	4 3/4
in cape, "foreign"	3 1/4
Standing Woman hands in pockets, blue glaze	6 1/2
Suffragette blue ink mark crown above H	10 1/4
Teddy Roosevelt majolica	13 1/2
Town Clerk	4 1/2
Welsh Lady	4 1/2

John Bull Toby Jug in two sizes

Monk, Falstaff, Friar, and Indian porcelain Toby Jugs

Standing Toby with hands in pockets and Welsh Lady Toby Jug

Old Salt Toby Jug

Tiny Ordinary Toby

Young Queeen Victoria Toby Jug

Suffragette Toby Jug

Modern reproduction of a Staffordshire Spaniel

Ramsey MacDonald, Earl Stanley Baldwin, and Harry Lauder Toby Jugs

Scotsman, Standing Man, and Welsh Lady three-quarter body Toby Jugs

Squat Toby jug

Standing Man in Majolica glaze ca. 1900; could be President Theodore Roosevelt

Six tiny Toby Jugs by unknown makers alongside a small Royal Doulton Happy John Toby Jug for size comparison (from the collection of Cliff Adkins)

Standing Toby and bisque Squire Toby

L
330

Collecting by Series, Sets and Pairs
Arranged alphabetically by maker

Applause

Dick Tracy (Movie) Set: Big Boy, Breathless Mahoney, Dick Tracy, Flat Top

Marvel Comics: Captain America, Dr. Doom, Incredible Hulk, Spiderman

Jim Henson Muppets Pair: Kermit, Miss Piggy

Star Trek Character Mug Series: Borg, Captain Janeway, Captain Kirk, Captain Sisko, Cardassian, Data, Dax, Deanna Troi, Dr. Crusher, Dr. McCoy, Gorn, Kazan, Geordie La Forge, Neelix, Odo, Q, Quark, Riker, Spock, Troi, Worf

Star Wars Character Mug Series: Bib Fortuna, Boba Fett, C-3PO, Chewbacca, Darth Vader, Emperor Palpatine, Gamorrean Guard, Han Solo, Luke Skywalker, Obi-Wan Kenobi, Princess Leia, Stormtrooper, Tusken Raider

Walt Disney Character Mug Series: Donald Duck, Dopey, Esmerelda, Goofy, Grumpy, Mickey Mouse, Minnie Mouse, Quasimodo, Queen, Rafiki, Scar, Simba, Ursula

Warner Brothers Character Mug Series: Bugs Bunny, Elmer Fudd, Foghorn Leghorn, Marvin the Martian, Michigan J. Frog, Pepe le Pew, Road Runner, Speedy Gonzales, Sylvester, Tasmanian Devil, Tweety Bird, Wiley Coyote

Arthur Bowker

Churchill Character Jug Pair: Clementine Churchill, Winston Churchill

Artone Pottery

Charles Dickens Character Jug Series (in two sizes): Artful Dodger, Buzz Fuzz, Cap'n Cuttle, Fagin, Mr. Beadle, Mr. Micawber, Mr. Pickwick, Oliver Twist, Scrooge, Uriah Heep

Charles Dickens Two-faced Character Jug Series (in two sizes): Josh, Mr. Micawber, Mr. Pickwick, Sarah Gamp,

Charles Dickens Toby Jug Series: Artful Dodger, Bill Sykes, Cap'n Cuttle, Fagin, Fat Boy, Mr. Pickwick, Oliver Twist, Tony Weller

Widecombe Fair Character Jug Series (in two sizes): Bill Brewer, Dan'l Whidden, Harry Hawke, Jan Stewart, Peter Davey, Peter Gurney, Tom Pearce, Uncle Tom Cobleigh

Working Man Toby Jug Series: Blacksmith, Cobbler, Cooper, Miner, Newspaper Seller, Postman, Saddler

Ashtead Potteries

Political Toby Jug Series: Douglas Hogg, David Lloyd George, S. M. Bruce, Stanley Baldwin

Avon Art Pottery

Charles Dickens Character Jug Series: Buzz Fuzz, Fagin, Fat Boy, Little Nell, Mr. Micawber, Mr. Pickwick, Tony Weller, Uriah Heep

Bairstow Manor Pottery

Charles Dickens Toby Jug Series: Artful Dodger, Bill Sykes, Fagin, Mr. Bumble, Mr. Pickwick, Nancy, Oliver Twist

Sporting Toby Jug Series: Bowler, Cricketer, Fisherman, Footballer, Golfer, Lady Golfer, Lady Tennis Player, Tennis Player

Traditional Toby Jug Series: Blacksmith, Cavalier, Coachman, Crusader, Friar, Highwayman, Inn Keeper, Jester, Medieval King, Puritan, Squire, Town Crier

Beswick

Armed Forces Character Jug Set: Air Force, Navy (Wink), Old Bill

Charles Dickens Character Jug Series (large size): Mr. Micawber, Sairey Gamp, Scrooge, Tony Weller

Charles Dickens Character Jug Series (medium size): Barnaby Rudge, Betsy Trotwood, Captain Cuttle, Little Nell's Grandfather, Martin Chuzzlewit, Mr. Bumble

1967 Character Jug Pair (large size): Falstaff, Henry VIII

Peter Rabbit Character Jug Series: Jemima Puddle-Duck, Jeremy Fisher, Mrs. Tiggy-Winkle, Old Mr. Brown, Peter Rabbit, Tom Kitten

Creamer and Sugar Bowl Pairs: Mr. Pecksniff, Mr. Pickwick, Mr. & Mrs. Varden, Mr. Micawber & Tony Weller

Bovey Pottery

The Doctor Who Toby Jug Series: The Doctor #1, The Doctor #2, The Doctor #3, The Doctor #4, The Doctor #5, The Doctor #6, The Doctor #7 (The last by Aidee Internatinal)

Burgess & Leigh

Charles Dickens Toby Jug Series: Charles Dickens, Dan'l Peggoty, Fat Boy, Mr. Micawber, Mr. Pecksniff, Mr. Pickwick, Mrs. Bardell, Nicholas Nickelby, Oliver Twist, Sairey Gamp, Sam

Weller, Scrooge, Tony Weller

London Toby Jug Pair: Beefeater, Chelsea Pensioner

William Shakespeare Toby Jug Series: William Shakespeare, Cardinal Wolsey, Ceasar, Falstaff, Juliet, Hamlet, MacBeth, Midsummer's Night Dream, Portia, Romeo, Shylock, Touchstone

Carlton Ware

Coronation Street Character Jug Series: Albert Tatlock, Ena Sharples, Stan Ogden, and others to be found (3)

Devonmoor Art Pottery

Ordinary Toby Series: Variety of sizes frin 1 1/2" to 23 1/4" in eight known colorways

Widecombe Fair Character Jug Series: Bill Brewer, Dan'l Whiddon, Harry Hawke, Jan Stewert, Old Uncle Tom Cobleigh, Peter Davey, Peter Gurney, Tom Pearce

Franklin Porcelain

Cries of London Toby Jug Series: Baked Potato Vendor, Chimney Sweep, Coalman, Door Mat Maker, Flower Girl, Milk Maid, Old Clothes Man, Orange Girl, Organ Grinder, Oyster Woman, Street Doctor, Umbrella Man

English Heritage Miniature Character Jug Collection Series: Alice, Artful Dodger, Captain Hook, Dick Turpin, Dr. Watson, Fagin, Friar Tuck, Henry V, Hornblower, Ivanhoe, King Arthur, Long John Silver, Mad Hatter, Merlin, Mr. Micawber, Mr. Pickwick, Moll Flanders, Peter Pan, Richard III, Robin Hood, Robinson Crusoe, Scrooge, Sherlock Holmes, Sir John Falstaff, Tom Jones

Famous Admirals Character Jug Set: Admiral Benbow, Admiral Lord Cunningham, Admiral Lord Hood, Admiral Lord Howe, Admiral John Lord Jellicoe, Admiral Lord Nelson, Admiral Lord St. Vincent, Earl Mountbatten, Admiral Robert Blake, Sir Francis Drake, Sir Richard Grenville, Sir Walter Raleigh

J. Fryer

Sherwood Forest Character Jug Series: Allan a'Dale, Friar Tuck, Little John, Robin Hood, Sheriff of Nottingham, Will Scarlet

Working Man's Character Jug Series: Crossing Sweeper, Fisherman, Poacher, Rat Catcher, Tramp, Woodcutter

Goebel

Friar Tuck Jug Series: Variety of Friar Tuck jugs, mugs and tankards in at least eight sizes ranging from 1 3/4" to 10" in height. It is also available in at least five sizes as Cardinal Tuck in a red colorway.

Modern Toby Jug Series: Bavarian Herr, Bavarian Frau, Bride, Chamber Maid, Clown, Devil, Dwarf, Innkeeper, King, Nightwatchman, Sailor, Vampire

Grimwades (Royal Winton)

National Symbols Character Jug Series (in multiple sizes): Canadian Mountie, John Bull, Indian Chief, Scotsman, Uncle Sam

WWII Heroes Character Jug Series (in multiple sizes): Franklin D. Roosevelt, General Douglas MacArthur, General Sir Archibald Wavell, Jan Christian Smuts, King George VI, Right Honorable Winston Churchill

Kevin Francis Ceramics

Artists and Potters Toby Jug Series: Bernard Leach, Charlotte Rhead, Clarice Cliff, David Winter, George Tinworth, Hannah Barlow, Josiah Wedgwood, Lucie Rie, Peggy Davies, Ralph Wood, Sandra Kuck, Sir Henry Doulton, Susie Cooper, William Moorcroft

Champagne Ladies Character Jug Set: Butterfly, Feathers, Masquerade, Paradise, Starlight Champagne

Classic Artist Toby Jug Series: Pablo Picasso, Salvador Dali, Vincent Van Gogh

Entertainers Toby Jug Series: Elvis Presley (prototype only), Kings of Comedy (Laurel and Hardy), Marx Brothers, Max Miller, Morecambe and Wise, Price of Clowns (Charlie Chaplin), Pavarotti (both seated and standing versions), Tommy Cooper

Great Generals Toby Jug Series: Duke of Wellington, Erwin Rommel, Field Marshall Montgomery, General Eisenhower, General G. S. Patton, General Grant, General Lee, General Norman Schwarzkopf, Napoleon Bonaparte, Stonewall Jackson

Lady Potters Character Jug Set: Clarice Cliff, Peggy Davies, Susie Cooper

Midshipmite Toby Jug Set: Fidel Castro, John Major, Kenneth Clarke, Winston Churchill

Miniature Animal Toby Jug Series: Alligator, Cat, Chicken, Dog, Duck, Elephant, Frog, Lion Cub, Monkey, Rabbit

Original Toby Jug Series designed by Peggy Davies: Clown, Cook, Doctor, Gardener, Shareholder

Political and Royalty Toby Jug Series: Boris Yeltsin, Helmut Kohl, John F. Kennedy, Nelson Mandela, Pope John Paul II, President Gorbachev, Princess Diana, Queen Elizabeth II, Queen Mother, variety of Winston Churchill jugs: Admiral, D-Day, Naval, Political, Seated, Standing, VE-Day

Queens of the Nile Character Jug Set: Cleopatra, Isis, Zenobia

Spitting Image Character Jug Series: Charles & Di, John Major, Margaret Thatcher, Neil Kinnock

Star Trek Toby Jug Series: Borg, Captain Kirk, Captain Picard, Dr. McCoy, Ferengi, Lieutenant Worf, Spock

Warner Brothers Cartoon Toby Jug Series: Bugs Bunny, Daffy Duck, Pepe Le Pew, Sylvester & Tweety, Tasmanian Devil

Kingston Pottery

Charles Dickens Character Jug Series: Artful Dodger, Betsy Trotwood, Bill Sykes, Convict (Provis), Fagin, Miss Havisham, Mr. Bumble, Mr. Dick, Mr. Micawber, Mr. Peggoty, Mrs. Bumble, Mrs. Micawber, Oliver Twist, Pickwick, Pip, Sam Weller

English Royalty Character Jug Series: Charles I, Charles II, Edward I, Edward III, Elizabeth I, George II, Henry VIII, King John, Richard I, Richard III, Victoria, William I

Irish Water Toby Jug Set: Danny Boy, Molly Malone, Mother Machree, Phil the Fluter

Lancaster and Sandland

Charles Dickens Character Jug Series: David Copperfield, Micawber, Pickwick, Sarah Gamp, Weller

Composer Character Jug Series: Beethoven, Bizet, Chopin, Grieg, Handel, Hayden, Liszt, Mozart, Schubert, Sibelius, Tchaikowsky, Verdi, Wagner

Dog Character Jug Series: Bloodhound, Boxer, Bulldog, Chow Dog, Collie, Dalmatian, King Charles Spaniel, Otter Hound, Poodle, St. Bernard, Water Spaniel

Gods Character Jug Series: Bacchus, Jupiter, Pan, Perseus, Pluto

Literary Character Jug Series: Burns, Dickens, Emerson, Longfellow, Lowell, E.A. Poe, Shakespeare, Tennyson, Thackery

Royalty Character Jug Series: Charles I, Edward VII, Henry VIII, Oliver Cromwell, Queen Bess, Victoria,

Silver Rim Tankard Series: Falstaff, Henry VIII, Highwayman, John Bull, John Peel, Long John Silver, Micawber, Pickwick, Puck, Robin Hood, Sarah Gamp, Scottie, Uncle Tom Cobleigh, Weller, William Shakespeare, Yeoman of the Guard

Statesmen Character Jug Series: Chamberlain, Disraeli, Franklin Roosevelt, Lincoln, Winston Churchill

Tiny Character Jug Series: Long John Silver, Micawber, Sarah Gamp, Scottie, Uncle Tom Cobleigh, Weller

Toby Jug Pair: Neville Chamberlain, Winston Churchill

Lefton

American Patriot Character Jug Series (in two sizes): Abraham Lincoln, Andrew Jackson, Benjamin Franklin, George Washington, John Adams, Robert E. Lee, Theodore Roosevelt, Thomas Jefferson, Ulysses S. Grant

H. G. Lesser & R. F. Pavey

Tinker, Tailor, Soldier, Sailor Toby Jug Series: Beggarman, Poorman, Richman, Sailor, Soldier, Tailor, Thief, Tinker

Mason's

Good Companions Character Jug Series: Doctor, Farmer, Farmer's Wife, Policeman, Policewoman, School Master, Secretary

Miniature Character Jug Series: Chef, Flower Seller, Gentleman, Grandmother & Child, Huntsman, Jolly Jack Tar, Lady Equestrian, Lady with muff, Little Girl, Maid of All Work, Old Lady, Postman, Scotsman, Squire, Undergraduate, Vicar

Minton

World War II Character Jug Pair: Franklin Roosevelt, Winston Churchill

Majolica Toby Jug Pair: Quaker Man (Barrister), Quaker Woman (Lady with Fan)

Noble Ceramics

Football Managers Character Jug Series: Alex Ferguson, Jack Charlton, Jeff Astle, Kevin Keegan, Ron Atkinson

Historical Legends Series: George Washington, Jackie Kennedy, John F. Kennedy, Margaret

Thatcher, Princess Diana, Richard Branson, Winston Churchill

Peggy Davies Ceramics

American Patriot Character Jug Series: Abraham Lincoln, Betsy Ross, George Washington, John F. Kennedy, Thomas Jefferson

US Civil War Character Jug Pair: Robert E. Lee, Ulysses S. Grant,

Roy Kirkham

Australain Toby Jug Set: Digger, Sheep Shearer, Swaggie

Charles Dickens Toby Jug Series: Artful Dodger, Bill Sykes, Fagin, Mr. Bumble, Mr. Pickwick, Mrs. Bumble, Oliver Twist, Sarah Gamp, Sam Weller, Scrooge

Sherwood Forest Toby Jug Series (in two sizes): Alan a'Dale, Friar Tuck, King John, Robin Hood, Sheriff of Nottingham, Will Scarlett

Tinker, Tailor, Soldier, Sailor Toby Jug Series: Beggarman, Poorman, Richman, Sailor, Soldier, Tailor, Thief, Tinker

Traditional Toby Jug Series (from Wedgwood & Co. molds): Beadle, Inn Keeper, Nightwatchman, Pedlar, Schoolmaster, Shepherd, Squire, Sweep, Town Clerk, Town Crier, Vicar

Royal Doulton

Alice in Wonderland Character Jug Series: Cook and Cheshire Cat, Mad Hatter, March Hare, Red Queen, Ugly Duchess, Walrus and Carpenter

Antagonists Character Jug Series: Chief Sitting Bull and George Armstrong Custer, Davy Crockett and Antonio Lopez de Santa Anna, George III and George Washington, Ulysses S. Grant and Robert E. Lee

Beatles Character Jug Set: George Harrison, John Lennon, Paul McCartney, Ringo Starr

Canadian Centennial Character Jug Set: Lumberjack, North American Indian, Trapper

Canadian On Guard for Thee Character Jug Set: Airman, Sailor, Soldier

Cartoon Character Jug Series: Dennis and Gnasher, Desperate Dan, Minnie the Minx, Plug of the Bash Street Kids

Celebrity Collection Character Jug Series: Clark Gable, Groucho Marx, Jimmy Durante, Louis Armstrong, Mae West, W. C. Fields; Elvis Presley, Humphrey Bogart, Marilyn Monroe

jugs prototyped but never released

Characters from Life Character Jug Series: Angler - version 1, Baseball Player, Bowls Player, Gardener - version 2, Golfer - version 2, Jockey - version 2, Master, Snooker Player

Characters from Literature Character Jug Series: Aramis, Athos, Captain Ahab, Cyrano de Bergerac, D'Artagnan, Don Quixote, Falstaff, Friar Tuck, Gulliver, Long John Silver, Merlin, Porthos, Rip Van Winkle, Robin Hood - version 2, Robinson Crusoe, Sancho Panca, Scaramouche - version 2, Touchstone

Characters from Williamsburg Character Jug Series: Apothecary, Blacksmith, Bootmaker, Cabinet Maker, Gaoler, Guardsman, Gunsmith, Night Watchman

Charles Dickens Characters Character Jug Series: Bill Sykes, Buz Fuz, Cap'n Cuttle, Charles Dickens, Fat Boy, Mr. Micawber (version 1), Mr. Pickwick, Sairey Gamp, Sam Weller, Tony Weller

Charles Dickens Commemorative Tiny Character Jug Set: Artful Dodger, Betsy Trotwood, Bill Sykes, Charles Dickens, David Copperfield, Fagin, Little Nell, Mr. Bumble, Mrs. Bardell, Oliver Twist, Scrooge, Uriah Heep

Christmas Miniature Character Jug Series: Angel, Caroler, Elf, Mrs. Claus, Santa Claus with wreath handle, Snowman

Circus Performers Character Jug Series: Clown - version 2, Elephant Trainer, Juggler, Ringmaster

Collecting World Character Jug Series: Antique Dealer, Auctioneer, Collector

Comrades in Arms Character Jug Set: Airman, Sailor, Soldier

Diamond Anniversary Tiny Character Jug Set: Dick Turpin, Granny, Jester, John Barleycorn, Parson Brown, Simon the Cellarer

Dickens Seated Toby Jug Set: Cap'n Cuttle, Fat Boy, Mr. Micawber, Mr. Pickwick, Sairey Gamp, Sam Weller

Doultonville Toby Jug Series: Albert Sagger the Potter, Alderman Mace the Mayor, Betty Bitters the Barmaid, Captain Prop the Pilot, Capt. Salt the Sea Captain, Charlie Cheer the Clown, Dr. Pulse the Physician, Flora Fuchsia the Florist, Fred Fearless the Fireman, Fred Fly the Fisherman, Len Lifebelt the Lifeboatman, Madam Crystal the Clairvoyant, Major Green the Golfer, Mike Mineral the Miner, Miss

Nostrum the Nurse, Miss Studious the Schoolmistress, Monsieur Chasseur the Chef, Mr. Brisket the Butcher, Mr. Furrow the Farmer, Mr. Litigate the Lawyer, Mr. Tonsil the Town Crier, Mrs. Loan the Librarian, Pat Parcel the Postman, Rev. Cossock the Clergyman, Sgt. Peeler the Policeman

Flambe' Character Jug Series: Aladdin's Genie, Confucius, Genie (pilot only), Pharaoh

Football Supporters Character Jug Series: Arsenal, Aston Villa, Celtic, Everton, Leeds United, Liverpool, Manchester United, Rangers, Sheffield Wednesday, Tottenham Hotspur

Great Composers Character Jug Series: Beethoven, Chopin, Elgar, Handel, Johann Strauss II, Mozart, Schubert, Tchaikovsky

Great Explorers Tiny Character Jug Set: Cook, Columbus, DeGama, Livingstone, Marco Polo, Scott

Great Generals Character Jug Series: Duke of Wellington, General Eisenhower, General Gordon, General Patton

Henry VIII and his Six Wives Character Jug Series: Anne Boleyn, Anne of Cleves, Catherine of Aragon, Catherine Howard, Catherine Parr, Henry VIII, Jane Seymour

Heroes of the Blitz Character Jug Set: ARP Warden, Auxiliary Fireman, Home Guard

Heroic Leaders Character Jug Set: Earl Mountbatten of Burma - version 1, Sir Winston Churchill, Viscount Montgomery of Alamein

Kings and Queens of the Realm Tiny Character Jug Set: Charles I, Edward VII, Elizabeth I, Henry V, Henry VIII, Victoria

London Collection Character Jug Series: Beefeater, Busker, Chelsea Pensioner, City Gent, Guardsman - version 2, London Bobby, Lord Mayor, Pearly King, Pearly Queen, Yeoman of the Guard

Monsters Character Jug Series: Count Dracula, Frankenstein's Monster, Phantom of the Opera, Quasimodo

Mystical Characters Character Jug Series: Genie, Witch, Wizard

National Service Character Jug Set: Airman, Sailor, Soldier

Original Tiny Character Jug Set: Arry, Arriet, Auld Mac, Cardinal, Fat Boy, John Peel, Mr. Micawber, Mr. Pickwick, Old Charley, Paddy,

Sairey Gamp, Sam Weller

Playing Card Toby Jug Series: King and Queen of Clubs, King and Queen of Diamonds, King and Queen of Hearts, King and Queen of Spades

Santa Claus Character Jug Series: large size handle variations - plain, doll, reindeer, stocking, red candy cane, wreath, red/green candy cane, Christmas tree; small size handle variations - plain, bells; miniature size handle variations - plain, wreath; tiny size handle variations - plain, candy cane, gift box, teddy bear

Shakespeare Character Jug Set: Hamlet, Henry V, Macbeth, Othello, Romeo, and William Shakespeare - version 1

Sherlock Holmes Tiny Character Jug Set: Dr. Watson, Inspector Lestrade, Jefferson Hope, Mrs. Hudson, Professor Moriarty, Sherlock Holmes

Small Toby Jug Series: Clown, Dr. Jekyll and Mr. Hyde (two sided jug), Father Christmas, Jester - version 1, Judge and Thief (two sided jug), Leprechaun, Town Crier

Sporting Heroes Character Jug Series: Dennis Compton, Dickie Bird M.B.E., Freddie Truman, Henry Cooper, Ian Botham, Johnners, Len Hutton, Murray Walker, W. G. Grace, Willie Carson

Star-crossed Lovers Character Jug Series: Anthony and Cleopatra, King Arthur and Guinevere, Napoleon and Josephine, Samson and Delilah

Three Musketeers Character Jug Series: Aramis, Athos, D'Artagnan, Porthos

Tiny Toby Jug Set: Best is Not Too Good, Happy John, Honest Measure, Jolly Toby, Old Charley, Toby XX

United States Presidents Character Jug Series: Abraham Lincoln, George Washington - version 2, Thomas Jefferson, Ronald Reagan (produced on special commission)

Wild West Collection Character Jug Set: Annie Oakley, Buffalo Bill - version 2, Doc Holliday, Geronimo, Wild Bill Hickock, Wyatt Earp

Other Character Jug Pairs: Ankhesenamun and Tutankhamen, Captain Bligh and Fletcher Christian, Charles I and Oliver Cromwell, Francis Rossi and Rick Parfitt, King Arthur and Merlin, King John and Richard III, King Phillip of Spain and Queen Elizabeth I, Napoleon and Wellington, Prince Albert and Queen Victoria, Ronnie Barker and Ronnie Corbett, Stan Laurel and Oliver Hardy

Other Toby Jug Pairs: Bearded Spook and Spook, Fire King and Ice Queen, Jester and Lady Jester

Shaw & Sons (Burlington Ware)

Nursery Rhyme Toby Jug Series: Bo Peep, Humpty Dumpty, Jack Horner, (Georgie) Porgy

Traditional Series: Oyez, Singer Sleeper, Spud, Squire, Winker

Shaw and Copestake (SylvaC)

Character Jug Pairs: George Bernard Shaw and Robert Burns, Mr. Pickwick and Mr. Micawber, Ann Hathaway and William Shakespeare (in two sizes)

Sherwood Forest Character Jug Series: Alan a'Dale, Friar Tuck, Little John, Maid Marian, Robin Hood, Sheriff of Nottingham

Toby Jug Pair (in two sizes): Sarah Gamp, Sam Weller

Shawnee Pottery

Toby Jug Pair (in two sizes): Little Bo Peep, Little Boy Blue

Shelley Potteries

Intarsio Toby Jug Series: Baby, Irishman, John Bull, Monk, Scotsman, Unkel Sam (rare)

Shorter & Son

1950s Character Jug Set: Dick Turpin, Hayseed, Pedro, Pirate Head, Sheikh, Sinbad

D'Oyly Carte Opera Toby Jug Set (in two sizes): Buttercup, Dick Dead-Eye, Don Alhambra, Duchess of Plaza Toro, Duke of Plaza Toro, Jack Point, Katisha, Ko Ko, Major General, Mikado, Pirate King, Pirate Maid, Pooh Bah, Sir John Porter

Large Character Jug Pair: Friar Tuck, Robin Hood

Queen's Men Toby Jug Set (in two sizes): Outrider, Royal Volunteer, Trumpeter

Toby Jug Pairs: John Bull and Uncle Sam, Mr. Farmer and Mrs. Farmer (in two sizes)

Toby Jug with corresponding Character Jug Pairs: Cavalier, Covent Garden Bill, Father Neptune, Fisherman, Highwayman, Huntsman, Irish Mike

Traditional Toby Jug Series (in three sizes): Beefeater, Chelsea Pensioner, Flower Seller, Gardener, Guardsman, Old Salt (Sailor, HMS Cheerio), Scottie

Staffordshire Fine Ceramics

Alice in Wonderland Character Jug Series (in two sizes): Alice, Cheshire Cat, Doormouse, King of Hearts, Mad Hatter, Mock Turtle, Queen of Hearts, White Rabbit

Charles Dickens Toby Jug Series: Fagin, Mr. Micawber, Mr. Peggotty, Mr. Pickwick, Scrooge

Country Folk Toby Jug Series: Farmer Giles, Farmer Nut Brown Ale, Game Keeper (large size), Highwayman, Martha, Robin Hood, Squire (large size), Toby Cartlidge

Days Gone By Character Jug Series: Dick Turpin, Jenny Jones, Mother Riley, Paddy, Rob Roy, Whiskers (small size)

Days of Olde Toby Jug Series: Coachman, Gaoler, Innkeeper, Lamp Lighter, Pedlar, Sweep

Jack of All Trades Toby Jug Series: Customs Man, Game Keeper, Hornblower, Collier, Smithy, Squire

Last Orders Toby Jug Series: Angus, Dart Player, Happy John, Jock, Ned (the Snufftaker), Toby

Little Brown Jug Toby Jug Series: Jolly Fred, Jolly Jock, 'Owd Jack, Sam Toby, Will Toby

Londen Toby Jug Series: Beefeater, Chelsea Pensioner, Grenadier Guardsman, Henry VIII, John Bull, Pearly King, Pearly Queen, Sir Winston Churchill (small size)

Muskateers Toby Jug Set: Aramis, Athos, D'Artagnan, Porthos

Olde Timers Character Jug Series: Beaky, Jolly, Say Again, Whiskers (miniature size)

Pirates and Lawmen Toby Jug Serier: Captain M. B. Sylvester, Customs Man, Judge, Long John Silver, Pirate, Smuggler

Royalty and Dignitaries Toby Jug Series: Archbishop, Earl Order of St. Patrick, King, Knight Order of the Garter, Lord Mayor, Queen

Sea Farers Toby Jug Series: Neptune, Sea Fisherman, Sir Francis Drake

Shakespeare Toby Jug Series: Falstaff, Hamlet, King Lear, MacBeth, Oberon, Othello, Shylock, Touchstone, William Shakespeare

Sherwood Forest Character Jug Series: Alan a'Dale, Friar Tuck, Little John, Maid Marian, Prince John, Robin Hood, Sheriff of Nottingham, Will Scarlett

Tinker, Tailor Toby Jug Set: Beggarman, Poorman, Richman, Sailor, Soldier, Tailor, Tinker, Thief

Toby Jug Pairs: Festival Mouse and Festival Rabbit, Mr. Diddy and Mrs. Diddy, Mr. Hawthorne and Mrs. Hawthorne

Traditional Toby Jug Series: Judge, Pub Orator Publican, Sleepy, Toby, Town Crier

Woodland Toby Jug Set: Dr. Swamp, Mr. Chips, Mr. Pickles, P. C. Brock, Peter Post, Reverend Pew

World War II Heroes Character Jug Set: Churchill, DeGaulle, Ike, MacArthur, Monty, Mountbatten, Rommel, Smuts

Syracuse China

1928 U. S. Election Pair: Al Smith and Herbert Hoover

Thorley China

Tiny Character Jug Series: Anne Boleyn, Churchill, Drake, Elizabeth I, Florence Nightengale, Friar Tuck, Henry VIII, Lincoln, Micawber, Peggotty, Pirate, Pirate's Wife, and possibly others

Small Political Character Jug Series: Abraham Lincoln, Dwight Eisenhower, Franklin Roosevelt, Winston Churchill

Tony Wood

Alice in Wonderland Toby Jug Series: Alice, Black Knight, Carpenter, Caterpillar, Jabberwockey, King of Hearts, Lion, Mad Hatter, March Hare, Queen of Hearts, Tweedle Dee & Tweedle Dum, Ugly Duchess, Unicorn, Walrus, White Knight, White Rabbit

Torquay Pottery

Widecombe Fair Character Jug Series: 'Arry 'Awk, Bill Brewer, Dan'l Whiddon, Jan Stewart, Peter Davey, Peter Gurney, Tom Pearce, Uncle Tom Cobleigh

Truscott Pottery

Royal Year Toby Character Jug Series: Bram Nicholson, Henry Porter, John Mulligan, Paul Smith, Robert McNeile (plus Lester Piggott produced by Melwood)

Wedgwood & Company

Royalty and Dignitaries Toby Jug Series: Archbishop, Earl Order of St. Patrick, Knight Order of the Garter, Lord Chief Justice, Lord Mayor, Prince Order of the Thistle

Tinker, Tailor Toby Jug Series: Beggar, Poorman, Richman, Sailor, Soldier, Tailor, Tinker, Thief

Traditional Toby Jug Series: Beadle, Coachman, Innkeeper, Nightwatchman, Pedlar, Schoolmaster, Shepherd, Squire, Town Clerk, Town Crier, Vicar

Westminster Pottery

Just So Character Jug Series: Big Chief, Gramp, Gran, Jock, Outlaw, Shiek, and others likely exist

Tavern Collection Toby Jug Series: Gaffer Jarge, Mine Host John, Mine Hostess, Watchman Jeremy, and others likely exist

A. J. Wilkinson

World War I Allied Commander Toby Jug Series: Admiral David Beatty, Admiral John Jellicoe, Field Marshall Douglas Haig, General Louis Botha, King George V, Lord John French, Lord Kitchener, Marshall Ferdinand Foch, Marshall Joseph Joffre, Right Honorable Lloyd George, Woodrow Wilson (World War II Winston Churchill is often included with this series)

William MacLean

Great Americans Character Jug Series: Abraham Lincoln, American Indian, Benjamin Franklin, Captain Ahab, Daniel Boone, Dwight Eisenhower, General George Custer, George Washington, Huckleberry Finn, Ichabod Crane, Robert E. Lee, Thomas Jefferson

Wood and Sons

Charles Dickens Toby Jug Series: Bob Cratchit & Tiny Tim, David Copperfield, Fagin, Little Nell, Miss Haversham, Mr. Micawber, Mr. Pickwick, Mrs. Gamp, Oliver Twist, Peggoty, Scrooge, Uriah Heep

Pride of Britain Portrait Character Jug Series: Admiral Lord Nelson, Anne Boleyn, Duke of Wellington, Henry VIII, Lord Montgomery, Winston Churchill

Traditional Toby Jug Series: Lord Howe, Martha Gunn, Ralph Wood Toby, Sailor, Squire, Toby Fillpot

Wood Potters of Burslem

Miniature Toby Jug Series: Clerk, Drunken Parson, Gamekeeper, Haymaker, Lover, Martha Gunn, Musician, Ralph Wood, Sailor, Shepherd, Shepherdess

About the Photographs

Most of the photos used in this book are by the authors, taken on location throughout England and the United States. Where whole individual collections were photographed the collectors are appropriately acknowledged in the text. Individual photos taken on location are acknowledged as "from the collection of". Photographs supplied by others are acknowledged as "courtesy of".

Illustration of how molds move around Stoke-on-Trent from one defunct pottery to the next. From left to right, top row – Pedlar by Wedgwood & Co. and Japanese pottery, Squire by Wedgwood, Roy Kirkham, Staffordshire Fine and Japanese pottery, and Schoolmaster by Wedgwood and Roy Kirkham; bottom row – Beadle by Wedgwood, Roy Kirkham and Japanese pottery, Innkeeper by Wedgwood and Roy Kirkham, and Vicar by Staffordshire Fine and Japanese pottery. These characters were undoubtedly produced by all three Staffordshire companies from the same molds; Japanese pieces obviously are direct copies.

Grouping of Jugs from the "Just So" series of Westminster Pottery, Ltd. and subsequent inheritors of the molds; left to right, top row – Jock by Westminster, Crown Clarence, Anton Potteries and (Rob Roy) Staffordshire Fine Ceramics; middle row – Gramp by Westminster and (Whiskers) Staffordshire Fine, Gran by Westminster and (Mother Riley) Staffordshire Fine; bottom row – Outlaw by Westminster, Crown Clarence, Anton Potteries and (Dick Turpin) Staffordshire Fine; last column, top to bottom – Indian Chief by Anton Potteries, Crown Clarence and (Hiawatha) Staffordshire Fine.

About the Authors

David Fastenau grew up in an antique filled household in Iowa, his mother being an antique dealer who bought more than she sold. He is a graduate Engineer from Iowa State University and Santa Clara University, and is currently a Marketing Manager with Hewlett-Packard in Northern California.

David's collecting passion for Toby Jugs was spurred when he inherited a small collection of Royal Doulton jugs from his grandmother. With these jugs, and memories of their comical and sometimes grotesque faces from his childhood, he set out to learn as much about Toby and Character Jugs as possible. His collection continues to grow and now numbers over 500 full bodied Toby Jugs.

For three years David edited and published *Tobies to Tinies*, a newsletter for the Toby and Character Jug enthusiast, which he discontinued in order to research and write this book. David also has spoken at Questers' groups, provided references for articles, and readily answers any toby related questions posed to him. He currently lives with his three children in Northern California.

Steve Mullins is a graduate of Dartmouth College and the University of Michigan Business School and is currently Chairman of a Chicago based real estate investment firm. He started collecting Toby and Character Jugs over fifty years ago when a camp counselor in Canada enticed him with a Royal Doulton brochure to spend the balance of his camp candy money, all of $9, to buy six small Character Jugs. Today the collection numbers over 2,000 Toby and Character Jugs from around the world, dating from those earliest produced in the 1760s to the latest jugs made. The collection is now on display in the American Toby Jug Museum in Evanston, Illinois, where Steve is the curator.

Steve regularly speaks before Royal Doulton collector's meetings around the country, as well as other interested groups, regarding the history of Toby and Character Jugs. He also has contributed to numerous books on the subject. Having raised three children, he currently resides in Evanston, Illinois with his wife and two Labrador Retrievers.

Together the authors have over seventy years of collecting experience and have spent over three years researching and compiling this book. Their travels have taken them to the far reaches of both the United States and the United Kingdom, and have included five separate visits to Stoke-on-Trent, the birthplace of Toby and Character Jugs.

Pirate King and Pirate Maid Toby Jugs from the Gilbert and Sullivan D'Oyly Carte Series by Shorter and Son.

Arcadian Arms China; *Arkinstall & Son Catalogue reprint.* (Hants, UK: Milestone Publications, 1980.)

Alfred Clough: From Pedlar to Potter; <u>Pottery Gazette and Glass Trade Review</u>. April 1959.

Atterbury, Paul and Batkin, Maureen; *The Dictionary of Minton.* (Suffolk, UK: The Antique Collector's Club Ltd., 1990.)

Atterbury, Paul and Irvine, Louise; *The Doulton Story.* (Stoke-on-Trent, England: Royal Doulton Tableware Ltd., 1979.)

Background to Denby. (England: The Artisan Press Ltd., ca 1960s.)

Barker, Ray; *The Crown Devon Collector's Handbook.* (London, UK: Francis Joseph Publishing Ltd., 1997.)

Bartlett, John A.; *British Ceramic Art 1870 - 1940.* (Atglen, Pennsylvania: Schiffer Publishing Ltd., 1993.)

Battie, David and Turner, Michael; *The Price Guide to 19th and 20th Century British Pottery.* (Suffolk, UK: Antique Collectors Club Ltd., 1990.)

Brammer, Geoffrey B.; *Toby Jugs.* (London, UK: Unpublished dissertation at London University, 1959.)

Brisco, Virginia; *Dartmouth Pottery.* (Devon, UK: The Torquay Pottery Collectors' Society, 1993.)

Chipman, Jack; *Collector's Encyclopedia of California Pottery.* (Paducah, Kentucky: Collector Books, 1995.)

Cieslik, Jurgen and Marianne; *German Doll Encyclopedia 1800 - 1939.* (Cumberland, Maryland: Hobby House Press, 1985.)

Colbert, Neva W.; *The Collector's Guide to Harker Pottery.* (Paducah, Kentucky: Collector Books, 1993.)

Coure, Elizabeth R.; *Collecting Burleigh Jugs.* (Leicestershire, UK: Letterbox Publishing Ltd., 1998.)

Crest of the Wave; A Visit to Grafton China. <u>Pottery and Glass</u>, December 1956.

Cunningham, Helen; *Majolica Figures.* (Atglen, Pennsylvania: Schiffer Publishing Ltd., 1997.)

Curran, Pamela Duvall; *Shawnee Pottery, The Full Encyclopedia.* (Atglen, Pennsylvania: Schiffer Publishing Ltd., 1995.)

Cushion, J. P.; *Pocket Book of British Ceramic Marks.* (England: Clays Ltd., 1994.)

Dale, Jean; *The Charlton Standard Catalogue of Royal Doulton Jugs*, Fourth Edition. (Ontario, Canada: The Charlton Press, 1997.)

Eberlein, Harold D. and Ramsdell, Roger W.; *The Practical Book of Chinaware.* (Cornwall, New York: The Cornwall Press, 1925.)

Eyles, Desmond; *Good Sir Toby.* (London, UK: Doulton & Co. Ltd., 1955.)

Eyles, Desmond; *Royal Doulton Character and Toby Jugs.* (London, UK: Royal Doulton Ltd., 1975.)

Flower Container Development; New Shapes by a Tunstall Teapot Firm. <u>Pottery Gazette and Glass Trade Review</u>. November 1961.

Godden, Geoffrey A.; *Encyclopaedia of British Pottery and Porcelain Marks.* (London, UK: Barrie & Jenkins Ltd., 1996.)

Hall, Douglas C.; *The Story of "Olde Staffordshire" Pottery by Kent of Burslem.* (Burslem, UK: William Kent Limited company brochure, 1960.)

Hallam, Edward; *Ashtead Potters Ltd.* (Surrey, England: Hallam Publishing, 1990.)

Halliman, Lincoln; *British Commemoratives.* (Suffolk, UK: The Antique Collectors Club Ltd., 1995.)

Hand-Painted Pottery from Devon; Progress by an 80-Year Old Honiton Firm. <u>Pottery Gazette and Glass Trade Review</u>. November 1961.

Haslam, Malcolm; *The Martin Brothers Potters.* (London, UK: Richard Dennis, 1978.)

Heckford, Brian; *Hornsea Pottery 1949 - 1989.* (UK; Hornsea Pottery Collectors and Research Society, 1998.)

The History of Crown Staffordshire China. <u>British Bulletin of Commerce</u>. November 1954, Volume 16, Number 7.

Hobbs, John; *The Devonmoor Art Pottery Liverton.* (Tavistock, UK: self published, 1998.)

Hopwood, Irene and Gordon; *The Shorter Connection.* (Somerset, UK: Richard Dennis, 1992.)

Huxford, Sharon and Bob; *The Collector's Encyclopedia of Brush-McCoy Pottery.* (Paducah, Kentucky: Collector Books, 1996.)

Jenkins, Steven; *Midwinter Pottery, A Revolution in British Tableware.* (Somerset, UK: Richard Dennis, 1997.)

Karmason, Marilyn G.: *Majolica A Complete History and Illustrated Survey.* (New York, New York: Harry N. Abrams, Inc., 1989.)

Klamkin, Marian; *American Patriotic and Political China*. (New York, New York: Charles Scribner's Sons, 1973.)

Knowles, Eric; *Miller's Royal Memorabilia*. (London, UK: Reed International Books Ltd., 1994.)

Lancaster and Sandland Limited company brochure. (England, 1960s.)

Lukins, Jocelyn; *Collecting Royal Doulton Character and Toby Jugs*, 3rd Edition. (London, UK: Venta Books, 1994.)

Mali, Millicent S.; *Three Hundred Years of Faience*. Old Quimper Review, July 1990.

Mansell, Colette; *The Collector's Guide to British Dolls Since 1920*. (London, UK: Robert Hale Limited, 1983.)

May, Harvey; *The Beswick Collectors Handbook*. (London, UK: Kevin Francis Publishing Ltd., 1988.)

McCaslin, Mary J.; *Royal Bayreuth, A Collector's Guide*. (Marietta, Ohio: Antique Publications, 1994.)

McIntyre, William N.; *Americraft and "Gesgesch" Tobies of Amercian Historical Figures*. The Antique Trader Weekly, August 26, 1981, Volume 25, Issue 34.

McIntyre, William N.; *Collecting Full-Figure Tobies Produced in the Last 125 Years*. The Antique Trader Weekly, .June 21, 1978, Volume 22, Issue 25.

McKeon, Julie; *Royal Doulton*. (Buckinghamshire, UK: Shire Publications Ltd., 1998.)

Melba Ware Flourishes at New Headquarters. Tableware International, December 1978/January 1979.

Miller, Muriel; *Collecting Royal Winton Chintz*. (London, UK: Francis Joseph Publishing Ltd., 1996.)

Murray, Pat; *The Charlton Standard Catalogue of Wade*, Volume 1, 2nd Edition. (Ontario, Canada: The Charlton Press, 1996.)

Niblett, Kathy; *Dynamic Design: The British Pottery Industry 1940 - 1990*. (Stafford, England: Stoke-on-Trent City Museum and Art Gallery, 1990.)

Pearson, Kevin; *Character Jug Collectors Handbook*, volume 4. (Kevin Francis Publishing Ltd., 1992.)

Peat, Allan; *Midwinter A Collector's Guide*. (Dumfriesshire, UK: Cameron & Hollis, 1992.)

Pine, Lynda and Nicholas; *William Henry Goss*. (Harts, UK: Milestone Publications, 1987.)

Poole, Keith; *The Art of the Torquay and South Devon Potters*. (Wilshire, England: The Torquay Pottery Collectors' Society and Bath Midway Litho Ltd., 1996.)

Rice, D. G.; *English Porcelain Animals of the 19th Century*. (Suffolk, UK: The Antique Collector's Club Ltd., 1990.)

Roberts, Gaye Blake; *Mason's, The First Two Hundred Years*. (London, UK: Merrell Holberton Publishers Ltd., 1996.)

Salmon, Francis; *Collecting Carlton Ware*. (London, UK: Francis Joseph Publishing Ltd., 1994.)

Salmon, Francis; *The New Character Jug Collectors Handbook*, Revised Edition. (London, UK: Francis Joseph Publishing Ltd., 1995.)

Sandon, Henry; *Royal Worcester Porcelain*. (Clarkson N. Potter, 1973.)

Scheider, Mike; *Grindley Pottery, A Menagerie*. (Atglen, Pennsylvania: Schiffer Publishing Ltd., 1996.)

Schneider, Robert; *Coors Rosebud Pottery*. (Seattle, Washington: Busche Waugh Henry Publications, 1984.)

Schroeder's Antiques Price Guide, 7th Edition, 1989.

Schuler, Vic; *British Toby Jugs*. (London, UK: Kevin Francis Publishing Ltd., 1988.)

Schuler, Vic; *Collecting British Toby Jugs*. (London, UK: Francis Joseph Publishing Ltd., 1994.)

Smith, Ronald A.; *Churchill: Images of Greatness*. (London, UK: Kevin Francis Publishing Ltd., unknown year)

Smith, Ronald A.; *The Premier Years of Margaret Thatcher*. (London, UK: Kevin Francis Publishing Ltd., 1991.)

Svec, J. J.; *New Plant Makes Parian and Bone Porcelain Collectibles*. Ceramic Industry, August 1977, Vol 109, Number 2.

Twitchett, John and Bailey, Betty; *Royal Crown Derby*. (Suffolk, UK: The Antique Collector's Club Ltd., 1988.)

Van Der Woerd; *Shaw & Copestake*. (Bath, UK: Georgian Publications, 1992.)

Vanstone, Graeme; *Have You Seen Any Manor Ware?* The Torquay Pottery Collectors' Society Magazine, November 1997.

Verbeek, Susan Jean; *The Sylvac Companion*. (London, UK: Pottery Publications, 1991.)

Verbeek, Susan Jean; *The Sylvac Story*. (London, UK: Pottery Publications, 1989.)

Watson, Howard and Pat; *The Clarice Cliff Colour Price Guide*. (London, UK: Francis Joseph Publishing Ltd., 1995.)

Watson, Howard and Pat; *Collecting Art Deco Ceramics*. (London, UK: Kevin Francis Publishing Ltd., 1993.)

Weiss, Princess and Barry; *The Original Price Guide to Royal Doulton Discontinued Character Jugs*, 6th Edition. (New York, New York: Harmony Press, 1987.)

White, Carole Bess; *Collector's Guide to Made in Japan Ceramics, Book II*. (Paducah, Kentucky: Collector Books, 1996.)

Wilkinson, Vega; *Copeland*. (Buckinghamshire, England. Shire Publications Ltd., 1994.)

Woodhouse, Charles Platten; *Old English Toby Jugs and Their Makers*. (London, UK: The Mountrose Press, 1949.)

This page is left blank intentionally

L

347

L